Lecture Notes in Computer Science 11203

Commenced Publication in 1973
Founding and Former Series Editors:
Gerhard Goos, Juris Hartmanis, and Jan van Leeuwen

More information about this series at http://www.springer.com/series/7407

Rio Yokota · Michèle Weiland
John Shalf · Sadaf Alam (Eds.)

High Performance Computing

ISC High Performance 2018 International Workshops
Frankfurt/Main, Germany, June 28, 2018
Revised Selected Papers

 Springer

Editors
Rio Yokota (iD)
Tokyo Institute of Technology
Tokyo, Japan

John Shalf
Lawrence Berkeley National Laboratory
Berkeley, CA, USA

Michèle Weiland (iD)
University of Edinburgh
Edinburgh, UK

Sadaf Alam
Swiss National Supercomputing Centre
Lugano, Switzerland

ISSN 0302-9743   ISSN 1611-3349 (electronic)
Lecture Notes in Computer Science
ISBN 978-3-030-02464-2   ISBN 978-3-030-02465-9 (eBook)
https://doi.org/10.1007/978-3-030-02465-9

Library of Congress Control Number: 2018944377

LNCS Sublibrary: SL1 – Theoretical Computer Science and General Issues

This Springer imprint is published by the registered company Springer Nature Switzerland AG
The registered company address is: Gewerbestrasse 11, 6330 Cham, Switzerland

Preface

A separate workshop day attached to the International Supercomputing Conference (ISC) High Performance, formerly known as the International Supercomputing Conference, was first added to the technical program in 2015 under the leadership of Bernd Mohr (Forschungszentrum Jülich GmbH). Supported by the success of the past 3 years, ISC High Performance renewed and further extended the workshop program in 2018, under the leadership of John Shalf (Lawrence Berkeley National Laboratory) and Sadaf Alam (Swiss National Supercomputing Center). Rio Yokota (Tokyo Institute of Technology) and Michele Weiland (The University of Edinburgh) joined the team as proceedings chair and deputy chair, respectively, and managed the organization of the proceedings for the workshops.

The 23 workshops at ISC High Performance 2018 provided a focused, in-depth platform with presentations, discussion, and interaction on topics related to all aspects of research, development, and application of large-scale, high-performance experimental and commercial systems. Workshop topics included HPC computer architecture and hardware; programming models, system software, and applications; solutions for heterogeneity, reliability, power efficiency of systems; virtualization and containerized environments; big data and cloud computing; artificial intelligence; as well as international collaborations. Workshops were selected with a peer-review process by an international committee of 16 experts in the field from Europe, the United States, and Asia.

Since 2016, ISC High Performance has provided a platform for workshops with their own call for papers and individual peer-review process through an early deadline in December 2017. In all, 13 workshop proposals were submitted before this deadline from organizers all over the world; the committee accepted 21 workshops (eight full-day and two half-day workshops) after a rigorous review process in which each proposal received three reviews. Additionally, each reviewer was given the possibility to discuss all the submissions. Workshops without a call for papers were invited to submit their proposals in February 2018. For this second deadline, 14 workshop proposals were submitted and 13 workshops (three full-day and ten half-day day workshops) were accepted by the committee with the same rigorous peer-review process as for workshops with proceedings.

The 23 workshops were held on Thursday, June 28, 2018, at the Frankfurt Marriott Hotel with 489 attendees in the morning and 419 in the afternoon, about 170 presentations, and over a dozen panel discussions. The workshop proceedings volume collects all the accepted papers of the workshops from the call for papers. Each chapter of the book contains the accepted and revised papers for one of the workshops. For some workshops, an additional preface describes the review process for that workshop and provides a summary of the outcome.

June 2018

Rio Yokota
Michèle Weiland
John Shalf
Sadaf Alam

Organization

ISC High Performance Workshops Co-chairs

John Shalf   Lawrence Berkeley National Laboratory, USA
Sadaf Alam   Swiss National Supercomputing Centre, Switzerland

ISC High Performance Workshops Committee

Rosa M. Badia   Barcelona Supercomputing Center, Spain
François Bodin   IRISA, France
Bronis R. de Supinski   Lawrence Livermore National Laboratory, USA
Simon McIntosh-Smith   University of Bristol, UK
Bernd Mohr   Jülich Supercomputing Centre, Germany
Michela Taufer   University of Delaware, USA
Antonino Tumeo   Pacific Northwest National Laboratory, USA
Didem Unat   Koç University, Turkey
Heike Jagode   University of Tennessee, USA
Diana Moise   Cray, Basel
Bilel Hadri   KAUST, Saudi Arabia
Carsten Trintis   TU Munich, Germany

ISC High Performance Workshops Proceedings Co-chairs

Rio Yokota   Tokyo Institute of Technology, Japan
Michèle Weiland   EPCC, The University of Edinburgh, UK

HPC I/O in the Data Center (HPC-IODC 2018)

Organizing Committee

Julian Kunkel   University of Reading, UK
Jay Lofstead   Sandia National Laboratories, USA

Program Committee

Jean-Thomas Acquaviva   DDN, France
Thomas Boenisch   HLRS, Germany
Jim Brandt   Sandia National Laboratories, USA
Sven Breuner   ThinkparQ, Germany
Matt Bryson   University of California, Santa Cruz, USA
Suren Byna   Lawrence Berkeley National Laboratory, USA
Sandro Fiore   CMCC, Italy
Wolfgang Frings   Jülich Supercomputing Centre, Germany

Javier Garcia Blas	Carlos III University of Madrid, Spain
Ann Gentile	Sandia National Laboratories, USA
Adrian Jackson	The University of Edinburgh, UK
Michael Kluge	TU Dresden, Germany
Julian Kunkel	University of Reading, UK
Jay Lofstead	Sandia National Laboratories, USA
George Markomanolis	KAUST, Saudi Arabia
Tiago Quintino	ECMWF, UK
Rob Ross	Argonne National Laboratory, USA
Brad Settleyer	Los Alamos National Laboratory, USA
Feiyi Wang	Oak Ridge National Laboratory, USA
Bing Xie	Oak Ridge National Laboratory, USA

Workshop on Performance and Scalability of Storage Systems (WOPSSS 2018)

Organizing Committee

Jean-Thomas Acquaviva	DDN, France
Jalil Boukhobza	University of Bretagne Occidentale, France
Phlippe Deniel	CEA/DIF, France
Pedro Javier García	University of LaMurcia-Castilla, Spain
Massimo Lamanna	CERN, Switzerland
Allen Malony	University of Oregon, USA

Program Committee

Julien Bigot	CEA, France
André Brinkmann	Mainz University, Germany
Jason Chun Xue	City University of Hong Kong, SAR China
Stefano Cozzini	CNR, Italy
Kaoutar El Maghraoui	IBM, USA
Jesus Escudero-Sahuquillo	University of Castilla-La Mancha, Spain
Maria E. Gomez	Polytechnic University of Valencia, Spain
Pilar Gonzalez Ferez	Universidad de Murcia, Spain
Denis Gutfreund	ATOS, France
Julian Kunkel	University of Reading, UK
J-Charles Lafoucrière	CEA, France
Duo Liu	Chongqing University, China
Manolis Marazakis	ICS-FORTH, Greece
Lars Nagel	Johannes Gutenberg-Universität Mainz, Germany
Ramon Nou	Barcelona Supercomputing Center, Spain
Franz-Josef Pfreundt	Fraunhofer ITWM, Germany
Juan Piernas Cánovas	Universidad de Murcia, Spain
Rekha Singhal	Tata Consultancy Services, India
Josef Weidendorfer	TU Munich, Germany
Soraya Zertal	University of Versailles, France

13th Workshop on Virtualization in High-Performance Cloud Computing (VHPC 2018)

Organizing Committee

Michael Alexander (Chair)	Institute of Science and Technology, Austria
Anastassios Nanos (Co-chair)	OnApp, UK
Romeo Kienzler (Co-chair)	IBM, Switzerland

Program Committee

Stergios Anastasiadis	University of Ioannina, Greece
Jakob Blomer	CERN, Europe
Eduardo César	Universidad Autonoma de Barcelona, Spain
Stephen Crago	USC ISI, USA
Tommaso Cucinotta	St. Anna School of Advanced Studies, Italy
Christoffer Dall	Columbia University, USA
Patrick Dreher	MIT, USA
Kyle Hale	Northwestern University, USA
Brian Kocoloski	University of Pittsburgh, USA
Uday Kurkure	VMware, USA
Nectarios Koziris	National Technical University of Athens, Greece
John Lange	University of Pittsburgh, USA
Giuseppe Lettieri	University of Pisa, Italy
Qing Liu	Oak Ridge National Laboratory, USA
Nikos Parlavantzas	INSA Rennes, France
Kevin Pedretti	Sandia National Laboratories, USA
Amer Qouneh	Western New England University, USA
Carlos Reaño	Technical University of Valencia, Spain
Borja Sotomayor	University of Chicago, USA
Craig Stewart	Indiana University, USA
Anata Tiwari	San Diego Supercomputer Center, USA
Kurt Tutschku	Blekinge Institute of Technology, Sweden
Yasuhiro Watashiba	Osaka University, Japan
Chao-Tung Yang	Tunghai University, Taiwan
Andrew Younge	Sandia National Laboratory, USA
Na Zhang	VMware, USA

Third International Workshop on in Situ Visualization: Introduction and Applications (WOIV 2018)

Organizing Committee

Kenneth Moreland	Sandia National Laboratories, USA
Guido Reina	University of Stuttgart, Germany
Thomas Theussl	KAUST, Saudi Arabia
Tom Vierjahn	RWTH Aachen University, Germany

Program Committee

Bartosz Borucki	University of Warsaw, Poland
Hadrien Calmet	Barcelona Supercomputing Center, Spain
Hank Childs	University of Oregon, USA
Steffen Frey	University of Stuttgart, Germany
Jens Henrik Göbbert	Forschungszentrum Jülich GmbH, Germany
Bernd Hentschel	RWTH Aachen University, Germany
Glendon Holst	KAUST, Saudi Arabia
Julien Jomier	Kitware, France
Joanna Leng	University of Leeds, UK
Kenneth Moreland	Sandia National Laboratories, USA
Benson Muite	University of Tartu, Estonia
Joachim Pouderoux	Kitware, France
Thomas Theussl	KAUST, Saudi Arabia
Tom Vierjahn	RWTH Aachen University, Germany
Gunther Weber	Lawrence Berkeley National Lab, USA
Ahmed Zawawi	Saudi Aramco, Saudi Arabia

4th International Workshop on Communication Architectures for HPC, Big Data, Deep Learning and Clouds at Extreme Scale (ExaComm 2018)

Organizing Committee

Hari Subramoni	Ohio State University, USA
Dhabaleswar K. Panda	Ohio State University, USA

Program Committee

Taisuke Boku	University of Tsukuba, Japan
Ron Brightwell	Sandia National Laboratories, USA
Hans Eberle	NVIDIA, Germany
Ada Gavrilovska	Georgia Tech, USA
Brice Goglin	Inria, France
Dror Goldenberg	Mellanox Technologies, Israel
R. Govindarajan	Indian Institute of Science, Bangalore, India
Ryan Grant	Sandia National Laboratories, USA
Hai Jin	Huazhong University of Science and Technology, China
Sven Karlsson	Technical University of Denmark, Denmark
Takeshi Nanri	University of Kyushu, Japan
Dimitrios Nikolopoulos	Queen's University of Belfast, UK
Antonio Pena	Barcelona Supercomputing Center, Spain
Sebastien Rumley	Columbia University, USA
Smruti Ranjan Sarangi	Indian Institute of Technology, Delhi, India
Martin Schulz	Lawrence Livermore National Laboratory, USA

John Shalf	Lawrence Berkeley National Laboratory, USA
Tor Skeie	Simula Research Laboratory, Norway
Sayantan Sur	Intel, USA
Xin Yuan	Florida State University, USA
Jidong Zhai	Tsinghua University, China

International Workshop on OpenPOWER for HPC (IWOPH 2018)

Organizing Committee

| Jack Wells | Oak Ridge National Laboratory, USA |
| Dirk Pleiter | Jülich Supercomputing Centre, Germany |

Program Committee

Zaid Al-Ars	TU Delft, The Netherlands
Manuel Arenaz	University of Coruña/Appentra, Spain
Hugh Blemings	OpenPOWER Foundation, USA
Carlo Cavazzoni	CINECA, Italy
Sunita Chandrasekaran	University of Delaware, USA
Barbara Chapman	Stony Brook University, USA
Norbert Eicker	Jülich Supercomputing Centre, Germany
Christoph Hagleitner	IBM Research, Switzerland
Oscar Hernandez (Co-chair)	Oak Ridge National Laborator, USA
Peter Hofstee	IBM, USA
Wen-Mei Hwu	University of Illinois, USA
Guido Juckeland	TU Dresden, Germany
Graham Lopez (Co-chair)	Oak Ridge National Laboratory, USA
Barney Maccabe	Oak Ridge National Laboratory, USA
Marek Michaelewicz	University of Warsaw, Poland
Rob Neely	Lawrence Livermore National Laboratory, USA
Duncan Poole	NVIDIA, USA
Stéphane Requena	GENCI, France
Vivek Sarkar	Rice University, USA
Fabio Schifano	University of Ferrara, Italy
Jim Sexton	IBM, USA
Gilad Shainer	Mellanox, Israel
Tjerk Straatsma	Oak Ridge National Laboratory, USA
Bronis de Supinski	Lawrence Livermore National Laboratory, USA
Michael Wolfe	NVIDIA/PGI, USA
Malgorzata Zimon	IBM Research, UK

IXPUG Workshop: Many-Core Computing on Intel Processors: Applications, Performance and Best-Practice Solutions

Organizing Committee

David Martin	Argonne National Laboratory, USA
John Pennycook	Intel, USA
Thomas Steinke	ZIB, Germany
Estela Suarez	Jülich Supercomputing Centre, Germany

Program Committee

Damian Alvarez-Mallon	Jülich Supercomputing Centre, Germany
Taisuke Boku	University of Tsukuba, Japan
Jeanine Cook	Sandia National Laboratories, USA
Douglas Doerfler	NERSC and Lawrence Berkeley National Laboratory, USA
Richard Gerber	Lawrence Berkeley National Laboratory and NERSC, USA
Clay Hughes	Sandia National Laboratories, USA
Juha Jaykka	The University of Cambridge, UK
Michael Klemm	Intel, Germany
David Martin	Argonne National Laboratory, USA
Simon McIntosh-Smith	Bristol University, UK
Kent Milfeld	TACC, USA
Hai Ah Nam	Los Alamos National Laboratory, USA
John Pennycook	Intel, USA
Hideki Saito	Intel, USA
Thomas Steinke	ZIB, Germany
Estela Suarez	Jülich Supercomputing Centre, Germany
Vit Vondrak	Technical University of Ostrava, Czech Republic
Zhengji Zhao	Lawrence Berkeley National Laboratory, USA

Workshop on Sustainable Ultrascale Computing Systems

Organizing Committee

Jesus Carretero	Carlos III University of Madrid, Spain

Program Committee

Carlos Jaime Barrios	Universidad Industrial de Santander, Colombia
Angelos Bilas	ICS FORTH, Greece
Harold Castr	Universidad de los Andes, Colombia
F. Javier García-Blas	Carlos III University of Madrid, Spain
J. Daniel Garcia	Carlos III University of Madrid, Spain
Alexey Lastoveysky	University College, Ireland
Laurent Lefevre	Ecole Normale Superiour Lyon, France

Svetozar Margenov	Bulgarian Academy of Science, Bulgaria
Radu Prodan	Alpen-Adria University of Klagenfurt, Austria
Gudula Ruenger	Technical University Chemnitz, Germany
Leonel Sousa INESC	Lisbon, Portugal
Xavier Vigoroux	ATOS-BULL, France
Vladimir Voevodin	Lomonosov Moscow State University, Russia
Zhiyi Huang	University of Otago, New Zealand

Approximate and Transprecision Computing on Emerging Technologies (ATCET 2018)

Organizing Committee

Cristiano Malossi	IBM Research GmbH, Switzerland
Costas Bekas	IBM Research GmbH, Switzerland
Luca Benini	ETH Zürich, Switzerland
Enrique S. Quintana Ortí	Jaume I University, Spain
Dimitrios S. Nikolopoulos	The Queen's University of Belfast, UK

Program Committee

Mahwish Arif	Queen's University of Belfast, UK
Henry-Pierre Charles	CEA, France
Dionysios Diamantopoulos	IBM Research, Switzerland
Andrew Emerson	CINECA, Italy
Luca Gammaitoni	University of Perugia, Italy
Frank K. Gurkaynak	ETH Zurich, Switzerland
Corine Lamagdeleine	GreenWaves Technologies, France
Michela Milano	University of Bologna, Italy
Andres Tomas-Dominguez	Jaume I University, Spain
Norbert Wehn	University of Kaiserslautern, Germany

First Workshop on the Convergence of Large-Scale Simulation and Artificial Intelligence

Organizing Committee

Christoph Angerer	NVIDIA, Germany
Axel Köhler	NVIDIA, Germany

Program Committee

Christoph Angerer	NVIDIA, Germany
Peter Dueben	ECMWF, UK
Axel Köhler	NVIDIA, Germany
Peter Messmer	NVIDIA, Switzerland
Christian Sigg	Google, Switzerland
Jean-Roch Vlimant	California Institute of Technology, USA

Third Workshop for Open Source Supercomputing (OpenSuCo 2018)

Organizing Committee

Anastasiia Butko	Lawrence Berkeley National Laboratory, USA
David Donofrio	Lawrence Berkeley National Laboratory, USA
Farzad Fatollahi-Fard	Lawrence Berkeley National Laboratory, USA
John Leidel	Texas Tech University and Tactical Computing Labs, USA
Sven Karlsson	Technical University of Denmark, Denmark

Program Committee

Anastasiia Butko	Lawrence Berkeley National Laboratory, USA
Sunita Chandrasekaran	University of Delaware, USA
David Donofrio	Lawrence Berkeley National Laboratory, USA
Glen Edwards	Micron Technology, Inc., USA
Farzad Fatollahi-Fard	Lawrence Berkeley National Laboratory, USA
Sven Karlsson	Technical University of Denmark, Denmark
Kurt Keville	Massachusetts Institute of Technology, USA
John Leidel	Texas Tech University and Tactical Computing Labs, USA
Martin Schulz	TU Munich, Germany
John Shalf	Lawrence Berkeley National Laboratory, USA
Noel Wheeler	Laboratory of Physical Science, USA
Sam Williams	Lawrence Berkeley National Laboratory, USA

First Workshop on Interactive High-Performance Computing

Organizing/Program Committee

Peter Messmer	NVIDIA, Switzerland
Sadaf Alam	Swiss National Supercomputing Centre, Switzerland
Albert Reuther	MIT Lincoln Laboratory, USA
Michael Ringenburg	Cray, USA
John Stone	University of Illinois at Urbana-Champaign, USA

Third International Workshop on Performance Portable Programming Models for Accelerators (P^3MA 2018)

Organizing Committee

Sunita Chandrasekaran	University of Delaware, USA
Graham Lopez	Oak Ridge National Laboratory, USA

Program Committee

Amit Amritkar	University of Houston, USA
Sridutt Bhalachandra	Argonne National Laboratory, USA
Kyle Friedline	University of Delaware, USA
Axel Huebl	Helmholtz-Zentrum Dresden-Rossendorf and TU Dresden, Germany
Adrian Jackson	The University of Edinburgh, UK
John Leidel	Texas Tech University, USA
Antonio J. Peña	Barcelona Supercomputing Center, Spain
John Pennycook	Intel, USA
Swaroop Pophale	Oak Ridge National Laboratory, USA
Suraj Prabhakaran	Intel, USA
Robert Searles	University of Delaware, USA
Ray Sheppard	Indiana University Bloomington, USA
Xiaonan Tian	NVIDIA, USA
Antonino Tumeo	Politecnico di Milano, Italy
Cheng Wang	University of Houston, USA
Sandra Wienke	RWTH Aachen University, Germany
Rengan Xu	Dell EMC, USA

Contents

13th Workshop on Virtualization in High-Performance Cloud Computing (VHPC 2018)

Third International Workshop on In Situ Visualization: Introduction and Applications (WOIV 2018)

**4th International Workshop on Communication Architectures
for HPC, Big Data, Deep Learning and Clouds at Extreme Scale
(ExaComm 2018)**

**International Workshop on OpenPOWER for HPC 2018
(IWOPH 2018)**

IXPUG Workshop: Many-Core Computing on Intel Processors: Applications, Performance and Best-Practice Solutions

Workshop on Sustainable Ultrascale Computing Systems

HPC I/O in the Data Center Workshop (HPC-IODC 2018)

HPC I/O in the Data Center Workshop
(HPC-IODC 2018)

Julian M. Kunkel[1,2], and Jay Lofstead[1,2]

[1] University of Reading
Whiteknights
Reading RG6 6AY, UK
j.m.kunkel@reading.ac.uk
[2] Center for Computing Research
Sandia National Laboratories
Albuquerque, USA

1 Introduction

Many public and privately funded data centers host supercomputers for running large scale simulations and analyzing experimental and observational data. These supercomputers run usually tightly coupled parallel applications that require hardware components that deliver the best performance. In contrast, commercial data centers, such as Facebook and Google, execute loosely coupled workloads with a broad assumption of regular failures. The dimension of the data centers is enormous. A 2013 article summarizes commercial data centers' dimensions [7]. It estimates, for example, that Facebook hosts around 100 PB of storage and Google and Microsoft manage around 1 million servers each – although the hardware is split among several physical data centers – a modus operandi not suitable for HPC centers. With the hunger for information, the globally installed storage capacity increases exponentially and is expected to hit 7,235 Exabytes by 2017 [4]. This trend is visible in the sales reports of companies such as the disk drive manufacturer Seagate. Within 5 years, they shipped 1 billion HDDs, which means 700.000 units every day [6]. With state-of-the-art 8 TB disks, this would already account for 5.5 exabyte of capacity by day.

Management of the huge amount of data is vital for effective use of the contained information. However, with limited budgets, it is a daunting task for data center operators, especially as design and storage system required hardware depends heavily on the executed workloads. A co-factor of the increasing difficulty is the increase in complexity of the storage hierarchy with the adoption of SSD and memory class storage technology. The US Department of Energy recognizes the importance of data management, listing it among the top 10 research challenges for Exascale [5].

There are several initiatives, consortia and special tracks in conferences that target RD&E audiences. Examples are the Storage Networking Industry Association (SNIA) for enterprises, the Big Data and Extreme-Scale Computing (BDEC) initiative[1],

---

[1] http://www.exascale.org/bdec/.

the Exascale10 workgroup [2], the Parallel Data Storage Workshop/Data Intensive Scalable Computing Systems (PDSW-DISCS) and the HEC FSIO workshop [1].

There are many I/O workloads studies and performance analysis reports for parallel I/O available. Additionally, many surveys of enterprise technology usage include predictions of analysis for future storage technology and the storage market such as [3]. However, analysis conducted for HPC typically focuses on applications and not on the data center perspective. Information about data center operational aspects is usually described in file system specific user groups and meetings or described partially in research papers as part of the evaluation environment.

In this workshop, we bring together I/O experts from data centers and application workflows to share current practices for scientific workflows, issues and obstacles for both hardware and the software stack, and R&D to overcome these issues. This year, we worked closely together with the *Workshop on Performance and Scalability of Storage Systems (WOPSSS)* in respect to the overall agenda organization and planned a joint morning session and split into two separate workshops in the afternoon.

2   Organization of the Workshop

The workshop was organized by

- Julian Kunkel, University of Reading, UK
- Jay Lofstead, Sandia National Lab, USA

The workshop is supported by the Centre of Excellence in Simulation of Weather and Climate in Europe (ESiWACE) and the Virtual Institute for I/O (VI4IO)[2].

The workshop covered three tracks:

- **Research paper presentations** – authors needed to submit a paper regarding relevant research for I/O in the datacenter.
- **Talks from I/O experts** – authors needed to submit a rough outline for the talk related to the operational aspects of the data center.
- A moderated **discussion** to identify key issues and potential solutions in the community.

The CFP has been issued beginning of January. Important deadlines were:

- Submission deadline: 2018-04-19 AoE
- Author notification: 2018-05-04
- Workshop: 2018-06-28
- Camera-ready papers: 2018-07-28

From all submissions, the program committee selected four talks from I/O experts and four research papers for presentation during the workshop.

---

[2] http://vi4io.org.

2.1 Program Committee

Adrian Jackson	The University of Edinburgh
Ann Gentile	Sandia National Laboratories
Bing Xie	Oak Ridge National Lab
Brad Settleyer	Los Alamos National Laboratory
Feiyi Wang	Oak Ridge National Lab
George Markomanolis	King Abdullah University of Science and Technology
Javier Garcia Blas	University Carlos III of Madrid
Jay Lofstead	Sandia National Lab
Jean-Thomas Acquaviva	DDN
Jim Brandt	Sandia National Laboratories
Julian Kunkel	DKRZ
Matt Bryson	University of California, Santa Cruz
Michael Kluge	TU Dresden
Rob Ross	Argonne National Laboratory
Sandro Fiore	CMCC
Suren Byna	Lawrence Berkeley National Laboratory
Sven Breuner	ThinkparQ
Thomas Boenisch	HLRS
Tiago Quintino	ECMWF
Wolfgang Frings	Jülich Supercomputing Center

3 Workshop Summary

Throughout the day, on average more than 40 participants attended the workshop. At a detailed level, we peaked at the following attendance in each of the four sessions (the first two shared with WOPSSS).

– First Session: 50
– After Morning Break: 45
– After Lunch: 30
– After Afternoon Break: 33

We had a good mix of talks from I/O experts, data center relevant research and two discussion sessions. A short summary of the presentations is given in the following. The slides of the presentations are available on the workshop's webpage: https://hps.vi4io.org/events/2018/iodc.

After a joint welcome message of HPC-IODC with WOPSSS, an invited keynote was given by Phil Carns (Argonne National Laboratory). In his talk "Understanding and Tuning HPC I/O", the OODA (Observe, Orient, Decide, and Act) loop was used to structure and illustrate challenges and tools in respect to I/O monitoring and analysis.

3.1 Research Papers

We received 10 research paper submissions, of which we accepted three papers for presentation and publication. Additionally, since analyzing and understanding I/O behavior and achieving consistent performance is still the top priority for researchers and data centers, we invited a community paper about Tools for Analyzing I/O.

The research session covered these papers:

- **I/O Interference Alleviation on Parallel File Systems Using Server-Side QoS-Based Load-Balancing** by Yuichi Tsujita, Yoshitaka Furutani, Hajime Hida, Keiji Yamamoto, Atsuya Uno, and Fumichika Sueyasu. Yuichi Tsujita gave an overview of the K computer and described the data staging methods to improve I/O performance. A slow metadata performance during the staging procedure was investigated by analyzing various statistics from the metadata server. To improve the behavior of the system, a quality-of-service using fair-share was introduced at the server and analyzed.
- **Analyzing the I/O scalability of a Particle-in-Cell parallel code** by Sandra Mendez, Nicolay Hammer, and Anupam Karmakar. In the talk, Sandra described the systems at LRZ, the PiC code for which the performance analysis study was made. The authors modeled exhibited application behavior mathematically to understand the relation between assessed performance and application activity better.
- **Cost and Performance Modeling for Earth System Data Management and Beyond** by Jakob Luettgau and Julian Kunkel. In the talk, example graph based and tabular models for communicating and visualizing system characteristics were introduced. The notion of the talk was to identify possibilities to standardize such visualizations and discuss the potential benefits.

3.2 Talks from Experts

The following talks from experts included some basic information about the site and typical application profiles but focuses on information regarding I/O tools and strategies applied to mitigate the pressing issues.

- First, Lionel Vincent introduced a strategy from Bull for **Self-Optimized Strategy for IO Accelerator Parametrization**. In this approach, the system learns to set tuning parameters that are unspecified by users. A gradient-free optimization method is used to determine the next candidate value for a parameter.
- Next, Patrick Widener talked about **Addressing data center storage diversity for high-performance computing applications using Faodel**. As data management service, it acts as a middleware between asynchronous or bulk-sychronous applications, resource manager, analysis, and data caching. The design and architecture is described together with use-cases.
- Then, Glenn Lockwood spoke about **Planning for the Future of Storage for HPC: 2020, 2025, and Beyond** for NERSC. Firstly, the current and planned infrastructure is introduced. An overall roadmap of NERSC is described discussing

issues with the current and future storage hierarchy alongside with technological trends.

- Next, Stephen Simms described a collaboration with DDN for **Lustre-On-ZFS**. After praising the benefits of ZFS a performance study is conducted. It turned out, that LDISKFS has compared to ZFS still a performance advantage in terms of the metadata operations getattr and setattr.
- Next, Simon Smart described the **Development of a high-performance distributed object-store for Numerical Weather Prediction and Climate model data**. After describing the ECMWF workflow, the MARS database is introduced that allows scientists to address data using scientific metadata from a fixed catalog. Additional insight about the usage of NVM is provided.
- Finally, Juan R. Herrera introduced approaches for **Exploiting Nonvolatile memory for HPC**. The talk illustrated the NextGenIO project which utilizing new hardware technology develops tools for analyzing I/O.

3.3 Discussion Sessions

The major distinguishing feature for this workshop compared to other venues is the discussion rounds. The opportunity for themed, open discussions about issues both pressing and relevant to the data center community facilitates sharing experiences, solutions, and problems.

In a first discussion, we focused on the possible community development of next generation semantic interfaces. Julian Kunkel provoked the community with a presentation about a possible approach that follows the successful approach of MPI which lead to a discussion how such a goal could be achieved. The community page is launched and supported by VI4IO, see https://ngi.vi4io.org. In the announced morning discussion, various topics have been briefly discussed.

In the afternoon discussion, we focused on community benchmark acceptance for newer workloads. For example, IOR and mdtest are both accepted as "good enough" to represent scale up workloads (Modeling and Simulation). For scale out workloads (e.g., data analytics), there are a variety of benchmarks, but no good exemplars that can represent a wide variety of workloads. The discussion generated the following ideas:

- Pynamic - because lots of Python is loaded on start for the analytics apps load. Lots of opens and closes for the Python packages. This is important when providing software on the storage.
- MDWorkbench - metadata latency testing tool
- LMDB - machine learning (MMAP IO)
- DASK - out of core Panda Frames (machine learning toolkits data representations)
- Graph 500
- Miraculus - Glen does not recommend
- BLAST IOR trace - pattern matching genomics
- Seven dwarves of data anaytics - mostly compute

Other thoughts brought up were:

Good idea: collect open source educational tools, but might be too specific to a site. Is there a good public available IO tutorial?

ATPESC has ANL IO tutorial materials, to a large degree.

How to run IO-500[3] when it is a shared storage array for the data center rather than just full access for a platform?

Splitting across platforms or just from a single platform?

These ideas will be incorporated into the IO-500 site as a guide for evaluating platform performance.

References

1. Bancroft, M., Bent, J., Felix, E., Grider, G., Nunez, J., Poole, S., Ross, R., Salmon, E., Ward, L.: Hec fsio 2008 workshop report. In: High End Computing Interagency Working Group (HECIWG), Sponsored File Systems and I/O Workshop HEC FSIO (2009)
2. Brinkmann, A., Cortes, T., Falter, H., Kunkel, J., Narasimhamurthy, S.: E10 – Exascale IO, June 2014
3. IDC: Enterprise storage services survey. http://www.idc.com/getdoc.jsp?containerId=254468
4. International Data Corporation. http://www.businesswire.com/news/home/20131021005243/en/IDCs-Outlook-Data-Byte-Density-Globe-Big
5. Lucas, R., Committee members: Top ten exascale research challenges, February 2014. http://science.energy.gov/~/media/ascr/ascac/pdf/meetings/20140210/Top10reportFEB14.pdf
6. Seagate: Storage Solutions Guide. http://www.seagate.com/files/www-content/product-content/_cross-product/en-us/docs/seagate-storage-and-application-guide-apac.pdf
7. StorageServers Blog: Facts and stats of world's largest data centers, July 2013. https://storageservers.wordpress.com/2013/07/17/facts-and-stats-of-worlds-largest-data-centers/

---

[3] For the IO-500 benchmark, see http://io500.org.

Analyzing the I/O Scalability of a Parallel Particle-in-Cell Code

Sandra Mendez$^{(\boxtimes)}$, Nicolay J. Hammer, and Anupam Karmakar

High Performance Systems Division, Leibniz Supercomputing Centre (LRZ) of the
Bavarian Academy of Sciences and Humanities, 85748 Garching bei München,
Germany
sandra.mendez@lrz.de

Abstract. Understanding the I/O behavior of parallel applications is
fundamental both to optimize and propose tuning strategies for improving the I/O performance. In this paper we present the outcome of an I/O
optimization project carried out for the parallel astrophysical Plasma
Physics application ACRONYM, a well-tested particle-in-cell code for
astrophysical simulations. ACRONYM is used on several different supercomputers in combination with the HDF5 library, providing the output
in form of self-describing files. To address the project, we did a characterization of the main parallel I/O sub-system operated at LRZ. Afterwards
we have applied two different strategies that improve the initial performance, providing a solution with scalable I/O. The results obtained show
that the total application time is 4.5x faster than the original version for
the best case.

1 Introduction

The Leibniz Supercomputing Centre (LRZ) operates a Top50 HPC system,
SuperMUC [1] accessible for users in Germany and Europe. SuperMUC has a
total peak performance of 6.8 Petaflops, 500 Terabyte main memory, 20 Petabyte
external data storage, and a high speed Infiniband interconnect. LRZ has a
strong focus on user support, in order to enable users to efficiently use all compute resources offered. As the installation of SuperMUC has increased LRZ's
compute capacities, users require more efforts for the parallel I/O of their applications. Therefore, we provide support for parallel I/O optimization to enable
high I/O scalability of applications that requires to analyze the application I/O
characteristics and its interaction with the I/O system. In the case of SuperMUC,
an additional complexity arises from the large diversity of scientific applications
which are actively used on the system.

The authors thank the ACRONYM developer team for their contributions and the good
teamwork. Special thanks goes to Gerald Mathias for reading the manuscript and
providing valuable feedback. Computations for this project were done on SuperMUC
at LRZ, a member of the Gauss Centre for Supercomputing (GCS).

R. Yokota et al. (Eds.): ISC 2018 Workshops, LNCS 11203, pp. 9–22, 2018.
https://doi.org/10.1007/978-3-030-02465-9_1

Since 2016 LRZ has build up structures to focus on domain specific community-oriented support and research infrastructure, to strengthen its support commitment. These so called *Application Labs* take the lead in supporting scientific communities in the following research areas: Astrophysics and Plasma Physics (AstroLab), Biology and Life Sciences (BioLab), Computational Fluid Dynamics (CFDLab) and Geosciences (GeoLab). Aside from first level support offered by the LRZ application support for technical problems with I/O implementations in scientific applications, the *Application Labs* offer project based high level support for tuning, optimization and refactoring I/O implementations for user applications.

In this paper, we present the work done during a project in the 2nd LRZ AstroLab Support Call. Its objective was to improve the I/O scalability of the astrophysical particle-in-cell Plasma Physics code ACRONYM [2], where scaling problems were observed for a larger number MPI tasks ($>10^4$, one SuperMUC's Island). It is a typical example for implementation related problems reported by SuperMUC users and how these problems can be overcome and can be seen as a blueprint for tackling and improving similar problems for other applications as well. Similar challenges were tackled in [3] using a different approach for the parallel Particle-in-Cell application VPIC.

The project consisted of three parts: (1) performance characterization of the I/O sub-system of SuperMUC with respect to I/O parameters at application user level; (2) Access pattern analysis of ACRONYM, to gain understanding of the application behavior and (3) Refactoring of ACRONYM's I/O implementation to enable data aggregation. First and second parts are the basis to explain the limitations of ACRONYM's I/O capabilities and to develop data aggregation strategies for performance improvement. We create I/O communicators for aggregation based on the application access pattern and system characterization. An own implementation for aggregation is proposed because the Two-Phase I/O technique reported poor performance in our GPFS file system and it does not support all two-phase I/O hints provided by ROMIO [4]. Tessier et al. [5] describes the limitations of two-phase I/O related with the problem of mapping aggregators in the topology and the data access pattern of the application.

The paper is organized as follows: in Sect. 2, we present a study of the I/O capabilities of the two SuperMUC GPFS file systems, Sect. 3 describes the methodology for analyzing the I/O scalability of parallel applications and Sect. 4 reviews the experimental evaluation. Finally, we present our conclusions in Sect. 5.

2   Characterization of the I/O System

In this section, we present the throughput evaluation of the SuperMUC file systems. Our aim is to evaluate the I/O performance behavior of the two file system under normal operation. We define two kinds of experiments for:

- *Throughput Evaluation as a Function of Request Sizes*: we evaluate request sizes which are `aligned/non-aligned` with file system block size (See Fig. 1). This decision is based on the experience that data sizes per MPI task in scientific applications are in most cases of arbitrary size and cannot be expressed as 2^n bytes. We use request sizes of $2^n \times 32$ kiB with $n \in (1..16)$ for `aligned` tests. For `non-aligned`, we use these (1.5 GiB, 729 MiB, 243 MiB, 81 MiB, 27 MiB, 9 MiB, 3 MiB, 1.4 MiB, 459 kiB, 153 kiB, 51 kiB, 17 kiB) request sizes.

– *Throughput Evaluation as a Function of the Number of Nodes*: we evaluate I/O aggregation using 32 to 2048 compute nodes for three request sizes: (a) 6.8 MiB, a request sizes slightly below the file system block size; (b) 13.6 MiB, a request sizes slightly above the file system block size and (c) 2 GiB, as maximum request size since the MPI I/O implementation based on 4 byte integers.

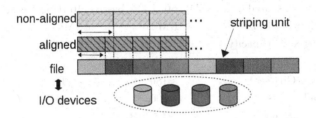

Fig. 1. Representation of request sizes `aligned`/`non-aligned` with the file system block size

Table 1 shows the compute system and I/O system description used for the experiments. Each measurement was rerun three times. We used an own benchmark based on MPI-I/O, in which every MPI task writes/reads its data consecutively in one block. The I/O tests was implemented in FORTRAN using MPI (IBM Parallel Environment 1.4.04). This benchmark has a long usage history on our system, which makes it easy to analyze the measured results. In several comparison tests our benchmark delivered consistent results with Livermore's IOR (see https://github.com/hpc/ior).

2.1   Throughput Evaluation as a Function of Request Sizes

In Fig. 2 we present the MPI-I/O throughput for the two available parallel filesystems of SuperMUC as a function of the request size. The measurements was done during user operation of SuperMUC, which may result in a "noisy" measurement due to I/O of other applications.

As can be observed, a general trend is the strong continuous increase of the throughput with growing request size. This is expected, since every I/O systems has a maximum number of IOPS, which naturally leads to smaller throughput at small request sizes and a higher throughput at larger request sizes.

Table 1. SuperMUC supercomputer

Compute system	Description	
Number of nodes	9216	
Nodes per Island	512	
Sockets per node	2	
Cores per node	16	
Memory per node (GByte)	32 (Usable 26)	
Communication network	FDR10 IB	
Intra-Island topology	Non-blocking tree	
Inter-Island topology	Pruned tree 4:1	
I/O system	WORK	SCRATCH
Parallel filesystem	IBM spectrum scale	
Network shared disk (NSD)	80 (DDN based)	16 (GSS based)
Stripe/block size	8 MiB	8 MiB
Filesystem capacity	12 PiB	5.2 PiB
Max. I/O performance		
Write(GiB/sec)	≈180	≈130
Read(GiB/sec)	≈200	≈150
Compute node	≈4.5 GiB/sec	

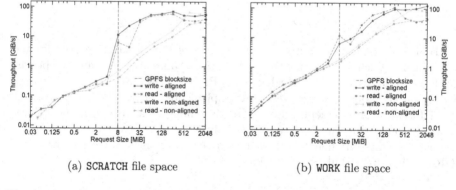

(a) SCRATCH file space   (b) WORK file space

Fig. 2. Throughput of our MPI-I/O benchmark as a function of request size. The job was executed on 512 compute nodes of the SuperMUC sandy bridge system with 1 MPI task per node. There are two cases shown, one (blue/red) for **aligned** requests and a second one (yellow/green) for **non-aligned**. Each point is the average of 3 independent measurements (Color figure online).

Discussion. For analyzing results, we sub-divided the graph in three regions, which mark different characteristics of the I/O sub-systems. We refer to the first region at the left end with limit in 4 MiB, as region of **small scale I/O**. Here the request sizes are smaller than the GPFS blocksize. To the third region at the right end, we refer as region of `large scale I/O` with request sizes larger than 512 MiB. To the second region located in between, we refer as `intermediate` region.

In the `large scale I/O` region, the throughput is given by the design specifications of the I/O sub-systems. Compared to that, in `small scale I/O` region the throughput is significantly smaller, because the filesystem was tuned for large throughput using large files and therefore a large blocksize is required and the IOPS limits of the I/O sub-system. In this region the `WORK` throughput is clearly higher than on the `SCRATCH`. The difference in throughput directly below the blocksize (8 MiB) is approximately a factor of 5 (`WORK` compared to `SCRATCH`). We associate this behavior with the larger number of NSD servers and the larger number of controller machines available on the I/O sub-system of `WORK`, compared to the `SCRATCH`. We therefore conclude that codes making I/O in that region, should rather use the `WORK` filesystem.

In the `intermediate` region, the throughput is strongly dependent on alignment with filesystem blocksize. If the data size can be expressed as an integer multiple of the blocksize, the throughput is high and, with increasing request size, it approaches the system maximum quite fast. If not, the throughput is significantly lower and straightly connects the `small` and `large` scale I/O regions. Only for request sizes in the order of GiB the throughput is on the same level for both cases. On both filesystems a dip in the read throughput curve at 16 MiB request size is visible which is connected to caching effects. However, currently we do not understand the root cause of this behavior.

2.2 Throughput Evaluation as a Function of the Number of Nodes

Fig. 3 shows the measured throughput as a function of the utilized number of nodes. The three measurements corresponds to request sizes slightly below and

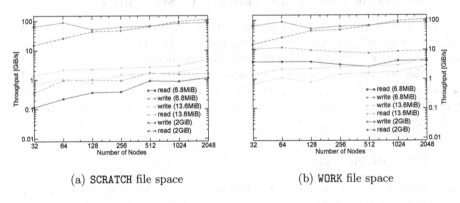

(a) SCRATCH file space   (b) WORK file space

Fig. 3. Throughput of our MPI-I/O benchmark on SuperMUC as a function of the number of I/O nodes (i.e. number of compute nodes). The benchmark was executed on SuperMUC Sandybridge system partion with 2 MPI task per node. The plot shows the write and read performance for a request size of 6.8 MiB (blue/red), 13.6 MiB (green/yellow) and 2 GiB (purple/brown) per task, respectively. Each point is the average of 3 independent measurements (Color figure online).

above the GPFS block size and a maximum request size. The general trend of all three measurements is a moderate increase of the throughput with increasing number of nodes (moderate compared to the increase of throughput with request size).

Discussion. The system behaviour observed explains quantitatively why aggregation is useful under certain conditions to improve the I/O performance of HPC applications. As can be seen in Figs. 2 and 3, the throughput improves strongly increases with request size in the region below and around the block size of the SuperMUC filesystems. At the same time the throughput does not strongly decrease with decreasing number of I/O nodes being used. This is true as long as the used number of nodes is large enough, i.e. greater/equal 256 nodes. An example to illustrate it is provided by the write values from Figs. 2 and 3(b). To make a conservative estimation, we take the read/write performance for a request size not matching a 2^n value, because the data size per MPI task in a lot of applications is defined by a dynamic domain decomposition scheme and it does not correspond to 2^n bytes.

In Fig. 2(b) it can be seen that the throughput increases by roughly a factor of 20 when scaling from a request size near 2 MiB to near 64 MiB. If the number of I/O nodes is down-scaled by a factor of 32, e.g. from 1024 nodes to 64 nodes, the I/O performance drops only by roughly a factor of 2 to 3 as seen in Fig. 3(b), so we "gain" a factor of 8. This example is not precise in it's numbers, but rather demonstrates the basic principles behind I/O aggregation. Moreover, one must take into account that the aggregation traffic imposes additional overhead to the communication costs of the application. However, due to the rather large gain factors (in our example approximately 8×) the I/O aggregation is still beneficial.

3 Analyzing the Application's I/O Scalability

In Sect. 2, we have presented a system I/O characterization for different I/O request sizes and compute nodes in a normal operation of the SuperMUC. This shows to users an initial idea about the I/O performance behavior.

In this section, we describe the proposed methodology to analyze the I/O scalability of parallel applications that is composed by three steps : (1) I/O Pattern Analysis, (2) Evaluation of the weight of I/O operations; and (3) Evaluation of I/O Strategies.

3.1 I/O Pattern Analysis

We perform two steps to analyze the I/O pattern with focus on the scalability:

1. Extracting temporal/spatial patterns to identify the dominant I/O phases.
2. Identifying the relation between application parameters and I/O phases.

ACRONYM made use of parallel HDF5 library to regularly write three-dimensional field datasets using collective operations with all processes participating. The ACRONYM users reported slow performance when using more than 10k MPI processes on SuperMUC. Initial tests revealed runtimes increasing superlinearly with the number of MPI ranks suggesting a growing communication overhead. Moreover, the data volume written by each process was small, exacerbating the problem. To understand the I/O pattern that produce that behavior, we evaluated the ACRONYM's I/O kernel, named IOSTEST, by using different number of MPI processes to extract the main properties of the I/O operations to analyze the scalability behavior. ACRONYM was evaluated by using a global simulation size $(52, 52, 66560)$ that means 52 cells along the x and y-direction and 66560 cells along the z-direction; 10 simulation steps and 6 fields.

Extracting Temporal/Spatial Patterns to Identify the Dominant I/O Phases. To extract the I/O pattern we use PIOM-MP (former knows as PAS2P-IO [6,7]) a tool that isolates the influence of the underlying I/O system allowing it to obtain the patterns in I/O phases and focus on the I/O routines. PIOM-MP depicts the global I/O pattern of a parallel application in two dimensions: the spatial and temporal patterns. The temporal pattern represents the order which the I/O operations are performed by the MPI processes and the spatial pattern represents the file logical view for each MPI process. Furthermore, a third dimension is added to show the weight of the I/O operations.

In Fig. 4 it is depicted the global I/O pattern by using 320 (small case) and 5120 (medium case) MPI processes. We can observe the same pattern in both cases, where the red point represent the I/O operations with bigger requests. The 3D picture depicts in the x-axis the process rank, in the y-axis the ticks that corresponds to the communication and I/O events of MPI, and in z-axis the file offset for each process in each tick. A heat map depicts the request size of each I/O operation in the 3D picture. Read operations in blue corresponds to small requests less than 512 Bytes that are independent on the application parameters. Write operations are in red and their request size is variable depending on the number of processes. As can be seen in Fig. 4, there are ten phases of writing operations, in which red points correspond to larger requests.

Additional read and view operations are done at MPI level, because ACRONYM uses parallel HDF5 that is built on top of MPI. Count of read operations is mainly related to the metadata operations of a HDF5 file. Additionally, the following metadata complements the pattern provided in Fig. 4: (a) Access type is shared that means that a file is accessed by all writer processes. The number of writer processes is equal to the number of compute nodes; (b) Access mode is strided that means each writer process accesses to non-contiguous positions of the file; (c) Read operations are independent, blocking and use explicit offset; (d) Write operations with more data to move are collective, blocking and use explicit offset; (e) Two view operations are called when a field is written to the file.

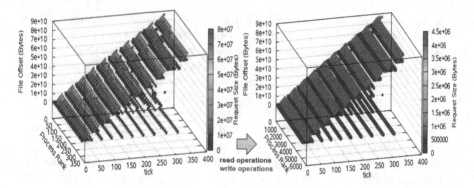

Fig. 4. Global I/O pattern of the Acronym's IOTEST at MPI-IO level using 320 (left) and 5120 (right) MPI processes. Write and read operations are represented in a 3D picture. x-axis corresponds to the MPI rank, y-axis represents calls to MPI-IO operations and z-axis represents the offset in the file for each MPI process. A heat map depicts the request size of each I/O operation. Read operations are represented in blue and write in red. Plots obtained with PIOM-MP [6,7] (Color figure online)

Identifying the Relation Between Application Parameters and I/O Phases. Focusing on a simulation step, we analyze its call tree that is shown in Table 2. Using the information of the global pattern and call tree we identify and define relation between the parameters of the application and the I/O pattern properties.

Table 2. Call tree for a simulation step

Order	MPI-I/O operation	Data access aspect
1	MPI_File_open	
2	Once only by rank 0	
	MPI_File_get_size	
3	From seven to twelve times	
	MPI_File_read_at	Blocking, noncollective, explicit offset
4	Six times (once for each field)	
	MPI_File_set_view	
	MPI_File_write_at_all	Blocking, collective, explicit offset
	MPI_File_set_view	
	MPI_File_read_at	Blocking, noncollective, explicit offset
5	Only for the first seven I/O ranks	
	MPI_File_write_at	Blocking, noncollective, explicit offset
6	MPI_File_set_size	
7	MPI_File_close	

The application parameters are shown in Table 3. As can be observed the request size (rs) depends on local simulation size that is based on the number of MPI processes (np). File size increases as writer processes (wp), rs, simulation steps (st) and fields (fi) increase. Each simulation step that corresponds with an I/O phase moves D_{st} bytes, which means that if we have a writer process per compute node, each compute node will write to the file system $rs \times fi$ bytes.

Table 3. I/O parameters of ACRONYM's I/O kernel.

I/O parameter	Values
Global simulation size	(x, y, z)
Local simulation size	$(x\_loc = x, y\_loc = y, z\_loc = \frac{z}{np})$
Compute nodes	cn
Simulation step	st
Fields	fi
Writer processes	$wp = cn$
Data size (bytes)	ds
RequestSize(bytes)	$rs = x\_loc \times y\_loc \times z\_loc \times ds$
FileSize(bytes)	$fz = cn \times rs \times st \times fi$
Data per st (Bytes)	$D_{st} = cn \times rs \times fi$
Data per 1 cn per st (Bytes)	$D_{cnxst} = rs \times fi$

In Table 4 we define the number of I/O operations based on the parameters that is performed to determine the scalability capacity of the I/O kernel. Request size corresponds to `write_at_all` operations, because they compose the I/O phase with more weight. Count of read operations is dependent upon the st, wp and fi. Furthermore, the rs of read operations is not dependent upon the parameters of the simulation and it is less than 512 Bytes.

The parameters and formula defined in Table 3 are applied to experimental design in Sect. 3.2 to evaluate I/O time impact on SuperMUC.

3.2 Evaluation of the Weight of I/O Operations

A strong scaling test is performed where the global simulation size stays fixed as the number of compute nodes grows. In this case, the request size is decreased and the count of I/O operations increases as the number of compute nodes increases. The used parameters were provided by the ACRONYM developers: the global simulation size in cells, with 52 cells along the x- and y-direction and 66560 cells along the z-direction $(52, 52, 66560)$; 10 simulation steps (st) and 6 fields (fi). The size of data (ds) is 128 Bytes. By using these values we determine the rs and D_{cnxst} (Data per compute node per simulation step). Table 5 presents the values for the experiments, which were calculated with the formulae shown in Table 3.

Table 4. Count of the MPI-IO operations for np processes and $cn = np/16$ based on ACRONYM's I/O parameters.

I/O operation	Count
MPI_File_open	$st \times cn$
MPI_File_write_at_all	$st \times fi \times cn$
MPI_File_write_at	$(fi + 1) \times st$
MPI_File_set_view	$st \times fi \times cn \times 2$
MPI_File_read_at	$2 \times fi \times st \times cn + 23 \times cn$
MPI_File_get_size	st
MPI_File_set_size	$st \times cn$
MPI_File_close	$st \times cn$

Table 5. ACRONYM IOTEST parameters. Global simulation size is (52,52,66560), File size = 82 GiB, 16 processes per compute node, 8.05 GiB per simulation step with a writer process per compute node.

Compute node (cn) or writer processes	Number of processes (np)	Local simulation size	Request size rs (MiB)	Data per 1 cn per st D_{cnxst} (MiB)
1	16	(52,52,4160)	1373.13	8238.75
5	80	(52,52,832)	274.63	1647.75
10	160	(52,52,416)	137.31	823.88
20	320	(52,52,208)	68.66	411.94
40	640	(52,52,104)	34.33	205.97
80	1280	(52,52,52)	17.16	102.98
160	2560	(52,52,26)	8.58	51.49
320	5120	(52,52,13)	4.29	25.75

To evaluate the I/O time for the different I/O operations of the call tree we use Darshan. Darshan [8] is a profiling tool for characterizing I/O workloads on the petascale systems.

Figure 5 shows the I/O time and the count of I/O operations per type of operation at MPI-IO level. In Fig. 5(a), the count of I/O operations is shown in a stacked histogram. It can be observed as write_at_all operations (green), read_at operations (cyan) and set_view operations (magenta) increase as the number of compute node grows. The percentage of operations is mainly represented by write_at_all with 17%, read_at with 40% and set_view with 34%. Although, count of write_at_all operations is less than read_at, the data transferred in write phases is more than 99% of the data transferred during the execution of the IOTEST.

The I/O operation time is shown in Fig. 5(b). write_at_all operations are representing more than 80% of the run time from 20 compute nodes. Despite read_at is representing 40% of the count of I/O operations in Fig. 5(a), this has less impact on the execution time, although its influence increases from 80 compute nodes. In the case of set_view (time included in the META time), that represent 34% in Fig. 5(a), it does not significantly increase running time.

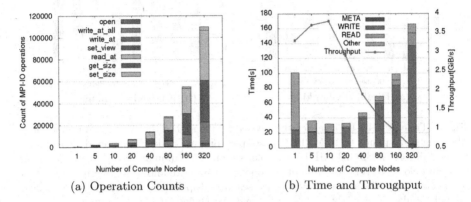

(a) Operation Counts   (b) Time and Throughput

Fig. 5. Time and count of operations at MPI-IO level for the I/O kernel of the ACRONYM application. Mapping corresponds to 16 MPI processes per compute node. Access mode is a shared file and file size is 82 GiB. META time corresponds to cumulative time spent in open, view and close. WRITE is cumulative time spent in write and sync. Global simulation size is x = 52, y = 52 and z = 66,560) (Color figure online)

These results show that ACRONYM is not scaling because the number of operations grows and the request size decreases, that means more I/O requests for the file system. Additionally, if the number of writer processes grows then the degree of I/O concurrency increases by generating more load for the file system. Experimental results achieve a transfer rate between 500 MiB/sec and 3.8 GiB/sec, the best result is using an I/O rank per 10 compute nodes where the request size is 137 MiB and the worst corresponds to 360 compute nodes with a request size of 4 MiB. These results affect the performance and it can be observed on the execution time. Using the parameters and formula defined in Table 3 it is possible to select the number of writer processes taking into account the global simulation size to have an appropriate request size to scale.

3.3   Evaluation of I/O Strategies

The original aggregation strategy implemented by ACRONYM developers created a new I/O communicator per compute node based on colors and keys to select the writer processes. Colors and keys are calculated by using the identifiers of island, rack and node where each MPI rank is running. This strategy allows to have an I/O communicator considering closeness of the MPI ranks. We have to mention that in SuperMUC by default the number of I/O aggregators is 1 per compute node when collective operations are used. Therefore the user could

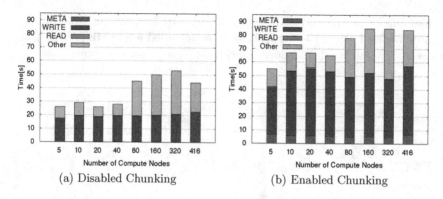

Fig. 6. Time at MPI-IO level for the revised I/O kernel of the ACRONYM application. Mapping corresponds to 16 MPI processes per compute node. Access mode is a shared file and file size is 82 GiB. META time corresponds to cumulative time spent in open, view and close. WRITE is cumulative time spent in write and sync. 5 writer processes for 5 compute nodes and 10 writer processes are setup for the rest of the experiments. Global simulation size is x = 52, y = 52 and z = 66,560) (Color figure online)

have used that strategy and not implement an own solution. However, we have observed the collective buffering report poor performance in SuperMUC.

Using the pattern analysis done we revised the original aggregation strategy removing unnecessary open calls and two aggregation strategies are implemented: (i) a small number of computational ranks also act as designated writer processes. These aggregate data from neighboring processes in simulated 3D space via MPI communication and the data is rearranged in memory; (ii) Enable HDF5 chunking based on a manual size selection or on an automatic selection where chunk size is equal to the output block size of writer processes. In both approaches, the data is subsequently written to disk, fewer processes are participating and larger blocks are sent to the filesystem. Moreover, the scheme is setup such that the number of writer along each dimension is configurable via simulation parameters.

Results for the first strategy is shown in Fig. 6(a). In this case the number of writer processes stays fixed to 10, except for 5 compute nodes where the writer processes are five. We can observe that the I/O time does not increase as increase the number of compute nodes which reduces the total execution time. Figure 6(b) shows execution time for the modified version with chunking strategy enabled and the same number of writers to Fig. 6(a). Chunking produces a fixed overhead for metadata and the I/O time does not grow as in original version.

By comparing the two strategies, we can observe better results for the first where the user can select the number of writers. This number of writers was selected considering the request sizes presented in Table 5 where the request sizes by using 5 and 10 writers obtain more performance in Fig. 2(b). In this case, we have selected the option with more writers because this value does not impact on the total time and provides a higher I/O parallelism degree.

4   Experimental Evaluation

In this section, we present the result of applying the modified I/O strategy on the ACRONYM for a weak scaling case. In order to avoid the overhead of thousands of processes accessing a single file, a small number of designated writer processes is chosen at the beginning of a simulation run. Through a setting in the configuration file, the number of MPI ranks taking part in the field output operation is selected. Communication occurs only between the computational nodes and their designated writer process as well as among the small number of writer processes.

Figure 7 shows the results of ACRONYM, the black continuous line represents the ideal scaling, the red line represent the time without I/O. The blue line represent the original strategy. We can clearly see the improvements with stronger aggregation factors, i.e. larger number of nodes sharing one writer process in yellow line with inverted-triangle. Results showed total time 4.5x faster than the original version for the best case.

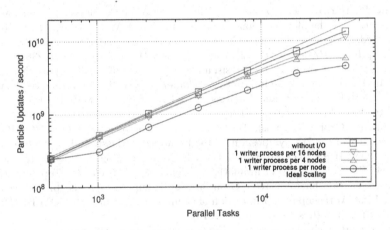

Fig. 7. Weak scaling of the ACRONYM PiC-Code with and without I/O by using the optimized I/O implementation (plot provided by ACRONYM developer team)

5   Conclusions

We have presented an analysis of the I/O scalability of ACRONYM parallel code and have shown promising results by using an I/O aggregation strategy taking into account the system topology of SuperMUC (i.e. island and node configuration of the system). We have defined the request size considering the simulation parameters and the I/O pattern that allows us to select an appropriate number of writer processes in the experimental design time.

We did a characterization of the I/O system and used the results to explain the behavior of the original I/O implementation of ACRONYM. Furthermore, we discussed a suitable range of aggregation factor for the implemented I/O aggregation scheme based on the characterization results. Moreover, the presented I/O characterization can provide guidelines for other users of SuperMUC encountering problems with I/O scalability.

Initial scaling tests of ACRONYM showed a sub-linear scaling with the number of MPI ranks suggesting a significantly growing communication overhead. Moreover, the data volume written by each MPI task was small by increasing the count of I/O operations, exacerbating the problem. This brought a complete redesign of the I/O routines into play. In latest code version, a small number of computational ranks act as designated I/O agents. This newly implemented method provides much better scaling even for simulations up to 32k cores by showing a total time 4.5x faster than the original version.

References

1. SuperMUC: Leibniz supercomputing centre (LRZ). Technical report, Bayerischen Akademie der Wissenschaften (2014)
2. Kilian, P., Burkart, T., Spanier, F.: The influence of the mass ratio on particle acceleration by the filamentation instability. In: Nagel, W.E., Kröner, D.B., Resch, M.M. (eds.) High Performance Computing in Science and Engineering 2011, pp. 5–13. Springer, Heidelberg (2012). https://doi.org/10.1007/978-3-642-23869-7_1
3. Byna, S., et al.: Parallel I/O, analysis, and visualization of a trillion particle simulation. In: Proceedings of the International Conference on High Performance Computing, Networking, Storage and Analysis SC 2012, vol. 59, pp. 1–12. IEEE Computer Society Press, Los Alamitos (2012)
4. Thakur, R., Gropp, W., Lusk, E.: Data sieving and collective I/O in ROMIO. In: Proceedings of the 7th Symposium on the Frontiers of Massively Parallel Computation FRONTIERS 1999, pp. 182–189. IEEE Computer Society, Washington (1999)
5. Tessier, F., Malakar, P., Vishwanath, V., Jeannot, E., Isaila, F.: Topology-aware data aggregation for intensive I/O on large-scale supercomputers. In: Proceedings of the First Workshop on Optimization of Communication in HPC COM-HPC 2016, pp. 73–81. IEEE Press, Piscataway (2016)
6. Mendez, S., Rexachs, D., Luque, E.: Modeling parallel scientific applications through their input/output phases. In: 2012 IEEE International Conference on Cluster Computing Workshops (CLUSTER WORKSHOPS), pp. 7–15, September 2012
7. Mendez, S., Panadero, J., Wong, A., Rexachs, D., Luque, E.: A new approach for analyzing I/O in parallel scientific applications. In: CACIC 2012, Congreso Argentino de Ciencias de la Computación, pp. 337–346 (2012)
8. Carns, P., et al.: Understanding and improving computational science storage access through continuous characterization. Trans. Storage 7(3), 8:1–8:26 (2011)

Cost and Performance Modeling for Earth System Data Management and Beyond

Jakob Lüttgau[1]([⊠]) and Julian Kunkel[1,2]

[1] Deutsches Klimarechenzentrum, 20146 Hamburg, Germany
{luettgau,kunkel}@dkrz.de
[2] University of Reading, Reading, UK

Abstract. Current and anticipated storage environments confront domain scientist and data center operators with usability, performance and cost challenges. The amount of data upcoming system will be required to handle is expected to grow exponentially, mainly due to increasing resolution and affordable compute power. Unfortunately, the relationship between cost and performance is not always well understood requiring considerable effort for educated procurement. Within the Centre of Excellence in Simulation of Weather and Climate in Europe (ESiWACE) models to better understand cost and performance of current and future systems are being explored. This paper presents models and methodology focusing on, but not limited to, data centers used in the context of climate and numerical weather prediction. The paper concludes with a case study of alternative deployment strategies and outlines the challenges anticipating their impact on cost and performance. By publishing these early results, we would like to make the case to work towards standard models and methodologies collaboratively as a community to create sufficient incentives for vendors to provide specifications in formats which are compatible to these modeling tools. In addition to that, we see application for such formalized models and information in I/O related middleware, which are expected to make automated but reasonable decisions in increasingly heterogeneous data centers.

Keywords: Storage · Data management · Earth systems · TCO · Cost

1 Introduction

As scientists are adapting their codes to take advantage of the next-generation exascale systems, the I/O bottleneck is becoming a major challenge [6,10,15] because storage systems struggle to absorb data at the same pace as it is generated. Large scale earth system simulations and workflows, as used in numerical weather prediction (NWP) and climate modeling, are especially I/O intensive. It is anticipated, that a growing proportion of the total budget for a supercomputer will be dedicated to storage systems. This raises the need to better understand the trade-offs associated with different technologies in short-, mid- and long-term perspectives. Technologies and applications are constantly influencing the research and development focus in one another.

© Springer Nature Switzerland AG 2018
R. Yokota et al. (Eds.): ISC 2018 Workshops, LNCS 11203, pp. 23–35, 2018.
https://doi.org/10.1007/978-3-030-02465-9_2

1.1   Data Growth and Access Requirements

From a scientific perspective, multiple factors contribute to increasing data volumes and velocities, soon requiring systems which are able to routinely handle exabytes of data. On the one hand Moore's Law and distributed computing allow generating more data in total, for example, by using higher resolution models or increasing the number of members in ensemble simulations. On the other hand sensors and data loggers have become more affordable so that more observational data is being gathered. This also shows in an increasing number of active satellites used for remote sensing which also feature higher resolutions and more instruments. Besides these two obvious trends, data sets are expected to be used interdisciplinary on a more regular basis, so that additional users coming from other scientific domains will be requesting data [7]. Simulations will need to read and write more data when being coupled to use and produce the data products from and for other sciences. As a result estimates for global and local archive capacity requirements are rising [16]. For example, the Climate Model Intercomparison Projects (CMIP) required a total of 35TB to store all CMIP3 data, while CMIP5 already required 3108TB. CMIP6 and CMIP7 are expected to experience comparable increases to capacity requirements now in the exabytes.

1.2   Existing and Emerging Technologies

From a systems perspective, it is sometimes hard to make predictions due to the impact of economic factors, technological breakthroughs or natural disasters which have shown profound impact in the past [8]. None the less, it is necessary to factor in these trends into the choice of architecture and the design of cost effective data centers in the future.

As vendors are growing their production capacities, NAND-based storage technologies are expected to become affordable enough to be feasible as an alternative to disk, despite its limited write endurance. Unfortunately, NAND-based memory's areal capacity for single-level cells can not be further improved, which drives the development of multi-level cells, 3D NAND and high-bandwidth memory – but those, while providing high throughput come with latency penalties for small random I/O. Finally, non-volatile memory technologies for burst buffers and network-attached memory (NAM) are being researched for integration into the next-generation of supercomputers [5].

As of 2018, the vast amount of online storage is provisioned using high performance, but expensive disks based storage systems. Object storage, instead of parallel file-systems, promises to offer a cost-effective alternative. Unfortunately, there is also a disconnect between how business and industry v. NWP and climate applications are using compute infrastructure, limiting direct benefit of commoditization for many HPC applications. Assuming more heterogeneous data centers, next-generation storage systems are likely requiring software stacks that play well with a variety of different interfaces to exploit storage technologies with new semantics.

Long-term archives and cold storage are typically realized using large automated tape library systems. The European Centre for Medium-Range Weather Forecasts (ECMWF) and the German Climate Computing Center (DKRZ) are among the institutions with the largest scientific archives world wide [9].

For NWP and climate users, upcoming infrastructure might be effected mainly by the following two modes of operation. Compute sites may specialize such that one site will focus on providing the required infrastructure to accommodate simulations, while another site might focus on infrastructure which is optimized for analysis tasks. A second model is collocation, where multiple services are consolidated into an external data center and potentially cloud providers. Both approaches can be observed within the climate and NWP communities and each approach comes with a number of benefits and drawbacks.

1.3 Addressing Domain Scientists and Their Workflows

Specialized centers may benefit from simplifications and assumptions that can be made about the user base and their workloads. For example, it is possible to relax security considerations when no personal data needs to be handled, which in turn can provide performance advantages. Specialized data centers in climate and NWP are operated by DKRZ, ECMWF, UK Met and others. Multipurpose data centers on the other hand benefit from economies of scale and they can make use of workload sharing, though in practice this is often not possible because applications are not yet designed with this in mind. But cloud environments already make extensive use of workload sharing. Fortunately, operating a larger system usually does no require a proportional increase in staff. Future solutions will need to fit current workflows for at least a intermediate period, while adding a number of advanced features for adoption by application developers.

More tools for automation will be required to operate even larger systems because component failures are expected to be more common in exascale systems. But also to perform common optimization transparently or automatically. This might allow to reduce staff on the one hand, but also frees up experts to focus on non-routine problems. Automation is also a prerequisite to realize data handling policies and service level agreements at scale. Which, in turn, enables resource sharing and allows prioritizing critical or rewarding well behaving applications. Finally, storage systems need to be more customizeable, on the one hand to support user specific workflows and automation which are not provided by default by the storage systems, but also to work well in heterogeneous architectures.

The remainder of this paper is structured as follows. Related work is presented in Sect. 2. Section 3 introduces a hierarchical modeling approach. Section 4 discusses the coarse model in detail and how it can also be used to model resilience and performance. In Sect. 5 considerations for the most important parameters of compute and I/O nodes are discussed. Section 6 analyses cost for the current DKRZ system and the impact of alternative deployment strategies for relatively new or merely anticipated technologies. Section 7 briefly explains how I/O middleware in the future may exploit cost models to improve performance or to reduce cost. The results of the paper are summarized in Sect. 8.

2 Related Work

Related work can be grouped into approaches analyzing and modeling system characteristics and storage systems on the one hand, and standardization on the other. Multiple approaches model HPC systems by implementing discrete event simulation (DES) of queuing systems, as this allows for more complex models and time dependency. Modeling of computer systems has a long history [18]. In the last decade, the analysis of supercomputers and storage gained attention. In the CODES Project, multiple use cases for storage have been implemented [14], which are using a simulation framework the Rensselaer's Optimistic Simulation System (ROSS) [4]. A similar effort is the Structural Simulation Toolkit (SST) [2]. These efforts are mostly focused on finding new architectures to cope with exascale workloads and do not consider initial and operation cost specifically. In Sect. 4 we also look at compatibility to a fine grained approach [13] which uses DES to determine cost and quality of service for hierarchical storage system including tape system in data centers. For the purpose of standardization and communication with users these models can be too fine-grained.

Modeling individual storage systems covers various characteristics like energy consumption, resilience, and performance. Llopis et al. [17] explored empiric means to determine power consumption for individual components with a focus on power consumption within the storage and I/O data paths. Various studies model resilience based on the distribution of data across storage devices and strategy; for example, in [21], resilience depending on RAID levels is investigated and visualized in 2D heatmaps depending on error rates of memory and storage. In [19], a formal method of investigating resilience depending on data replication strategy and hardware is described and explored on several use cases.

The topology of storage systems and their characteristics is documented by most data centers and experts. While they can typically be understood by experts and serve the purpose of communication, the representations vary significantly in terms of abstraction, detail and style. An attempt to document the I/O path in a more standardized fashion has been made in [12]. A recent approach to collect the topology of data centers and their hardware characteristics is the Data Center List on the Virtual Institute for I/O[1]. It provides a template for different hardware components that can be filled. While this could standardize the descriptive nature of HPC systems, it does not allow to derive conclusions.

There have been various attempts to use and extend UML diagrams for performance prediction, mostly for use in computer aided software engineering. For example, UML activity diagrams are candidates to apply analysis techniques from PetriNets [20] and an assessment of parallel programs is described in [3]. The analysis of system performance is not covered as it depends on the use case.

Performance of parallel file systems have been subject to modeling, and for most file systems at least one attempt has been made. Examples are models for PVFS2 [1] and Lustre [22]. Both use a graphical representation and are based on

---

[1] https://www.vi4io.org.

various system parameters as well as file system-specific configurable parameters like stripe size.

The work in this paper aims to provide abstractions that ease communication between experts and deriving conclusions while relying on a hardware model independent of the storage system and its tunable parameters. As such, the approach outlined in this paper aims to provide a performance estimate that is easy to understand by non-experts.

3   Cost Modeling

With all of the challenges and trends outlined in Sects. 1 and 2 it is apparent that there is a demand for better tools to conduct cost modeling of storage infrastructure in data centers. A common challenge to cost modeling is, that it is often only possible to make assumptions and best estimates. This may be due to changing release road-maps of vendors, due to unreliable technological breakthroughs but also because workloads might differ on a new systems as bottlenecks or user behavior are changing. Unfortunately, highly granular models quickly become not only overwhelmingly complex to maintain but also get prohibitively expensive to compute. Yet, for novel architectures it is not possible to turn to empiric data which would allow to simply measure the emerging behavior of a complex system. As it is not easy to find a balance here, a hierarchical approach is proposed. Starting from a coarse grained model, individual sub-components can use more detailed models where further insight is needed.

The coarse grained model would be covering relevant components and related metrics for a data center as well as an abstract workload description and optimization strategies related to system technology and workload organization. The goal of the model is to provide a heuristics to quickly determine promising combinations of data centre layouts and their associated costs. It is not our aim to provide a cent-accurate model. This level of the model ignores temporal and spatial factors of the workload runtime behavior.

For additional insight, parts of a coarse grained model can be refined with more detailed models. For example, by mimicking workload execution using DES and workload traces in combination with the actual data center topology, taking temporal behavior into account (see Sect. 2 and [13]). This way one can narrow down on uncertain areas in the general model. Typically, one might implement a fine grained model for promising coarse grained model or for an existing system to get further insight for optimization.

Ideally, using these models it should be possible to provide a workload mix, e.g., the behavior of multiple typical user and estimate the inherent costs, performance and required fault tolerance. While this paper focuses on data center cost, performance and cost considerations are intimately related to each other. It allows to explore different data center designs in respect to storage given a fixed budget or required features for hardware and software.

4   Coarse Grained Model

This section introduces the coarse grained modeling considerations in more detail. In the coarse grained model a graph of components is assumed which models also how components relate to each other. The graph of components is the foundation to compute different emerging properties. Graphs for an abstract case and a cost example are shown in Fig. 1. Component 1 and 2 have dependencies to a root component, and the Subcomponent to Component 1. Edges and components can hold key value pairs which describe the characteristics and which also allows to add custom annotations. The cost example features cost information for the major components and also includes specification details such as performance or annual power consumption. This approach is flexible to model system characteristics beyond cost such as resilience and performance.

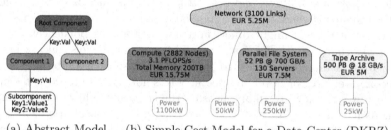

(a) Abstract Model   (b) Simple Cost Model for a Data Center (DKRZ)

Fig. 1. Example for relationships and characteristics for system components.

4.1   Resilience Model

To model resilience, components need to feature failure metrics, for example, derived using empirical methods. Error propagation of failures follows a directed graph. This also allows to account for cascades as well as mitigation measures.

A simple example to model resilience is shown in Fig. 2. A failing data center power supply may result in subsequent switch failures, but selected subsystems may be kept operational for 20 min due to the presence of an uninterrupted power supply (UPS). Mitigation strategies usually depend on redundancy, for example, replication of data usually adds costs but may either reduce or improve performance as can be the case for RAID systems. Besides topological relationships, annotations allow to associate components with common error measures such as mean-time between failures (MTBF), or mean-time to recovery (MTTR). To allow calculating reliability metrics of parent components, error metrics for sub-components should be independent. Mitigation strategies can become rather complex, and it is not always obvious if a architecture decisions mainly serves as a resilience or a performance feature. Similarly, an uninterrupted power supply might be deployed to ensure high availability, but could also only serve to shutdown a system into a consistent state.

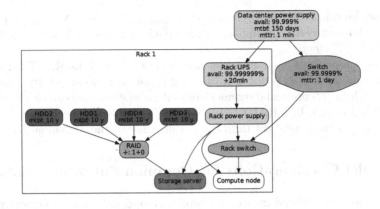

Fig. 2. Component dependency graph to model resilience.

4.2 Performance Model

The performance model also uses a graph based description, again using annotation for relevant components featuring throughput and latencies. Using the hardware graph it is easy to determine theoretic peak performance for individual components. But also in more complex scenarios, it is possible to gauge the performance that can be obtained from using components in parallel.

Figure 3 shows an example graph with performance metrics for compute nodes, network and storage media added. For example, it is easy to see that node to node communication can not exceed bandwidths of 10 GB/s, while the storage server will be happy to handle incoming bandwidths of up to 15 GB/s. Unlike networks, storage media require a more granular approach to account for different transfer rates for read or writes. The throughput for paths to the net-

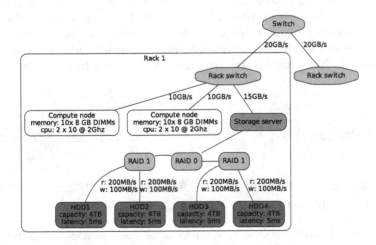

Fig. 3. Component dependency graph to model performance.

work may be simply defined by $max(edge0_{throughput}, ..., edgeN_{throughput})$. Similarly the latency is the accumulation of latencies attached edges and nodes on the path $\sum_{item}^{path} item_{latency}$.

Some components such as disks are commonly used in RAID arrays or another combination. It is not always useful to model this complexity explicitly even though the theoretical dynamics are well understood and can be abstracted as described in [12]. In a RAID 1+0 group, for example, the performance of the RAID group is more relevant than the performance of the individual HDDs.

5   Model Considerations for Common Subcomponents

As the approach outlined in Sect. 3 assumes components and sub-components, this section discusses the most important building blocks for cluster systems in more detail. In particular compute nodes Sect. 5.1 and I/O nodes Sect. 5.2 affect the cost and the performance of a system. For both a breakdown by subcomponents is provided to illustrate impact on cost and power consumption.

5.1   Compute Nodes

Compute nodes come in various configurations depending on the tasks most commonly performed. For climate simulation, nodes usually require substantial amount of compute power and memory in combination with a low latency network. Other use cases, such as visualization or increasingly big data and machine learning applications, may be less dependent on synchronous communication but make use of accelerators. Figure 4 illustrates the initial cost as well as the power consumption per sub-component. CPUs, GPUs and potentially FPGAs determine how fast data can be processed or generated. They also account for most of the power consumption of the node. If there is spare processing power, it may be invested into data reduction or more intelligent data handling. The system memory affects the problem size that can be held for quick access on the node. More main memory allows to improve storage performance by use of caching. However, memory is usually contended, for exmaple by network components that require buffers. Nodes may feature storage, which is local to the node. Usually,

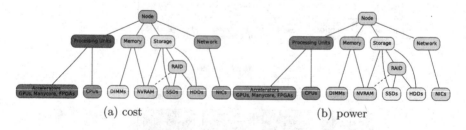

(a) cost   (b) power

Fig. 4. Cost and power footprint by component for compute nodes. A darker shade represents a larger share relative to the total node configurations.

node local storage is considered too slow for large amounts of data in comparison to PFS/Object Storage. There is potential for this to change as node local NVRAM and burst buffers become more affordable. Network interface cards of a node determine how fast nodes may communicate with each other, but also how fast data can be drained away from the compute nodes, e.g., when writing snapshots. The network also affects how quickly a compute node, which needs to load parts of datasets or shared libraries first, can start to perform useful work.

5.2 I/O Nodes

Scalable storage systems often feature different types of I/O nodes, each subsystem specialized to handle a different class of requests. Figure 5 illustrates the main contributors to initial cost as well as the power consumption in I/O nodes. In I/O nodes processors determine the number of requests that can be handled by a single node. Increasingly, GPUs may be used for data reduction and other in-transit transformations. I/O nodes typically feature considerate amounts of memory, for use as a quick cache layer, but most importantly they accommodate a large amount of disks or SSDs, with data of objects or files strided across multiple devices for fault tolerance and higher performance. In many cases, the storage devices are bundled in so called JBODs which then are connected to the I/O nodes, while an I/O node itself has no storage devices. I/O nodes in HPC systems, commonly use advanced interconnects in fail-over configurations. Depending on the application this maybe high-bandwidth for data storage or low-latency interconnects for metadata access.

Metadata Handlers and Targets: Parallel file systems provide dedicated metadata targets optimized to perform many I/O operations. Metadata servers commonly utilize different storage media than data targets. For example, they often have faster and more expensive solid state disks, and may be candidates for storage class memory (SCM).

Data Handlers and Targets: Data targets are configured for capacity and high throughput. Data targets may feature a lot of memory for caching but the cost is dominated by the amount of hard drives. For HPC systems, usually larger reads

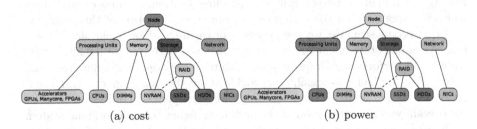

(a) cost   (b) power

Fig. 5. Cost and power footprint by component for I/O nodes. A darker shade represents a larger share relative to the total node configurations.

and writes are observed, for database systems also the data targets might profit substantially from the usage of SSDs. RAID controllers can also be a cost factor but software-based RAID is becoming very popular for being more flexible.

6 Cost Study for Alternative Deployments

This section discusses alternative architecture deployments for upcoming data centers. As described in Sect. 1 research institutions tend to organize compute and storage capabilities either by specializing at different locations or by collocating and consolidating different services into a single site, as is the case with DKRZ. In this paper only the summary of a larger case study is presented, a more detailed report [11] is available separately.

The DKRZ system (Mistral) operates 3.300 compute nodes in a 3.1 petaflop compute cluster attached to a 52 Petabyte disk based PFS distributed across over 10.000 disks. Besides online storage there is also an archive with capacity of up to 500 petabyte on tape (more for next-generation LTO tapes). In the current deployment I/O related investments are 7.5M Euro for two Lustre based PFS, 5.25M Euro for the network and 5M Euro for the archive. Figure 1(b) illustrates this setup using the graph approach introduced in Sect. 4. Together with Table 1 this preserves the relationship between components while allowing to use additional visual cues. With these numbers as a baseline for each subsystem and a total budget of roughly 39M Euro, it maybe interesting to see what half the storage budget might achieve given current technology. Table 1 compares two alternative deployment scenarios and offers a breakdown of cost, performance and power consumption including the factor with respect to the actually deployed system to gauge the impact on each subsystem for different metrics.

The first scenario, not diverting from the topology of the actual deployment, explores the potential trade-off when altering the ratio of offline storage to online storage. The general motivation for this scenario being that timely data staging from tape to PFS might preserve quality of service at lower cost. This would, however, require transparent automated staging mechanisms which integrate with batch scheduling system like Slurm or workload specifications. The example calculation does not take licensing costs into account, and somewhat optimistically assumes performance and power consumption scale linearly. Finally, any remaining budget is used to procure additional compute capabilities, which is responsible for the higher overall power consumption of this scenario.

In a second scenario we use object storage instead of a parallel file system. Assuming state of the art hardware this has a performance penalty, as the throughput performance drops to about a third of the original system. Yet, using only half the budget it is possible to provide about the same capacity and also to conserve energy. Again, as the remaining budget is spent on additional compute, the overall power consumption of the system is higher than the original system.

Burst buffers promise to compensate for some of the lost throughput performance of the previous two scenarios. Unfortunately, only a number of experimental commercial products for burst buffers are available at the moment and price estimates may be subject to non-disclosure agreements. Non-volatile memory maybe integrated into compute nodes, which can be attractive for data locality, e.g. in case of node failures, which potentially takes load off the network. Alternatively burst buffers could be integrated similar to network attached memory (NAM), which allows to dynamically allocate remote memory which provides a high degree of flexibility.

Given the recent rise of cloud technologies and popularity of object storage, some might anticipate a possible displacement of parallel file systems and tape archive in future data centers. The integration of clouds, can reduce some burdens on application developers and add flexibility to applications, but current rates charged by cloud service providers do not justify moving away from on-premise deployments.

7 Application in Cost-Aware I/O Middleware

Besides better understanding the relationship of cost, performance and resilience when procuring and designing new systems, these models can also support I/O middleware to make better decisions. In the ESiWACE [6] project, the *Earth System Data Middleware* (ESDM) is developed. It is designed to address multiple I/O challenges simultaneously, such as: (1) automatic seperation of data and metadata when using data description frameworks (2) the distributing data accross different storage tiers and services in the data center using a description of the site configuration and (3) adaptive I/O strategies and data representations depending on anticipated workflows and service level agreements. A prerequisite for such automatic optimization is a capable software infrastructure on the one hand, but more importantly, this requires adequate and light-weight models to derive reasonable decisions and policies tunable to a data centers demands.

8 Summary

Modeling data center cost and performance is a complicated task but by approaching cost modeling in a systematic way it is possible to reuse and adapt existing models more easily. The paper presented a methodology and considerations relevant for modeling data centers intended for the climate and NWP community. In Sect. 1 domain and technological trends are discussed which are then accommodated in the hierarchical model presented in Sect. 3. It was demonstrated how to construct a coarse grained model not only for cost but also, with some limitations, for resilience and performance. In a case study of the DKRZ system, the paper briefly explored how alternative deployments may allow to prioritize cost reductions or performance improvements. In future work we want integrate cost models with I/O middleware such as with ESDM, to allow addressing the challenges of multiple stakeholders.

Table 1. Summary of the expected impact of two alternative deployment scenarios. Comparison of mistral as installed, a deployment with a reduced disk system and a deployment using object storage instead of a file system.

	Mistral	Scale-down PFS, spent leftovers on compute		Switch to object storage, leftovers spent on compute	
Characteristics	Value	Factor	New value	Factor	New value
Performance	3.1 PF/s	1.17	3.6 PF/s	1.19	3.7 PF/s
Nodes	2882	1.17	3370	1.19	3430
Node performance	1.0 TF/s				
System memory	200 TB	1.17	234 TB	1.19	238 TB
Network links	3100	1.12	3450	1.15	3565
Storage capacity	52 PB	0.5	26 PB	0.9	47 PB
Storage throughput	700 GB/s	0.5	350 GB/s	0.375	262 GB/s
Storage servers	130	0.5	65	0.75	98
Disk drives	10600	0.5	5300	0.74	7800
Archive capacity	500 PB				
Archive throughput	18 GB/s				
Compute costs	15.75 M EUR	1.17	19.53 M EUR	1.24	19.53 M EUR
Network costs	5.25 M EUR	1.10	6.04 M EUR	0.98	5.15 M EUR
Storage costs	7.5 M EUR	0.5	3.75 M EUR	0.5	3.75 M EUR
Archive costs	5 M EUR				
Building costs	5 M EUR				
Investment	38.5 M EUR		38.41 EUR		38.43 M EUR
Compute power	1100 kW	1.19	1290 kW	1.10	1309 kW
Network power	50 kW				
Storage power	250 kW	0.5	125 kW	0.75	188 kW
Archive power	25 kW				
Power consumption	1.20 MW		1.49 MW		1.57 MW

Acknowledgment. The ESiWACE project received funding from the EU Horizon 2020 research and innovation programme under grant agreement No 675191.

References

1. Performance Evaluation of the PVFS2 Architecture. Napoli, Italy
2. SST Simulator - The Structural Simulation Toolkit. http://sst-simulator.org/
3. Arjona, J.O.: Using UML state diagrams for modelling the performance of parallel programs. Computación y Sistemas **11**(3), 199–210 (2008)
4. Carothers, C.: ROSS: rensselaer's optimistic simulation system, November 2017. https://github.com/carothersc/ROSS
5. DEEP Projects. http://www.deep-projects.eu/

6. ESiWACE: Centre of excellence in simulation of weather and climate in Europe. https://www.esiwace.eu/
7. ExtremeEarth. http://www.extremeearth.eu/
8. Fontana, R.E., Decad, G.M., Hetzler, S.R.: The impact of areal density and millions of square inches (MSI) of produced memory on petabyte shipments of TAPE, NAND flash, and HDD storage class memories. In: 2013 IEEE 29th Symposium on Mass Storage Systems and Technologies (MSST), pp. 1–8. IEEE (2013). http://ieeexplore.ieee.org/xpls/abs_all.jsp?arnumber=6558421
9. HPSS collaboration: list of sites (2018). http://www.hpss-collaboration.org/customersT.shtml
10. Intel, T.: HDF Group, EMC, Cray: Fast Forward Storage and I/O, June 2014
11. Luettgau, J., Kunkel, J., Jensen, J., Lawrence, B.: ESIWACE D4.1 business model with alternative scenarios. Technical report. https://www.esiwace.eu/results/deliverables/d4-1-business-model-with-alternative-scenarios
12. Kunkel, J.M., Ludwig, T.: IOPm - modeling the I/O path with a functional representation of parallel file system and hardware architecture. In: 20th Euromicro International Conference on Parallel, Distributed and Network-Based Processing (2012). https://doi.org/10.1109/PDP.2012.13
13. Luettgau, J., Kunkel, J.: Simulation of hierarchical storage systems for TCO and QoS. In: Kunkel, J.M., Yokota, R., Taufer, M., Shalf, J. (eds.) High Performance Computing, pp. 132–144. Springer International Publishing, Cham (2017). https://doi.org/10.1007/978-3-319-67630-2_12
14. Mubarak, M., Carothers, C.D., Ross, R., Carns, P.: Modeling a million-node dragonfly network using massively parallel discrete-event simulation. In: 2012 SC Companion: High Performance Computing, Networking Storage and Analysis, pp. 366–376. November 2012. https://doi.org/10.1109/SC.Companion.2012.56
15. NEXTGenIO: next generation I/O for the exascale. http://www.nextgenio.eu/
16. Overpeck, J.T., Meehl, G.A., Bony, S., Easterling, D.R.: Climate data challenges in the 21st century. Science 331(6018), 700–702 (2011)
17. Llopis, P., Dolz, M.F., Blas, J.G., Isaila, F., Heidari, M.R., Kuhn, M.: Analyzing the energy consumption of the storage data path. J. Supercomput. 72(11), 4089–4106 (2016). https://doi.org/10.1007/s11227-016-1729-4
18. Pentzaropoulos, G.: Computer performance modelling: an overview. Appl. Math. Model. 6(2), 74–80 (1982)
19. Pereverzeva, I., Laibinis, L., Troubitsyna, E., Holmberg, M., Pöri, M.: Formal modelling of resilient data storage in cloud. In: Groves, L., Sun, J. (eds.) ICFEM 2013. LNCS, vol. 8144, pp. 363–379. Springer, Heidelberg (2013). https://doi.org/10.1007/978-3-642-41202-8_24
20. Tribastone, M., Gilmore, S.: Automatic extraction of PEPA performance models from UML activity diagrams annotated with the MARTE profile. In: Proceedings of the 7th International Workshop on Software and Performance, WOSP 2008, pp. 67–78. ACM (2008). https://doi.org/10.1145/1383559.1383569
21. Zhang, Y., Myers, D.S., Arpaci-Dusseau, A.C., Arpaci-Dusseau, R.H.: Zettabyte reliability with flexible end-to-end data integrity, pp. 1–14. IEEE May 2013. https://doi.org/10.1109/MSST.2013.6558423, https://ieeexplore.ieee.org/document/6558423/
22. Zhao, T., March, V., Dong, S., See, S.: Evaluation of a performance model of Lustre file system. In: 2010 Fifth Annual ChinaGrid Conference (ChinaGrid), pp. 191–196. IEEE (2010)

I/O Interference Alleviation on Parallel File Systems Using Server-Side QoS-Based Load-Balancing

Yuichi Tsujita[1](✉), Yoshitaka Furutani[2], Hajime Hida[3], Keiji Yamamoto[1], Atsuya Uno[1], and Fumichika Sueyasu[2]

[1] RIKEN Center for Computational Science, Kobe, Hyogo, Japan
yuichi.tsujita@riken.jp
[2] Fujitsu Limited, Minato-ku, Tokyo, Japan
[3] Fujitsu Social Science Laboratory Limited, Kawasaki, Kanagawa, Japan

Abstract. Storage performance in supercomputers is variable, depending not only on an application's workload but also on the types of other concurrent I/O activities. In particular, performance degradation in meta-data accesses leads to poor storage performance across applications running at the same time. We herein focus on two representative performance problems, high load and slow response of a meta-data server, through analysis of meta-data server activities using file system performance metrics on the K computer. We investigate the root causes of such performance problems through MDTEST benchmark runs and confirm the performance improvement by server-side quality-of-service management in service thread assignment for incoming client requests on a meta-data server.

Keywords: Lustre · FEFS · MDS · OSS · Data-staging · QoS
K computer

1 Introduction

I/O performance is one of the most prominent contributors in supercomputing, and many parallel file systems, such as GPFS [15] and Lustre [5], have been developed. Meta-data servers (MDSs) are among the most significant performance bottlenecks for Lustre and its enhanced file systems. Since a large number of concurrent file I/O operations at the same storage may lead to high MDS load, poor file I/O performance may be experienced in not only the root-cause user application but also other applications that access the same storage system. In the worst case, unstable file system operation may occur due to such high MDS load. We can easily detect such high MDS loads and root-cause applications through monitoring the associated performance metrics of the MDS, and stable operation can be achieved by terminating such root-cause applications, for instance.

© Springer Nature Switzerland AG 2018
R. Yokota et al. (Eds.): ISC 2018 Workshops, LNCS 11203, pp. 36–48, 2018.
https://doi.org/10.1007/978-3-030-02465-9_3

On the other hand, it is difficult to detect slow MDS response caused by a large number of file accesses under a large stripe count. Once an I/O request is processed by an MDS, the MDS sends associated requests to corresponding object storage servers (OSSes), where the number of requests issued by the MDS is proportional to the stripe count and the number of accessed files. Consequently, setting the stripe count to be large and having a huge number of concurrent file accesses lead to high OSS load, and service threads of the MDS continue to wait for responses from associated OSSes for a long time. As a result, the performance of MDS operations for new incoming I/O requests is degraded, and such a situation leads to poor storage performance.

Knowing the I/O patterns for such slow MDS response is an urgent issue for better file system operation. In order to examine the root causes of slow MDS response, we conducted performance evaluations using MDTEST [6] version 1.9.3. The results indicate that a similar file I/O performance degradation occurs due to the problematic file access patterns. File I/O performance degradation was caused by a mismatched stripe count configuration with respect to the file I/O pattern. Once we introduced quality-of-service-based (QoS-based) service thread management to an MDS, such degradation was minimized.

The main contributions of this paper are as follows:

- Analysis of meta-data accesses to find the root causes of slow storage performance
- Server-side QoS-based management to achieve fair-share service thread allocation on an MDS

Section 2 describes the research background of this research work, including a brief introduction of the K computer, its asynchronous data-staging scheme, and the QoS-based service thread management adopted herein. The analysis of the performance degradation of an MDS is explained in Sect. 3. Section 4 reports the I/O performance evaluation associated with root-cause I/O patterns that led to performance degradation of an MDS and performance improvements using QoS-based management in file system accesses. Related work is discussed in Sect. 5, followed by concluding remarks in Sect. 6.

2   Research Background

This section presents research background and a system overview of the K computer. Since our analysis and I/O performance evaluation were performed using the K computer, we briefly describe the K computer and its file systems before discussing our analysis and performance evaluation.

2.1   K Computer and Its File Systems

The K computer consists of 82,944 compute nodes, where each system rack consists of 96 compute nodes. Figure 1 shows an overview of the K computer system including its two-staged parallel file system. The Fujitsu Exabyte File System

(FEFS), which is an enhanced Lustre file system created by FUJITSU [14,16], has been used in parallel file systems. The layered file system consists of a local file system (LFS) and a global file system (GFS). The LFS, which provides high performance I/O during computation. is intended for performance-oriented use, whereas the GFS is intended for capacity-oriented use, e.g., to keep users' permanent files such as user programs and data files.

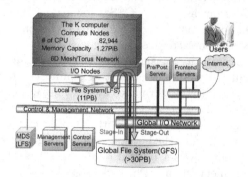

Fig. 1. Overview of the K computer

The number of available OSTs at the LFS is uniquely configured based on the shape of assigned compute nodes according to the I/O zoning scheme [16] of the LFS, where the I/O zoning scheme mitigates I/O interference on OSTs among user jobs by isolating the OSTs assigned for each job. Although the default stripe count of the LFS is 12, users can change the stripe count up to the maximum number of assigned OSTs for newly created files or directories, or can simply set the stripe count to −1, which ensures that the maximum number of assigned OSTs will be used. Moreover, although the default stripe count of the GFS is four, the stripe count of the GFS can be set to the maximum number of OSTs for each target GFS volume.

A subset of I/O nodes, called global-I/O (GIO) nodes, accesses an MDS and the OSSes of each GFS volume via the global I/O network using 4×QDR Infini-Band links. I/O nodes, including GIO nodes, each consist of a single FUJITSU SPARC64 VIIIfx and 16 GB memory. GIO nodes are also responsible for asynchronous data-staging [4] between the LFS and the GFS as shown in Fig. 2(a). This scheme guarantees sufficient I/O performance for programs running on compute nodes and effective job scheduling. An MDS server of the LFS consists of two Intel Xeon E5-2690 CPUs and 256 GB of memory, whereas a subset of I/O nodes, called local I/O (LIO) nodes, is dedicated for an OSS of the LFS. The MDS of the LFS is accessed by GIO nodes and compute nodes in data-staging and local file I/O, respectively.

In order to achieve higher scalability in LFS accesses, loopback file systems, called rank-directories, are created for each rank in the stage-in phase, as shown in Fig. 2(b). Localizing file I/O by rank in each rank-directory can reduce the MDS load.

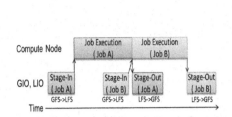
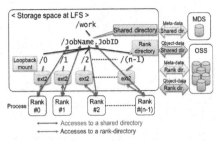

(a) Asynchronous data-staging scheme   (b) Overview of rank-directories

Fig. 2. Data-staging and rank-directories at the K computer

2.2 Performance Problems of File I/O on the K Computer

During the course of our K computer operation, which exceeds file years, we have faced various types of problems related to file systems, as well as problems related to both hardware and software components. Although most of these problems have been addressed, recently we have faced file system problems, including performance degradation due to user applications. Among the file system problems encountered, solutions of the problems of slow file I/O due to inefficient MDS operations is among the highest priorities. In this context, we focus on the analysis of MDS activities and file I/O operations in order to improve file I/O performance.

The numbers of MDS operations per second (OPS) observed for typical high MDS load and quite low MDS response cases in the K computer operation are shown in Figs. 3(a) and (b), respectively. The scales of both axes are different between Figs. 3(a) and (b) because we need to clearly show the focused MDS load.

In the high MDS load case in Fig. 3(a), the horizontal axis covers approximately 24 h, which includes the focused MDS activities. A user job with 8,000 processes on 1,000 compute nodes accesses a large number of files on a shared space of the LFS during a 23 h period. (Although 1,008 compute nodes were assigned for the job due to the topological layout, only 1,000 nodes were used for the job.) Such a file access pattern led to a high MDS load, and consequently there was a tremendous negative impact on the I/O operations of other user jobs due to the high MDS load.

On the other hand, Fig. 3(b) shows the low MDS load case for a period of 14 min near the middle of the graph due to a large number of concurrent file accesses by 12,096 processes on the same number of compute nodes. The horizontal axis of this figure covers approximately three hours in order to focus on the low MDS load. Although this job also accessed a shared space of the LFS, the MDS load was quite low during concurrent file accesses for a larger number of files, as compared with the previous case. As a result, the file access performance of every user job that included this job was degraded during this time.

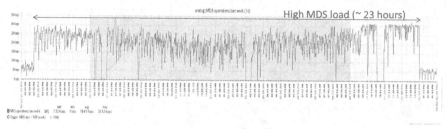

(a) High MDS load due to a large number of file accesses, continuing for approximately 23 hours

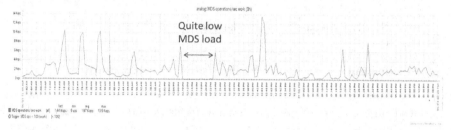

(b) Low MDS response due to congestion between an MDS and the associated OSSes

Fig. 3. MDS activity during slow file I/O at the LFS of the K computer

A high MDS load is easily detected by monitoring MDS activities, and stable operation can be achieved by terminating root-cause jobs for example. However, root causes of the slow MDS response cannot be detected only by monitoring MDS activities. Two problematic MDS activities have led to not only performance degradation in file I/O by user jobs but also a large increase in the time required for rank-directory creation prior to stage-in operation. Note that such long times for rank-directory creation have led to delays in start-up of stage-in operation. As a result, slow file I/O or long delays in stage-in operation have led to ineffective job scheduling, despite asynchronous data-staging. Therefore, we need to investigate the root causes of the above MDS performance problems, and finding an effective way to mitigate I/O interference is an urgent problem.

2.3   QoS-Based Management at an MDS

Although the FEFS is based on Lustre version 1.8, the file system has been still extended to cope with high I/O demands at the K computer. One feature of the FEFS is QoS-based service thread sharing among client nodes or among user jobs on each MDS or OSS. The QoS function limits the number of available threads for multiple pre-defined client groups in one of the two modes, static or dynamic. The static case involves the use of a single rate relative to the total number of threads, whereas the dynamic case involves the use of lower and higher rates to advance the demand-based dynamic assignment scheme. Note that this QoS scheme prevents the lack of free service threads due to a heavy workload, which occurs in the two above-mentioned problematic cases.

Figure 4(a) shows the I/O request flow using the QoS function. Assume that we have two groups, group-A and group-B, for the QoS control, and that client jobs, Job-1 and Job-2, belong to the former and latter groups, respectively. An I/O request is placed in a queue of `ptlrpcd`, and its associated information is placed in another queue associated with a client job. In this case, a new request from Job-1 is placed in a `ptlrpcd` queue, and its associated information including a reference index, which indicates the position of a corresponding request in the `ptlrpcd` queue, is stored in a queue for Job-1. Therefore, a target request is referenced in an indirect manner from queues for client jobs to the `ptlrpcd` queue. The observer task of the QoS function checks the number of free and working service threads. According to the QoS ratio between groups, an I/O request is dispatched to a service thread.

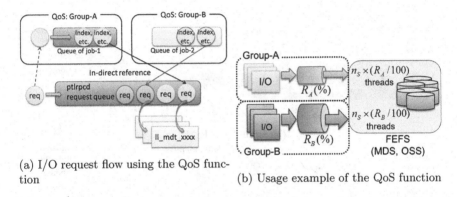

(a) I/O request flow using the QoS function

(b) Usage example of the QoS function

Fig. 4. Schematic diagram of (a) the I/O request flow using QoS function and (b) an example of its usage

Figure 4(b) shows an example of fair-share management among two groups, group-A and group-B, in accessing the same target file system by limiting the maximum number of service threads of an MDS and/or an OSS to each registered group. Assume that we have n_S service threads on each MDS/OSS, the QoS configuration limits up to $R_A\%$ of the n_S service threads for group-A. Thus, group-A can use up to $n_S \times (R_A/100)$ service threads. In contrast, up to $n_S \times (R_B/100)$ service threads can be used for group-B, where its available rate is $R_B\%$. On the other hand, the dynamic configuration can give upper and lower rates in each group.

3   Investigation of Internal File Server Activities

High MDS load has been caused by a large number of concurrent file accesses. At present, the K computer limits the maximum number of service threads to 24 on the MDS of the LFS without any load-balancing, which leads to a high MDS load. Moreover, quite a slow MDS response has been caused by high contention in OSS operations due to a large stripe count in conjunction with a huge number of concurrent file accesses. Such contention is the result of an existing Lustre implementation. Once an MDS receives an I/O request from a client, associated requests to corresponding OSSes are issued by the MDS. The number of associated requests on each OSS is absolutely proportional to the product of the stripe count and the number of concurrent file accesses. Moreover, user jobs specifying a stripe count of −1 use all available OSTs. Once a large number of OSTs are assigned based on the shape of the allocated compute nodes, a large stripe count is provided unexpectedly. Once associated OSSes becomes very busy in managing incoming requests, service threads on an MDS are blocked in order to await responses from the OSSes. During the time of the contention, the MDS has a very difficult time for processing new I/O requests. Therefore, such contention leads to quite slow MDS operation, as shown in Fig. 3(b).

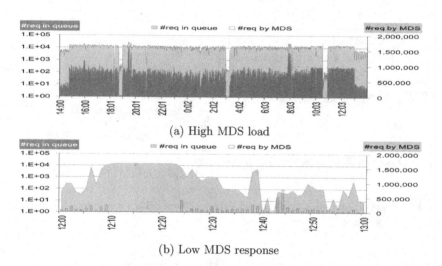

(a) High MDS load

(b) Low MDS response

Fig. 5. Numbers of requests in queue and processed by an MDS over time in the two MDS load cases at the LFS of the K computer

In order to investigate the root causes of the above problem, we have examined the performance statistics of the MDS in detail. Figure 5 shows the average number of requests in a queue and the average number of requests processed by the MDS in one-minute intervals for the two cases shown in Fig. 3. Note that the horizontal axis of Fig. 5(a) covers 24 h, whereas that of Fig. 5(b) covers one hour in order to focus on the target activities. Moreover, the vertical axes on the left-hand side differ scale in order to more clearly show the two operations. We selected the statistics of the MDS in each given interval using the procedure of Lustre llstat. In the high MDS load case shown in Fig. 5(a), a very high number of requests are continuously processed over 23 h, whereas, in the slow MDS response case shown in Fig. 5(b), MDS activity is quite low for 14 min starting from 12:10, when the root-cause job started file I/O.

4 Performance Evaluation

In order to examine the file access patterns that led to slow MDS response and the effectiveness of the QoS function of the FEFS, we conducted a performance evaluation using MDTEST version 1.9.3 at the K computer. In this section, the following three evaluations were conducted in order to examine the MDS of the LFS:

- Stripe count impact on MDS performance using MDTEST
- Impact of QoS management on the MDS for fair-share execution among concurrent MDTEST jobs
- I/O interference alleviation in data-staging using QoS management at the MDS

Through the three evaluations, we demonstrate which types of file I/O access pattern lead to poor MDS response in terms of stripe count configuration and effectiveness of QoS management with respect to MDS performance problems.

4.1 MDS Response Evaluation Using MDTEST

This section discusses performance impact on MDS response regarding stripe count. We evaluated MDS response at the LFS using an MDTEST benchmark code on 192 compute nodes in logical 3D layout of 4 × 6 × 8. We deployed four or eight processes per compute node, and every process accessed 100 files per iteration in each individual directory on the LFS. Mean performance results were obtained from six iterations.

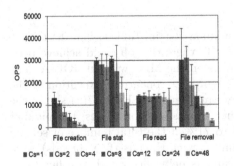 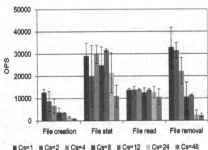

(a) 768 processes on 192(4 × 6 × 8) nodes (b) 1,536 processes on 192(4 × 6 × 8) nodes

Fig. 6. MDTEST evaluation results for various stripe count values, where C_S represents the stripe count

Figure 6 shows the performance results. We have examined seven sets of stripe counts, which are described by C_S in the figure, ranging from 1 to 48 with respect to the target directories on the LFS. The figure shows the mean values of four file-specific operations with variances shown by error bars. Based on the results, we can see a performance degradation in each of the three operations, except for "File read", as the stripe count increased.

4.2　QoS Impact in Fair-Share Execution Among Concurrent Running Jobs

Fair-share execution using the QoS function was evaluated using two concurrently running MDTEST jobs, JOB-A and JOB-B, on the LFS. JOB-A with 6,144 processes on the same number of compute nodes in a $16 \times 12 \times 32$ layout imitated a root-cause job of slow MDS response under a stripe count of 96. While JOB-B with 768 processes on 192 compute nodes in an $8 \times 12 \times 2$ layout imitated an affected job under a stripe count of four. In both cases, 100 files were created by each process in an individual directory per iteration. We measured the performance of the JOB-B from three iterations during 200 iterations of JOB-A.

Table 1. Configuration of two MDTEST jobs for the examination of fair-share job execution

Notation	Executed jobs	# processes	C_S	# threads	User fair-share
Reference	JOB-B	768	4	17	None
Off	JOB-A	6,144	96		None
	JOB-B	768	4		
On	JOB-A	6,144	96		JOB-A:JOB-B = 50%:50%
	JOB-B	768	4		(up to 90% each if available)

The measurement configuration is summarized in Table 1. The first case, "reference", is the reference case for JOB-B, where the job could achieve peak performance by using all 17 service threads on the MDS without JOB-A. The following two cases, i.e., "on" and "off", represent concurrent execution of the two jobs with and without user fair-share management. Figure 7(a) shows the QoS setup for the MDTEST performance results. In both cases, the number of available service threads was limited to 71% of the total number of service threads (17 threads), while the remaining service threads (five threads) were separated in order to simulate service threads being dedicated to other tasks by GIO nodes to simulate real QoS use. Competition among the two jobs for 17 service threads led to contention on the MDS in the "off" case, whereas in the "on" case, each job could use up to 50% of the 17 service threads. If the counterpart job did not run or did not operate I/O, up to 90% of the 17 threads was available, i.e., up to 15 threads.

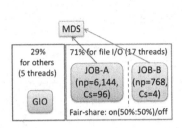

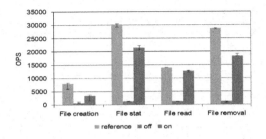

(a) QoS setup in MDTEST eval- (b) Performance results for the JOB-B group with
uation for fair-share manage- and without fair-share management during job ex-
ment ecution of the JOB-A group

Fig. 7. MDTEST evaluation for fair-share management, where (a) shows the QoS setup
and (b) shows the performance results

Figure 7(b) shows the MDTEST performance results of JOB-B for four file-
specific operations at the LFS with and without fair-share management, where
the bar charts show mean values with bars indicating the maximum and minimum performance values from three iterations. Performance of the "off" case
was greatly degraded due to I/O interference by JOB-A because MDS accesses
by 6,144 processes under a stripe count of 96 led to slow response of the MDS.
By comparing the "off" case with the "on" case, the performance of every operation was improved effectively. For instance, the "on" case was around 16 times
faster than the "off" case for "File stat" operation. By comparing the performance of the "on" case with that of the "reference" case, JOB-A also degraded
the performance of the "on" case, however the fair-share management mitigated
the performance decrease dramatically.

We also found such performance improvements in the JOB-B case in CPU
utilization at the MDS, as shown in Fig. 8. With fair-share management, as
indicated by "Fair-Share ON," we can see a higher CPU utilization of up to
approximately 70%, whereas a lower CPU utilization of approximately 20% is
observed without the fair-share management, as indicated by "Fair-Share OFF".
Therefore, the high CPU utilization for the "Fair-Share ON" case was due to
improved MDS activities for JOB-B.

4.3 QoS Impact in Data-Staging

We measured the times for rank-directory creation in the stage-in phase under
high MDS load by an I/O heavy MDTEST job with and without QoS management for MDS service threads. We increased the total number of service threads
of the MDS from 24 to 32, two of which were used for file system monitoring. Therefore, the remaining 30 threads were used for data-staging and file I/O.
Here, the lower and higher rates of QoS management were 20% and 94%, respectively, for the data-staging job, and 4% and 69%, respectively, for the I/O heavy
MDTEST job.

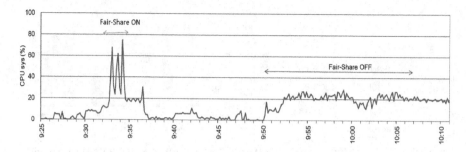

Fig. 8. CPU system use of an MDS during MDTEST runs with and without fair-share management over time

We executed a job for data-staging evaluation by changing the number of compute nodes during a high MDS load caused by an MDTEST job by running 6,144 processes on the same number of compute nodes under a stripe count of 96. Every process accessed 100 files per iteration in an individual directory. Due to the limited time for the evaluation setup without any other user jobs, only one data-staging operation was carried out in each configuration.

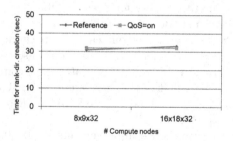

Fig. 9. Times for rank-directory creation in the stage-in phase under QoS control for service threads on an MDS

Figure 9 shows the times for rank-directory creation for two node layouts. The horizontal axis describes the number of assigned compute nodes in the 3D layout. "Reference" indicates the times without the high MDS load job, which were measured as reference values. Note that rank-directory creation in the stage-in phase under the high MDS load job did not finish within five minutes after start-up of the rank-directory creation. In the smaller case of $8 \times 9 \times 32$, only up to four rank-directories were created, none of which was created in the case of $16 \times 18 \times 32$. On the other hand, rank-directory creation with QoS control described by "QoS = on" in Fig. 9 showed approximately the same performance as the "Reference" case.

Based on the results, QoS control is considered to be very effective for stable rank-directory creation in stage-in operation even if high MDS load jobs processed are at the same time.

5   Related Work

Performance optimization in Lustre file systems has been investigated in various research works [2,3,7,12,13]. These works tuned parameters based on empirical data or operation profiles. In such cases, monitoring tools are important in order to clarify activities of MDSs, OSSes, and associated components and future aspects of the target file system [1,17,18]. Uselton et al. [17] demonstrated server-side monitoring using Lustre Monitoring Tools (LMT) [8]. Although LMT monitors the storage server status, such as the CPU utilization, memory usage, and disk I/O bandwidth, the LMT does not provide detailed I/O tracing information, which is useful for systematic analysis such as file system statistics.

A number of studies have investigated load-balancing or contention-aware optimization including QoS management. Zhang et al. [19] introduced machine learning into a QoS parameter setup scheme and implemented the scheme in PVFS2. Qian et al. [11] proposed a dynamic I/O congestion control algorithm for Lustre. They proposed a token bucket filter [10] in the network request scheduler (NRS) framework [9]. However, the token bucket filter does not guarantee free service threads for numerous incoming I/O requests. On the other hand, the proposed QoS-based approach available on the FEFS provides server-side management by limiting the number of service threads to each pre-assigned group for fair-share I/O bandwidth utilization. The QoS function controls RPC request dispatching to service threads based on the IP addresses of RPC request senders or a user grouping scheme. Even in the slow response of an MDS, the QoS function maintains a pre-defined number of free service threads for registered clients, independent of the I/O load by other clients on an MDS. In this context, the QoS approach is more realistic manner for stable file system operation.

6   Concluding Remarks

We have investigated the root causes of high MDS load and slow MDS response through analysis of several performance metrics and benchmark runs on the K computer. Our analysis of the two problematic MDS activities has revealed distinct I/O patterns accessing a large number of files on a parallel file system, i.e., the FEFS, on the K computer. A high MDS load originated from a large number of concurrent file accesses, whereas a slow MDS response was caused by a larger stripe count configuration in accessing a large number of files. Such a stripe count configuration led to congestion in sending requests from an MDS to associated OSSes and every service thread on the MDS waited for a long time. Consequently, the MDS could not process new incoming requests. We observed the same situation in MDTEST benchmark runs.

Even in the case of such a slow MDS response, the QoS function of the FEFS mitigated performance degradation in file I/O of the MDTEST benchmark runs. Interference in rank-directory creation during data-staging operation was also dramatically alleviated by the QoS function. In the future, we intended to consider adoption of the QoS function for OSSes of the LFS on the K computer. Such an approach is expected to mitigate I/O interference on OSSes among file I/O by user jobs and the data-staging phase.

Acknowledgment. The results of this paper were obtained using the K computer.

References

1. Brim, M.J., Lothian, J.K.: Monitoring extreme-scale Lustre toolkit. In: Proceedings of the International Workshop on the Lustre Ecosystem: Challenges and Opportunities (2015). http://arxiv.org/html/1506.05323
2. Crosby, L.D., Mohr, R.: Petascale I/O: challenges, solutions, and recommendations. In: Proceedings of the Extreme Scaling Workshop, BW-XSEDE 2012, pp. 7:1–7:7. University of Illinois at Urbana-Champaign (2012)
3. Ezell, M., Mohr, R., Wynkoop, J., Braby, R.: Lustre at petascale: experiences in troubleshooting and upgrading. In: 2012 Cray User Group Meeting (2012)
4. Hirai, K., Iguchi, Y., Uno, A., Kurokawa, M.: Operations management software for the K computer. Fujitsu Sci. Tech. J. **48**(3), 310–316 (2012)
5. Lustre. http://lustre.org/
6. MDTEST. https://github.com/hpc/ior
7. Mohr, R., Brim, M., Oral, S., Dilger, A.: Evaluating progressive file layouts for Lustre (2016). http://lustre.ornl.gov/ecosystem-2016/
8. Morrone, C.: LMT Lustre monitoring tools. In: Lustre User Group 2011 (2011)
9. Qian, Y., Barton, E., Wang, T., Puntambekar, N., Dilger, A.: A novel network request scheduler for a large scale storage system. Comput. Sci. - Res. Dev. **23**(3), 143–148 (2009)
10. Qian, Y., et al.: A configurable rule based classful token bucket filter network request scheduler for the Lustre file system. In: Proceedings of the International Conference for High Performance Computing, Networking, Storage and Analysis, SC 2017, pp. 6:1–6:12. ACM (2017)
11. Qian, Y., Yi, R., Du, Y., Xiao, N., Jin, S.: Dynamic I/O congestion control in scalable Lustre file system. In: IEEE 29th Symposium on Mass Storage Systems and Technologies (MSST 2013), pp. 1–5, May 2013
12. Reed, J., Archuleta, J., Brim, M.J., Lothian, J.: Evaluating dynamic file striping for Lustre. In: Proceedings of the International Workshop on the Lustre Ecosystem: Challenges and Opportunities (2015). http://arxiv.org/html/1506.05323
13. Saini, S., Rappleye, J., Chang, J., Barker, D., Mehrotra, P., Biswas, R.: I/O performance characterization of Lustre and NASA applications on Pleiades. In: 19th International Conference on High Performance Computing (HiPC), pp. 1–10 (2012)
14. Sakai, K., Sumimoto, S., Kurokawa, M.: High-performance and highly reliable file system for the K computer. Fujitsu Sci. Tech. J. **48**(3), 302–309 (2012)
15. Schmuck, F., Haskin, R.: GPFS: a shared-disk file system for large computing clusters. In: Proceedings of the 1st USENIX Conference on File and Storage Technologies, FAST 2002, USENIX Association (2002)
16. Sumimoto, S.: An overview of Fujitsu's Lustre based file system. In: Lustre User Group 2011 (2011)
17. Uselton, A.: Deploying server-side file system monitoring at NERSC. In: 2009 Cray User Group Meeting (2009)
18. Uselton, A., Wright, N.: A file system utilization metric for I/O characterization. In: 2013 Cray User Group Meeting (2013)
19. Zhang, X., Davis, K., Jiang, S.: QoS support for end users of I/O-intensive applications using shared storage systems. In: Proceedings of 2011 International Conference for High Performance Computing, Networking, Storage and Analysis, SC 2011, pp. 18:1–18:12. ACM (2011)

Tools for Analyzing Parallel I/O

Julian Martin Kunkel[1]([✉]), Eugen Betke[2], Matt Bryson[3], Philip Carns[4],
Rosemary Francis[5], Wolfgang Frings[6], Roland Laifer[7], and Sandra Mendez[8]

[1] University of Reading, Reading, UK
j.m.kunkel@reading.ac.uk
[2] German Climate Computing Center (DKRZ), Hamburg, Germany
[3] University of California, Santa Cruz, USA
[4] Argonne National Laboratory, Lemont, USA
[5] Ellexus Ltd., Cambridge, UK
[6] Jülich Supercomputing Centre (JSC), Juelich, Germany
[7] Karlsruhe Institute of Technology (KIT), Karlsruhe, Germany
[8] Leibniz Supercomputing Centre (LRZ), München, Germany

Abstract. Parallel application I/O performance often does not meet
user expectations. Additionally, slight access pattern modifications may
lead to significant changes in performance due to complex interactions
between hardware and software. These issues call for sophisticated tools
to capture, analyze, understand, and tune application I/O.

In this paper, we highlight advances in monitoring tools to help
address these issues. We also describe best practices, identify issues in
measurement and analysis, and provide practical approaches to translate
parallel I/O analysis into actionable outcomes for users, facility operators, and researchers.

1 Introduction

The efficient use of I/O systems is of prime interest for data-intensive applications, since storage systems are increasing in size and the use case of a single system is so diverse, especially in the scientific community. As computing
centers grown in size, and the high-performance computing (HPC) community
approaches exascale [1,2], it has become increasingly important to understand
how these systems are operating and how they are being used. Additionally,
understanding system behavior helps light the path for future storage system
development and allows the purveyors of these systems to ensure performance is
adequate to allow for work to continue unimpeded. While industry systems are
typically well understood, shared storage systems in the HPC community are
not as well understood. The reason is their sheer size and the concurrent usage
by many users, which typically submit disparate workloads. Most applications
achieve only a fraction of theoretically available performance. Hence, optimization and tuning of available knobs for hardware and software are important.

The U.S. government retains certain licensing rights. This is a U.S. government work
and certain licensing rights apply.

© Springer Nature Switzerland AG 2018
R. Yokota et al. (Eds.): ISC 2018 Workshops, LNCS 11203, pp. 49–70, 2018.
https://doi.org/10.1007/978-3-030-02465-9_4

This requires that the user to understand the I/O behavior of the interaction between application and system, since it determines the runtime of the applications.

However, measuring and assessing observed performance are already nontrivial tasks and raise various challenges around hardware, software, deployment, and management. This paper describes the current state of the practice with respect to such tools.

The paper is structured as follows: First, an introduction to concepts in performance analysis is given in Sect. 2. Various tools and concepts are described in Sect. 3. In Sect. 4 small example studies illustrate how these tools could be used to identify inefficient system behavior. In Sect. 5 we discuss common issues and sketch potential roads to overcome these issues. In Sect. 6 we summarize our conclusions.

2   Introduction to Performance Analysis

In computer science, *performance analysis* refers to activity that fosters understanding in timing and resource utilization of applications. Understanding resource utilization includes understanding runtime behavior of the application and the system. For parallel applications, the concurrent computation, communication, and parallel I/O increase the complexity of the analysis.

In industry, the process of system and application tuning is often referred to as *performance engineering*. Software engineers design special methods to embed performance engineering into the application development. With these approaches, performance is considered explicitly during the application design and its implementation. Tools and methodologies such as *Computer-aided software engineering* (CASE) serve the developer in the phases of the software lifecycle, namely, requirement engineering, analysis, design, coding, documentation, and testing. Such tools try to encourage software engineers to incorporate the performance relevant aspects early in the development cycle. Unfortunately, the research and processes in industry are not integrated in state-of-the-art HPC application development, although a few tools do assist in the development of parallel applications. Instead, a closed loop of performance tuning is applied that optimizes programs after a running version exists.

So far, we discussed the situation from the point of view of the user or application. For facility operators or file system administrators, the I/O performance of the whole system or of one parallel file system is the primary concern: Does the system provide the expected or degraded performance, is the system is efficiently used, or do some applications create such a high load that other applications see a significant performance impact?

2.1   Closed Loop of Performance Tuning

The localization of a performance issue on an existing system is a process in which a hypothesis is supported by measurement and theoretic considerations.

Measurement is performed by executing the program while monitoring runtime behavior of the application and the system. In general, tuning is not limited to source code; it can be applied to any system. The typical iterative optimization process is the *closed loop of performance tuning* consisting of the phases:

Measurement of performance in an experiment. The environment, consisting of hardware and software including their configuration, is chosen; and the appropriate input (i.e., problem statement) is decided. Since monitoring is limited to instances of program input, optimizations made for a particular configuration might degrade performance on a different setup or program input. Typically, the measurement itself perturbs the system slightly by degrading performance. Picking the appropriate measurement tools and granularity can reveal the relevant behavior of the system.

Analysis of obtained empirical performance data to **identify issues** and optimization potential in the source code and on the system. Particularly, hot spots—code regions where execution requires significant portions of runtime (or system resources)—are identified. Then, the optimization potential of the hot spots is assessed based on potential performance gains and the estimated time required to modify the current solution.

Changing a few code lines to improve runtime by 5% is more efficient than recoding the whole input/output of a program, especially if I/O might account for only 1% of the total runtime. However, care must be taken when the potential is assessed; depending on the overall runtime, a small improvement might be valuable. From the view of the computing facility, decreasing by 1% the runtime of a program which runs for millions of CPU hours yields a clear benefit by saving operational costs in form of 10,000 CPU hours (about 1.5 CPU years).

Generation of Alternatives. Based on the insight gained by the analysis, alternative implementation and tuning options are explored, and system modifications are considered that may mitigate the observed performance issue. This is actually the hardest part of the tuning because it requires that the behavior of the new system can be predicted or estimated. In practice, however, multiple potential options often are evaluated; and, based on the results, the best one is chosen. With increasing experience and knowledge of the person tuning the system, the number of options is reduced as the future behavior can be better anticipated.

Implementation. At the end of a loop the current system is modified; that is, one of the performance relevant layers is adjusted, to realize the potential improvement of the new design. The system is re-evaluated in the next cycle until the time required to change the system outweighs potential improvements or potential gains are too small because the performance measured is already near-optimal. In practice, however, in most cases the efficiency of the current solution is not estimated; instead, the current runtime is considered to be potentially saved.

These phases are then repeated until the desired performance is achieved or until further tuning is not cost effective.

2.2   Measurement

In the closed loop, data is collected that characterizes the application run and system utilization. Many types of data can be collected. For example, the operating system provides a rich set of interesting characteristics such as memory, network, I/O, and CPU usage. These characterize the activity of the whole system, and sometimes usage can even be assigned to individual applications.

The semantics of this data can be of various kinds. Usually, a *metric* defines the measurement process and the way subsequent values are obtained. For example, *time* is a simple metric that indicates the amount of time spent in a program, function or hardware command. The *throughput* of a storage system, that is, the amount of data transferred per second, is another metric.

One way of managing performance information is to store *statistics*, for example, absolute values such as number of function invocations, utilization of a component, average execution time of a function, or floating-point operations performed. Statistics of the activity of a program are referred to as a **profile**. A profile aggregates events by a given metric, for example by summing up the inclusive duration of function calls. Many tools exist that generate profiles for applications.

In contrast to a profile, a **trace** records events of a program together with a timestamp. Thus, it provides the exact execution chronology and allows analysis of temporal dependencies. External metrics such as hardware performance can be integrated into traces as well. Tracing of behavior produces much more data, potentially degrading performance and distorting attempts of the user to analyze observation. Therefore, in an initial analysis, often only profiles are recorded. A combination of both approaches can be applied to reduce the overhead while still offering enough information for the analysis. Events that happen during a timespan can be recorded periodically as a profile for an interval, thus allowing analysis of temporal variability. By generating profiles for disjoint code regions, behavior of the different program phases can be assessed. Another approach is to enable tracing conditionally, for example by capturing the coarse-grained I/O behavior of the application with statistics and starting tracing when observed performance drops.

The performance data must be correlated with the interesting application's behavior and source code. Depending on the measurement process, assigning information to the cause can be impossible. For example, a statistic cannot reveal the contribution of concurrent activity. Some low-level tools exploit compiler-generated debug symbols to localize the origin of triggered events in the source code.

Several approaches can be used to measure the performance of a given application. A *monitor* is a system that collects data about the program execution. Approaches can be classified based on *where*, *when* and *how* runtime behavior is monitored. A monitor might be capable of recording activities within an application (e.g., function calls), across used libraries, activities within the operating system such as interrupts, or it may track hardware activities; in principle, data can be collected from all components or layers. For I/O analysis, monitors rely on software to measure the state of the system. Data from available hardware sensors is usually queried from the software on demand. Hardware monitors are too expensive, complicated, and inflexible to capture program activity in detail, yet some metrics such as network errors may be provided by the hardware itself.

File system administrators typically measure on the file system server side. Many measurements are independent from the file system type, for example, the load on the servers or the summarized throughput on network adapters or on storage subsystems. Some statistics, however, are only available with special file system types (e.g., Lustre, Spectrum Scale, BeeGFS, NFS).

2.3   Preparation of Applications

Although the Linux operating system offers various statistics in the /proc file system, this information is often insufficient for I/O analysis. Usually, changes are made to the program under inspection in order to increase analysis capabilities; the activity that alters a program is called *instrumentation*. Popular methods are to modify source code, to relink object files with patched functions, overriding dynamic library calls at execution time with *LD_PRELOAD*, or to modify machine code directly [3]. During execution, such a modified program invokes functions of the monitoring environment to provide additional information about the program execution and the system state. This instrumentation functionality could also be supported directly by the (operating) system, and hence one could collect performance data without modifying the application.

Since a software monitor requires certain resources to perform its duty (those can be considered as overhead), monitoring an application perturbs the original execution. Observed data must be kept in memory and might be flushed to disk if memory space does not suffice. Additionally, computation is required to update the performance data. The overhead depends on the characteristics of the application and system: it might perturb behavior of the instrumented application so much that an assessment of the original behavior is impossible. In I/O analysis, particularly storing the profile or trace in memory and flushing it to secondary storage incurs considerable overhead that causes additional I/O.

Several techniques can be used to combat potential overhead (and thus application perturbation) in I/O instrumentation. Some tools constrain their instrumentation to summary statistics [4] or compressed representations [5] to minimize overhead. Others may automatically filter activity if an event is fired too often or if the overhead of the measurement system itself grows too high. If filtering still incurs too much overhead, then interesting functions can be manually instrumented, i.e., by inserting calls to the monitoring interface by hand.

Additionally, a selective activation of the monitor can significantly reduce the amount of recorded data. A monitor could sample events at a lower frequency, reducing the overhead and the trace detail level on the same extent.

2.4   Analysis of Data

Users analyze the data recorded by the monitoring system in order to localize optimization potential. Performance data can be recorded during program execution and assessed after the application has finished; this approach of *postmortem* analysis is also referred to as *offline* analysis. An advantage of this approach is that data can be analyzed multiple times and compared with older results. Another approach is to gather and assess data *online*, while the program runs. In this approach, feedback is provided immediately to the user, who could adjust settings to the monitoring environment depending on the results.

Because of the vast amount of data, sophisticated tools are required in order to localize performance issues of the system, correlate them with application behavior, and identify the source code causing them. Tools operate either manually (i.e., the user must inspect the data) or automatically. A *semi-automatic tool* could give hints to the user where abnormalities or inefficiencies are found. Tool environments that localize and tune code automatically, without user interaction, are on the wishlist of all programmers. Because of the system and application complexity, however, such tools are only applicable for a very small set of problems. Usually, tools offer analysis capability in several *views* or *displays*, each relevant to a particular type of analysis.

At best a system-wide monitoring of all applications can be conducted to reveal issues; in other words, all applications running on a supercomputer are constantly monitored in a non-intrusive fashion while additional analysis is triggered upon demand. In order to better understand the behavior of a single application, separate analysis runs may be conducted, since it is important to reduce the complexity of scientific software in order to find the cause of the behavior.

The performance analysis is usually done in an ad hoc manner because of the nature of the logs produced by these large scale machines: they are machine specific, and despite having similar attributes, do not share a single format for their trace behavior. This situation extends past HPC storage, and applies more broadly to HPC in general and, additionally, to individual application traces.

Because of this difference in log/trace format, system analysis is usually done per system. Such analysis can produce useful results on the behavior of a particular system, but sheds no light on how it compares to other similar systems, HPC or otherwise [6–9]. Additionally, programmer effort is wasted analyzing each system when the generated analytics are the same or similar for each system. Because of the difference in traces and techniques, these are not typically comparable, leading to most systems being analyzed in a vacuum, never compared to one another.

3 Tools

This section gives an overview of existing tools.

3.1 Darshan

Darshan [10,11] is an open source I/O characterization tool for post mortem analysis of HPC applications' I/O behavior. Its primary objective is to capture concise but useful information with minimal overhead. Darshan accomplishes this by eschewing end-to-end tracing in favor of compact statistics such as elapsed time, access sizes, access patterns, and file names for each file opened by an application. These statistics are captured in a bounded amount of memory per process as the application executes. When the application shuts down, it is reduced, compressed, and stored in a unified log file. Utilities included with Darshan can then be used to analyze, visualize, and summarize the Darshan log information. Because of Darshan's low overhead, it is suitable for system-wide deployment on large-scale systems. In this deployment model, Darshan can be used not just to investigate the I/O behavior of individual applications but also to capture a broad view of system workloads for use by facility operators and I/O researchers. Darshan is compatible with a wide range of HPC systems.

Darshan supports several types of instrumentation via software modules. Each module provides its own statistical counters and function wrappers while sharing a common infrastructure for reduction, compression, and storage. The most full-featured modules provide instrumentation for POSIX, MPI-IO and standard I/O library function calls, while additional modules provide limited PNetCDF and HDF5 instrumentation. Other modules collect system information, such as Blue Gene runtime system parameters or Lustre file system striping parameters. The Darshan eXtended Tracing (DXT) module can be enabled at runtime to increase fidelity by recording a complete trace of all MPI-IO and POSIX I/O operations.

Darshan uses *LD_PRELOAD* to intercept I/O calls at runtime in dynamically linked executables and link-time wrappers to intercept I/O calls at compile time in statically linked executables. For example, to override POSIX I/O calls, the GNU C Library is overloaded so that Darshan can intercept all the read, write and metadata operations. In order to measure MPI I/O, the MPI libaries must be similarly overridden. This technique allows an application to be traced without modification and with reasonably low overhead.

3.2 Vampir

Vampir[1] [12] is an open source graphical tool for post mortem performance analysis of parallel systems. It supports off-line analysis of parallel software (MPI, OpenMP, multi-threaded) and hardware-accelerated (CUDA and OpenCL) applications. The analysis engine allows a scalable and efficient processing of

---

[1] http://www.paratools.com/Vampir.

large amounts of data. Vampir uses the infrastructure of Score-P[2] for instrumenting applications. Score-P stores events in a file, which can be analysed by Vampir and converted to different views; for example, events can be presented on a time axis or compressed to different statistics. Some views have elaborate filters and zoom functions that can provide an overview but can also show details. Effective usage of Vampir requires a deep understanding of parallel programming. Although the program enables one to capture and analyze sequences of POSIX I/O operations, it gives little or no information about the origin or evaluation of I/O.

3.3   Mistral/Breeze

Mistral is commercial command-line tool from Ellexus[3] used to report and resolve I/O performance issues of misbehaving complex Linux applications on HPC clusters. It has real-time monitoring abilities and can change the I/O behavior of applications in order to delay I/O operations and prevent overloading of shared storage. Rules for monitoring and throttling I/O are stored as plain text in configuration files called contracts, which can be modified at runtime by privileged users for systemwide changes and by users application-wide. A sophisticated logging mechanism registers monitoring and throttling events and stores them in files; but with an appropriate plug-in, the logging information can be redirected to any location, for example, in a central database such as Elasticsearch or InfluxDB so that the results can be viewed with Grafana.[4] Administrators can use Mistral to identify applications that are running with bad I/O patterns and harming performance of shared file systems. It can also be used outside of production to run quality assurance tests on complex applications prior to deployment. The key idea behind Mistral is that the information collected is configurable and easily aggregated so that Mistral can be run at scale. Mistral supports POSIX and MPI (MPICH, MVAPICH, OpenMPI) I/O interfaces.

Ellexus Breeze is a user-friendly, self-explained, and well-documented off-line analysis tool with command-line, GUI, and HTML reporting modes. All the information gathered during the application runtime is presented in a comprehensive format and can be of great help to developers. The detailed information about environment can help support teams reproduce and understand problems. The most valuable piece of information is the list of application dependencies so that users and administrators can get a list of every file, library, program, and network location used by an application. Breeze also includes a breakdown of how each program accessed each file so that performance issues such as inefficient metadata access can be found and resolved.

The analysis tool is delivered with a tool called *"trace-program.sh"* that can capture MPI-IO and POSIX function calls and information about the environment and store them in binary trace files. It uses $LD\_PRELOAD$ to wrap original

---

[2] http://www.vi-hps.org/projects/score-p/.

[3] https://www.ellexus.com/products/.

[4] https://grafana.com/.

I/O function and, therefore, works only with dynamically linked I/O libraries. Breeze uses either a proprietary binary trace format or plain text output files reported similar to the popular diagnostic tool *strace*. The binary format has some performance advantages and can be decoded to a human readable representation by the included *decode-trace.sh* tool.

Another feature is the ability to compare two different application runs, thereby identifying changes in an application's behaviour and providing valuable feedback to the application's developers.

3.4 SIOX

SIOX [13] is a highly modular instrumentation, analysis, and profiling framework. It contains an instrumentation tool *"siox-inst"*, a trace reader *"siox-trace-reader"*, and a set of plug-ins and wrappers.

It has wrappers for MPI, POSIX, NetCDF, and HDF5 interfaces that contain reimplementations of the original I/O functions. Inside a reimplemented function is a call to the original function or syscall, and instrumentation code, that generates an activity after each execution. Activities in SIOX are structures that contain various information about the calls. The wrappers can be dynamically linked to an application by using *LD_PRELOAD* and the creation of wrappers during link-time.

Extreme modular design is a key feature of SIOX. The tools *siox-inst* and *siox-trace-reader* can be considered as pure plug-in infrastructures. In other words, there is no functionality inside until some plug-ins and wrappers are loaded. Usage of different sets of plug-ins and wrappers may result in "new" tools that exactly fit the problem. There is no restriction on the number of wrappers and plug-ins that can be loaded simultaneously, so that the functionality of SIOX can be easily extended to perform complex tasks. It has been used to research various aspects such as triggering tracing depending on unusual system behavior, the creation of replayers for recorded behavior, the mutation of I/O calls rerouting targets or replacing system calls, and online analysis. Online analysis can be done by *siox-inst*, by collecting activities from the wrappers and forwarding them to the registered plug-ins. Off-line analysis is based on both tools. Most of the SIOX plug-ins use plug-in interfaces that are supported by *siox-inst* and *siox-trace-reader*, and consequentially these plug-ins can be used by both tools. SIOX has also been coupled with OpenTSDB and Grafana to support online monitoring [14].

By using an instrumented version of FUSE, we found that the complexity of I/O tracers can be reduced and one can monitor `mmap()` of applications. Note that because of the popularity of other tools, SIOX is primarily maintained as a research vehicle.

3.5 PIOM-MP

PIOM-MP (formerly known as PAS2P-IO [15,16]) represents the MPI application's I/O behavior by using I/O phases. A phase is a consecutive sequence of similar access patterns into the logical view of a file. Because HPC scientific applications show a repetitive behavior, m phases will exist in the application. PIOM-MP identifies applications" phases with their access patterns and weights. By using phases of the applications, the analysis focuses on the functional model of the applications.

The I/O phases are used as units for analyzing the performance and scalability of parallel applications. Our approach [17] depicts the global access pattern (spatial and temporal) at the MPI-IO and POSIX-IO level. Figure 1 shows different components of PIOM-MP. It comprises three modules: PIOM-MP Tracer, PIOM-MP Analyzer, and PIOM-MP Visualizer. The first module must be in the HPC system in which the parallel application is executed; the other modules can be in a different system.

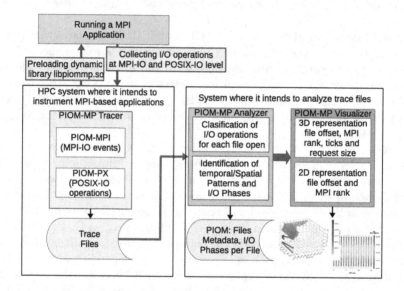

Fig. 1. PIOM-MP modules

With PIOM-MP, the user can define the relation between the phase's pattern and the I/O system configuration by using the concept of the I/O requirement in order to explain the I/O performance in a specific system [18]. Furthermore, the user can extrapolate the phases for another number of MPI processes and workloads to evaluate the parallel application I/O scalability.

3.6   Additional User-Level Tools

The Linux kernel monitors various statistics and provides them in the /proc file system. These statistics are updated with a certain frequency—typically 1 s— and can be queried by various Linux tools to monitor system and application behavior. Since these counters are incremented, they can be used to derive certain statistics for any interval such as the amount of data accessed during the execution of an application. For example, *collectl*[5] can be used to capture and analyse Lustre throughput or metadata statistics or throughput on an InfiniBand network. Other similar tools include Ganglia and Nagios.

Additional user-level tools can be executed to get a basic understanding of what the application is doing. For example, one can compare the capacity and node quotas before and after job execution to check how much permanent data and how many files have been created. Some tools work only for special file system or network types and need to be executed on client nodes where the application is running.

Additional tools of note are the Integrated Performance Monitoring for HPC[6], IOSIG [19], RIOT [20], ScalaIOTrace [5], and Linux blktrace.

3.7   Further Administrative Tools

Most preassembled parallel file system appliances provide a monitoring system with a GUI. It displays various aspects of the servers such as load and I/O activity for current and previous time slots. Typically, it also shows a number of file-system-specific statistics. In many cases, the monitoring systems are only accessible by system administrators, and hence only a few HPC sites expose such information to their users.

However, statistics can be gathered from either each client node or the server nodes. Correlation of a parallel application with the triggered activities on I/O servers is non-trivial since these are shared. With Lustre, *jobstats* [21] provide a way to easily collect I/O statistics of batch jobs with little overhead, for example, the number of open operations or total amount of written data. To activate *jobstats*, a system administrator selects the environment variable that holds the batch job ID on the client nodes. Lustre clients send the content of this variable with the standard Lustre protocol to the servers, and the servers sum up all I/O activity on this content. An example of how these statistics can be easily made available for users is described in [22]. The Lustre Monitoring Tool (LMT) [23] is also available for collecting server-side time series statistics from Lustre file systems, although data produced with LMT does not distinguish traffic from different applications.

The first tool that combined actual client and server traces of I/O into one view to show a comprehensive timeline of activities was PIOviz [24].

3.8   Tools for Unifying Trace Formats

The diversity of file formats for profiles and tracing is approached by tracing formats such as OTF [25], TAU, and EXTRAE by providing converters between the formats. Since the formats differ slightly, sometimes some information is lost. Besides such generic trace formats, various specialized trace formats exist.

---

[5] collectl, http://collectl.sourceforge.net/.
[6] IPM, https://github.com/nerscadmin/IPM.

Work is being done at the University of California, Santa Cruz, to produce a tool that provides field per record access to traces with the ability to convert them to another trace schema format on the fly. By giving the ability to translate traces directly to other formats, there is the expectation that analysis will not be done ad hoc for different storage systems. This enables the creation of a standard set of tools for analyzing the behavior of parallel file systems without converting typically large traces.

While the database community has allowed programmable data presentation for some time [26], through views and computed columns, these techniques have not worked their way into trace analysis, despite many system traces being stored in database formats, such as `Parquet`, a Spark SQL queryable columnar format [27]. Presenting data in a uniform format, similar to a trace, is essential but does not require the overhead of a database, since most analysis is done in place, usually in a time series format.

The trace unification tool being developed borrows techniques from NoDB systems as well as from the database community at large. Because of the sequential nature and read-only analysis properties of trace analysis, our aim is a way to enable low-latency translation from one format to another. This approach can be used to unify traces based on the information they share and allow for the information to be analyzed directly, either from a storage system trace analysis tool that we plan to create or from an API that we plan to add in future work.

This system ingests minimal information about each file in order to allow for field-per-record addressing, which is a good interface for analysis tools to access trace data. This mechanism of trace addressing is used to create field and record primitives, which serve as the basis for our schema translation language. By allowing for records and fields to be used as primitives, a simple mechanism for traces to be unified is provided. This is achieved with a simple translation language based on s-expressions that allows for simple translation to occur, with more functionality coming in future work.

Other projects, such as TOKIO [28,29], have explored the possibility of synthesizing normalized data on demand via modular libraries rather than standardizing on an at-rest trace format. This approach is well-suited to integration of vendor instrumentation tools that utilize proprietary formats or are otherwise difficult to modify. It also enables the integration of multiple data sources simultaneously for holistic analysis and correlation.

4   Example Studies

This section gives examples about how the aforementioned tools can be used to identify performance issues. First, we describe some performance issues that can arise.

System administrators typically try to identify users with the highest I/O activity because of the huge impact that can be realized by helping such users reduce their I/O. Often users are not aware of what they are doing; for example, a user may forget to remove debugging output, and the application will write many times more data than normal. Sometimes this is sufficient to crash the storage completely.

Many sites have different options for storing data: local SSDs on the cluster nodes, burst buffers, different parallel file systems, and so forth. Frequently, application runtime can be improved by selecting an appropriate storage device. For example, with the application OpenFoam [30], one usually can use local disks to store scratch data. Doing so increases the scalability of the application and reduces the load on the central parallel file system, thus helping accelerate other applications. While these optimizations are simple to apply, users commonly store data in the wrong place and hence increase the load on the file system inadvertently.

With Lustre *jobstats* and a simple perl script [22], one can display all jobs with I/O activity above a high-water mark, for example, jobs that have done more than 5 million open operations. Huge amounts of metadata operations should be omitted because each operation requires communication with the responsible server. Lots of small read and write operations have a similar effect and additionally might cause numerous slow seeks on the file system disks. Again, *jobstats* can be used to find jobs doing a huge number of read or write operations with a small average I/O size. For more detailed information about job I/O patterns one would need to combine the file system metrics with application-level tracing from a tool such as Mistral.

Metadata operations are often a source of performance degradation. Common issues include trawling the file system looking for a file, which results in lots of failed stat or open operations. Programs also commonly check the existence of a file before opening it, producing an extra stat for every open. A better approach would be to try to open the file and to fail gracefully if it is not there. Users also can significantly slow metadata servers by opening a file every time it is written to. This usually happens when the open operation has been placed inside a for loop.

In general, parallel file systems show better performance with large sequential read/write operations than with small random operations (huge IOPS rates). Therefore, applications should read or write data in huge chunks. One area of HPC that is known for small I/O operations is the life-sciences industry [31] where applications often use one-byte reads and writes and almost always use 32 kB reads and writes. Although small I/O operations may be justifiable when the algorithms employed in mapping genomes lend themselves to the generation of lots of small files of around 4 kB, often the I/O operations are far smaller, leaving room for improvement.

Another easy improvement with parallel file systems can be achieved by setting the appropriate stripe count. If many files are used and if they are not accessed at the same time by many tasks, a stripe count of 1 is appropriate. On the other hand, if files are shared by many tasks or if only a few tasks use huge files, increasing the stripe count usually improves performance.

With MPI-IO, the MPI library, underlying libraries, and its adaption for the underlying file system can make a huge difference. For example, some vendors provided MPI versions with activated Lustre support providing further optimizations. With the main optimization each collective buffering node collects the I/O for one OST, in other words, small I/O buffers are collected into bigger buffers, and there are no locking conflicts between different nodes which try to access the same area of data. Thus, selecting the right number of collective buffering nodes for a given application and problem size might improve its runtime.

4.1 I/O Performance Analysis at the Application Level

The interaction between the I/O system and the application pattern can report poor performance in some HPC systems. In order to identify the root cause of the problem, the I/O pattern along the I/O path needs to be analyzed. Because the I/O system spans between user (compute nodes) and administrator domains, sometimes it is very difficult to coordinate work to find a possible solution.

On the one hand, administrators have several monitoring tools and commands to control, identify, and solve problems. Usually, these tools are not accessible by the users, however. Problems on this level are related mainly to parallel file systems, the network, and storage devices.

On the other hand, users have several performance analysis tools that, depending on the problem, can be used as profiling or tracing to identify or analyze the I/O. At this level, I/O issues are related mainly to application pattern and I/O libraries. The user needs to understand the impact that a specific access pattern can have on the performance. Achieving such understanding is not simple, however, because a real application can use several files and the user must evaluate each file to weigh the impact of each one, which not always is related directly with file size. An appropriate tool to start with for I/O performance analysis is Darshan, which provides I/O time and throughput for each file opened by a parallel application.

To illustrate this, Fig. 2a shows the I/O time and the relation with total time for a strong scaling case that was obtained using Darshan. Two files are selected for analyzing the application scalability: (1) the fieldgrid.h5 (red line) is the file that the user considers more important for the application because move a total of 400 GiB, which after optimizations shows a scalable behavior; and (2) a small file that corresponds to ghost cells (gc_stencils.h5 in black line) that is avoiding scaling to the application. Figure 2b shows the offset for the ghost file, whose size is 2.9 G. Concurrent accesses can be observed in Fig. 2c for all the MPI processes in lowest and highest offsets, which serialize the I/O as can be seen in Fig. 2d. The application presents an I/O imbalance observed for the first 1024 MPI processes. The I/O pattern represented in Fig. 2b is similar for the different cases showed in Fig. 2a in which there are several rewriting operations that are moving more data into the file system as the number of MPI processes increases. In this case, one must redesign the I/O pattern in order to remove the problem.

4.2 Online Monitoring

DKRZ maintains a monitoring system that gathers various statistics from 3,340 client nodes, 24 login nodes, and Lustre servers. The monitoring system is real-

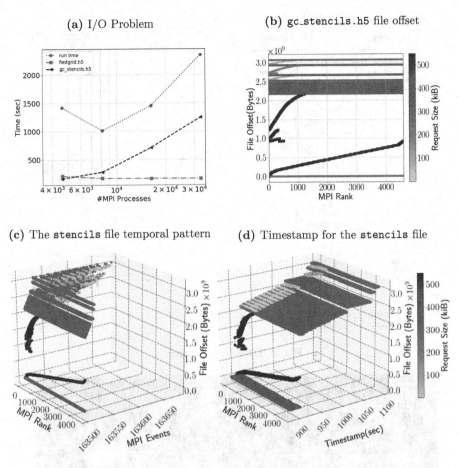

(a) I/O Problem

(b) `gc_stencils.h5` file offset

(c) The `stencils` file temporal pattern

(d) Timestamp for the `stencils` file

Fig. 2. Example of I/O performance analysis. (a) Identifying the file with more impact on run time using Darshan. (b) Analyzing the I/O pattern with a focus on the `gc_stencils.h5` file offset for 4608 MPI processes using PIOM-MP. (c) The `gc_stencils.h5` file temporal pattern based on the application logical using MPI events as ticks. (d) The `gc_stencils.h5` file temporal pattern using system timestamps. (Color figure online)

ized mainly by open source components such as Grafana, OpenTSDB,[7], and Elasticseach but also includes a self-developed data collector. Additionally, the monitoring system obtains various information from the Slurm workload manager. A schematic overview is provided in Fig. 3.

The data is aggregated and visualized by a Grafana web interface, which is available to all DKRZ users. The information is structured in three sections: login nodes, user jobs, and queue statistics.

---

[7] Consists of various additional components from the Hadoop Stack.

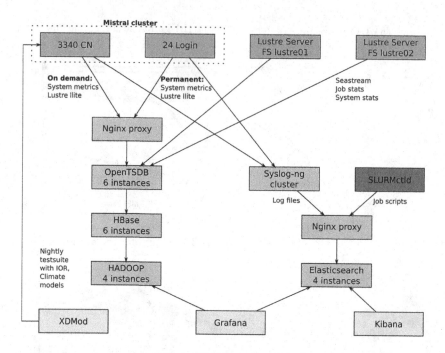

Fig. 3. DKRZ-monitoring

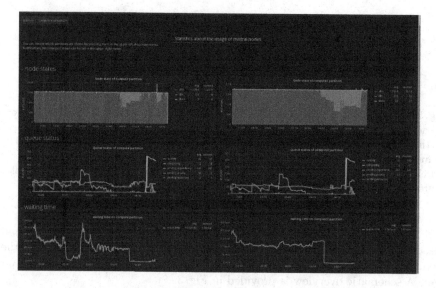

Fig. 4. Statistics about the usage of Mistral nodes

In the first place, a monitoring service gives the users an overview of the current state of the system, namely, the current load of login nodes and number of used nodes on Slurm partitions. For each single machine, a detail view also provides information about system load, memory consumption, and Lustre statistics, as well as historical data. Job monitoring is enabled by default in a coarse-grained mode but can be modified by a Slurm parameter. When enabled, the monitoring system gathers information about CPU usage and frequency, memory consumption, Lustre throughput, and network traffic for each client node. Statistics about the usage of *Mistral* nodes (Fig. 4) show the current state and history of node allocation, queue status, and waiting time of both Slurm partitions. Additionally, DRKZ runs xdmod on the client nodes for viewing historical job information as well as real-time scientific application profiling.

4.3   Online Monitoring with LLview

In 2004 the Jülich Supercomputing Centre (JSC) began to develop LLview [32], an interactive graphical tool to monitor job scheduling for various resource managers such as SLURM or LoadLeveler. In its stand-alone and web-based clients LLview provides information about currently running jobs and how they are mapped on the individual nodes of an HPC cluster, using an intuitive visual representation of the underlying cluster configuration. In addition, it includes statistical information on completed jobs as well as a prediction for scheduled future jobs [33]. LLview is client-server based. Internally it uses an XML schema named LML [34] as an extensible abstraction layer to encode monitor data. The data itself is obtained from various server and application interfaces and subsequently transferred to the clients of LLview. LML is a simple, extensible, and independent description of node- and job-related information. A subset of the LLview dashboard elements are also integrated in Parallel Tools Platform, an extension to Eclipse to develop, run, and debug parallel programs on a remote HPC system [35].

Recently, a number of extensions to LLview have been designed and implemented that allow users to acquire, store, and display job performance metrics such as node CPU load, memory usage, interconnect activity, and I/O activity. In practice at JSC these have greatly facilitated the analysis of HPC codes that either show unsatisfactory performance or behave incorrectly. With regard to metrics about I/O, the subject of this paper, LLview uses performance data generated with the GPFS mmpmon command [36] within the framework of the IBM Spectrum Scale (GPFS) file system. At JSC, all GPFS clients running on cluster compute nodes are configured to frequently write (every 1–2 min) such mmpmon data to a log file that itself resides in a local GPFS files system. The LLview server components collect the I/O performance data (e.g., number of bytes written/read, number of open/close calls) from these files and match it to user jobs that are running on these nodes. This mapping is possible because node sharing is not applied on JSC systems. The job-based data is then stored in an internal database, from which individual performance reports are generated.

Since the minimum update frequency of LLview is not more than once a minute, JSC has integrated this to help users monitor job behavior on a coarse level and to help detect performance issues while jobs are running on the system. Within a web portal (*LLview jobreports*) access is provided to timeline-based performance data of current and recently finished jobs on the system, ranging two weeks into the past. In addition to interactive charts displaying the various performance data, the portal provides PDF reports for all jobs, which can be collected and archived by users to document their production runs. These extensions of LLview have proven useful as a first step of performance analysis and code tuning, thanks to the integrated coarse view on the most essential performance metrics of user jobs. In this way it greatly facilitates the detection of situations where deeper performance analysis and tuning should be started with additional tools such as Darshan or SIOX (Sect. 3).

5   Challenges in Analyzing I/O

The following list represents issues that we see as a community that must be overcome to ensure effective and efficient monitoring in future HPC systems.

- **Ability to monitor I/O at all levels:** The involvement of many layers in the I/O stack that are not instrumented limits the ability to identify issues. Today, parallel file systems typically have disks, storage controllers, storage servers, and clients. All are connected with different network types. Hardware and firmware or software can cause performance degradation at each layer. Above the parallel file systems are MPI-IO, MPI libraries, and upper-level libraries such as HDF5. In many cases administrative power and deep knowledge are required in order to capture data from certain layers. In an ideal case, one should be able to easily investigate the I/O at each level.
- **Adaption of tools to new programming models:** The HPC application community has long been (and still is) dominated by MPI simulations written in Fortran or C. However, other paradigms such as deep learning and big data use their own programming models, languages, and runtime environments. Parallel I/O analysis tools must adapt to keep pace as these models are more widely adopted in HPC.
- **Adaption to new hardware technologies:** Analyzing parallel I/O at the moment basically means analyzing I/O access to a parallel file system, but a number of emerging technologies call for a broader interpretation of I/O. Future systems may include nonvolatile memory (which may be accessed as a memory device or a file system) and multiple tiers of storage that hold the simulation working set, campaign data, or archival data. The performance of each subsystem is best interpreted in the context of the complete storage hierarchy. These new technologies must provide means to systematically report performance data for the analysis.
- **Integrating analysis data:** Data analysis of performance data is often an afterthought, done after the application was executed (post mortem). Projects such as TOKIO[8] are working toward integrating data from multiple components of the storage system, but this remains a pressing problem. Each storage

---

[8] http://www.nersc.gov/research-and-development/storage-and-i-o-technologies/tokio/.

system component is typically designed by a specialized vendor and is serviced by its own instrumentation framework. Aligning and synthesizing data from job schedulers, applications, file systems, storage devices, and network devices remain a significant challenge.

- **Feature replication and sustainability:** Many of the technologies included in this survey serve overlapping purposes and implement their own variation of tasks such as function interception, time series indexing, and visualization. Increased standardization and code sharing could potentially reduce the engineering effort involved in each project while at the same time increasing portability.

- **Performance assessment:** Monitoring and recording performance data are part of the process. However, it is often hard for experts to assess whether the observed behavior and performance is acceptable or not. End users typically do not understand what a runtime of X seconds or an achieved performance of Y GiB/s means. Guidance for assessing the quality is a necessary step.

- **Correlation of I/O monitoring with other metrics:** In parallel applications it is often essential to observe more than only one performance metric such as I/O activity in an isolated manner. Rather, bringing I/O activity in correlation with other metrics such as CPU activity, memory usage, and interconnect usage is needed in order to identify root causes of faulty behavior and to distinguish between causes and effects.

- **User guidance:** A gap remains between what can be learned from expert I/O analysis and what can be readily adapted by end users. The data produced by today's I/O analysis tools requires significant expertise to interpret, and little guidance is provided as to what I/O performance a user should expect in a given application scenario.

- **Small developer community:** I/O tools for HPC suffer from the fact that the HPC community is small and I/O is often neglected. Massive amounts of traces are being generated from user applications and other sources outside the HPC community but not covered by tools. We have to make the base of tools (at least) useful outside the HPC community, for example, to CERN [37,38], in order to speed the development.

We believe that the **standardization of monitoring APIs and infrastructure** is a necessary step facing the overall community. At the moment no standard API exists to ease the reporting of data; instead, vendors and tool developers build their own solution. A standard would be beneficial to several issues mentioned in this list, and might help encourage hardware and software developers to provide the necessary data. Indeed, we must standardize our approaches to system analysis, both to allow comparison between like systems and to avoid the programming overhead of repeatedly creating the same analytics code again and again. By creating a standardized method of analyzing storage systems, as well as other system traces, we hope to light the path ahead to exascale and help computing centers deal with massive growth and data-driven analysis.

Additionally, by creating a general-purpose method of trace analysis, we can provide optimizations and features that would be too costly to develop for individual tools or systems.

6 Conclusions

In this paper, we have provided an overview of the state-of-the-art in I/O monitoring tools, motivated by our own involvement in the development of the described tools. We then gave examples of how monitoring can be used to reveal I/O issues; because of space limitations, this list is intended as an appetizer for the reader to study the tools and mentioned papers further. Furthermore, we discussed challenges we see as a community that are currently not well addressed and must be resolved further in future research, development, and engineering. One step forward for the community is to work on standardization.

Acknowledgments. PIOM-MP is a work partially supported by the MICINN/ MINECO Spain under contracts TIN2014-53172-P and TIN2017-84875-P. This material is based in part on work supported by the U.S. Department of Energy, Office of Science, under contract DE-AC02-06CH11357. We thank Felicity Pitchers for the proofreading.

References

1. Benson, T., Anand, A., Akella, A., Zhang, M.: Understanding data center traffic characteristics. SIGCOMM Comput. Commun. Rev. **40**(1), 92–99 (2010)
2. Bergman, K., et al.: Exascale computing study: technology challenges in achieving exascale systems. Technical report 15, Defense Advanced Research Projects Agency Information Processing Techniques Office (DARPA IPTO) (2008)
3. Shende, S., Malony, A.D., Ansell-bell, R.: Instrumentation and measurement strategies for flexible and portable empirical performance evaluation. In: International Conference on Parallel and Distributed Processing Techniques and Applications, PDPTA, pp. 1150–1156 (2001)
4. Carns, P., Latham, R., Ross, R., Iskra, K., Lang, S., Riley, K.: 24/7 characterization of petascale I/O workloads. In: Proceedings of 2009 Workshop on Interfaces and Architectures for Scientific Data Storage. IEEE (2009)
5. Vijayakumar, K., Mueller, F., Ma, X., Roth, P.C.: Scalable I/O tracing and analysis. In: Proceedings of the 4th Annual Workshop on Petascale Data Storage, pp. 26–31. ACM (2009)
6. Adams, I., Madden, B., Frank, J., Storer, M.W., Miller, E.L.: Usage behavior of a large-scale scientific archive. In: Proceedings of the 2012 International Conference for High Performance Computing, Networking, Storage and Analysis (SC 2012) (2012)
7. Adams, I.F., Storer, M.W., Miller, E.L.: Analysis of workload behavior in scientific and historical long-term data repositories. ACM Trans. Storage **8**(2), 6:1–6:27 (2012)

8. Wang, F., et al.: File system workload analysis for large scale scientific computing applications. In: Proceedings of the 21st IEEE/12th NASA Goddard Conference on Mass Storage Systems and Technologies, College Park, MD, pp. 139–152, April 2004

9. Grawinkel, M., Nagel, L., Mäsker, M., Padua, F., Brinkmann, A., Sorth, L.: Analysis of the ECMWF storage landscape. In: 13th USENIX Conference on File and Storage Technologies (FAST 2015), Santa Clara, CA, pp. 15–27. USENIX Association (2015)

10. Carns, P., et al.: Understanding and improving computational science storage access through continuous characterization. ACM Trans. Storage (TOS) 7(3), 8 (2011)

11. Carns, P.: Darshan. In: High Performance Parallel I/O. Computational Science Series, pp. 309–315. Chapman & Hall/CRC (2015)

12. Knüpfer, A., et al.: Score-P: a joint performance measurement run-time infrastructure for Periscope, Scalasca, TAU, and Vampir. In: Brunst, H., Müller, M., Nagel, W., Resch, M. (eds.) Tools for High Performance Computing 2011, pp. 79–91. Springer, Heidelberg (2012). https://doi.org/10.1007/978-3-642-31476-6_7

13. Kunkel, J.M., et al.: The SIOX architecture – coupling automatic monitoring and optimization of parallel I/O. In: Kunkel, J.M., Ludwig, T., Meuer, H.W. (eds.) ISC 2014. LNCS, vol. 8488, pp. 245–260. Springer, Cham (2014). https://doi.org/10.1007/978-3-319-07518-1_16

14. Betke, E., Kunkel, J.: Real-time I/O-monitoring of HPC applications with SIOX, elasticsearch, Grafana and FUSE. In: Kunkel, J.M., Yokota, R., Taufer, M., Shalf, J. (eds.) ISC High Performance 2017. LNCS, vol. 10524, pp. 174–186. Springer, Cham (2017). https://doi.org/10.1007/978-3-319-67630-2_15

15. Mendez, S., Rexachs, D., Luque, E.: Modeling parallel scientific applications through their input/output phases. In: 2012 IEEE International Conference on Cluster Computing Workshops (CLUSTER WORKSHOPS), pp. 7–15, September 2012

16. Mendez, S., Panadero, J., Wong, A., Rexachs, D., Luque, E.: A new approach for analyzing I/O in parallel scientific applications. In: CACIC 12, Congreso Argentino de Ciencias de la Computación, pp. 337–346 (2012)

17. Gomez-Sanchez, P., Mendez, S., Rexachs, D., Luque, E.: PIOM-PX: a framework for modeling the I/O behavior of parallel scientific applications. In: Kunkel, J.M., Yokota, R., Taufer, M., Shalf, J. (eds.) ISC High Performance 2017. LNCS, vol. 10524, pp. 160–173. Springer, Cham (2017). https://doi.org/10.1007/978-3-319-67630-2_14

18. Mendez, S., Rexachs, D., Luque, E.: Analyzing the parallel I/O severity of MPI applications. In: Proceedings of the 17th IEEE/ACM International Symposium on Cluster, Cloud and Grid Computing, CCGRID 2017, Madrid, Spain, 14–17 May 2017, pp. 953–962 (2017)

19. Yin, Y., Byna, S., Song, H., Sun, X.H., Thakur, R.: Boosting application-specific parallel I/O optimization using IOSIG. In: Proceedings of the 2012 12th IEEE/ACM International Symposium on Cluster, Cloud and Grid Computing (CCGRID 2012), pp. 196–203. IEEE Computer Society (2012)

20. Wright, S.A., et al.: Parallel file system analysis through application I/O tracing. Comput. J. 56(2), 141–155 (2012)

21. Intel (2011–2017), Oracle(2010–2011): Lustre Software Release 2.x, Operations Manual. Chapter 12.2

22. Lustre-Community: Lustre Monitoring and Statistics Guide. Chapters 6.2.7 and 6.2.8. http://wiki.lustre.org/Lustre_Monitoring_and_Statistics_Guide

23. Uselton, A.: Deploying server-side file system monitoring at NERSC. In: Proceedings of the 2009 Cray User Group (2009)
24. Ludwig, T., Krempel, S., Kuhn, M., Kunkel, J., Lohse, C.: Analysis of the MPI-IO optimization levels with the PIOViz jumpshot enhancement. In: Cappello, F., Herault, T., Dongarra, J. (eds.) EuroPVM/MPI 2007. LNCS, vol. 4757, pp. 213–222. Springer, Heidelberg (2007). https://doi.org/10.1007/978-3-540-75416-9_32
25. Eschweiler, D., Wagner, M., Geimer, M., Knüpfer, A., Nagel, W.E., Wolf, F.: Open Trace Format 2: the next generation of scalable trace formats and support libraries. In: PARCO, vol. 22, pp. 481–490 (2011)
26. Smith, I.: Guide to using SQL: computed and automatic columns. Rdb J. (2008)
27. Armbrust, M., et al.: Spark SQL: relational data processing in Spark. In: Proceedings of the 2015 ACM SIGMOD International Conference on Management of Data, SIGMOD 2015, pp. 1383–1394. ACM, New York (2015)
28. Lockwood, G.K., et al.: UMAMI: a recipe for generating meaningful metrics through holistic I/O performance analysis. In: Proceedings of the 2nd Joint International Workshop on Parallel Data Storage and Data Intensive Scalable Computing Systems, pp. 55–60. ACM (2017)
29. Lockwood, G.K., Snyder, S., Brown, G., Harms, K., Carns, P., Wright, N.J.: TOKIO on ClusterStor: connecting standard tools to enable holistic I/O performance analysis. In: Proceedings of the 2018 Cray User Group (2018)
30. Jasak, H., Jemcov, A., Tukovic, Z., et al.: OpenFOAM: a C++ library for complex physics simulations. In: International Workshop on Coupled Methods in Numerical Dynamics, vol. 1000, pp. 1–20. IUC Dubrovnik, Croatia (2007)
31. Ellexus, Alces-Flight: Maximising HPC performance on AWS public cloud. https://www.ellexus.com/wp-content/uploads/2017/07/white_paper_alces_ellexus.pdf
32. Frings, W., Karbach, C.: LLview: graphical monitoring of batch system controlled cluster (2004, 2018). http://www.fz-juelich.de/jsc/llview/
33. Karbach, C.: A highly configurable and efficient simulator for job schedulers on supercomputers. PARS-Mitt. **30**(1), 25–36 (2013)
34. Karbach, C.: LML: large-scale system markup language (2013). http://llview.fz-juelich.de/LML/OnlineDocumentation/lmldoc.html
35. Watson, G.R., Frings, W., Knobloch, C., Karbach, C., Rossi, A.L.: Scalable control and monitoring of supercomputer applications using an integrated tool framework. In: 2011 40th International Conference on Parallel Processing Workshops, pp. 457–466, September 2011
36. IBM: Monitoring GPFS I/O performance with the mmpmon command (2018). https://www.ibm.com/support/knowledgecenter/STXKQY_5.0.0/com.ibm.spectrum.scale.v5r00.doc/bl1adv_mmpmonch.htm
37. Peters, A., Sindrilaru, E., Adde, G.: EOS as the present and future solution for data storage at CERN. J. Phys.: Conf. Ser. **664**(4), 042042 (2015)
38. Peters, A.J., Janyst, L.: Exabyte scale storage at CERN. J. Phys.: Conf. Ser. **331**(5), 052015 (2011)

Workshop on Performance
and Scalability of Storage Systems
(WOPSSS 2018)

Workshop on Performance and Scalability of Storage Systems (WOPSSS 2018)

Jean-thomas Acquaviva[1], Jalil Boukhobza[2], Philippe Deniel[3],
Massimo Lamanna[4], Pedro Javier Garcia[5], and Allen D. Malony[6]

[1] DDN Storage
[2] Univ. Bretagne Occidentale
[3] CEA/DIF
[4] CERN
[5] University of Castilla-La Mancha
[6] University of Oregon

WOPSSS is a place to discuss and present research results in the area of storage and IO with a specific twist on performance. The notion of performance is large and can be declined in different sub-topics, from scalability, robustness, or quality of service, and so on. The initial motivation for this workshop relies in the emergence of new hardware technologies which had held promises of dramatic performance improvements. These expectations had an hard time to be fulfilled. Which in turn has increased the interest for performance analysis of the legacy software from storage systems.

For instance, Fig. 1 displays the write efficiency of 3 different storage systems, all of them using flash device[1]. On these graphics I/O patterns are defined by 3 parameters:

– I/O size: from 4KB (small), to 32KB (medium) and 1MB (large),
– Spatial locality: either sequential or random,
– Congestion factor: Shared file or one File Per Process (FPP).

It appears that depending on the I/O pattern each system responds differently in term of performance. Overall each system has a distinct robustness profile in respect to the I/O patterns.

For its third edition, WOPSSS had seven papers presented this year. These contributions address: performance analysis, application of performance analysis to on-line optimization, evaluation of the new hardware and also new performance monitoring frameworks. On the field of performance analysis, the first article is addressing the specific problem of metadata perceived performance. Quite often meta-data results are presented as throughput measurements. However, from an end-user perspective meta-data is primarily about latency. The work presented in *Understanding Metadata Latency with MDWorkbench* propose to enrich the way metadata are measured in order to capture this latency parameter.

Performance analysis is not necessarily an off-line process, and the paper *Self-Optimized Strategy for IO Accelerator Parametrization* is displaying research results

---

[1] Intel NVMe P3520 model.

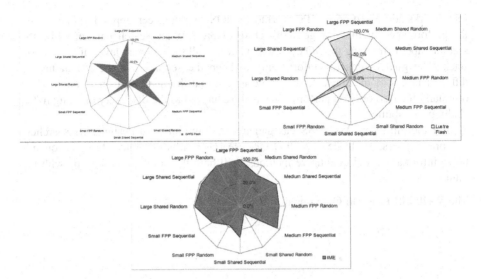

Fig. 1. Write efficiency: ability of storage systems to deliver performance when confronted to various I/O patterns. Spectrum Scaler (top), Lustre (middle) and IME (bottom). The 3 systems have been tested using identical NMVe drives as storage devices. The impact of the software layer clearly appears in the way these 3 systems respond to the different I/O patterns. For instance Lustre has some difficulties to cope with small shared write accesses, while Spectrum Scaler is more sensitive to random accesses. IME is more robust but it is not a file system per se, more an acceleration layer. All figures were obtained using 140 MPI processes to generate the write workload.

where a machine learning algorithm is involved to dynamically characterize the IO pattern of an application. Based on the dynamic characterization various optimization policies can be triggered on the storage architecture. Characterization is specifically focused on the spatial locality of the IO accesses.

Two papers are investigating the performance impact of new hardware platform. Firstly, *Performance study of non-volatile memories on a high-end supercomputer* is presenting measurements obtained using non-volatile-memory directly within a compute node. Such an architecture offers a deeper storage hierarchy, with a local fast storage, and a remote-fabric attached storage more oriented toward capacity and resilience. The second hardware paper *Benefit of DDN IME-Fuse and IME-Lustre file systems for IO intensive HPC applications* is discussing the performance impact of DDN's IME storage system. This approach also leads to a deeper storage hierarchy, but this time behind the fabric, the remote storage becomes tiered between a flash layer and a capacity one using hard drives.

While not being strictly an hardware analysis *Exploring Scientific Application Performance Using Large Scale Object Storage* could be considered as an infrastructure analysis, where the impact of the paradigm shift from files to objects is discussed. Two performance monitoring frameworks are also introduced, *IOscope: A Flexible IO Tracer for Workloads IO Pattern Characterization* and *From Application to Disk: Tracing IO Through the Big Data Stack*. Interestingly enough both frameworks addressed none-HPC workloads. IOScope has been applied to understand the performance of the storage architecture of the QWant Search engine, while the second paper is tracking the I/O cycles spent across all the software layer of an Hadoop stack. The goal in this last effort being to keep the semantic of the I/O along the different layers of the stack. It should be noted, that the last effort on Hadoop while originally focused only on performance analyse has led to the discovery of a bug in the Hadoop distribution.

For the third year WOPSSS has gathered a community of designers, researchers and practitioners. With the hope that the research results presented, bringing quantitative information and qualitative methods, will help the community to cope with the future storage.

The WOPSSS Program Committee.

Understanding Metadata Latency
with MDWorkbench

Julian Martin Kunkel[1]([✉]) and George S. Markomanolis[2]

[1] University of Reading, Reading, UK
j.m.kunkel@reading.ac.uk
[2] KAUST Supercomputing Laboratory, Thuwal, Saudi Arabia

Abstract. While parallel file systems often satisfy the need of applications with bulk synchronous I/O, they lack capabilities of dealing with metadata intense workloads. Typically, in procurements, the focus lies on the aggregated metadata throughput using the MDTest benchmark (https://www.vi4io.org/tools/benchmarks/mdtest). However, metadata performance is crucial for interactive use. Metadata benchmarks involve even more parameters compared to I/O benchmarks. There are several aspects that are currently uncovered and, therefore, not in the focus of vendors to investigate. Particularly, response latency and interactive workloads operating on a working set of data. The lack of capabilities from file systems can be observed when looking at the IO-500 list, where metadata performance between best and worst system does not differ significantly.

In this paper, we introduce a new benchmark called MDWorkbench which generates a reproducible workload emulating many concurrent users or – in an alternative view – queuing systems. This benchmark provides a detailed latency profile, overcomes caching issues, and provides a method to assess the quality of the observed throughput. We evaluate the benchmark on state-of-the-art parallel file systems with GPFS (IBM Spectrum Scale), Lustre, Cray's Datawarp, and DDN IME, and conclude that we can reveal characteristics that could not be identified before.

1 Introduction

The benchmarking of storage systems fosters understanding of performance behavior in order to identify performance bottlenecks in the storage landscape and to tune applications towards the capabilities of the systems. The benchmarking of metadata operations of a parallel file system characterizes the performance when creating, accessing and searching directories and files. Typical user workloads on HPC systems include the bulk creation of output files from a parallel application, intensive I/O operations on a single file, the post-processing of a subset of files, and the interactive navigation/searching for relevant output files. Since HPC file systems are designed to deal with large files, they typically do not perform well on workloads involving many small files. Such workloads are, however, common and not the exception. This pattern emerges, for example, when

© Springer Nature Switzerland AG 2018
R. Yokota et al. (Eds.): ISC 2018 Workshops, LNCS 11203, pp. 75–88, 2018.
https://doi.org/10.1007/978-3-030-02465-9_5

home directories and software packages are stored on the shared file system, as some sites manage them. Container solutions also suffer from metadata issues. Additionally, some domain-specific workflows, e.g., from genomics involve many small files. This lack of performance has been finally recognized by the vendors and, for example, in the US CORAL pre-exascale initiative, IBM improved the metadata performance of Spectrum Scale (GPFS) significantly. However, there is still the need to drive the effort in the right direction.

Procurement procedures for HPC systems cover metadata requirements often by declaring a certain minimal throughput when running the MDTest benchmark. However, deployed systems still lack mandatory requirements of the users. For example, access to files is sensitive to latency; waiting up to 10 s to list 100 files or touch a new file is hindering the interactive data navigation and preparation of scientific software. The high latency is also apparent when hosting software on a shared file system. To overcome the metadata bottleneck, data centers implement workarounds like storing a container or a local file system image on the parallel file system, for example, by serving the software tree as a (read-only) EXT4 image on a Lustre file system. An image can then be mounted (typically read-only) on the clients turning the metadata workload into a well-aligned data workload for the parallel file system. The container solution Singularity[1] uses this approach, too. However, concurrent modifications to such image from multiple nodes are not possible for consistency reasons. Unfortunately, the burst buffer solution IME from DDN and Cray's DataWarp utilize the metadata infrastructure from the backend file system depending on the underlying file system's capabilities.

Besides latency, the phase oriented execution of MDTest leads to several shortcomings: First of all, a production file system will rarely see a phase oriented pattern ever in practice because typically several jobs run concurrently (acceptance testing is an exception). A phase execution of, e.g., file creates or stats in isolation, however, may lead to a different performance behavior as some resources of the parallel file system are not used within a phase, and internal locks are often not utilized. For example, in Lustre, the creation of files does mostly affect the metadata server – the MDT pre-creates a pool of zero-length objects. Moreover, bulk synchronous workloads of many benchmarks are well optimized even for disk-based storage technology, allowing benchmarks to report metrics that are artificially high and not achievable in any production environment as background processes cause interference. Additionally, a storage system that offers separated path for the individual metadata operations (which is desirable) has a disadvantage when performance of each phase is measured individually. Depending on the optimization in place, e.g., the caching strategy, results of a benchmark may vary significantly.

The contributions of this paper are: the introduction of the MDWorkbench benchmark to reveal relevant characteristics of storage systems; and the investigation of latency factors on existing parallel file systems.

---

[1] http://singularity.lbl.gov/.

This paper is organized as follows: First, related work is provided in Sect. 2. Next, the benchmark MDWorkbench is introduced together with its workload description in Sect. 3. In the evaluation (Sect. 4), we first describe the experimental setup together with four different platforms where the evaluation of the benchmark is conducted, and then present and discuss the results in Sect. 5. Finally, the paper is wrapped up in Sect. 6.

2   Related Work

The main reasons for benchmarking a computer system is to understand its performance behavior and compare it with other systems. From the user perspective, benchmarks are of interest that are representative for the applications run on a system. The importance of analyzing and improving metadata performance is illustrated in various studies, for example, in [1] and [2].

In [5], standards for building a good benchmark are discussed. According to Huppler, any good benchmark should have the most of the following criteria: to be relevant, i.e., represent something important, to be repeatable – that the benchmark can deliver same results across various executions, to be fair – not to be optimized for specific platform only, to be able to verify the output, and to be affordable for any user. In [7], an I/O system evaluation is proposed that takes into account both application requirements and the I/O configuration. The methodology is constituted of three phases: In the first one, the characterization of the application I/O requirements is extracted by measuring bandwidth and I/O operations per second (IOPs). In the second phase, the I/O configuration analysis, factors that impact the I/O system performance are identified, such as file system and I/O node connection. Finally, important metrics of application execution are collected in the evaluation phase under different configurations.

Several metadata benchmarks have been used to investigate parallel file systems. MDTest is the most common MPI benchmark for evaluating the metadata performance of a file system. The benchmark runs in phases, measuring bulk-synchronous workloads. It can be executed on any POSIX-compliant file system; the newest version is integrated into the IOR benchmarking suite supporting additional interfaces. The benchmark can create various workloads, file-only tests, and nested directory trees. Fs_mark[2] is a multi-threaded benchmark for measuring concurrent activity on a POSIX file system, e.g., mimicking a mail server. It measures the time for each operation individually and reports an average throughput for each operation type. PostMark [6] is similar but primarily aims to simulate workload of a mail server by utilizing a stochastic model for the operations like creating, reading and deleting of files.

In the web server market, for OLTP workloads and low-latency applications like banks, latency is very important as, e.g., customers tend to leave slow responding web pages. Therefore, the Storage Performance Council[3] designed the SPC-1 benchmark [8]. This specification defines a workload, benchmark,

---

[2] https://sourceforge.net/projects/fsmark/.
[3] http://www.storageperformance.org/.

and a test methodology to ensure reproducible results. A standardized workload is modeled based on real-world applications and the benchmark measures and reports response time and IOPS that are crucial. However, the benchmark is designed to measure a single storage system connected to a client; it is not applicable to an HPC environment.

The Yahoo Cloud Serving Benchmark (YCSB) is widely used to measure the response time of a web application on top of a NoSQL interface offering CRUD operations. YCSB varies the number of requests issued concurrently and measures the latency. However, when responses take unexpectedly long, the threads are unable to create the necessary request rate. As a consequence, it typically reports a too optimistic value. The issue of stragglers hiding latency issues has been well summarized by Schuetze from Azul systems in a presentation[4]. The NoSQLMark [3] is an extended version of the YCSB intended to fix this issue.

3   MDWorkbench

This MPI parallel benchmark[5] mimics the concurrent access to typically small objects. It comes with the following features: deterministic access pattern mimicking interactive users or producer/consumer queues; configurable working set size to fit into a cache of a given size or exceed it; performance regression testing by preserving the working set between runs; support for various storage backends (POSIX, MPI-IO, S3, MongoDB, PostgreSQL), and report of throughput and latency statistics including timing individual I/O operations. Since the benchmark supports object storage, the naming conventions for the pattern are datasets (directories in POSIX) and objects (files in POSIX).

The benchmark executes three phases: precreation, benchmark, and cleanup. The precreation phase setups the working set and the cleanup phase removes it. A precreated environment that is not cleaned can be reused for subsequent benchmarks to speed up regression testing, i.e., constant monitoring of performance on a production system. During the benchmark run, the working set is kept constant: in each iteration, a process produces one new object and then consumes a previously created object in FIFO order. The pattern is parameterized with the following variables:

N: The number of MPI processes
D: Working set size: number of datasets to create per process
P: Working set size: number of objects to create per dataset
I: Benchmarking phase – iterations to perform per dataset
S: Size per object
O: Offset in ranks between writer and reader

For the ease of understanding, the created working set is illustrated as directory tree in Fig. 2. During the precreation phase the structure is created; each

---

[4] https://www.azul.com/files/HowNotToMeasureLatency_LLSummit_NYC_12Nov20 13.pdf.

[5] MDWorkbench is available under: https://github.com/JulianKunkel/md-workbench.

```
1  for(p=0; p < P; p++){
2    for(d=0; d < D; d++){
3      dataset = (rank, d)  // POSIX namespace is: rank/d/p
4      write(dataset, p)
5    }
6  }
```

Fig. 1. Pseudocode: creation phase

process generates a directory labeled with its rank and with D datasets, each of the datasets is populated with P objects, each of size S. On object storage, the rank directory is virtual – the D datasets are typically prefixed by the rank. The objects are created in order of their number (0 to $P-1$), see Fig. 1. After the benchmarking phase, each process is responsible for cleanup its datasets. Since I objects have been created per dataset in the meantime, the offset of these objects is shifted by I (see the files in Fig. 2).

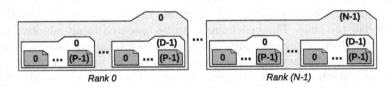

Fig. 2. The content of the working set (directory tree) after pre-creation phase, the ranks responsible for creating/deletion are indicated on the datasets. After benchmark phase all files (red boxes) are offset by I (Color figure online)

```
1  for(i=0; i < I; i++){
2    for(d=0; d < D; d++){
3      // The "rank" directories owning the files
4      read_rank = (rank - 0 * (d+1)) % N
5      write_rank = (rank + 0 * (d+1)) % N
6      // Access previously created data in FIFO order
7      dataset = (read_rank, d)
8      stat(dataset, i)
9      read(dataset, i)
10     delete(dataset, i)
11     // Append new data to increase the working set size
12     dataset = (write_rank, d)
13     write(dataset, P + i)
14   }
15 }
```

Fig. 3. Pseudocode: benchmarking phase

In the benchmarking phase, each process iterates over $D \cdot I$ objects as described in Fig. 3. In each iteration, file information from a previously created object is fetched[6], then the object is retrieved and deleted. Then a new

---

[6] A backend like MPI-IO may implement this operation as NoOp if it is not supported.

object is created. A process reads from datasets created by the D ranks before him and writes to those D ranks after him appending a new object. Objects of a rank's initially created dataset are accessed by $2D$ other ranks. It is assumed that $N > D \cdot O$ to prevent that datasets previously created by a rank are accessed later by itself, but users may test this pattern intentionally.

The outer loop iterates over the object number, thus, if all processes proceed at the same speed, a FIFO pattern of object accesses emerges. Since the successful run of the benchmarking phase, the working set looks identical besides that all objects are shifted by I, the benchmark run can be repeated on the same working set simply using an offset to the object number. The pattern can be interpreted as N users working concurrently on shared project directories or as a producer/consumer system where each process retrieves jobs from D waiting queues, processes them and issues them into D further queues.

The benchmark supports an additional *waiting factor* (throttling) parameter $T \geq 0$, that forces a process to wait T times the observed runtime after each operation. Thus, it simulates a processing time and reduces the number of submitted requests; a waiting factor of 1 effectively means that a process performs I/O only half the time. The benchmark can be executed in an adaptive mode that uses this feature several times that scans various waiting factors allowing to investigate the latency of storage depending on the number of concurrent requests (not discussed in this paper). As we will see, this allows identifying overloaded servers.

4   Experimental Setup

Benchmark Configuration: The MDWorkbench is executed from a script where several runs are executed individually: 1. Precreation of the working set; 2. Benchmarking phase; 3. Benchmarking phase (this one serves the purpose to verify the results); 4. Benchmarking phase in read-only mode; 5. Cleanup phase. Each benchmark run repeats the measurement three times with a file size of 3901 bytes[7] and reports the individual latencies of each operation. We vary: processes per node (PPN = 1 or 10), the number of datasets (D = 1 or 10), and the working set size per process (either 10k objects precreated and 2k objects for the benchmarking phase or 1k and 200 objects). Most tests were executed with 10 nodes as these typically suffice to extract near peak performance. In all cases, we run during production, so we cannot exclude interference of concurrent jobs in individual measurements. However, since each measurement is repeated 3 times and the benchmarking phase is repeated several times, outliers can be identified.

Cooley at ACLF: Cooley is the visualization cluster of Mira on the Argonne Leadership Computing Facility. It provides 126 nodes with two Intel Haswell processors (E5-2620v3 @2.4 GHz). Interconnected with FDR Infiniband, the GPFS (v3.5.0) home directory is used.

---

[7] This value is used in the IO-500 benchmark as it prevents inode stuffing; for comparison, we choose it.

Mistral at DKRZ: The supercomputer Mistral provides 3000 compute nodes each equipped with an FDR Infiniband interconnect and a Lustre storage system with 54 PByte capacity distributed across two file systems. DKRZ's Lustre version is based on a Seagate fork of Lustre 2.5 with several backports from 2.7. We harness DNE phase I, thus have several metadata servers. However, in the experiments, we use only one metadata server for comparison reasons. The directories are configured with a stripe count of 1; data is stored on 62 Cluster-Stor L300 appliances providing 124 OSTs. The nodes used for the testing are equipped with two Intel Broadwell processors (E5-2695v4 @2.1 GHz).

IME at Düsseldorf: DDN provided access to their test cluster in Düsseldorf on which 8 nodes could be used for testing. Each node is equipped with two Sandy Bridge processors (8 cores, E5-2650v2 @2.60 GHz). They are interconnected with a Mellanox Connect-X-3 card providing 100 Gb/s (4x EDR). As storage, a DDN ES14K (Exascale 3.1) with 2 metadata servers and Lustre 2.7.19.12 is provided; the storage is complemented by an IME system consisting of 4 servers. The flash native data cache of IME acts as a burst buffer and is drained to the ES14K Lustre, performance reported with IOR is 85 GB/s in write mode. In the conducted tests, IME is used via its FUSE mount.

Systems at KAUST and NERSC: Both KAUST Supercomputing Laboratory and NERSC provide access to Cray XC-40 supercomputers, called Shaheen II [4] and Cori, respectively. Both systems deploy Lustre and Cray DataWarp (DW) technologies. Also, a Sonexion 2000 is installed with a peak performance of 500 GB/s and 700 GB/s of throughput for KAUST and Cori, respectively. Shaheen II is constituted of 268 DW nodes, amounting to 1.5 PB capacity and peak performance 1.6 TB/s, while Cori uses 288 DW nodes with 1.6 PB and 1.7 TB/s peak performance. In both installations, each of DW nodes is constituted by 2 Intel P3608 SSDs. On Cori the latest Cray Linux Environment (CLE v6.0.4) is installed, while Shaheen uses CLE v5.2; this comparison is relevant for us.

5   Results

5.1   Impact of Concurrent Execution of Several Metadata Operations

This experiment fosters the understanding of the impact when running different operations concurrently vs. the execution in phases. Additionally, it demonstrates how fine grained measurements provide insights into the understanding of behavior. Therefore, we analyze the performance when bulk is creating the files, i.e., starting at an empty directory tree, each process generates 10k files in an explicitly owned private directory. Additionally, the creation rate during the mixed workload of the benchmarking phase is computed with maximum performance and one with a waiting factor of 4. The throughput as computed by overall benchmark runtime is shown in Table 1. Note that during the benchmark phase not only files are created but also read, delete, and their information is queried using stat, so the observed metadata throughput of this mixed work-load is 4x the creation rate listed in the table. With a waiting factor of 4, after each operation, we wait 4x the execution time. This, in essence, throttles the load on the metadata server to 1/5, i.e., instead of 100 processes issuing operations, roughly 20 issue requests at any time. Therefore, we compute a corrected (virtual) creation rate by multiplying the measured creation rate by 5.

From the table, it can be observed that for Lustre based systems the performance of the benchmarking phase with $T = 0$ is <1/4 precreation phase, where for Mistral it drops to 10%. KAUST with one DataWarp node is not able to provide enough metadata throughput while 8 nodes do. The GPFS on Cooley does not suffer much during the benchmarking phase and, thus, allows overlapping the different operation types more efficient than Lustre. The new hardware of the DDN system at Düsseldorf yields the best performance since it uses DNE2 and utilizes two metadata servers. However, the IME performance is significantly lower than the underlying Lustre system. The reason is the FUSE mount and that IME uses a Lustre file system for the metadata handling and needs to manage the flash storage.

Now comparing the benchmarking phase with $T = 0$ and $T = 4$, there are several cases: The virtual creation rate of $T = 4$ is higher, this is caused by a decrease in request latency since the load to the file system is reduced to one fifth – the servers have a small queue of pending operations. GPFS benefits minimal (25%), while other systems the rate increases to 3x. Mistral is different: its performance decreases when the request rate is throttled. The reason for this performance loss of Mistral is that the file system is accessed by many users and background operations issued by other users still lead to waiting queues. The burst buffers at KAUST and NERSC deliver similar results albeit different client nodes are deployed. More details are discussed in the next sections.

Table 1. Aggregated performance comparing precreation and benchmarking phase. Benchmarking phase using a waiting factor T of 0 or 4.

System	Nodes	PPN	D	Creation rate (creates/s)		
				Precreate	Benchm. $T = 0$	Benchm. $T = 4$
ALCF Cooley (GPFS)	10	10	1	6,500	5,640	8,300
Düsseldorf (Lustre)	8	10	1	47,600	12,600	30,700
Düsseldorf (IME+Lustre)	8	10	1	4,500	1,550	4,460
DKRZ Mistral (Lustre)	10	10	1	21,800	2,380	2,220
KAUST (1 DataWarp BB)	10	10	1	3,800	3,390	14,600
KAUST (8 DataWarp BB)	10	10	1	25,600	8,190	32,000
NERSC (8 DataWarp BB)	10	10	1	19,000	8,560	35,100

This alone is not sufficient to illustrate the difference in precreation and benchmarking phase. Therefore, the density of each individually timed create operation is plotted for selected systems and these phases in Fig. 4. A density graph can be considered a smoothened histogram – x-axes shows the observed runtime and the y-axes the number of occurrences, the x-axes uses the same scale for all three examples, the first diagram is printer larger for better exploration. It can be seen, that the overall system behavior changes between precreate and benchmarking phase. For Mistral, the change is minimal, while for the benchmark run they are executed typically below 1ms, the precreation phase shows a right shift in the response time and some operations take now up to 10 ms; however, the computed average performance on the benchmarking phase is lower compared to precreate! As we will see, this is due to the fact that delete and read operations of the mix take longer while create speeds up in the mix. The GPFS system behaves totally different between precreate and benchmarking phase. This is presumably caused by the locking strategy that has an issue with shared directories. The throttled benchmark run with $T = 4$ leads to a similar latency distribution than $T = 0$ for Mistral and GPFS. Furthermore, for IME+Lustre the pattern changes, here precreation and benchmark run look similar but $T = 4$ decreases latency of the creates significantly. The reason is again to be examined in the complex interplay with the FUSE client, IME and that some operations cause a delay on IME.

We investigated many cases for 10 and 100 nodes (except for the Düsseldorf cluster which had only 8 usable nodes), and from this analysis, it can be concluded that the impact of the concurrent metadata access pattern is significant. The typically significantly higher throughput of bulk creation demonstrates that preserving a fixed working set by MDWorkbench is able to investigate more real behavior and reveals caching and locking issues. To measure a system, one cannot run a single phase alone as a production system will see a mixed workload.

5.2   Overview of Results for the Benchmark Phase

An overview of the performance of all systems (and $T = 0$) is given in Table 2. Note, we exceptionally include results of DKRZ's Mistral first file system (phase 1) for comparison. The table describes the parameters for running the benchmark and provides several metrics: The creation rate of the mixed workload – the actual metadata performance is 4x the creation rate, but since so far we discussed the creation rate, we sticked with it; the balance across processes which is (t_{min}/t_{max}) – a value of 100% means all processes finish at the same time; next is the maximum time for any individual operation across all processes; finally, the latency in seconds of the 3rd quartile (Q3), i.e., below which 75% of all observations are – is given for each operation type. Albeit not a density diagram, this enables a quantitative understanding of latency.

First, we look at the balance: Most runs achieve a balance of 90%, i.e., all clients finish at the same time. However, the Mistral Lustre yields worse results, just above 70%; even for 10 client processes (Nodes = 10, PPN = 1), the balance is worse. The Düsseldorf DDN Lustre also is unbalanced, but significantly faster. Looking into the rates, the DDN Lustre system yields the best results followed by the Lustre systems with 8 DataWarp nodes. IME and the GPFS achieve the worst performance. There are several remarkable observations that

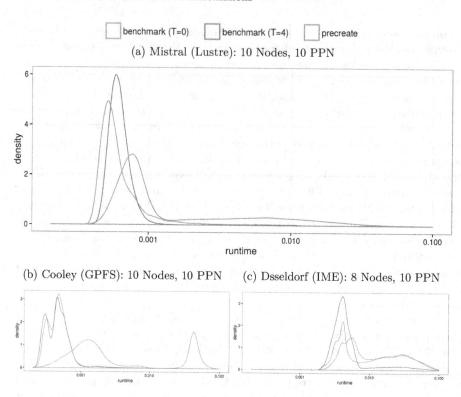

Fig. 4. Density of create operations: creation phase compared to the benchmark phase with waiting factor of 0 and 4. Parameters: $D = 1$, $I = 2000$, $P = 10000$

can only be made analyzing the latencies: (1) First of all, on several systems a maximum operation latency of one second is observable, which impacts users that work interactively; (2) At Mistral, using Nodes $= 100$ and PPN $= 10$ doubles the overall throughput of the benchmark from 2200 creates/s. But, at the same time, the maximum waiting time increases to 16 s and the waiting time of individual operations of the third quartile is increased by an order of magnitude (except for stat which increases slightly). Since in all other cases for Mistral Q3 is similar, this is a clear indicator of an overloaded file system and metadata server. This is expected at some point since the servers need to queue up pending requests increasing their latencies; (3) Q3 for IME system read is worse than for the underlying Lustre system, particularly when running multiple processes per node, so for small files, there is no benefit from the flash based solution, yet. The reason is presumably the overhead in FUSE and particularly the thread handling within FUSE where other operations delay the execution of the read operation; (4) The KAUST burst buffer can deal with a working set of 100k files well, but with 1 million files, the performance drops. This affects all Q3 statistics and the drop is more severe for 8 burst buffer nodes than for one; (5) For all Lustre systems, the number of directories does not influence the performance

Table 2. Result overview; several performance metrics for the individual systems

Nodes	PPN	D	O	P	Rate cre-at/s	balan-ce %	op_max in s	Latency of quartile 3			
								read	stat	create	delete
ACLF Cooley GPFS											
10	1	1	2000	10k	1530	95.5	0.13	9.2E-3	8.4E-4	3.9E-4	3.0E-4
10	1	10	200	1k	500	99.8	0.17	1.4E-2	8.5E-4	8.1E-3	4.5E-3
10	1	10	2000	10k	540	100	0.17	1.4E-2	9.8E-4	7.6E-3	4.1E-3
10	10	1	2000	10k	5280	60.7	0.20	1.8E-2	8.3E-4	5.6E-4	2.8E-4
DKRZ Mistral Lustre											
10	1	1	2000	10k	290	86.3	3.60	4.8E-3	6.4E-4	6.4E-4	5.8E-4
10	10	1	2000	10k	2180	68.2	3.50	4.6E-3	4.0E-4	6.7E-4	4.9E-4
10	10	10	2000	10k	2140	78.4	7.90	5.6E-3	4.2E-4	6.3E-4	3.4E-4
100	1	1	2000	10k	1610	72.2	4.60	4.8E-3	6.4E-4	6.5E-4	6.2E-4
100	10	1	2000	10k	4890	77.3	16.00	3.3E-2	6.9E-4	1.1E-2	9.9E-3
DKRZ Mistral Lustre (Procurement phase 1 file system)											
10	1	1	2000	10k	1640	100	0.54	1.0E-3	5.9E-4	7.3E-4	5.3E-4
10	1	10	2000	10k	980	100	3.90	3.8E-3	4.4E-4	7.9E-4	2.9E-4
10	10	1	2000	10k	2660	100	7.40	1.2E-2	8.7E-4	5.4E-3	5.7E-3
Dsseldorf DDN Lustre											
8	1	1	2000	10k	4750	92.4	0.00	5.0E-4	3.1E-4	4.5E-4	3.3E+4
8	1	10	200	1k	4980	95	0.01	5.6E-4	3.2E-4	4.5E-4	3.4E-4
8	10	1	2000	10k	11850	49.5	1.00	1.5E-3	8.1E-4	1.7E-3	1.7E-3
8	10	10	200	1k	10390	40.1	0.10	1.8E-3	9.7E-4	2.0E-3	2.0E-3
Dsseldorf DDN IME											
8	1	1	2000	10k	820	94.9	0.05	7.4E-4	5.5E-4	4.2E-3	4.4E-3
8	1	10	200	1k	820	96.1	0.06	7.3E-4	5.5E-4	4.1E-3	4.4E-3
8	10	1	2000	10k	1540	89.7	0.86	5.4E-3	2.0E-2	2.6E-2	1.2E-2
8	10	10	200	1k	1460	93.4	0.20	8.8E-3	2.3E-2	2.8E-2	1.4E-2
Kaust DataWarp 1 burst buffer node											
10	1	1	2000	10k	3170	99.2	0.03	6.7E-4	3.3E-4	2.2E-3	3.7E-4
10	1	10	200	1k	3130	98.8	0.06	7.5E-4	3.5E-4	2.1E-3	3.8E-4
10	10	1	2000	10k	3340	94.4	0.18	4.7E-3	7.6E-4	1.6E-2	7.9E-3
10	10	10	200	1k	3340	98.2	0.16	5.1E-3	7.3E-4	1.6E-2	8.3E-3
10	10	10	2000	10k	2190	98.4	0.43	5.0E-3	3.9E-3	2.3E-2	2.2E-2
Kaust DataWarp 8 burst buffer nodes											
10	1	1	2000	10k	4650	97.6	0.01	5.3E-4	3.3E-4	1.2E-3	3.0E-4
10	1	10	200	1k	5000	96.9	0.01	4.7E-4	2.9E-4	1.1E-3	2.9E-4
10	10	1	2000	10k	7250	82.1	0.16	1.2E-3	4.8E-4	4.1E-3	1.3E-3
10	10	10	200	1k	6510	91.3	0.16	1.2E-3	3.9E-4	3.9E-3	1.2E-3
10	10	10	2000	10k	1860	91.9	0.43	1.2E-2	1.1E-3	1.8E-2	4.9E-3
NERSC DataWarp 8 burst buffer nodes											
10	1	1	2000	10k	4000	95.3	0.03	5.2E-4	1.4E-4	8.8E-4	9.7E-5
10	1	10	200	1k	6670	93.4	0.02	4.2E-4	1.8E-4	8.2E-4	1.2E-4
10	10	1	2000	10k	8770	84.9	0.15	2.4E-3	2.0E-3	5.3E-3	1.2E-3
10	10	10	200	1k	8730	96.8	0.08	2.7E-3	1.9E-3	6.4E-3	1.3E-3

much, as long as the total working set is the same (D = 1, P = 10k, I = 2k vs. D = 10, P = 1k, I = 200). For GPFS, however, the performance behavior changes significantly, for PPN = 1, the case with D = 1 is 3x faster than D = 10. The Q3 for the stat does not change, but all other operations are one order of magnitude slower. For interactive usage, the importance of latency analysis is apparent when comparing GPFS and Mistral 100 nodes, the creation rate is similar; however, the maximum waiting time for Mistral is 16 s! For Lustre, the Q3 is slower by an order of magnitude for most operations, but it also faces extreme slow stragglers (not shown).

5.3   Understanding Latencies

To understand the density diagrams better, the timelines for the individual operations can be analyzed. In Fig. 5, we selected timelines to investigate interesting issues. A point represents a measured latency from any of the processes[8].

(a) Mistral: 10 PPN, D=1, I=2000, P=10k, Precreation phase (b) Mistral: 10 PPN, D=1, I=2000, P=10k, creates of the benchmark phase

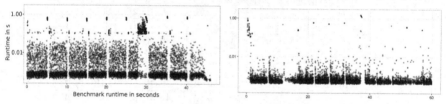

(c) GPFS: 10 PPN, D=1, I=2000, P=10k, Precreation phase (d) GPFS: 1 PPN, D=1, I=200, P=1000, creates of the benchmark phase

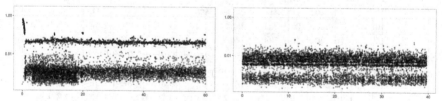

Fig. 5. Timeline of individual measurements for 10 nodes; sparse plot with random points, but every point above 0.1 s is added (qualitative view).

First, we briefly investigate the difference in creation rate between precreation phase (Fig. 5a) and benchmarking phase with T = 0 (Fig. 5b) for Mistral. One can see a periodic pattern – every 5 s, the operation execution stalls and take about a second. This could be explained by the behavior of the underlying LDISKFS (EXT4), e.g., the metadata commit timer. When running the mixed workload of the benchmark phase, intermediate waiting times are reduced and

---

[8] The plot is sparse, e.g., 100k data points of 1 million creates have been randomly selected. Additionally, all measurements about 0.1 s have been added.

slow operations are less likely. Still, the 5 s commit rate remains. Actually, the waiting time only appears for metadata modifying operations, when running the read-only workload the periodic stalls disappear. Again this shows the importance of running a mixed workload and the complexity of file systems.

For GPFS, two graphs are included: In Fig. 5c, the timeline for the precreation phase is shown. One can also see two classes of latency bands, one at 50 ms and one at 1ms. Additionally, in the beginning, with a nearly empty directory, the latency is substantially higher. Operating on multiple directories, i.e., increasing parameter D to 10 reduces performance significantly. For example, with PPN = 1 it falls from 1,500 creates/s to 500 creates/s. Figure 5d shows the timings for $D = 10$, here two bands can be observed at 10ms and at 1ms. With same total working set size but $D = 1$, the upper band vanishes (not shown). Presumably, the reason is the locks involved in the directories (tokens in GPFS speech). With $D = 10$, each directory is written and read by 10 processes increasing the looking overhead. During the precreation, each process operates on its directory but periodically flushes the data leading to the higher latencies.

6   Conclusions

In this paper, we discussed several issues for metadata benchmarking and for 10 and 100 nodes showed the importance of latency measurements. Experiments and the introduced methodology shows that with 10 nodes metadata servers of all file systems (except on Mistral) are well utilized. We demonstrated that phase-wise execution of a single operation type is unable to capture certain characteristics like contention caused by metadata changes. MDWorkbench offers an alternative workload emulating the sharing of datasets and objects combined with several features useful for regression testing and data analysis. For example, we identified issues and could understand the relation between observed throughput and latency characteristics on several state-of-the-art systems better. In the future, we will experiment with machine learning to mine interesting patterns.

Acknowledgements. Thanks for DDN providing access to their facility and the discussion with Jean-Thomas Acquaviva and Jay Lofstead. This research used resources of the KAUST Supercomputing Core Laboratory, of the Argonne Leadership Computing Facility and NERSC, which are under DOE Office of Science User Facilities supported under Contract DE-AC02-06CH11357 and DE-AC02-05CH11231 respectively.

References

1. Alam, S.R., El-Harake, H.N., Howard, K., Stringfellow, N., Verzelloni, F.: Parallel I/O and the metadata wall. In: Proceedings of the Sixth Workshop on Parallel Data Storage, pp. 13–18. ACM (2011)
2. Carns, P., Lang, S., Ross, R., Vilayannur, M., Kunkel, J., Ludwig, T.: Small-file access in parallel file systems. In: Proceedings of the 2009 IEEE International Symposium on Parallel and Distributed Processing, pp. 1–11 (2009)

3. Friedrich, S., et al.: NoSQL OLTP benchmarking: a survey. In: GI-Jahrestagung, pp. 693–704 (2014)
4. Hadri, B., Kortas, S., Feki, S., Khurram, R., Newby, G.: Overview of the KAUST's cray X40 system-Shaheen II. In: Proceeding of Cray User Group (2015)
5. Huppler, K.: The art of building a good benchmark. In: Nambiar, R., Poess, M. (eds.) TPCTC 2009. LNCS, vol. 5895, pp. 18–30. Springer, Heidelberg (2009). https://doi.org/10.1007/978-3-642-10424-4_3
6. Katcher, J.: PostMark: a new file system benchmark. Technical report, TR3022, NetApp (1997)
7. Méndez, S., Rexachs, D., Luque, E.: Methodology for performance evaluation of the input/output system on computer clusters. In: 2011 IEEE International Conference on Cluster Computing (CLUSTER), pp. 474–483 (2011)
8. Storage Performance Council: SPC BENCHMARK 1 (SPC-1) - Rev. 3.5, September 2017

From Application to Disk: Tracing I/O Through the Big Data Stack

Robert Schmidtke$^{(\boxtimes)}$ ⓘ, Florian Schintke, and Thorsten Schütt

Zuse Institute Berlin, 14195 Berlin, Germany
{schmidtke,schintke,schuett}@zib.de

Abstract. Typical applications in data science consume, process and produce large amounts of data, making disk I/O one of the dominating—and thus worthwhile optimizing—factors of their overall performance. Distributed processing frameworks, such as Hadoop, Flink and Spark, hide a lot of complexity from the programmer when they parallelize these applications across a compute cluster. This exacerbates reasoning about I/O of both the application and the framework, through the distributed file system, such as HDFS, down to the local file systems.

We present SFS (Statistics File System), a modular framework to trace each I/O request issued by the application and any JVM-based big data framework involved, mapping these requests to actual disk I/O.

This allows detection of inefficient I/O patterns, both by the applications and the underlying frameworks, and builds the basis for improving I/O scheduling in the big data software stack.

Keywords: Distributed File Systems · I/O analysis
Big data ecosystems

1 Introduction

The I/O behavior of big data applications is often a key aspect for the overall system performance, but is complex and hard to reason about. The involved software stack ranges from low and middle storage layers (GFS (Google File System) [8], HDFS (Hadoop Distributed File System), Bigtable [4], Apache HBase) via simple parallelization techniques (MapReduce [9], Apache Hadoop) to high level abstractions (Apache Hive and Pig). While facilitating application development through many layers of abstraction, the hidden complexity makes I/O behavior hard to reason about, trace, and debug.

The aggregate file system statistics of HDFS or the underlying persistent file systems provide limited insights. They only report the volume of read/written data for a whole application run and do not allow tracing back I/O requests to their originating process. Furthermore, these statistics can differ tremendously from the expectations application developers might have, even if they are familiar with the inner workings of the big data software stack.

© Springer Nature Switzerland AG 2018
R. Yokota et al. (Eds.): ISC 2018 Workshops, LNCS 11203, pp. 89–102, 2018.
https://doi.org/10.1007/978-3-030-02465-9_6

Previous studies have examined the levels of I/O in isolation by modeling the local file systems [12], tracing I/O of single file systems [14], or investigating I/O routing within them [20,21]. Even sufficient logging of each component [5, 15,26] on the server-side may not capture causal relationships between events of different systems and discards the notion of client applications.

Approaches such as Pivot Tracing [16] have been developed to mitigate these issues, however they require expert source-level knowledge of the system under test, as well as modifications to their source codes, which may not be possible.

To obtain more detailed insights into the I/O caused by each component in the aforementioned deep big data stack (examined in Sect. 2), down to the disk-level, we present a framework that can readily be used with HDFS and any JVM (Java Virtual Machine)-based big data framework (open or closed source). Specifically, we introduce SFS (Statistics File System) in Sect. 3, which:

1. wraps each I/O request at the topmost HDFS level entering the big data stack and logs statistics such as duration and amount of data involved,
2. wraps each I/O request at the lowest JVM level leaving the stack and incurring actual disk I/O, logging similar statistics for each low-level request.

Using these statistics we are able to:

- trace I/O requests from the moment they are issued by the application or any framework involved, down to the individual disk in the individual machines comprising the compute cluster (Sect. 3.2),
- tell, for each point in time over the entire application run the caused I/O of each component to discern and evaluate their particular I/O impact with greater detail than previously possible,
- analyze the popular TeraSort benchmark on Hadoop, Flink and Spark and present and evaluate the insights obtained using SFS (Sect. 4),
- optimize Hadoop's default configuration to reduce I/O by 48% for reads, and 40% for writes compared to the default configuration (Sect. 4.4),
- further optimize data access inside big data frameworks, e.g. an accepted patch to reduce Hadoop's shuffle I/O by 50% in certain scenarios (Sect. 6).

2   Big Data Software Stack

The big data software stack consists of several levels of abstraction [12] to hide the complexity of distributed systems programming. However, these layers offer different I/O paths down to the actual disks (Fig. 1), which makes reasoning about and influencing an application's I/O throughout the stack a challenging task. Local Applications access Disks via Local File Systems, such as XFS or ext4. DFSes (Distributed File Systems), such as HDFS, expose these disks as a single logical volume with their aggregate capacity to Distributed Applications. Files are split into large blocks (64 MiB and upwards) and distributed in the DFSes for load balancing, fault tolerance and fast parallel access. Distributed Processing Frameworks (e.g. Hadoop, Flink, Spark) use Resource Managers (e.g. YARN (Yet

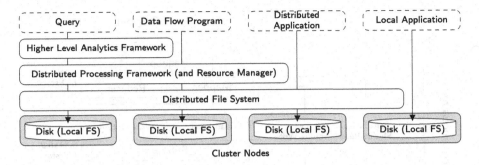

Fig. 1. Possible ways applications can access files through the big data software stack.

Another Resource Negotiator)) to distribute computation and data access of Data Flow Programs among nodes, favoring data local processing. Finally, Higher Level Analytics Frameworks (e.g. Hive, Pig) support SQL-like Queries as data flow programs. Reasoning about, predicting or debugging an application's I/O (and any of the involved layers') in this complex setting is not trivial.

3   Methodology

In order to understand the I/O behavior of an application run on this software stack, examining statistics collected by the DFS and the underlying file system is a natural first step to take. However, these statistics are aggregates, and if not sampled throughout the application run, they only provide accumulated data. It is therefore tedious, if possible at all, to examine I/O for specific, and potentially overlapping, phases of an application, or for specific components in the stack.

As a motivating example we use a MapReduce application on Hadoop/YARN with HDFS as persistence layer, which uses the local file system XFS on each node to store its data. This is shown in Fig. 2, along with how SFS (Statistics File System) integrates into this stack (highlighted as gray boxes, see Sect. 3.2).

3.1   Status Quo

Aggregate statistics can be obtained for some components by dumping them before and after the application run (*whole run I/O stats* in Fig. 2). Hadoop has designated counters for MapReduce, such as bytes read and written during shuffle and spilling phases. Hadoop's DFS abstraction tracks the number of bytes read and written for each file system used, i.e. per used URIs, e.g., `hdfs://` and `file://`. XFS counts the total number of bytes read from and written to disk.

However, HDFS's statistics may deviate from the local file system's statistics (Sect. 4). Furthermore, these statistics do not distinguish originators of I/O and permit limited inference of each component's share in the aggregate I/O.

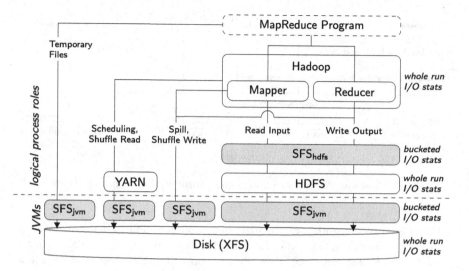

Fig. 2. SFS (gray boxes) integrated into Hadoop/HDFS on YARN with XFS as file system on a single node with a single disk for simplicity.

3.2 Statistics File System

To obtain more details on the I/O behavior, we developed SFS (Statistics File System).[1] SFS is integrated at two levels of the big data software stack (gray boxes in Fig. 2): (1) the topmost level to intercept all high-level I/O to HDFS, and (2) the lowest level to intercept all low-level I/O to the underlying file system.

Capturing I/O at those two levels allows a precise mapping for each I/O request issued to actual disk I/O, both *bucketed* over the entire application execution time $t_0, ..., t_n$, and for each component/ JVM (see Fig. 2).

The top layer of SFS (SFS_{hdfs}) records for each HDFS I/O request: hostname, process ID, custom identifier (see below), start time, duration, custom file descriptor, number of bytes read or written, and local or remote access. To this end, SFS extends Hadoop's abstract `FileSystem` class, transforming `sfs://` URIs to `hdfs://` URIs before invoking the wrapped file system implementation (e.g. HDFS), and vice versa for returned URIs.

The bottom layer of SFS (SFS_{jvm}) records per filesystem I/O request: hostname, process ID, custom identifier, start time, duration, custom file descriptor, and number of bytes read or written. Collecting the same attributes in both layers allows correlating I/O inside the big data stack in later analysis.

As all components involved run within dedicated JVMs, SFS_{jvm} uses Java bytecode instrumentation via an agent to wrap the relevant I/O methods of core Java classes for each of the components' JVMs, add logging instructions similar to SFS_{hdfs}, and asynchronously write the statistics to disk.

---

[1] GitHub: https://github.com/robert-schmidtke/hdfs-statistics-adapter.

The instrumenting agent is added to each JVM involved by passing a command line option to each JVM invocation, either directly, or by specifying it in environment variables (HADOOP_OPTS, YARN_OPTS), or via Hadoop configuration options (mapreduce.[map|reduce].java.opts). We currently discard mmap invocations (see Sect. 6), and only instrument read and write file operations.

We perform **runtime aggregation** of statistics before flushing them to disk to decrease I/O overhead and to speed up subsequent analysis of the log files. Specifically, we aggregate statistics per $S = (host, custid, pid, source, type, time)$ tuple, where *custid* is a configurable string to group JVMs that belong to the same component, e.g. yarn or hdfs. *source* is either SFS_{hdfs} or SFS_{jvm}. *type* is one of read, write or other. *time* specifies the granularity of the collected statistics: currently we use time bins of one second.[2] For each S, the aggregation sums up CPU time, bytes read/written, and number of operations. Section 5 details overheads of this runtime aggregation.

4   A Case Study: TeraSort

In order to evaluate SFS, we used the Hadoop TeraSort benchmark, shown in Fig. 3, since it is both popular, and well documented [3,17,18,23].

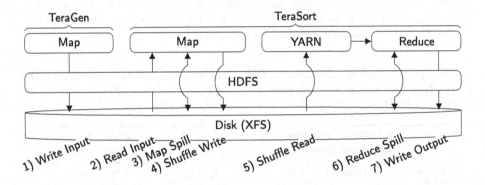

Fig. 3. The Hadoop TeraGen/TeraSort benchmark, for simplicity on a single disk.

TeraGen Map (step 1) generates about $1.1 * 10^{10}$ 100-byte-long records and stores them in HDFS to form the $1.1 * 10^{12}$ bytes (1,024 GiB) of input data. **TeraSort Map** (step 2) reads the input, and samples 100,000 keys to define a key range for each reducer. **TeraSort Reduce** (step 7) sorts the non-overlapping partitions of the output data and stores them in HDFS.

In the theoretical case, this benchmark should incur 2,048 GiB worth of data written to (steps 1 and 7), and 1,024 GiB worth of data read from persistent storage (step 2). Anticipating otherwise, we will discuss steps 3–6 in greater detail later in the next sections.

---

[2] We assume NTP synchronized clocks for JVMs/CPUs and nodes.

4.1 Setup

We ran this benchmark on 16 nodes, fully connected via 10 Gbit Ethernet, running Ubuntu 16.04.2, with two 8-core Xeon E5-2630v3 CPUs, 64 GiB of memory and 421 GiB of local HDD storage (XFS). We used Hadoop/YARN/HDFS/ TeraSort r2.7.4 on OpenJDK 8u131-b11 for all experiments.[3] YARN was configured to allocate 56 GiB of memory and 16 cores per node. This resulted in a compute capacity of 256 cores, 896 GiB of memory and 6.6 TiB of storage.

To assess Hadoop's vanilla configuration, we ran TeraSort without SFS, where only the following parameters have been changed from their defaults. We used a `dfs.blocksize` of 256 MiB (default: 128 MiB), and a `dfs.replication` factor of 1 (in accordance with the original TeraSort configuration [3], default: 3). Furthermore, we configured 2,048 `mapreduce.job.[maps|reduces]` Mappers and Reducers (default: 2 and 1), and 2,048 MiB of `mapreduce.[map|reduce].memory.mb` for each Mapper and each Reducer (default: 1,024 MiB each).

4.2 Vanilla Hadoop Results

Table 1 shows our theoretical expectations and the aggregate statistics reported by the Hadoop components for the baseline run without SFS. Furthermore, we present data from the underlying XFS counters, aggregated over all nodes, which form the ground truth for further analysis. These are the only numbers that the typical user/administrator has access to.

Table 1. Theoretical TeraSort I/O (GiB), Hadoop's counters in the vanilla configuration; XFS as reference.

		TeraGen		TeraSort	
		Read	Write	Read	Write
	Theory	0	1,024	1,024	1,024
Hadoop	hdfs://	0	1,024	1,024	1,024
	Shuffle	–	–	1,065	1,065
	Spill	0	0	3,072	3,072
	file://	0	0	2,194	3,196
	XFS	17	1,037	4,471	4,238

Table 2. Vanilla Hadoop TeraSort I/O (GiB) through SFS, by layer/component.

		TeraGen		TeraSort	
		Read	Write	Read	Write
SFS_hdfs	Map	0	1,025	1,024	0
	Reduce	0	0	0	1,028
SFS_jvm	HDFS	0	1,033	1,046	1,038
	Map	4	0	1,148	2,132
	Reduce	0	0	1,127	1,076
	YARN	7	0	1,208	0
	Total	11	1,033	4,528	4,247

We discuss the difference of more than 3 TiB of additional reads and writes for just 1 TiB of input data between the theoretical optimum and the actual I/O reported by XFS in Sect. 4.3, and now briefly touch on the other metrics.

---

[3] We successfully tested SFS on Oracle Java 1.8.0_45-b14 as well.

Hadoop's `hdfs://` counter indicates data (in GiB) that Mappers and Reducers read from/wrote to HDFS [24], and equals the theoretical values expected during TeraGen and TeraSort (steps 1, 2, 7 in Fig. 3). Considering Hadoop's *Shuffle* steps 4 and 5 in Fig. 3, the shuffle counters agree with expected I/O.

Hadoop's spill counter reported that a total of $3.3 * 10^{10}$ records had been spilled by all Mappers and Reducers, without further distinction. From this we calculated the spill I/O, using the fact that each record is 100 bytes long. However, there were no further details whether this spilling was due to memory exhaustion, or part of regular program execution, which is why we cannot map the spill I/O to any of the steps 2–7 in Fig. 3.

Hadoop's `file://` counters are similar in nature to `hdfs://`, except their counters refer to the local file system instead of HDFS. It is not clear whether shuffle and/or spill I/O was counted using the `file://` counters as well.

Because of the uncertainties with respect to how Hadoop's counters correlate, we refrain from presenting any summation or correlation of these counters at this point. In Sects. 4.3 and 4.4, we use SFS to shed light onto these uncertainties.

4.3   SFS Insights

We ran the benchmark again with the same configuration, except with SFS enabled, to get more detailed insights into I/O over time.

Table 2 shows the aggregate SFS results. The top two rows show the top level I/O incurred by the Mapper and Reducer JVMs via the `hdfs://` interface (SFS$_{hdfs}$ in Fig. 2). These numbers approximately agree with our theoretical expectations, as well as with the Hadoop `hdfs://` counters in Table 1.

The next five rows show the low level I/O incurred by the HDFS JVMs (`NameNode` and `DataNode`), the Mapper and Reducer JVMs and the YARN JVMs (`ResourceManager` and `NodeManager`) (obtained through SFS$_{jvm}$ in Fig. 2). We omitted the XFS total as it lies at most 0.3% above the totals in Table 1. Note that SFS matches XFS to more than 98%, except for TeraGen Read, which is dominated by loading dependencies.

For Map, Reduce and YARN it is instructive to examine their I/O as it occurred over time, traced by SFS, as shown in Fig. 4. The upper graph plots the statistics collected by SFS$_{hdfs}$, the lower graph plots the SFS$_{jvm}$ statistics.

The SFS$_{hdfs}$ plot agrees with our theoretical expectations, as well as the `hdfs://` counters presented in Table 1. The SFS$_{jvm}$ plot, however, reveals deviations from our expectations.

For Map, 1 TiB of writes would be expected due to the shuffle phase during TeraSort (step 4 in Fig. 3). However, we observe more than 2 TiB of writes, and more than 1 TiB of reads. The bottom graph in Fig. 4 shows that reading and writing in the Map JVMs started almost immediately after TeraSort had begun, and increased until the Reduce JVMs had picked up. This indicates a lot of I/O before the shuffle phase, hinting at suboptimal buffer and memory settings, forcing the Map JVMs to spill to disk unnecessarily often (step 3).

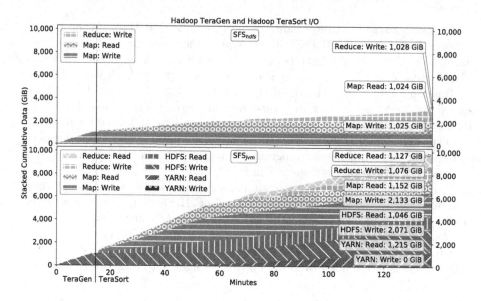

Fig. 4. I/O over the entire run of Hadoop TeraGen and TeraSort with vanilla configuration.

Knowing that reading the shuffled Map outputs does not occur within Reduce JVMs, but within YARN `NodeManagers` [24] (step 5), observing any I/O at all in the Reducers is unexpected. This indicates spilling during step 6 as well.

Finally, YARN behaved as expected, incurring 1 TiB of reads during the shuffle phase (step 5), with the remaining reads likely being due to resource distribution of JAR files and configurations, as well as speculative execution of Reduce tasks, which is enabled by default to reduce the impact of stragglers [24].

The observed read and write bandwidths per host were 35 and 41 MiB/s, the latter one plotted using SFS$_{jvm}$ in Fig. 5, which were well below the HDD's 115 MiB/s maximum bandwidth, due to the high number of small I/O operations: average request sizes were between 2 and 32 KiB. Figure 6 shows the total data read and written for SFS$_{hdfs}$ and SFS$_{jvm}$, as well as the first three nodes in the job allocation which would identify stragglers.

4.4   Optimized Hadoop Results

Having identified Map and Reduce as causes for unexpected I/O, we were able to select three parameters to tune, out of the 232 available parameters for Map and Reduce alone [2]. Specifically, we:

1. set `mapreduce.task.io.sort.mb` to 1,024 MiB (default: 100 MiB) to avoid spilling Map output prematurely and therefore on-disk sorting,
2. set `mapreduce.reduce.input.buffer.percent` to 50% (default: 0%) to allow Reducers to use up to half of their memory to store Map outputs, instead of spilling them to disk directly,

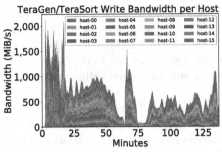

Fig. 5. Write bandwidth per host over the entire run of Hadoop TeraGen and TeraSort with vanilla configuration (SFS$_{jvm}$).

Fig. 6. Total data per host over the entire run of Hadoop TeraGen and TeraSort with vanilla configuration.

Table 3. Optimized Hadoop Tera-Sort I/O (GiB) through SFS, by layer/component; XFS as reference.

		TeraGen		TeraSort	
		Read	Write	Read	Write
SFS$_{hdfs}$	Map	0	1,026	1,024	0
	Reduce	0	0	0	1,026
SFS$_{jvm}$	HDFS	0	1,035	1,047	1,035
	Map	4	0	16	1,065
	Reduce	0	0	61	13
	YARN	7	0	1,206	0
	Total	11	1,035	2,330	2,113
	XFS	23	1,035	2,302	2,115

Table 4. Overhead of using SFS, based on the median of average `collectl` metrics from five runs of several benchmarks.

Benchmk.	Metric	Orig	SFS	Diff
TeraSort	Time (s)	1,280	1,462	+14.2%
	CPU (%)	1,258	1,840	+46.3%
	Mem. (MiB)	55,560	55,640	+0.1%
NNBench	Time(s)	367	371	+1.1%
	CPU (%)	234	250	+6.8%
	Mem. (MiB)	28,588	26,542	−7.2%
DFSIO	Time (s)	1,606	1,605	−0.1%
	CPU (%)	137	149	+8.8%
	Mem. (MiB)	5,054	5,523	+9.3%

3. disabled `mapreduce.reduce.merge.inmem.threshold` (default: 1,000) to allow an unlimited number of Map outputs during in-memory merge and only have the available memory determine when to start spilling.

The SFS results when running Hadoop TeraSort using the new configuration are shown in Table 3. The run incurred 48% less data being read (2,164 GiB less) and 40% less data being written (2,135 GiB less). With the unnecessary spilling eliminated, the new XFS I/O observed came close to the optimum for Hadoop TeraSort, reporting a total of 2.3 TiB of reads and 3.1 TiB of writes.

Now we can resolve the uncertainties mentioned in Sect. 4.2 with respect to spilling and Hadoop's `file://` counters, as during TeraSort we observed 1 TiB each for (a) shuffle read and write, (b) spill, and (c) `file://` writes. Having configured the Mappers and Reducers not to spill to disk any longer, we conclude that Hadoop's spill counter not only reports records written to and read from disk during the Map and Reduce phases, but also the records written to disk during the shuffle phase. Hence, in the optimal case, the number of shuffled and spilled records are equal. This also means that the I/O reported for shuffle is part of the spilling I/O. We can therefore conclude, that the `file://` counter reports I/O during the shuffle phase, as well as any additional spilling, which is in agreement with the numbers in Table 1.

We successfully ran TeraSort on Apache Flink 1.3.2 and Spark 2.2.0 with SFS as well. Using SFS in a Flink application implementing peak picking of proteomics data [6], we identified and eliminated unfortunate local file usage due to jmzML [7] library API restrictions, and resolved load imbalances incurred by HDFS file placement in certain situations, attaining an overall 4x speedup.

5   SFS Overhead

In order to assess the overhead of using SFS, we ran TeraGen/TeraSort, as well as the HDFS NNBench and DFSIO benchmarks.

We measured total application execution times, as well as average CPU and memory utilization for five runs, both with and without SFS using `collectl` (`collectl.sf.net`). Table 4 shows the median values for each of the benchmarks. HDFS was configured to use SSDs, accounting for the shorter execution times.

The largest overhead in both execution time and CPU utilization is found in the TeraSort benchmark. This is because of the many small I/O requests (see Sect. 4.3), the statistics of each of which are asynchronously aggregated in a thread pool. We estimate this to be a worst-case scenario for I/O, and are therefore confident that SFS should not incur more than the observed 14% increase in execution time in the average case.

The NNBench and DFSIO benchmarks do not show significant increases in execution time since there are enough CPU resources available to handle aggregation, as exemplified by the increased CPU utilization when using SFS. Recall that each node in the system has 16 real cores, so utilization above 1,600% should increase runtime significantly, as seen for TeraSort.

In order to perform live aggregation of statistics and avoid object creation overhead in the JVM, each instrumented SFS JVM performs its own memory management, using an extra of at most 27 MiB per Map or Reduce process; the other processes require only between 1 and 5 MiB additional memory. For Tera-Sort, the resources available permit no more than 20–30 concurrently running Map or Reduce processes per node. NNBench and DFSIO exhibit a much smaller degree of parallelism, thus they should result in less memory overhead.

The observed large differences result from a high variance in memory consumption between runs, especially for NNBench and DFSIO: Without SFS, the standard deviation is as large as 2,001 MiB (NNBench) and 1,277 MiB (DFSIO). With SFS, however, the standard deviation is much lower: 1,502 MiB for NNBench and 7 MiB for DFSIO. The storage overhead for the SFS logs over all nodes was 2 GiB (TeraGen/TeraSort), 13 MiB (NNBench), and 50 MiB (DFSIO).

Comparing different problem sizes showed that SFS scales with the underlying system, with some constant overhead, which is plausible, given that SFS does not introduce any inter-process communication.

6   Discussion and Limitations

SFS provides the best insight when used with HDFS (or any other Hadoop compatible file system) and other JVM-based analytics frameworks, because then both the highest and lowest levels of I/O abstraction are captured. However when Java code invokes non-Java routines that perform I/O, such as external processes, or native methods via JNI, SFS misses these I/O operations.

A limitation inherent to I/O tracing is the usage of mmap: there are no guarantees as to when I/O on an mmaped file region causes actual disk I/O. mmap may be the result of some FileChannel.transfer[To|From] implementations, which are used throughout Hadoop, Flink and Spark for transferring data across the network. HDFS and Hadoop provide two options to disable transfer[To|From] calls, and instead rely on regular read/write I/O: dfs.datanode.transferTo.allowed and mapreduce.shuffle.transferTo.allowed.

We ran TeraSort with these options set to false to learn about Hadoop's mmap usage and made two observations: (1) mmap was not used in our setup, and (2) with mmap disabled, YARN performed almost 100% more read I/O than expected. Using SFS, we traced the issue to YARN's shuffle algorithm when handling small partitions, and provided a fix merged in Hadoop r2.9.0.[4]

7   Related Work

Sampling as a means of gathering execution information about applications has been in use for more than four decades, most notably as the monitor/prof combination [22]. Lacking timing information and parameter/result values, such as request size for I/O operations, tracing provides more detailed information, either directly [19], or via tools such as gprof [10]. Sampling, tracing and hardware counters form the basis of many analysis tools available in UNIX/Linux [11].

An operating system tracing method that additionally supports Windows is described in [13], using FiST to model file systems [25]. A tracing framework allowing prioritization of I/O in a single-node I/O stack is described in [14]. Advanced sampling tools have been proposed to support multiprocessor systems [1].

Software stacks managing distributed systems have become deep and complex. In order to profile these stacks, zero-overhead solutions have been developed, processing the already available log files [5,15,26]. These approaches assume that every 'important' event has been logged across all systems, otherwise they cannot be correlated throughout the stack. This assumption may

---

[4] https://issues.apache.org/jira/browse/MAPREDUCE-6923.

not hold for each operation, e.g. for small or implicit I/O, and requires verbose logging.

Tracing with explicit focus on I/O in distributed systems has been performed in [12], with a similar approach to high-level instrumentation of HDFS I/O. The authors propose a model and simulation that maps HDFS to local I/O, while we have presented an additional layer of instrumentation for detailed insight.

A versatile approach using bytecode instrumentation that can be used for I/O tracing is presented in [16], using runtime queries that execute with low overhead. However, precise knowledge of the sources of the instrumented frameworks is necessary. SFS is a drop-in component for open and closed source systems, does neither require knowledge of, nor modifications to the frameworks' sources, and provides similarly meaningful I/O statistics at comparable overheads.

Another, Windows-centered, approach considering I/O in the entire distributed big data stack is presented in [20]. The I/O stack is modeled as a network, where packets can be traced and routed, based on IOFlow [21].

8   Future Work

We identified two immediate improvements to SFS. First, we do not distinguish between different files per node (see Sect. 3.2), and only report overall I/O. Future work will examine I/O per file per process per node, and thus we will gain insight into hotspot files, different I/O access patterns, and shared resource contention, among others. This may form the basis for live I/O rescheduling transparent to the application. Second, exploiting the fact that we instrument JVM code, instead of wrapping the JVM, we will obtain stack traces of the JVM state. To reduce the resulting overhead, these traces will be sampled.

9   Conclusions

Typical data science applications process large amounts of data, making disk I/O a relevant optimization factor. Distributed processing engines like Hadoop, Flink and Spark hide a lot of complexity when executing these applications, exacerbating reasoning about I/O from the application, via the underlying frameworks, through the distributed file system (e.g. HDFS), down to the local file systems.

We have presented a holistic approach to I/O analysis for these frameworks, from formulating expectations, to analyzing available file system counters, and obtaining detailed insight in every involved component's I/O. To this end we developed SFS (Statistics File System), an I/O analysis framework that can be used with any JVM-based data processing framework. SFS allows fine-grained tracing of I/O through the big data software stack over time, from high level applications down to actual disks at low overheads. Using SFS requires no development effort, and can be used as a drop-in wrapper around HDFS at the high level, and as a Java agent instrumenting core classes at the low level.

We showed generality by using SFS to monitor I/O incurred by Hadoop, Flink and Spark on YARN/HDFS during the popular TeraSort benchmark, for which we reduced I/O by 44%. Using SFS with Flink for a medical application revealed optimizations giving a 4x speedup. Finally, SFS helped us fix an issue in YARN's shuffle step causing 100% read overhead, included in Hadoop r2.9.0.

Acknowledgments. This work received funding from the BMBF projects *Berlin Big Data Center (BBDC)* under grant 01IS14013B and *GeoMultiSens* under grant 01IS14010C.

References

1. Anderson, J.M., et al.: Continuous profiling: where have all the cycles gone? ACM Trans. Comput. Syst. **15**(4), 1–14 (1997)
2. Apache Software Foundation: Mapreduce default configuration (2017). https:// github.com/apache/hadoop/blob/branch-2.7.4/hadoop-mapreduce-project/ hadoop-mapreduce-client/hadoop-mapreduce-client-core/src/main/resources/ mapred-default.xml
3. Apache Software Foundation: org.apache.hadoop.examples.terasort package description (2017). https://hadoop.apache.org/docs/r2.7.4/api/org/apache/ hadoop/examples/terasort/package-summary.html#package.description
4. Chang, F., et al.: Bigtable: a distributed storage system for structured data. ACM Trans. Comput. Syst. **26**(2), 4:1–4:26 (2008). https://doi.org/10.1145/1365815. 1365816
5. Chow, M., Meisner, D., Flinn, J., Peek, D., Wenisch, T.F.: The mystery machine: end-to-end performance analysis of large-scale Internet services. In: 11th USENIX Symposium on Operating Systems Design and Implementation (OSDI 2014), Broomfield, CO, pp. 217–231. USENIX Association (2014). https://www.usenix. org/conference/osdi14/technical-sessions/presentation/chow
6. Conrad, T.O.F., et al.: Sparse proteomics analysis - a compressed sensing-based approach for feature selection and classification of high-dimensional proteomics mass spectrometry data. BMC Bioinform. **18**(1), 160 (2017). https://doi.org/10. 1186/s12859-017-1565-4
7. Côté, R.G., Reisinger, F., Martens, L.: jmzML, an open-source Java API for mzML, the PSI standard for MS data. Proteomics **10**(7), 1332–1335 (2010). https://doi. org/10.1002/pmic.200900719
8. Dean, J., Ghemawat, S.: MapReduce: simplified data processing on large clusters. Commun. ACM **51**(1), 107–113 (2008). https://doi.org/10.1145/1327452.1327492
9. Ghemawat, S., Gobioff, H., Leung, S.T.: The Google file system. SIGOPS Oper. Syst. Rev. **37**(5), 29–43 (2003). https://doi.org/10.1145/1165389.945450
10. Graham, S.L., Kessler, P.B., Mckusick, M.K.: Gprof: a call graph execution profiler. In: ACM SIGPLAN Notices, vol. 17, pp. 120–126. ACM (1982)
11. Gregg, B.: Linux performance, August 2017. http://www.brendangregg.com/ linuxperf.html
12. Harter, T., et al.: Analysis of HDFS under HBase: a Facebook messages case study. In: Proceedings of the 12th USENIX Conference on File and Storage Technologies, FAST 2014, pp. 199–212. USENIX Association, Berkeley (2014). http://dl.acm. org/citation.cfm?id=2591305.2591325
13. Joukov, N., Traeger, A., Iyer, R., Wright, C.P., Zadok, E.: Operating system profiling via latency analysis. In: Proceedings of the 7th Symposium on Operating Systems Design and Implementation, pp. 89–102. USENIX Association (2006)

14. Kim, S., Kim, H., Jonwoon, L., Jeong, J.: Enlightening the I/O path: a holistic approach for application performance. In: Proceedings of the 15th USENIX Conference on File and Storage Technologies, FAST 2017, pp. 345–358. USENIX Association, Berkeley (2017). https://www.usenix.org/system/files/conference/fast17/fast17-kim-sangwook.pdf

15. Liu, Y., Gunasekaran, R., Ma, X., Vazhkudai, S.S.: Automatic identification of application I/O signatures from noisy server-side traces. In: Proceedings of the 12th USENIX Conference on File and Storage Technologies (FAST 2014), Santa Clara, CA, pp. 213–228. USENIX (2014). https://www.usenix.org/conference/fast14/technical-sessions/presentation/liu

16. Mace, J., Roelke, R., Fonseca, R.: Pivot tracing: dynamic causal monitoring for distributed systems. In: Proceedings of the 25th Symposium on Operating Systems Principles, SOSP 2015, pp. 378–393. ACM, New York (2015). https://doi.org/10.1145/2815400.2815415

17. O'Malley, O.: Terabyte sort on Apache Hadoop, May 2008. http://sortbenchmark.org/YahooHadoop.pdf

18. O'Malley, O., Murthy, A.C.: Winning a 60 second dash with a yellow elephant, April 2009. https://pdfs.semanticscholar.org/176b/c836e106bfdfe818adfc9dc1c0b150d85e54.pdf

19. Ousterhout, J.K., Da Costa, H., Harrison, D., Kunze, J.A., Kupfer, M., Thompson, J.G.: A trace-driven analysis of the UNIX 4.2 BSD file system, vol. 19. ACM (1985)

20. Stefanovici, I., Schroeder, B., O'Shea, G., Thereska, E.: Treating the storage stack like a network. Trans. Storage **13**(1), 2:1–2:27 (2017). https://doi.org/10.1145/3032968

21. Thereska, E., et al.: IOFlow: a software-defined storage architecture. In: Proceedings of the Twenty-Fourth ACM Symposium on Operating Systems Principles, SOSP 2013, pp. 182–196. ACM, New York (2013). https://doi.org/10.1145/2517349.2522723

22. Thompson, K., Ritchie, D.M.: Unix Programmer's Manual, 5 edn, June 1974

23. Transaction Processing Performance Council: TPC Express Benchmark[TM]HS, June 2017. http://www.tpc.org/tpc_documents_current_versions/pdf/tpcx-hs_v2.0.1.pdf

24. White, T.: Hadoop: The Definitive Guide, 4th edn. O'Reilly Media Inc., Sebastopol (2015)

25. Zadok, E., Nieh, J.: Fist: a language for stackable file systems. In: Proceedings of the Annual Conference on USENIX Annual Technical Conference, ATEC 2000, p. 5. USENIX Association, Berkeley (2000). http://dl.acm.org/citation.cfm?id=1267724.1267729

26. Zhao, X., Rodrigues, K., Luo, Y., Yuan, D., Stumm, M.: Non-intrusive performance profiling for entire software stacks based on the flow reconstruction principle. In: 12th USENIX Symposium on Operating Systems Design and Implementation (OSDI 2016), pp. 603–618. USENIX Association (2016). https://www.usenix.org/conference/osdi16/technical-sessions/presentation/zhao

IOscope: A Flexible I/O Tracer for Workloads' I/O Pattern Characterization

Abdulqawi Saif[1,2(✉)], Lucas Nussbaum[1], and Ye-Qiong Song[1]

[1] Université de Lorraine, CNRS, Inria, LORIA, 54000 Nancy, France
abdulqawi.saif@gmail.com
[2] Qwant Enterprise, 88000 Épinal, France

Abstract. Storage systems are getting complex to handle *HPC* and Big Data requirements. This complexity triggers performing in-depth evaluations to ensure the absence of issues in all systems' layers. However, the current performance evaluation activity is performed around high-level metrics for simplicity reasons. It is therefore impossible to catch potential I/O issues in lower layers along the Linux I/O stack. In this paper, we introduce *IOscope* tracer for uncovering I/O patterns of storage systems' workloads. It performs filtering-based profiling over fine-grained criteria inside Linux kernel. *IOscope* has near-zero overhead and verified behaviours inside the kernel thanks to relying on the *extended Berkeley Packet Filter* (eBPF) technology. We demonstrate the capabilities of *IOscope* to discover patterns-related issues through a performance study on *MongoDB* and *Cassandra*. Results show that clustered *MongoDB* suffers from a noisy I/O pattern regardless of the used storage support (HDDs or SSDs). Hence, *IOscope* helps to have better troubleshooting process and contributes to have in-depth understanding of I/O performance.

1 Introduction

Storage systems become complex to keep pace with the requirements of both *HPC* and Big Data. The current way of evaluating storage systems, especially the data stores, has not changed adequately. It still focuses on high-level metrics which completely ignores potential issues in lower interfaces. For instance, studies like [1,8,11,12] use *YCSB* [5] benchmark. Their core evaluation metrics are limited to workloads' throughput and execution time. One would know more why a given system achieves modest or strange results, but unfortunately such metrics cannot explain I/O performance. They only give indications that something goes wrong. Hence, in-depth evaluations such as evaluating I/O activities and interactions in lower layers is required. It leads to explain high-level measurements and to examine production workloads. Thus, our main concern here is to analyze how data files are accessed during workloads' execution, investigating if such experience leads to discover potential I/O issues.

© Springer Nature Switzerland AG 2018
R. Yokota et al. (Eds.): ISC 2018 Workshops, LNCS 11203, pp. 103–116, 2018.
https://doi.org/10.1007/978-3-030-02465-9_7

Henceforth, we define workloads' I/O pattern as the order of files' offsets targeted by I/O requests during accessing on-disk data. Potential I/O issues may appear due to various reasons. For instance, reordering I/O requests in lower layers of I/O stack or a content distribution issue in the applicative layers may transform a sequential access into a random access or vice versa. However, analyzing I/O pattern is less practiced during evaluations for two reasons. Firstly, there is a lack of specific tools to directly analyze in-production I/O workloads. Secondly, this is considered as an internal testing procedure which is often faced by a convention that all storage systems are well tested internally.

Tracing is highly used for evaluating storage systems [23]. Tracing tools often collect generic I/O traces from several layers of I/O stack. This leads not only to incur high overheads regarding the large number of diversified interceptions inside and outside the Linux kernel, but also to generate large quantity of tracing files that need huge effort for post-analysis. In contrast, multiple tracing tools are specific enough to collect precise data. However, they partially cover the dominant methods the storage systems use for issuing I/O workloads.

The key contributions of this paper are as follows. Firstly, we introduce the *IOscope*[1] tracer. *IOscope* applies both tracing and filtering techniques by relying on the *eBPF* which incurs a negligible overhead [20,21]. *IOscope* addresses the above-mentioned limitations by generating specific and ready-to-visualize traces about workloads' I/O patterns; it also covers the dominant methods of issuing I/O workloads including *mmap I/O*. Secondly, we describe original experiments on *MongoDB* and *Cassandra* using *IOscope*. The results show that a pattern-related issue in clustered *MongoDB* is behind the performance variability of experiments. We then propose an ad hoc solution to fix that issue.

The rest of this paper is organized as follows. We describe *IOscope* design and validation is Sect. 2, before describing the performed experiments on *MongoDB* and *Cassandra* in Sect. 3. We present the related work of *IOscope* in Sect. 4. Finally, we conclude with Sect. 5.

2   IOscope Design and Validation

This sections presents *eBPF* before describing the *IOscope* design and validation.

2.1   Foundation: eBPF

The basic idea of *eBPF* is to inject byte-code programs into the kernel for extending a given kernel functionality. For example, injecting a program to perform statistics on a specific kernel function. *eBPF* consists of a virtual machine and a syscall called *bpf syscall*. The virtual machine has three major features. Firstly, it has eleven 64-bit registers. One of them is only readable for holding the frame pointer of the injected *eBPF* program. Secondly, it has an extended verifier which checks that the *eBPF* byte code is free of loops, has no side effect behaviors (e.g.,

---

[1] https://github.com/LeUnAiDeS/IOscope.

could not lead to crashing the kernel), and terminates without problems. It also has an in-kernel data structures (*eBPF-maps*), which are accessible by user-space processes, suitable to use for data communications between *eBPF* and userspace programs [19]. Through those data structures, the *bpf syscall* bidirectionally transfers the data between the kernel/userspace pair. It carries out both injecting the *eBPF* byte code into the kernel, and communicating the target kernel data towards a userspace process.

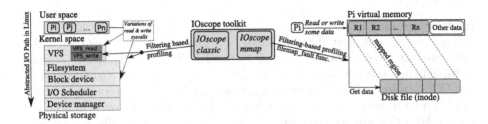

Fig. 1. *IOscope* tools and their instrumentation points inside the Linux kernel

EBPF and Tracing

eBPF can be used to do in-kernel tracing thanks to the aforementioned features as well as its ability to connect to various data sources. Whenever an *eBPF* program is attached to a data source (e.g. a kernel function), the *bpf syscall* introduces a breakpoint on the target function. This allows *eBPF* stack-pointer to capture the functions' context. The *eBPF* program is then supposed to run as configured, i.e., before and/or after every single event on the target function). This program cannot alter the execution context of traced functions because the context is held by a not-writable register as mentioned in Sect. 2.1.

2.2   IOscope Design

IOscope contains two tools: *IOscope_classic* and *IOscope_mmap* (see Fig. 1). The key idea of *IOscope* is to construct the workloads I/O patterns by tracing and filtering the sequences of workloads' I/O requests. Both tools work with files offsets. An offset is a placement value (in byte) held by an I/O request. It indicates where is the beginning placement in the target file to read from or to write into. The tools apply many filters in earlier steps, e.g., reporting the I/O activities of a specific process or a specific data file. They aim at performing a precise-objective tracing and incurring less overhead. They are injected into the kernel via the *bpf syscall*. They are attached to the targets functions using the *kprobe & kretprobe* modes which allow to execute the tracing code before and after the target functions' body, respectively. Indeed, tracing based on internal kernel functions is dependent on kernel changes. However, the target functions of *IOscope* tools seem to be stable over multiple kernel releases.

IOscope tools are designed using the Python frontend of the *BCC* [18] project (a project that facilitates the development of eBPF-based tools). This implies having two processes for each tool. The first process which runs in userspace is responsible for (1) injecting the *IOscope*-core code into the kernel and (2) performing posterior filtering tasks on the received data from the kernel. The injected program runs as a second process inside the kernel. It intercepts the target functions to perform the filtering-based profiling task. It regularly exposes the matched traces into a ring buffer for which the userspace process is connected as a consumer.

(a) IOscope_classic

IOscope_classic addresses different kinds of I/O methods. For instance, synchronous I/O, asynchronous I/O, and vectored I/O (scatter/gather I/O from multiple buffers). It obtains the tracing data from both (1) the *virtual file system* (*VFS*) as many I/O *syscalls* terminate at this layer in the kernel I/O path, and (2) from different *syscalls* that bypass the *VFS*. Thus, it covers almost all I/O methods that are based on the variations of *read, write syscalls* (e.g., *pread, pwritev, read, preadv, pwritev2*). This tool catches the mixed I/O workloads (read & write workloads) even if targeting the same file. It reports a pure view of how the analyzed system is accessing data over the execution time.

The tool should run for a specific userspace process in order to prevent profiling all the I/O requests found in the kernel. Thus, the *PID* of the target process must be provided to allow *IOscope* to check every issued request if it belongs to that process or not. If so, the tracing code of *IOscope_classic* will be executed, otherwise the I/O request continues its path without being traced.

IOscope_classic collects various informations from the target function parameters. The principal ones are the *offsets* of I/O requests, their *data size*, their *target file name* or *file identifier*, and the *request type* (read or write). This is done before executing the target function body. This information is stored in a hash map (a type of *eBPF-maps*). The tool also measures the latency for every I/O request as the elapsed time to execute the body of the target function. This indicates the time taken to write into or to read from a given offset on a target file. This is done by the *kretprobe* mode, which allows running a part of *IOscope_classic* code before the closing bracket of the target function.

(b) IOscope_mmap

IOscope_mmap tackles the I/O activities that access the *memory mapped files* (*mmap*). This method allows the system to map the data files into its private address space, manipulating data like it is already located in memory. The CPU and some internal structures of the kernel bring out the data from the physical storage each time requested by a given process. Because of the absence of *syscalls* that carry the data access, the effective way to obtain the I/O access patterns would be to trace inside the kernel. However, the main challenge is to find a stable instrumentation point through which the I/O patterns can be obtained.

We find that the kernel function *filemap_fault* can serve as an instrumentation point. This function is responsible for processing the memory faults of mapped files. When a process attempts to read or to write some data, a generated memory fault occurs. The CPU investigates if the data is already in memory (during previous retrieval) or not yet loaded. Each memory fault has an offset that indicates where the required data is found inside a memory page. The offset is still helpful in case of having several memory regions of the mapped file.

The typical workflow of using this tool is to provide either the *inode* number or a data path with an extension of target files. The first is required in case of targeting only one file while the path and extension are required to trace the matched files. *IOscope_mmap* then starts to examine only the memory faults over the given file/files thanks to its preliminary filter. Its mechanism for connecting to the target function is similar to the *IOscope_classic* tool (*kprobe* and *kretprobe*). *IOscope_mmap* also reports the same data as the *IOscope_classic* tool.

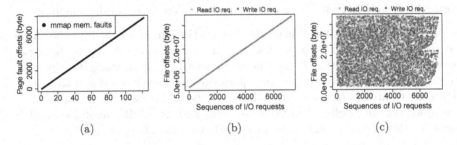

(a)   (b)   (c)

Fig. 2. Selected results from the experimentation campaign of validating *IOscope* via *Fio* benchmark, over a 32 MB file. (a) shows I/O patterns of a read workload on *Mmap IOengine*, (b) Shows I/O patterns of a readwrite workload on *Posixaio IOengine*, and (c) presents I/O patterns of a random readwrite workload on *Psync IOengine*

Table 1. Validated I/O access modes and workloads

Fio IOengine	Target syscalls	Tested workloads: *read, write, randread, randwrite, readwrite,* and *randreadwrite*
Sync	read, write	All
Psync	pread, pwrite	All
Pvsync	preadv, pwritev	All
Pvsync2	preadv2, pwritev2	All
posixaio	aio_read, aio_write	All
Mmap	mmap, memcpy	All

2.3 IOscope Validation

IOscope is experimentally validated over synthetic workloads. The flexible I/O benchmark (*Fio*) is used to generate workloads that encompass the applied workloads by real systems and applications. These workloads are tested against the *Fio IOengines* which represents various I/O methods for accessing data (e.g., direct access, vectored I/O, memory-mapped access). Table 1 lists those engines, the *syscalls* through which the I/O requests pass, and the tested workloads.

The validation experiments are executed on a single machine running *Ubuntu 14.04 LTS, Linux kernel 4.9.0* and *Fio-v2.1.3*. Figure 2 shows some validation results. The flow of sequential workloads is always represented as a diagonal line of file offsets. The random workloads are represented as scratch dots, indicating that the I/O requests target random offsets during the workload execution. It is noticeable from Fig. 2c that the *Fio* random workloads are totally shapeless.

IOscope Overhead. We measure the overhead of using *IOscope* over the realistic workloads described in the next section. This is done by getting the difference between the execution time of an experiment with & without using *IOscope*. The maximum overhead obtained for an experiment was less than 0.8% of the execution time regardless of analyzing millions of I/O requests. In terms of memory overhead, the ring buffer of *IOscope* is limited up to 8 MB. No single event is lost with this configuration even in case of having high frequency I/Os.

3 Experiments

This section describes a set of experiments on two NoSQL storage databases (*MongoDB* and *Cassandra*) for which *IOscope* is used to analyze I/O patterns. It starts by presenting the environmental setup, and the applied experimental scenarios. It then describes the experiments done on *MongoDB* and its revealed performance issue before describing how *IOscope* is used to explain that issue. It ends by describing the experiments done on *Cassandra*.

3.1 Setup, Datasets, and Scenarios

Environmental Setup. We perform those experiments on the *Grid'5000* [2] testbed. Each machine has two Intel Xeon E5-2630 v3 CPUs (8 cores/CPU), 128 GB of RAM, and a 10 Gbps Ethernet. Every machine is equipped with an *HDD* of 558 GB, and an *SSD* of 186 GB. The disks are connected as *JBOD*, using Symbios Logic MegaRAID SAS-3 3008 (rev 02). We deploy *Ubuntu 14.04 LTS* with *Linux 4.9.0* in which a resident *eBPF* virtual machine is enabled. The *Ext4* filesystem is used. The *deadline* I/O scheduler is used by default. Linux I/O schedulers (*Noop, deadline,* and *CFQ*) are interchangeable in our experiments due to the absence of concurrent I/O processes. The *Native Command Queuing* (*NCQ*) of disks is 2^6 by default; it minimizes the mechanical seeks of disks via rescheduling groups of concurrent I/O requests. We clean out the cache data including the memory-resident data of *MongoDB* and *Cassandra* between experiments. No more than one experiment is executed at the same time.

MongoDB v3.4.12[2] is used. It is tested with default configuration in which *WiredTiger* is the main storage engine. We use *Cassandra v 3.0.14* with its default configuration too. In both databases, nodes hold equal portions of data in case of cluster experiments, thanks to the built-in partitioner/balancer.

Datasets. Two equally sized datasets are created (each has 71 GB) to perform our experiments on *MongoDB* and *Cassandra*. Their contents are randomly generated to eliminate data-biased results. Each dataset has 20,000,000 data elements (called documents in *MongoDB* and rows in *Cassandra*) with 3.47 kB as an average size. Each element consists of (1) one integer with random values, (2) a timestamp, (3) two string fields, (4) and one array which has a random number of fields up to four. *MongoDB* stores the dataset as a single file. In contrast, the number of *Cassandras' SSTables* depends on how many times the data is flushed into disks (one or more SSTables).

Workload and Scenarios. The experiments are executed on either a single server or a distributed cluster of two shard nodes. In both scenarios, one client running on another node performs an indexation workload. The workload aims at indexing an integer field, pushing the target databases to read the entire datasets in order to construct a corresponding index tree. The objective is to look at how each database is accessing data and to see if some hidden issues could be revealed. This does not necessarily mean that the results of both databases are comparable due to an absence of a tuning phase for making an *apple-to-apple* comparison. In each scenario, All experiments cover both technologies of storage: *HDDs* and *SSDs*. They are executed one time using *HDDs* as principal storage of the involved machines, and another time on *SSDs*. We test the data contiguity on disks by profiling their physical blocks using filesystem `FIBMAP` command. Each data file resides on about 99.9% of contiguous blocks.

For the distributed experiments, the data is distributed using a hash-based mechanism. This is achieved over the _id field in *MongoDB* and over the primary key in *Cassandra* (*uuid* field), both in order to obtain evenly distributed data. In the rest of the paper, *executions* means that the experiment is re-performed from the step of pushing the dataset into the distributed cluster.

3.2   MongoDB Experiments

This section describes the high-level results of executed workloads before showing *IOscope* results. High-level results are presented to convince that they only give insights into understanding I/O performance but cannot explain issues. The section ends by describing an *ad hoc* solution to the discovered issue by *IOscope*.

---

[2] A major version of *MongoDB* (v3.6) has been released during writing this paper. It suffers from the same performance issue discussed in Sect. 3.2, regardless of the optimized throughput.

Table 2. Average throughputs of single-server and clustered experiments. Results of clustered *MongoDB* show a performance variability issue

		HDD (MB/s)	SSD (MB/s)
Single-server experiment		48.4	306.7
Two-Shards cluster	1st shard (51% of data)	25.5	161.2
	2nd shard (49% of data)	11.8	182.6
Another execution of Two-Shards cluster	1st shard (50.27% of data)	47.8	539.6
	2nd shard (49.72% of data)	30.6	401.4

(a) High-Level Results

The indexation workload described in Sect. 3.1 is executed. This workload is an intensive read workload in *MongoDB*. The dataset must be entirely retrieved from the storage support to be parsed document by document. Table 2 shows average throughputs of single-server and distributed experiments.

Single-server Experiments. The execution time is reduced by a factor of 6.3 when using SSD as a principal storage instead of HDD. This indicates how the storage technology can improve accessing data. Repeating these experiments makes no changes over the execution time and throughput values. Hence, we use them as a reference for the distributed experiments to investigae *MongoDB* scalability.

Distributed Experiments. For the two-shards experiments, we expect to decrease the execution time by half as an ideal case of linear scalability. However, the performance results of several runs are not as expected (see Table 2). *MongoDB* reports variable performance over both *HDDs* and *SSDs*. Performing other executions over the same dataset brings out variable results too.

There is a hidden issue behind obtaining variable performance results. This issue can not be explained using high-level metrics as shown. This implies to go beyond those results by doing further investigations with *IOscope*.

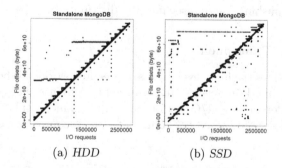

(a) *HDD*   (b) *SSD*

Fig. 3. I/O patterns of the single-server experiments described in Table 2

(b) IO Pattern Analysis Using IOscope

We expect that *IOscope* reports a clear diagonal line of file offsets if the data is sequentially accessed. Otherwise, a noisy access pattern or even a shapeless one is obtained. The size of collected trace files of experiments is 1 GB.

For the single-server experiments, both I/O patterns over the *HDD* and the *SSD* are acceptable. The files are sequentially accessed as shown in Fig. 3. The diagonal lines are present in both sub-figures regardless of the tiny noises that might refer to file alignments operations.

IOscope uncovers the reasons behind the performance variability of the distributed experiments. Figures 4 and 5 show the I/O patterns of these experiments. The same analysis can be done for *HDDs* and *SSDs* experiments as the obtained I/O patterns of each shard correspond to its execution time. In regard to the *SSDs* experiments, Fig. 5a shows that both shards have totally-random I/O patterns. Thy take about 97%, 82% of the execution time of the single-server experiment. In contrast, the I/O patterns of both shards shown in Fig. 5b are sequential. The shards reach the required performance (near 50% of execution time obtained in the single-server experiment). Hence, it is obvious to see the shards patterns as diagonal lines indicating that the data is accessed as it should be. This example shows that *IOscope* is able to explain issues even over recent storage support like *SSDs* and over a fine-grain execution time. This leaves no doubt that the I/O patterns are behind the reported performance variability.

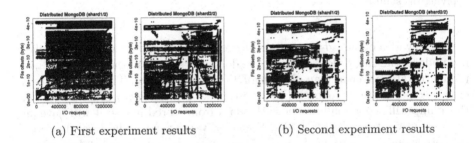

(a) First experiment results   (b) Second experiment results

Fig. 4. I/O patterns of the distributed experiments on *HDDs* described in Table 2

We performed further experiments with three and four sharding nodes, but the random access patterns are still present. As a result, the inefficient way used by *MongoDB* for accessing data is the main reason of obtaining that issue.

(c) An Ad Hoc Solution to Fix MongoDB Issue

A mismatch between the order applied by *MongoDB* to retrieve data and the order of stored data is behind the above described issue. *MongoDB* tries to sequentially traverse the documents based on its view of pre-stored $\_id_s$. This occurs even if its retrieval plan does not follow the exact order of documents in the collection file. As described, the symptoms of this issue are (1) incurring mechanical seeks and (2) having noisy I/O patterns.

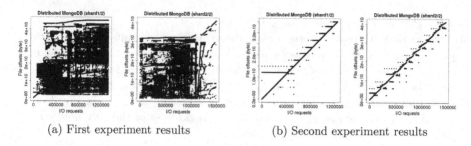

(a) First experiment results   (b) Second experiment results

Fig. 5. I/O patterns of the distributed experiments on *SSDs* described in Table 2

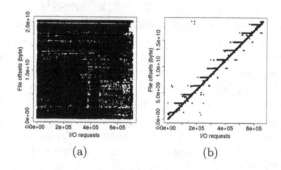

(a)   (b)

Fig. 6. I/O pattern of a *MongoDB* shard with 20 GB of data (a) before, and (b) after applying the solution

The key idea of our *ad-hoc* is to re-write the shards data locally. This implicitly updates the $\_id_s$ order regarding the documents order in the stored file, i.e., the inaccurate traversal plan of *MongoDB* will be replaced. The detailed steps of this solution are as follows. Firstly, we make a local dump of shards' data; this dump will sequentially retrieve the data from stored file, so it will have an accurate view of documents' order. Secondly, we re-extract the local dump on the corresponding shard, so *MongoDB* takes into account the novel documents' order. Of course, it is unrealistic to perform this solution every time encountered by similar issue due to the enormous overhead of rewriting data. But it gives insights to *MongoDB* community to fix that issue in upcoming versions.

Figure 6 shows a worst I/O pattern obtained on a shard node over an *HDD*. After applying our *ad hoc* solution, the execution time becomes 12.4 times faster (it is reduced from 1341 s to 108 s). On *SSD*, the performance is enhanced with a speedup factor of 2.5 (time is reduced from 89 s to 32 s). This might be related to the nature of the used *SSD* (Toshiba PX04SMQ040) which is optimized for sequential reading workloads.

3.3   Cassandra Experiments

This section describes the results of experiments performed on *Cassandra*.

(a) Results

Single-server Experiments. *Cassandra* maintains a stable throughput during the workload execution as shown in Fig. 7. However, the workload execution depends more on CPU as the stacked CPU sub-figure shows; the peak CPU reaches more than 150% of a core capacity. We only show the I/O patterns of the biggest *SSTable* in the same figure. In fact, the other *SSTables* have the same clear sequential access (the dataset is represented by five different-size *SSTables*).

The peak value of the disk utilization is near 30%, indicating that the indexing operations are not I/O bounded. Hence, the factor that stresses the performance is the amount of used memory. If we limit the available memory for *Cassandra*, the performance in terms of execution time will increase to some extent. This occurs due to an increase of memory operations being performed such as freeing memory pages. However, the access patterns will not be changed thanks to the metadata that are used to regulate accessing data.

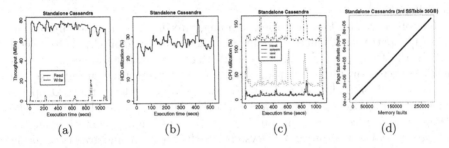

Fig. 7. Cassandra single-server experiment results on *HDD*. (a) shows the I/O throughput, (b) shows the disk utilization, (c) presents the CPU mode, and (d) shows the I/O pattern of the largest SSTable

Distributed Experiments. *Cassandra*'s nodes still reach the same throughput of the single-server configuration both over *HDDs* and *SSDs*. As a result, the execution time is optimized as expected on both nodes of *Cassandra*. Each node takes near 50% out of the single-server execution time. *IOscope* shows sequential I/O patterns for both experiments (similar results of Fig. 7d). Because of space limitation, those results are not shown here.

4   Related Work

Betke and Kunkel [3] proposed a framework for real-time I/O monitoring. It does not implement a filtering mechanism like *IOscope* during the interception of I/O traces, leading to collecting a huge number of generic traces. Daoud and Dagenais [6] proposed a *LTTng*-based framework for collecting disks metrics. Their framework only analyses generated traces of *HDDs*, and no information is provided about its applicability on *SSDs*. In addition, it does not collect file offsets, which is our main metric for analyzing workloads' I/O patterns. Jeong et al. [10] proposed a tool to generate I/O workloads and to analyze I/O performance for Android systems. Their I/O performance analyzer requires a modified kernel and runs only for custom filesystems (ext4, fat32). In contrast, *IOscope* needs no kernel modification and mainly works on the *VFS* layer to support wide number of filesystems. Other tools [4,14,15,22,24] aim to predict and extrapolate the I/O performance for large scale deployments by analyzing and replaying small set of traces. In contrast, our work focuses on collecting fine-grained traces of I/O workloads under study for discovering and explaining I/O issues.

Several tracing tools such as SystemTap [9], Dtrace [17], LTTng tools [7] load tracing scrip as dynamic modules into the kernel (e.g., using *dkms* package). This makes them unsuitable for usage in some situations, e.g., in case of signed kernels. Using them also implies doing posterior efforts for analyzing massive quantity of collected traces. In contrast, *eBPF* is formally adopted by the Linux kernel [13]. It is mainly known for its filtering capabilities that we leveraged to build *IOscope*.

IOscope performs four activities: profiling, filtering, tracing, and direct analysis of I/O patterns. Its filtering and tracing activities are comparable to several tools of the BCC project [18]. In general, they give an instantaneous view of matched events on target instrumentation points, presenting outputs like the top command of Linux. BCC *Slower* tools are built to filter the I/O operations with large latencies. They work on higher layers of Linux I/O stack. The *fileslower* tool traces operations on the VFS layer of Linux I/O stack while the *ext4slower* tool works on *Ext4* filesystem. Both bring out fine-grained filtering of I/Os (e.g., reporting I/Os per process), but deal with partial I/O contexts. The *fileslower* does not work with *pvsync*, *pvsync2*, and *mmap* I/Os, while the *ext4Slower* lacks supporting *mmap* I/Os. Extracting I/O patterns is still possible for the supported I/O contexts. However, this requires much post-analysis effort compared with *IOscope* which needs nothing to prepare final results.

Several tools collect traces from the block I/O layer on Linux I/O stack. For instance, BCCs' *biotop*, BCCs' *bIOsnoop*, DTraces' *IOsnoop*. These tools generate traces in terms of *accessed sectors* of disks. They do not link those sectors to workloads' accessed files, being more close to studying hardware issues rather than analyzing I/O patterns. To explain, collecting disks sectors do not specify how applications access data files. The reason is that I/O requests are expected to be re-ordered in intermediate layers (e.g., in the I/O scheduler layer). A modified tracer [16] of *blktrace* addresses that issue by combining traces from block I/O and VFS layers. However, it lacks supporting *mmap* I/O, and it needs an additional effort to analyze I/O patterns. Hence, replacing *IOscope* by any of these tools cannot explain I/O issues. Analyzing I/O flow in terms of disk sectors has no sense as there is no constraints to allocate data on successive or random sectors. *IOscope* addresses that by working with files offsets. Over a given file, the offsets specify the order of all read/written data throughout workloads' I/Os.

5   Conclusions

Performing in-depth analysis of storage system workloads is necessary to reveal potential I/O issues in lower levels. Robust and flexible tools are needed to perform such detailed evaluations. In this paper, we first described *IOscope* which uncovers I/O patterns of storage workloads. It has less than 1% overhead and inherits other features from *eBPF* technology, being suitable for analyzing production workloads. We then showed use case experiments over *MongoDB* and *Cassandra* using *IOscope*. The results from *MongoDB* experiments reinforce our hypothesis for going beyond high-level evaluations. *IOscope* was able to report the main reasons behind the performance variability of *MongoDB*, over executed workloads. The issue is raised due to unexpected mismatch between the order of the allocated data on disks, and the traversal plan used by *MongoDB* in case of distributed experiments. Moreover, *IOscope* was able to confirm the occurrence of that issue over *HDDs* and *SSDs*. Based on the insights provided by *IOscope*, we proposed an *ad hoc* solution to fix that issue by re-writing the shards data. This allows achieving anew linear and scalable results of the concerned experiments.

References

1. Abramova, V., Bernardino, J.: NoSQL databases: MongoDB vs cassandra. In: Proceedings of the International C* Conference on Computer Science and Software Engineering, pp. 14–22. ACM (2013)
2. Balouek, D., et al.: Adding virtualization capabilities to the Grid'5000 testbed. In: Ivanov, I.I., van Sinderen, M., Leymann, F., Shan, T. (eds.) CLOSER 2012. CCIS, vol. 367, pp. 3–20. Springer, Cham (2013). https://doi.org/10.1007/978-3-319-04519-1_1
3. Betke, E., Kunkel, J.: Real-time I/O-monitoring of HPC applications with SIOX, elasticsearch, Grafana and FUSE. In: Kunkel, J.M., Yokota, R., Taufer, M., Shalf, J. (eds.) High Performance Computing, pp. 174–186. Springer, Cham (2017). https://doi.org/10.1007/978-3-319-67630-2_15
4. Chahal, D., Virk, R., Nambiar, M.: Performance extrapolation of IO intensive workloads: work in progress. In: Proceedings of the 7th ACM/SPEC on International Conference on Performance Engineering, pp. 105–108. ACM (2016)
5. Cooper, B.F., Silberstein, A., Tam, E., Ramakrishnan, R., Sears, R.: Benchmarking cloud serving systems with YCSB. In: Proceedings of the 1st ACM Symposium on Cloud Computing, pp. 143–154. ACM (2010)
6. Daoud, H., Dagenais, M.R.: Recovering disk storage metrics from low-level trace events. Softw.: Pract. Exp. **48**(5), 1019–1041 (2018)
7. Desnoyers, M., Dagenais, M.R.: The LTTng tracer: a low impact performance and behavior monitor for GNU/Linux. In: OLS (Ottawa Linux Symposium), vol. 2006, pp. 209–224. Citeseer, Linux Symposium (2006)
8. Gandini, A., Gribaudo, M., Knottenbelt, W.J., Osman, R., Piazzolla, P.: Performance evaluation of NoSQL databases. In: Horváth, A., Wolter, K. (eds.) EPEW 2014. LNCS, vol. 8721, pp. 16–29. Springer, Cham (2014). https://doi.org/10.1007/978-3-319-10885-8_2
9. Jacob, B., Larson, P., Leitao, B., Da Silva, S.: SystemTap: instrumenting the Linux kernel for analyzing performance and functional problems. IBM Redbook (2008)

10. Jeong, S., Lee, K., Hwang, J., Lee, S., Won, Y.: Androstep: Android storage performance analysis tool. Software Engineering (Workshops), vol. 13, pp. 327–340 (2013)
11. Jung, M.G., Youn, S.A., Bae, J., Choi, Y.L.: A study on data input and output performance comparison of MongoDB and PostgreSQL in the big data environment. In: 2015 8th International Conference on Database Theory and Application (DTA), pp. 14–17. IEEE (2015)
12. Klein, J., Gorton, I., Ernst, N., Donohoe, P., Pham, K., Matser, C.: Performance evaluation of NoSQL databases: a case study. In: Proceedings of the 1st Workshop on Performance Analysis of Big Data Systems (2015)
13. Manual page on Linux, B.: (2017). http://man7.org/linux/man-pages/man2/bpf.2.html
14. Luo, X., et al.: HPC I/O trace extrapolation. In: Proceedings of the 4th Workshop on Extreme Scale Programming Tools. p. 2. ACM (2015)
15. Luo, X., et al.: ScalaiOExtrap: elastic I/O tracing and extrapolation. In: 2017 IEEE International Parallel and Distributed Processing Symposium (IPDPS), pp. 585–594. IEEE (2017)
16. Mantri, S.G.: Efficient in-depth IO tracing and its application for optimizing systems. Ph.D. thesis, Virginia Tech (2014)
17. McDougall, R., Mauro, J., Gregg, B.: Solaris performance and tools: DTrace and MDB techniques for Solaris 10 and OpenSolaris. Prentice Hall (2006)
18. Collection project, B.C.: https://github.com/iovisor/bcc
19. Schulist, J., Borkmann, D., Starovoitov, A.: Linux socket filtering aka Berkeley Packet Filter (BPF) (2016)
20. Sharma, S.D., Dagenais, M.: Enhanced userspace and in-kernel trace filtering for production systems. J. Comput. Sci. Technol. 6, 1161–1178 (2016)
21. Starovoitov, A.: (2014). https://lwn.net/Articles/598545/
22. Tak, B.C., Tang, C., Huang, H., Wang, L.: PseudoApp: performance prediction for application migration to cloud. In: 2013 IFIP/IEEE International Symposium on Integrated Network Management (IM 2013), pp. 303–310. IEEE (2013)
23. Vef, M.A., Tarasov, V., Hildebrand, D., Brinkmann, A.: Challenges and solutions for tracing storage systems: a case study with spectrum scale. ACM Trans. Storage 14(2), 1–24 (2018). https://doi.org/10.1145/3149376
24. Virk, R., Chahal, D.: Trace replay based I/O performance studies for enterprise workload migration. In: 2nd Annual Conference of CMG India, Page Online (2015)

Exploring Scientific Application Performance Using Large Scale Object Storage

Steven Wei-der Chien[1(✉)], Stefano Markidis[1], Rami Karim[1], Erwin Laure[1], and Sai Narasimhamurthy[2]

[1] KTH Royal Institute of Technology, Stockholm, Sweden
{wdchien,markidis,ramik,erwinl}@kth.se
[2] Seagate Systems UK, Havant, UK
sai.narasimhamurthy@seagate.com

Abstract. One of the major performance and scalability bottlenecks in large scientific applications is parallel reading and writing to supercomputer I/O systems. The usage of parallel file systems and consistency requirements of POSIX, that all the traditional HPC parallel I/O interfaces adhere to, pose limitations to the scalability of scientific applications. Object storage is a widely used storage technology in cloud computing and is more frequently proposed for HPC workload to address and improve the current scalability and performance of I/O in scientific applications. While object storage is a promising technology, it is still unclear how scientific applications will use object storage and what the main performance benefits will be. This work addresses these questions, by emulating an object storage used by a traditional scientific application and evaluating potential performance benefits. We show that scientific applications can benefit from the usage of object storage on large scales.

Keywords: Scientific applications · Object storage · Parallel I/O
HPC · HDF5

1 Introduction

Parallel I/O is becoming one of the most serious performance bottlenecks in HPC applications as the number of processes writing/reading to/from the supercomputer I/O system keeps increasing at a considerable pace. An exascale supercomputer will likely support billions of processes [4] that can potentially access and update shared files, all at the same time. The implementation of existing HPC parallel interfaces, such as MPI I/O, HDF5 and NetCDF are all based on and complaint to the POSIX standard. The POSIX standard requires strong consistency when accessing and updating a file. In a parallel environment, strong consistency is achieved by a process acquiring a lock on the file, completing the operation and releasing the lock. One reason for the performance bottleneck of

© Springer Nature Switzerland AG 2018
R. Yokota et al. (Eds.): ISC 2018 Workshops, LNCS 11203, pp. 117–130, 2018.
https://doi.org/10.1007/978-3-030-02465-9_8

HPC parallel I/O interfaces is the strong consistency POSIX requirement, and its implementation.

One of the possible disruptive solutions to address the lack of scalability of traditional parallel I/O would be the adoption of object storage technology [11]. Object storage is a well-spread technology in cloud computing and is currently being utilized by large tech companies. For instance, Amazon and Google, to mention a few, have implemented Amazon S3 and Google Cloud object storage; services which are used by many companies today. Object storage abandons traditional POSIX I/O concepts, such as directories, files, and certain file operations. Unlike many other parallel file systems, object storage provides a single flat global name space and supports only a few operations, among which are the PUT and GET operations. Performance scalability of object storage is partly due to the concept of *object immutability* and also due to the semantics of the PUT and GET operations. Objects are *immutable*, as in-place changes to the data in the object are not possible. A PUT operation creates an object, adds data to it and returns an object Universally Unique Identifier (UUID). A simple hash function or a combination of them can then be used to determine the location of the object in Object Storage Device (OSD). The main two advantages of object storage when compared to traditional approaches are:

1. Because objects are immutable, it is impossible for a node to write to an object that is being read by others. This allows removal of locks while reading data from an object, providing a lock-free data access.
2. Because physical object locations can be determined by object UUID and hashing function, it possible to directly access data without any locational metadata.

The main limitation of the object storage is that it requires additional software for metadata. In fact, metadata, such as the object name, creation time, etc., that is not comprised in the object storage needs to be stored and managed outside the object storage. For this reason, objects stores are usually equipped with a key-value store, providing users with a front-end interface and mapping object UUID to metadata.

A simplified diagram of object storage is presented in Fig. 1, showing an application putting two objects in the object storage, similar to CEPH object storage [27]. With the PUT operation, two objects are created and their UUIDs are retrieved. A hash function is used to determine the placement group (an object pool) and then the physical location on the OSDs. The PUT operation also inserts associated metadata to the metadata server.

While object storage is a promising technology that could potentially replace parallel file systems in the future, it is unclear how current scientific applications running on supercomputers will use object storage and what the potential benefits are. To the best of our knowledge, there are no large scale supercomputers that are directly using object storage. For this reason, our goal is to take an application with similar workload to typical HPC applications, and emulate object storage on it. We emulate object storage to write both individual and shared

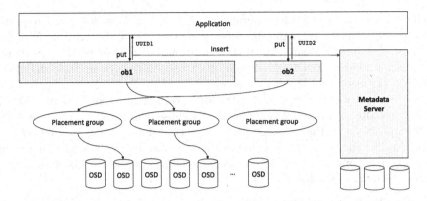

Fig. 1. Simplified diagram of an application writing two objects to the object store, similar to CEPH [27].

objects and to compare the I/O performance with existing parallel HDF5 implementations [12].

The paper makes the following contributions:

- We propose a methodology to evaluate the scalability of object storage at scale and develop a simple emulator to write and read objects on an object store serving large supercomputers.
- We deploy the object storage emulator in a representative massively parallel application and measure the I/O performance.
- We analyze the emulated object storage performance at scale, compare it with performance of parallel HDF5 and evaluate the object storage potential for extreme scale systems.

The paper is organized as follows. First, we provide background to this study and present related work in Sect. 2. Section 3 presents the design and implementation of an emulator for object storage at scale. Section 4 introduces the benchmarking environment. Section 5 presents the results. Finally, Sect. 6 summarizes the results, discusses the limitations of this work and outlines future work.

2   Background and Related Work

In this section, we provide an overview of common parallel I/O libraries and file systems, together with the related work.

POSIX I/O. POSIX (Portable Operating System Interface) is a specification defined by IEEE Computer Society for a standardized operating system interface and environment. Among other operations and concepts, POSIX defines the interaction between file descriptors and standard I/O streams [3]. From a programmer's perspective, POSIX I/O is characterized by the following interfaces: open(), close(), read(), write(), and lseek(). Additionally, the POSIX standard specifies the semantics of such operations. POSIX I/O is stateful and requires the operating system to maintain persistent states. In order to modify a file one must first open a descriptor, seek a location and read or write from there. File descriptors are not shared between processes and the system must maintain every descriptor opened by all processes.

Another feature of POSIX I/O is the strict consistency requirement. POSIX defines that after a successful write() call, any subsequent read() operations from the byte positions in the modified file must return data written by that write() operation [3]. The consistency semantics is often implemented with some form of locking mechanism [20]. In the case of parallel file systems, this is often implemented via distributed locking [14].

Parallel File Systems. Parallel file systems such as *Lustre* [2], *GPFS* [20] and *VPFS* [9] are created to support parallel I/O in a cluster environment. These file systems implement I/O forwarding at an extra layer between the storage system and computing system, which handles I/O on behalf of the computing systems. One of the widely adopted parallel file systems is Lustre. Lustre Metadata Servers (MDS) handles information such as physical locations, file names, permissions and timestamps. Data is striped and sent to different Object Stores Servers (OSS) [21]. Although Lustre is object store based, it exposes itself through POSIX I/O interface and is near POSIX compliant. POSIX consistency semantics is enforced through distributed locking. One performance bottleneck of Lustre lies on metadata management. Another bottleneck lies in file locking, which it is required to preserve consistency. Excessive striping can also negatively impact performance [28,29]. Performance of parallel writing to a single file can be improved by explicit configuration of striping, yet it increases failure risk and worsen performance of writes to non-shared files [5].

Parallel I/O Libraries. It is common to use parallel file systems with parallel I/O libraries. *MPI-IO* [23], *Parallel HDF5* [24] and *Parallel netCDF* [13] are parallel I/O libraries that work on top of parallel file systems. MPI-IO aims to provide a portable interface which addresses common parallel I/O patterns, such as collective I/O and non-contiguous access. MPI-IO exposes several POSIX like I/O interfaces with relaxed consistency requirements. MPI-IO guarantees that a write from one process is immediately visible to processes in the same communicator group in which the file was opened with atomic mode. Otherwise the content is only visible after explicit synchronization. Many I/O libraries, such as HDF5 and Parallel netCDF, are built upon MPI-IO to take advantage of portable parallel I/O. However, MPI-IO provides little performance improvement for contiguous access [5]. Due to its similarity to POSIX I/O, the performance of these two APIs is often similar.

Object Storage System. Object storage system is an architecture which manages data as objects instead of files [11]. Due to their scalability, object stores are widely adopted in cloud based systems. Object store operations are stateless and in object store semantics there are only two basic operations: GET and PUT. A PUT operation returns an ID which uniquely represents the object. Object store implementations usually provides a facility to map an assigned name to an ID, together with metadata which describes the object. This is often implemented with a key-value store. All objects are stored without structure and clients communicate directly to the storage node where data physically resides without requiring location lookup by hashing the object's ID [27]. Objects are immutable and it is impossible to concurrently create or update the same object. This eliminates the bottleneck caused by locking. In contrary to POSIX I/O, object stores support a weak form of consistency: eventual consistency. This means that a successfully returned PUT operation does not necessary require that the object will be visible immediately. Deterministic placement of object through ID hashing leads to the elimination bottleneck due to lookup.

CEPH [27] is one of the most commonly known object storage system. It exposes itself as through a POSIX interface and at the same time provides a number of POSIX I/O extensions which provides relaxed consistency. Unlike Lustre, any party can compute the physical location of an object by hashing its ID. For this reason, location metadata is completely eliminated. This reduces the stress on the metadata cluster. Additionally, it is possible to manipulate the underlying object store directly through librados [1]. Additional emerging object storages, targeting HPC workloads, are Seagate's Mero [15,16], DAOS [6] and DDN's Web Object Store (WOS) [10]. Studies have also been made on how HPC applications can interact with these transaction based storage systems [19]. The adoption of these systems enabled a wider range of underlying storage technologies to be used, such as hybrid-memory storage systems and Non-volatile memory storage systems [17,18].

I/O Pattern in Scientific Applications. The majority of scientific applications perform a large number of write operations to preserve intermediate states and final outcome of simulation variables for post-processing (visualization and data analysis) and check-pointing. In scientific applications, these operations occur typically at a given computational cycle, defined by users. Because of the computational cost of parallel I/O, I/O operations are kept at minimum in scientific applications. Typically, these outputs are only for the purpose of archiving, later post-processing and check-pointing for restarting simulations.

Parallel I/O operations either:

1. Write/Read one file per process (independent parallel I/O), or
2. Write/Read to the same shared file (cooperative parallel I/O). In this case, parallel I/O is performed using parallel I/O libraries, such as MPI-IO, Parallel HDF5 and NETCDF.

Studies have shown that parallel write to the same file often results in worse performance than writing to individual non-shared files [5,7,26], implying that existing parallel file systems are not well suited for parallel I/O. For Lustre, custom striping configuration can result in similar performance between the two approaches, but also results in higher failure risk.

In terms of concurrent write, it is rarely the case that a process requires the latest update through a read operation immediately after a write operation. This can be efficiently implemented through MPI point-to-point or collective where data is in-memory if data sharing is needed. Therefore, the strict read-after-write consistency requirement imposed by POSIX I/O is rarely required.

By decoupling metadata management and relaxing consistency requirements, object stores can potentially provide extreme scalability for parallel I/O. Scalability is achieved through deterministic placements and lock-free accesses. Since most scientific applications are write intensive and do no rely on POSIX consistency guarantees, we argue that object stores will be extremely valuable for scientific applications.

3   Emulating Scientific Applications Using Object Storage

Our goal is to assess the impact of object storage system on supercomputers in HPC scientific applications. In particular, we are interested in how object stores can improve scalability of such applications. Yet, HPC-ready object stores are not widely adopted. For this reason, we have designed and implemented a simple library that emulates the workings of an object storage system. Specifically, we emulate four key features of object storage systems, namely: flat namespace structure, object immutability, deterministic object placement and metadata management. We implement the API according to object store semantics. A GET operation retrieves an object and a PUT operation creates a new object as shown in Fig. 2. Metadata are stored as serialized binary files to mimic a key-value store where the file name is the key. Furthermore, we support chunking operations. This implies that it is possible to create an object concurrently by different processes.

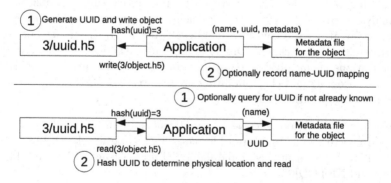

Fig. 2. Illustration of how our emulator mimics object store PUT (top) and GET (bottom) operations in an application.

3.1   Emulator Implementation

We implement an emulator to mimic an object storage serving a large scale supercomputer as a C library. For the purpose of the experiment, we support the storage of multidimensional arrays in 64-bit double, 32-bit float and 32-bit integer data-type as objects. Objects are stored in one or more HDF5 files. These HDF5 files are represented by UUID and a part number. Metadata are represented in protobuf serialized data format. Furthermore, we emulate different Object Storage Devices (OSD) as different folders. Our emulator employs a weak form of consistency: eventual consistency. This means that an object being written will not be immediately visible to other processes, but will eventually be. We define that an object is visible after the metadata is written and synchronized to disk. The writing of metadata is performed after all data is successfully written. This is to support wait-free read by other processes to an object with the same name. In this way, processes will retrieve the ID of the object from existing metadata, which point to an existing object, while the new object is being written to another location with another ID. We also write a HDF5 virtual dataset which links all the chunks together and present a unified view of the entire object. HDF5 virtual datasets can be opened as a single dataset with existing HDF5 dataset APIs as if it is one single file. How our emulator writes an object chunk and correspondent metadata is shown in Fig. 3.

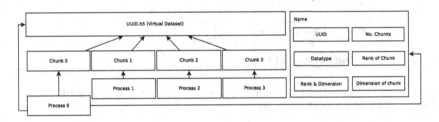

Fig. 3. Illustration of how the emulator uses object chunks and metadata.

Objects Creation. A new object is created with a PUT operation. A PUT operation receives object name, data and metadata which describes the object, and performs operations. We support multidimensional data in a variety of datatypes. Additionally, we represent descriptive information such as size and dimension as metadata. When a PUT request is received, a new UUID is generated to uniquely represent the object. We use a hash function to determine in which object storage device the object will the be placed. A new HDF5 dataset will be created to store the structured input data and stored in an HDF5 file with the UUID as filename.

Object Chunking. During object chunking, the object is divided into equal sized portions and stored individually with many HDF5 files. Multidimensional chunks are supported. A chunk ID is appended to the filename for reconstruction. Immediately before the metadata is being written, a HDF5 Virtual Dataset (VDS) is created to provide a high level overview of the object being written [7, 25]. Thus, the object chunks can be retrieved as a single object thereafter. Figure 4 shows our object store design, where individual object chunks are represented as individual HDF5 files and are linked via VDS according to part number.

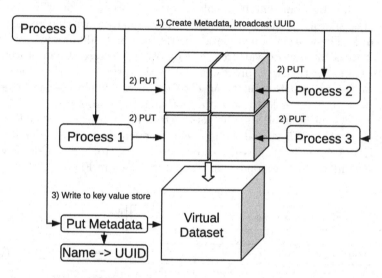

Fig. 4. In our emulated object storage, object chunks are stored as HDF5 files and metadata as Virtual Data Sets (VDS).

Metadata Management. We represent object metadata using protobuf, which is a serialization mechanism developed by Google. Our emulated object storage supports data in multi-dimensional tensors. So, in our particular case, we store the rank of the tensor, the size for each tensor dimension and the UUID. If the object is chunked, then the chunk size, dimension and chunk count will be also stored. The protobuf object will be serialized and written to a temporary file on disk. After the file is synchronized to disk, we perform a POSIX rename() and synchronization to rename the temporary file to the user defined object name. This ensures that a third party client who is accessing the metadata file with the same name will either get a new or an old copy of the metadata. A client who is holding a file descriptor to the old metadata will still be able to read the old copy of the metadata. In the case where multiple clients are creating different chunks of the same object, the master process must initiate a PUT process by obtaining a copy of the metadata and UUID from the library. The UUID will be broadcast to other processes and they can perform their own chunked PUT by supplying the data, UUID and part number. When all processes have completed their respective chunked PUT, the master process performs a commit to write the metadata to disk so that the new object will be visible. It is the application's responsibility to ensure that all chunked PUT operations by different processes are complete. When two processes perform PUTs with the same object name concurrently, the most up-to-date version of the object is the object of the last process writing the metadata.

4   Experimental Environment

Our experiments are performed on the Beskow supercomputer at KTH. Beskow is a Cray XC40 system, consisting of 2,060 compute nodes, equipped with two Xeon E5-2698v3 Haswell 2.3 GHz CPUs (16 cores per CPU) per node and high speed network Cray Aries. The storage employs a Lustre parallel file system (client v2.5.2) with 165 OST servers. Beskow OS is SUSE LINUX (Release 11). We use GCC version 4.9.1, Cray-MPICH v7.0.4 and HDF5 v1.10.1.

To measure the I/O performance, we use the Darshan profiler [8]. Darshan is a low-overhead tool to investigate the I/O performance of parallel applications. Darshan provides bandwidth and measured time spent on I/O. Measurement is done at MPI I/O and POSIX level. For this reason, the Darshan tool is capable of profiling both our emulated library and parallel HDF5 as our library is implemented through HDF5 which is based on POSIX I/O; and parallel HDF5 which is based on MPI I/O.

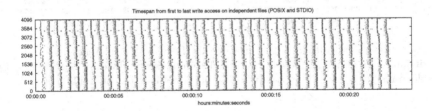

Fig. 5. Different processes writing to individual object chunks.

We implemented a skeleton application iterating over 200 computational cycles. Every five cycles, we perform parallel I/O. Therefore, the whole execution cycle consists of 40 I/O phases. The computation and I/O phases take approximately 75% and 25% of the total execution time respectively. We perform weak scaling test, keeping the amount of data to be written by each process constant while varying number of processes. For every I/O phase, we output a two dimensional integer array where the size is a multiple of chunk size with the number of processes. A broadcast of UUID is performed by rank 0, processes

write their chunk and sign-in to a barrier. Rank 0 commits metadata to disk
after all processes are signed-in. To compare the I/O performance with parallel
HDF5, a separate experiment that utilizes HDF5 was created. The set-up consists of the same skeleton application performing calculations at each iteration
and I/O with parallel HDF5 to write to a shared file every five cycles. MPI hints
are provided to utilize Lustre striping with a stripe count equal to the number
of MPI processes in use divided by the number of processes per stripe.

We created test configuration with different chunk sizes. We tested 16 × 4096,
32 × 4096 and 64 × 4096. For parallel HDF5, we additionally test for different
number of processes per stripe. We tested 16, 32 and 64, where 32 is the number
of processors on one computing node of Beskow. For each configuration we repeat
the tests 5 times and report the median, minimum and maximum bandwidth in
MiB/s. For time spent on I/O operation we report the average value in seconds.

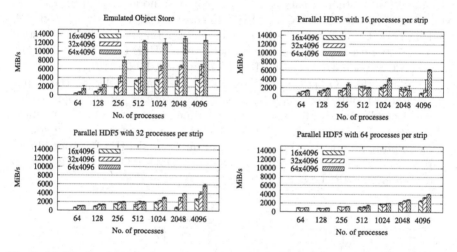

Fig. 6. Median bandwidth in MiB/s measured by Darshan for different configurations.
Maximum and minimum bandwidth recorded are represented by error bars. Scaling of
workload results in increase of bandwidth in both methods but on a different scale.

5   Evaluation

We perform scaling tests up to 4,096 processes. We measure both time spent on
I/O operations and bandwidth of write operations. Figure 5 shows I/O patterns
of different processes of a particular configuration using our emulator where
processes perform putting of their data chunk. Figure 6 shows the bandwidth
under different chunk sizes and stripe configuration by the application with the
two I/O methods: emulated object storage and parallel HDF5 to a shared file.
Our emulator outperforms parallel HDF5 in terms of bandwidth. Comparing
to the emulator, parallel HDF5 only provides moderate scaling in bandwidth.

We also noticed that the performance of parallel HDF5 is extremely sensitive to configurations. Figure 7 shows the maximal and minimal bandwidth measured from writing operations among all configurations.

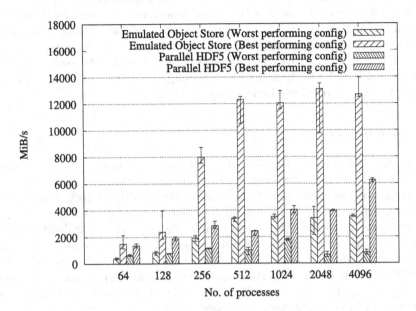

Fig. 7. Configurations with maximal and minimal bandwidth in MiB/s measured by Darshan among different configurations. Both methods provide comparable bandwidth with small number of processes.

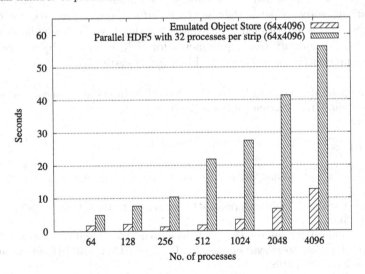

Fig. 8. Average total time spent on I/O in seconds with chunk size 64 × 4096. For parallel HDF5 32 processes per strip is set.

We find that our emulated object store implementation provides better scalability than writing to shared file. Although still outperforming parallel HDF5, after more than 2,048 processes are used, we observe saturation and slight decline in bandwidth. We also observed that the bandwidth scales together with increasing chunk size with our emulator. The same is observed with parallel HDF5. Yet the scaling comparing with the emulator is only moderate. Figure 8 shows the total time spent on I/O during application execution. We observe a large increase of time spent on I/O relative to number of processes used for the implementation with parallel HDF5. On the other hand, the implementation with our emulated object store shows relatively little change in terms of time spent.

6   Conclusion

One of the performance and scalability bottlenecks in large scientific applications is parallel I/O to file systems. In fact, the usage of parallel file systems and consistency requirements of POSIX (that all the traditional HPC parallel I/O interfaces adhere to) poses limitations to scientific applications. Object storage is a promising technology that could address the parallel I/O scalability issues at extreme scale. In this work, we designed and implemented a library to emulate the object storage operation semantics with the goal of understanding the scalability benefit of scientific HPC applications, using object storage on large scale supercomputers. We showed that scientific applications can benefit from the usage of object storage on large scales.

In the future, we would like to apply our library to HPC applications with heavy I/O workload patterns and investigate further for potential improvements. In particular, we would like to implement a submodule with IOR [22], an I/O benchmarking software such that we can perform qualitative studies of how object store I/O semantics can contribute to scalability. Through these studies, we also hope to identify the requirements for HPC oriented object stores and how they can contribute to future highly parallel systems.

Acknowledgments. Funding for the work is received from the European Commission H2020 program, Grant Agreement No. 671500 (SAGE).

References

1. Introduction to Librados. http://docs.ceph.com/docs/master/rados/api/librados-intro/
2. Lustre: A scalable, high-performance file system. Cluster File Systems Inc., White Paper (2002)
3. IEEE standard for information technology-portable operating system interface (POSIX(R)) base specifications, issue 7. IEEE Std 1003.1-2017 (Revision of IEEE Std 1003.1-2008) (2018)
4. Bergman, K., et al.: Exascale computing study: technology challenges in achieving exascale systems. Defense Advanced Research Projects Agency Information Processing Techniques Office (DARPA IPTO), Technical Report 15 (2008)

5. Borrill, J., Oliker, L., Shalf, J., Shan, H.: Investigation of leading HPC I/O performance using a scientific-application derived benchmark. In: Proceedings of the 2007 ACM/IEEE Conference on Supercomputing, SC 2007, pp. 1–12 (2007)

6. Breitenfeld, M.S., et al.: DAOS for extreme-scale systems in scientific applications. arXiv preprint arXiv:1712.00423 (2017)

7. Byna, S., Chaarawi, M., Koziol, Q., Mainzer, J., Willmore, F.: Tuning HDF5 subfiling performance on parallel file systems (2017)

8. Carns, P., Latham, R., Ross, R., Iskra, K., Lang, S., Riley, K.: 24/7 characterization of petascale I/O workloads. In: IEEE International Conference on Cluster Computing and Workshops, CLUSTER 2009, pp. 1–10. IEEE (2009)

9. Carns, P.H., Ligon III, W.B., Ross, R.B., Thakur, R.: PVFS: a parallel file system for Linux clusters. In: Proceedings of the 4th Annual Linux Showcase and Conference, vol. 4. p. 28 (2000). https://www.usenix.org/legacy/publications/library/proceedings/als00/2000papers/papers/full_papers/carns/carns_html/#foot9

10. Data Direct Networks: WOS: Object storage. https://www.ddn.com/products/object-storage-web-object-scaler-wos/

11. Factor, M., Meth, K., Naor, D., Rodeh, O., Satran, J.: Object storage: the future building block for storage systems. In: Local to Global Data Interoperability-Challenges and Technologies, pp. 119–123. IEEE (2005)

12. Folk, M., Heber, G., Koziol, Q., Pourmal, E., Robinson, D.: An overview of the HDF5 technology suite and its applications. In: Proceedings of the EDBT/ICDT2011 Workshop on Array Databases, pp. 36–47. ACM (2011)

13. Li, J., et al.: Parallel netCDF: a high-performance scientific I/O interface. In: 2003 ACM/IEEE Conference on Supercomputing, p. 39 (2003)

14. Mohindra, A., Devarakonda, M.: Distributed token management in Calypso file system. In: Proceedings of 1994 6th IEEE Symposium on Parallel and Distributed Processing, pp. 290–297 (1994)

15. Narasimhamurthy, S., et al.: The SAGE project: a storage centric approach for exascale computing. In: Proceedings of Computing Frontiers. ACM (2018)

16. Narasimhamurthy, S., et al.: SAGE: percipient storage for exascale data centric computing. Parallel Comput. (2018). https://doi.org/10.1016/j.parco.2018.03.002

17. Peng, I.B., Gioiosa, R., Kestor, G., Cicotti, P., Laure, E., Markidis, S.: Exploring the performance benefit of hybrid memory system on HPC environments. In: 2017 IEEE International Parallel and Distributed Processing Symposium Workshops (IPDPSW), pp. 683–692. IEEE (2017)

18. Peng, I.B., Markidis, S., Laure, E., Kestor, G., Gioiosa, R.: Exploring application performance on emerging hybrid-memory supercomputers. In: 2016 IEEE 18th International Conference on High Performance Computing and Communications, IEEE 14th International Conferenceon Smart City, IEEE 2nd International Conference on Data Science and Systems (HPCC/SmartCity/DSS), pp. 473–480. IEEE (2016)

19. Rivas-Gomez, S., et al.: MPI windows on storage for HPC applications. In: Proceedings of the 24th European MPI Users' Group Meeting, p. 15. ACM (2017)

20. Schmuck, F.B., Haskin, R.L.: GPFS: a shared-disk file system for large computing clusters. In: Proceedings of the Conference on File and Storage Technologies, FAST 2002, pp. 231–244 (2002)

21. Schwan, P., et al.: Lustre: building a file system for 1000-node clusters. In: Proceedings of the 2003 Linux Symposium, vol. 2003, pp. 380–386 (2003)

22. Shan, H., Antypas, K., Shalf, J.: Characterizing and predicting the I/O performance of HPC applications using a parameterized synthetic benchmark. In: Proceedings of the 2008 ACM/IEEE Conference on Supercomputing, p. 42. IEEE Press (2008)
23. Thakur, R., Gropp, W., Lusk, E.: On implementing MPI-IO portably and with high performance. In: Proceedings of the Sixth Workshop on I/O in Parallel and Distributed Systems, pp. 23–32 (1999)
24. The HDF Group: Hierarchical Data Format, version 5 (1997). http://www.hdfgroup.org/HDF5/
25. The HDF Group: HDF5 Virtual Dataset (2014). https://support.hdfgroup.org/HDF5/Tutor/vds.html
26. Wang, F., et al.: File system workload analysis for large scale scientific computing applications. Technical report (2004)
27. Weil, S.A., Brandt, S.A., Miller, E.L., Long, D.D., Maltzahn, C.: Ceph: a scalable, high-performance distributed file system. In: Proceedings of the 7th symposium on Operating systems design and implementation, pp. 307–320. USENIX Association (2006)
28. Xu, C., et al.: LIOProf: exposing Lustre file system behavior for I/O middleware (2016). https://cug.org/proceedings/cug2016_proceedings/at_a_glance.html
29. Yu, W., Vetter, J., Canon, R.S., Jiang, S.: Exploiting Lustre file joining for effective collective I/O. In: Seventh IEEE International Symposium on Cluster Computing and the Grid (CCGrid 2007), pp. 267–274 (2007)

Benefit of DDN's IME-FUSE for I/O Intensive HPC Applications

Eugen Betke[1]([⊠]) and Julian Kunkel[2]([⊠])

[1] Deutsches Klimarechenzentrum, Hamburg, Germany
betke@dkrz.de
[2] University of Reading, Reading, UK
j.m.kunkel@reading.ac.uk

Abstract. Many scientific applications are limited by I/O performance offered by parallel file systems on conventional storage systems. Flash-based burst buffers provide significant better performance than HDD backed storage, but at the expense of capacity. Burst buffers are considered as the next step towards achieving wire-speed of interconnect and providing more predictable low latency I/O, which are the holy grail of storage.

A critical evaluation of storage technology is mandatory as there is no long-term experience with performance behavior for particular applications scenarios. The evaluation enables data centers choosing the right products and system architects the integration in HPC architectures.

This paper investigates the native performance of DDN-IME, a flash-based burst buffer solution. Then, it takes a closer look at the IME-FUSE file systems, which uses IMEs as burst buffer and a Lustre file system as back-end. Finally, by utilizing a NetCDF benchmark, it estimates the performance benefit for climate applications.

Keywords: Lustre · FUSE · Evaluation · Flash-based storage

1 Introduction

The dilemma of conventional high-performance storage systems based on HDDs is that they must maximize the throughput to reduce application run times and at the same time they shall minimize the provided bandwidth to reduce costs. The first requirement is often prioritized to the detriment of the second one, which typically ends up in the oversizing and in a low average usage of the bandwidth procured. The prioritization is motivated by the requirement to process large performance peaks particular due to checkpoint/restart workloads, that often occur in large-scale applications. However, since these systems are optimized for sequential I/O, data-intense workloads that are not following this pattern are unable to saturate the network – reducing the effective utilization.

Traditional parallel file systems can be deployed on flash-based storage instead of HDDs, increasing performance for random workloads. A nice work in

© Springer Nature Switzerland AG 2018
R. Yokota et al. (Eds.): ISC 2018 Workshops, LNCS 11203, pp. 131–144, 2018.
https://doi.org/10.1007/978-3-030-02465-9_9

this direction was done in [3]. Typically, data is accessed via POSIX interfaces but can be accessed using MPI-IO [14]. MPI-IO is a widely accepted middleware layer for parallel I/O that relaxes the POSIX semantics and is designed for parallel I/O. In an alternative storage architecture, a burst buffer [8,11] is placed between compute nodes and the storage. Acting as an intermediate storage tier, it's goal is to catch the I/O peaks from the compute nodes. Therefore, it provides a low latency and high bandwidth to the compute nodes, but also utilizes the back-end storage by streaming data constantly at a lower bandwidth.

In-memory systems, like the Kove® XPD® [7], provide byte-addressable storage with better latency, endurance and availability as flash chips. Flash-based systems, like DDN IME [13], are also byte-addressable, but have different characteristics than an in-memory storage, for example, flash offers a better costs per gigabyte ratio.

Accessing a fast storage over a POSIX compliant file system or MPI-IO interface is an interesting option for many users, because neither changes in source code, nor software recompilation is required as long as it doesn't degrade the performance too much. Closed source and pre-compiled applications could also benefit from that. For that purpose, DDN developed a fuse module (IME-FUSE) which uses IME as a burst buffer and stores data on a parallel file system. In this evaluation we used Lustre as back-end.

Our **contributions** are: (1) we investigate peak performance of IME-native and IME-FUSE, and compare it to Lustre, (2) we estimate the performance behaviour for HPC applications, that access data using NetCDF library.

This paper is structured as follows: Section 2 discusses related work, then Sect. 3 describes the test environment. Sections 4 and 5 show the test setup and performance results. Finally, the paper is summarized in Sect. 6.

2   Related Work

Relevant state-of-the-art can be grouped into performance optimization, burst buffers to speedup I/O and in-memory storage solutions.

Optimization and tuning of file systems and I/O libraries is traditionally an important but daunting task as many configuration knobs can be considered in parallel file system servers, clients and the I/O middleware. Without tuning, typical workloads stay behind the peak-performance by orders of magnitude. With considerable tuning effort a well fitting problem can yield good results: [15] reports 50% peak performance with a single 291 TB file. In [4] MPI-IO and HDF5 were optimized and adapted to each other, improving write throughput by 1.4x to 33x.

Many existing workloads can take benefit of a burst buffer as a fast write-behind cache that transparently migrates data from the fast storage to traditional parallel file system. Burst buffers typically rely on flash or NVRAM to support random I/O workloads. For flash based SSDs, many vendors offer high-performance storage solutions, for example, DDN Infinite Memory Engine (IME) [2], IBM FlashSystem [5] and Cray's DataWarp accelerator [1]. Using comprehensive strategies to utilize flash chips concurrently, these solutions are powerful and robust to guarantee availability and durability of data for many years.

The integration of Cray DataWarp burst buffer into the NERSC HPC architecture [10] increased the I/O performance of Chumbo-Crunch simulator by 2.84x to 5.73x, compared to Lustre. However, for the sake of efficient burst buffer usage, the serial simulator workflow had to be split into single stages (i.e., simulation, visualization, movie encoding), which then were executed in parallel. The research group at JSC uses DDN IME burst buffer [12] and GPFS to identify requirements for the next HPC generation. The main purpose is to accelerate the I/O performance of the NEST ("NEural Simulation Tool"). The preliminary IOR experiments show, that I/O performance can be increased upto 20x. BurstFS [16] uses local NVRAM of compute nodes, instead of dedicated remote machines. An elaborated communication scheme interconnects the distributed NVRAM and provides a contiguous storage space. This storage is allocated at beginning and exists for the lifetime of the job. In the experiments, BurstFS outperforms OrangeFS and PLFS by several times.

The usage of DRAM for storing intermediate data is not new and RAM drives have been used in MSDOS and Linux (with tmpfs) for decades. However, offered RAM storage was used as temporary local storage and not durable and usually not accessible from remote nodes. Exporting tmpfs storage via parallel file systems has been used mainly for performance evaluation but without durability guarantees. Wickberg and Carothers introduced the RAMDISK Storage Accelerator [18] for HPC applications that flushes data to a back-end. It consists of a set of dedicated nodes that offer in-memory scratch space. Jobs can use the storage to pre-fetch input data prior job execution or as write-behind cache to speedup I/O. A prototype with a PVFS-based RAMDISK improved performance of 2048 processes compared to GPFS (100 MB/s vs. 36 MB/s for writes). Burst-mem [17] provides a burst buffer with write-behind capabilities by extending Memcached [6]. Experiments show that the ingress performance grows up to 100 GB/s with 128 BurstMem servers. In the field of big data, in-memory data management and processing has become popular with Spark [19]. Now there are many software packages providing storage management and compute engines [20].

The Kove XPD [7] is a robust scale-out pooled memory solution that allows aggregating multiple Infiniband links and devices into one big virtual address space that can be dynamically partitioned. Internally, the Kove provides persistence by periodically flushing memory with a SATA RAID. Due to the performance differences, the process comes with a delay, but the solution is connected to a UPS to ensure that data becomes durable in case of a power outage. While providing many interfaces, the XPD does not offer a shared storage that can be utilized from multiple nodes concurrently.

3   Test Environment

DDN provided access to their test cluster in Düsseldorf on which 10 nodes could be used for testing. Each node is equipped with two Sandy Bridge processors (8 cores, E5-2650v2 @2.60 GHz) and 64 GB RAM. They are interconnected with a Mellanox Connect-X-4 card providing 100 Gb/s (4x EDR). As storage, a DDN ES14K (Exascale 3.1) with two metadata servers and Lustre 2.7.19.12 is provided; additionally, an IME system consisting of 4 servers is provided. The flash native data cache of IME acts as a burst buffer and is drained to the Lustre system, the performance reported with IOR is 85 GB/s in write mode. The DDN IME provides byte-addressable flash-based storage space with high performance characteristics. It can be addressed directly (IME-native) in a fast and efficient way, but DDN also provides a number of convenient solutions, that require less integration effort. (1) The applications can be re-linked to the MPI-IO implementation with IME support, which was developed by DDN. (2) Then, DDN provides a fuse module (IME-FUSE) with IME support, which are convenient ways to access a shared storage. Both file systems are POSIX compliant and can be used by the applications without any source code modification, recompilation, or re-linking. In the conducted tests, IME is used via its FUSE mount and backed by the DDN Lustre. We assume during the write experiment, data is kept inside the burst buffer and not written back, albeit we cannot ensure this.

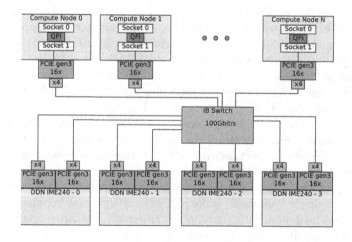

Fig. 1. DDN test cluster

The DDN cluster is a experimental system with a lightweight software setup. Especially, the exclusive access to the IME was not guaranteed, so that some results could be affected by other users. Therefore, we don't draw conclusions from outliers, since we don't know the origin of them.

3.1 Benchmarks

As our primary benchmark, IOR [9] is used varying access granularity, processes-per-node, nodes and access pattern (random and sequential). The official version of IOR allows us to measure the real performance without considering open/close times (see Eq. (1)). To synchronize the measurements and capture time for open, close and I/O separately, inter-phase barriers are turned on (IOR option -g). The DDN version (IME-IOR) supports IME-native interface, but doesn't allow measuring real I/O performance. Therefore, the performance values include open/close times (see Eq. (2)).

$$\text{perf}_{\text{Lustre, IME-FUSE}} = \frac{\text{filesize}}{t_{\text{io}}} \tag{1}$$

$$\text{perf}_{\text{IME-native}} = \frac{\text{filesize}}{t_{\text{total}}} = \frac{\text{filesize}}{t_{\text{open}} + t_{\text{io}} + t_{\text{close}}} \tag{2}$$

Since the IOR benchmarks does not support NetCDF, and HDF5 is only supported with limited configuration of the pattern, additionally, the NetCDF-Bench has been used[1]. This benchmark uses the parallel NetCDF interface to read/write patterns on a 4D dataset into a NetCDF4/HDF5 file. It decomposes a domain geometry of (t, x, y, z), e.g., $(100, 16, 64, 4)$ across the processes of an MPI parallel program. The processes partition the geometry in x and y direction and one time step is accessed per iteration of each parallel process. Various options to control the optimizations and data mappings from NetCDF are exported by the benchmark (chunking vs. fixed layout, unbound dimensions, chunk size, pre-filling).

Finally, to measure performance of individual operations to investigate variability, the sequential benchmark io-modelling is used[2]. It uses a high-precision timer and supports various access patterns on top of the POSIX interface.

4 Experiment Configuration

On the DDN cluster, we use NetCDF-Bench, IOR, and IME-IOR to measure the IME's throughput, and use io-modelling for testing variability. Each test configuration is repeated 10 times. All experiments are conducted with block sizes 16, 100, 1024, and 10240 KiB.

To find the performance limits of the test system we use the IOR benchmarks. For that purpose, we conduct a series of experiments with various parameters, where we measure the performance for {read, write} × {random, sequential} × {POSIX, MPIIO} × {Lustre, IME-FUSE, IME-native} × {collective, independent}. The stripe count on Lustre is twice as large as the number of nodes.

The purpose of NetCDF-Bench is to investigate the I/O behaviour of typical scientific application, that access large variable through NetCDF4. In the

---

[1] https://github.com/joobog/netcdf-bench.
[2] https://github.com/JulianKunkel/io-modelling.

experiment, we varied the following parameters: {Lustre, IME-FUSE} × {read, write} × {chunked, contiguous} × {collective, independent}.

With `io-modelling` benchmark we looked at the variability of individual I/O accesses {Lustre, IME-FUSE} × {read, write} × {random, sequential}.

4.1   Open/Close Times

The time of open/close reduces the reported performance of IME. They are dropped whenever possible for two reason. Firstly, in our experiments the test file size is variable (filesize = 100·blocksize·NN·PPN), it affects small experiments more than the larger ones. Additionally, it should be noted, that for production runs, larger files and capacities are assumed, reducing this overhead. Unless otherwise stated, the performance reported in this paper was measured without open/close times.

The goal of our evaluation is to systematically investigate the scaling behavior of the DDN IME's, IME-FUSE and Lustre. In the following experiments we use 1–10 client nodes (NN) and 1–8 processes per node (PPN) to push hardware to the limits. On each compute node only one CPU is used, that is connected directly to the Infiniband adapter, to avoid the QPI overhead. To provide reliable results, each experiment was repeated 10 times.

4.2   Performance

Table 1 shows the best and the average performance values that were observed with IME-IOR during the test runs on a single node and on 10 nodes for random and sequential I/O. Based on average performance for random I/O with NN = 1 and PPN = 8, 10 client nodes can achieve a throughput of 61 GB/s and of 80 GB/s for write and read, respectively. As Table 1 shows, the measured write performance is similar to expected values, which indicates that the compute nodes are the bottlenecks. But the measured read performance is significantly lower than expected. This indicates, that the bottleneck here are the IMEs. The same considerations apply to sequential performance.

5   Evaluation

IME-Native (Figs. 2 and 3): Characteristic for IME-native is that for each block size, there is a linear dependency between read and write accesses. The performance behavior for each block size can be approximated by a linear function and that small block sizes tend to have better write behaviour.

The complete set of performance results for random I/O is shown in Fig. 3. Firstly, it confirms the linear scalability. Secondly, there is also no regression of the curves, probably because the experiment setup couldn't push the IMEs to the limits. Further observations are: (1) writing small blocks is more efficient than reading small blocks; reading large blocks is more efficient that writing large

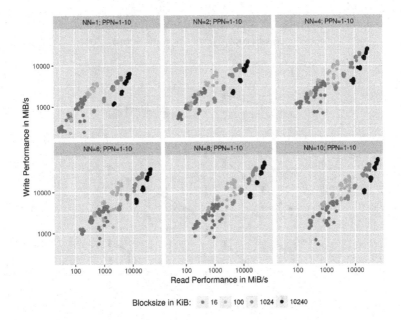

Fig. 2. Random access performance depending on blocksize and PPN

Table 1. The best and mean performance measured with IME-IOR (blocksize: 10MiB) (NN: number of nodes; PPN: processes per node).

NN	PPN	Best performance in [MiB/s]		Mean performance in [MiB/s]		I/O type	File size in [MiB]
		read	write	read	write		
1	1	2,560	1,240	2,400	1,180	rnd	1000
1	1	2,290	1,230	2,000	870	seq	1000
1	8	8,500	6,390	8,100	6,120	rnd	8000
1	8	8,700	6,380	7,100	4,530	seq	8000
10	1	22,300	10,700	21,200	10,000	rnd	10000
10	1	23,200	10,800	22,200	8,430	seq	10000
10	8	67,500	60,200	65,300	58,400	rnd	80000
10	8	67,500	62,900	61,700	54,300	seq	80000

blocks, (2) performance increases with increasing access granularity. (3) with 1 or 4 PPN the available network bandwidth is not utilized. With PPN=8, we are close to the available network bandwidth for 1 and 10 MiB accesses. Hence, the I/O path involves relevant latencies.

Lustre (Fig. 4a): Firstly, a single node can profit from caching, when reading data. In this case observable performance can rise up to 37 GiB/s (not shown in the figure). The caching effects disappear for NN > 1, hence we ignore them in further discussion. Secondly, the read performance don't exceed 17.4 GiB/s, and is achieved with NN = 10, PPN = 8, BS = 100 KiB. This is a contra-intuitive, because usually large block size show better performance. The best write performance is 11.8 GiB/s, and is achieved with NN = 4, PPN = 6, BS=1000 KiB. This

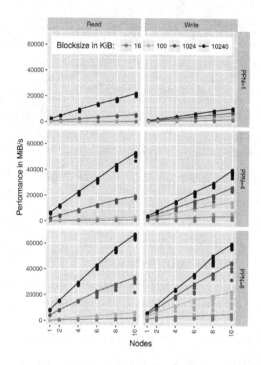

Fig. 3. IME-native random I/O performance (lines go through max. values)

measurement and the incrementally flattening curve indicate a poor scalability of Lustre. Generally speaking, Lustre has a lot of internal overhead, especially to make it POSIX compliant, e.g. distributed lock management. Thirdly, a particular striking point is the result for MPI-IO write performance. It is significantly lower than for other configurations. For this behaviour we have no explanation at the moment. It is also a confusing result, because it is in contradiction to our later experiment with NetCDF-Bench (Fig. 5). NetCDF4 uses MPI-IO as back-end, but achieves better results.

IME-FUSE (Fig. 4b): The file system shows a linear scalability, similar to the IME-native, but provides less I/O performance, especially for reading. This is probably caused by the FUSE overhead, which includes moving I/O requests from user space to kernel space, and then from kernel space to IME-FUSE.

Table 2. NetCDF-Bench configuration used in during the benchmark.

Parameter ($-d$) ($t{:}x{:}y{:}z$)	Data size [in GiB]	Block size [in KiB]
(100:16:64:4)	0.5	16
(100:16:64:25)	3.1	100
(100:16:64:256)	7.8	1024
(100:16:64:2560)	78.1	10240

(a) Lustre

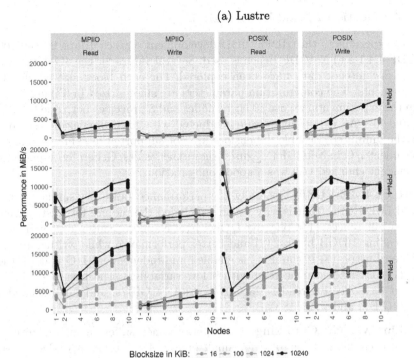

Blocksize in KiB: — 16 — 100 — 1024 — 10240

(b) IME-FUSE

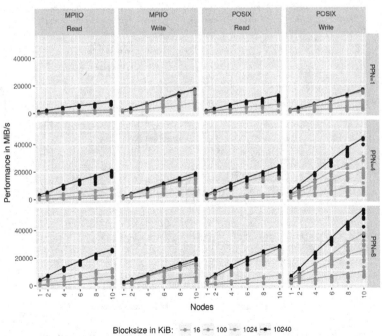

Blocksize in KiB: — 16 — 100 — 1024 — 10240

Fig. 4. Random I/O performance (lines go through max. values)

5.1   Application Kernel Using HDF5

In this experiment, the HDF5 VOL development branch (date 2016-05-09), NetCDF 4.4.1 and NetCDF-bench is used. Several values for the 4D data geometry of raw integer data have been explored. For each block size we did 100 measurements. The configuration parameters are summarized in Table 2.

In the experiments, we use 10 client nodes and 8 processes per node to access a shared file. All experiments were conducted with fixed dimension sizes only, since the unlimited/variable dimensions are not supported in combination with independent I/O in NetCDF4. Figure 5 shows the results. Generally, as expected, independent chunked I/O was a good configuration.

Lustre vs. IME-FUSE: Generally, the performance looks very similar for Lustre and IME-FUSE, that is why we only included the picture for Lustre. There are a few differences: (1) Collective I/O without chunking causes large variability while reading 16 KiB blocks, (2) and better performance while writing 10 MiB blocks on Lustre. (3) If chunking is enabled and independent I/O is used, then 10 MiB block sizes can be read with a low variability. The best performance achieved for collective read is 23 GiB/s write 14 GiB/s, and for independent read 40 GiB/s and write 18 GiB/s.

Chunking vs. No Chunking: Read performance suffers a lot on both file systems, if chunking is enabled for small blocks. The probability, that several

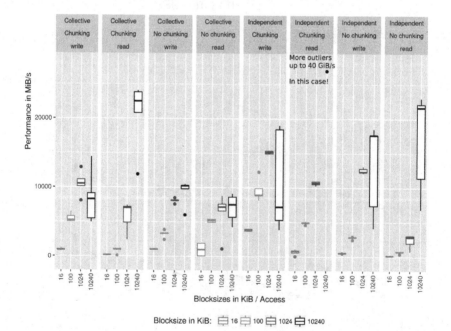

Fig. 5. NetCDF performance for Lustre (similar to IME-FUSE)

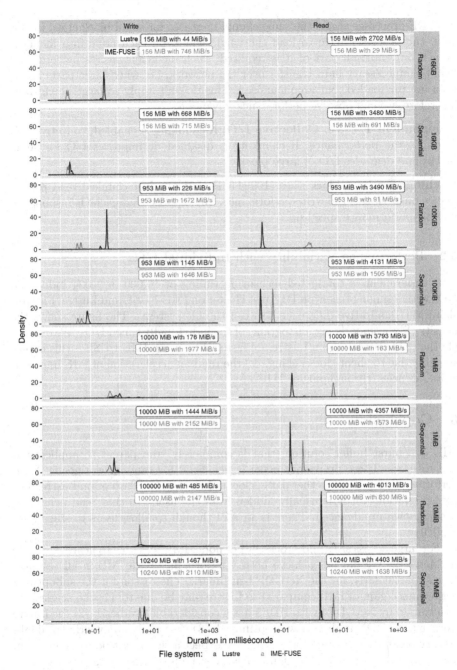

Fig. 6. Density of timing individual I/O operations

NetCDF processes access the same chunk, increases for small block sizes. In this case, the processes have to load the whole chunk on each node into memory, even if only a small part of it is required. Such inefficient access patterns can lead to unnecessary data transfer over the network, i.e. when large parts of the data are pre-loaded, but aren't unused. This doesn't apply to large block sizes. Therefore, we can observe performance advantages.

Independent I/O vs. Collective I/O: If chunking is enabled, collective I/O degrades the performance. If chunking is disabled, it improves I/O for small blocks and degrades I/O of large blocks.

Caching: For large block sizes (10204 KiB) independent chunked read performance outperforms the write performance. We suppose that cache is responsible for this performance speed-up.

5.2   Performance Variability with Individual I/Os

This experiment is conducted measuring timing of 10,000 or 1,024 individual I/Os with a single process on IME test cluster on IME-FUSE and Lustre. Figure 6 shows the qualitative difference between the file systems. The figure shows the density (like a smoothened histogram) of the individually timed I/Os. We observe (1) the read operations on Lustre are faster than using IME-FUSE – this is presumably due to client-side caching. (2) the random acceleration of IME improves write latencies/throughput for IME.

6   Conclusion

IME is a burst buffer solution, that is completely transparent to applications and to users. These properties make it beneficial for random workloads. Read performance depends whether data is located on the IME flash or on Lustre. The data migration policy is usually hidden from the users, so that read behaviour is not known in advanced. There is an API though to allow users to stage data explicitly.

For large access sizes and processes per node, IME was able to nearly saturate the network. We did not achieve better performance with IME in all test scenarios, particularly, for the NetCDF benchmark. The reason for the suboptimal performance gain of IME compared to Lustre may be due to: (1) the access pattern caused by NetCDF4 with HDF5 has a considerable overhead; (2) the Lustre storage from DDN is already well optimized; (3) the small and experimental laboratory setup that we used for testing. We expect a significant performance gain once more clients access IME. Further large-scale investigation is necessary.

Acknowledgment. Thanks to DDN for providing access to the IME test cluster and to Jean-Thomas Acquaviva for the support.

References

1. Cray: CRAY XC40 DataWarp Applications I/O Accelerator. http://www.cray. com/sites/default/files/resources/CrayXC40-DataWarp.pdf
2. DDN: Worlds's most advanced application aware I/O acceleration solutions. http://www.ddn.com/products/infinite-memory-engine-ime14k
3. Hebenstreit, M.: Performance evaluation of Intel SSD-based Lustre cluster file systems at the Intel CRT-DC. Technical report, Intel (2014). http://www.intel. com/content/dam/www/public/us/en/documents/performance-briefs/lustre-cluster-file-system-performance-evaluation.pdf
4. Howison, M., Koziol, Q., Knaak, D., Mainzer, J., Shalf, J.: Tuning HDF5 for lustre file systems. In: Workshop on Interfaces and Abstractions for Scientific Data Storage (IASDS 2010), Heraklion, Crete, Greece, 24 September 2010 (2012)
5. IBM: Flash Storage. http://www-03.ibm.com/systems/storage/flash
6. Jose, J., et al.: Memcached design on high performance RDMA capable interconnects. In: 2011 International Conference on Parallel Processing, pp. 743–752. IEEE (2011)
7. KOVE: about xpress disk (xpd) (2015). http://www.hamburgnet.de/products/ kove/Kove-XPD-L3-4-datasheet.pdf
8. Liu, N., et al.: On the role of burst buffers in leadership-class storage systems. In: Proceedings of the 2012 IEEE Conference on Massive Data Storage (2012)
9. Loewe, W., McLarty, T., Morrone, C.: IOR benchmark (2012)
10. Ovsyannikov, A., Romanus, M., Straalen, B.V., Weber, G.H., Trebotich, D.: Scientific workflows at datawarp-speed: accelerated data-intensive science using NERSC's burst buffer (2016). http://conferences.computer.org/pdswdiscs/2016/ papers/5216a001.pdf
11. Romanus, M., Parashar, M., Ross, R.B.: Challenges and considerations for utilizing burst buffers in high-performance computing. arXiv preprint arXiv:1509.05492 (2015)
12. Schenck, W., El Sayed, S., Foszczynski, M., Homberg, W., Pleiter, D.: Early evaluation of the "Infinite memory engine" burst buffer solution. In: Taufer, M., Mohr, B., Kunkel, J.M. (eds.) ISC High Performance 2016. LNCS, vol. 9945, pp. 604–615. Springer, Cham (2016). https://doi.org/10.1007/978-3-319-46079-6_41
13. Storage, D.: Burst buffer & beyond; I/O & Application Acceleration Technology. DDN Storage, September 2015
14. Thakur, R., Gropp, W., Lusk, E.: On Implementing MPI-IO Portably and with High Performance. In: Proceedings of the Sixth Workshop on I/O in Parallel and Distributed Systems, pp. 23–32 (1999)
15. The HDF Group: A Brief Introduction to Parallel HDF5. https://www.alcf.anl. gov/files/Parallel_HDF5_1.pdf
16. Wang, T., Mohror, K., Moody, A., Sato, K., Yu, W.: An ephemeral burst-buffer file system for scientific applications. In: Proceedings of the International Conference for High Performance Computing, Networking, Storage and Analysis, SC 2016, pp. 69:1–69:12. IEEE Press, Piscataway (2016). http://dl.acm.org/citation.cfm? id=3014904.3014997
17. Wang, T., Oral, S., Wang, Y., Settlemyer, B., Atchley, S., Yu, W.: BurstMem: a high-performance burst buffer system for scientific applications. In: 2014 IEEE International Conference on Big Data (Big Data), pp. 71–79. IEEE (2014)

18. Wickberg, T., Carothers, C.: The RAMDISK storage accelerator: a method of accelerating I/O performance on HPC systems using RAMDISKs. In: Proceedings of the 2nd International Workshop on Runtime and Operating Systems for Supercomputers, p. 5. ACM (2012)
19. Zaharia, M., et al.: Resilient distributed datasets: a fault-tolerant abstraction for in-memory cluster computing. In: Proceedings of the 9th USENIX Conference on Networked Systems Design and Implementation, p. 2. USENIX Association (2012)
20. Zhang, H., Chen, G., Ooi, B.C., Tan, K.L., Zhang, M.: In-memory big data management and processing: a survey. IEEE Trans. Knowl. Data Eng. **27**(7), 1920–1948 (2015)

Performance Study of Non-volatile Memories on a High-End Supercomputer

Leonardo Bautista Gomez[(⊠)], Kai Keller, and Osman Unsal

Barcelona Supercomputing Center (BSC-CNS),
Carrer de Jordi Girona, 29-31, 08034 Barcelona, Spain
{leonardo.bautista,kai.keller,osman.unsal}@bsc.es

Abstract. The first exa-scale supercomputers are expected to be operational in China, USA, Japan and Europe within the early 2020's. This allows scientists to execute applications at extreme scale with more than 10^{18} floating point operations per second (exa-FLOPS). However, the number of FLOPS is not the only parameter that determines the final performance. In order to store intermediate results or to provide fault tolerance, most applications need to perform a considerable amount of I/O operations during runtime. The performance of those operations is determined by the throughput from volatile (e.g. DRAM) to non-volatile stable storage. Regarding the slow growth in network bandwidth compared to the computing capacity on the nodes, it is highly beneficial to deploy local stable storage such as the new non-volatile memories (NVMe), in order to avoid the transfer through the network to the parallel file system. In this work, we analyse the performance of three different storage levels of the CTE-POWER9 cluster, located at the Barcelona Supercomputing Center (BSC). We compare the throughputs of SSD, NVMe on the nodes to the GPFS under various scenarios and settings. We measured a maximum performance on 16 nodes of 83 GB/s using NVMe devices, 5.6 GB/s for SSD devices and 4.4 GB/s for writes to the GPFS.

1 Introduction

Supercomputers' performance has been increasing exponentially for decades, however the I/O performance has only increased linearly over the same time. This has generated an I/O bottleneck that can cause large overheads when large amounts of data have to be written in the parallel file system (PFS). To alleviate this issue, multiple intermediary storage layers have been added between the main dynamic random-access memory (DRAM) and the PFS. Among others, the solid-state drives (SSD) and the more recent non-volatile memories (NVM) offer different performance/reliability/capacity trade offs.

In this paper we analyze the performance of a computing cluster with these three levels of storage. We use the widely recognized IOR I/O benchmark [5] for our measurements. In addition to baseline read/write speed we also perform weak-scaling experiments that emulate large checkpoints being performed by scientific applications. Our results show that NVM offer over an order of magnitude higher writing speed than the PFS and SSD.

© Springer Nature Switzerland AG 2018
R. Yokota et al. (Eds.): ISC 2018 Workshops, LNCS 11203, pp. 145–156, 2018.
https://doi.org/10.1007/978-3-030-02465-9_10

The rest of this article is organized as follows. Section 2 presents the related work. Section 3 explains the test methodology and specification of the platform. Section 4 shows the results of our evaluation and Sect. 5 concludes this work.

2 Related Work

In recent years, there has been multiple works exploring the benefits of NVM for supercomputers as well as studying the current software limitations with respect to NVMs. Mittal et al. [6] did a survey of the software approaches to take advantage of NVM and to cope with the existing limitations. The survey first gives a brief overview of the different memory technologies, then it focuses on the management techniques that has been proposed for NVM; and it also explores attempts to combine multiple types of memory.

Vetter et al. [7] study the advantages of using NVM in terms of reduced power consumption, increased storage capacity and lower costs. A detailed comparison in terms of data retention, cell size, access granularity, endurance, speed and power is given from multiple storage technologies. Possible architectural and functional integrations are explored as well. It also shows that these devices open new opportunities in terms of application checkpointing and resilience.

The above state-of-the-art is based on qualitative comparison of proposed NVMe devices. In contrast, this work focuses on a practical experimentation with real NVM devices, in which we stress them under multiple different configurations and measure its performance and limitations. We compare multiple storage levels all integrated in the same computing cluster.

3 Methodology and Technical Specifications

3.1 The Device Specifications

The experiments were performed on the CTE-POWER9 (IBM) cluster at the BSC. We were granted 16 nodes where each node was equipped with:

- 2 × IBM Power9 8335-GTG @ 3.00 GHz (20 cores, 160 threads)
- 512 GB DRAM
- 2 × Micron 5100 Series 1.9 TB SATA SSD
- 2 × Samsung PM1725a 3.2 TB NVMe SSD
- 4 × GPU NVIDIA V100 (Volta) with 16 GB HBM2
- Single Port Mellanox EDR
- GPFS via one fiber link of 10 GBit

The node configuration is shown in Fig. 1. The GPFS operates on 4 IBM Elastic Storage Servers (ESS) [1]. The performance (measured internal at the BSC) has been observed to be about 30 GB/s per ESS, thus, the expected maximum performance of the GPFS is expected to be at 120 GB/s. However, The bandwidth/node is limited by the 10 Gbps connection (1.25 GB/s). The cluster in turn is connected to the GPFS via 8 links of 10 Gbps each. Hence the maximum performance of the cluster is limited to 80 Gbps (10 GB/s).

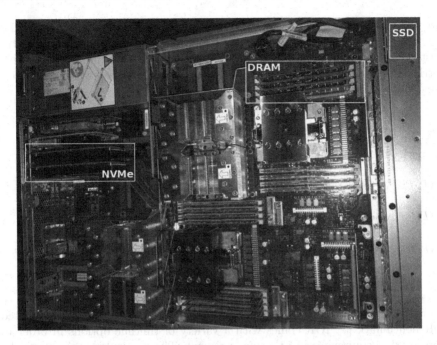

Fig. 1. Node configuration CTE-POWER9 cluster. The Micron SSDs are installed in front of the blades, near to the ventilation and are not visible in the picture. The 4 GPU Volta are installed under the copper heatsinks (orange colour in the picture). The NVMe controller are installed in the top left corner (2 black devices). (Color figure online)

The expected I/O bandwidths for read and write operations are given in Table 1. The bandwidth for the GPFS results from the one 10 Gbps (1.25 GB/s) ethernet on the nodes. The bandwidths for the NVMe and SSD devices are taken from [2,3] respectively.

Table 1. Expected I/O performance for the three different storage layer GPFS, SSD (local) and NVMe (local).

Storage type	write (seq.)	read (seq.)	write (rand. 4K)	read (rand. 4K)
GPFS	1.25 GB/s		-	
SSD	520 MB/s	540 MB/s	24,000 IOPS	93,000 IOPS
NVMe	3 GB/s	6.4 GB/s	170,000 IOPS	1,080,000 IOPS

The scaling per additional node for the local devices is expected to behave linearly. This does not apply for the GPFS. In contrast to the on-node devices, adding a compute node does not add another GPFS storage device. The transfer rate per node indeed is expected to be linear, but, the achievable total bandwidth is limited by the maximum performance of the GPFS storage servers or the cluster-to-GPFS network connection. Also we have to take into account other bottlenecks and the fact that the I/O performance is shared with other users using the GPFS.

3.2 Experimental Methodology

We performed three different kinds of measurements.

EXP.TS, we kept the problem size constant and varied the transfer size.

EXP.FS, we kept the number of processors constant and varied the file size

EXP.WS, we kept the file size constant and varied the number of processors.

3.3 Benchmarking

In order to measure the I/O performance, we applied the well known and tested IOR benchmark [5]. IOR comes with a variety of runtime options in order to align to the requirements of the measurement. The particular options may be read in the IOR user manual available inside the git repository [5]. Some tests were done with IOzone leading to similar results as IOR.

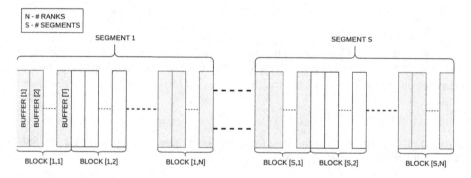

Fig. 2. IOR file structure if -F option omitted. Block[i, j] denotes the ith block written by rank j, S corresponds to the IOR parameter `segmentCount` or -s. The block size (`blockSize` or -b) is equal to the accumulated buffer sizes that account to one block. The buffer size may be set by `transferSize` or -t. The block size has to be a multiple of the transfer size.

IOR provides control about the file access patterns by setting the following parameters:

– `blockSize` -b: Size of a contiguous data segment in the test files

- `transferSize` -t: Size of contiguous memory transfered in one I/O call
- `segmentCount` -s: Number of file segments
- `filePerProc` -F: Every process creates its own file
- `randomOffset` -z: Apply a random access pattern for I/O calls

Additional parameters that we applied are:

- `useO_DIRECT` -B: Provide O_DIRECT to open calls
- `fsync` -e: Call `fsync()` after I/O operation
- `intraTestBarriers` -g: Synchronize open and close calls
- `repetitions` -i: Number of test repetitions
- `testFile` -o: Set output/input file name

If we omit the option -F, IOR will create one single file for all processes. Figure 2 shows the file structure of such a single file. Setting -F causes that the several blocks are located just next to each other in the files of each process. Since we write to devices that are local to the nodes and thus not accessible by processes that are on a different node, we will always write into single files per process (i.e. -F set). Thus, varying the block size should not affect our measurements, however, the setting is important for simulating a random access pattern for read and write operations. IOR computes the file offsets for the I/O calls using the parameters for the `transferSize` and `blockSize` (and the rank for the case of a single shared file). The offsets are kept inside an array local to the ranks. Passing the parameter -z triggers a randomization of the offsets by a random mixing of the offset-array entries. The `transferSize` might influence the performance, since it corresponds to the size of the contiguous memory buffers allocated by IOR. These buffers are directly passed to the I/O interface calls.

In order to measure the actual I/O speed of each device, we need to by-pass the library and kernel buffers. This can be accomplished by setting the -B option. This option causes the O_DIRECT flag to be set in the `open()` calls. This ensures that the read and write operations address the device directly. To ensure that the data has been stored in stable storage and not inside a device buffer we append a call to `fsync` by providing the -e flag.

4 Evaluation

In this section we present the results of the experiments we described in Sect. 3. These are the variation of the transfer size (EXP.TS), the variation of the file size while keeping the number of processes constant (EXP.FS) and the variation of the number of processes while keeping the file size constant (EXP.WS).

In addition to that, we will present performance measurements that are typically performed by vendors in order to give an estimation of the overall performance of the storage devices. These measurements incorporate the response time (latency) for 512B and 4 KB packages, the performance of sequential read and write operations for 128 KB blocks and random access read and write operations for 4 KB blocks depending on the query depth (processes per file).

Table 2 shows the latencies measured for the three devices. We can see that the average times for the GPFS are slightly higher than those for the node storage devices. The latencies for the SSD and NVMe devices are very low, in the order of 1 μs. But also the latency of the GPFS is not significantly higher.

Table 2. Response time (latency) for the request of 512B and 4KB packages measured for GPFS, SSD and NVMe (measured with ioping).

Size	Minimum	Average	Maximum	Deviation
GPFS				
512 B	3.26 μs	3.89 μs	7.11 μs	354 ns
4 KB	3.24 μs	4.39 μs	13.5 μs	579 ns
SSD				
512 B	865 ns	1.14 μs	4.28 μs	202 ns
4 KB	932 ns	1.18 μs	3.92 μs	198 ns
NVMe				
512 B	793 ns	1.02 μs	4.13 μs	228 ns
4 KB	869 ns	1.17 μs	4.69 μs	223 ns

The sequential write and read performance at a transfer size of 128 KB was measured using 64 processes per node and 120 GB file size. We observed for the SSD's, 449 ± 2 MB/s write and 448 ± 1 MB/s read performance and for the NVMe's 2634 ± 60 MB/s write and 5887 ± 21 MB/s read performance. However, as we will see in the next paragraph, the performance is not the same for all the SSD's on the cluster. We noticed that the performance of the devices, SSD's and NVMe's, differ for different nodes.

The peak performance measured for a transfer size of 16 MB for the SSD's was 504 MB/s for write and 515 MB/s for read operations. For the NVMe we measured 3035 MB/s for write and 5231 MB/s for read operations. The individual performance for the devices was not the same on all the nodes. Figure 3 shows the individual speeds measured on the particular nodes. Since we depended on the job scheduler to assign the executing nodes, we do not have measurements for all nodes and each of the devices (blank regions in the plots).

The fluctuations of the write performance for the SSD's was about 11% of the average. The fluctuations for the NVMe's are with 4% a bit lower. Table 3 summarizes the results for the measured speeds on different nodes.

Figure 4 shows the result of the measurements we performed for random access operations using a transfer size of 4 KB.

4.1   Transfer Size Impact

Figure 5 shows the results of the EXP.TS measurements, where we kept the file size constant and varied the transfer size. The behavior of I/O depending

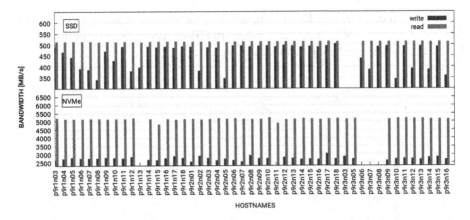

Fig. 3. Performance measurements performed on particular nodes for the SSD and NVMe devices.

Table 3. Average values of read and write performances for SSD and NVMe devices on the cluster.

Operation	SSD		NVMe	
	Bandwidth	sdev	Bandwidth	sdev
write	456 MB/s	53 MB/s	2740 MB/s	115 MB/s
read	514 MB/s	1 MB/s	5126 MB/s	73 MB/s

(a) Write   **(b)** Read

Fig. 4. Random access for read and write operations (4 KB packages). Query depth corresponds to the number of processors participating in the operation.

on the transfer size is important in order to estimate I/O performance in scientific applications in HPC. According to the study [4] of the storage clusters Spider and Spider II at the Oak Ridge Leadership Facility (OLCF), about 50% of the requested transfer sizes are below 16 KB and 50% between 512 KB and 1 MB in size. In Fig. 5 we can see that for 1 MB transfer size, both local storage layers already have reached a region of maximal performance. Both local storage devices experience a decrease in performance for transfer sizes below 32 KB. However, the effective performance for both relevant transfer sizes is higher than the performance of the GPFS. The bandwidth for transfer sizes of 1 MB for the GPFS is below half of that for the peak at 16 MB transfer size. The performance for both relevant regimes is summarized in Table 4.

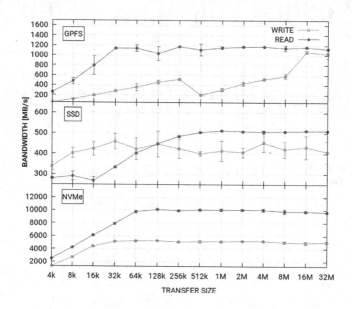

Fig. 5. Results of the EXP.TS measurements for the three tested devices. The plot for the NVMe device were performed using the two devices on the node. All measurements were performed on one node using 64 processes.

Table 4. Performance comparison for most relevant transfer sizes between the three storage layers.

Transfer size	GPFS		SSD		NVMe	
	write [MB/s]	read [MB/s]	write [MB/s]	read [MB/s]	write [MB/s]	read [MB/s]
4 KB	60.51	261.30	338.24	279.12	1323.62	2528.76
8 KB	118.16	480.68	402.67	290.24	2720.43	4220.36
16 KB	196.94	794.66	423.96	267.79	4416.42	6092.37
1 MB	308.02	1153.72	413.50	511.84	5178.11	10068.27

It is remarkable that the NVMe's show quite a stable performance for transfer sizes above 64 KB. Also, the NVMe performance even for very small transfer sizes is above the peak performance for the GPFS at 16 MB transfer size.

We can see in this figure that the measured 1 node performance of the GPFS does fit quite well to the expected one for transfer sizes above 16 MB. The nodes are equipped with one 10 Gbps ethernet card, thus we a bundled maximum of 1.25 GB/s. The measured maximum speed was slightly below at 1 GB/s for both I/O modes, read and write.

Also the SSD performance is slightly below our expectations. The read and write performance at 128 KB transfer size is expected to be 540 and 520 MB/s respectively. We can see in the figure that we have about 450 MB/s for both modes. However, we have seen earlier, that the performance differs for the SSD's depending on which node we are executing, thus, we might encounter the expected performance on another nodes SSD. The important observation in this experiment is how the devices react on changing the transfer size.

Although as well slightly below our expectations, the NVMe's still outperform both, SSD and GPFS. We reach a read and write speed of 10 and 5 GB/s respectively, which is for operating with two NVMe's on the nodes. This is a remarkable I/O performance for a stable storage device.

4.2   Weak Scaling

Figure 6 shows the results for the EXP.WS measurements. We have performed this experiment with 160 processes and 64 processes per node. As we can see in the figure, the results are very similar. This indicates that the maximum I/O performance is below a query depth of 64 processes per node for all tested devices. We expect a noticeable decrease in performance for 32 and less processes per node (see Fig. 4).

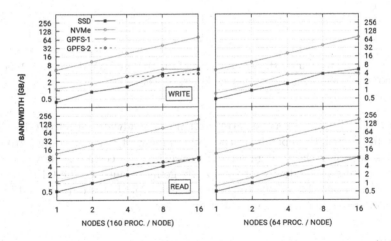

Fig. 6. Results of the EXP.WS measurements for the three tested devices. The 1st row shows the write operation for 160 and 64 processors per node respectively. The second row the read operations. The black dotted lines in the left plots correspond to a second measurement. It indicates the relatively large fluctuation for the maximum performance on the GPFS.

According to Fig. 4 we expected to see an increased performance for 160 towards 64 processes for read operations of the NVMe device. This has not been observed. We have a saturation below 64 processes per node also for this device.

However, the measurements use different transfer sizes. The measurement in Fig. 4 was performed with 4 KB packages, the weak scaling on the other hand was performed with 32 MB packages. The larger transfer size might cause the earlier saturation. Also, Fig. 4 uses random access and the weak scaling was performed with sequential access patterns.

The scaling of the NVMe devices is almost perfectly linear. The scaling for the SSD's is not as good as for the NVMe. This is most likely connected to the varying performance for the SSD's on different nodes. Figure 7 shows the linear regression for the on node devices. Here it is apparent that the linearity of the NVMe devices is indeed remarkable. We can expect a continuation of this linearity and thus great performance for large scale. This also applies for the SSD's, however, at large scale there might be higher performance fluctuations.

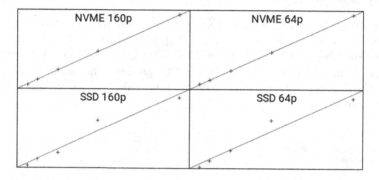

Fig. 7. Linear regression for the weak scaling of the SSD and NVMe devices. 160p and 64p denotes 160 and 64 processes per node respectively.

For the GPFS, we observe a saturation of the bandwidth at 3 to 5 GB/s. The maximum bandwidth depends on the total amount of requests coming from all the users accessing the storage servers. However, at a certain scale the performance of local storage devices is eventually going to outpace the GPFS performance of any large cluster due to the linear behavior that is only limited by the amount of available nodes (i.e. local storage devices).

4.3   File Size Impact

In this section we analyse the behavior of the local storage layers upon heavy usage. In order to do this, we submitted jobs that performed measurements for a long time using a single storage device. The measurements aimed to record the I/O performance for writing and reading files of varying sizes, until a maximum file size that is close to the maximal capacity of the device. For the SSD device we write up to 1200 GB (1600 GB available) and for the NVMe 2800 GB (3200 GB available). For each file size we repeated the read and write of the file 5 times. Figure 8 shows the results of this measurements.

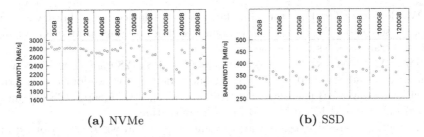

(a) NVMe   (b) SSD

Fig. 8. Results for the EXP.FS write measurements. The measurements were performed 5 times for each file size.

We can see that for the NVME's, for file sizes up to 400 GB, the bandwidth is very stable. This is about 8 GB/process, which is more than the common amount of I/O that a single process performs in an usual I/O heavy application. Above 800 GB the aggregate bandwidth for the whole file starts to fluctuate significantly. But even for the largest file size this accounts for a maximum deviation of less than 10 min for writing the file. The bandwidth for the read operations were again remarkably stable for all file sizes. We recorded an average of 5870 MB/s with the corresponding standard deviation of only 15 MB/s. The results for read performance were so stable that we decided to not add the figures for brevity (i.e., no unusual pattern).

For the SSD's we observe a similar behavior. The dispersion of the bandwidth starts a bit earlier, at 400 GB file size. Interesting is that the fluctuations of the bandwidth are rather towards higher bandwidths. Hence it seems to be rather beneficial to write large files. Again, the read performance is quite stable at the average value of 513 MB/s and the corresponding standard deviation of 1 MB/s.

5   Conclusion

In this article we analyzed the I/O behavior of three different storage layers accessible within the CTE-POWER9 cluster located at the BSC. Each node has access to the GPFS, as well as local NVMe and SSDs. We focus in this article mostly on the performance of the node-local storage layers.

We performed a scaling experiment see Sect. 4.2) that showed an excellent linear scaling for the NVMe's with a maximum bandwidth of 82,607 GB/s for write operations and 185,443 GB/s for read operations on 16 nodes and 64 processes per node. This corresponds to a bandwidth scaling per node of 5,153 MB/s for write and 11,586 MB/s for read operations. This provides potentially an extremely high gain of I/O performance for large scale applications that run on several hundreds of nodes. The execution time of I/O heavy applications may be decreased significantly by using this kind of local storage. The same is valid for the local SSD's. However, the bandwidth of these is one order of magnitude below the NVMe devices (read and write gain per node was 513 and 378 MB/s).

We demonstrated that the node-local storage devices have both very low latency (see Table 2) and the performance is superior than that of GPFS for common transfer sizes (see Table 4).

The SAMSUNG NVMe's deliver 1,149,696 IOPS (128 query depth) for random access read and 290,048 IOPS (64 query depth) for random access write operations using 4 KB packages. The Micron SSD's show 76,800 IOPS (32 query depth) for read and 103,168 IOPS for write operations.

The average speed measured for sequential read and write operations using 128 KB packages was 5,887 MB/s and 2,634 MB/s for the NVMe's and 448 MB/s and 447 MB/s for the SSD's respectively.

We have observed significant performance differences for SSD's located on different nodes (see Fig. 3). This could lead to a low effective performance for collective I/O operations limited by the slowest SSD device. The fluctuations range from under 350 MB/s to about 500 MB/s. We have observed this also for the NVMe's, however, the fluctuations were smaller regarding the average bandwidth of the respective devices.

Acknowledgements. This project has received funding from the European Union's Horizon 2020 research and innovation programme under the Marie Sklodowska-Curie grant agreement No 708566 (DURO). Part of the research presented here has received funding from the European Union's Seventh Framework Programme (FP7/2007-2013) and the Horizon 2020 (H2020) funding framework under grant agreement no. H2020-FETHPC-754304 (DEEP-EST). The present publication reflects only the authors' views. The European Commission is not liable for any use that might be made of the information contained therein.

References

1. IBM Elastic Storage Server Overview and Datasheet. https://www.ibm.com/us-en/marketplace/ibm-elastic-storage-server. Accessed 06 June 2018
2. Micron 5100 series SATA NAND flash SSD. https://4donline.ihs.com/images/VipMasterIC/IC/MICT/MICT-S-A0003387673/MICT-S-A0003387673-1.pdf. Accessed 28 May 2018
3. SAMSUNG Samsung PM1725a NVMe SSD. http://www.samsung.com/semiconductor/insights/tech-leadership/brochure-samsung-pm1725a-nvme-ssd/. Accessed 28 May 2018
4. Gunasekaran, R., Oral, S., Hill, J., Miller, R., Wang, F., Leverman, D.: Comparative I/O workload characterization of two leadership class storage clusters. In: Proceedings of the 10th Parallel Data Storage Workshop, PDSW 2015, pp. 31–36. ACM, New York (2015). https://doi.org/10.1145/2834976.2834985
5. Lawrence Livermore National Laboratory (LLNL), Loewe, W., McLarty, T., Morrone, C.: IOR - parallel filesystem I/O benchmark (2018). https://github.com/hpc/ior
6. Mittal, S., Vetter, J.S.: A survey of software techniques for using non-volatile memories for storage and main memory systems. IEEE Trans. Parallel Distrib. Syst. **27**(5), 1537–1550 (2016)
7. Vetter, J.S., Mittal, S.: Opportunities for nonvolatile memory systems in extreme-scale high-performance computing. Comput. Sci. Eng. **17**(2), 73–82 (2015)

Self-optimization Strategy
for IO Accelerator Parameterization

Lionel Vincent, Mamady Nabe, and Gaël Goret[✉]

ATOS-Bull, BDS R&D-Software Data Management, 38130 Échirolles, France
{lionel.vincent.external,mamady.nabe,gael.goret}@atos.net

Abstract. Exascale reaching imposes a high automation level on HPC supercomputers. In this paper, a self-optimization strategy is proposed to improve application IO performance using statistical and machine learning based methods.

The proposed method takes advantage of collected IO data through an off-line analysis to infers the most relevant parameterization of an IO accelerator that should be used for the next launch of a similar job. This is thus a continuous improvement process that will converge toward an optimal parameterization along iterations.

The inference process uses a numerical optimization method to propose the parameterization that minimizes the execution time of the considered application. A regression method is used to model the objective function to be optimized from a sparse set of collected data from the past runs.

Experiments on different artificial parametric spaces show that the convergence speed of the proposed method requires less than 20 runs to converge toward a parameterization of the IO accelerator.

Keywords: HPC · Supercomputing · IO · Optimization
Regression · Inference · Machine learning · Auto-tuning
Parameterization · Data management

1 Introduction

To reach exascale [1], future HPC supercomputers will require more and more automation [2] to overcome growing complexity in their administration and usage. All levels of supercomputers will be affected by automation: power consumption, network, data management, etc.

Nowadays, such automation solutions are already in use to predict breakdown events [3]. However, the next generation solutions will be able to not just predict events but also automatically reconfigure the supercomputer to maintain the operating performance in an optimal state. Such reconfigurations, that will affect all levels of the supercomputer, induce an on-line monitoring of metrics and a dynamic adjustment of its operating state.

This work aims to address this point on the data management side. Software products are developed to work together and make a continuously improving

© Springer Nature Switzerland AG 2018
R. Yokota et al. (Eds.): ISC 2018 Workshops, LNCS 11203, pp. 157–170, 2018.
https://doi.org/10.1007/978-3-030-02465-9_11

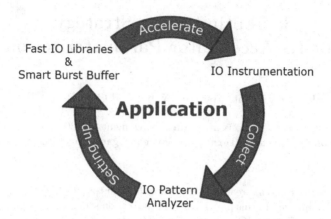

Fig. 1. Continuous improvement of IO efficiency in HPC applications through three classes of products (Instrumentation, Analyzer, Accelerators).

loop as described in Fig. 1. Three classes of products form this loop to collect, analyze and accelerate the applications. First, the Bull IO Instrumentation [4] monitors the IO produced by the runs of jobs and collects them in a database. Then, the Bull IO Pattern Analyzer parametrizes our IO accelerator products (Bull Fast IO Libraries [4] and Bull Smart Burst Buffer) from the knowledge of the collected data.

However, the accelerators can have multiple parameters (e.g. three parameters for the Fast IO Libraries) that can take a wide range of values. The challenge is to determine the best parameterization that enables to reach the best application performance, i.e. that minimizes the execution time of the application.

Several approaches can be envisioned to tackle the problematic of parameterization (Fig. 2). The static solution fixes permanently the parameters of the accelerator, in such a way that all the jobs are launched with the same parameterization. In this case, the parameterization is globally chosen to provide a mean performance for a wide range of jobs, but is rarely optimal. On the other hand, a dynamic approach will monitor and adapt on-line the parameterization to provide the optimal performance at any moment of the execution of the jobs. However, the dynamic approach requires a lot of computational resources, to perform all this monitoring and adaptation on-line, that could lead to mitigate the potential performance gain.

An adaptive solution, trade-off between the static and dynamic approaches (Fig. 2) is developed. It determines before the launch of the job the best static parameterization. To do that, the job submission is intercepted and the Bull IO Pattern Analyzer analyzes it and all the past runs of this job. From this knowledge of the past, the Bull IO Pattern Analyzer proposes the best parameterization that should be used to improve the execution time of the submitted job, and the job is launched. The data collected during this new run will feed the knowledge of the job behavior to make the loop converge iteratively toward an optimal parameterization of the IO accelerator products for this job.

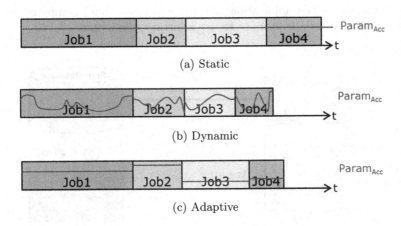

Fig. 2. Different parametrization approaches

In this paper the principle of the self-optimization method designed to converge toward the best parameterization of the accelerators products will first be described in Sect. 2. Then, in Sect. 3, a focus on the inference step will be developed in two parts: the regression of an objective function and an optimum search on this function. The proposed convergence method will be validated in Sect. 4, and the convergence speed will be demonstrated. Finally, the Sect. 5 will conclude.

2   Self-optimization Strategy

A method is proposed to self-optimize the IO accelerator parameters that should be used to launch an application to improve its performance. In the HPC context, the optimal parameterization minimizes the execution time of the application. The performance criterion that the method tries to optimize is then the execution time of an application.

A Job is represented here by a set of metadata associated to the way an application is launched on a HPC cluster. The metadata that define a Job are, a discriminator $\mathcal{D}$ of the launched application (binary name, slurm info, accessed files, first stack frames,...), the hardware topology $\mathcal{T}$ that is used (computation and storage), and, in our case, the IO accelerator parameters, or more generally the execution context parameters $\mathcal{P}$.

As described in Fig. 3 at the step 1, the proposed method will intercept the metadata during the submission of a job. The user can choose to fix some metadata and can let the other ones free to be optimized. Typically, the user wants to launch a specific application (metadata $\mathcal{D}$ fixed) with a specific topology (metadata $\mathcal{T}$ fixed), but he has no idea of what could be the more relevant parameters of an IO accelerator that could be used (metadata $\mathcal{P}$ free). The self-optimization method aims to propose the user a parameterization that improves the performance of the application (i.e. the execution time) compared to the launch without the accelerators or to use arbitrary parameters.

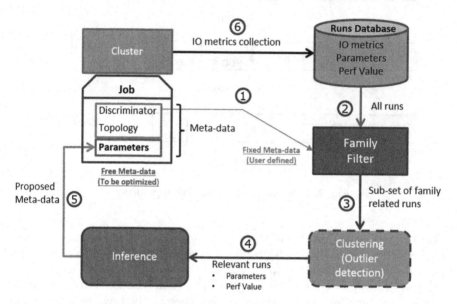

Fig. 3. The self-optimize loop proposed to converge globally to optimal values for the accelerator parameters (in red). (Color figure online)

Since it is not possible to model the performance/accelerator parameters relationship of a job *a priori* (i.e. without launching several runs of a job), the proposed method is based on the observation, *a posteriori*, of the performance of a set of runs of the same job family (i.e. jobs with same fixed metadata than the ones submitted), see step 2 in Fig. 3. If this set of runs used different accelerator parameterizations, then it describes sparsely the space of the parameters of this job family.

Nevertheless, some outliers (e.g. runs that aborted during their executions) can distort the performance value/parameters relationship, because the performance of these runs is not representative of the real behavior of the job. While being optional, the step 3 in Fig. 3 aims to detect potential outliers using clustering methods. This discrimination of non-relevant runs is based on the analysis of the mismatch of the IO timing behavior of the runs. If this step is not used steps 3 and 4 in Fig. 3 are identical, and provide a set of relevant runs for the inference step.

The inference step aims to propose a parameterization at the step 5 of the Fig. 3. This is the core of the proposed method, and the technical choices of this step will be detailed in Sect. 3. The principle is to take advantage of the past runs of jobs from the same family to predict the best parameterization that should be used to launch the current job. The more runs with different parameterizations are collected, the more the variation of the performance in the parameters space is representative of the whole continuous space for the considered job family. That is why the proposed method is based on a loop, to explore efficiently (i.e. with the minimal number of needed runs) this space of parameters and find the optimal accelerator parameterization.

The research of the optimal solution of the parameterization is, then, an iterative process [5], where each iteration will feed the method to enrich the knowledge of the characteristics of the family (i.e. the performance/accelerator parameters relationship). Indeed, in step 6 of Fig. 3, the job is finally launched with the inferred parameterization. If few runs from the same job family were available in the database, the knowledge of the relationship performance/accelerator parameters would probably be too sparse to infer the best parameterization (i.e. the global optimal). However, the inferred solution will improve the performance of the run, and will improve the space of parameter coverage with a new entry.

At each iteration, the proposed parameterization is used to launch the submitted job. This new run of the job is in turn instrumented and the data collected feed the database, improving the knowledge of the performance value of this job according to parameter variations. This loop permits to explore efficiently the space of parameters, performing a continuous improvement process and converging towards the global optimum.

In the following section, the inference part of the proposed method will be described.

3   Inference of the Accelerator Parameters

Through IO Instrumentation, various data are collected which describe the runs of the applications. Those data can then be used by the analytics system, IO Pattern Analyzer (IOPA), in the ultimate goal to improve the IO performance. The aim of the inference is to propose a parameterization for the accelerator by analyzing the collected data. Iteration after iteration, the proposed solution will converge toward an optimal parameterization.

At the launch of a new job, the optimal values for the accelerator parameters should be to suggested to minimize the execution time of the given job. To perform this optimization (i.e. in our case a minimization of the execution time) the relationship accelerator parameters/performance value need to be modeled. This model can then be used as an objective function that will be optimized using a numerical optimization algorithm.

Because no material is available to model theoretically the objective function, the chosen approach is to perform a mathematical regression using the past runs as a sparse description of the objective function.

3.1   Regression of the Objective Function

The mathematical regression methods aim to model the relationship between explained variables (a.k.a dependent variables) and explanatory ones (a.k.a independent variables). In our case, the explained variable is the execution time of the job, and the explanatory ones are the accelerator parameters. By nature, the explanatory variables are the ones used to infer an optimal value.

Regression techniques can be classified according to:

- the type of relation (linear or non-linear),
- the number of independent variables (simple or multiple),
- the number of dependent variables (univariate or multivariate).

In our case, the goal is to determine a set of accelerator parameters with respect to a single performance measure, the execution time. Thus, the problematic includes a multiple univariate regression. Because *a priori* the type of relation that links the accelerator parameters to the execution time is not known, different regression techniques have been considered to compare their efficiency.

Introduction of the Different Methods. The following regression techniques were experimented:

- A simple linear regression which uses the L2-norm for regularization.
  - Bayesian Ridge Regression (BRR) [6] has the advantage to provide a simple and explainable model, however in our use-cases, it does not describe enough the complexity of the true relationship between the different variables.
- Two advanced methods which use the kernel trick, a technique used to transform non-linear problems in one space to a linear problem in another space called the feature space.
  - Support Vector Machine for Regression (SVR) [7] is the regression version of the support vector machine for classification. It makes it possible to obtain a sparse model based solely on support vectors which help define the hyperplane to fit the data. Since the support vectors are just a subset of the available data, this model allows for a fast prediction.
  - Gaussian Process Regression (GPR) [8] is the kernelized version of the Bayesian ridge regression. It has the advantage to use a probabilistic approach which makes it more robust to missing data and it is fast to train.

The kernel based methods are based on a function (kernel) that is a similarity measure between two points in the feature space. In this study, the same kernel function was used for all the non-linear regression method used: the Radial Basis Function (RBF) kernel. This function k describes the relationship between two feature vectors x and y by:

$$k(x,y) = \exp(-\gamma \left\| (x-y) \right\|^2)$$

where γ is a free parameter. Unlike the polynomial kernel, which requires determining the degree required for the model function, the RBF kernel operates without *a priori*.

The ultimate goal of the regression is to obtain at the end a function which gives an approximate value of the performance measure for any accelerator parameter set.

Comparison of the Different Methods. To evaluate the quality of a regression model, some statistics were computed to inform how good the model is. In this part, two of them will be discussed: the root mean square error (RMSE) and the coefficient of determination (R^2).

- The RMSE is the square root of the average of squared errors in a set of predictions. It is the sample standard deviation of the residuals, defined as follows:

$$RMSE = \sqrt{\frac{1}{n}\sum_{i=1}^{n}(y_i - p_i)^2},$$

with y_i and p_i the values of the explained variable, respectively, for the sample y of n input data and the sample p of n predicted data from the regressed function.
- The coefficient of determination indicates the percentage of change in the dependent variable that is explained by the changes in the independent variables. It gives an idea about how well the model accounts for the variance in the response variable that is predictable from the explanatory variables. It is defined as follows:

$$R^2 = 1 - \frac{\sum_{i=1}^{n}(y_i - p_i)^2}{\sum_{i=1}^{n}(y_i - y_{mean})^2},$$

with the same notation as used in the previous formula, and y_{mean} the mean of the y input sample.

An experiment was conducted on real data collected with our IO Instrumentation product. The data was obtained running 168 runs of an IO simulation application with different values of accelerator parameters.

To perform the regression and assess its quality, it is important to divide the set of data into two sets, one for training to obtain the model and another to test the obtained model. By the way, the quality metrics can be computed from the two sets of data. Tables 1 and 2 present respectively the $RMSE$ and R^2 metrics for the different regression method considered.

Table 1. Results on training set

Train	RMSE	R^2
BRR	2.2936	0.002289
SVR	0.0914	0.9984
GPR	0.1768	0.9940

Table 2. Results on test set

Test	RMSE	R^2
BRR	2.4058	0.00232
SVR	1.226	0.7406
GPR	0.5848	0.9410

From the results presented in the Tables 1 and 2, it is obvious that the simple linear regression model does not model well the relationship between the dependent and independent variables. However, it is not that easy to distinguish between the other two methods.

To choose among these methods, another important criterion is the time required to perform the training (i.e. the regression of the function) and prediction (i.e. evaluation of the explained variables for given explanatory variables). The Table 3 presents the time, in seconds, required to perform training and prediction, for the two non-linear regression methods, SVR and GPR, considered previously.

Table 3. Results for training and predicting time

Method	Train	Prediction
SVR	0.169 s	0.001 s
GPR	0.068 s	0.001 s

Even though they take approximately the same time for prediction, GPR outperforms SVR in training time. It is thus natural to choose GPR as a good solution for the regression step of the optimization loop.

Once the objective function has been evaluated using a regression method, the optimum of this function can be searched. In the next section, the optimization process in the search of the optimal solution will be discussed.

3.2 Search for the Optimal Parameterization

Optimization algorithms can then be applied to the objective function, built thanks to regression, to find its optimum. It corresponds to the optimal parameters the user should use to launch its job.

Note that what it is called "the optimal parameters" here is relative to the current knowledge of the parametric space; i.e. if few runs are available in the database, the proposed optimal solution is probably not the "real theoretical" one that could be found with the knowledge of the exhaustive sampling of the parametric space. However, our proposed self-optimization loop aims to reach this "real theoretical" solution, converging toward it iteration after iteration.

Optimization algorithms use heuristics to resolve optimization problems in a reasonable time. Optimization algorithms can be classified into two categories:

- The methods based on the gradient: they use the derivatives of the objective function to quickly find the extrema.
- The gradient-free methods: These are methods that work without any information related to the differentiability of the objective function.

For the search for parameters, whose space often has multiple local optima, gradient-free methods offer more possibilities to converge towards the global optimum, contrary to the gradient methods that are often trapped by local optima.

Various methods which do not use the gradient computation were experimented. Our work was focused on three algorithms: the Nelder-Mead algorithm, the Particle Swarm Optimization algorithm and the Covariance Matrix Adaptive - Evolution Strategy algorithm.

The Nelder-Mead Algorithm (NM) [9]. Nelder-Mead algorithm is an optimization algorithm for continuous functions in a multidimensional space. Also called the downhill simplex method, it is built upon the notion of simplex which is a polytop of $N+1$ vertices in an N dimensional space. It is an iterative process where at each step, the simplex undergoes simple mathematical transformations: it deforms, moves and decreases progressively until its vertices are closer to a point where the function is locally minimal.

Particle Swarm Optimization Algorithm (PSO) [10]. Unlike the Nelder-Mead algorithm, the Particle Swarm Optimization adopts a stochastic approach, using multi-agent modeling. This method spreads multiple agents in the parametric space, which share the evaluated values of the objective function at different points, contributing to the global knowledge of the particle swarm. This sharing of information can be done either locally, that limits the exchange to the particles of the close neighborhood, or globally, which ensures a privileged sharing between the particle having the best evaluation of the objective function and the others ones.

Covariance Matrix Adaptive - Evolution Strategy (CMA-ES) [11]. This method searches the optimum in many directions by randomly generating points within the search space, rather than searching from one direction. It uses three main principles coming from biological evolution ideas: mutation, recombination, selection, to converge toward the optimum of the function.

All these methods have the advantage of being gradient-free, making them famous for various real world problems. They each have advantages and disadvantages that will be discussed next.

PSO and CMA-ES are stochastic and handle the issue of local optimum fairly well. They have the advantage to not base the search on only one point at each iteration, rather on many points. That makes them computationally demanding, particularly for ill-conditioned problems. CMA-ES in contrast with PSO has a mathematical proof of convergence and is currently the state-of-the-art of numerical optimization algorithms.

Nelder-Mead evaluates only on some points, depending on the dimension of the problem. For high dimensions, it could be impractical since there will be too many evaluations required for each iteration. But, it has the benefit of performing deterministic transformations, one at each iteration.

Taking into account the advantages of each method, CMA-ES was chosen as the optimization algorithm. In the next section, the results for the experiments using this algorithm and the regression method chosen in Sect. 3.1 will be presented.

4   Experiments and Results

The self-optimization method is an iterative process which gradually improves the execution time performance of a job each time a new parameterization is suggested. The convergence speed, i.e. the number of needed runs to reach the optimal parameterization, is then a key point that must be investigated to conclude on the usability of the proposed method.

To validate this method, an experiment is set up where the regression process is performed on artificial parametric spaces built from theoretical functions f. From the theoretical function, n parameter sets $P_n^{init} = \{p_1, p_2, \ldots, p_n\}$ (representing the n initial runs in database needed to start the loop) are sampled randomly in order to perform the regression to build the objective function $\hat{f}_n$. Then, the objective function is used to find the optimal parameters p_{n+1}, i.e. the parameters that correspond to the minimum of the objective function. These new parameters and their corresponding performance value $f(p_{n+1})$ will be used to run the next inference iteration with $n + 1$ parameter sets $P_{n+1} = \{p_1, p_2, \ldots, p_{n+1}\}$.

One of the goals of the experiment is to identify a good number n of initial parameter sets to start the inference process. Moreover to assess how fast the self-optimization method converges, it is also important to quantify, for each initial parameter set P_n^{init}, how many iterations i the optimization process takes. This is a measure of the speed of convergence.

To evaluate the influence of the value n on the convergence speed, the protocol is the following: for N different initial parameter sets P_n^{init}, the looped inference process (regression and optimization) is run. The process ends on a termination criterion based on a tolerance on the function evaluation $\hat{f}_n$ between two consecutive iterations:

$$|\hat{f}_n(p_{i+1}) - \hat{f}_n(p_i)| < TOL$$

where TOL is the convergence criterion, or on a maximal number of iteration criterion (e.g. $i < 50$) to avoid having an optimization which runs for a long time. Once the termination criterion is reached, i_{end} the number of iteration needed is stored, and so the total number of runs $R_n^{tot} = n + i_{end}$ needed to reach the optimal parameterization can be computed.

For each considered value of n the convergence experiment is performed 1000 times, such that some statistic metrics to evaluate the convergence speed (mean and standard deviation values of the 1000 R_n^{tot}) can be computed. The set of initial parameters P_n^{init} is randomly chosen for each of the 1000 experiments.

Three theoretical functions (Sphere, Rosenbrock and Styblinski-Tang functions, Fig. 4) have been used in this study aiming to give an idea about the different situations that the self-optimization method may have to face when coping with different kinds of problems, while searching for an optimum [12]. The three functions represent different hardness levels of optimization with in the increasing order:

- the Sphere function which presents a single localized minimum (Fig. 4a),
- the Rosenbrock function that has a single minimum but with a large *straight valley* of close values (Fig. 4b),
- the Styblinski-Tang function that has multiple local minima with one of them being the global minimum (Fig. 4c).

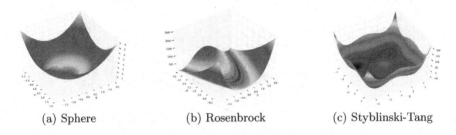

(a) Sphere   (b) Rosenbrock   (c) Styblinski-Tang

Fig. 4. Artificial parametric spaces built on theoretical functions.

The Fig. 5 illustrates the convergence speed results for the three functions presented previously. The figures present the total number of runs R_n^{tot} needed to reach the optimal parameterization according to the number of initial runs n. The black line represents the mean value of R_n^{tot} obtained for the 1000 experiments, and the red and green lines represent the standard deviation.

All the results of the Fig. 5 are obtained considering the objective function f in a three dimensional parametric space to consider an accelerator with three parameters. However, the values are chosen in specific interval in a such way that the considered functions present interesting topologies, leading to choose $p \in \mathbb{R}^3_{[-5,5]}$.

To evaluate fairly the convergence speed, the tolerance TOL must be chosen relatively to a reference performance value. In a real case, a good reference could be the execution time of a non-accelerated run, considering this run presents the worst performance value compared to using the accelerator. As a consequence, for our experiment, the convergence criterion can then be defined in terms of the tolerance TOL as a percentage of the maximal value of the objective function, since the objective function f is bounded in the defined parametric space. This is a hyper-parameter to be fixed a priori and for the experiments, in this experiment it is chosen at $TOL = 10\% \times \max f(p)$. This way, the convergence criterion is set the same for any test functions in the parametric space of interest.

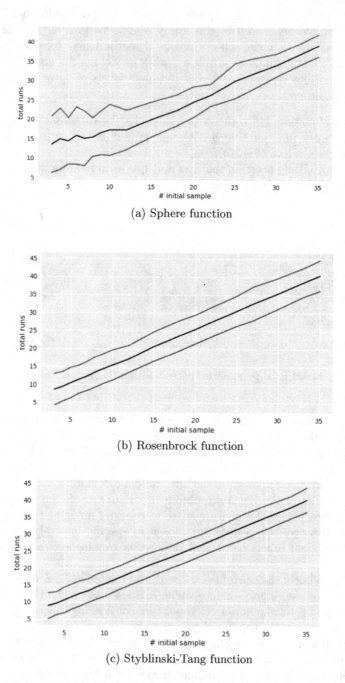

(a) Sphere function

(b) Rosenbrock function

(c) Styblinski-Tang function

Fig. 5. Influence of the number of initial runs (n) on the convergence speed in terms of the total number of runs R_n^{tot} (Color figure online)

For the real problem, the user could define the criterion in such a way that it improves of 10% the application's execution time between two consecutive iterations when using the accelerator. For a non-accelerated application which takes one hour to run completely, fixing the tolerance to 10% will lead to gain a minimum of 6 min between two consecutive iterations. Of course, the user can set the tolerance according to his own constraints, with the trade-off convergence speed/optimum accuracy.

All the results of the Fig. 5 have the same trend: an increasing number of the total number of runs R_n^{tot} with the number of initial runs n used in the inference process. The method converges fast (i.e. it takes less number of iterations) as the number of initial runs is important. Having then an important number of initial runs does not necessarily increase the profitability of the method.

Furthermore, analyzing more carefully the number of additional runs needed to reach the convergence criterion, the number of initial runs n has an influence on R_n^{tot}. For example, in the case of the sphere function, the self-optimization method converges in only about 5 more iterations when the number of initial runs $n = 35$, while it takes 10 more iterations when $n = 5$. This means the method converges faster when the initial number of runs is considerable, but overall it takes less iterations even if the initial number of runs is small. This is due to the fact that more data are available to perform the regression at the first iteration, leading to a faster convergence. Nevertheless, the gain in term of convergence iterations is not mitigated by the high number of initial required runs.

Another point is, in all the cases the standard deviation of the number of total runs before convergence is about 5. This shows the robustness of the method, since the difference in terms of iterations before convergence for the thousand experiences in each case of initial number of runs is small.

5   Conclusion

The proposed method aims to automatically optimize the performance of HPC applications, by collecting data (IO metrics, performance values, etc.) and meta-data (parameters, etc.), analyzing them and parameterizing IO accelerators to perform an inference that produces parameters as relevant as possible. It is a continuous improvement process, that takes part of the increasing data collection along iterations to converge toward an optimal parameterization.

The result of experiments on theoretical functions have shown that the self-optimization method converges in a reasonable number of iterations, regardless the number of initial runs. For example, considering a complex parametric space such as the Rosenbrock function one, only 6 iterations are needed to reach a convergence stability under 10% in term of performance value, with only 3 initial runs.

Future work will focus on finding a good strategy of the placement of the initial points in the parametric space. Indeed, the choice of the parameters of the initial runs has an influence on the accuracy of the objective function. The more homogeneously spread the initial parameter set, the more representative the regressed objective function compared to the theoretical continuous one. As a consequence, in such a case the convergence speed should be improved.

Another point of interest will aim at detecting outlier runs, in order to use the relevant runs of a job family only. This selection will be performed by a clustering step before the inference.

References

1. Bergman, K., et al.: Exascale computing study: technology challenges in achieving exascale systems. Defense Advanced Research Projects Agency Information Processing Techniques Office (DARPA IPTO), Technical report 15 (2008)
2. Abrahm, E., et al. Preparing HPC applications for exascale: challenges and recommendations. In: 2015 18th International Conference on Network-Based Information Systems (NBiS). IEEE (2015)
3. Gainaru, A., et al.: Failure prediction for HPC systems and applications: current situation and open issues. Int. J. High Perform. Comput. Appl. **27**(3), 273–282 (2013)
4. https://atos.net/en/products/high-performance-computing-hpc/extreme-data
5. Vu, K.K., D'Ambrosio, C., Hamadi, Y., Liberti, L.: Surrogate-based methods for blackbox optimization. Int. Trans. Oper. Res. **24**, 393–424 (2017). https://doi.org/10.1111/itor.12292
6. Mackay, D.J.C.: Bayesian interpolation. Neural Comput. J. **4**, 415–447 (1992)
7. Cortes, C., Vapnik, V.: Support vector networks. Mach. Learn. J. **20**(3), 273–297 (1995)
8. Rasmussen, C.E., Williams, C.K.I.: Gaussian Processes for Machine Learning. MIT press, Cambridge (2006)
9. Nelder, J., Mead, R.: A simplex method for function minimization. Comput. J. **7**, 308–313 (1965)
10. Kennedy, J., Eberhart, R.: Particle swarm optimization. IEEE (1995)
11. Hansen, N., Müller, S.D., Koumoutsakos, P.: Reducing the time complexity of the derandomized evolution strategy with covariance matrix adaptation (CMA-ES). Evol. Comput. **11**(1), 1–18 (2003)
12. Jamil, M., Xin, X.-S.: A literature survey of benchmark functions for global optimisation problems. Int. J. Math. Model. Numer. Optim. **4**, 150–194 (2013)

13th Workshop on Virtualization in High-Performance Cloud Computing (VHPC 2018)

13th Workshop on Virtualization in High-Performance Cloud Computing (VHPC 2018)

Michael Alexander, Anastassios Nanos, and Romeo Kienzler

Virtualization technologies constitute a key enabling factor for flexible resource management in modern data centers, and particularly in cloud environments. Cloud providers need to manage complex infrastructures in a seamless fashion to support the highly dynamic and heterogeneous workloads and hosted applications customers deploy. Similarly, HPC environments have been increasingly adopting techniques that enable flexible management of vast computing and networking resources, close to marginal provisioning cost, which is unprecedented in the history of scientific and commercial computing.

Various virtualization technologies contribute to the overall picture in different ways: machine virtualization, with its capability to enable consolidation of multiple under-utilized servers with heterogeneous software and operating systems (OSes), and its capability to live–migrate a fully operating virtual machine (VM) with a very short downtime, enables novel and dynamic ways to manage physical servers; OS-level virtualization (i.e., containerization), with its capability to isolate multiple user-space environments and to allow for their co-existence within the same OS kernel, promises to provide many of the advantages of machine virtualization with high levels of responsiveness and performance; I/O Virtualization allows physical network interfaces to take traffic from multiple VMs or containers; network virtualization, with its capability to create logical network overlays that are independent of the underlying physical topology is furthermore enabling virtualization of HPC infrastructures.

This year's workshop featured a paper on memory elasticity by Aimilios Tsalapatis et al. with an emphasis on the side-by-side of hypervisor and VM memory management. Here, Userspace Trancendent Memory (utmem) is proposed as an extension over the existing Transcendent Memory concept. A paper by Radostin Stoyanov and Martin Kollingbaum gave a review of container live migration and looked at a new Linux CRIU feature called image cache/proxy to address the case of the rate of new dirty memory pages exceeding interconnect bandwidth during migration. Invited talks were given by Andrew Younge, Dimitrios Nikolopoulos, Gregorz Kurtzer and Josh Simmons which were all very well received by the audience.

The chairs would like to thank the ISC workshop organizers and the members of the program committee along with the speakers and attendees, whose interaction contributed to a stimulating environment.

utmem: Towards Memory Elasticity
in Cloud Workloads

Aimilios Tsalapatis[(✉)], Stefanos Gerangelos[(✉)], Stratos Psomadakis[(✉)],
Konstantinos Papazafeiropoulos[(✉)], and Nectarios Koziris[(✉)]

Computing Systems Lab, National Technical University of Athens, Athens, Greece
{etsal,sgerag,psomas,kpapazaf,nkoziris}@cslab.ece.ntua.gr

Abstract. In environments where multiple virtual machines are colo-
cated on the same physical host, the semantic gap between the host and
the guests leads to suboptimal memory management. Solutions such as
ballooning are unable to modify the amount of memory available to the
guest fast enough to avoid performance degradation. Alternatives such
as Transcendent Memory allow the guest to use host memory instead
of swapping to disk. All these techniques are applied at the memory
management subsystem level, resulting in cases where abrupt changes in
memory utilization cause unnecessary guest-side swapping. We propose
Userspace Transcendent Memory (utmem), a version of Transcendent
Memory that can be directly utilized by applications without interference
from the guest OS. Our results demonstrate that our approach succeeds
in allowing the guests to rapidly adjust the amount of memory they use
more efficiently than both ballooning and Transcendent Memory.

Keywords: Virtualization · Virtualized memory management
Transcendent Memory

1 Introduction

In cloud computing environments, the lack of cooperation between the guest
OSes and the hosts incurs systemwide performance penalties. Because each guest
has its own internal mechanisms for managing its resources, unaware of the environment it is running in, all VMs concurrently try to optimize the resources allocated to them as if they were running alone in a physical server. Moreover, hosts
are oblivious to any resource management on the guests' side, unless there are
paravirtualization mechanisms in the system with which the two can coordinate
[10].

In the case of paravirtualized memory management, the guests and the host
use approaches such as memory balloons, which let them pass ownership of
physical pages to one another. The balloon, which resides in the guest, tries to use
as much guest physical memory as possible. Since the balloon never actually uses
the memory that it allocates, the guest's maximum memory usage is reduced.

As a result, it cannot put as much memory pressure on the host. When the
guest is in need of memory, it signals to the balloon to free some of the pages it

© Springer Nature Switzerland AG 2018
R. Yokota et al. (Eds.): ISC 2018 Workshops, LNCS 11203, pp. 173–183, 2018.
https://doi.org/10.1007/978-3-030-02465-9_12

has been given. These can then be once again used by the guest, and the host once again needs to back them with actual memory.

Ballooning allows for dynamically modifying the amount of guest memory, but it is often inefficient for a number of reasons. One of them is that traditional operating systems tend to use as much memory as they can, because they are designed to be the sole tenants of their machine. As a result, the balloon driver constantly competes with the rest of the system for guest physical memory. This causes slow reaction times to spikes in memory usage, degrading overall performance [3]. Apart from that, ballooning also tends to fragment the guest's physical memory map by grabbing free memory areas that rest between used ones, creating holes in the address space [6].

An alternative method for dynamically adjusting the size of guest memory is Transcendent Memory [2] (tmem). Tmem modifies the amount of memory available to the guest without deconstructing and reconstructing the virtual machines' physical address space. The core of the idea is that the guest directly manages only part of the memory allocated to it, and has to indirectly use the rest through requests to the host. As a result, the host can more easily impose policy, since it does not need to wait for the guests to comply to its requests to redistribute the machine's resources, as in the case of ballooning [4]. This method has up to now found applications as part of the guest's memory subsystem. An example is the *frontswap* module [1] for Linux guests, which intercepts attempts to swap a page to disk and tries to store it in a tmem pool in the host. Another one is *cleancache* [1], which functions as a page cache for the guest, but is managed by the host.

While efficient, tmem suffers from the limitation that it cannot be used directly by applications. This in turn means that every tmem request must pass through the memory subsystem before being serviced. Moreover, the usage patterns of the memory pool are dictated by the subsystem, with the workloads being unable to directly determine which data gets sent to the pool. Current tmem implementations are also confined in the that part of the kernel, and can therefore only be used for storing the kinds of data present there, like disk blocks and physical pages.

In this paper we present Userspace Transcendent Memory (utmem), a mechanism which can be leveraged by guest workloads to achieve memory elasticity without the need of balloon drivers. Due to utmem's design, memory does not change ownership between the host and the guests. Performance thus does not degrade as guest memory usage rises, and in fact stays fixed regardless of the total amount of memory that the guest uses throughout the system.

We also demonstrate that, for guests which consume large amounts of memory, our design performs better under sustained memory pressure than existing tmem mechanisms. The cause of this speedup is that our solution completely avoids traversing the I/O stack, in contrast to ordinary tmem.

In this work we implement the utmem mechanism and prove its efficiency, providing the following contributions:

- We expand the KVM hypervisor to support tmem operations. We do so by adding a new hypercall, as well as support for directly manipulating the system's tmem pools from userspace. We also introduce tmem backend functionality directly to the Linux operating system.
- We construct a device on the guest kernel that exposes the aforementioned pools' functionality in a way directly usable by workloads. We demonstrate this functionality by introducing it to the Redis key-value store.
- We demonstrate that applications which can utilize the utmem mechanism ("utmem-capable") demonstrate significant speedups over unmodified applications in cases where guest memory consumption is close to its memory limit.

2   Background

The tmem mechanism can be used to streamline memory management in systems with multiple guests. It specifically addresses the problem of fluctuating guest memory usage, which causes significant performance penalties in systems that rely solely on ballooning. The concept is described in the paper by Magenheimer et al. [7].

Tmem is a key-value store that is accessed by the guests through explicit requests to the host. This store is created by gathering spare memory in the host to create a shared resource called a pool. One of the defining properties of tmem is having its data gated off behind its two main calls: PUT and GET . By having well-defined entry points, tmem is able to decouple the implementation of its pools from the interface to the users. As a result, the data in the pools can be represented in arbitrary ways, like for example in a compressed form [5]. Even if the data is stored locally and as-is (as in the case of the Xen hypervisor [8]), the guests still cannot access them without a request to the hypervisor. This means that the host remains in control of the system's memory at all times.

Figure 1 demonstrates the location of the tmem pools and the guest-side buffers in the Xen implementation. Each guest has its own tmem frontend (a), which is the only guest-side component aware of the tmem mechanism. It communicates with the host via hypercalls (b), which are then serviced by the hypervisor in the backend (c). The backend in turn stores the data to (or retrieves it from) its tmem pools.

These pools can be private or shared, depending on whether the data of a guest can be accessed by another one. The tmem specification also describes ephemeral and persistent pools, depending on the permanence of the data stored in them. Because ephemeral pools may discard the data stored in them at any given time in order to service the rest of the system's memory needs, they can be used to build entities such as victim caches. In contrast, persistent pools are guaranteed to keep the information stored indefinitely, and are more appropriate for creating high-speed tmem alternatives to more costly storage methods. In this paper we focus on persistent memory pools.

Tmem frontends include the *frontswap* and *cleancache* modules for Linux guests running on top of Xen. These consist of hooks on the I/O subsystem that

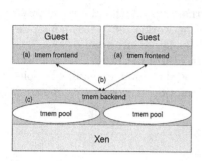

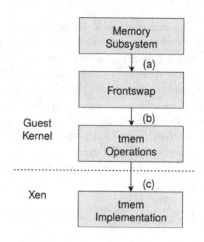

Fig. 1. The location of the pools in the Xen tmem implementation

Fig. 2. The layers of a typical frontswap-capable system

can be used to make a tmem call to the host, instead of a costlier operation like a disk access.

Frontswap's purpose is to avoid guest swapping during periods of especially high guest-side memory pressure [1]. Figure 2 demonstrates the relationship between the guest's memory subsystem, frontswap, and tmem. Before the guest resorts to swapping to disk, it first sends a request to frontswap (a) to save the page. The module attempts to do so by performing a PUT which amounts to looking up the implementation of the operation, typically a hypercall (b). It then makes the appropriate request to the backend (c), which stores the page if it has enough memory, or denies the request, if it does not. The result is passed to frontswap, which then informs the guest kernel whether the operation succeeded. If it did, then there is no need to write the page to swap. As a result, the cost of accessing the guest's disk is replaced by the cost of a single VM exit.

3   Overview

3.1   Design

The limits of tmem are currently defined by its use cases. More specifically, the whole mechanism has been used exclusively in the confines of the memory management subsystem of the guest. As a result, every tmem call presently incurs a performance overhead due to traversing the I/O stack of the guest.

This is not a penalty inherent to the tmem mechanism. In fact, one of its main advantages over approaches like swapping to host-side ramdisks is that successful stores simply consist of a hypercall, without passing through the swap I/O subsystem. One of the main goals of our framework is to completely bypass the I/O stack of the guest and access host memory through hypercalls, resulting in an overall faster and simpler system.

The main design objective of utmem is to integrate easily with applications which access data by means of explicit storage and retrieval API calls. The mechanism can be interposed between the application and the API, replacing the functions which store or retrieve information. Our goal is to have a design where the host provides a backing store for arbitrary data. The store should be completely opaque to the guests, comprised of discrete tmem pools, and accessible only through tmem calls.

Utmem is split into three parts, which communicate with each other using tmem requests. These parts are:

- The utmem device, which exposes the utmem API to userspace and dictates policy
- The tmem frontend, which implements the communication method with the backend (hypercalls, networking, etc.)
- The tmem backend, which implements the store and services requests

The present implementation is generic and can work with arbitrary data, including physical pages and key-value pairs. It is also superior to both native applications and existing tmem-based solutions in terms of performance. We achieve this speedup without utilizing domain-specific information, like for example the nature of the data being stored. Given a specific client workload, the mechanism can be configured to utilize this kind of information, in order to deliver additional performance gains with little effort.

3.2 Implementation

For the implementation of utmem, we choose to use the KVM hypervisor. Since it does not currently support tmem, we opt to implement that functionality by adding a hypercall. The additions to the hypervisor are about 150 lines of code, most of it due to the hypercall added. The only modification of existing code is an extra 3 lines of code in the main hypercall servicing loop.

Requests propagate across the components of the utmem mechanism, until they reach a tmem backend which can store the data. In our implementation we create a frontend in the guest, which makes a hypercall for each request. This call is received by the hypervisor in the host, which forwards it to a backend that actually possesses tmem pools. After the value is stored, the hypervisor is notified, and in turn notifies the client in the guest that initiated the operation.

The exact series of calls to be made for a utmem request is described in Fig. 3. This stack is usable both by guest userspace processes through the utmem mechanism, as well as from kernel space tmem users like frontswap.

We have chosen Redis as the workload to be used for the evaluation of this mechanism. As an in-memory key-value store, its access semantics are very similar to those of tmem. Our application communicates with the mechanism using a device that can be controlled using the `ioctl()` system call. This device is responsible for copying the key-value pairs received from userspace into the buffers used by the guest tmem frontend, and vice versa.

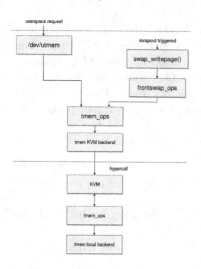

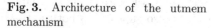

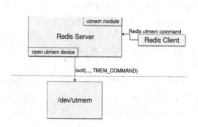

Fig. 3. Architecture of the utmem mechanism

Fig. 4. Architecture of the Redis workload

The additions to Redis are shown in Fig. 4. They are implemented in a Redis module, which holds the functions which turn the client's requests into `ioctls` to be sent to the utmem device.

4   Evaluation

To assess our approach, we use the Redis benchmark for the reasons noted above. The utmem mechanism is evaluated on two fronts:

- How well it performs under significant memory pressure. The results confirm our claim that the utmem-capable system is oblivious to guest-side memory pressure, while the unmodified one experiences performance degradation due to swapping.
- How well it performs in situations where memory is abundant. Our results show a slight performance penalty, due to the extra memory copies in our implementation.

To further analyze the behaviour of our approach, we look into a breakdown of the latency for the two basic operations. Our experimental evaluation shows a discrepancy between the latency of PUT and GET , which stems from their implementation.

We have set up our testbed on a machine with an Intel Xeon X5650 processor with 48 GB of RAM. Both the host and the guest are running Linux 4.9.

4.1 Evaluation of utmem Under Memory Pressure

The first set of experiments we performed showcases the advantage of a utmem-capable system against a conventional one, when under pressure. We also demonstrate that utmem exhibits better performance than existing tmem designs.

In the experiment, we fill up the Redis server or the utmem backing store with values of collective size 100% that of the guest's total memory. We keep executing the Redis benchmark until its results converge.

Looking at the results in Fig. 5 we confirm that the utmem-capable system is approximately 2x-3x times as fast as the unmodified one, depending on the size of the values being stored with each operation. The native case suffers heavy performance degradation due to swapping, even if it is not over its memory limit. On the other hand, utmem's throughput does not decrease. Utmem also outperforms systems running unmodified Redis instances that also use tmem by means of the frontswap mechanism. This demonstrates that avoiding disk I/O by using frontswap is not enough to completely avoid performance degradation.

We also benchmarked the guests for working sets of different sizes, with the latter being fractions of total system memory close to unity. Again, by looking at Fig. 5 we can see that the performance multiplier of the utmem mechanism against the native case rises together with the size of the working set. Once again, we confirm that frontswap is not suitable for totally mitigating the performance penalties associated with high memory pressure.

4.2 Evaluation of utmem Under Nonexistent Memory Pressure

The next experiment we performed concerns the throughput of a system that does not swap. More specifically, we tested the performance of an unmodified and a utmem-capable Redis server. The Redis client is executed outside the guest, in order to avoid influencing the Redis server's performance. There is no memory pressure, because the same key is used for each operation. The benchmark used is the Redis builtin benchmark.

From the graph in Fig. 6, we observe that both servers exhibit similar performance. The difference between the two commands is due to the extra copies needed by utmem to finish the storage/retrieval of the value. The performance penalty hovers around 85%, irrespective of the value size. This is expected, considering that the only difference between the operations of different sizes is the number of hypercalls per KB of data moved to the host. The cost of these is negligible compared to the data transfer, so it does not show up in the graph.

In order to look further into the sources of latency for the utmem operation, we create a microbenchmark which is similar to the Redis benchmark. Its function is to continually perform the same operation for 10^5 iterations, using only one key-value pair of size 1024 KB. We have normalized the results for the time needed for the microbenchmark to complete for PUT , which was 992 ms.

Going back to Fig. 6, it is obvious from the graph that the costliest part of the operation is copying the data to and from the backend. The difference between the internal guest call and the guest-to-host communication demonstrates that the major factor of the operations' latency is the memory copies. Another interesting observation is that there is a slight discrepancy between the two basic operations: PUT has a small amount of latency coming from the host backend itself, while the GET operation does not. This is because the PUT hypercall needs to allocate memory in order to finish it. GET does not, because the guest itself provides the buffer into which the data will be written.

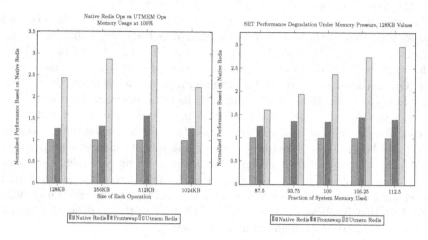

Fig. 5. Performance of native, frontswap-capable, and utmem-capable Redis server for memory usage exactly at and close to unity.

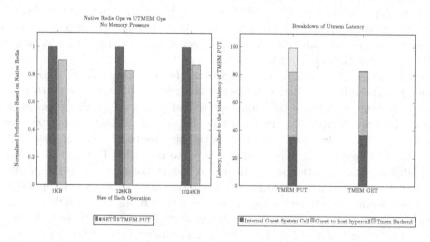

Fig. 6. Left figure: performance of native and utmem-capable Redis for no memory pressure. Right figure: breakdown of the latency of the basic utmem operations.

5   Related Work

Transcendent Memory is an idea that has been mainly used to build caches by being able to reserve system memory, which it then uses to serve clients. These can be the guest kernel, or a userspace process. Instances of this design include a two-level cache for systems with nonvolatile memory, as described in [12]. Another example is MemFlex [13], which like frontswap is a cache for swapped-out pages. Unlike frontswap, it is combined with a balloon which deflates when the tmem pool starts getting used, in order to swap the pages in the cache back in, thus freeing host memory.

Another design that draws from the aforementioned work is Mortar [3], which focuses on pools similar to those created by ephemeral tmem. The memory accumulated in the pools is used to build shared caches, which store data that also exists elsewhere. As a result, the caches can shrink instantaneously when memory pressure intensifies. The goal of this approach is to maximize memory utilization by making use of spare resources.

Research efforts have been made to make ballooning more responsive and efficient. These designs aim to avoid needing what amounts to a memory buffer that absorbs spikes in memory demand, in the form of tmem and similar mechanisms. One such approach includes introducing ballooning at the application level [11], so that applications in the guest that manage their own memory, like language runtimes and other middleware, directly control the balloon that exists in the kernel. Another effort to make ballooning more efficient is iBalloon [9], where efficient ballooning is treated as a learning task, with reinforcement techniques being applied to teach the mechanism to reach the desired state in the shortest amount of time.

6   Conclusion and Future Work

6.1   Future Work

While the mechanism presented is already competitive in regards to its performance, there are possible improvements that can be made. An example would be having different backends in the host, each of them with its own tradeoffs, depending on the use case. Another potential expansion is to add a deduplication mechanism for the data stored. Since the values can be objects other than pages, guests running on the same host that store values of the same kind could end up sharing a lot of data, which in turn means that the system's memory limits could be expanded further.

While our approach is appropriate for handling large amounts of data, when used for storing smaller structures the performance penalty from the hypercall may become more apparent. A possible solution to that is to coalesce multiple tmem requests into larger ones, and only flush the data when needed. This would aid in avoiding superfluous VM exits, by keeping inside the guest values that do not take up significant space in memory.

When it comes to combining in-guest storage with utmem, another extension could be an adaptive mechanism that determines whether a value will be stored in guest or host memory. This mechanism would take into account how often a value is accessed, as well as the guest's and the host's memory load.

6.2 Conclusion

In this paper we present utmem, a mechanism for enabling the host to efficiently and flexibly manage system memory. We design utmem by extending the tmem architecture to include a device for communicating directly with userspace. This approach enables the utilization of existing tmem users in KVM, like frontswap.

In order to implement the mechanism, we create a backing store for the tmem service that can reside in Linux itself. We add a new hypercall to the KVM hypervisor, and implement a module in the guest that we can use to send tmem requests from guest userspace to the host.

We evaluate our mechanism and demonstrate that in setups where the guest is under significant memory pressure, the applications which use utmem outperform their native counterparts by a factor up to 3. In the worst case scenario, utmem-aware applications are shown to incur an overhead of 20%, due to the extra data copy needed by our implementation.

References

1. Cleancache and Frontswap. https://lwn.net/Articles/386090/. Accessed 26 Feb 2018
2. Transcendent Memory in a Nutshell. https://lwn.net/Articles/454795/. Accessed 26 Feb 2018
3. Hwang, J., Uppal, A., Wood, T., Huang, H.: Mortar: filling the gaps in data center memory. ACM SIGPLAN Not. 49(7), 53–64 (2014)
4. Hwang, W., Roh, Y., Park, Y., Park, K.W., Park, K.H.: Hyperdealer: reference-pattern-aware instant memory balancing for consolidated virtual machines. In: 2010 IEEE 3rd International Conference on Cloud Computing (CLOUD), pp. 426–434. IEEE (2010)
5. Jennings, S.: Transparent memory compression in linux (2013)
6. Liu, H., Jin, H., Liao, X., Deng, W., He, B., Xu, C.: Hotplug or ballooning: a comparative study on dynamic memory management techniques for virtual machines. IEEE Trans. Parallel Distrib. Syst. 26(5), 1350–1363 (2015)
7. Magenheimer, D., Mason, C., McCracken, D., Hackel, K.: Transcendent memory and linux. In: Proceedings of the Linux Symposium, pp. 191–200. Citeseer (2009)
8. Magenheimer, D., et al.: Transcendent memory on xen. Xen Summit, pp. 1–3 (2009)
9. Rao, J., Bu, X., Wang, K., Xu, C.Z.: iBalloon: self-adaptive virtual machines resource provisioning
10. Russell, R.: virtio: towards a de-facto standard for virtual I/O devices. ACM SIGOPS Oper. Syst. Rev. 42(5), 95–103 (2008)
11. Salomie, T.I., Alonso, G., Roscoe, T., Elphinstone, K.: Application level ballooning for efficient server consolidation. In: Proceedings of the 8th ACM European Conference on Computer Systems, pp. 337–350. ACM (2013)

12. Venkatesan, V., Qingsong, W., Tay, Y.: Ex-Tmem: extending transcendent memory with non-volatile memory for virtual machines. In: 2014 IEEE International Conference on High Performance Computing and Communications, 2014 IEEE 6th International Symposium on Cyberspace Safety and Security, 2014 IEEE 11th International Conference on Embedded Software and System (HPCC, CSS, ICESS), pp. 966–973. IEEE (2014)
13. Zhang, Q., Liu, L., Su, G., Iyengar, A.: MemFlex: a shared memory swapper for high performance VM execution. IEEE Trans. Comput. **66**(9), 1645–1652 (2017)

Efficient Live Migration of Linux Containers

Radostin Stoyanov and Martin J. Kollingbaum[✉]

University of Aberdeen, Aberdeen, UK
r.stoyanov.14@aberdeen.ac.uk, m.j.kollingbaum@abdn.ac.uk

Abstract. In recent years, operating system level virtualization has grown in popularity due to its capability to isolate multiple userspace environments and to allow for their co-existence within a single OS kernel instance. Checkpoint-restore in Userspace (CRIU) is a tool that allows to live migrate a hierarchy of processes – a container – between two physical computers. However, the live migration may cause significant delays when the applications running inside a container modify large amounts of memory faster than a container can be transferred over the network to a remote host. In this paper, we propose a novel approach for live migration of containers to address this issue by utilizing a recently published CRIU feature, the so-called "image cache/proxy". This feature allows for better total migration time and down time of the container applications that are migrated by avoiding the use of secondary storage.

Keywords: Linux containers · CRIU · Live migration
Cloud computing

1 Introduction

Live migration of containers is the act of detaching a set of processes that run in the context of a container, transfer them to a remote host, and reattach them back to the new OS kernel. Checkpoint-restore in Userspace (CRIU) [4] is a tool that allows such live migration of a hierarchy of processes (container) between two physical computers. Live migration techniques are used for moving a container instance from one physical host to another, while preserving the running state of the containerized applications and maintain open network connections. Live migration across distinct physical hosts has several benefits, such as dynamic load balancing, fault tolerance, data access locality, and it makes low-level system maintenance easy by allowing a clean separation between hardware and software. Migration can be used to improve power efficiency by gathering containers together on a physical machine, and to enable the suspension of currently-unused hardware resources.

During migration, several resources are transferred over the network – CPU state, memory state, network state and disk state. The transfer of the disk state can be circumvented by having a shared storage (SAN, NAS, NFS, etc.) between

© Springer Nature Switzerland AG 2018
R. Yokota et al. (Eds.): ISC 2018 Workshops, LNCS 11203, pp. 184–193, 2018.
https://doi.org/10.1007/978-3-030-02465-9_13

hosts participating in the live migration process. The size of the memory state depends on the type of applications that are being migrated. For example, an HTTP server such as Nginx[1] might use only a few hundreds megabytes of memory, whereas an in-memory data store such as Redis[2] might be associated with several gigabytes of data. The transfer of the whole memory state during migration can take too long to be a practical solution [14]. This problem is specifically hard when containerized applications modify large amounts of memory faster than a container can be transferred over the network.

The technique used to send the memory state to a remote host is, therefore, a major concern in live migration algorithms.

Improving the performance of live migration algorithms mainly focuses on reducing the *total migration time* and *down time*. The total migration time is the time between the start and the end of the migration process. Down time is the time when the migrated application is not running neither on the source nor on the destination server. Live migration algorithms aim to minimize the down time period, during which the application service is totally unavailable, while keeping the total migration time as small as possible.

Many live migration algorithms have been proposed over the years [18]. In terms of the way they transfer the memory state, these algorithms are classified into three categories:

1. **Pre-copy** migration starts by copying the memory state to the destination host. While copying, the source host remains responsive and keeps progressing all running applications. As memory pages may get updated on the source system, even after they have been copied to the destination system, the approach employs mechanisms to monitor page updates.
2. **Post-copy** first suspends the migrated application at the source host, copies a minimal processor state to the destination host, where the migrated application is resumed, and begins fetching memory pages over the network from the source.
3. **Hybrid-copy** works by combining both pre and post copy algorithms. It first starts pre-copy migration of the application, which keeps running on the source host, while all the memory pages are copied to the destination host. The application is then suspended and its processor state is copied over, without the remaining memory pages. Then, the application is resumed at the destination immediately, and the post-copy algorithm is used to synchronize the rest of the memory pages.

Two main implementations of container migration, Docker [6] and LXD [7] currently only use pre-copy migration. There are no container runtime systems that currently use image-cache/image-proxy for migration. In this paper, we report on our migration implementation that uses Image Cache and Image Proxy for container migration, which are two options in development in the CRIU (Checkpoint Restore In Userspace) tool. We show that live migration of Linux

---

[1] https://www.nginx.com/.

[2] https://redis.io/.

containers based on the image-cache and image-proxy components of CRIU, currently available in its development branch, provides better performance and time savings in migrating containers. The pre-copy migration algorithm has been implemented by performing one or more pre-dump iterations with CRIU Sect. 2.1. This approach allows the automation of the transfer of image files and reduces the total migration time and down time by keeping all memory pages in a cache buffer rather than storing them on disk. The results of our evaluation show that the performance of pre-copy migration with CRIU depends on the memory intensity of applications, and the total migration time and down time increase proportionally to the amount memory used by the migrating process.

In Sect. 2, we describe in detail the particular features of checkpoint/restore mechanisms relevant to our work. In Sect. 3, we point out how we improve live migration. In Sect. 4, we provide a performance analysis of process live migration. In Sect. 5, we discuss future work and conclude the paper with Sect. 6.

2   Live Migration with CRIU

With the increased interest in Linux container technology, the checkpoint/restore mechanism has attracted more attention. This mechanism can be used for fault tolerance or dynamic load balancing by migrating a running process from one system to another. Live migrating a process is nothing more than checkpointing a process, transferring it to a destination system, and restoring the process back to its original running state. The checkpoint/restore mechanism can be applied to a hierarchy of processes, thus it is a perfect base technology for container migration. Early implementations of checkpoint/restore were implemented as an in-kernel approach [10,16]. As pointed out in [3], these implementations did not focus on upstream inclusion in the Linux kernel. As a result, there was no agreement in the Linux kernel community on the design of a checkpoint/restore mechanism, which led to the adoption of solutions that were not officially accepted by the Linux community [3]. The CRIU project solves this problem by implementing checkpoint/restore in user space, using available kernel interfaces. As pointed out in [3], one of the most important kernel interfaces for checkpointing is the *ptrace* (see ptrace manual pages) system call. It provides means for a process to control the execution, and examine and change the memory allocated to another process and its registers. Another important kernel feature, *last_pid* control, that is used to implement the restore functionality of CRIU allows the restored process to receive the same process identifier (PID) it had during checkpointing. In order to achieve this, CRIU writes one number less of the desired PID to /proc/sys/kernel/ns_last_pid. Then, it verifies that the newly created process has the correct PID, otherwise the restoration of this process is aborted.

2.1   Pre-copy Migration with CRIU

Iterative pre-copy live migration is one of the most reliable live migration algorithms. By *"iterative"* we mean that pre-copying occurs in *rounds*, during which the memory pages to be transferred in round n are those that are modified after round n - 1 (all pages are transferred in the first round). The pre-copy support in CRIU is implemented as an incremental pre-dump [1] by using the concept of "soft-dirty bit" on a Page Table Entry (PTE) [13]. The soft-dirty bit feature is implemented in the Linux kernel to enable tracking of memory changes [12]. CRIU starts the tracking of memory by writing the integer 4 to /proc/$PID/clear_refs. This operation instructs the kernel to clear the soft-dirty and the writable bits from all PTEs of the specified process. After this, every first write operation on a memory page associated with this process will set the soft-dirty flag. Modified PTEs are identified in a subsequent pre-copy iteration by reading /proc/$PID/pagemap, where $PID is a process identifier of the migrated process. The modified PTEs are those that have a soft-dirty (the 55'th) bit reported. CRIU enables pre-copy iterations with the pre-dump action. This allows CRIU to extract only part of the information (i.e. the memory pages) associated with a container.

2.2 Post-copy Migration with CRIU

Post-copy minimizes the application down time during live migration. In contrast to pre-copy, this algorithm transfers all memory pages until after the CPU state has already been moved and resumed on the destination host. Concurrently, when the migrated application accesses a missing memory page, CRIU handles this page fault by transferring the required page from the source node and injects it into the running task memory address space. This demand paging approach ensures that each memory page is sent over the network *at most once*. However, the network delay might cause a performance degradation of the migrated process, as well introduce additional, high-priority network traffic. Residual dependencies are being removed from the source host as quickly as possible by pro-actively pushing the remaining memory pages to the destination.

The post-copy algorithm is implemented in CRIU by utilizing a recently added user-space page fault feature in the Linux kernel – userfaultfd [2]. The post-copy migration can be started by providing a --lazy-pages flag to the *dump* action, as well as during restore to skip the injection of memory pages into the processes address space and register lazy memory areas with userfaultfd [2]. This option instructs CRIU to not extract memory pages during checkpoint, and to allow the lazy-pages daemon to request them via TCP connection. Memory page fault notifications are handled by a *lazy-pages* daemon that receives a userfault file descriptor from the restore process via UNIX socket.

2.3 Automatic Transfer of Image Files

Recently, CRIU has been extended with a new feature that automates the transfer of image files [8]. This feature enables live migration of Java applications from one Java runtime environment (the so-called "Java Virtual Machine") to another without performing expensive I/O operations. This extension introduces the "image-cache" and "image-proxy" actions for CRIU, as well as the --remote option for dump and restore. The automatic transfer of image files enables simplified implementation for live migration of containers.

Two main implementations of container migration, Docker [] and LXD [] currently only use pre-copy migration. There are no container runtime systems that would use image-cache/image-proxy for migration. In this paper, we report on a migration implementation that uses Image Cache and Image Proxy for container migration, using image cache and image proxy for live migrating containers. The pre-copy migration algorithm has been implemented by performing one or more pre-dump iterations with CRIU Sect. 2.1. The pre-dump CRIU feature allows to extract relevant memory pages of a hierarchy of processes (container) that is being migrated. The pre-dump CRIU feature is described in the Patent Specification US9621643B1 [11] and is implemented by injecting a parasite code, which is used to execute CRIU service routines inside the address space of the migrated process. The parasite code is a binary blob of code built in PIC (position-independent code) format for execution inside another process address space. PIC is a body of machine code that, being placed somewhere in the primary memory, executes properly regardless of its absolute address.

There are two modes the parasite can operate in - *trap mode* and *daemon mode*. In trap mode, the parasite executes one command at a time. Right after a call is executed, a trapping instruction is placed to trigger a notification to the caller and indicate that the parasite has finished. When the parasite runs in daemon mode, it opens a command socket that is used to communicate with the caller. Once the socket is opened, the daemon will wait for commands in sleep mode. When everything is done, the parasite code is being removed, and the migrated process is left back into the state it was before the injection.

2.4   Design of Post-copy Memory Migration

The current Post-copy implementation in CRIU begins with a "normal" checkpoint (`criu dump`) with provided `--lazy-pages` option. By using this option, the process memory is collected into pipes and non-lazy pages are stored into image files or transferred over to the destination host via page-server. The lazy pages are kept in pipes for later transfer. After the checkpoint is completed (at the dump_finish stage), a TCP server is started to handle page requests from the restore host. In other words, the lazy memory pages are transferred on-demand via TCP connection rather than being stored into image files. At the destination side, a lazy-pages daemon has to be started to create two sockets – a UNIX socket that is used to receive page-faults from the restore; and a TCP socket to forward page requests to the source host. The checkpoint image files are used by the restore action to create memory mappings, registers memory areas with userfaultfd and fill the VMAs that cannot be handled by the userfaultfd mechanism. All lazy memory pages are handled by a dedicated daemon. On page-fault, the restore action sends the userfaultfd to the lazy-pages daemon, which sends a command to the source host. The source side extracts the requested memory pages from the pipe and send them over via the TCP socket, and the lazy-pages daemon copies the received pages into the restored process address space. The lazy-pages daemon knows which pages exist on destination host, and therefore it can identify when all pages have been migrated. CRIU implements the *active pushing* mechanism [15] for post-copy migration by copying the remaining memory pages of the migrated process in the background while no network page faults are being requested [2].

2.5 Combining Pre-copy and Post-copy Migration

Both Pre-copy and Post-copy migration algorithms have advantages and disadvantages. Application down time can be significantly decreased by pre-copying relevant memory pages from the address space of the migrating process hierarchy before the final freeze. However, in the case of write-memory-intensive applications, such pre-copy iterations have negative effects and increase the total migration time without improving the application down time. A solution to this problem is provided with post-copy migration. The post-copy algorithm transfers only the minimal application state that is required during down time in order to resume execution on the destination host. This approach greatly improves the application down time and ensures that each memory page is transmitted over the network at most once. However, this approach has two major drawbacks. First, the performance of the application during migration time is affected significantly due to the network latency that slows down memory access. Second, the reliability of this migration algorithm is reduced due to the impossibility to recover the running state of the application on neither the source or the destination host in case of network problems.

Fortunately, both pre- and post-copy algorithms can be used together with CRIU [19]. This approach is also known as *hybrid-copy*. The benefits of this combination are the following:

1. Application downtime is minimized by transferring memory pages that are being frequently modified on-demand.
2. Performance degradation of the application, after it has been moved over to the destination host, is minimized by providing as much memory pages as possible on the destination side prior the start of the post-copy phase. For example, read-only areas of the application's memory address space are being transfered over prior the post-copy phase.
3. Reliability is significantly improved, in comparison with Post-copy, by reducing the number of pages that are being transfered on-demand.

3   Using Image Cache and Image Proxy for Container Live Migration

Originally, CRIU was designed to store the running state of a checkpointed process as a collection of image files to persistent storage. In a live migration scenario, this approach has two major disadvantages. First, all image files are written to persistent storage twice – once when dumping the container on the source host, and once when receiving the images on the destination host. Second, these image files are read from disk twice – once when sending the images to destination host, and once when performing the restore operation. A simple solution of this issue is outlined in the CRIU documentation [5] as *disk-less migration*, which stores image files on a temporary file system instead of persistent storage.

A better solution has been proposed by introducing two new components to CRIU – image-cache and image-proxy [8]. These components allow a decoupling of the saving/reading of image files from dumping/restoring a process tree. The communication between these two components is achieved over a TCP socket and the running state of the checkpointed/restored process is transferred via Unix sockets from the CRIU process. This approach decreases the total migration time and down time for live container migration by keeping image files in cache rather than on persistent storage. Another major advantage of this approach is the automated transfer of image files, which allows a simplification of the implementation of live migration with CRIU.

4   Evaluation

Qualitative evaluation between pre- and post-copy migration algorithms would give some indication of their potential value for migrating memory-intensive applications. The image-cache/proxy implementation is compared with total-copy, which transfers (using rsync) the entire process state before the process execution resumed on the destination machine.

All evaluation tests were performed by live migrating the memhog process between two VMs with pre-installed Fedora 27 Cloud Edition and CRIU compiled from the criu-dev git branch – commit 8340e64137e. Both VMs have an identical hardware configuration – 4 vCPUs (Intel(R) Xeon(R) CPU E5-2650 v4 @ 2.20 GHz), 30 MB cache size, and 8 GB RAM.

The results show that the performance of pre-copy migration with CRIU depends on the memory intensity of applications, and the total migration time and down time increase proportionally to the amount memory used by memhog. The total migration time and down time for the post-copy migration do not increase significantly with the increase of memory used by memhog.

The image-cache/proxy mechanism does not have significant improvement in terms of decreased total migration time. In contrast, when compared with the total-copy using rsync, the image-cache/proxy technique shows higher migration time, which increases proportionally with the amount of memory used by memhog.

5   Discussion and Future Work

Several techniques, borrowed from live migration of virtual machines, are applicable for Linux containers. These techniques can be used to extend CRIU to further optimize the pre- and post-copy migration (Fig. 1).

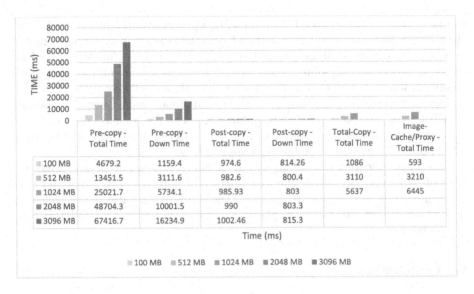

Fig. 1. Comparison of the live migration algorithms for the memory intensive application (*memhog*) used with different size of allocated memory.

In identifying the Writable Working Set, each process will have some (hopefully small) set of memory of pages that it updates very frequently and which are therefore poor candidates for pre-copy migration. This concept of *writable working set* (WWS) was first introduced in [9]. Based on the analysis of the behavior of server workloads (the WWS), the number of pre-copy iterations can further improve the efficiency of the migration. The writable working set can be identified by reading /proc/$PID/pagemap between pre-copy iterations and keep track of the modified memory pages since the last iteration that have not been send over to the new host yet. A similar idea was demonstrated with a Markov model applied to forecast the memory access pattern to adjust the memory page transfer order and reduce the number of unnecessary transfers [17].

A crucial concern for live migration is the impact on active services. Resource usage control during live migration may provide performance enhancements. For instance, iteratively extracting and sending memory pages between two hosts in a cluster can easily consume the entire bandwidth available between them and hence starve the active services of resources. This issue needs to be addressed by carefully controlling the network and CPU resources used by CRIU during the migration process, thereby ensuring that it does not interfere excessively with active traffic or processing.

Another improvement may be achieved through Delta Compression Based Memory Transfer. In order to live migrate a virtual environment (container), all memory pages need to be transferred across the network to the destination host. However, a typical memory page occupies 4 KB, a standard Ethernet network packet can only transport 1 KB (including header). Therefore to transfer a unique memory page, we need to send a minimum of 5 packet over the networks. When the memory pages are frequently updated, and the changes must be propagated over some transport medium it is undesirable to transmit the full new page due to its size. An effective solution to this I/O bottleneck is a delta compression algorithm for live migration of KVM virtual machines [14]. By using a simple and fast compression algorithm such as XORed Binary Run Length Encoding (XBRLE) [14] on the original and updated memory pages, and transmit only the delta file, the amount of down time can be reduced drastically, making live migration a suitable for large business applications.

The characteristics of this algorithm of being very small (a few hundred lines of code) and fast, allow the maintenance of both memory pages and the executable code in CPU cache. However, the compression ratio performance is limited since information entropy plays a role as a measure on how well data can be compressed.

6   Conclusion

In this paper, we discuss an implementation of the use of Image Cache and Image Proxy for container migration (CRIU). Originally, CRIU was designed to store the running state of a checkpointed process as a collection of image files to persistent storage. In a live migration scenario, this approach has major disadvantages as image files have to be stored and retrieved multiple times from persistent storage. In this paper, we presented the implementation of a *disk-less migration*, which stores image files on a temporary file system instead of persistent storage, using two new components to CRIU – image-cache and image-proxy. The results show that the performance of pre-copy migration with CRIU depends on the memory intensity of applications, and the total migration time and down time increase proportionally to the amount memory of the migrating process. More work is needed to improve the migration performance of our implementation of an image-cache/proxy mechanism. Although it should perform better then a total-copy migration, the evaluation results show that our implementation is not yet optimized. The pre- and post-copy algorithms were compared by migrating a memory intensive process – memhog. The results show that post-copy performs better for this type of application.

References

1. Memory changes tracking - CRIU documentation. https://criu.org/Memory_changes_tracking
2. Userfaultfd - CRIU documentation. https://criu.org/Userfaultfd
3. CRIU - Checkpoint/Restore in User Space, October 2016. https://access.redhat.com/articles
4. CRIU (2018). https://criu.org/
5. CRIU disk-less migration (2018). https://criu.org/Disk-less_migration
6. Docker, July 2018. https://docs.docker.com/engine/reference/commandline/checkpoint/

7. Lxd, July 2018. https://github.com/lxc/lxd
8. Bruno, R., Ferreira, P.: ALMA: GC-assisted JVM live migration for java server applications. In: Proceedings of the 17th International Middleware Conference, p. 5. ACM (2016)
9. Clark, C., et al.: Live migration of virtual machines. In: Proceedings of the 2nd Conference on Symposium on Networked Systems Design & Implementation-Volume 2, pp. 273–286. USENIX Association (2005)
10. Documentation, O.: Checkpointing and live migration (2018). https://wiki.openvz. org/Checkpointing_and_live_migration
11. Emelyanov, P.: System and method for joining containers running on multiple nodes of a cluster. https://patents.google.com/patent/US9621643
12. Emelyanov, P.: Ability to monitor task memory changes, April 2013. https://lwn. net/Articles/546966/
13. Emelyanov, P.: Soft-Dirty PTEs - Linux Kernel Documentation, April 2013. https://www.kernel.org/doc/Documentation/vm/soft-dirty.txt
14. Hacking, S., Hudzia, B.: Improving the live migration process of large enterprise applications. In: Proceedings of the 3rd International Workshop on Virtualization Technologies in Distributed Computing, pp. 51–58. ACM (2009)
15. Hines, M.R., Deshpande, U., Gopalan, K.: Post-copy live migration of virtual machines. ACM SIGOPS Oper. Syst. Rev. 43(3), 14–26 (2009)
16. Laadan, O., Nieh, J.: Transparent checkpoint-restart of multiple processes on commodity operating systems. In: 2007 USENIX Annual Technical Conference on Proceedings of the USENIX Annual Technical Conference, ATC 2007, pp. 25:1–25:14. USENIX Association, Berkeley (2007). http://dl.acm.org/citation. cfm?id=1364385.1364410
17. Lei, Z., Sun, E., Chen, S., Wu, J., Shen, W.: A novel hybrid-copy algorithm for live migration of virtual machine. Future Internet 9(3), 37 (2017)
18. Milojičić, D.S., Douglis, F., Paindaveine, Y., Wheeler, R., Zhou, S.: Process migration. ACM Comput. Surv. (CSUR) 32(3), 241–299 (2000)
19. Reber, A.: Combining pre-copy and post-copy migration, October 2016. https://lisas.de/~adrian/posts/2016-Oct-14-combining-pre-copy-and-post-copy-migration.html

Third International Workshop on In Situ Visualization: Introduction and Applications (WOIV 2018)

Third International Workshop on In Situ Visualization: Introduction and Applications (WOIV 2018)

Kenneth Moreland[1], Guido Reina[2], Thomas Theußl[3], and Tom Vierjahn[4]

[1] Sandia National Laboratories, USA
[2] University of Stuttgart, Germany
[3] KAUST, Saudi Arabia
[4] RWTH Aachen, Germany

1 Introduction

Large-scale HPC simulations with their inherent I/O bottleneck have made *in situ* an essential approach for data analysis. In situ coupling of analysis and visualization to a live simulation circumvents writing raw data to disk. Instead, data abstracts are generated that capture much more information than otherwise possible.

The workshop series "In Situ Visualization: Introduction and Applications" provides a venue for speakers to share practical expertise and experience with in situ visualization approaches. This 3rd edition of the workshop, WOIV'18, took place as a full-day workshop on 28 June 2018 in Frankfurt, Germany, after two half-day workshops in 2016 and 2017. The goal of the workshop in general is to appeal to a wide-ranging audience of visualization scientists, computational scientists, and simulation developers, who have to collaborate in order to develop, deploy, and maintain in situ visualization approaches on HPC infrastructures.

For WOIV'18 we additionally encouraged submissions on approaches that either did not work at all or did not live up to their expectations. We therefore expected to get first-hand reports on lessons learned. Speakers should detail if and how the application drove abstractions or other kinds of data reductions and how these interacted with the expressiveness and flexibility of the visualization for exploratory analysis or why the approach failed.

2 Organization of the Workshop

The workshop content was built on two tracks:

Invited talks experts in the field were invited to share their thoughts and insights

Research paper presentations authors were required to submit a full paper before the workshop, which was then reviewed for inclusion in the conference proceedings

After the submission deadline in mid-May 2018, eight final manuscripts were submitted. Having the time of a full-day workshop at their disposal, the organizing committee was able to select all eight submissions for presentation at the workshop. After a full review cycle by an international program committee, all papers were selected for inclusion in the conference proceedings as well. Additionally, four internationally recognized researchers agreed to each give an invited talk at the workshop. All slides of the talks can be downloaded from the conference web page at http://woiv.org.

2.1 Organizing Committee

Kenneth Moreland	Sandia National Laboratories, USA
Guido Reina	University of Stuttgart, Germany
Thomas Theußl	KAUST, Saudi Arabia
Tom Vierjahn	RWTH Aachen, Germany

2.2 Program Committee

Bartosz Borucki	University of Warsaw, Poland
Jose Camata	Federal University of Juiz de Fora, Brasil
Hadrien Calmet	BSC-CNS, Spain
Hank Childs	Lawrence Berkeley Laboratory, USA
Steffen Frey	University of Stuttgart, Germany
Jens Henrik Goebbert	Jülich Supercomputing Centre, Germany
Glendon Holst	KAUST, Saudi Arabia
Julien Jomier	Kitware, France
Joanna Leng	University of Leeds, UK
Samuel Li	National Center for Atmospheric Research, USA
Benson Muite	University of Tartu, Estonia
Joachim Pouderoux	Kitware, France

3 Workshop Summary

3.1 Invited Talks

In the first invited talk, David Keyes from King Abdullah University of Science and Technology (KAUST) shared his "Observations on the Role of Visualization in Large-scale Simulation". He presented the four paradigms for understanding (theory, experiment, simulation, big data) and discussed combining the third and fourth paradigms.

Next, Peter Messmer from NVidia talked about "In-situ vis in the age of HPC+AI" and projects at NVidia to meet these demands. He described how recent work in AI could be applied to solve in situ visualization problems like anomaly detection and classical visualization algorithms like marching cubes. He also described recent advances in image rendering and compression.

Jim Jeffers from Intel in his talk on "The Path Forward to In Situ Visualization At Scale" on the other hand described strategies at Intel towards in situ processing and visualization. He remarked that Exascale is at our doorstep, but that in situ is an HPC and not a Visualization problem. He called on the in situ visualization community to actively seek collaborations with computational scientists.

Finally, Matt Larsen from Lawrence Livermore National Laboratory (LLNL) talked about "The changing balance in HPC and in situ visualization challenges". In this talk he outlined some of the reasons and importance for employing in situ visualization in his work. He also described Ascent, a lightweight in situ visualization library he is developing.

3.2 Research Papers

Sanderson et al. in their paper "Coupling the Uintah Framework and the VisIt Toolkit for Parallel In Situ Data Analysis and Visualization and Computational Steering" have, coupled the Uintah Framework for simulation of chemical and physical reactions to the visualization tool VisIt. This allows scientists to perform parallel in situ visualization of simulation and runtime performance data. In addition they introduce to their simulation a dashboard to read/write parameters and present performance data that can be used to steer as well as debug a simulation.

Kress et al. in "Binning Based Data Reduction for Vector Field Data of a Particle-In-Cell Fusion Simulation" present a technique to drastically reduce the amount of particle data through an in situ data binning approach. Massive particle data is generated by a fusion simulation software at a rate of 0.5 TB per time step. The data binning approach produces twelve configurations from four different mesh sizes and three different particle sampling densities. They compare the associated errors of these data reductions with different tests such as streamline and pathline integration. With the best result, i.e the best compromise between data reduction and associated error, a reduction of the data set by a factor of 109 could be achieved while maintaining a low error percentage.

The paper "In Situ Analysis and Visualization of Fusion Simulations: Lessons Learned" by Kim et al. describes two setups for combining simulations using in situ processing for code-coupling and analysis. It sketches out the frameworks and technologies used to combine simulation, analysis, and visualization. The paper outlines two simulation campaigns, and discusses the gained experiences and lessons learned from performing in situ analysis and visualization.

Ono et al. in "Design of an In Transit Framework with Staging Buffer for Flexible Data Processing and Visualization of Time-Varying Data" describe an in transit visualization framework that is deployed on the ITO HPC system in Kyushu University. Using this framework, the HPC system comprises a powerful "back-end" for simulation runs, a less powerful but still very capable "front-end" for data processing and visualization, and a "client" from which users interact with the system. Thus, this paper presents a successful use of an in transit visualization system with the various considerations discussed being also applicable to in situ applications.

Sdeo et al. in "In-Situ Visualization of Solver Residual Fields" present an approach to visualize the operation of numerical solvers for field-based simulations in high-performance computing environments. Their motivation is to provide more information to the users and developers of such solvers than just the traditional residual. To this end, they first introduce the approach of residual field stacking and accumulation, which provides detailed insight into residual dynamics but does not lend itself for monitoring. Motivated by this limitation they introduce the concept of residual curves to monitor the dynamics of residual fields and demonstrate their technique at 2D flow simulation runs.

In "Streaming Live Neural Simulation Data Into Visualization and Analysis", Oehrl et al. describe an ad-hoc in situ pipeline for analysis and visualization of neuronal simulation data. They present a data model (NESCI) based on the Conduit technology, and a transport model (CONTRA) which they implemented for a shared memory context. Finally, they describe an application based on a NEST simulation which is analyzed and visualized using Matplotlib in 2D and VTK in 3D.

Marsaglia et al. in "Enabling Explorative Visualization With Full Temporal Resolution Via In Situ Calculation Of Temporal Intervals" presents a technique for performing in situ processing for spatio-temporal simulation. They use "compressor objects" designed to guarantee error bounds over temporal intervals. Finally, they present their findings on four different data sets from scientific simulations.

The last paper, "An In-Situ Visualization Approach for the K computer using Mesa 3D and KVS" by Hayashi et al., focuses on the utilization of Mesa 3D and the Kyoto Visualization Library in order to enable in situ visualization applications to run on the K computer. They describe some software engineering-level work to be successful on K, reporting on the frontline experiences that visualization practitioners at a large HPC center face.

Coupling the Uintah Framework and the VisIt Toolkit for Parallel In Situ Data Analysis and Visualization and Computational Steering

Allen Sanderson[1]([✉]), Alan Humphrey[1], John Schmidt[1], and Robert Sisneros[2]

[1] Scientific Imaging and Computing Institute, University of Utah, Salt Lake City, UT 84112, USA
{allen,ahumphrey,jas}@sci.utah.edu
[2] National Center for Supercomputing Applications, University of Illinois at Urbana-Champaign, Urbana, IL 61801, USA
sisneros@illinois.edu

Abstract. Data analysis and visualization are an essential part of the scientific discovery process. As HPC simulations have grown, I/O has become a bottleneck, which has required scientists to turn to in situ tools for simulation data exploration. Incorporating additional data, such as runtime performance data, into the analysis or I/O phases of a workflow is routinely avoided for fear of excaberting performance issues. The paper presents how the Uintah Framework, a suite of HPC libraries and applications for simulating complex chemical and physical reactions, was coupled with VisIt, an interactive analysis and visualization toolkit, to allow scientists to perform parallel in situ visualization of simulation and runtime performance data. An additional benefit of the coupling made it possible to create a "simulation dashboard" that allowed for in situ computational steering and visual debugging.

Keywords: In situ visualization · Runtime performance data
Visual debugging · Computational steering

1 Introduction

When discussing techniques for in situ visualization, the focus is typically on the infrastructure for efficiently utilizing the simulation data generated by the application. However, other more ephemeral data is also of interest. We define ephemeral data as that which is generated by the application, optionally written to disk for post hoc analysis, but not otherwise saved or utilized by the application in subsequent time steps. Examples of ephemeral data include in situ simulation analysis (i.e., analysis routines that are directly incorporated into the application) and runtime performance data. For the work presented in this paper, it is this data and the infrastructure required for efficiently utilizing it that are of primary interest.

© Springer Nature Switzerland AG 2018
R. Yokota et al. (Eds.): ISC 2018 Workshops, LNCS 11203, pp. 201–214, 2018.
https://doi.org/10.1007/978-3-030-02465-9_14

We also introduce the concept of a simulation dashboard to present parameters and resulting performance data that may be used to control or drive the simulation. The parameters are supplied to the application by the user as part of the *Uintah Problem Specification*. Measured performance data is rarely written to disk and is therefore an excellent target for incorporation in an in situ framework.

In the context of in situ terminology [8], we are interested in data access, and more specifically how the application makes data available to the in situ infrastructure. Because of the heterogeneity of the data generated and parameters utilized by the application, different approaches were required. In some cases, direct access was possible. In other cases, data access was accomplished via a series of lightweight data structures and wrappers. The lightweight data structures replaced the previous infrastructure within the Uintah framework, and the wrappers were used when it was necessary to work within the current infrastructure.

2 Background

In this paper, we present a hybrid approach that intersects the state-of-the-practice in in situ data analysis and visualization with the use of collected runtime performance data. In this section the foundational background for in situ techniques is outlined, followed by a description of the state-of-the-practice in utilizing diagnostic data in general, of which runtime performance data is a subset.

2.1 In Situ Data Analysis and Visualization

The integration of visualization in HPC workflows relies heavily on supported software. The visualization software staples at HPC centers are those that are open-source, actively developed, and scalable. The difficulties arising from large-scale computing as well as the expected inadequacy of postprocessing due to overwhelming data sizes are well documented [12,13]. So far, the accepted answer for these challenges, with respect to data analysis and visualization, is in situ processing [4,8,19].

The standard software suites for data analysis and visualization, VisIt [9] and ParaView [16], offer in situ libraries [5,11,28] in addition to client/server execution models, batch mode processing, and a complete scripting interface. In this work, we instrument the Uintah framework using VisIt's in situ library, *libsim* [28]. Although not quite a middleware approach [10], our implementation does indeed alleviate some of the burden associated with libsim's tightly coupled instrumentation. We direct the interested reader to a state-of-the-practice report [6] for additional, general details regarding in situ techniques.

2.2   Utilization of Diagnostic Data

At the two ends of the HPC community are the large computing hardware and the users who run applications on them. Between are the systems administrators and engineers who maintain that hardware and are focused on maximizing throughput of users' codes, and is critical given the cost of operation of these large machines. Monitoring system diagnostic data can benefit this effort in a number of ways, and there are many systems in place to do so [1–3,20].

The tendency toward heavily visual systems as well as the common visual paradigms bolster motivation for inclusion of system visualizations we use in this work. In particular, we integrate a visualization of the high-speed network fabric favoring a machine layout [27] over purely graphical representations [15,25]. A defining differentiation of this work is its in situ deployment. The tools and approaches mentioned above rely on mechanisms of collecting, storing, and retrieving stored data external to the application; see OVIS [7] for a representative framework. We sidestep this approach and do it within the application because these external tools can not tap into Uintah's custom debugging streams in the way presented in this paper, which at times is the best and only way to get Uintah-specific diagnostic data.

Furthermore, in this case there is an uncommon, but natural coupling of diagnostic data to scientific simulation data that has allowed us to create novel visualizations leveraging this coupling. That is, we view system diagnostic data in both spatial contexts: job layout on the machine as well as compute layout on the simulation mesh. While there are examples of recent work visualizing diagnostic data on the mesh [14], even in situ [29], frameworks serving such data are still reliant on an additional data management solutions, i.e. databases. In such situations the flexible, user-defined data we serve in situ is not as practical.

3   Methods

One of the objectives of this research was to efficiently communicating ephemeral data, data that is typically not visualized or otherwise presented to the user in an in situ framework. To accomplish this objective, lightweight data structures and wrappers were developed and deployed that allowed for direct memory access to the data. The lightweight data structures replaced existing data collection and storage structures in Uintah to reference simulation parameters and global analysis data in a minimally intrusive manner.

3.1   Per-Rank Runtime Performance Data

Per-rank runtime performance may be collected by different parts of the application infrastructure at different stages of the execution path and written to disk for post hoc analysis. Within the Uintah infrastructure runtime performance data is collected by the simulation controller, memory manager, scheduler, load balancer, AMR regridder, and data archiver (I/O). The data collected range from memory usage to MPI wait times. In addition, the Uintah application also collects runtime performance data that is specific to the simulation physics, such as the solver performance.

Gaining access to runtime performance data for in situ communication required that the data be collected centrally and in a generic manner. To facilitate the centralized collection of data, we leveraged Uintah's Common Component Architecture [17]. The simulation controller is the central component in Uintah and interfaces with all of the other underlying infrastructure components (Scheduler, Load Balancer, I/O, etc.) as well as the application component. As the central component, the simulation controller owned and shared the runtime performance data collected with all of the other components.

Data Collection. To manage the collecting of the per-rank runtime performance data, we created an extended map class. Maps are associative containers that are a combination of a key value and a mapped value. Our extended class maintained the core map abstraction while allowing for generic indexed based access. This allowed the Uintah infrastructure to continue to have the flexibility to utilize a key value, in this case an enumerator specific to the runtime performance measure. When the data needed to be communicated to VisIt, the indexed-based access method was utilized. Iterators were not used as they required the key value type, which was not available to middleware utilized between Uintah and VisIt.

The collecting of runtime performance data was done on a per-rank basis, allowing utilization of our extended map class. However, it was also useful to present global values. To address this need, global MPI reduce operations were built into the extended map class. The Uintah infrastructure also supports multithreading, which required a reduction over the shared resource on each node. To facilitate this reduction, the extended map class also incorporated a MPI reduce that utilized a split communicator based on the ranks on each node (i.e., all ranks on a node had the same communicator). These reduced values could then be accessed as additional node-level mapped values in our extended map class.

Spatial Granularity. Now that the runtime performance data could be collected and reduced at different processor levels, we address the issue of visualizing the data at different spatial granularities. The global values could be shown in a tabular fashion or as a series of strip charts as part of the simulation dashboard (see Sect. 3.2). Of greater interest was the ability to visualize the runtime performance data.

The Uintah infrastructure utilizes a patch-based structured grid. Each patch contains multiple cells and is assigned to a specific rank. This patch-rank assignment was used to map the runtime performance data to the simulation mesh with all patches on the same rank displaying the same value (Fig. 1a). In a similar fashion, the per-node runtime performance data was also mapped to the simulation mesh with all patches on the same node displaying the same value (Fig. 1b).

(a) (b)

Fig. 1. A simple visualization of (a) the per-rank task execution times for 192 ranks and (b) the per-node task execution times for nine nodes mapped onto the simulation mesh (Blue - fast, Red - slow). Of the nine nodes, eight nodes were 20-core nodes, and one node was a 12-core node. Thus the summed time for the 12-core node, in blue is substantially less than the other nodes. (Color figure online)

The ability to map the runtime performance data to the simulation mesh at different granularities allowed us to check the mesh layout against the raw performance statistics reported (e.g., load balancing, communication patterns, etc.) and provided insight not usually possible. For instance, the ability to see the patch layout on particular ranks gave insight into the load balancer assignment.

It was also possible to gain insight by visualizing runtime performance data using the physical machine layout. For instance, the runs presented were done on a heterogeneous HPC system comprised of 253 - 12 core nodes, 164 - 20 core nodes, and 48 - 24 core nodes (7468 total cores) connected using an InfiniBand network (For Figs. 1, 2, 3, 4, eight 20 core nodes and one 12 core node were used). To obtain the network layout, the 'ibnetdiscover' command was utilized to discover the InfiniBand subnet, which was then visualized based on the switch connections (Fig. 2).

Via a series MPI queries, a mapping between the nodes and cores being utilized by Uintah and the machine layout was created (Fig. 2).

Utilizing this mapping and the ability to easily collect rank based runtime performance data using our new map class, performance data could now be visualized using the machine layout. As with the simulation mesh, both the per-rank and per-node runtime performance data could be mapped directly to the machine layout (Figs. 3, 4). Visualizing the runtime performance data on the machine layout gave insight into how the machine layout affected the runtime performance, for instance, which ranks or tasks were taking the most time for MPI waits or parallel collections.

Per-Task Runtime Performance Data. The Uintah runtime infrastructure utilizes dynamic task scheduling for its execution [22]. For a typical CFD simulation, 10 to 50 tasks were assigned uniformly to each patch across the domain. These tasks may be created by the simulation (e.g., solver) or the infrastructure (e.g., I/O) and are able to monitor their runtime performance in the form of

Nodes

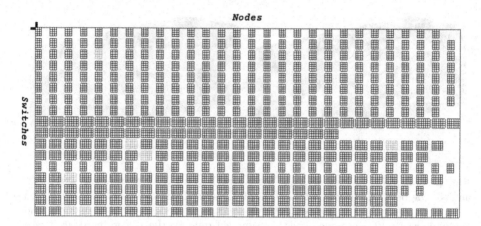

Fig. 2. A visualization of the machine layout based on the switch connections. Each row represents a switch (17 total), each block represents a processor node, and each cell within a block represents a core. Highlighted in red are the nine nodes and 192 ranks used by the simulation. (Color figure online)

Nodes

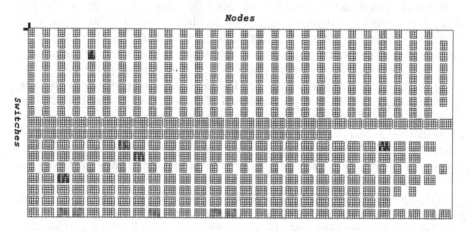

Fig. 3. A visualization of the per-rank task execution time for 192 ranks mapped onto the machine layout (Blue - fast, Red - slow). Compare the figure to the same times mapped onto the simulation mesh in Fig. 1a. (Color figure online)

execution and wait times. These times can be saved as a series of per-task/per-rank text files for later post hoc analysis, but previously were not otherwise visualized.

To facilitate access to this data for in situ visualization, a map structure utilizing two keys was constructed. The first key mapped the task and the second key mapped the patch. Taking advantage of Uintah's one-to-one mapping between patches and tasks visualizing the per-task runtime performance data in situ on the simulation mesh was a straightforward process. Visualizing the

Nodes

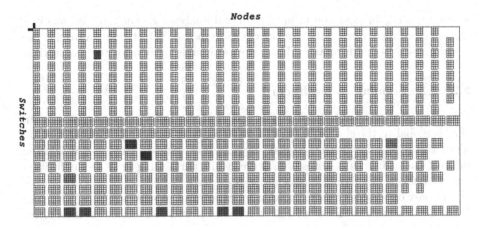

Fig. 4. A visualization of the per-node task execution times mapped onto the machine layout (Blue - fast, Red - slow). Compare the figure to the same times mapped onto the simulation mesh in Fig. 1b. (Color figure online)

per-task runtime performance data on the simulation mesh gave users the ability to understand hot spots and their possible cause, for instance, the time between the end of the execution of one task to the beginning of the execution of the next task for each thread (Fig. 5a).

If desired, the per-task runtime performance data could also be summed over all tasks for each patch. For instance, the sum of task exection times utilized by Uintah's load balancer's dynamic cost modeler [18], that previously, had not been possible to visualize (Fig. 5b). With the implementation of this map, users were able to visualize these sums and see load imbalances.

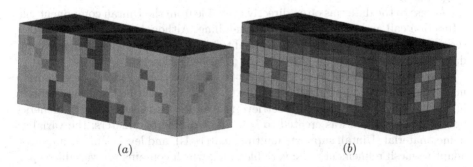

(a)   (b)

Fig. 5. A simple visualization of (a) the per patch task wait times and (b) the per patch load balancer costs for 1344 patches (Blue - fast, Red - slow). (Color figure online)

Initially, the per-task runtime performance data was accessed only for in situ visualization. However, after seeing the utility of visualizing this data, users requested that the data be stored in Uintah's data warehouse [21] so it could be written to disk for post hoc visualization and analysis. As such, a task was created to store the collected data in the data warehouse. Which being a task, it too could monitor its performance. Thus, it was possible to monitor the monitoring.

3.2   The Simulation Dashboard

When performing in situ visualization, it is often desirable to have access to data that is global to the simulation, such as the reduced runtime performance data, all of which may be written to disk for post hoc analysis. However, it is often impractical to analyze a series of text files while performing in situ visualization and therefore a simulation dashboard was created.

As part of VisIt's *libsim* [28], an application can provide a Qt [24] Designer XML file defining a series of widgets that can be used to generate an interactive user interface on the fly. This user interface forms the basis for the simulation dashboard and is fully customizable by the user. Communication from the application to VisIt was accomplished through an interface function that, in general, requires little more than the widget name and a value. Communication from VisIt to the application was accomplished via callback functions that were registered by the application during the in situ initialization process.

General Simulation Data. When running a simulation, a plethora of data can be reported to the user. Some of the data may be read-only or may be read-/write. When the data is read/write, a callback function is required to update the values. Examples of read-only data are the simulation time and time increment (Fig. 7b(1)). Read-only data also includes wall time intervals (Fig. 7b(3)) and AMR grid information (Fig. 7b(6)). Examples of read/write data are the simulation time increments in which the user can change most all of the values (Fig. 7b(2)).

Access to the data was often directly available from the Uintah component via a function call and required no special handling. Although simple, it required a series of singular calls to VisIt, as opposed to looping through a list of lightweight data structures pointing to the data (as described below).

Uintah also contains in situ methods to calculate both general, (e.g., min/-max) and simulation specific values, (e.g., total momentum) that are stored in Uintah's data warehouse. To retrieve the values for in situ usage, a generic lightweight structure was created to hold the required parameters; the variable name, material (Uintah supports multiple materials), and level (Uintah supports adaptive mesh refinement), the variable label, which contains the variable type, (e.g., scalar or vector) and the variable reduction type, (e.g., min, max, or sum).

An application developer coding an analysis module utilized the lightweight structure to wrap the values of interest. This structure was then registered with the in situ middleware when the analysis module was initialized. At the end of each time step, the situ interface looped through each registered structure, retrieved the analysis data from the data warehouse, and passed it on to VisIt to display (Fig. 7b(5)).

Strip Charts. In addition to a tabular display of analysis data (Fig. 7b(5)) and runtime performance data (Fig. 8a(1–3)), visualizations over time are possible using a series of multivalued strip charts (Fig. 6). Although integral to the simulation, the strip charts were not integrated into the simulation dashboard but were instead integrated into VisIt's simulation control window for generiazed use by expanding VisIt's in situ interface to manage strip charts and utilized the QWT [26] library's 2D plotting widget.

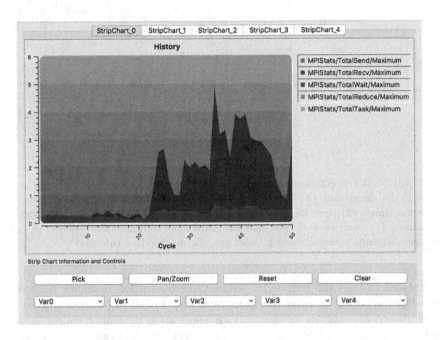

Fig. 6. A strip chart showing MPI runtime performance stats over 50 time steps.

Computational Steering. Computational steering allows the user to modify simulation parameters on the fly to change a simulation's outcome [23]. As noted above, data such as the simulation time increment is read/write and thus can be interactively modified by the user. Although computational steering is not typically available in in situ frameworks, it is a natural extension. One of the goals of in situ visualization is to provide real-time feedback to the user, which can then be used to interactively steer the computation.

Uintah simulations are defined via a series of parameters that are part of the *Uintah Problem Specification*. These parameters are used to describe the initial simulation and are typically not changed during the life of the simulation, but may be tuned beforehand via a series of exploration runs.

Changing some of the variables may have side effects, such as requiring new tasks to be performed and forcing the task graph to be recompiled [18]. To facilitate the modification of these parameters in situ, a lightweight structure

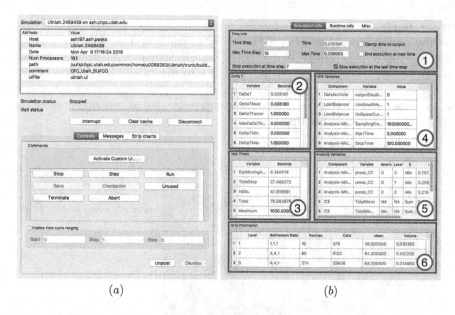

(a)   (b)

Fig. 7. (a) VisIt's simulation control window, which allows the user to issue commands to the simulation. (b) The simulation dashboard with general information; (1) simulation times, (2) time stepping, (3) wall times, (4) Uintah problem specification parameters, (5) analysis variables, and (6) AMR information. Values shown in light gray are read-only, whereas those in black may be modified by the user.

was created to hold the parameter name, type description, memory reference, and a flag indicating whether the task graph would need to be recompiled.

Similar to an analysis component, an application developer coding a simulation component utilized the lightweight structure to wrap the parameter. This structure was then registered with the in situ middleware when the component was initialized. At the beginning of each time step, the situ interface looped through each registered structure, retrieved the simulation parameter, and passed it to Uintah, where it was utilized for the subsequent time step (Fig. 7b(4)).

Visual Debugging. As part of VisIt's Simulation window, it is possible for the user to issue commands to the simulation to stop, run, step, save, checkpoint, abort, etc., the simulation (Fig. 7a). These commands are defined by the simulation and give the user some level of control. However, when debugging, the user may want finer grained control. For instance, for a simulation that is known to crash at particular time step, the user may want to stop the simulation just before that time step and begin debugging (Fig. 7b(1)). This ability is especially important because the overall state of the application would be maintained as long as possible, thus not perturbing the debug condition.

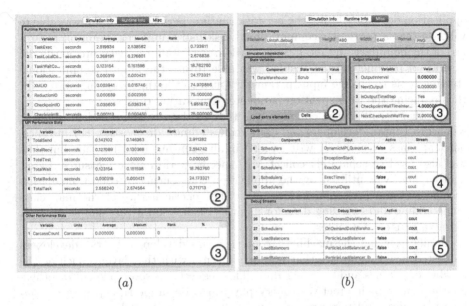

(a)   (b)

Fig. 8. The simulation dashboard with (a) runtime performance data; (1) infrastructure, (2) MPI, and (3) application specific, and (b) other information; (1) image generation, (2) state variables, (3) output and checkpointing frequency, and (4) and (5) debug streams. Values shown in light gray are read-only, whereas those in black may be modified by the user.

Debugging may require changing the output frequency, turning on debug streams, (e.g., text-based output), or exposing intermediate data values. To facilitate access to the debug streams, they were rewritten to self-register when constructed. Once registered, the debug streams can then be accessed by the in situ interface via a centralized list (Fig. 8b(4–5)).

To expose state variables, the lightweight structure developed for exposing the *Uintah Problem Specification* parameters was utilized (Fig. 8b(2)). One such state variable controlled the scrubbing of intermediate variables from Uintah's data warehouse. To reduce memory, intermediate variables not needed for checkpointing are deleted at the completion of a time step and not normally visualized. However, visualizing these variables can be an important part of code verification.

4   Results

The main result of coupling the Uintah Framework with the VisIt toolkit is allowing for Uintah developers and users to visualize and explore empheral data. For instance, Uintah infrastructure developers using per-rank runtime performance data were for the first time able to visualize the load balancing on the simulation mesh and machine layout insteading of resorting to text output. A Uintah application developer, using the per-task runtime performance data, was able to validate that a particular computational task had a uniform execution regardless of the boundary and mesh configuration. A Uintah user, who previously did a series of parameter runs, instead was able to use the in situ computational steering tools to change input parameters such as the time stepping on the fly, thus reducing the time spent on parameter exploration runs.

Another result of the coupling was that as data was exposed in different scenarios, Uintah developers and users requested new diagnostics. For instance, our map class was initially written for Uintah's runtime infrastructure but then was also used to separately collect MPI-specific performance measures. Later, another map was utilized by the application components to collect simulation specific runtime performance measures. The generic nature of the map class made adding and exposing data for in situ visualization a very simple process, taking a matter of minutes.

Similarly, when the machine layout view was developed, Uintah developers requested new diagnostics that only made sense with that layout, such as the number of patches and tasks per rank. This request was soon followed by others for the ability to interactively query physical node properties such as the on-board memory and temperature. At the same time, the lightweight wrappers made adding and exposing parameters for computational steering a very simple process. Users could add the needed code in a matter of minutes, re-run their simulation, and interactively explore while asking "what if questions."

From a more practical point of view, code maintainability became easier when it was necessary to modify the Uintah infrastructure, whether for new data collections or for managing debug streams. At the same time, it became clear that visualization developers needed to have a more integral role in the development of the Uintah Framework.

5   Conclusion

In this paper, we have presented work to couple the Uintah Framework with the VisIt toolkit to allow scientists to perform parallel in situ analysis and visualization of runtime performance data and other ephemeral data. Unique to the system is the ability to view the data in different spatial contexts: job layout on the machine and the compute layout on the simulation mesh. We have also introduced the concept of a "simulation dashboard" to allow for in situ computational steering and visual debugging. The coupling relied on incorporating lightweight data structures and wrappers in a minimally intrusive manner into Uintah to access the data and communicate it to VisIt's in situ library.

In several cases, the Uintah developers found the infrastructure changes to be beneficial beyond the need for in situ communication. The developers were able to collect data more easily and visualize it in ways not previously possible thus gaining new insight.

From this experience, two lessons were learned, the coupling of a simulation to an in-situ framework will require changes to its infrastructure, and is a chance to re-evaluate previous design decisions. When infrastructure changes are not possible, other mechanisms such as lightweight wrappers are key.

Going forward, as more ephemeral data is collected and communicated to the in situ framework scalability will need to be assured. In addition, the collection and communication of emphermal data must continue to have a minimal impact on the simulation physics. For instance, currently there is litte impact on memory resources when compared to those being used by the simulation physics. However, that could certainly change as additional diagnostics are incorporated.

Acknowledgment. This material was based upon work supported by the Department of Energy, National Nuclear Security Administration, under Award Number(s) DE-NA0002375. The authors wish to thank the Uintah and VisIt development groups.

Disclaimer. This report was prepared as an account of work sponsored by an agency of the United States Government. The views and opinions of authors expressed herein do not necessarily state or reflect those of the United States Government or any agency thereof.

References

1. Bright-computing cluster manager. http://www.brightcomputing.com/Bright-Cluster-Manager.php
2. Cacti. http://www.cacti.net/
3. Nagios. http://www.nagios.com/
4. Ahern, S., et al.: Scientific discovery at the exascale. Report from the DOE ASCR 2011 Workshop on Exascale. Data Management (2011)
5. Ayachit, U., et al.: ParaView catalyst: enabling in situ data analysis and visualization. In: Proceedings of the First Workshop on In Situ Infrastructures for Enabling Extreme-Scale Analysis and Visualization, pp. 25–29. ACM (2015)
6. Bauer, A.C., et al.: In situ methods, infrastructures, and applications on high performance computing platforms. Comput. Graph. Forum **35**, 577–597 (2016)
7. Brandt, J., et al.: The OVIS analysis architecture. Sandia Report SAND2010-5107, Sandia National Laboratories (2010)
8. Childs, H.: The in situ terminology project. http://ix.cs.uoregon.edu/~hank/insituterminology. Accessed 06 Apr 2018
9. Childs, H., et al.: VisIt: an end-user tool for visualizing and analyzing very large data. In: High Performance Visualization-Enabling Extreme-Scale Scientific Insight, pp. 357–372. CRC Press, October 2012
10. Dorier, M., Sisneros, R., Peterka, T., Antoniu, G., Semeraro, D.: Damaris/Viz: a nonintrusive, adaptable and user-friendly in situ visualization framework. In: 2013 IEEE Symposium on Large-Scale Data Analysis and Visualization (LDAV), pp. 67–75. IEEE (2013)
11. Fabian, N., et al.: The ParaView coprocessing library: a scalable, general purpose in situ visualization library. In: 2011 IEEE Symposium on Large Data Analysis and Visualization (LDAV), pp. 89–96. IEEE (2011)
12. Geist, A., Lucas, R.: Major computer science challenges at exascale. Int. J. High Perform. Comput. Appl. **23**(4), 427–436 (2009)
13. Hoisie, A., Getov, V.: Extreme-scale computing - where 'just more of the same' does not work. Computer **42**(11), 24–26 (2009)

14. Huck, K.A., Potter, K., Jacobsen, D.W., Childs, H., Malony, A.D.: Linking performance data into scientific visualization tools. In: 2014 First Workshop on Visual Performance Analysis, pp. 50–57 (2014)
15. Isaacs, K.E., Landge, A.G., Gamblin, T., Bremer, P.-T., Pascucci, V., Hamann, B.: Exploring performance data with boxfish. In: 2012 SC Companion High Performance Computing, Networking, Storage and Analysis (SCC), pp. 1380–1381. IEEE (2012)
16. KitWare. ParaView. http://www.paraview.org/
17. Kumfert, G., et al.: How the common component architecture advances computational science. J. Phys.: Conf. Ser. **46**(1), 479 (2006)
18. Luitjens, J., Berzins, M.: Improving the performance of Uintah: a large-scale adaptive meshing computational framework. In: Proceedings of the 2010 IEEE International Symposium on Parallel and Distributed Processing, IPDPS 2010, pp. 1–10, May 2010
19. Ma, K.-L.: In situ visualization at extreme scale: challenges and opportunities. IEEE Comput. Graph. Appl. **29**(6), 14–19 (2009)
20. Massie, M.L., Chun, B.N., Culler, D.E.: The ganglia distributed monitoring system: design, implementation, and experience. Parallel Comput. **30**(7), 817–840 (2004)
21. Meng, Q., Berzins, M.: Scalable large-scale fluid-structure interaction solvers in the Uintah framework via hybrid task-based parallelism algorithms. Concurr. Comput.: Pract. Exp. **26**, 1388–1407 (2014)
22. Meng, Q., Luitjens, J., Berzins, M.: Dynamic task scheduling for the Uintah framework. In: 2010 3rd Workshop on Many-Task Computing on Grids and Supercomputers, pp. 1–10 (2010)
23. Mulder, J.D., van Wijk, J.J., van Liere, R.: A survey of computational steering environments. Future Gener. Comput. Syst. **15**(1), 119–129 (1999)
24. Nord, H., Chambe-Eng, E.: The Qt company. https://www.qt.io. Accessed 06 Apr 2018
25. Padron, O., Semeraro, D.: TorusVis: a topology data visualization tool (2014)
26. Rathmann, U., Wilgen, J.: Qwt user's guide. http://qwt.sourceforge.net. Accessed 06 Apr 2018
27. Sisneros, R., Chadalavada, K.: Toward understanding congestion protection events on blue waters via visual analytics. In: Proceedings of the Cray User Group meeting (2014)
28. Whitlock, B., Favre, J.M., Meredith, J.S.: Parallel in situ coupling of simulation with a fully featured visualization system. In: Proceedings of the 11th Eurographics Conference on ParallelGraphics and Visualization, EGPGV 2011, Aire-la-Ville, Switzerland, pp. 101–109. Eurographics Association (2011)
29. Wood, C., Larsen, M., Gimenez, A., Harrison, C., Gamblin, T., Malony, A.: Projecting performance data over simulation geometry using SOSflow and ALPINE. In: 2017 Forth Workshop on Visual Performance Analysis, pp. 1–8, November 2017

Binning Based Data Reduction for Vector Field Data of a Particle-In-Cell Fusion Simulation

James Kress[1,2(✉)], Jong Choi[1], Scott Klasky[1], Michael Churchill[3], Hank Childs[2], and David Pugmire[1]

[1] Oak Ridge National Laboratory, Oak Ridge, TN 37831, USA
kressjm@ornl.gov
[2] University of Oregon, Eugene, OR 97403, USA
[3] Princeton Plasma Physics Laboratory, Princeton, NJ 08543, USA

Abstract. With this work, we explore the feasibility of using in situ data binning techniques to achieve significant data reductions for particle data, and study the associated errors for several post-hoc analysis techniques. We perform an application study in collaboration with fusion simulation scientists on data sets up to 489 GB per time step. We consider multiple ways to carry out the binning, and determine which techniques work the best for this simulation. With the best techniques we demonstrate reduction factors as large as 109x with low error percentage.

Keywords: In situ · Data reduction · Visualization

1 Introduction

As leading-edge supercomputers get increasingly powerful, scientific simulations running on these machines are generating ever larger volumes of data. However, the increasing cost of data movement, in particular moving data to disk, limits the ability to process, analyze, and fully comprehend simulation results [1]. Specifically, while I/O bandwidths regularly increase with each new supercomputer, they are well below corresponding increases in computational ability and data generated. Further, this trend is predicted to persist for the foreseeable future.

Given this reality, many large-scale simulation codes are attempting to bypass the I/O bottleneck by using in situ visualization and analysis, i.e., processing simulation data when it is generated. In situ processing can be difficult however, as it is generally not known a priori all of the analysis tasks that will be done on simulation output. One method supporting unanticipated analysis, or exploration, is to produce a reduced representation which can be written to disk. Examples of data reductions include compression techniques (both lossy and

© Springer Nature Switzerland AG 2018
R. Yokota et al. (Eds.): ISC 2018 Workshops, LNCS 11203, pp. 215–229, 2018.
https://doi.org/10.1007/978-3-030-02465-9_15

lossless), reduced precision representations, data subsets and extracts, spatial resampling, and summary data. Here care must be taken in order to preserve the information content in the data while at the same time, minimizing the size.

With this research, we consider the model where in situ processing is used to produce an information preserving reduced data representation of the simulation data that can be saved to disk. This reduced representation data can then be used for post processing analysis, visualization, and exploration. Additionally, we evaluate the errors introduced when doing a variety of analysis and visualization operations on these reduced data representations.

In this paper we apply this in situ model to XGC1 [3], a plasma fusion simulation code that runs at scale on supercomputers. XGC1 is a gyrokinetic particle-in-cell code that is used for modeling the physics of plasmas in fusion tokamak devices. XGC1 uses a large number of particles to represent the kinetic behavior of the plasma. Summarizations of these particles are imposed upon an unstructured grid, which is small enough that it can be saved to disk. Currently, the particles, which are the representation of the plasma, are too large to save out at each time step.

In this paper we study and apply multiple data binning techniques to these particles to extract a vector field representation from the individual particle trajectories. The resulting vector field, which is orders of magnitude smaller than the entire set of particles, can be easily saved to disk and used for post processing analysis and visualization. To evaluate this method, we use streamlines and Poincaré analysis using particle advection on the vector field representations for the full and reduced representation data, and examine the errors associated with different binning techniques. One of the best binning techniques operates on 500 GB of data per time step, achieving a reduction of 109x with an average error of 1.15% in under 140 s.

In the remainder of this paper, we discuss related works in Sect. 2, describe the binning of fusion particle data in Sect. 3, describe our in situ workflow in Sect. 4, and present the results from our analyses in Sect. 5.

2   Related Work

We present the related work for information preserving in situ data reduction and visualization of particles in three sub-categories: (1) in situ visualization, (2) XGC1 visualization, and (3) large-scale particle visualizations.

2.1   In Situ Visualization

Visualization algorithms are particularly sensitive to I/O bandwidth [4,5], causing the community to turn to in situ techniques to alleviate this growing problem. There has been significant work and successes with the in situ visualization paradigm. For instance, ParaView Catalyst coprocessing [6] and VisIt LibSim [22] are frameworks that are tightly-coupled to the simulation, i.e, the visualization runs at scale with the simulation. Alternatively, visualization and analytics can be performed during the transport of the simulation data to the I/O layer. Three examples of this loosely coupled approach are Nessie [16], GLEAN [21], and ADIOS [11]. For a more thorough overview of the three loosely-coupled in situ visualization frameworks, we refer the reader to [2].

2.2 XGC1 Visualization

Early work on production visualization for XGC1 mainly focused on addressing the immediate data needs of scientists during the course of a simulation run. One example of this was an online dashboard that was developed for XGC1 simulation monitoring called eSimon [20]. This dashboard was launched in conjunction with each simulation run, and was responsible for performing common visualization and analysis tasks in XGC1.

More recent work has focused on expanding the visualization capabilities and opportunities for XGC1 through the utilization of in situ methods. For example, they utilized the features of ADIOS and EAVL [17], and demonstrated the effectiveness of loosely coupled in situ visualization for large scale simulation codes using a workflow with dedicated data staging nodes. In that work, they focused on the performance, scalability, and ease of use of visualization plugins that were used on the output of the XGC1 simulation code. One component of this study looked at optimizing the parallel rendering pipeline in situ, and gave insight into getting high performing renderings in continuing studies.

Recent research with XGC1 has cataloged their common visualization and analysis tasks, analyzed their workflow, and captured common data sizes produced by the simulation [8], in an effort to prepare for their challenges at exascale. Further research has also done preliminary work at identifying areas of interest and some of the challenges associated with information preserving data reductions within XGC1 [7]. This work points out how data reductions must be done carefully in order to preserve the integrity of the underlying data when post-hoc analysis will need to generate derived quantities from reduced data. These derivations can end up with completely inaccurate information if data reductions are not done carefully.

2.3 Large-Scale Particle Visualization

There have been several works in recent years that focus on visualizing large-scale particle data sets. The first set of works that will be described tackle this problem as a post-hoc task. The first work looked at the visualization of trillion particle data sets, and utilized a multi-scale rendering architecture which enabled hierarchical views of the data [19]. This approach enabled interactive speeds for users exploring and querying the dataset. A second example utilized bandlimited OLAP cubes which were based on kernel density plots [18]. This approach created an artifact free visualization at interactive speeds. The defining characteristics of these two techniques however, are that they are post-hoc, requiring the full particle data set to be saved to disk, so they did not address our need for in situ data reduction.

Another approach is to consider particle visualization as an in situ task. One approach in this area was to use spatially organized 2D histograms for viewing large data set in situ [15]. This work looked at several different application domains and was able to demonstrate that features within the data could be visualized by creating many different histograms for different regions of the data. This approach is similar to ours in that it creates a velocity representation. That said, it does not describe data reduction results, or if the histograms could be used for more than just visualization, such as post-hoc analysis. A second approach performs two different steps in situ to first create probability distribution functions and then a second step to specially reorganize particles for faster post-hoc access [23]. The difference between this work and our current work is that they are still saving subsets of particles. We are utilizing all of the simulation's particles in creating our data representations, which reduces the data that we have to save. Further, this technique currently lacks an analysis of the errors introduced through their subsampling process on post-hoc visualization and analysis routines.

All of these techniques are interesting reduction operators. That said, our domain scientist collaborators are interested in binning since the code already uses a finite element mesh internally for some calculations, and so our study focused on tradeoffs within binning. Comparisons with other techniques is an interesting topic for future work.

3   Binning of Fusion Data

Fusion scientists for the XGC1 fusion simulation are interested in looking at particle data coming from the simulation at a finer temporal fidelity than is currency possible in a post-hoc workflow. In the post-hoc workflow particle data is only saved out at each of the simulation checkpoints, which only occur between every 100 and 1,000 time steps [8], leaving a large temporal gap. This gap reduces the fidelity of their analysis techniques and leaves the very real possibility that something interesting in the data will be lost due to the turbulent nature of the data. Historically however, this temporal gap was necessary due to the shear size of the particle data at each time step, which is up to 20 TB.

To address the issue of the large temporal gap, some sort of in situ data reduction technique is required for this workflow due to both the size of the data generated per time step, and the short amount of time between individual time steps. To overcome this issue we created a workflow for the in situ application of a data binning technique to the particle data from the simulation. This binning technique generates vectors in each of the bins that represents the speed and direction of particles within that cell's region. Furthermore, this technique allows the scientists to tune the binning code for both specific accuracy and speed requirements by modifying the size of the binning grid, and the number of particles used to extract the vector field.

3.1   Generating the Binned Data

In creating this vector field, there are two different control points for tuning the accuracy of the vector representation: (1) the size of the binning mesh, and (2) the number of particles sampled from the simulation to extract the vector field.

In this paper we looked at four different mesh sizes and three different particle sampling counts for each of the four mesh representations.

Mesh Representations. An unstructured mesh representation was used for this study. Figure 1 shows an example of the representation. The reduced representations of the unstructured mesh were generated by performing a quadratic clustering decimation on the unstructured mesh from the XGC1 simulation itself, and setting the number of divisions argument for the clustering to be equal for height and width.

The five different mesh sizes used are shown in Table 1. In this study we use the original mesh as our *Ground Truth Mesh* comparator against the four reduced representations. We chose these reduced mesh sizes in order to have a spectrum of reduced mesh cell sizes which reduces the amount of work required to generate the vector representations, saving time during the in situ calculation.

Fig. 1. Example of the unstructured mesh used. The unstructured mesh is a decimated version of the simulation mesh.

Table 1. A Breakdown of the four reduced mesh sizes used in the study compared to the original simulation mesh. The reduced meshes were generated using quadratic clustering. The dimensions used by quadratic clustering are listed in the left-hand column.

		Number of cells	Percent reduction
Unstructured mesh	45×45	2,903	98.6%
	90×90	11,154	94.7%
	200×200	52,707	74.9%
	450×450	186,609	1.1%
	Original	209,576	0.0%

Sampling Particles. Due to the size of the particle data generated by the simulation at each time step, it was important to perform a subsample operation on the simulation particle data to reduce the number of particles transfered from the simulation to our binning routines. We used three different particle counts in our tests in order to get a sampling of the spectrum in terms of vector representation accuracy and speed. The three particle counts we used in our subselection operation were: 3 million, 30 million, and 300 million. Each of these values represents an order of magnitude reduction from the total particle count at each simulation time step, which is 3.3 billion.

The particle subsampling was performed by uniformly selecting particles from the original XGC1 mesh. Table 2 shows a breakdown of the statistics for each of these three particle selections.

Table 2. A breakdown of each of the different factors of merit for the three reduced particle counts we tested. The final output of our method is the "Binned Data" and its size is always the same, as the binning grid was fixed.

Total particles	Particle reduction amount	Reduced particle size (GB)	Particle subselection time (sec)	Binning time (sec)	Binned data size (MB)
3M	1092x	0.609	15	67	89
30M	109x	2.0	25	115	89
300M	11x	18.0	40	345	89

Two of the most important values from this table is the amount of data reduction, and the binning time. The amount of data reduction represents the data reduction size on disk of the subsampled particles versus the size of all of the particles on disk. The binning time is the amount of time that it took to create our binned data representation after the data subsampling took place. This number can be fine tuned during a simulation run to be lower or higher based on the vector accuracy needs, and the amount of time available to perform the binning transformation. Even when only performing a one order of magnitude reduction on the number of particles and subselecting 300 million particles it only took a maximum of 345 s to create the binned representation, which lies within the average time per time step for XGC1 at full scale, which lies between 5 to 10 min [8].

4   Experimental Overview

This section presents an overview description of the in situ workflow, explains the evaluation metrics for the vector data, and how the accuracy from those metrics was evaluated.

4.1   Workflow Description

The workflow consists of three primary elements: (1) the simulation code; (2) a data transfer system to move data from the simulation to the visualization nodes; and (3) an efficient parallel visualization library. The workflow is launched as three separate binaries, with resources for each partitioned as follows: (1) 1024 XGC1 nodes; (2) 12 Staging nodes; and (3) 32 visualization nodes. A diagram of the workflow is shown in Fig. 2. This study was conducted on the Rhea cluster at the Oak Ridge Leadership Computing Facility. Rhea consists of 512 nodes each with 128 GB of ram and dual Xeon processors with 16 cores each.

Each of the three elements of the workflow are described below, followed by a description of how the components of the workflow interact.

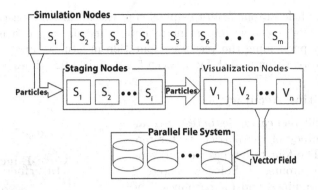

Fig. 2. Experimental setup and data flow between each of the three separate workflow components.

XGC1 Simulation Code. The simulation code, XGC1, is a 5D gyrokinetic ion-electron particle in cell (PIC) code used to study fusion of magnetically confined burning plasmas. XGC1 is used in particular to study turbulence in the outer region of the plasma called the *edge*. The simulation proceeds by computing the interactions of a very large number of particles (ions and electrons) at each simulation time step.

For this study we are interested in using the particle data from the simulation. All of the simulation's particles can be very large, generally ranging from 400 GB to nearly 20 TB per time step. To get good particle velocity vector fields as the particles move around the tokamak, we were required to access the particles at each time step of the simulation.

ADIOS Data Staging. The Adaptable I/O System (ADIOS) [9], is a componentization of the I/O layer that is accessible via a posix-style interface. ADIOS enables a loosely coupled paradigm for a clean interface and separation from XGC1 that provides ease of use, and fault tolerance. The ability to control the concurrency of the visualization tasks independent of the concurrency of XGC1 is important for ensuring good scalability on the visualization nodes

The particle subsampling operation occurred on the simulation side, with particles being uniformly subselected from the simulation's total particles before they were sent over the network with ADIOS. In our study we were only interested in examining ions from the simulation, so only they were selected and transmitted.

Visualization Library. We designed our visualization routines based on an emerging community standard, VTK-m [14], which is a project building upon the success of three existing visualization frameworks, Dax [13], PISTON [10], and EAVL [12]. The VTK-m framework is targeted to emerging computational systems where parallelism and the use of accelerators are dramatically increasing, and memory per core is decreasing.

The vector field output from this portion of the workflow is written to disk for post hoc analysis. It is important to note that this step is a major data reduction. By performing the vector computation in situ, we are reducing the amount of data written to disk by between 5,494 and 11,926 times, see Table 2.

4.2   Evaluating Accuracy

We ran four different categories of tests to evaluate the accuracy of the particle vector representation. The four test types we ran were: (1) Poincaré contours, (2) Poincaré centers of mass, (3) streamlines, and (4) pathlines. Due to the turbulent nature of the XGC1 code, we further broke each of these tests down into three different regions, based on the turbulence in the code. The three regions we used are shown in Fig. 3, and are (1) the core of the tokamak, (2) the core-edge interface, and (3) the edge of the tokamak. The core region is generally less turbulent than the core-edge interface, which is generally less turbulent than the edge. This breakdown allowed us to quantify what error we were getting in each of these three regions, which may be important if we are going to do an analysis that specifically cares about a given region of the plasma. Each of these tests was conducted on each of the different mesh sizes, with four different particle counts each.

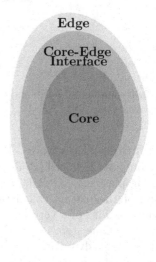

Fig. 3. The three test regions projected onto a slice of the XGC1 tokamak.

We compared the results from each of the tests against what the test produced when performed on *Ground Truth* data. We defined ground truth data to be the vector field that was created when all of the particles from the simulation were used to construct the vector field using the original unstructured XGC1 mesh. We take this vector representation to be the best possible representation when using a vector representation. An overview of each of these test types is given below.

Poincaré Tests. We conducted the Poincaré tests based on the guidance of our fusion partners, as the motion of particles is something that they often study, so it has to be accurate. The Poincaré test on XGC1 data is particularly informative about the accuracy of a reduction method, because Poincaré plots can be used to track the magnetic field lines within the tokamak. The field lines are the magnetic surfaces that particles generally follow around the toroidal shape of the tokamak. Therefore, if a reduced data set has a similar Poincaré outline and center of mass, the reduction method was successful at preserving the magnetic surfaces.

To conduct this test we advected 50 particles from random locations in the core, 25 particles from random locations in the core-edge interface, and 25 particles from random locations on the edge. We then collected the puncture locations for each test and created a contour line that connected all of the punctures to form a closed shape. Using these contours then we were able to calculate the area in the contour as well as the center of each contour.

For each test we compared the contour and contour center we got from the reduced vector representation against that of the ground truth representation. This comparison gave the difference in the area of the contour and difference in location of the centers of the contours. We then used this value as the error associated with that test.

Streamline/Pathline Tests. The second series of tests we conducted were streamlines and pathlines. The streamline and pathline tests also utilized the three different test regions that the Poincaré tests used, giving three different errors for each individual test.

The streamline tests advected particles a random distance around the tokamak, returning the end position of each streamline. The end positions obtained from the ground truth data sets were compared against the reduced representations, giving a difference in end point location as our error metric. For this test we advected 2,000 particles from random locations in the core, 1,000 particles from random locations in the core-edge interface, and 1,000 particles from random locations on the edge.

The pathline tests worked the same as the streamline tests, except particles were advected over time. For this test we advected 200 particles from random locations in the core, 100 particles from random locations in the core-edge interface, and 100 particles from random locations on the edge.

5 Results

The results are organized into three subsections. Section 5.1 does an initial summary and general discussion of results. Section 5.2 examines the Poincaré test results in detail, and Sect. 5.3 examines the streamline and pathline results in detail.

5.1 Test Result Summary

Many different tests were run and analyzed with this work in order to find an optimal configuration for XGC1. In order to make this evaluation intuitive, we created a *lookup table* that can be used in selecting a binning configuration based on the amount of error that is acceptable in each of the three regions of the tokamak.

Table 3 is our *lookup table* and shows the errors of all four of our tests together, presented as percent errors. This table is showing the average percentage error from each of our test configurations compared against *Ground*

Truth. The table is colored according to the percent error, where the darkest blues represent low errors.

One of the most notable observations is the occasional large variation in the performance of the tests from the core to the core-edge interface to the edge of the plasma. This is an interesting feature of this reduced data representation, and can actually be exploited in certain circumstances depending on the location and type of the post-hoc visualization operation we want to run on the reduced data. For example, it is possible to use a 1092x reduction in particles on the 90×90 mesh, and maintain an error on the edge of the plasma for a Poincaré analysis under 2%.

Table 3. Percentage errors in the core, interface and edge regions, for each of the four evaluation metrics used. These percentages represent the average error for each test for each mesh size and particle count compared against the *Ground Truth* data. The color scale highlights the areas where good test configurations are found.

Reduced Mesh Size	Particle Reduction Factor	Poincare Contour Error			Poincare Center Error			Streamline End Point Error			Pathline End Point Error		
		Core	Interface	Edge	Core	Interface	Edge	Core	Interface	Edge	Core	Interface	edge
45x45 Mesh	1092x	3231.60%	11.80%	3.47%	1.30%	1.01%	1.00%	4.08%	4.23%	15.09%	5.82%	13.50%	59.18%
	109x	60.20%	7.70%	3.04%	1.06%	0.89%	1.22%	3.75%	3.31%	17.66%	7.47%	12.41%	38.07%
	11x	2132.95%	11.09%	3.09%	1.19%	1.00%	1.02%	3.85%	3.17%	20.27%	9.84%	5.72%	48.63%
	All Par.	10066.79%	8.58%	2.51%	1.38%	0.94%	0.87%	4.18%	3.18%	12.93%	10.48%	14.19%	60.32%
90x90 Mesh	1092x	81.10%	4.10%	1.88%	0.89%	0.57%	1.03%	1.88%	2.66%	14.38%	8.22%	12.28%	36.90%
	109x	30.61%	2.17%	2.02%	0.61%	0.59%	0.99%	1.44%	1.54%	6.18%	2.44%	4.47%	18.88%
	11x	26.14%	2.47%	1.67%	0.55%	0.41%	1.08%	1.52%	1.90%	3.48%	4.50%	3.41%	16.43%
	All Par.	41.26%	2.80%	2.07%	0.63%	0.57%	1.01%	0.98%	1.32%	3.29%	1.79%	3.14%	28.10%
200x200 Mesh	1092x	1591.39%	11.54%	6.47%	3.13%	2.25%	3.86%	19.96%	29.19%	50.08%	50.09%	79.29%	120.35%
	109x	4.78%	1.39%	1.17%	0.45%	0.32%	0.67%	1.05%	0.96%	5.85%	13.29%	18.73%	9.17%
	11x	2.52%	1.06%	1.06%	0.35%	0.37%	0.66%	0.50%	0.60%	1.81%	1.05%	1.44%	3.73%
	All Par.	3.49%	0.75%	1.63%	0.44%	0.29%	0.72%	0.35%	0.34%	1.95%	0.60%	0.72%	2.31%
450x450 Mesh	1092x	2572.48%	33.95%	3044.93%	5.93%	2.40%	15.25%	166.58%	169.19%	167.28%	117.68%	164.07%	142.75%
	109x	126.75%	1.98%	1.29%	2.73%	2.55%	2.39%	4.10%	2.03%	13.81%	19.93%	27.30%	19.18%
	11x	2.71%	1.08%	0.95%	0.40%	0.35%	0.73%	0.98%	0.46%	3.07%	1.86%	1.85%	9.56%
	All Par.	2.37%	0.87%	0.65%	0.27%	0.29%	0.52%	0.11%	0.10%	3.07%	0.26%	0.40%	7.14%

5.2   Poincaré Test Results

Two separate features were tacked in the Poincaré tests:

– Difference in area of the ground truth data versus the binned representations.
– Differences in the centers of mass of the two representations.

The test results from the Poincaré test for the difference in areas of the ground truth and reduced representations are presented in Fig. 4. This figure presents the results for each of the four unstructured reduced mesh representations and each of the different particle counts as boxplots in a single figure.

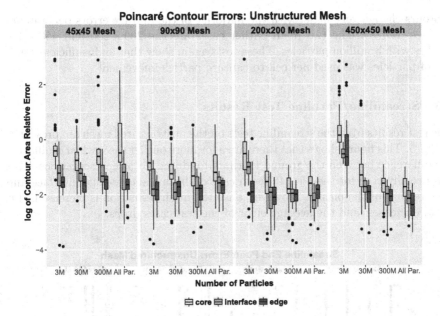

Fig. 4. Boxplots of the difference in areas of contours generated from Poincaré method on the ground truth and reduced representation data for the unstructured mesh.

The first thing to note in this figure is that some of the tests performed very well while some did not. Consider the 45 × 45 mesh for example. In this series of tests, the core of the plasma across all of our tests had a high median and variation in error, including the test that used the reduced 45 × 45 vector mesh created by averaging all particles from the simulation. From these large variations in error, we were able to figure out that the 45 × 45 mesh representation created too large of a decimation in the core of the plasma to create good vector averages from the particles. The core-edge interface and the edge however did perform well for all of those tests.

Moving on to the 90 × 90 and 200 × 200 mesh tests, the variation in error drops significantly, with the average core error dropping below 3% in the test case with the 200 × 200 mesh and 300 million particles. In the 450 × 450 test case the 3 million particle test jumps out, with all of the core, core-edge interface, and edge region errors jumping dramatically. This jump is due to the mesh being too refined for the number of particles that were used to generate it. In that case, it takes more than 3 million particles to create an accurate representation of the motion of the plasma. Thus, it is important to tune the number of particles to be a high enough ratio to adequately cover the number of bins in the mesh representation.

Similar results and trends were observed in the Poincaré test on the unstructured meshes for the difference in centers of mass of the ground truth and reduced representations. The main difference is that in almost all tests, the centers of the contours change very little, with the majority of the average errors being under 1%, see Table 3. The two main outlier cases are the 200×200 and 450×450 meshes with 3 million particles. These tests again show that an insufficient number of particles was used per cell to capture particle movement.

5.3 Streamline/Pathline Test Results

The test results from the streamline tests on the unstructured mesh are presented in Fig. 5. This figure shows that there are a lot more outlier cases when evaluating the difference between the ground truth and reduced data representations. This is especially true for the 45×45 mesh case on both the core-edge interface and edge regions of the plasma. However, once the mesh resolution is increased, this trend decreases, and the average error of the test cases drops.

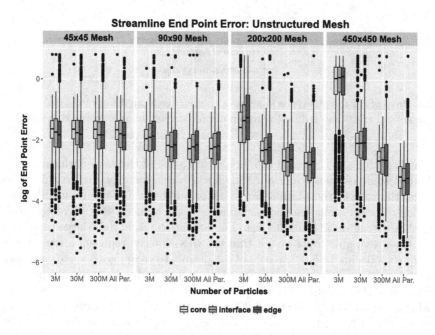

Fig. 5. Boxplots of the difference in end position of the streamlines generated from the ground truth and reduced representation data for the unstructured mesh.

One trend that persists from the Poincaré analysis are the cases where too few particles were used in the 3 million particle case for both the 200×200 and 450×450 meshes. Once the particle count was increased however, the errors dropped significantly, with errors under 1% in both the core and core-edge interface regions using 30 and 300 million particles with the 200×200 mesh.

The test results from the pathline tests on the unstructured mesh show the same general trends, with the largest difference being on the edge of the plasma, see Table 3. This result, though, is not surprising due to the very turbulent nature of the edge of the plasma in the XGC1 code, meaning that particles are bound to act erratically in that region.

6   Conclusions and Future Work

With this paper we have shown that large scale particle data can be binned in situ at every simulation time step in order to increase the temporal fidelity of the output particle data, while also reducing the amount of data transmitted over the network and subsequently saved to disk. We have further demonstrated that with domain specific knowledge it is possible to create multiple different configurations for the binning operation that enable it to be tuned for both accuracy of representation and the shortest time-to-solution. Our binning approach is capable of reducing the size of the particle data every time step from 489 GB down to 81 MB as a final output. Furthermore, we have shown through multiple post-hoc analysis operations that it is possible to generate reduced representations with known errors under 1% for certain regions of the plasma.

In future we would like to apply our binning technique to XGC1 at even larger simulation scales, and then expand to other particle codes to see if the technique remains valid and predictable. Further, while this application paper focused on in depth evaluation of our collaborators' preferred reduction technique, we think an expanded study that compared between more reduction operators would be very interesting.

Acknowledgements. This research used resources of the Oak Ridge Leadership Computing Facility, which is a DOE Office of Science User Facility supported under Contract DE-AC05-00OR22725.

References

1. Ahern, S., et al.: Scientific discovery at the exascale. In: Report from the DOE ASCR 2011 Workshop on Exascale Data Management (2011)
2. Bauer, A.C., et al.: In Situ Methods, Infrastructures, and Applications on High Performance Computing Platforms, a State-of-the-art (STAR) Report. In: Computer Graphics Forum, Proceedings of Eurovis 2016, vol. 35, no. 3, June 2016. lBNL-1005709
3. Chang, C., et al.: Compressed ion temperature gradient turbulence in diverted tokamak edge. Phys. Plasmas (1994-Present) **16**(5), 056108 (2009)
4. Childs, H., et al.: Extreme scaling of production visualization software on diverse architectures. IEEE Comput. Graph. Appl. **30**(3), 22–31 (2010)
5. Childs, H., et al.: Visualization at extreme scale concurrency. In: Bethel, E.W., Childs, H., Hansen, C. (eds.) High Performance Visualization: Enabling Extreme-Scale Scientific Insight. CRC Press, Boca Raton (2012)
6. Fabian, N., et al.: The paraview coprocessing library: a scalable, general purpose in situ visualization library. In: 2011 IEEE Symposium on Large Data Analysis and Visualization (LDAV), pp. 89–96. IEEE (2011)

7. Kress, J., Churchill, R.M., Klasky, S., Kim, M., Childs, H., Pugmire, D.: Preparing for in situ processing on upcoming leading-edge supercomputers. Supercomput. Front. Innov. **3**(4), 49–65 (2016)
8. Kress, J., Pugmire, D., Klasky, S., Childs, H.: Visualization and analysis requirements for in situ processing for a large-scale fusion simulation code. In: Proceedings of the 2nd Workshop on In Situ Infrastructures for Enabling Extreme-scale Analysis and Visualization, pp. 45–50. IEEE Press (2016)
9. Liu, Q., et al.: Hello adios: the challenges and lessons of developing leadership class i/o frameworks. Concurr. Comput.: Pract. Exp. **26**(7), 1453–1473 (2014). https://doi.org/10.1002/cpe.3125
10. Lo, L., Sewell, C., Ahrens, J.P.: Piston: a portable cross-platform framework for data-parallel visualization operators. In: EGPGV, pp. 11–20 (2012)
11. Lofstead, J.F., Klasky, S., Schwan, K., Podhorszki, N., Jin, C.: Flexible io and integration for scientific codes through the adaptable io system (adios). In: Proceedings of the 6th International Workshop on Challenges of Large Applications in Distributed Environments, CLADE 2008, pp. 15–24. ACM, New York (2008). https://doi.org/10.1145/1383529.1383533
12. Meredith, J.S., Ahern, S., Pugmire, D., Sisneros, R.: EAVL: the extreme-scale analysis and visualization library. In: Eurographics Symposium on Parallel Graphics and Visualization, pp. 21–30. The Eurographics Association (2012)
13. Moreland, K., Ayachit, U., Geveci, B., Ma, K.L.: Dax toolkit: a proposed framework for data analysis and visualization at extreme scale. In: 2011 IEEE Symposium on Large Data Analysis and Visualization (LDAV), pp. 97–104, October 2011
14. Moreland, K., et al.: VTK-m: accelerating the visualization toolkit for massively threaded architectures. IEEE Comput. Graph. Appl. (CG&A) **36**(3), 48–58 (2016)
15. Neuroth, T., Sauer, F., Wang, W., Ethier, S., Ma, K.L.: Scalable visualization of discrete velocity decompositions using spatially organized histograms. In: 2015 IEEE 5th Symposium on Large Data Analysis and Visualization (LDAV), pp. 65–72. IEEE (2015)
16. Oldfield, R.A., Widener, P., Maccabe, A.B., Ward, L., Kordenbrock, T.: Effcient data-movement for lightweight i/o. In: 2006 IEEE International Conference on Cluster Computing, pp. 1–9, September 2006. https://doi.org/10.1109/CLUSTR.2006.311897
17. Pugmire, D., Kress, J., Meredith, J., Podhorszki, N., Choi, J., Klasky, S.: Towards scalable visualization plugins for data staging workows. In: Big Data Analytics: Challenges and Opportunities (BDAC 2014) Workshop at Supercomputing Conference, November 2014
18. Reach, C., North, C.: Bandlimited olap cubes for interactive big data visualization. In: 2015 IEEE 5th Symposium on Large Data Analysis and Visualization (LDAV), pp. 107–114. IEEE (2015)
19. Schatz, K., Müller, C., Krone, M., Schneider, J., Reina, G., Ertl, T.: Interactive visual exploration of a trillion particles. In: 2016 IEEE 6th Symposium on Large Data Analysis and Visualization (LDAV), pp. 56–64. IEEE (2016)
20. Tchoua, R., et al.: Adios visualization schema: a first step towards improving interdisciplinary collaboration in high performance computing. In: 2013 IEEE 9th International Conference on eScience (eScience), pp. 27–34. IEEE (2013)
21. Vishwanath, V., Hereld, M., Papka, M.: Toward simulation-time data analysis and i/o acceleration on leadership-class systems. In: 2011 IEEE Symposium on Large Data Analysis and Visualization (LDAV), pp. 9–14 (2011). https://doi.org/10.1109/LDAV.2011.6092178

22. Whitlock, B., Favre, J.M., Meredith, J.S.: Parallel in situ coupling of simulation with a fully featured visualization system. In: Proceedings of the 11th Eurographics conference on Parallel Graphics and Visualization, pp. 101–109. Eurographics Association (2011)
23. Ye, Y.C., et al.: In situ generated probability distribution functions for interactive post hoc visualization and analysis. In: 2016 IEEE 6th Symposium on Large Data Analysis and Visualization (LDAV), pp. 65–74. IEEE (2016)

In Situ Analysis and Visualization of Fusion Simulations: Lessons Learned

Mark Kim[1]([✉]), James Kress[1,5], Jong Choi[1], Norbert Podhorszki[1],
Scott Klasky[1], Matthew Wolf[1], Kshitij Mehta[1], Kevin Huck[5], Berk Geveci[3],
Sujin Phillip[3], Robert Maynard[3], Hanqi Guo[2], Tom Peterka[2],
Kenneth Moreland[4], Choong-Seock Chang[6], Julien Dominski[6],
Michael Churchill[6], and David Pugmire[1]

[1] Oak Ridge National Laboratory, Oak Ridge, TN 37831, USA
kimmb@ornl.gov
[2] Argonne National Laboratory, Lemont, IL 60439, USA
[3] Kitware Inc., Clifton Park, NY 21065, USA
[4] Sandia National Laboratories, Albuquerque, NM 87185, USA
[5] University of Oregon, Eugene, OR 97403, USA
[6] Princeton Plasma Physics Laboratory, Princeton, NJ 08543, USA

Abstract. The trends in high performance computing, where far more data can be computed that can ever be stored, have made in situ techniques an important area of research and development. Simulation campaigns, where domain scientists work with computer scientists to run a simulation and perform in situ analysis and visualization are important, and complex undertakings. In this paper we report our experiences performing in situ analysis and visualization on two campaigns. The two campaigns were related, but had important differences in terms of the codes that were used, the types of analysis and visualization required, and the visualization tools used. Further, we report the lessons learned from each campaign.

Keywords: In situ · Scientific · Visualization

1 Introduction

The traditional *post hoc* model for analysis and visualization has been for the simulation to write data to disk, and for a set of tools to read the data back into memory at a later time to perform analysis and visualization. Because supercomputers can produce far more data than can be saved, this traditional model is breaking down. This imbalance in supercomputers has made it very attractive to perform the analysis and visualization operations *in situ*, as soon as the data are produced and resident in memory.

Because the traditional model is breaking down, new models, frameworks, and tools need to be developed that allow simulations to make use of *in situ* visualization. These same models, frameworks and tools, where possible, need to

© Springer Nature Switzerland AG 2018
R. Yokota et al. (Eds.): ISC 2018 Workshops, LNCS 11203, pp. 230–242, 2018.
https://doi.org/10.1007/978-3-030-02465-9_16

be able to work with existing analysis and visualization tools, or provide a foundation for the development of the next generation of libraries and tools. While *in situ* visualization is a straightforward concept, the implementation details, constraints, and requirements for resilience make this much harder to achieve for production use. Much of the difficulty is a result of the visualization being much closer to the running simulation. In a *post hoc* model, where communication between the simulation and visualization is done through files, there are far fewer constraints on time and resource utilization, as well as resilience. In an *in situ* model, strict constraints are placed on the analysis and visualization routines. Further, any error in the analysis or visualization that causes the simulation to crash are unacceptable. Requirements like these, and many others, make robust deployment of in situ visualization a challenge.

In this paper we describe our experience performing analysis and visualization with two different simulation campaigns. The two campaigns were performed with a plasma physics simulation that each had different analysis and visualization requirements. In addition, each campaign used performance tools to monitor the simulation while it was running and report different statistics. Finally, data compression techniques were used on the simulation outputs. The performance of these compression techniques was also monitored and reported. Each campaign used a different set of analysis and visualization tools. We discuss the workflows that were constructed, the resulting visualizations, and the lessons learned from each. Also, each the visualization of each campaign was focused on different aspects of the simulation. We discuss these requirements, and the lessons learned.

We begin with a brief review of related work in Sect. 2. In Sect. 3 we provide some motivation and background on the structure of each campaign. In Sect. 4 we describe how the simulation, analysis and visualization components of each campaign were configured. In Sect. 5 we show the analysis and visualization results that were produced for each campaign. Finally, in Sects. 6 and 7 we discuss the lessons learned throughout both simulation campaigns, and make some concluding remarks, and thoughts for future work.

2 Related Work

Current and future trends in high performance computing continue to point to systems where the ability to produce data far exceeds the ability to save that data. This system imbalance has made in situ methods an important topic for simulation science. Bauer et al. [6] provides a detailed survey of the broad and long history of in situ visualization.

A number of frameworks for in situ visualization have been developed and used over the years. These include SCIRun [19], a problem solving environment that supports in situ visualization and computational steering. LibSim [23] is a library that allows simulations to connect to the VisIt [9] visualization tool. Catalyst [5] allows a simulation to connect to ParaView [1] for visualization.

ADIOS [17] is an I/O middleware library that exposes in situ processing to a simulation through a POSIX-like API. ADIOS supports memory-to-memory coupling through a number of different transports methods, including DataSpaces [12], DIMES [24], and FlexPath [10].

Several studies have been done to explore using these frameworks with simulations. Bennett et al. [7] do in situ visualization and analysis using the ADIOS. Ayachit et al. [4] use the SENSEI framework to study in situ visualization using ADIOS, LibSim and Catalyst.

3 Motivation

The two simulation campaigns in this paper were motivated by trying to understand new approaches for simulation science on HPC systems. These efforts were focused in several directions. First, as mentioned previously, the growing compute and I/O imbalance, and a need to monitor running simulations is necessitating the use of in situ methods for analysis and visualization. Second, there is a need to monitor and understand the different performance aspects of the simulation, including FLOPS, memory usage, network bandwidth, compression ratios, and I/O throughput. Third, the physics teams are focusing on using code coupling to solve the multi-scale, multi-physics aspects of the simulations. Code coupling is a powerful technique for using multiple simulation codes to work together on difference pieces of the problem, and then coordinate their results for whole-physics solution. In this context, the simulation team was interested in analysis and visualization, performance, and compression for the individual codes, as well as the coupled solutions.

The code coupling was performed in an environment enabled by in-memory communication. The analysis and visualization also made use of this in-memory environment for access to simulation data. This environment enabled the launching of executables to perform the various operations (simulation, performance monitoring, analysis and visualization). A workflow system was used that launched the various executables. These executables include the two simulations, the performance monitoring executables, and the analysis and visualization executables. The workflow also specified the connectivity between these executables. This environment allows flexibility in what operations are executed, where they are executed, and what types of pipelines are constructed.

4 Setup

This section describes the components, and their configurations for each of the two simulation campaigns. In each of the simulation campaigns, two physics codes were used to simulate plasma physics in a tokamak device. One code was responsible for the core region of the tokamak, while the other code was responsible for the edge region of the tokamak. The particular codes used in each campaign are discussed in Sects. 4.1 and 4.2.

Each campaign was initiated using the Savanna [15] workflow system. Savanna is a python-based workflow composition and dispatch engine that to composes and orchestrates complex workflows that consist of multiple applications. Savanna specifies the parameters for each component in the workflow, as well as how the components are configured and connected to one another. These components all make use of the ADIOS middleware layer for memory-to-memory data transfer, and I/O operations. Two different memory-to-memory data transport methods were used. FlexPath [10], a peer-to-peer data staging service, and DIMES [24], a client-server based model data transfer service. These transport methods in ADIOS enabled the coupling of the physics codes, as well as the transport of simulation output to other data consumers in the workflow. The TAU [20] performance tool was used to monitor the running simulations, and used ADIOS for memory-to-memory data transfer to visualization resources. The in situ analysis and visualization operations use ADIOS to obtain the data from both simulations, as well as the performance tools. The data compression capability in ADIOS was also used to reduce the amount of data transfered in situ, as well as written to disk. Two different lossy compression methods were used in the two campaigns; MGARD [2,3], and SZ [11]. To assess the quality of the compression, Z-checker [21] was also used.

For analysis and visualization, two different tools were used: VisIt [9], and VTK-m [18]. VisIt is a fully featured parallel production tool for scientific analysis and visualization. VTK-m is a scientific visualization toolkit that is enabled to take advantage of the multi/many-core nodes in HPC systems. Small, lightweight analysis and visualization services were built using VTK-m to perform specific tasks. These services used the ADIOS in situ environment, and the ADIOS visualization schema [22] to ingest simulation data, and to output data extracts for subsequent processing. The visualization schema is a convenience layer in ADIOS that allows an application to add additional markup to data as it is being written. This additional markup then allows the reader application to know exactly how to ingest the data. For example, it could specify that it was writing a rectilinear mesh, and that mesh had two fields, one called "energy" which is cell centered, and one called "velocity" which is point centered (Fig. 1).

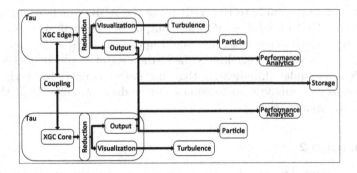

Fig. 1. Simulation 1 code coupled fusion simulation diagram.

4.1   Campaign 1

In the first campaign, two instances of the same code were coupled together. This choice permitted to focus on the code coupling model when avoiding the extra-complications related to the use of different codes. Two instances of a single code, XGC1 [8] were used, each configured for a specific region of the computational domain, see reference [13] for a description of the coupling scheme. TAU was used performance monitoring, and both VisIt and VTK-m were used for analysis and visualization.

Computation Code. The XGC1 computation code is a highly scalable physics code used to study plasmas in fusion tokamak devices. XGC1 is a particle-in-cell code. The simulation will solve for the motion of very large number of charged particles inside the plasma, and then statistically deposit the particles onto the mesh. Scientists are interested in both the field variables on the mesh, and the particles.

In this example, two instances of XGC1 were run. One instance was configured for the core region of the plasma, and another instance was configured for the edge region of the plasma. There was a coupling region of the mesh where the core and edge codes would communicate the state of the physics. The ADIOS memory-to-memory data transport is used for the simulations to communicate this coupling data.

Visualization. In this demo, VisIt was used as the dashboard to display the progress of the running simulation through different visualizations. First, the simulation and the visualization services were launched. Subsequently, the VisIt GUI interface would be launched and it would connect to the running simulation, and display the simulation progress in real time.

VisIt was configured using a Python script which setup the different windows and positions of each of the visualizations within the dashboard, as well as handling the updating of plots as new data became available. Due to time constraints, we were unable to run VisIt using the ADIOS memory-to-memory data transport, and we used ADIOS files output by the analysis services, and the simulation. Each analysis service would update a ".visit" file as soon as it had new data ready to be visualized. The Python script would then check for a ".visit" file to be updated, indicating that new data was ready to be visualized, and as soon as each analysis application had new data available, VisIt was able to perform an update (Fig. 2).

4.2   Campaign 2

In the second campaign, two different codes were used coupling. GENE [16] was used for the core region, and XGC1 was used for the edge region. The same coupling model that was used for coupling two instance of XGC and described

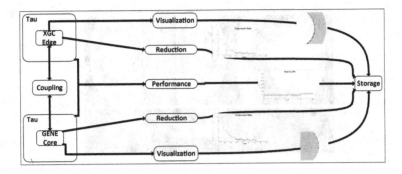

Fig. 2. Simulation 2 code coupled fusion simulation diagram.

in Ref. [13] has been used. Additional difficulties, including the extra compli-cations of having different grids in GENE and XGC, will be described in an upcoming publication [14]. As in campaign 1, TAU was used performance mon-itoring. MGARD, and SZ were used for compression of simulation data, and Z-checker used to monitor the compression quality. Lightweight in situ analysis and visualization services were used for all of the visualizations.

Computation Code. GENE is an Eulerian gyrokinetic code that is used to simulate the core region of the tokamak. The same code in Campaign 1, XGC1 is used to simulate the edge region of the tokamak. As before, a coupling region is used between the core and edge for both codes to communicate the state of the physics. The ADIOS memory-to-memory data transport is used for the simulations to communicate this coupling data.

Visualization. The analysis and visualizations for Campaign 2 were generated using a collection of lightweight services. Each service used the ADIOS environ-ment, ADIOS visualization schema, and memory-to-memory data transport for the communication of data. At each timestep of the simulation, data would flow through the ADIOS environment to each services where analysis and visualiza-tions were performed. The terminal rendering services would produce output images that are saved to disk.

5 Results

5.1 Campaign 1

The code coupled fusion simulation was run on OLCF Titan, with XGC1 utiliz-ing 2048 MPI processors and GENE using: 2048 MPI processors. Each visual-ization and analysis process is assigned an MPI processor as well.

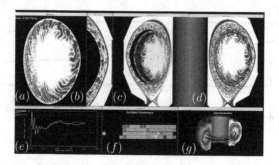

Fig. 3. Dashboard for Campaign 1.

Visualization. The fusion scientists were interested in visualizations of several physics quantities, and performance metrics. First, they were interested in the energy concentrations that form within the plasma. This quantity, called the *scalar potential*, is derived from the particles, and is a field variable on the core and edge meshes (Fig. 3(a–b), respectively). Second, they are interested in the behavior of the particle data in the simulation. This was visualized using a reduction technique where the bulk particle velocity field was computed from the motion of the particles. The bulk velocity field was then visualized using streamlines. Third, in order to understand the convergence, they wanted to see a time varying 1D plot of the heat flux. Finally, to monitor the system performance, a visualization of the total FLOPS and memory usage for each node was done.

Streamline Visualization. Particles from XGC1 are the largest data produced by the simulation. There are too many particles to save to disk every timestep, so they are only saved during simulation checkpointing. This means that performing any analysis or visualization on the particles is essentially impossible, since once a new checkpoint is saved, the old one is deleted to clear space. To overcome this limitation, we processed the particles coming from the simulation every simulation cycle in situ. This processing consisted of a spatial reduction of the particles by binning. All particles from the simulation were binned into a decimated version of the simulation mesh. Due to the large number of particles, 3 billion++, this operation was performed in parallel across several nodes. This process allowed every particle from the simulation to contribute to the final binned values. Following binning the binned representation of the particles was saved to disk for visualization and analysis. Using this approach we gained a high temporal frequency view of the particles as they progressed during the simulation. After the data was saved to disk it was loaded into VisIt were a streamline operation was performed, with the final rendered image (Fig. 3(f)) showing up on the simulation dashboard.

5.2   Campaign 2

The code coupled fusion simulation was run on OLCF Titan, with XGC1 utilizing 3072 MPI processors and GENE using: 1024 MPI processors. Each visualization and analysis process is assigned an MPI processor as well.

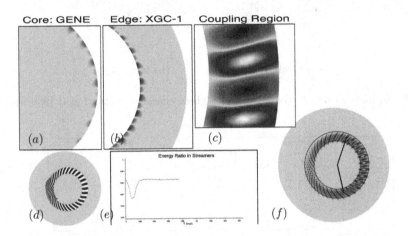

Fig. 4. The dashboard visualizations for Campaign 2.

Visualization. Similar to the visualization performed for Simulation 1 in Sect. 5.1, scientists needed to visualize the potential energy of the simulation. The potential energy is visualized for the core, edge, and coupling (Fig. 4(a–c)) of the fusion simulation.

Further, the scientists were looking for a specific energy interaction between the streamers in the coupling region of the simulation. The two circular black lines denote the coupling region of the simulation where XGC1 and Gene interact. The two lines emanating from the center of the tokomak plane, resembling clock hands, change dynamically as the simulation progresses, and denote the region where the highest 70% of streamer energy lies. In the beginning of the simulation this region is large, and as the simulation progresses the region shrinks (Fig. 5), and the area denoted by the hands is essentially the strong side of the plasma. This visualization helps researchers to confirm that the simulation is progressing normally and that things have converged.

Analytics. The analytic services in this demo were broken into four light-weight visualization services. First was the SZ visualization service. SZ was used to perform compression on data coming from XGC. The visualization service connected to staging and read ten individual scalar values each cycle from the simulation. These scalars values were then plotted as line graphs using the VTK-m software rasterizer, and an image was stored to disk at each time step. Second, MGARD

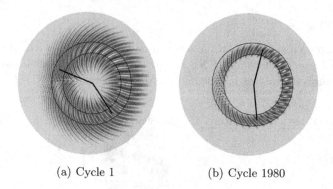

(a) Cycle 1   (b) Cycle 1980

Fig. 5. (a) and (b) denote the regions of highest energies at step 1 and 1980, respectively.

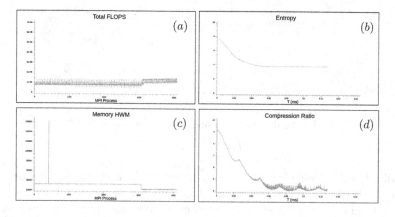

Fig. 6. The dashboard graphs for Campaign 2.

was used to perform compression on data coming from GENE. The visualization service connected to staging and read five individual scalar values each cycle from the simulation. These scalar values were then plotted as line graphs using the VTK-m software rasterizer, and an image was stored to disk at each time step. Third was the TAU visualization service. Finally, Z-checker provided further analytics for the compression, the ratio and the entropy (Fig. 6(b) and (d), respectively). TAU was used to gather simulation performance data from XGC1 and GENE. The visualization service connected to staging and read eight scalar arrays from staging each simulation cycle. The length of these arrays were 4096, and gave performance data for each simulation process in XGC1 and GENE. The data was then plotted as a line graph (Fig. 6(a)), and an image was stored to disk for each time step.

The TAU visualization service allowed us to see when failures were occurring during our testing runs. Specifically, the ability to monitor the memory usage per process in the simulation aided in finding a bug in a different visualization service.

During a test run, there were several nodes that consumed all the memory as the simulation ran, until it eventually crashed the simulation itself. This can be seen in the spike in the graph in Fig. 6(c). As it turns out, this memory increase was due to a leak in the Z-checker compression service in ADIOS. The memory usage visualization was useful in this case because we could see that the simulation crash was only due to a small number of nodes running out of memory, which narrowed down where the issue could be coming from.

The fourth and final analysis service was a feature detection service for extracting streamers in the plasma. The streamers, shown in Fig. 4(d) are areas of high energy density, and are a key driver in the evolution of the plasma.

6   Discussion

In this section we discuss the lessons learned from the two campaigns. The backbone of both campaigns was the ADIOS environment. It provide the memory-to-memory data transport, as well as the I/O for all the components in both campaigns. Using a single environment made it much easier to setup the workflows, and provide the connections between individual components. This was especially important in Campaign 2 where the analysis and visualization requirements were changing, and the plug-and-play nature of the system made it easy to develop a service that would easily work.

A significant advantage of the ADIOS environment is that it is easily configurable to use either files, or memory-to-memory data transfer. Because of this, services could be developed and tested using files, and then deployed in situ by setting a flag. This was invaluable in the development, testing, and debugging of services. This also enabled the development of services to be performed independent of the simulation, and the supercomputer. It also made it easier to groups of developers to build services independently, and the coordinate at the end. Once the services run independently in a development environment using files, a parameter is modified, and the services will run on the HPC system.

The ADIOS environment also made it trivial to chain multiple services together for more complex operations. Because we were using the ADIOS visualization schema to annotate the semantics of the data being transported, the services could easily communicate to each other. The ability also made it trivial to chain multiple services together, as was done with the streamer detection algorithm in Campaign 2.

Another advantage of the ADIOS environment is the runtime resilience provided. ADIOS is designed to allow the dynamic connection and disconnection of services from the ADIOS stream. That is, the simulation that is writing data via ADIOS will not crash if the process consuming that data crashes. A process can then reconnect to the ADIOS data stream after it has recovered from the failure. It is important to note that the analysis process itself is responsible for being resilient enough to be restarted and reconnected to the ADIOS stream, ADIOS will not maintain any state for a crashed analysis process.

An example of the resilience in ADIOS comes from Campaign 2. In Campaign 2, there was a memory leak in the base layer used by VTK-m services. Each time a service read in a timestep, tens of megabytes of memory would leak. After enough timesteps, the node would run out of memory and crash. However, since the simulation and visualization are not directly connected, the simulation continued to run.

Because of time constraints, and technicalities associated with Campaign 1, we were not able to connect VisIt to the ADIOS environment using the memory-to-memory data transfer. As a workaround, VisIt read ADIOS files from disk. There were three different files ready by VisIt that were generated by the simulation, and analysis services: simulation output, TAU performance data, vector field data produced by the in situ particle reduction services. The ability to avoid disk altogether would have provided flexibility for the visualization, and made it more efficient.

For visualization, each campaign used different modes. In Campaign 1, VisIt, a fully featured visualization tool was used. In Campaign 2, a set of lightweight visualization services were used. At a high level, VisIt is designed for interactive visualization while a lightweight visualization service is not. This can affect how scientists interface with a simulation as it runs. With the service oriented strategy, the output is either a data extract, or an image. This means that scientists are limited with exploring the dataset beyond the visualizations they have invoked through the framework. Understanding these limitations, and the requirements by the scientists can inform which choice is most appropriate.

Further, VisIt is a mature, full featured tool, while the lightweight visualization service is based on VTK-m, which is a relatively young, and growing library. Because of this, some more advanced visualizations are possible using VisIt, as shown in Fig. 3(c), (d). However, the flexibility provided by lightweight service model makes it much easier to provide custom visualizations, like the ballooning angle visualization in Fig. 5.

Most of the visualizations done in each of the two campaigns were not performance intensive. They ran one a single node, and were easily able to keep up with the output frequency of the simulations. The particle visualization was the most time and resource intensive analysis that was run. It was launched with multiple nodes and multiple processes per node in order to keep up with the simulation output. However, there were times when it did not maintain pace with the simulation. When the particle visualization was unable to keep up, some simulation steps were dropped, but it would continue by reading the next available one once it had caught up. Again, the simulation continued regardless of the whether the particle visualization kept up. This demonstrated the important resilience of ADIOS and the visualization services.

Finally, one problem encountered was rendering on the HPC resource using lightweight services. This is because of the challenges having system administrators install and maintain OpenGL and EGL drivers on the compute nodes. To get around this problem, we used a software based rasterizer in VTK-m to visualize the graphs, and a software based ray casting algorithm to render the visualizations.

7 Conclusion and Future Works

The growing complexity in high performance computing has led to new frameworks, models, and tools for simulation codes. These tools need to be able to work with existing visualization tools, or provide a way forward to enable new models and frameworks to be implemented. One attractive approach to allow this is to perform visualization *in situ*, where the data resides in memory.

In this paper, we discussed various aspects of performing *in situ* visualization for two plasma physics simulation campaigns. Each campaign had varying visualization and analysis requirements and used different visualization and analysis algorithms. We discussed two different workflows, one that is interactive and another that is service oriented. Finally, we discussed the resulting visualizations and the lessons learned.

In the future, we would like to further explore this interactive versus service oriented paradigms. In particular, when one strategy is beneficial over the other, and vice versa. Finally, we would like to explore a mix of interactive and service oriented visualization, as well. Ultimately, we believe that a combination of both interactive, and a service oriented visualization provides the most flexibility to scientists.

References

1. Ahrens, J., Geveci, B., Law, C.: Visualization in the paraview framework. In: Hansen, C., Johnson, C. (eds.) The Visualization Handbook, pp. 162–170 (2005)
2. Ainsworth, M., Tugluk, O., Whitney, B., Klasky, S.: MGARD: a multilevel technique for compression of floating-point data. In: DRBSD-2 Workshop at Supercomputing 2017, Colorado, USA (2017)
3. Ainsworth, M., Tugluk, O., Whitney, B., Klasky, S.: Multilevel techniques for compression and reduction of scientific data-the univariate case. Comput. Vis. Sci. (2017, submitted)
4. Ayachit, U., et al.: The SENSEI generic in situ interface. In: 2016 Second Workshop on In Situ Infrastructures for Enabling Extreme-Scale Analysis and Visualization (ISAV), pp. 40–44, November 2016. https://doi.org/10.1109/ISAV.2016.013
5. Ayachit, U., et al.: ParaView catalyst: enabling in situ data analysis and visualization. In: Proceedings of the First Workshop on In Situ Infrastructures for Enabling Extreme-Scale Analysis and Visualization, pp. 25–29. ACM (2015)
6. Bauer, A.C., et al.: In situ methods, infrastructures, and applications on high performance computing platforms, a state-of-the-art (STAR) report. In: Computer Graphics Forum, Proceedings of EuroVis 2016, vol. 35, no. 3, June 2016. LBNL-1005709
7. Bennett, J.C., et al.: Combining in-situ and in-transit processing to enable extreme-scale scientific analysis. In: Proceedings of the International Conference on High Performance Computing, Networking, Storage and Analysis, SC 2012, pp. 49:1–49:9. IEEE Computer Society Press, Los Alamitos (2012). http://dl.acm.org/citation.cfm?id=2388996.2389063
8. Chang, C., et al.: Compressed ion temperature gradient turbulence in diverted tokamak edgea. Phys. Plasmas (1994-present) **16**(5), 056108 (2009)

9. Childs, H., et al.: VisIt: an end-user tool for visualizing and analyzing very large data. In: High Performance Visualization-Enabling Extreme-Scale Scientific Insight, pp. 357–372, October 2012

10. Dayal, J., et al.: Flexpath: type-based publish/subscribe system for large-scale science analytics. In: 2014 14th IEEE/ACM International Symposium on Cluster, Cloud and Grid Computing (CCGrid), pp. 246–255. IEEE (2014)

11. Di, S., Cappello, F.: Fast error-bounded lossy HPC data compression with SZ. In: 2016 IEEE International Parallel and Distributed Processing Symposium, IPDPS 2016, Chicago, IL, USA, 23–27 May 2016, pp. 730–739 (2016)

12. Docan, C., Parashar, M., Klasky, S.: Dataspaces: an interaction and coordination framework for coupled simulation workflows. Cluster Comput. **15**(2), 163–181 (2012)

13. Dominski, J., et al.: A tight-coupling scheme sharing minimum information across a spatial interface between gyrokinetic turbulence codes. Phys. Plasmas **25**(7), 072308 (2018). https://doi.org/10.1063/1.5044707

14. Dominski, J., Merlo, G., et al.: Gyrokinetic core-edge coupling of the continuum code GENE with the particle-in-cell code XGC (temporary title). (in preparation)

15. Foster, I., et al.: Computing just what you need: online data analysis and reduction at extreme scales. In: Rivera, F.F., Pena, T.F., Cabaleiro, J.C. (eds.) Euro-Par 2017. LNCS, vol. 10417, pp. 3–19. Springer, Cham (2017). https://doi.org/10.1007/978-3-319-64203-1_1

16. Görler, T., et al.: The global version of the gyrokinetic turbulence code gene. J. Comput. Phys. **230**(18), 7053–7071 (2011). https://doi.org/10.1016/j.jcp.2011.05.034. http://www.sciencedirect.com/science/article/pii/S0021999111003457

17. Liu, Q., et al.: Hello ADIOS: the challenges and lessons of developing leadership class I/O frameworks. Concurrency Comput.: Pract. Exp. **26**(7), 1453–1473 (2014). https://doi.org/10.1002/cpe.3125

18. Moreland, K., et al.: VTK-m: accelerating the visualization toolkit for massively threaded architectures. IEEE Comput. Graph. Appl. **36**(3), 48–58 (2016)

19. Parker, S.G., Johnson, C.R.: SCIRun: a scientific programming environment for computational steering. In: Proceedings of the 1995 ACM/IEEE Conference on Supercomputing, p. 52. ACM (1995)

20. Shende, S.S., Malony, A.D.: The tau parallel performance system. Int. J. High Perform. Comput. Appl. **20**(2), 287–311 (2006)

21. Tao, D., Di, S., Guo, H., Chen, Z., Cappello, F.: Z-checker: a framework for assessing lossy compression of scientific data. Int. J. High Perform. Comput. Appl. 1094342017737147 (2017). https://doi.org/10.1177/1094342017737147

22. Tchoua, R., et al.: ADIOS visualization schema: a first step towards improving interdisciplinary collaboration in high performance computing. In: 2013 IEEE 9th International Conference on e-Science, pp. 27–34, October 2013. https://doi.org/10.1109/eScience.2013.24

23. Whitlock, B., Favre, J., Meredith, J.: Parallel in situ coupling of simulation with a fully featured visualization system. In: Proceedings of the 11th Eurographics Conference on Parallel Graphics and Visualization, pp. 101–109 (2011)

24. Zhang, F., et al.: In-memory staging and data-centric task placement for coupled scientific simulation workflows. Concurrency Comput.: Pract. Exp. **29**(12), e4147 (2017)

Design of a Flexible In Situ Framework with a Temporal Buffer for Data Processing and Visualization of Time-Varying Datasets

Kenji Ono[1,2]([✉])(iD), Jorji Nonaka[2](iD), Hiroyuki Yoshikawa[3](iD), Takeshi Nanri[1], Yoshiyuki Morie[2], Tomohiro Kawanabe[2](iD), and Fumiyoshi Shoji[2](iD)

[1] Research Institute for Information Technology, Kyushu University, Fukuoka, Japan
keno@cc.kyushu-u.ac.jp
[2] RIKEN Center for Computational Science, Kobe, Japan
[3] Fujitsu Limited, Tokyo, Japan

Abstract. This paper presents an in situ framework focused on time-varying simulations, and uses a novel temporal buffer for storing simulation results sampled at user-defined intervals. This framework has been designed to provide flexible data processing and visualization capabilities in modern HPC operational environments composed of powerful front-end systems, for pre-and post-processing purposes, along with traditional back-end HPC systems. The temporal buffer is implemented using the functionalities provided by *Open Address Space (OpAS)* library, which enables asynchronous one-sided communication from outside processes to any exposed memory region on the simulator side. This buffer can store time-varying simulation results, and can be processed via in situ approaches with different proximities. We present a prototype of our framework, and code integration process with a target simulation code. The proposed in situ framework utilizes separate files to describe the initialization and execution codes, which are in the form of Python scripts. This framework also enables the runtime modification of these Python-based files, thus providing greater flexibility to the users, not only for data processing, such as visualization and analysis, but also for the simulation steering.

Keywords: Temporal buffer · Time-varying data
Heterogeneous architecture

1 Introduction

High-performance simulations are widely used in a variety of fields, including science, engineering, medicine, and big data, where huge computational resources are required. Since large-scale computations can generate enormous amounts of data, even the transfer of the simulation output from the computing environment

© Springer Nature Switzerland AG 2018
R. Yokota et al. (Eds.): ISC 2018 Workshops, LNCS 11203, pp. 243–257, 2018.
https://doi.org/10.1007/978-3-030-02465-9_17

to the attached storage system can be a resource intensive and time consuming task. The data movement even using high-speed network based parallel file system, such as Lustre file system, has gradually become impractical due to the ever increasing resource and time requirements. This issue has motivated the research and development of in situ processing to overcome and replace the traditional file-based post-processing approach [2]. Considering that the in situ approach can bypass the bottleneck of the time-consuming I/O operations, we can expect an increase in the scalability and throughput when dealing with small amounts of metadata such as rendered images or extracted subsets of the data such as the extracted region of interest (ROI) subsets of the original data. The in situ approach has been shown to be effective when handling non-time-varying datasets. However, there still exist some methodological obstacles when trying to handle dynamic data that vary in time. Here, we can consider the following two main issues:

1. Inconvenience caused by the producer/consumer speed mismatch between the data generation and processing;
2. Difficulty in optimizing the rendering parameters when dealing with time-varying datasets.

In the first issue, the rate at which data are generated by the simulator depends on the allocated and utilized computing resources: the performance of the applications and the selected parameters for generating the temporal outputs at the user determined intervals used in the data processing. On the other hand, although the speed of the data processing has the same dependencies, there is an important additional constraint: human intervention during the interactive visual exploration. If data are generated much faster than they are being processed and visualized, then there is a risk that simulation results will be overwritten before they are processed. On the other hand, if the time required for the data generation is large, this will impact the efficiency of the data processing.

The second issue is to determine the optimal rendering parameter for the time-varying datasets. To find the optimal rendering parameters over some period of time, a mechanism for accessing the simulation results at multiple time steps is highly desirable. However, these time-varying datasets are generated sequentially, and the data are overwritten when new simulation results become available. To overcome this issue, we introduce a temporal buffer mechanism to handle the abovementioned time-varying datasets which are being continuously simulated and updated.

In addition to the abovementioned issues, we need to consider the heterogeneity of the hardware infrastructure of modern HPC operational environments. For instance, in our case, the computational environment includes a powerful homogeneous HPC cluster, a GPU combined heterogeneous cluster, and a large-memory many-core system. Recently there has been a shift in the development of HPC systems from simply maximizing the computational performance to providing enhanced usability, and in this context, we consider the application of our method to powerful front-end sub-systems in addition to the traditional back-end HPC systems.

In this paper, we propose a novel in situ framework with a temporal buffer to handle the time-varying datasets during the data processing and visualization. We introduce the proposed temporal buffer in the next section.

2   Temporal Buffer

In this section, we present an outline of the temporal buffer utilized in the proposed in situ framework.

2.1   Description

The temporal buffer can be described as a sequentially allocated memory region (array) for storing time-dependent simulation results, which are continuously generated from a running simulator at user-defined time intervals. Figure 1 shows an overview of the temporal buffer and how it is used by the simulator to store the sampled simulation results. Once a time series of computed simulation results is stored in the temporal buffer, the users are able to freely explore the time-varying datasets to find the optimal rendering parameters, or to find a period of interest (POI) in the underlying simulated physical phenomena. If a POI is not found in the current set of sampled time series, then the users can purge the contents stored in the temporal buffer and restart the sampling process. It is worth noting that the users are able to use more than one temporal buffer at the same time if there are sufficient memory resources available on the processing machine for storing and processing. As a result, the maximum number of time steps that can be processed directly depends on the available resources, and this is discussed in more detail in Sect. 4.2. In addition, the temporal buffer can either be allocated on the same memory region to be handled by the same processes (the in situ approach) or on a different memory region to be handled by different processes (the in transit approach).

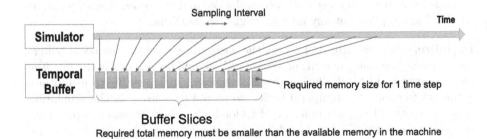

Fig. 1. Overview of the proposed temporal buffer, and its use by the simulator. The blue arrows indicate the copying/transfer of the simulation data to the temporal buffer (Color figure online)

2.2   Buffer Operations

Some of the API functions for manipulating the temporal buffers include the buffer creation, purging, copy, arithmetic operations, deletion, and output to files. The fundamental operations, such as creation and deletion, will be automatically processed by the `initialize()` and `finalize()` functions (see List 1.1). In addition, the users are able to include additional features and functionalities by manually manipulating the functions provided by the API. It is worth noting that the temporal buffers can be treated as variables, and as a result, we can apply some of the arithmetic operations to these temporal buffers as follows:

$$A = B + \frac{1}{2} C^2,$$

where A, B, and C represent different temporal buffers.

2.3   Code Integration

The code integration represents a significant part of the effort required by the users during the elaboration of a loosely coupled in situ [6] processing application. Therefore, it is important to reduce or minimize the labor costs when integrating the proposed in situ framework into simulation applications with well-established code. For this purpose, we have adopted the approach to code integration used by SENSEI [1] generic in situ interface. At this initial stage, we have used our own API for facilitating the code integration with our own simulation code. However, we kept in mind the importance of using a de facto standard API for facilitating the portability and reuse; thus, as an area for future work, we aim to merge this framework into SENSEI framework. List 1.1 shows an example of code integration within our framework, named *MicroEnv*, where the main functions necessary for the code integration are as follows: Initialize; Copy; Execute, and Finalize. The parameters are sent using JSON files, which also contain the necessary code for the initialization and processing (visualization, analysis, or simulation steering). This approach provides a great deal of flexibility to the users, since it avoids the need for recompilation, and the processing step can be modified and replaced at any time through the JSON file.

Initialize. The Initialize API allows the users to prepare the temporal buffers for the post-processing, and the necessary code should be included in the *init.json* file as shown in List 1.2. During the initialization, it is possible to instantiate an object to create the temporal buffer, to map a data array in the simulation onto the created temporal buffer, and to load any other necessary parameters. In the example described in List 1.2, the object *pressure* has variable p in the simulation code mapped onto the temporal buffer *prs*. Here, *float32* means that the temporal buffer element has 4-byte floating-point precision, and the allocated element size for one time step is *1,234,567* bytes. The *buff_slice: 150* means there are 150 allocated time slices, and thus the data array p is saved every *10* time steps as defined by the *interval* variable. Therefore, by using this initialization setting, the generated temporal buffer will be capable of holding the simulation results for 150 time steps out of a total of 1,500 time steps.

Listing 1.1. An example of *MicroEnv* code integration, where the array *p*, mimicking the simulation result, is processed by the visualization code written in the *exec.json* file. This pseudo code also shows the flexibility of *MicroEnv* API since the *exec.json* can be replaced at any time, and can also be used for the simulation steering

```
#include <stdio.h>
#include <sys/stat.h>
#include <time.h>
#include <cstdio>
#include <unistd.h>
#include "MicroEnv.h"

int main(int argc, char **argv){
  size_t z=1234567;
  float *p=new float[z]; // declare pressure
  const char* fpath = "./exec.json";
  struct stat sbuf;

  MicroEnv* me;
  me->initialize(..., "init.json");

  for (int step=0; step<MaxTimeStep; step++) {
    // update parameters
    if ( stat(fpath, &sbuf) ) {
      fprintf(stderr, "file not found: %s\n", fpath);
      return 1;
    }
    load_parameter(); // read user's parameter

    // simulation procedure
    ...
    prs_update(p,...); // update pressure
    me->copy("p",...); // copy data from array p to buffer
    ...
    me->execute(fpath);
  }

  me->finalize();
  return 0;
}
```

Data Copy. The copying of the simulation results to the temporal buffer starts after the calling of the copy() API, which should be called right after the update of the variable array *p* in the simulation. The copying of the data can be run in either *sync* or *async* mode, and in the case of the *sync* mode, MPI barrier occurs implicitly, and in the case of the *async* mode, MPI_Waitall is called inside the execute() API, allowing us to hide the communication during the processing of extra tasks.

Listing 1.2. An example of the initialization file (JSON file) for the Initialize API

```
{
  "pressure" {
    "buf_name":"prs",
    "buf_precision":"float32",
    "buf_element":1234567,
    "buf_slice":150,
    "src_name":"p",
    "interval":10
  },
  "mode":"in_situ", // "both"
  ...
}
```

Listing 1.3. Example of a JSON file for data transfer and execution. In this example, *draw.py* indicates matplotlib [4] code to visualize 2D data objects

```
{
  "transfer" {
    "sync":"async",
    "source": p
  },
  "exec" {
    "exec_file":"draw.py"
  }
}
```

Execute. The Execute API executes the procedures described in the *exec.json* file, such as shown in the example in List 1.3. In this example, the variable *transfer* sets the transfer mode to be asynchronous between the array p in the simulator and in the corresponding temporal buffer. Meanwhile, the variable *exec* refers to the file *draw.py*, which contains the actual code to be executed. Figure 2 shows a 2D cross-section of the 3D cavity flow simulation results, obtained by executing *draw.py*.

Finalize. The Finalize API tells the application to finish the utilization of the in situ framework, and removes all of the temporal buffers.

2.4 Update Parameters and Steering

The proposed framework also provides a checking function to verify whether a specified file was updated, by using the *stat()* system call, which returns the timestamp of the checked file. This function gives the necessary information to update the most recent contents during the simulation runs and provides a flexible steering functionality. Figure 3 shows the procedure of this update mechanism, where the users are directly manipulating the *exec.json* file from

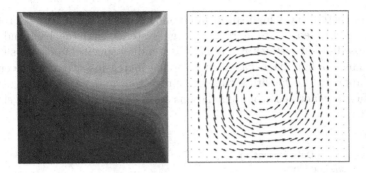

Fig. 2. Some rendering examples of the cavity flow simulation generated by *draw.py* by using matplotlib [4] functionalities. The left figure shows a pressure contour map, and the right figure shows the velocity vector

their clients, via an ssh connection. If the *exec.json* file is updated inside the time step loop, the JSON file content is loaded and reflected in the application during the execution. Although this mechanism is simple, it is worth mentioning that it is powerful enough to steer both the application and the in situ processing.

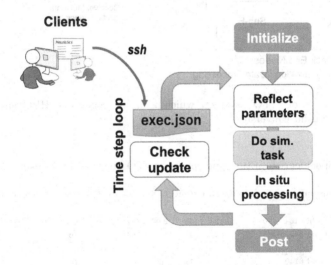

Fig. 3. Flowchart of the proposed in situ framework. The corresponding code is shown in List 1.1

3   Computational Environment and Implementation

3.1   Computational Environment

Our target HPC environment [5] for the proposed framework is a heterogeneous system that combines a back-end HPC system with a powerful front-end subsystem connected via a high-speed interconnect as shown in Fig. 4. Front-end nodes are composed of standard and large systems, and the back-end nodes are composed of subsystems A and B. The detailed specifications are shown in Table 1. This configuration has been receiving increasing attention recently as a viable approach to facilitate the data processing and visualization of large-scale datasets generated from simulations with constantly increasing size and complexity.

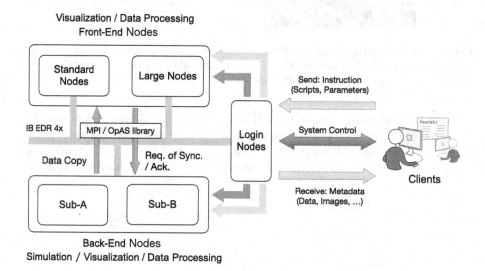

Fig. 4. Overview of "ITO" system, which is a heterogeneous HPC environment, installed at Kyushu University

Table 1. Specification of the supercomputer ITO operated by Kyushu University

	Architecture	Clock [GHz]	CPU	Core	Node	Memory [GB]	Network [Gbps]	GPU
Back-end								
Sub-A	Xeon Gold 6154	3.0	2	18	2,000	192	100	–
Sub-B	Xeon Gold 6140	2.3	2	18	128	384	100	P100×4
Front-end								
Standard	Xeon Gold 6140	2.3	2	18	160	384	10	Quadro×1
Large	Xeon E7-8880 v4	2.2	16	22	4	12,000	10	Quadro×1

3.2   Software System

The following description considers the in transit case, using different computing resources in the viewpoint of proximity, although it is also valid for the in situ case if the main processing is conducted with the same processes used for the simulation. The in situ functionalities provided by the proposed framework are based on Open Address Space (OpAS) library [7] as shown in Fig. 5. OpAS library is a PGAS-based one-sided communication library. This library provides an API to enable asynchronous access to the exposed memory region from the simulation code (indicated by the *Addrs* in the figure) to outside applications. In some cases, the number of nodes allocated for running the simulation can differ slightly from those allocated for the data processing, and in such cases it becomes necessary to efficiently map the data between them. In our proposed framework, *xDMlib* data management library is used [8] for this purpose. An example of the data redistribution is shown in Fig. 5, where the data are placed on a node, on the simulator side, and are split and sent to two different nodes on the data processing side.

Figure 5 shows an example of an implementation using OpAS library, which is composed of OpAS Target, OpAS Server, and OpAS Client. OpAS Target implies the application, OpAS Client implies the external process, such as a visualization process, which interacts with the application, and OpAS Server works as a manager between the application and the external process. OpAS Target and Server are invoked at the same time and OpAS Client is able to connect to the server at any time. In the example shown here, the simulator generates results and the framework copies the results from the application to the temporal buffers asynchronously at the specified intervals. Users explore the accumulated data in the buffer through a visualization application, which is built using the APIs provided by the framework and is implemented with OpAS Client. Then, we obtain the metadata such as the rendered images or the extracted ROI portion of the data. Finally, the metadata are sent to the clients.

Libsim is a widely used in situ library, which provides similar functionality to OpAS libray via a set of high level API functions. OpAS library was developed by one of the co-authors, and through a thorough evaluation OpAS library was found to be able to execute more detailed interactions between the application and the external processes than Libsim. OpAS library also allows other types of interactions, and thus the OpAS library can provide completely independent access from the external processes. This means that OpAS library has a smaller computational overhead and requires less modification to the original applications.

3.3   Use In Situ and in Transit Scenarios

Figure 6 shows a use case in the in situ processing scenario. In this use case, both the application and the processing are executed on the same computing resources, represented by the process groups #0 and #1, respectively, in the figure. Since the application and analysis processes share the memory region on the same node, the data communication will be replaced by the data copying operations. The use case for the in transit processing scenario is shown in Fig. 7. In this use case, different computational resources are assigned to handle the application and the visualization and data processing; thus, a more flexible utilization is possible.

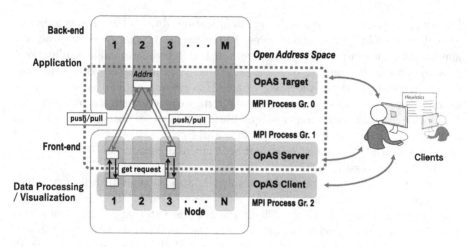

Fig. 5. Implementation of OpAS library on both back-end and front-end systems. In this figure, OpAS Client is invoked on the same node as OpAS Server. However, it is possible to assign OpAS Client on different nodes in the front-end system or even on the nodes in the back-end system. MPI process groups 0,1,2 are formed of OpAS Target, Server, and Client, respectively

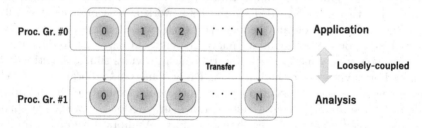

Fig. 6. An example use case for the in situ processing scenario

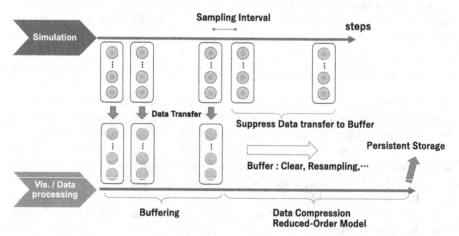

Fig. 7. An example use case of the in transit processing scenario

4 Evaluation and Discussion

4.1 Target Application

We consider RIAM-COMPACT simulator for the 3D incompressible Navier-Stokes equations, which is used to investigate the airflow over a terrain to predict the power generated by a wind turbine [9], and is discretized by a finite-difference method on a structured grid system with large eddy simulation (LES) turbulence modeling. This simulation uses a Cartesian grid system, which is regularly spaced in the horizontal (X-Y) directions and is stretched in the vertical (Z) direction, and all variables are defined on a node (collocated). This simulator solves four primitive variables, that is, the pressure and three velocity components. However, this simulator requires 16 additional scalar arrays, thus, 20 words per point are required in total.

4.2 Considerations on the Number of Time Steps to Hold

The number of time steps which can be stored on the system for the post-processing is directly dependent on the available computing resources. In the case of RIAM-COMPACT application running on ITO system, we make the following considerations. From the viewpoint of performance, we can assign 2 million points for each of the CPU cores, and this will give a total of 640 MB of memory usage per core.

$$2\,M \times 4\,\text{components} \times 20\,\text{words} \times 4\,\text{byte(float)} = 640\,\text{MB/core}$$

Since each node in ITO subsystem A has 36 cores, the application will occupy 23 GB on a single node. Assuming that the Linux system uses around 20 GB, the remaining memory will be around 150 GB. As a result, if we store four primitive variables as a snapshot, it will require 1 GB per node, and consequently, a total of 150 time steps can be stored in this situation.

$$2\,M \times 4\,\text{components} \times 4\,\text{byte(float)} \times 36\,\text{cores} = 1\,\text{GB/node}.$$

4.3 Target Processing Examples

Visualization Parameter Searching. During the optimization of the visualization parameters for the time-varying simulation results, the user can use a trial-and-error approach via interactive visual exploration using the collected simulation time steps at user-specified time intervals. After finding the optimal parameters, the user can also switch to the offline batch mode and use the obtained visualization parameters for submitting large-scale visualization oriented batch jobs.

The proposed temporal buffer can alleviate the inconvenience caused by the producer/consumer speed mismatch between the data generation and processing. If the data processing is slow compared to the data generation, then unless we have a way to preserve the time series data, such as the proposed temporal buffer, the users may face the risk of losing data due to overwriting of data during the simulation run. On the other hand, if the data processing is faster than the data generation, then the users will need to wait until the completion of the simulation run before continuing with the processing, and as a result, the data processing throughput will greatly decrease during the rendering parameter exploration considering the human-in-the-loop process.

Since the maximum number of time steps which can be stored in the buffer is constrained by the memory capacity of the computing resources, the advantage of our approach is that different data processing steps, including the rendering parameter search, can be performed on the data accumulated in the temporal buffer. In addition, the accumulated data will be available until it is explicitly deleted; thus, it is independent of the data generation speed on the simulator side. Therefore, the inconvenience caused by the producer/consumer speed mismatch is eliminated as well as the risk of losing data each time the dataset is updated.

Steering and Flexible Data Processing. Thanks to the update mechanism of the control file (*exec.json*) provided by the proposed framework, as described in detail in Sect. 2.4, it is possible to arbitrarily change the in situ processing parameters, even during the simulation, by modifying the contents of the control file. Therefore, this approach gives a great flexibility to the users not only for the post processing, but also for the simulation steering.

Data Compression. If a user wants to investigate the time-varying data after the simulation, as in conventional post-hoc processing, several data reduction techniques can be applied to the accumulated data in the temporal buffer. For instance, we can subset the data region by specifying a ROI, by applying data compression techniques, or by extracting only the necessary variables, or by selecting a specific POI. Afterwards, the reduced data can be stored on the persistent storage for light-weight post-hoc processing.

Construction of a Reduced-Order Model. A reduced-order model (ROM) can be built, for instance, by applying principal component analysis (PCA) to the number of time steps accumulated in the temporal buffer, and by choosing the time step that has the largest eigenvalue, it becomes possible to optimize the data reduction factor while taking into consideration the reproduction precision. Then, after saving the calculated eigenvalues and eigenvectors, we can remove the contents of the temporal buffer, update the data, and repeat this process. By instantiating two buffers, that is, by using a double buffer, continuous processing becomes possible, and from the set of obtained eigenvalues and eigenvectors, it becomes possible to generate a ROM over all simulated time steps, allowing detailed post-processing analysis. In order to support this work, incremental POD [3] plays an important role.

4.4   Data Transfer Performance (In Transit Scenario)

We are aware that in the in transit scenario, the data transfer time between OpAS Target and OpAS Server may be a potential bottleneck when using the proposed framework. Therefore, we evaluated the data transfer performance on ITO system. Table 2 shows the timings for the data transfer when using five processes: four processes (two nodes) run on Subsystem A were as OpAS Targets and one process on the front-end node as OpAS Server. Although the data transfer performance varies depending on the data size, the obtained data transfer rate for 4 MB of data was 1,428 MB per second. Therefore, it theoretically requires about 0.7 s to transfer 1 GB of data. Meanwhile, if we consider that the simulation time for a single time step is usually of the order of few seconds, we can conclude that the data transfer in this in transit scenario will not be a serious bottleneck in the workflow.

Table 2. Measurement of the data transfer performance (in transit scenario) on ITO system

Data	Size	Bandwidth [MB/s]
4	[B]	0.2
4	[KB]	150
4	[MB]	1,428

5   Conclusion

This paper proposes a novel and flexible in situ framework targeting traditional time-varying simulations executed in a modern heterogeneous HPC operational environment composed of traditional HPC back-end nodes in addition to powerful cluster-based front-end nodes. We propose a temporal buffer to absorb the producer/consumer time mismatch between the simulation and data processing. The main contribution of this work is the detailed design of the in situ framework with a temporal buffer. The temporal buffer was introduced to enable the accumulation of time-varying data from the simulator running on back-end HPC nodes. These accumulated time-varying data, sampled at user defined time intervals, can be accessed for the data processing using the same processes (in situ approach), as well as using different processes (in transit approach). The proposed framework is implemented sing the MPI and OpAS libraries, and can be used in both the in situ and in transit processing scenarios.

We also present *MicroEnv* API which provides the necessary functionalities for the code integration, as well as for manipulating the temporal buffers. This API provides an option to utilize an external JSON file for handling the initialization and the main processing. Since this JSON file can be modified and replaced during operation, flexible data processing including simulation steering becomes possible. In addition, this API also provides a checking functionality for the file update, which can be highly useful for the asynchronous steering of both the simulation and data processing, such as the visualization and analysis. To consider the performance of the framework in practical application scenarios, we described the visualization parameter exploration, data compression, and the construction of reduced-order models. In the specific case of ITO system environment, we also confirmed that the data transfer has minimal interference with the throughput of the in transit processing scenario. Therefore, the proposed framework enables us to completely separate the time required for simulating from the time required for data processing/visualization, and as a result, we believe that the proposed framework can significantly improve the flexibility of in situ data processing.

Although we are still in the initial concept and testing stage, we present some of the early evaluation results. In future work, we are planning to use SENSEI generic interface in order to improve the portability and reuse.

Acknowledgement. This research has used the computational resources of the K computer at RIKEN Center for Computational Science (R-CCS) in Kobe, Japan. This work is partially supported by the "Joint Usage/Research Center for Interdisciplinary Large-scale Information Infrastructures" in Japan (Project ID: jh180060-NAH), and also by the Japanese Ministry of Education, Culture, Sports, Science and Technology (MEXT) as a social and scientific priority issue (Development of Innovative Design and Production Processes that Lead the Way for the Manufacturing Industry in the Near Future) to be tackled by using the post-K supercomputer.

References

1. Ayachit, U., et al.: The SENSEI generic in situ interface. In: Proceedings of the 2nd Workshop on In Situ Infrastructures for Enabling Extreme-scale Analysis and Visualization, ISAV 2016, pp. 40–44. IEEE Press, Piscataway (2016). https://doi.org/10.1109/ISAV.2016.13
2. Bauer, A.C., et al.: In situ methods, infrastructures, and applications on high performance computing platforms. Comput. Graph Forum **35**(3), 577–597 (2016). https://doi.org/10.1111/cgf.12930. https://onlinelibrary.wiley.com/doi/abs/10.1111/cgf.12930
3. Fareed, H., Singler, J.R.: Error Analysis of an Incremental POD Algorithm for PDE Simulation Data. ArXiv e-prints, March 2018
4. Hunter, J.D.: Matplotlib: a 2D graphics environment. Comput Sci Eng. **9**(3), 90–95 (2007). https://doi.org/10.1109/MCSE.2007.55
5. Research Institute for Information Technology, K.U.: Supercomputer System ITO. https://www.cc.kyushu-u.ac.jp/scp/eng/system/01_into.html. Accessed 15 May 2018
6. Kress, J., Klasky, S., Podhorszki, N., Choi, J., Childs, H., Pugmire, D.: Loosely coupled in situ visualization: a perspective on why it's here to stay. In: Proceedings of the First Workshop on In Situ Infrastructures for Enabling Extreme-Scale Analysis and Visualization, pp. 1-6. ISAV 2015. ACM, New York (2015). https://doi.org/10.1145/2828612.2828623, http://doi.acm.org/10.1145/2828612.2828623
7. Nanri, T.: Proposal of interface for runtime memory manipulation of applications via PGAS-based communication library. In: Workshop on PGAS programming models: Experiences and Implementations, HPC Asia 2018, 31 January 2018

8. Ono, K., Kawashima, Y., Kawanabe, T.: Data centric framework for large-scale high-performance parallel computation. Procedia Comput. Sci. **29**, 2336–2350 (2014). https://doi.org/10.1016/j.procs.2014.05.218, http://www.sciencedirect.com/science/article/pii/S1877050914003950. 2014 International Conference on Computational Science
9. Uchida, T.: LES investigation of terrain-induced turbulence in complex terrain and economic effects of wind turbine control. Energies **11**(6), 1530 (2018). https://doi.org/10.3390/en11061530

Streaming Live Neuronal Simulation Data into Visualization and Analysis

Simon Oehrl[1,5]([✉]) [ID], Jan Müller[1] [ID], Jan Schnathmeier[1] [ID],
Jochen Martin Eppler[2] [ID], Alexander Peyser[2] [ID], Hans Ekkehard Plesser[3,4,6] [ID],
Benjamin Weyers[1,5] [ID], Bernd Hentschel[1,5] [ID], Torsten W. Kuhlen[1,5] [ID],
and Tom Vierjahn[1,5] [ID]

[1] Virtual Reality and Immersive Visualization, RWTH Aachen University, Aachen,
Germany
{oehrl,kuhlen}@vr.rwth-aachen.de, tom.vierjahn@acm.org
[2] SimLab Neuroscience, Forschungszentrum Jülich GmbH,
Institute for Advanced Simulation, Jülich Supercomputing Centre (JSC),
Jülich, Germany
[3] Institute of Neuroscience and Medicine (INM-6) and Institute for Advanced
Simulation (IAS-6), Forschungszentrum Jülich GmbH, Jülich, Germany
[4] Faculty of Science and Technology, Norwegian University of Life Sciences,
Ås, Norway
[5] JARA-HPC, Aachen, Germany
[6] JARA-BRAIN Institute I, Jülich, Germany
https://www.vr.rwth-aachen.de,
https://www.fz-juelich.de/ias/jsc/slns.html,
http://www.csn.fz-juelich.de, http://www.nmbu.no/imt,
http://www.jara.org/en/research/hpc,
http://www.jara.org/en/research/brain

Abstract. Neuroscientists want to inspect the data their simulations
are producing while these are still running. This will on the one hand
save them time waiting for results and therefore insight. On the other, it
will allow for more efficient use of CPU time if the simulations are being
run on supercomputers. If they had access to the data being generated,
neuroscientists could monitor it and take counter-actions, e.g., parameter adjustments, should the simulation deviate too much from in-vivo
observations or get stuck.

As a first step toward this goal, we devise an in situ pipeline tailored
to the neuroscientific use case. It is capable of recording and transferring
simulation data to an analysis/visualization process, while the simulation
is still running. The developed libraries are made publicly available as
open source projects. We provide a proof-of-concept integration, coupling
the neuronal simulator NEST to basic 2D and 3D visualization.

Keywords: Neuroscientific simulation · In situ visualization

© Springer Nature Switzerland AG 2018
R. Yokota et al. (Eds.): ISC 2018 Workshops, LNCS 11203, pp. 258–272, 2018.
https://doi.org/10.1007/978-3-030-02465-9_18

1 Introduction

In order to understand the complex in-vivo processes inside the human brain, neuroscientists work on creating realistic in-silico simulations of subsets of it running on a computer. They create models consisting of individual neurons and their connections. Furthermore, they set the neurons' and the connections' parameters to values that have been determined via prior experiments – either in vivo or in silico. They also use values that they consider reasonable first guesses in order to determine ones that lead to realistic behaviour. A simulation is then run and reveals the behaviour of the neuronal network with the current set of parameters. Due to the complexity of the neuronal networks, the simulations are often run in a massively parallel fashion on supercomputers.

Neuroscientists analyse the acquired data once the simulation has terminated. They compare the simulated data to in-vivo data. For this purpose, they apply statistics and visualizations, for instance, line plots revealing the individual neurons' membrane potentials or raster plots presenting the spikes emitted by the neurons. From observed differences between simulated and the in-vivo data the neuroscientists devise updates to the model and the set of parameters. The updated neuronal model is then again simulated, analysed and re-assessed.

This iterative process of simulation and subsequent analysis (e.g., [20]) requires the neuroscientists to wait for the simulation to be finished before the model and its parameters can be adjusted. Interactive simulations are still very primitive, non standardized, and ad-hoc: means of looking into a running simulation exist (e.g., [16]), but they are limited. Neuroscientists can hardly take counter-actions to simulations that deviate too much from real-life behaviour or that show erratic behaviour beyond recovery. If this happens early during a simulation, scarce CPU time is wasted, without yielding new insight. On the contrary, that time cannot be used for other experiments waiting in the job queue – submitted by other scientists or for simulations using updated parameters.

If the neuroscientists were able to visualize their measurements during a live simulation, they could adjust parameters on the fly. That way, the parameters could be adjusted more frequently, using the allotted compute time more efficiently, providing insight earlier. To date, the only way mimicking such an interactive simulation requires to run it for very short intervals, halt it, analyse/visualize the data, adjust the model and its parameters, and eventually resume the simulation. This is tedious since the neuroscientists have frequently to restart even well-behaving simulations without applying any changes. More importantly, resuming a simulation introduces an overhead due to additional initialization time spent inside the simulator. This overhead will add up, so that currently the neuroscientists trade interactivity for better CPU time usage.

To overcome this, we devise a framework for streaming simulation data from a simulator to a separate analysis/visualization process. The framework is separated into two lightweight parts. The one converts the simulation data into a simulator-agnostic transfer format and provides the analysis/visualization process with means to access that data. The other provides a thin layer for transporting data packets in the transfer format. This separation facilitates adaptation of the framework to other simulators. Furthermore, we expect that the transport layer will be useful to in situ applications in fields other than neuroscience.

In the remainder of this paper Sect. 2 gives an overview of the related work. Section 3 presents the in situ framework we propose, Sect. 4 outlines our proof-of-concept integration of simulation and visualization, Sect. 5 evaluates the performance of the proposed framework. Section 6 concludes the paper and gives an outlook on future work.

2 Related Work

Simulating a neuronal network in the computer resembles an electrophysiological experiment. The neuroscientist builds a neuronal system by creating one or more model neurons and connecting them via synapses to form a network. After running the simulation, they analyse the measured data.

The NEST simulator [8] is able to work with large, heterogeneous networks of spiking neurons – either point neurons or neurons with a small number of compartments. NEST can represent spikes in continuous time [14]. It allows for simulating different types of model neurons and synapse models in one network. Arbor [5] is a new multi-compartment neuronal network simulator currently under active development. It is specifically designed for many-core architectures and provides optimized backends for CUDA, KNL, and AVX2. Arbor features asynchronous spike exchange that overlaps compute and communication, and therefore hides latencies. It will enable new scales and classes of morphologically detailed neuronal network simulations on current and future supercomputing architectures. NEURON [9,12] is capable of simulating individual neurons and networks of neurons. The related models are closely linked to experimental data. NEURON supports the neuroscientist in gaining insight without requiring in-depth expertise in numerical methods or programming by providing convenient tools for constructing, exercising, and managing neuron models.

Neuroscientists will look at the simulation results using statistical analysis tools as well as visualizations. They use either file I/O to write the simulation data to disk and read it back, or they use more elaborate transport mechanisms. MUSIC [7] is a standard API for exchanging data between simulators. It provides mechanisms to synchronize the simulations and map their data models to each other. NEST and NEURON provide interfaces to MUSIC. However, MUSIC primarily facilitates inter-operability between neuronal simulators within a parallel computer during runtime. This paper therefore provides a lightweight alternative specifically tailored to coupling simulations and visualizations. Nett[1] [17] provides a similar approach in this regard, building on top of ZeroMQ[2]. Furthermore, it can be used to steer simulations [16]. ZeroEQ[3] follows a similar approach.

---

[1] https://devhub.vr.rwth-aachen.de/VR-Group/nett.

[2] http://zeromq.org.

[3] https://github.com/HBPVis/ZeroEQ.

The scientific visualization (SciVis) community is facing similar in situ visualization challenges as the neuroscience community, albeit on significantly larger scales: while large-scale neuronal network simulations today typically operate on several tens of thousands to a few million neurons with only few recorded attributes, for SciVis the simulation data of a single timestep nowadays easily exceeds hundreds of gigabytes. In order to deal with these amounts of data efficiently, several in situ frameworks have emerged. ParaView Catalyst [2] provides data processing and visualization for in situ analysis and visualization. It works seamlessly with the visualization toolkit VTK [19] and ParaView [1]. LibSim [22] takes a similar approach and facilitates in situ computations within simulation codes. It interfaces VisIt [4] for data analysis and visualization, also building upon VTK. Catalyst and LibSim are pipelines specifically tailored to their visualization applications ParaView and VisIt, respectively. More general pipelines have emerged recently. SENSEI [3] provides a generic in situ interface promoting code portability and reusability, building upon an extended VTK data model. ALPINE [11] is targeting modern supercomputer architectures. It supports Catalyst and LibSim but also provides ALPINE Ascent as its own runtime. Conduit[4] provides a model describing hierarchical scientific data. It provides access to simulation mesh data structures and basic communication functionality. Among others, ALPINE Ascent and VisIt are using Conduit.

All of the above in situ frameworks focus more on the "established" HPC simulations, like computational fluid dynamics or climate simulations, than on the ones used in the field of neuroscience. Therefore, we devise a custom pipeline, developed along use cases emerging from the Human Brain Project [13]. We use Conduit for data description, due to the convenience it provides. We add a lightweight transport layer in order to connect simulation and analysis/visualization. By using Conduit, we expect the pipeline to be compatible to at least some of the existing, mature in situ frameworks, most notably ALPINE. We can therefore later adopt one of them if need be.

3   Method

The devised framework for streaming simulation data from a live simulation to a separate analysis/visualization process consists of two parts. The one Subsect. 3.1 plugs into the neuronal simulation, takes the recorded data and converts it into a simulator-agnostic transfer format; on the analysis/visualization side this part provides access to the stored data. The other part Subsect. 3.2 handles data transport.

3.1   NESCI – Neuronal Simulator Conduit Interface

Neuronal simulators provide means to record the simulated data. NEST [8], for instance, provides among others multimeters and spike detectors as instruments

---

[4] https://software.llnl.gov/conduit/.

that the neuroscientist can connect to either individual neurons or populations of them [21]. Arbor [5] provides similar methods. These instruments are optimized to efficiently work with the respective simulator. Consequently, the interfaces of their associated classes and methods to be called during simulation differ. In order to facilitate connecting any simulator to analysis/visualization, we propose a simulator-agnostic transfer data format.

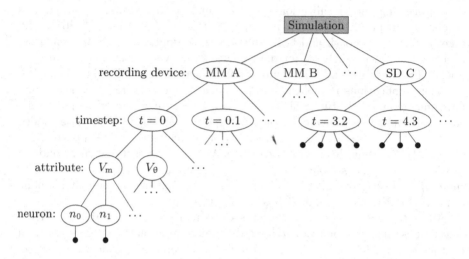

Fig. 1. Hierarchical data layout used for transfer: each recording device defines a subtree containing data for the stored timesteps. Multimeters (MM A, MM B) store measurements (black circles) of an attribute (V_m, V_θ, ...) for every neuron (n_0, n_1, ...). Spike detectors (SD C) store a list of neurons that fired in the respective timestep.

In this transfer format, data is arranged hierarchically in a tree, since this layout emerges naturally from the concept of data recording in neuronal simulation. Figure 1 presents an overview. The simulation acts as the root node of the data. Each recording device then establishes a subtree immediately underneath the root node. Since all the currently considered recording devices record data that is related to the simulation time, each recording device comprises again several subtrees – one per recorded timestep.

Multimeters record time series data of certain attributes for individual neurons. Those attributes are, for instance, the membrane potential (V_m) or the voltage threshold (V_θ) for firing. Each attribute constitutes a separate subtree underneath the respective time step. For a multimeter, data of each attribute is recorded in every timestep. The data is stored per neuron in the tree's leaves.

Spike detectors record neurons' firing events, i.e., spikes. Typically, these data are sparse: spikes occur only in few timesteps and only few neurons fire in a timestep. Consequently, only those timesteps that contain spikes are stored in the tree. The firing neurons' ids are immediately stored as a list in the leaves of underneath the timestep.

We use Conduit for data handling. Conduit provides intuitive means to write and retrieve hierarchical data. The hierarchical layout of a block of raw memory can be described to Conduit via JSON. An individual datum is addressed via its path. A valid path consists of the names of the tree's nodes, concatenated along the path from the root node to the respective datum. Furthermore, Conduit provides convenient means to serialize/deserialize the stored data for transport. Finally, Conduit efficiently facilitates updating existing data. The update is encoded as another Conduit tree and fed into the existing one. If a path exists, data are updated. If a path does not yet exists, the respective memory is allocated and data from the update is incorporated into the existing tree. This updating mechanism facilitates implementation of thread safe recording device adapters: each holds its own Conduit tree to record the data, consequently not requiring synchronization. Data is then transported off each device individually, again not requiring synchronization except for the transport layer. The analysis/visualization side in turn holds its own Conduit tree to collect the data to be visualized. It receives the individual trees and gathers them into its tree via Conduit's update mechanism.

On the simulation side, we provide base classes to facilitate implementation of simulator-specific adapters. These then tap into the recording methods of the simulator and feed the data into the hierarchical storage for transfer. On the analysis/visualization side, we provide base classes to facilitate implementation of reader classes that provide access to the stored data. Since each recording device in each simulator may provide different recordings, those reader classes again have to be simulator-specific.

We have implemented the described data layer, converting simulation data to and from the transfer format, as the C++ library `nesci` (pronounce 'nɛsi) – Neuronal Simulator Conduit Interface.

`Nesci` currently contains recording devices for NEST and a prototypic multimeter for Arbor. We provide Python bindings for the analysis/visualization side of `nesci` for convenient integration into existing scripts. `Nesci` is publicly released[5] under the terms and conditions of the Apache v2.0 license.

3.2 CONTRA – Conduit Transport

The data generated by the simulator and recorded via `nesci` has to be transported to the analysis/visualization side. Since `nesci` encoded the data using Conduit into a simulator-agnostic transfer format, we provide a general purpose transport layer for Conduit trees. We expect this transport layer to be therefore also useful for domains other than neuroscience.

The transport layer provides an abstraction from the specific transport technology, e.g., shared memory or network connections. Inspired by Conduit, we offer a relay that acts as the interface to the data producers and consumers, respectively. The former sends Conduit trees via the relay interface. The latter

---

[5] https://devhub.vr.rwth-aachen.de/VR-Group/nesci.

is provided by the relay with a list of Conduit trees that can then be aggregated into a single data set via Conduit's update mechanism (cf. Subsect. 3.1).

A relay constructs an instance of an accessor to the selected transport technology. On sending, the Conduit tree is serialized into a data packet comprising the tree's data as raw bytes and its schema as a JSON string. The packet is then handed over to the selected transport technology via the accessor. On receiving, the arrived packets are deserialized into individual Conduit trees, one per packet. That way, the consuming application can implement application-specific data aggregation using Conduit's update mechanism.

We provide a relay implementation that can use a variety of transport technologies. For each technology an accessor needs to be implemented. This accessor has to be able to handle the specified data packets by providing suitable send and receive methods. Consequently, environment specific transport technologies can be added in a straightforward way.

We have implemented the described transport layer as the C++ library `contra` – CONduit TRAnsport. `Contra` currently executes data transport via shared memory provided by `boost::interprocess`[6]. That way, `contra` can be used for coupling simulations to analysis/visualization processes both running on a neuroscientist's local workstation. A ZeroMQ-based and a GPRC-based transport will be added in the near future enabling simulation and analysis/visualization to be run on separate machines. MPI-based transport will be added afterwards, possibly relying on Conduit's existing MPI support. We provide Python bindings for the transport interfaces for convenient integration into existing scripts. `Contra` is publicly released[7] under the terms and conditions of the Apache v2.0 license. The LGPL will apply for ZeroMQ-based transport.

4 Application

As a proof-of-concept application we couple a small NEST simulation to both a 2D and a 3D visualization. Both simulation and visualization are supposed to run on a single machine, so that neuroscientists can immediately inspect a running simulation at their desk. This, however, deliberately limits the simulatable network size. Nevertheless, simulations of larger networks to be run on a supercomputer are left for future work. Simulation and visualization are supposed to run in different processes, having simulation and analysis loosely coupled. This split is furthermore expected to simplify later deployment to other platforms using different means of transportation.

4.1 NEST Simulation

The simulated network consists of two layers of neurons containing $4n$ excitatory and n inhibitory neurons, respectively. The neurons are simulated using

---

[6] https://www.boost.org.

[7] https://devhub.vr.rwth-aachen.de/VR-Group/contra.

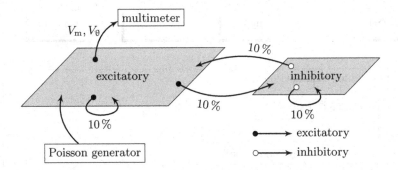

Fig. 2. Neural network used for the proof-of-concept application. A layer of $4n$ excitatory neurons and a layer of n inhibitory neurons are connected with both intra- and inter-layer connections. The excitatory neurons are fed a noise signal. They are connected to a multimeter for visualization.

a leaky integrate-and-fire model with exponential shaped postsynaptic currents [6,10,18]. With a 10% probability each neuron creates intra- and inter-layer connections to other neurons. A Poisson generator is connected to each excitatory neuron, feeding them a noise signal, serving as input to the neuronal network. The structure of the network is visualized in Fig. 2. A multimeter is connected to the excitatory neurons, recording their membrane potentials V_m and their firing threshold V_θ.

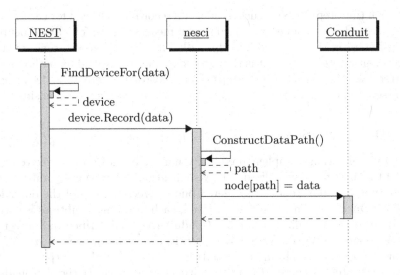

Fig. 3. Data flow for writing data from the NEST simulation to the Conduit node of a nesci device (e.g., a multimeter or spike detector).

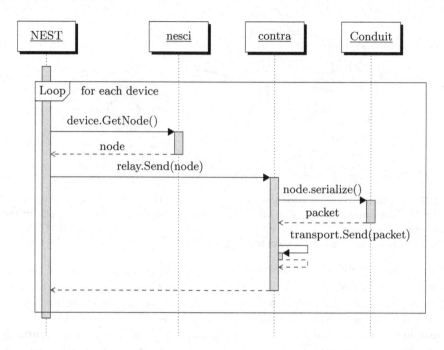

Fig. 4. Data flow for sending data stored in the Conduit nodes of each nesci device via contra.

In each timestep, NEST issues a call to its recording backend for each recording device and each connected neuron. The measurements for all the neuron's recorded attributes are passed into this call. This data is passed to `nesci` using a convenient interface where it is then stored at the corresponding path in a conduit tree Fig. 3. After some timesteps being recorded – here 10 – the recorded data is sent via `contra`'s transport layer to the analysis/visualization side Fig. 4.

4.2   2D Visualization

The 2D visualization is implemented in Python. It has a Conduit tree to aggregate all the data to be visualized. The visualization is run as a separate process and continuously polls `contra` for new Conduit trees (cf. top of the outer loop in Fig. 5). Once new data has been received, each of the new subtrees is used as an update to the visualization's main Conduit tree as described in Subsect. 3.1 (cf. inner loop in Fig. 5). After having received new data, the 2D plot of the simulated neurons' membrane potentials is updated. For this purpose a list of available timesteps is queried from the multimeter. Afterwards, the neuron ids for which the requested attribute (here the membrane potential) has been recorded during the timesteps is determined. Then, the time-series data is queried for each neuron and passed to Matplotlib for plotting (cf. bottom of the outer loop in Fig. 5).

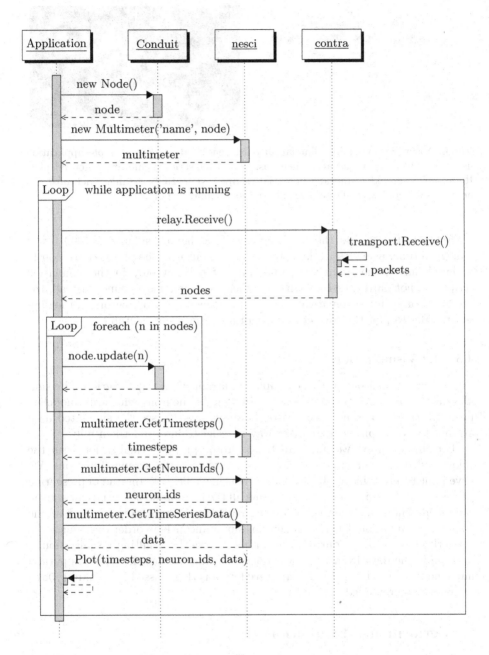

Fig. 5. Structure of the visualization applications. A single nesci multimeter device is created and used to query the data from the main conduit node for the visualization. The relay polls for nodes containing new data via the transport layer (the shared memory) and adds each subtree to the main conduit tree.

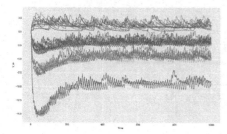
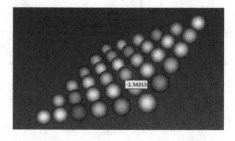

Fig. 6. Visualization of live simulation data generated for the example application using $n = 9$, i.e., 36 excitatory neurons. Left: time-series membrane-potential plot. Right: colour-coded membrane potential mapped to spatially arranged neurons; one neuron is selected with the tooltip showing its membrane potential.

Figure 6, left, shows the resulting plot after having simulated 1000 ms of biological time, using $n = 9$, i.e., 36 excitatory neurons. The plot is continuously updated during the simulation. The value of n is set only in the simulation script and not hard-coded anywhere in the nesci-contra pipeline. Instead, the visualization script automatically determines the number of neurons in the data set in order to plot the correct number of lines – one per neuron.

4.3 3D Visualization

Physically, the neurons in this example are arranged on regular grids. The simulation requires only the connections between the neurons which are modelled probabilistically. The neuroscientists, however, need to see the simulated data arranged in their physically correct way in order to interpret them fully.

For this purpose, we have created a prototypic 3D visualization with the colour-coded membrane potential mapped onto spatially arranged neurons. We have implemented this application in C++ using VTK [19]. Instead of presenting time-series data, this application presents all the membrane potentials for a given time step. The neuroscientists can then navigate the time steps to look at the respective simulation data for all neurons simultaneously in order to evaluate the network's spatial behaviour. Figure 6, right, shows the resulting visualization.

Polling the data from contra is done the same way as the previous python implementation (c.f. Fig. 5). The retrieved data is then passed to a vtkPolyData in order to be rendered.

5   Performance Evaluation

An important question is how much overhead this adds to the simulation when using our proposed pipeline as the benefits of in situ visualization vanish if it slows down the simulation too much. The neuronal network described in the previous section was simulated on a machine equipped with two Intel® Xeon® CPU E5-2695 v3 @ 2.3 GHz for $n = 9$, $n = 25$, and $n = 81$. We connected a simple python client similar to Fig. 5 to poll – and thus clear – the shared memory to avoid running to create a realistic scenario. However, the display of the plots was removed from the application to reduce the impact on the simulation as both run on the same machine. We do not focus on the performance of the visualization but rather the overhead added to the simulation by adding our custom recording backend to the NEST simulator.

Table 1. The total time to run the simulation without any recording backend attached, with the ASCII recording backend attached and with our streaming recording backend attached. The percentages in brackets denote the relative duration of the simulation with the corresponding recording backend attached compared to the baseline.

	Baseline	ASCII	NESCI & CONTRA
$n = 9$	21.5 ms	98.2 ms (457%)	543.7 ms (2528 %)
$n = 25$	62.2 ms	281.1 ms (452%)	1559.0 ms (2506 %)
$n = 81$	206.7 ms	940.5 ms (455%)	5293.2 ms (2560 %)

First, we ran the simulation without any recording backend attached to get a baseline of how long the simulation takes on this specific machine. Second, we ran the same simulation attached with the ASCII recording backend that is provided alongside the NEST simulator. It is used to compare the overhead of our streaming backend to other recording backends. Last, we ran the same simulation attached with our custom streaming recording backend that uses nesci and contra. Table 1 shows the total simulation time for the three presented scenarios. For each scenario the network was simulated for 1000 ms of biological time. The simulation time denotes how long it took the simulation to finish. Each test was repeated 5 times only counting the minimum result.

Currently, our custom recording backend adds to much overhead to the simulation for practical usage in real world applications. However, it should be noted that the current implementation is only a proof-of-concept and not a finished product because at this point in time no effort has been put into optimizing the performance of the pipeline. To determine where the performance can be improved the simulation was profiled using the Valgrind instrumentation framework [15].

Profiling revealed two major bottlenecks in the recording backend: writing new data into the Conduit tree as described in Fig. 3 and writing the data into the shared memory as described in Fig. 4. These two functions contribute to over 90% of the total simulation time (46% and 45% respectively). In the remaining part of this section, we focus on a more detailed analysis of these two functions and suggests possible optimizations.

The main operations that contribute to the bad performance of writing data to the Conduit tree (c.f. Fig. 3) are constructing the path to the data (16 % of the total simulation time) and inserting the data into the Conduit tree (22 % of the total simulation time). Constructing the path currently involves numerous costly `std::stringstream` operations to convert floating point values to strings.

The 2017 standard of C++ provides the alternative function `std::to_chars` which is optimized for performance instead of flexibility and usability. The second operation – inserting the data into the tree – involves numerous costly string operations to extract the path and dynamic allocations for the newly added nodes. Conduit supports preallocating a block of memory that can be used to store the data directly. On the one hand, this would drastically reduce the number of allocations when adding new nodes to the tree. On the other hand, the data cen be now written directly to the raw memory by calculating the offset. This saves the costly string operations introduced by parsing the path to the data.

The second major bottleneck is writing the conduit tree to the shared memory (c.f. Fig. 4). Like in the previous scenario, two operations take the majority of the time: serializing the Conduit tree (22% of the total simulation time) and actually writing the data to the shared memory (20% of the total simulation time). The serialization of the tree is done by Conduit itself so there is no direct way to optimize this step. However, preallocating blocks of memory as discussed before should also accelerate the serialization process as Conduit is able to just copy the block instead of traversing every single node of the tree. In the second limiting operation – writing to the shared memory – almost the whole time is spent acquiring the mutex that synchronizes the writing and the reading process. This could be done in a separate thread so it does not block the simulation.

6   Conclusion and Future Work

We have proposed a lightweight streaming framework for connecting neuronal simulators to analysis/visualization. We have demonstrated its applicability by a proof-of-concept application coupling a simple NEST simulation to 2D and 3D visualizations. Both present the data while it is being simulated without having to continuously pause and resume the simulation. The current state of the pipeline adds too much overhead, but we provided a lot of suggestions to improve its performance in future work.

The two developed libraries (`nesci` and `contra`) work hand in hand, providing concise APIs for integration into neuroscientific workflows. We have demonstrated this property by outlining a typical data flow. Both libraries are publicly available under the terms and conditions of the Apache v2.0 license. While `nesci` is specifically developed for neuroscientific applications, we expect `contra` to be useful in other domains that are using Conduit for describing their data.

We plan to add ZeroMQ-, GRPC-, and MPI-based transport mechanisms to `contra` in the near future. That way, the proposed pipeline will become applicable to large-scale neuronal simulations. Furthermore, we plan to extend `nesci`'s Arbor support. We currently have only a rudimentary implementation available. Working in close collaboration with the Arbor developers will help streamline this implementation and greatly improve performance. In the long run, we will add support for other widely used neuronal simulators.

Acknowledgements. This project has received funding from the European Unions Horizon 2020 research and innovation programme under grant agreement Nos 720270 (HBP SGA1) and 785907 (HBP SGA2), and from the Excellence Initiative of the German federal and state governments.

References

1. Ayachit, U.: The ParaView Guide: A Parallel Visualization Application. Kitware Inc., New York (2015)
2. Ayachit, U., et al.: ParaView catalyst: enabling in situ data analysis and visualization. In: Proceedings of 1st Workshop In Situ Infrastructures for Enabling Extreme-Scale Analysis and Visualization, pp. 25–29 (2015). https://doi.org/10.1145/2828612.2828624
3. Ayachit, U., et al.: The SENSEI generic in situ interface. In: Proceedings of 2nd Workshop In Situ Infrastructures for Enabling Extreme-scale Analysis and Visualization, pp. 40–44 (2016). https://doi.org/10.1109/ISAV.2016.13
4. Childs, H., et al.: VisIt: an end-user tool for visualizing and analyzing very large data. In: High Performance Visualization-Enabling Extreme-Scale Scientific Insight, pp. 357–372 (2012)
5. Cumming, B., Yates, S., Klijn, W., Peyser, A., Karakasis, V., Perez, I.M.: Arbor: A morphologically detailed neural network simulator for modern high performance computer architectures. Proc. Neurosci. (2017). http://juser.fz-juelich.de/record/840405
6. Diesmann, M., Gewaltig, M.O., Rotter, S., Aertsen, A.: State space analysis of synchronous spiking in cortical neural networks. Neurocomputing **38–40**, 565–571 (2001). https://doi.org/10.1016/S0925-2312(01)00409-X
7. Djurfeldt, M., et al.: Run-time interoperability between neuronal network simulators based on the MUSIC framework. Neuroinformatics **8**(1), 43–60 (2010). https://doi.org/10.1007/s12021-010-9064z
8. Gewaltig, M.O., Diesmann, M.: NEST (neural simulation tool). Scholarpedia **2**(4), 1430 (2007)
9. Hines, M.L., Carnevale, N.T.: NEURON: a tool for neuroscientists. Neuroscientist **7**(2), 123–135 (2001). https://doi.org/10.1177/107385840100700207
10. Kobayashi, R., Tsubo, Y., Shinomoto, S.: Made-to-order spiking neuron model equipped with a multi-timescale adaptive threshold. Front Comput. Neurosci. **3**, 9 (2009). https://doi.org/10.3389/neuro.10.009.2009
11. Larsen, M., et al.: The ALPINE in situ infrastructure: ascending from the ashes of strawman. In: Proceedings of 3rd Workshop In Situ Infrastructures on Enabling Extreme-Scale Analysis and Visualization, pp. 42–46 (2017). https://doi.org/10.1145/3144769.3144778
12. Lytton, W.W., Seidenstein, A.H., Dura-Bernal, S., McDougal, R.A., Schürmann, F., Hines, M.L.: Simulation neurotechnologies for advancing brain research: parallelizing large networks in NEURON. Neural Comput. **28**(10), 2063–2090 (2016). https://doi.org/10.1162/NECO_a_00876
13. Markram, H., et al.: Introducing the human brain project. Procedia Comput. Sci. **7**, 39–42 (2011). https://doi.org/10.1016/j.procs.2011.12.015
14. Morrison, A., Straube, S., Plesser, H.E., Diesmann, M.: Exact subthreshold integration with continuous spike times in discrete-time neural network simulations. Neural Comput. **19**(1), 47–79 (2007). https://doi.org/10.1162/neco.2007.19.1.47

15. Nethercote, N., Seward, J.: Valgrind: a framework for heavyweight dynamic binary instrumentation. SIGPLAN Not. **42**(6), 89–100 (2007). https://doi.org/10.1145/1273442.1250746

16. Nowke, C., et al.: Toward rigorous parameterization of underconstrained neural network models through interactive visualization and steering of connectivity generation. Front Neuroinf. (2018). Provisionally accepted

17. Nowke, C., Zielasko, D., Weyers, B., Peyser, A., Hentschel, B., Kuhlen, T.W.: Integrating visualizations into modeling NEST simulations. Front Neuroinf. **9**, 29 (2015). https://doi.org/10.3389/fninf.2015.00029

18. Rotter, S., Diesmann, M.: Exact digital simulation of time-invariant linear systems with applications to neuronal modeling. Biol. Cybern. **81**(5), 381–402 (1999). https://doi.org/10.1007/s004220050570

19. Schroeder, W., Martin, K., Lorensen, B.: The Visualization Toolkit-An Object-Oriented Approach To 3D Graphics, 4th edn. Kitware Inc., New York (2006)

20. Schuecker, J., Schmidt, M., van Albada, S.J., Diesmann, M., Helias, M.: Fundamental activity constraints lead to specific interpretations of the connectome. PLoS Comput. Biol. **13**(2), 1–25 (2017). https://doi.org/10.1371/journal.pcbi.1005179

21. Schumann, T., Frings, W., Peyser, A., Schenck, W., Thust, K., Eppler, J.M.: Modeling the I/O behavior of the NEST simulator using a proxy. In: Proceedings of 3rd ECCOMAS Young Investigators Conference (2015). http://nbn-resolving.de/urn/resolver.pl?urn=urn:nbn:de:hbz:82-rwth-2015-039806

22. Whitlock, B., Favre, J.M., Meredith, J.S.: Parallel in situ coupling of simulation with a fully featured visualization system. In: EG Symposium Parallel Graphics and Visualization (2011). https://doi.org/10.2312/EGPGV/EGPGV11/101-109

Enabling Explorative Visualization with Full Temporal Resolution via In Situ Calculation of Temporal Intervals

Nicole Marsaglia[1]([✉]) [iD], Shaomeng Li[2] [iD], and Hank Childs[1]([✉]) [iD]

[1] University of Oregon, Eugene, OR 97403, USA
{marsagli,hank}@cs.uoregon.edu
[2] National Center for Atmospheric Research, Boulder, CO 80305, USA
shaomeng@ucar.edu

Abstract. We explore a technique for saving full spatiotemporal simulation data for visualization and analysis. While such data is typically prohibitively large to store, we consider an in situ reduction approach that takes advantage of temporal coherence to make storage sizes tractable in some cases. Rather than limiting our data reduction to individual time slices or time windows, our algorithms act on individual locations and save data to disk as temporal intervals. Our results show that the efficacy of piecewise approximations varies based on the desired error bound guarantee and tumultuousness of the time-varying data. We ran our in situ algorithms for one simulation and experienced promising results compared to the traditional paradigm. We also compared the results to two data reduction operators: wavelets and SZ.

1 Introduction

Traditionally, scientific simulations have enabled their data to be visualized by saving many "time slices" to disk. That is, at regular (or irregular) intervals, a simulation code will store the current state of the simulation to a file (or group of files). Visualization programs then operate on this data by loading it from the disk. In this model, the simulation code performs a temporal sampling, meaning that it contains accurate information about the simulation's state for the time slices that were stored, but no information about what happened for the intervals between its time slices. As a result, information between time slices is lost, creating a risk of lost science.

The purpose of our research is to enable the storage of full spatiotemporal data, and our research idea is enabled by an emerging processing paradigm for visualization on high-performance computers. This paradigm uses a combination of in situ processing and post hoc processing. First, in situ routines transform—and often reduce—data, which is then saved to disk. Second, the post hoc routines are then used for explorative visualization after the simulation has finished running. While this paradigm has emerged to enable explorative use

---

© Springer Nature Switzerland AG 2018
R. Yokota et al. (Eds.): ISC 2018 Workshops, LNCS 11203, pp. 273–293, 2018.
https://doi.org/10.1007/978-3-030-02465-9_19

cases in the face of I/O limitations, we believe it also creates opportunities for better preserving full spatiotemporal data. This is the case with our own work, which is less about data reduction than it is about increasing temporal resolution. That said, saving full spatiotemporal data requires prohibitive storage capabilities, and so data reduction is still necessary; we demonstrate reduction factors that reduce storage needs to being equal to the storage needs of the traditional paradigm—with the benefit of having full temporal access.

Our research approach depends on the concept of temporal intervals. However, raw temporal interval data is too large to store to disk—just as the traditional model would be if it stored all time slices—so it is only feasible if the intervals are compressed as they are stored. With our approach, we compress the data in a way that guarantees accuracy, e.g., 95% accurate, 99% accurate, etc. Our approach, then, has the benefit of being able to present known error bounds to stakeholders. However, the storage to achieve this accuracy guarantee is variable, and, for some types of data, may require more storage than the stakeholder is willing to allocate. For this research, we decided to embrace this decision (fixed error rate with unknown storage requirements) rather than consider the alternative (fixed storage requirements with unknown error rates), since we feel the former proposition is more desirable to stakeholders.

This work implemented an in situ algorithm with the choice of three different compressors that compress data temporally with a guaranteed error rate. For the chosen algorithm and user defined error rate, the algorithm operates individually on every grid point within a simulation. Within each grid point, for every generated value, the algorithm decides whether its current approximation sufficiently captures the value, or whether the approximation should be reset. We ran our algorithm on multiple data sets both post-hoc and in situ. We then analyzed the storage differences of our method compared to other known data reduction techniques. By implementing temporal data reduction in situ, this research has shown an improvement over saving at fixed intervals in the traditional paradigm. By compressing data temporally, the algorithm provides full temporal resolution of the simulation data and is a viable compression option compared to other techniques, namely wavelets and SZ.

2 Related Work

This section begins by classifying related work into categories of compression algorithms and what type of temporal data they operate on:

- Individual Time Slice Data (Sect. 2.1)
- Multiple Time Slice Data (Sect. 2.2)
- Complete Temporal Data (Sect. 2.3)

The remainder of this section considers the impact of introducing error during compression (Sect. 2.4) and how our approach differs from previous work (Sect. 2.5).

2.1 Individual Time Slice Data

This approach to data reduction disregards the temporal coherence between data points. Most of these data reduction techniques do, however, use spatial coherence to perform compression.

One approach to compress individual time slice data is to use *lossless* data compressors. Such compressors include FPC [7] for 64-bit floating-point scientific data; FPZIP [33] for generic scientific data; a framework by Fout and Ma [14] for floating-point volumetric data; and the approach by Chen et al. [9] for compressing irregular grids. Certain operations (e.g., sorting, mutation, etc.) can be applied to "precondition" the data to improve compression effectiveness. Such preconditioners include MAFISC [17] which consists of five individual filters; ISOBAR [40] which statistically separates data based on compressability; and a binary mask approach developed by Gomez et al. [15]. MPC [44] and FPcrush [6] are compressors built on top of preconditioners. However, lossless compression techniques can usually only reduce data by modest amounts and can be computationally intensive, and thus less attractive for in situ data reduction.

Another approach to compressing individual time slices is *lossy* data compression. ZFP [31] achieves high compression via spatial coherence and bit reduction, but this technique strongly favors smooth data. Similarly, the RBD algorithms [19] utilize spatial locality by viewing data point grids as graphs and representing subgraphs as singular values based on a user defined error bound. The lossy version of FPZIP [33] uses predictive encoding with a relative error bound. The newly emerged SZ compressors [12,41] use multiple predictive approaches to achieve effective compression.

Lossy wavelet compression has also been used in many visualization studies. 3D wavelet transforms have been shown to provide random access of voxels [18,38], level of detail [5,36,39], and fast volume rendering [16,21]. Data reduction achieved by wavelets has also been used to visualize large data in real time, for example, at a cost of $5\,\mathrm{s}$ per time slice on a $1,024^3$ turbulent-flow data set [42]. Work by Li et al. [28] improves the time cost of wavelet compression using parallel primitives on heterogeneous architectures, making wavelets a viable option for in situ compression [27]. These wavelet-based compression schemes, however, do not guarantee an error bound, and users often need to try their data before knowing the amount of deviation.

2.2 Multiple Time Slice Data

This approach to data reduction takes into account multiple time slices, utilizing the temporal coherence present in many scientific data sets, and potentially spatial coherence as well.

ISABELA [22] takes advantage of monotonic inheritance of points over time by first sorting a time slice, applying B-spline curves, and then representing multiple temporal windows with a reconstructed curve. It is reported to compress tumultuous data by nearly 85% with a 99% average correlation between the original and compressed data with little overhead in runtime [23]. Lehmann et al. [25] extended ISABELA by adding corrective computations to the sorted data and loosening the restrictions of when to write a window to memory. Additionally, their technique added support for selective loading of regions with varying levels of resolution.

Wavelet compression is also reported to operate across multiple time slices, making it a spatio-temporal compressor [30]. Here time slices after traditional spatial wavelet transforms are grouped into "windows" to perform additional temporal wavelet transforms, making use of the temporal coherence. The authors reported an approximately 2:1 benefit of incorporating temporal compression.

While these works take into account both spatial and temporal coherency, they do not provide full spatiotemporal resolution as their compression only applies to several consecutive time slices, and not every time slice.

2.3 Complete Temporal Data

This section encompasses full temporal resolution at the same spatial resolution as the native grid.

IDEALEM [24] relies on statistical similarities and breaks streams of data into windows, then compresses those windows based on point distribution to reduce data in situ. IDEALEM does well with tumultuous data as it provides a heavy distribution of points. However, it performs poorly with smooth curves as the data distribution is sparse within each window.

The work by Fernandes et al. [13] improved upon volumetric depth images (VDIs) by exploiting temporal coherence and utilizing delta encoding, allowing them to achieve both data reduction and explorable time-varying imagery.

Our work also falls under this category of compression.

And finally, we remind our readers that a more comprehensive survey on scientific data reduction techniques was done by Li et al. [29].

2.4 Impact of Error in Compression

Some work has been done to study the extent of error and error propagation on simulations utilizing compression techniques or the errors present in the subsequent analysis.

Lindstrom [32] researched error distributions of lossy compression, and found that the choice of compressors affects the error distribution and subsequent autocorrelation. Baker et al. [3,4] developed a methodology to evaluate the compression impact on climate data using ensembles of data, and later argued that multiple compression schemes applied on different variables can achieve the best compression on such data [2]. Woodring et al. [43] also looked at climate data compression, and argued that the maximum error (L^∞-$norm$) being most effective in communicating compression error.

With respect to visualization, Ma et al. [34] informed users the compression variations by encoding them into marching cubes. Li et al. [26] researched into the impact of data compression to visual analytics in regard to turbulent flow data.

2.5   How Our Approach Differs from Previous Work

Our work is specifically focused on providing complete temporal resolution at the same spatial resolution of the simulation. Since this data is assumed to be too large to store, we compress the data to make storage feasible. This is, of course, related to previous compression work, although we place a particular focus on guaranteeing accuracy—without guaranteed accuracy our approach has little meaning. As an example, it would be possible to use the traditional approach, temporal sampling, and interpolate between adjacent time slices. But such an approach would not actually be especially informative, since it would miss features that fell outside the interpolation. We experimented with this approach, and found that more than 1% of all interpolated values were more than 5% away from their correct values (see Table 5); we believe this rate of inaccuracy is unacceptable.

Our work operates on each grid point's continuous stream of data, attempting to compress every incoming value. Our research includes three in situ compressors that reduce temporal data into piecewise approximations. Each compressor uses a sliding window similar to the SWAB [20] data mining technique for segmenting time series data.

3   Algorithm

The objective of this work is to provide full temporal resolution with spatial resolution identical to the native grid, that is feasible enough to store on disk, and comes with an error bound guarantee; this is accomplished via a tailored compression technique.

Our algorithm was designed to work in situ and works as follows. Our algorithm creates an instance of a compression object for each grid point in the simulation. Each such object reduces its respective time series into piecewise approximations. The compression object at a given grid point runs independent of the compression objects at other grid points. For every generated value at a grid point, there are two possible outcomes. One, the simulation's current value falls within the error bound of the current approximation. Or two, the simulation's current value does not fall within the error bound of the current approximation. In this case, the former approximation is written to disk or memory and the process begins anew with the current value.

3.1   Error Bound

For most of the research presented in Sect. 2, a user defined error is realized as a maximum error bound. Maximum error can either mean a maximum absolute error (all reconstructed values must be within X units of the original values) or a relative absolute error (all reconstructed values must be within $X\%$ of the original values). In our case, we focus on relative absolute error, because maximum absolute error can lead to loss of important information when a value is near zero.

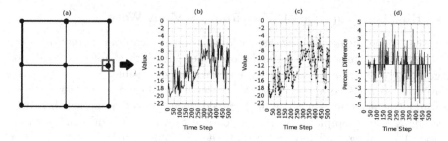

Fig. 1. Image (a) represents a simulation mesh with nine grid points. As the simulation runs, it generates a stream of data at each grid point. In our notional example, we consider the data stream at the grid point indicated with the red square. We apply a compressor object at each grid point which independently compresses its time series into a piecewise approximation. Image (b) shows the original time series of one grid point with 500 values, (c) is the piecewise approximation, and (d) is the per point difference of the two. In the example, the error bound is selected to be 5%, and image (d) shows our approximation to be within that error bound. (Color figure online)

However, by using a maximum relative error bound rather than an absolute error bound, we are imposing a stricter threshold on our compression algorithms. But we believe this guarantee, that results in no post-hoc artifacts, is important to domain scientists. Future work could involve relaxing this error guarantee, which would undoubtedly result in better compression.

3.2   Compression Approaches

As discussed earlier, our overall algorithm instantiates a compressor object for each grid point. We considered three types of compression approaches, each of which could be instantiated as the compressor objects for our algorithm. The three compression approaches are:

- Piecewise Linear (PL)
- Piecewise Constant (PC)
- Piecewise Constant Mean (PCM)

While each compression approach is similar, they are differentiated by how they approximate the time series. Each compression object approximates a stream of data by attempting to compress each value it encounters one by one.

Figure 1 shows an instance of a compressor object on a single grid point, the resulting approximation, and the difference between the original and approximated time series.

Piecewise Linear (PL). This compression approach transforms consecutive grid point values into piecewise linear approximations as the simulation progresses.

Struct *PC_CompressorObject_state***contains**
| float prediction;
end
void PiecewiseConstant_AddToStream(PC_CompressorObject_state *s, float cur_value,
                                   int cycle, int grid_point_index, float error_target)
if *(cycle == 0)* **then**
| s→prediction = cur_value;
else
| float allowable_diff = abs(cur_value)*error_target;
| float actual_diff = abs(cur_value − s→prediction);
| **if** *(actual_diff > allowable_diff)* **then**
| | s→prediction = cur_value;
| **end**
end

Algorithm 1. The pseudocode for the PC compressor object for a single grid point. This object will approximate the grid point's stream of values with a guaranteed error bound.

The approximation begins by taking the first value of the stream and assigning it to the starting value of the approximation. When the subsequent value is encountered, the slope (i.e. rate of change) is calculated. Using the starting value and the associated slope, it's possible to calculate the predicted value for a given time step. If $f(n)$ is a valid linear approximation up to time step n with x_i being the start of this approximation, and if t is the different in simulation time between two cycles, then the $slope = \frac{x_{i+1} - x_i}{t}$. Let n be the current time step and i be the starting time step of the approximation, let k be the difference between the current time step and the approximation's starting time step. In this case, $k = (n - i) * t$. The prediction for time step n becomes

$$f(n) = slope * k + x_i \tag{1}$$

From the starting value, the slope is extended one unit for every time step, creating our approximation as seen in Eq. (1). For each time step, the prediction is compared to the current value. If the difference between the approximated value and the current value is within the error bound, ϵ, then this process continues. If the difference between the current value and the approximated value does not fall within the error bound then the starting value, slope, and previous time step are saved. Once an approximated line has been saved, the approach then restarts with a new starting point.

$$f(n + 1) = \begin{cases} slope * k + x_i & \text{Error}(x_{n+1}, f(n + 1)) \leq \epsilon \\ x_{n+1} & \text{Error}(x_{n+1}, f(n + 1)) > \epsilon \end{cases} \tag{2}$$

The new starting point is the last value that was not within the error bound of the approximation, as seen in Eq. (2). A new slope will then be calculated using the starting point and the subsequent value.

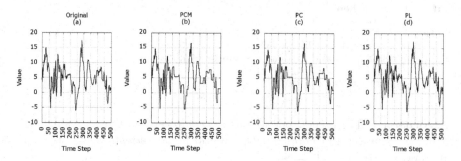

Fig. 2. Image (a) shows the original values. Images (b)–(d) are approximations created by our compression approaches using a 5% error bound. Image (b) is the piecewise approximation created by the PCM compression approach. Image (c) is the piecewise approximation created by the PC compression approach. And image (d) is the piecewise approximation created by the PL compression approach.

Piecewise Constant (PC). Piecewise Constant, our second approach and the approach described in Algorithm 1, is similar to Piecewise Linear. However, in the Piecewise Constant compression approach, a single value represents an interval of the time series, as in Eq. (3). If $f(n)$ is a valid constant approximation up to time step n and if x_i is the start of this approximation, then the prediction for time step n becomes

$$f(n) = x_i \tag{3}$$

The approximated line is extended until the difference between the predicted value and the current value exceeds the error bound, ϵ.

$$f(n+1) = \begin{cases} x_i & \text{Error}(x_{n+1}, f(n+1)) \leq \epsilon \\ x_{n+1} & \text{Error}(x_{n+1}, f(n+1)) > \epsilon \end{cases} \tag{4}$$

Once the error bound is exceeded, the compression approach saves the previous reference value and last valid time step, and the value that could not be represented by the approximation becomes the reference value going forward, as in Eq. (4).

Algorithm 1 shows the pseudocode of the PC compressor object at a single grid point and how this particular approach approximates each individual value encountered. For each incoming point in the stream, the compressor object makes a decision based on the error bound. If the incoming point and the predicted value are within an error bound then the prediction is valid and no actions are taken. Otherwise, the compression object saves the previous prediction and begins a new approximation with the current value.

Piecewise Constant Mean. The third compression approach, Piecewise Constant Mean, is similar to the first two, but takes the average of the encountered values per approximation interval. If $f(n)$ is a valid constant approximation up to time step n and if x_i is the start of this approximation, then the approximation is the average of all encountered points from x_i to x_n. The prediction for time step n becomes

$$f(n) = AVG(x_i, x_{i+1}, \ldots, x_{n-1}, x_n) \tag{5}$$

With each new incoming value, the compression approach calculates an approximation. The approximation is the mean of all the encountered values in the current interval, as in Eq. (5). The compression approach also makes sure that no point in the interval range falls outside the error bound in relation to the mean, as in Eq. (6).

$$f(n+1) = \begin{cases} AVG[x_i, x_{n+1}] & \begin{array}{c} Error(range\_max, f(n+1)) \leq \epsilon \\ \textbf{and} \\ Error(range\_min, f(n+1)) \leq \epsilon \end{array} \\ x_{n+1} & \text{o.w.} \end{cases} \tag{6}$$

That is, for every new value the approach checks to make sure that all represented points of the interval are within $[mean - \epsilon, mean + \epsilon]$ where ϵ is the error bound. This error bound needs to be checked for the minimum and maximum value of the current interval mean approximation. If the current minimum and maximum are within the error bound of the mean, which can change with every added value, then all values within the minimum and maximum are within their relative error bound to the approximated mean.

Figure 2 shows our three compression approaches approximating the same time series.

3.3   Memory Requirements

Within memory, each grid point is required to save several values that facilitate the compression process. Table 1 lists all the necessary data that each grid point must store.

3.4 Reconstruction

Constructing an approximation of the original data requires the desired time slice along with the compressed data.

The reconstruction process from the compressed data works as follows. The data from every grid point is written and subsequently available in its own file. Better organization of this data, for example, in one file, is future work. This information consists of the saved data values and their corresponding time steps. In addition to the time step and value, the PL approach also saves the associated slope.

Given the desired time slice, it is straightforward to find the corresponding value within each grid point's file. If the desired time slice falls within an approximation interval, we know that the value associated with that interval represents the desired time slice at some grid point. For reconstructing the PL approach, it is necessary to determine where the desired time slice falls within the approximation interval, this information can then be used to calculate the approximation value using the starting value and slope for that interval.

Table 1. The data members for each compressor object. For each approximation, it is necessary to have either the starting value or the current approximation value. For the PL approach, each object stores the slope associated with the current approximation. The PL and PCM also require the count, or number, of time steps they are approximating. The PL needs the count for post-hoc reconstruction, in order to calculate the current position of the line using the slope and starting value, and the PCM needs it to calculate the mean of all relevant values for the line. Note that an unsigned short could be sufficient for the count variable. Additionally, PCM requires the local range to be stored in order to guarantee the error bound criteria.

Algorithm	Memory
Piecewise Linear (PL)	4 Byte Slope 4 Byte Starting Value 4 Byte Count
Piecewise Constant(PC)	4 Byte Approx. Value
Piecewise Constant Mean (PCM)	4 Byte Min and Max 4 Byte Approx. Value 4 Byte Count

Reconstruction Time. Due to the rudimentary file organization, with each location having its own approximation file, the reconstruction time is proportional to the size of each file. With 250,000 time steps, reconstructing the later time steps takes longer than reconstructing earlier time steps due to searching individual files for the desired approximation interval and respective value. The reconstruction time of the compressed data set in Phase 3 of our research ranged from 30 s to 2 min. We aim to decrease reconstruction time in future work by implementing a more sophisticated way to save the approximation data.

4   Evaluation

Our experiments were designed to quantitatively evaluate our technique. This section outlines the parameters of the research conducted.

Our study was divided into three phases. In the first phase, we evaluated our technique in various configurations, including multiple data sets and error bounds. Phase one helped determine the potential and viability of our approaches as well as what type of data is best suited for our experiments. In the second phase, we compared our method with data reduction techniques that focus solely on spatial coherence. In the third phase, we ran an in situ study using our technique to demonstrate its viability as an in situ compressor.

The discussion of experiment factors is organized into configuration parameters (Sect. 4.1), measurement and metrics (Sect. 4.2), computing environment (Sect. 4.3), and software (Sect. 4.4).

4.1   Experiment Configuration

We varied the following factors:

- Compression Approaches (3 options)
- Data Sets (4 options)
- User Defined Error Bounds (3 options)

In the first phase of our study, the cross product of these factors was explored. In the second and third phases, only a subset of the cross product was considered.

Compression Approaches. We evaluated the three compression approaches described in Sect. 3: Piecewise Constant (PC), Piecewise Linear (PL), and Piecewise Constant Mean (PCM).

Data Sets. The first phase focused on time series data, with each time series coming from a spatial location within a simulation. The times series data we considered is as follows:

- LULESH [1]: A collection of 8 time series (i.e. from 8 different spatial locations) from an explosion data set. Each time series has 4,561 single-precision data points; each time series is 18.244 kB.
- Tornado [37]: A collection of 10 time series from a tornado data set. Each time series has 500 single-precision data points; each time series is 2 kB.
- XGC1 Ion Particles [8]: A collection of 25 time series from a tokamak data set. Each time series has 818 single-precision data points; each time series is 3.272 kB.
- GHOST [35]: A collection of 15 time series from a turbulent rotational flow data set. Each time series has 5,000 single-precision data points; each time series is 20 kB.

For the second phase we compared our algorithm results on 10,000 time slices of GHOST with two spatial compression techniques: wavelets and SZ-1.4. Each time slice of GHOST is roughly 8 MB in size, with each time slice being comprised of 128^3 single-precision floating point values.

For the third phase, we ran our algorithm in situ on the GHOST simulation for 250,000 time steps.

User Defined Error Bound. We applied three user defined error bounds: 1%, 3%, and 5%. Our error bound is a point-wise relative error bound, and is the same error bound that SZ-1.4 provides as a compression option. The point-wise relative error bound acts on individual grid points. If a grid point has value v, and the point-wise error bound is set at 5%, then the reconstructed value will be abs$(0.05 * v)$ away from v.

From here on we will refer to this error bound approach as *point-wise error bound*.

4.2   Phase Overview and Measurements

The first phase was comprised of applying our algorithm to the four data sets, LULESH, Tornado, XGC1 Ion Particles and GHOST. For each data set we ran our algorithm with each compression approach and each user defined error bound. This means we ran 36 experiments each with multiple measurements. For each data set we calculated the maximum compression ratio, the minimum compression ratio, and average compression ratio.

For the second phase, we compared our compression approach with two other compressors: wavelets and SZ-1.4. In this phase, we fixed certain aspects of each compression operator, compressed 10,000 time slices of GHOST, and measured the results. Because our method produces results with full temporal resolution that allow for post-hoc exploration, we applied wavelets and SZ-1.4 to every time step to mimic the temporal resolution that our algorithm produces.

For the wavelet compressor, we fixed the compression ratio and measured the average point-wise error, maximum point-wise error, and average compression time. We ran four wavelet configurations that guaranteed compression size, namely, 32:1, 64:1, 128:1, and 256:1 compression.

For SZ-1.4, we fixed the point-wise error bound to be 1%, 3%, and 5% and then measured the average point-wise error, maximum point-wise error, average compression ratio, and average compression time.

We also applied our approach to the 10,000 time slices of GHOST and measured the average point-wise error bound, maximum point-wise error bound, average compression ratio, and average compression time. We note that we did not run the SZ-1.4 or wavelet compression operators in situ, but applied the compressors to each of the 10,000 time slices of GHOST post-hoc.

In the third phase, our algorithm was run in situ on GHOST with each compression approach and each error bound. The GHOST simulation setup has 128^3 grid points oriented as a cube. We instantiated a tightly coupled compressor object on each grid point and ran each simulation configuration for 250,000 time steps. The measurements on GHOST include the number of values saved per time step and resulting average compression, as well as the average computation time and average I/O time for all three compression approaches at each error bound.

For all experiments, we only consider a single scalar value per grid point per time step. While this may not be in line with current simulations, we decided to explore the feasibility of in situ compression on individual scalar values and save implementing in situ compression on multiple scalar values for future work.

4.3 Hardware

This research was done on Alaska, our in-house research cluster. Alaska is composed of a dual-Xeon E5-2667v3 (16 core) head node and four Intel Xeon E5-1650v3 (6 core) cluster nodes.

4.4 Software

Besides our proposed algorithm, we used two other compressors as comparators: a wavelet compressor from VAPOR [10,11] and SZ-1.4 [41].

VAPOR is an open-source visualization package for the geoscience community that adopts wavelet transforms to achieve compression. It utilizes coefficient prioritization as its compression strategy, which means wavelet coefficients are prioritized based on their information content, and the ones containing less information are discarded. We used the best wavelet configurations reported in [26] in our study.

SZ-1.4 is an open-source lossy compression code that uses a multidimensional prediction model. The model compresses each data point using the prediction of nearby values in multiple dimensions. From here on we will refer to SZ-1.4 as SZ.

For all three softwares, we compiled them using gcc with the -O2 optimization on for a fair comparison.

5 Results

This results section is organized as follows: Phase One (Sect. 5.1) of our evaluation applies our compression algorithm on time series data. Phase Two (Sect. 5.2) compares our compression results with two other compression methods: wavelets and SZ. Phase Three (Sect. 5.3) evaluates our algorithm in situ for the GHOST simulation and compares our compression results with temporal sampling.

5.1 Phase One: GHOST, LULESH, XGC1 Particle Ions, and Tornado

The four data sets displayed a wide range of compression ratios compared to the size of the original time series data. Table 2 displays the minimum, average, and maximum compression ratios achieved for each data set using the PCM compressor with a 5% error bound.

The best results were for GHOST. Over the fifteen time series, the worst compression was 11:1 and the best compression was 2500:1. The average over the time series was just under 41:1. Assuming the time series were representative, this means we could save all temporal data using the same storage requirements as the traditional temporal sampling technique when saving every 41st time slice.

The results for the Tornado and XGC1 data sets were much worse. The time series for these data sets were much more turbulent temporally, and they do not seem to be appropriate for our technique. As a result, we eliminated them from further consideration, recognizing that our technique works best with smooth data. Further, although the LULESH results were better than the Tornado and XGC1 data sets, we decided to focus on GHOST for our in situ experiments, since it produced the best results.

Table 2. The minimum, maximum, and average compression ratios of all four data sets using the PCM approach and an error bound of 5%.

Data set	Min CR	Max CR	Avg. CR
GHOST	11:1	2500:1	40.99:1
LULESH	16.89:1	21.51:1	18.6:1
Tornado	1.11:1	3.7:1	1.07:1
XGC1	.63:1	2.11:1	.845:1

5.2   Phase Two: Comparison with Wavelets and SZ

Wavelets are fundamentally different from our approach in that wavelets allow the end user to pick an arbitrary compression level with no consideration to accuracy. In contrast, our approach and SZ both guarantee an error bound, but they are unable to guarantee a given level of data reduction. We found the best way to compare wavelets and our approach was to find configurations where they achieve similar data reductions, and then compare their respective accuracies. Results for wavelets are in Table 3 and for our compression algorithm using the PCM approach are in Table 2 in Fig. 3.

Table 3. The results from Phase 2 using wavelet compression on 10,000 time slices of the GHOST data set.

Time	0.327 s	0.327 s	0.327 s	0.327 s
Space	32:1	64:1	128:1	256:1
Avg error	10.89%	15.46%	23.67%	34.6%
Max error	352k%	443k%	776k%	980k%

For 5% error, our PCM approach achieved a compression ratio of 34:1, whereas the wavelet approach with fixed 32:1 compression had an average error of 10.89%. This is a bigger contrast than initially appears, as the maximum error for our approach is twice as good as the average error for wavelets in this case. As a result, we conclude that our method is superior for spatiotemporal data with high temporal frequency.

Our approach produced better compression rates for each error bound compared to SZ (Table 1 in Fig. 3). We believe this is due to the fact that SZ is based on spatial coherency, whereas our method is based on temporal coherency. For example, with a 5% error guarantee, SZ achieved a compression ratio of 4:1, whereas our approach using PCM achieved 34:1 compression (Fig. 3).

Time	0.155s	0.156s	0.156s
Space	2.37:1	3.46:1	4.01:1
Relative Error	1%	3%	5%
Avg Error	.0254%	0.051%	0.102%
Max Error	1.01%	3%	5%

Table 1: SZ

Time	0.364s	0.325s	0.304s
Space	9.61:1	21.0:1	35.0:1
Relative Error	1%	3%	5%
Avg Error	0.481%	1.79%	2.3%
Max Error	1%	3%	5%

Table 2: Intervals: PCM

Fig. 3. Results from Phase 2. In this phase, 10,000 time slices of the GHOST data set were compressed using SZ and using our interval compression with the PCM approach.

SZ had the best runtime, taking roughly half the compression time experienced by both the parallelized wavelet implementation and our interval approach. Overall, all three compression approaches have runtime overhead that we feel are acceptable for in situ.

5.3   Phase Three: In Situ Experimentation

Phase Three ran our algorithm in situ and measured the number of values saved per time step. We then calculated the compression ratio based on the size of an entire time slice.

Figure 4 shows an example of decompressed data and how close it is to the original data. With our technique, the reconstructed data is always within the user defined error bound.

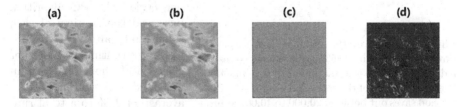

Fig. 4. Image (a) is the original data at time slice 25,000. Image (b) is the reconstructed data that used the PCM algorithm with a 5% error. Image (c) is a data comparison of their difference. And image (d) is the absolute value of their difference. Both the dark and light blue in image (d) represents minimal differences between the original and reconstructed data, differences well within the 5% error. (Color figure online)

Table 4. The average compression ratio of the reduced data per time step of each algorithm and each user defined error percent over 250,000 time steps.

Algorithm	1%	3%	5%
PCM	11.27:1	29.6:1	45.59:1
PL	14.56:1	49.9:1	63.55:1
PC	6.64:1	16.38:1	25.45:1

With a 5% user defined error, GHOST, on average, saves between 11,000 and 41,200 values per time step depending on the approach, as shown in Fig. 5. With the PCM and PC algorithms this means saving a 4 byte single precision floating point value and a 4 byte integer time step. Whereas the PL algorithm also needs to save the 4 byte single precision floating point value, 4 byte integer time step, as well as an 4 byte single precision floating point value for the slope. This is an improvement of 25.45:1-63.55:1 per time step as opposed to saving the entire time slice.

Table 4 lists the average compression ratio each approach achieves per error percent.

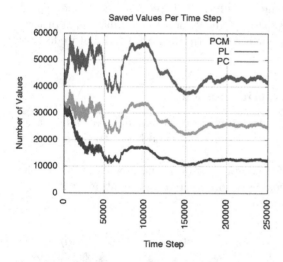

Fig. 5. For each of the 250,000 time steps, the three methods, with a 5% error bound, saves out reduced data that is a fraction of the original data. For instance, out of the total grid of 128^3, the PCM method saves out between 20,000 to 40,000 approximation values per time step.

Runtime. Our algorithm does affect simulation runtime. Typically, the algorithm adds roughly 30–35% to the runtime depending on the compression approach when running on a single core. On average, each time step of GHOST executes in 1.10 s per cycle. With minor percentage variations depending on the error bound, the PCM algorithm increased the runtime by an average of 34% to a total runtime of 1.48 s per cycle. The PC algorithm increased the runtime of each time step by an average of 31% to a total runtime of 1.44 s per cycle. And the PL algorithm increased the runtime by an average of 27% to a total runtime of 1.40 s per cycle.

These results are based on a single scalar value being approximated at each grid point. But many simulations have multiple scalars at each grid point. We ran our algorithms with two scalar values being approximated independently at each grid point. We found that an additional scalar approximation added negligible strain to the simulation. For instance, the PL run time increased from a total of 1.40 s to 1.44 s when approximating one scalar value and two scalar values, respectively. We believe this is due to the fact that adding scalar values does not increase the number of cache misses since each approximation can be in the same data structure. But approximating additional scalars means adding, and in most cases doubling, the memory requirements for the approximations.

I/O. We consider efficient I/O to be an area of future work for this method. Since our current implementation has many small writes, I/O times could be as much as six seconds per time step. We believe this slowdown is unacceptable in practice, but could be mitigated in the future by staging data in a deep memory hierarchy with occasional saves of large numbers of temporal intervals en masse.

Scalability. Our algorithm is embarrassingly parallel, i.e., it can proceed on a per node basis with no coordination across nodes. Therefore, we expect excellent scalability. One point of contention, however, would be in coordinating the way we write to disk.

Our Approach vs. Temporal Sampling. Although users rarely want to output every time slice, our approach, with a 5% error bound, would lead to a 63.55:1 improvement. In a more common case of temporal sampling, such as saving every 50th time step, the algorithm has an improvement of 1.27:1. This is calculated by comparing the amount of data of necessary to save a complete time slice every 50th time step, as in the traditional model, compared to saving intervals intermittently for 50 time steps with our in situ compression. But our method provides full temporal resolution at the same spatial resolution as the native grid for the entirety of the simulation with a guaranteed error bound. Whereas temporal sampling does not provide full spatiotemporal resolution and can only accurately depict the saved time slices.

With temporal sampling, linear interpolation can be used to reconstruct the missing time slices. We reconstructed a time slice using linear interpolation between time slices fifty time steps apart and measured the error compared to the original time slice, as shown in Table 5. While the majority of points in the reconstruction had a point-wise relative error less than or equal to 1%, there was still an occurrence of errors greater

Table 5. The percentage of points with a point-wise error less than or equal to 1%, 3%, 5%, and greater than 5% for the reconstructed data using linear interpolation between two time slices of GHOST fifty time steps apart.

Error	Percentage of points
<=1%	98.1146%
<= 3%	0.475788%
<= 5%	0.141287%
> 5%	1.26834%

than 5%. With linear interpolation there is no guarantee that the reconstructed slices will be similar to the ground truth and may introduce higher than anticipated error rates. In the context of this example, our algorithm provides information (with guaranteed error) for an additional 49 time slices for every individual time slice saved using the traditional model, all while saving less data overall.

6 Conclusion

With this work, we consider a new approach for visualization of time-varying data, namely temporal intervals. We introduced an algorithm that uses several compressors that use the temporal interval approach. Our findings show that the algorithm is effective enough to create feasible storage requirements for some data (but not others). Temporal intervals are a different paradigm than the traditional technique. They provide complete temporal information, as opposed to the traditional method of temporal sampling. But, to make the technique practical, the displayed results include error. Our approach adapts to this error by providing firm limits on the total amount of error that can be presented to an end user. In all, we believe this approach has merit, as it provides domain scientists certainty that they are not missing important science—which can be a pitfall with temporal sampling.

In terms of specific findings, this work presents three piecewise approximation compressors that guarantee an error bound and provides full temporal resolution for post-hoc exploration. We found that, depending on the data set and specifically for GHOST, the compression algorithms can reach a compression ratio greater than 2500:1 for individual grid points, and upwards of 63:1 for an entire simulation. The compression approaches achieved these results on a data set with smooth temporal coherence with data fluctuation spread out over time. On the other hand, this algorithm did not achieve high compression rates on the XGC1 or Tornado data sets, although it did show decent compression with the LULESH times series.

7 Future Work

The biggest area of future work is to develop new compression operators that improve the value proposition for stakeholders. New compression operators could include more elaborate encoding strategies with higher-order reconstruction, this would undoubtedly require more memory per grid point but may result in better compression. If compression operators can be developed that produce, for example, 1000:1 reductions in data storage, then we believe this technique could be very useful in the future to address shortcomings in supercomputer I/O and scenarios where domain scientists would typically opt to save data less and less often.

We will continue to evaluate these approaches on other data sets and simulations to determine the extent of their capabilities on both smooth and tumultuous time varying data. We will also work on reducing the I/O and reconstruction time, in particular the way we store our approximations to disk. A final point of evaluation is on the effects resulting from transitioning from one temporal interval to another. In the worst case, this could lead to "flickering" when animating over time. We have not observed this in our own experiments, and we believe that the phenomenon is prevented by our error bound guarantee. Regardless, more evaluation is needed.

References

1. Hydrodynamics Challenge Problem, Lawrence Livermore National Laboratory. Technical report LLNL-TR-490254
2. Baker, A.H., Xu, H., Hammerling, D.M., Li, S., Clyne, J.P.: Toward a multi-method approach: lossy data compression for climate simulation data. In: Kunkel, J.M., Yokota, R., Taufer, M., Shalf, J. (eds.) ISC High Performance 2017. LNCS, vol. 10524, pp. 30–42. Springer, Cham (2017). https://doi.org/10.1007/978-3-319-67630-2_3
3. Baker, A.H., et al.: Evaluating lossy data compression on climate simulation data within a large ensemble. Geosci. Model Dev. **9**(12), 4381–4403 (2016)
4. Baker, A.H., et al.: A methodology for evaluating the impact of data compression on climate simulation data. In: Proceedings of the 23rd International Symposium on High-performance Parallel and Distributed Computing, HPDC 2014, pp. 203–214. ACM, New York (2014)
5. Bertram, M., Duchaineau, M.A., Hamann, B., Joy, K.I.: Bicubic subdivision-surface wavelets for large-scale isosurface representation and visualization. In: Proceedings of the Conference on Visualization 2000, pp. 389–396. IEEE Computer Society Press (2000)
6. Burtscher, M., Mukka, H., Yang, A., Hesaaraki, F.: Real-time synthesis of compression algorithms for scientific data. In: International Conference for High Performance Computing, Networking, Storage and Analysis, SC 2016, pp. 264–275, November 2016
7. Burtscher, M., Ratanaworabhan, P.: FPC: a high-speed compressor for double-precision floating-point data. IEEE Trans. Comput. **58**(1), 18–31 (2009)
8. Chang, C., et al.: Compressed ion temperature gradient turbulence in diverted tokamak edge. Phys. Plasmas (1994-present) **16**(5), 056108 (2009)
9. Chen, D., Chiang, Y.J., Memon, N., Wu, X.: Lossless geometry compression for steady-state and time-varying irregular grids. In: Santos, B.S., Ertl, T., Joy, K. (eds.) EUROVIS - Eurographics/IEEE VGTC Symposium on Visualization. The Eurographics Association (2006)
10. Clyne, J., Mininni, P., Norton, A., Rast, M.: Interactive desktop analysis of high resolution simulations: application to turbulent plume dynamics and current sheet formation. New J. Phys. **9**(8), 301 (2007)
11. Clyne, J., Rast, M.: A prototype discovery environment for analyzing and visualizing terascale turbulent fluid flow simulations. In: Electronic Imaging 2005, pp. 284–294. International Society for Optics and Photonics (2005)
12. Di, S., Cappello, F.: Fast error-bounded lossy HPC data compression with SZ. In: Proceedings of the IPDPS. IEEE (2016)
13. Fernandes, O., Frey, S., Sadlo, F., Ertl, T.: Space-time volumetric depth images for in-situ visualization. In: 2014 IEEE 4th Symposium on Large Data Analysis and Visualization (LDAV), pp. 59–65, November 2014
14. Fout, N., Ma, K.L.: An adaptive prediction-based approach to lossless compression of floating-point volume data. IEEE Trans. Vis. Comput. Graph. **18**(12), 2295–2304 (2012)
15. Gomez, L.A.B., Cappello, F.: Improving floating point compression through binary masks. In: 2013 IEEE International Conference on Big Data, pp. 326–331. IEEE (2013)
16. Guthe, S., Strasser, W.: Real-time decompression and visualization of animated volume data. In: Proceedings of IEEE Visualization (VIS 2001), pp. 349–572, October 2001

17. Hübbe, N., Kunkel, J.: Reducing the HPC-datastorage footprint with mafisc—multidimensional adaptive filtering improved scientific data compression. Comput. Sci. - Res. Dev. **28**(2), 231–239 (2013)

18. Ihm, I., Park, S.: Wavelet-based 3D compression scheme for interactive visualization of very large volume data. In: Computer Graphics Forum, vol. 18, pp. 3–15. Wiley Online Library (1999)

19. Iverson, J., Kamath, C., Karypis, G.: Fast and effective lossy compression algorithms for scientific datasets. In: Kaklamanis, C., Papatheodorou, T., Spirakis, P.G. (eds.) Euro-Par 2012. LNCS, vol. 7484, pp. 843–856. Springer, Heidelberg (2012). https://doi.org/10.1007/978-3-642-32820-6_83

20. Keogh, E., Chu, S., Hart, D., Pazzani, M.: An online algorithm for segmenting time series. In: Proceedings of the 2001 IEEE International Conference on Data Mining, pp. 289–296 (2001)

21. Kim, T.Y., Shin, Y.G.: An efficient wavelet-based compression method for volume rendering. In: Proceedings of the Seventh Pacific Conference on Computer Graphics and Applications, pp. 147–156. IEEE (1999)

22. Lakshminarasimhan, S., et al.: Compressing the incompressible with ISABELA: in-situ reduction of spatio-temporal data. In: Jeannot, E., Namyst, R., Roman, J. (eds.) Euro-Par 2011. LNCS, vol. 6852, pp. 366–379. Springer, Heidelberg (2011). https://doi.org/10.1007/978-3-642-23400-2_34

23. Lakshminarasimhan, S., et al.: ISABELA for effective in situ compression of scientific data. Concurr. Comput.: Pract. Exp. **25**(4), 524–540 (2013)

24. Lee, D., Sim, A., Choi, J., Wu, K.: Novel data reduction based on statistical similarity. In: Proceedings of the 28th International Conference on Scientific and Statistical Database Management, p. 21. ACM (2016)

25. Lehmann, H., Jung, B.: In-situ multi-resolution and temporal data compression for visual exploration of large-scale scientific simulations. In: 2014 IEEE 4th Symposium on Large Data Analysis and Visualization (LDAV), pp. 51–58, November 2014

26. Li, S., Gruchalla, K., Potter, K., Clyne, J., Childs, H.: Evaluating the efficacy of wavelet configurations on turbulent-flow data. In: 2015 IEEE 5th Symposium on Large Data Analysis and Visualization (LDAV), pp. 81–89 (2015)

27. Li, S., Larsen, M., Clyne, J., Childs, H.: Performance impacts of in situ wavelet compression on scientific simulations. In: Proceedings of the In Situ Infrastructures for Enabling Extreme-Scale Analysis and Visualization Workshop, ISAV 2017. ACM, New York (2017)

28. Li, S., Marsaglia, N., Chen, V., Sewell, C., Clyne, J., Childs, H.: Achieving portable performance for wavelet compression using data parallel primitives. In: Telea, A., Bennett, J. (eds.) Eurographics Symposium on Parallel Graphics and Visualization. The Eurographics Association (2017). https://doi.org/10.2312/pgv.20171095

29. Li, S., Marsaglia, N., Garth, C., Woodring, J., Clyne, J., Childs, H.: Data reduction techniques for simulation, visualization and data analysis. Comput. Graph. Forum, March 2018. https://doi.org/10.1111/cgf.13336

30. Li, S., Sane, S., Orf, L., Mininni, P., Clyne, J., Childs, H.: Spatiotemporal wavelet compression for visualization of scientific simulation data. In: 2017 IEEE International Conference on Cluster Computing (CLUSTER), pp. 216–227, September 2017

31. Lindstrom, P.: Fixed-rate compressed floating-point arrays. IEEE Trans. Vis. Comput. Graph. **20**(12), 2674–2683 (2014)

32. Lindstrom, P.: Error distributions of lossy floating-point compressors. In: Joint Statistical Meetings, October 2017

33. Lindstrom, P., Isenburg, M.: Fast and efficient compression of floating-point data. IEEE Trans. Vis. Comput. Graph. **12**(5), 1245–1250 (2006)
34. Ma, J., Murphy, D., O'Mathuna, C., Hayes, M., Provan, G.: Visualizing uncertainty in multi-resolution volumetric data using marching cubes. In: Proceedings of the International Working Conference on Advanced Visual Interfaces, pp. 489–496. ACM (2012)
35. Mininni, P., Alexakis, A., Pouquet, A.: Large-scale flow effects, energy transfer, and self-similarity on turbulence. Phys. Rev. E **74**(1), 016303 (2006)
36. Olanda, R., Pérez, M., Orduña, J.M., Rueda, S.: Terrain data compression using wavelet-tiled pyramids for online 3D terrain visualization. Int. J. Geogr. Inf. Sci. **28**(2), 407–425 (2014)
37. Orf, L., Wilhelmson, R., Wicker, L.: Visualization of a simulated long-track EF5 tornado embedded within a supercell thunderstorm. Parallel Comput. **55**, 28–34 (2016)
38. Rodler, F.F.: Wavelet based 3D compression with fast random access for very large volume data. In: Seventh Pacific Conference on Computer Graphics and Applications, pp. 108–117. IEEE (1999)
39. Sakai, R., Sasaki, D., Obayashi, S., Nakahashi, K.: Wavelet-based data compression for flow simulation on block-structured Cartesian mesh. Int. J. Numer. Methods Fluids **73**(5), 462–476 (2013)
40. Schendel, E.R., et al.: ISOBAR preconditioner for effective and high-throughput lossless data compression. In: Proceedings - International Conference on Data Engineering, pp. 138–149 (2012)
41. Tao, D., Di, S., Chen, Z., Capello, F.: Significantly improving lossy compression for scientific data sets based on multidimensional prediction and error-controlled quantization. In: IEEE International Parallel and Distributed Processing Symposium (2017, to appear)
42. Treib, M., Burger, K., Reichl, F., Meneveau, C., Szalay, A., Westermann, R.: Turbulence visualization at the terascale on desktop PCs. IEEE Trans. Vis. Comput. Graph. **18**(12), 2169–2177 (2012)
43. Woodring, J., Mniszewski, S., Brislawn, C., DeMarle, D., Ahrens, J.: Revisiting wavelet compression for large-scale climate data using jpeg 2000 and ensuring data precision. In: IEEE Symposium on Large Data Analysis and Visualization (LDAV), pp. 31–38. IEEE (2011)
44. Yang, A., Mukka, H., Hesaaraki, F., Burtscher, M.: MPC: a massively parallel compression algorithm for scientific data. In: 2015 IEEE International Conference on Cluster Computing, pp. 381–389, September 2015

In-Situ Visualization of Solver Residual Fields

Kai Sdeo$^{(\boxtimes)}$, Boyan Zheng, Marian Piatkowski, and Filip Sadlo

Heidelberg University, Heidelberg, Germany
{kai.sdeo,boyan.zheng,marian.piatkowski}@iwr.uni-heidelberg.de
sadlo@uni-heidelberg.de

Abstract. Whereas the design and development of numerical solvers for field-based simulations is a highly evolved discipline, and whereas there exists a wide range of visualization techniques for the (in-situ) analysis of their numerical results, the techniques for analyzing the operation of such solvers are rather elementary. In this paper, we present a visualization approach for in-situ analysis of the processes within numerical solvers. That is, instead of visualizing the data that result from such solvers, we address the visualization of the processes that generate the data. We exemplify our approach using different simulation runs, and discuss its in-situ application in high-performance computing environments.

Keywords: Residual analysis · Solver analysis · In-situ visualization

1 Introduction

During the last decades, numerical simulation has been more and more replacing physical experiments in science and engineering—providing various advantages, including reproducibility, simplified setup, and reduced cost. The wide application of simulation techniques has, on the other hand, led to an intense increase in compute demands, necessitating ever-growing supercomputing facilities. This development is currently at the threshold to exascale computing, where the limited communication bandwidths and storage resources inhibit storage and subsequent analysis of finely space-time resolved results. By employing preprocessing and data reduction at the compute nodes during simulation, and thus enabling transfer of only the essential information to the user, in-situ visualization is considered a main solution to this dilemma in today's and tomorrow's computing.

In this paper, we do not follow the typical track of in-situ visualization techniques, i.e., we do not process the data that a compute node produces. Instead, it is our aim to complement these techniques by providing a tool to support the effective operation of numerical solvers in high-performance computing. Traditionally, numerical solvers are monitored in terms of a defect, or *total residual*, which is typically a single value for each iteration of a solver. This residual is traditionally plotted (Fig. 1) during operation of the solver, to monitor its convergence behavior and accuracy. However, whereas such simple plotting is good

© Springer Nature Switzerland AG 2018
R. Yokota et al. (Eds.): ISC 2018 Workshops, LNCS 11203, pp. 294–309, 2018.
https://doi.org/10.1007/978-3-030-02465-9_20

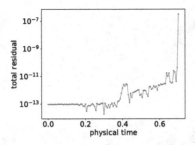

Fig. 1. Diverging simulation (Kármán Run I dataset), monitored with traditional residual plot. Solver fails to converge after last time step (physical time step 112). While such plots can indicate problems, they do not support the reasoning of their causes.

at indicating the trend of the residual and thus at indicating convergence problems, it is typically not sufficient to help in understanding the structure and the causes of such problems. In this paper, we examine approaches to provide more information to the user, to give a better picture of solver behavior, and to support in-situ operation, and development of numerical solvers in general.

Our approach addresses field-based simulations, with the Navier–Stokes equations being a prominent example, and is based on residual *fields*. Residuals can be seen as the discrepancy of an (intermediate) solution with respect to the discretized formulation of the underlying problem and the employed numerical scheme. That is, the solver minimizes some norm of these residuals to obtain a solution. Instead of plotting the total residual, i.e., the norm of such intermediate residuals, we map the residuals back to the domain, and thus obtain spatial fields. Consequently, such *residual fields* are available for all quantities a solver computes in such a manner (Fig. 2).

In this work, we investigate the analysis of residual fields to obtain additional insights into solver dynamics, also w.r.t. slow (or failing) convergence. Our overall approach is designed for in-situ operation in field-based solvers. Nevertheless, our current prototype is implemented and evaluated only on a single compute node—integration and evaluation in a high-performance compute environment is to be carried out as future work. That is, this work researches the basics for in-situ residual field visualization.

2 Related Work

Surprisingly, we have not been able to find any previous work on the visualization of residual fields. Whereas there is virtually no numerical solver that does not perform a plotting of a residual, the spatiotemporal structure of residual fields has been ignored so far, at least from a visualization research point of view.

Convergence analysis [3] is a very broad and mature field, which, however, does typically not make use of (advanced) visualization techniques, and does not consider residual fields. Less closely related, but more graphical, are techniques that visualize the "state space" of numerical algorithms, such as Newton fractals [6], which depict the convergence behavior of Newton's method. Convergence

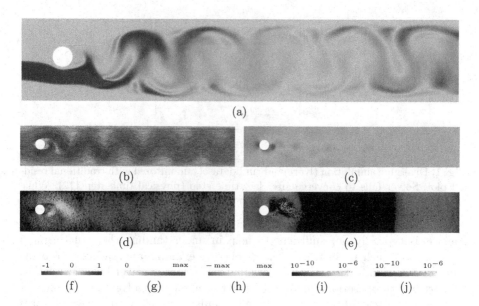

Fig. 2. 2D flow around a cylinder (white), inlet on the left, outlet on the right. Last physical time step ($t_{112} = 0.7$ s) of Kármán Run I dataset, before simulation diverges. (a) Visualization by a tracer c (seeded at dark region on left boundary). (b) Velocity $\mathbf{u}$ by line integral convolution [2], with color-coded magnitude. (c) Pressure field p. (d) Residual field of velocity $\mathbf{r(u)}$ indicates severe problems just behind the cylinder. (e) Residual field of pressure $r(p)$ exhibits some high-valued noise just behind cylinder. (f)–(j) Respective color maps where max represents the maximum value in the field. (Color figure online)

analysis of integration schemes, e.g., with respect to A-stability [3,4] is also an example of weakly related work, where a, however, simple graphical representation is involved. On the other hand, there is only one work that we are aware of, which visualizes technical processes within a solver, i.e., our visualization of piecewise linear interface calculation inherent to two-phase flow simulation [7]. That work, however, does also not investigate residual fields, and rather focuses on geometric and quantitative analysis.

Another related field, where solver-specific representation is taken into account, is the visualization of higher-order data, such as in the case of discontinuous Galerkin [5,10], finite-element [9], or particle-partition of unity [12] simulation. Similar to these approaches is the incorporation of simulation models into interpolation techniques to accomplish model-consistent interpolation [11].

Various approaches have been presented so far in the general field of in-situ visualization. Kress [8] can provide an introduction to the topic. Contributions in this field range, e.g., from particle-based simulations [13] to climate research [14].

3   Method

Our overall approach consists of several building blocks, which we present here in the order of increasing solver process detail. These building blocks complement each other, and make up our overall approach for in-situ analysis of residual fields. Section 3.1 gives some background on typical solver processes, establishes terminology with respect to solver iterations and physical time, and details the concept of residual fields. Since direct investigation of these data, e.g., as animations of residual fields, would lead to issues with perception, exploration, and I/O bandwidth, we present in Sect. 3.2 aggregation of residual fields. Because such aggregations provide an overview of the convergence behavior of simulations, but at the same time suffer from temporal "averaging", we complement them with the concept of residual curves, presented in Sect. 3.3. These curves are obtained by dimensionality reduction of sets of residual fields—either representing sets of solver iterations or sets of physical time steps—and enable qualitative analysis of such sets. For detailed inspection of the sets, the approach is complemented with residual stacks (Sect. 3.4), which provide them in space-time or space-iteration representation. Finally, in-situ context is discussed in Sect. 3.5.

3.1   Solvers and Residual Fields

The addressed solvers for field-based simulations discretize the space domain $\Omega \subset \mathbb{R}^n$ into cells defined by nodes $\mathbf{x}_i \in \Omega$, and the time domain $\mathrm{T} \subset \mathbb{R}$ into physical time steps $t_j \in \mathrm{T}$. Each physical time step gives rise to (a set of) fields, such as a velocity $\mathbf{u}(\mathbf{x}, t_j)$ and a pressure $p(\mathbf{x}, t_j)$ field (Fig. 2(b) and (c)). Note that we exemplify our approach by means of 2D flow simulations, i.e., $n = 2$, position $\mathbf{x} \in \Omega \subset \mathbb{R}^2$, and $\mathbf{u} : \Omega \times \mathrm{T} \to \mathbb{R}^2$.

Each of these physical time steps (i.e., fields) is the result of a process that minimizes some norm of the residuals. Since many underlying problems are inherently nonlinear, this minimization is often accomplished by iterative techniques. In other words, each physical time step t_j is typically the result of a sequence of iterations. We name them *solver iterations* and denote them t_j^k, i.e., the kth solver iteration for physical time step j. The solver stops iteration when the total residual drops below a user-defined threshold. Thus, at the example of the velocity field for physical time step t_j, the first intermediate solution is $\mathbf{u}(\mathbf{x}, t_j^1)$, and assuming that 11 iterations are needed to reach the total residual threshold, the resulting solution is $\mathbf{u}(\mathbf{x}, t_j) := \mathbf{u}(\mathbf{x}, t_j^{11})$.

By mapping the residuals back to the domain, we obtain, on the one hand, for each physical time step t_j the corresponding residual fields $\mathbf{r}(\mathbf{u}(\mathbf{x}, t_j))$ and $r(p(\mathbf{x}, t_j))$, and on the other hand, for each solver iteration t_j^k, the residual fields $\mathbf{r}(\mathbf{u}(\mathbf{x}, t_j^k))$ and $r(p(\mathbf{x}, t_j^k))$. Notice that the residual fields inherit the dimensionality from the quantity that is being solved, e.g., the residual field of velocity is a vector field, too. For the remaining part of this paper, we focus on velocity residual fields, and defer investigation of the pressure residual to future work.

Figure 3 provides selected velocity residual fields for two different simulation runs, a diverging one (Kármán Run I) and a non-diverging one (Kármán Run II).

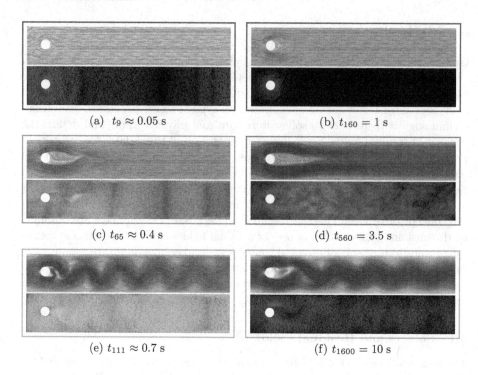

(a) $t_9 \approx 0.05$ s   (b) $t_{160} = 1$ s

(c) $t_{65} \approx 0.4$ s   (d) $t_{560} = 3.5$ s

(e) $t_{111} \approx 0.7$ s   (f) $t_{1600} = 10$ s

Fig. 3. Exemplary fields for diverging Kármán Run I (left column) and non-diverging Run II (right column), with velocity $\mathbf{u}(\mathbf{x}, t_j)$ (top, color map from Fig. 2) and residual field $\|\mathbf{r}(\mathbf{u}(\mathbf{x}, t_j))\|$ (bottom, color map from Fig. 4. The colored frames correspond to the clusters of solver behavior in Fig. 5 (ellipses with corresponding colors). (Color figure online)

One can see, that residual fields for these simulations have a rather noisy structure in space and time, but also that the magnitude at the last physical time step (t_{112}) that still converged in Kármán Run I is overall high, and that it is particularly high directly behind the obstacle (Fig. 3(e)). Thus, this region may be considered the "ignition spark" of solver divergence in the computation of the subsequent time step.

3.2   Aggregated Residual Fields

Although residual fields can provide insights in solver dynamics (as will be further investigated in Sect. 4), their visual analysis at full time resolution would suffer from perceptual issues, and—even more important—it would exceed the available bandwidth (and storage) if all residual fields for all physical time steps would be communicated. On the other hand, it is a common approach in field-based numerical simulation to discard most physical time steps and store, e.g., only every 100th for later analysis. However, assuming that the available bandwidth would allow us to also communicate every corresponding 100th residual field for analysis (which might, however, often not be feasible, in particular in high-scale computing), the behavior of the solver during the 99 time steps in between would still remain unknown. This would be in particular a problem because the probability that the solver experiences issues during the 99 discarded time steps is much higher than during the communicated one.

This motivates aggregation of residual fields, i.e., the combination of the information from sets of residual fields. In the abovementioned scenario, we could combine the residual fields for the 99 time steps that are discarded. For example, for a set $\mathcal{R}_\mathbf{u}$ of velocity residual fields, we define the maximum-aggregated residual field $r_{\max}^{\mathcal{R}_\mathbf{u}}(\mathbf{x})$ as follows:

$$r_{\max}^{\mathcal{R}_\mathbf{u}}(\mathbf{x}) := \max_{\mathbf{r}_j \in \mathcal{R}_\mathbf{u}} \|\mathbf{r}_j(\mathbf{x})\|. \tag{1}$$

Assume that the solver fails to converge, e.g., at time step 50, in such a scenario. In this case, this time step will typically exhibit very high residual field magnitude (Fig. 2(d)), and thus it would dominate $r_{\max}^{\mathcal{R}_\mathbf{u}}(\mathbf{x})$. Therefore, in case of solver divergence, we omit the diverging time step from $\mathcal{R}_\mathbf{u}$, and communicate both the aggregated $r_{\max}^{\mathcal{R}_\mathbf{u}}(\mathbf{x})$, as well as the residual field of the diverging time step for analysis. The maximum-aggregated residual field enables the identification of spatial regions that exhibited low residual magnitude over the entire set, or regions that exhibited at least for one moment large residual magnitude.

Since aggregation is a local operation, and since the aggregated field is of the size of a single residual field and thus (the respective part) should typically fit into a compute node's memory, it lends itself well for in-situ visualization. As motivated above, aggregated residual fields can be computed for series of physical time steps that are not communicated for analysis, and in case of solver problems, they can give insight about the reasons of the problems. In Fig. 4(a), i.e., the diverging Kármán Run I example, $r_{\max}^{\mathcal{R}_\mathbf{u}}(\mathbf{x})$ shows that the region behind the cylinder exhibited (at least for short times) large velocity residual magnitude, whereas in the upstream region of the cylinder, residual magnitude has always been lower. This, for example, indicates that the solver problem is not related to the inlet, but is rather related to the obstacle. In contrast, for the non-diverging Run II, Fig. 4(b) shows that the velocity residual has always been low behind the obstacle during the aggregated time interval, and that velocity residual magnitude is overall lower and more spatially uniform than in Fig. 4(a). Such distributions are typical for simulation runs that do not exhibit problems.

3.3 Residual Curves

So far, we introduced residual fields and their aggregation. Whereas these approaches can be used to obtain detailed insight into the dynamics of a solver with respect to its residuals, their rich structure impedes their application for monitoring, quick qualitative overview, and context. This motivates our next complementing concept, which we denote *residual curves*.

We obtain these curves by computing from each residual field a vector

$$\rho_l(t_j) := \ln \|\mathbf{r}(\mathbf{u}(\mathbf{x}_l, t_j))\|, \tag{2}$$

10^{-10}

10^{-17}

(a)   (b)

Fig. 4. Maximum-aggregated velocity residual field $r_{\max}^{\mathcal{R}_u}(\mathbf{x})$ for time steps t_1–t_{111} of diverging the Kármán Run I (a), and for time steps t_1–t_{1600} of the non-diverging Run II (b). In the diverging case, residual magnitude is overall higher, and particularly high just behind the obstacle. The non-diverging case, in contrast, exhibits low residual magnitude behind the cylinder, and in general a more uniform distribution. (Color figure online)

where $\mathbf{x}_l$ is the respective node of the simulation grid. Note that we employ logarithmic mapping of the individual residual element magnitude to avoid clutter, i.e., to obtain more expressive residual curves.

This way, each residual field consisting of m nodes provides an m-dimensional vector $\boldsymbol{\rho}$, which in turn represents a point in m-dimensional space. As a consequence, series of residual fields represent polylines in this m-dimensional space. We take all points $\boldsymbol{\rho}$ of such a series, and apply dimensionality reduction by means of principal component analysis (PCA). That is, we project the polylines to 2D space spanned by the two major PCA eigenvectors.

Remember that residual fields can be computed for both series of physical time steps t_j and series of solver iterations t_j^k. Whereas series of physical time steps (e.g., the discarded ones) provide analysis of solver behavior over physical time, one can investigate the computation of a single physical time step by means of series of solver iterations. Thus, respective residual curves can provide an overview of the dynamics during both physical time steps and solver iterations. We visualize the residual curves in their 2D projection, with a color map that encodes the order of the individual residuals, to provide a notion of succession. Figure 5 gives an example for residual curves with respect to physical time, whereas Fig. 6 provides an example for residual curves of solver iterations.

In Fig. 5, we can identify clusters w.r.t. simulation behavior, which are marked by ellipses and exemplified in Fig. 3. Residual fields within such clusters turn out to look similar. In Fig. 6, which visualizes solver iterations, we additionally indicate the start of each iteration stage with a black box glyph, and the start of each Newton iteration with a triangle glyph. This nicely reveals the similarity of solver behavior in the two iteration stages in this example.

3.4   Residual Stacks

So far, we have seen that residual curves can provide a qualitative overview of sequences of physical time steps and sequences resulting from solver iterations. However, once, e.g., a cluster in these curves has been identified, a more detailed analysis of the residual fields is required. One could color-map each residual field and compose the respective sub-sequences into animations, the observation

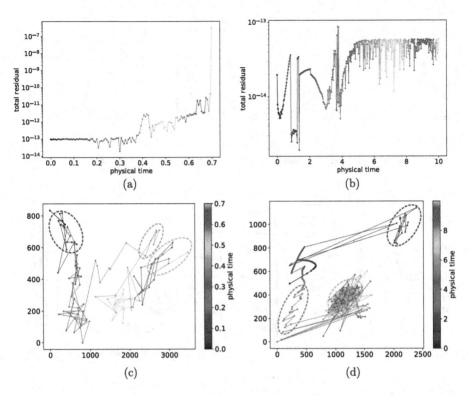

Fig. 5. Traditional total residual plots (top) and our residual curves (bottom), for the diverging Kármán Run I (left) and non-diverging Run II (right), w.r.t. physical time steps t_j. The residual curves reveal clusters of simulation behavior, some indicated with ellipses, in which residual fields exhibit similarities, see Fig. 3 for respective residual fields. The non-diverging run exhibits more compact clusters and a more regular curve. (Color figure online)

of these animations would, however, involve perceptual difficulties. For time-dependent 2D simulations, space-time representation, i.e., treatment of the time axis as an additional spatial dimension, is a common approach that at least partially avoids these issues. We name the resulting representations of sequences of residual fields *residual stacks*. Figure 7 provides physical-time residual stacks for the Kármán Run I and II cases, i.e., stacked with respect to physical time steps t_k. Note that in all visualizations of the stacks, the x-axis is visualized in red, the y-axis green, and the physical time or solver iteration axis blue.

Whereas physical-time residual stacks serve well for understanding long-term behavior of a solver, e.g., to understand how residual structure develops over physical time and eventually leads to divergence, solver-iteration residual stacks provide the analog with respect to solver iterations. Since the residual fields tend to be rather noisy in space and (iteration) time, we employ smoothing prior to, e.g., isosurface extraction.

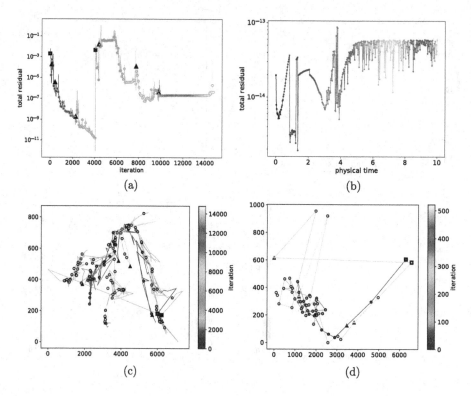

Fig. 6. Total residual plots (top) and residual curves (bottom) for the diverging Kármán Run I (left) and non-diverging Run II (right) w.r.t. solver iterations t_j^k for the computation of physical time step t_{112} (left) and physical time step t_{1600} (right). For the diverging run, the residual curve exhibits several phases, each with substantial perturbations. For the non-diverging run, the shape of the residual curve is more ordered, and both stages (starting at black square glyphs) exhibit a similar behavior. (Color figure online)

In Fig. 5, we have identified clusters for both simulation runs (light green ellipse in the diverging, and teal green in the non-diverging case) which correspond to a temporal peak in the total residual plots. Using residual stacks, these clusters can be investigated by means of isosurfaces. We observe a large red structure at the center of Fig. 7(a), and a cloud-shaped horizontal structure at the lower third of Fig. 7(b), which is related to the structure in Fig. 3(d).

In Fig. 8, we analyze the computation of the last physical time step t_{112}, which did not converge, in the diverging run, and the last physical time step t_{1600} that was computed in the non-diverging run. Since the underlying solver performs the computation of a physical time step in two stages, we provide a solver-iteration residual stack for both stages separately. While the first stage of the diverging run (Fig. 8(a)) still converged, we can see the cylindrical structures of too high residual in the vicinity of the obstacle during the second stage (Fig. 8(c)). The non-diverging run (Fig. 8(b) and (d)), in contrast, exhibits structures similar to

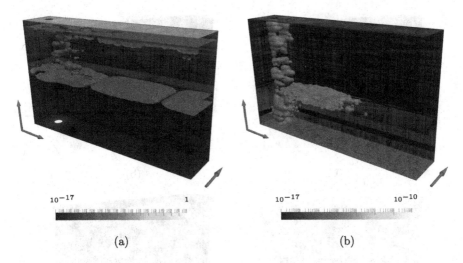

Fig. 7. Isosurfaces of physical-time residual stacks for diverging Kármán Run I (a) and non-diverging Run II (b). The structure at the center of (a) corresponds to the light green peak/ellipse in Fig. 5(a) and (c). The dominant structure at the lower third of (b) corresponds to the teal green peak/ellipse in Fig. 5(b) and (d). As in all stacks, x-axis by red arrow, y-axis by green, and physical time/solver iteration by blue. (Color figure online)

those of the first stage in the diverging run. Additionally, there seems to be more solver dynamics in the second stage of the non-diverging run, which might relate to the used higher-order time integration scheme.

The approach of residual field stacking provides quite detailed insight into residual dynamics, and motivates further analysis with feature extraction techniques. On the other hand, the runtime and memory overhead, especially for the iteration stacks, is large compared to the other building blocks of our approach.

3.5   In-Situ Application

So far, we have identified aggregated residual fields (Sect. 3.2) to fit well into in-situ environments because their computation is local and well-suited for, e.g., domain decomposition. However, residual curves (Sect. 3.3) and residual stacks (Sect. 3.4) are global constructs in space-(iteration-)time, therefore require entire sets of residual information, and are thus not straightforward to employ in-situ.

In our implementation, we follow a sliding-window approach for these constructs. That is, we maintain the residual fields (i.e., physical-time residual stacks) of a fixed number of most recent physical time steps, as well as a fixed number of most recent solver-iteration residual stacks. These data are, however, not communicated for analysis by default. Only if issues are determined, either because the simulation diverged, or based on the regularly communicated aggregated residual fields, the user can request these data for computation of residual curves as well as composition of residual stacks.

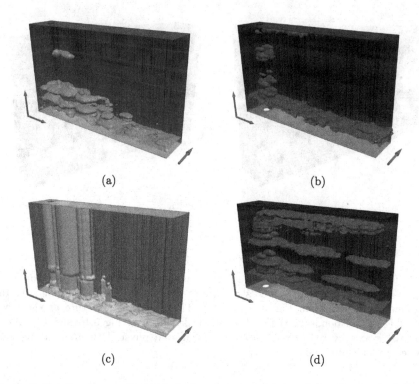

(a)   (b)

(c)   (d)

Fig. 8. Solver-iteration residual stacks for stage one (top) and two (bottom) of diverging Kármán Run I (left, $t_{112} = 0.7\,\mathrm{s}$) and non-diverging Run II (right, $t_{1600} = 10\,\mathrm{s}$). Whereas the first stage exhibits similar structure in both runs, the second stage shows very high residuals for the diverging run, which eventually leads to divergence. Please refer to Fig. 7(a) for the color maps. (Color figure online)

4   Results

We start with some details on the implementation and a performance analysis (Sect. 4.1). Then, we describe the two simulation runs that were used to present our technique (Sect. 4.2), followed by an experiment investigating the impact of grid resolution on residual fields (Sect. 4.3), and some experiments on mesh refinement based on residual fields (Sect. 4.4).

4.1   Implementation and Timings

The simulation code underlying our experiments is based on DUNE [1], which we extended to access and export the residual fields and our derived representations. In our experiments, we export $\mathbf{u}(\mathbf{x}, t_j)$ and $\mathbf{r}(\mathbf{u}(\mathbf{x}, t_j))$ every fourth time step, and $\mathbf{r}(\mathbf{u}(\mathbf{x}, t_j^k))$ at every tenth iteration. The aggregation of $r_{\max}^{\mathcal{R}_\mathbf{u}}(\mathbf{x})$ is computed also within the solver, but from consecutive time steps. The overhead of our technique can be obtained from Table 1—and the absolute overhead is rather small. For larger grids, however, exporting the solver iterations becomes expensive, especially due to the memory overhead that grows with the number of iterations. In our prototype, the computation of the residual curves was accomplished using a separate Python program. For the PCA, the sklearn Python library was used. Note that our naive implementation writes and reads thousands of residual fields (one for each solver iteration) in this case, and could be optimized substantially. Still, the method was, in our experiments, fast enough to be used for monitoring.

4.2   Kármán Runs

This experiment consists of two simulation runs (Kármán Run I and Kármán Run II) of a 2D flow around a cylinder, which exhibits vortex shedding, and is used to demonstrate the interplay of the presented building blocks. It is simulated with a physical time step size of 0.00625 s, a triangular simulation grid consisting of 17552 nodes and 34422 cells, and features an inlet along its left boundary, and an outlet along its right boundary (Fig. 2). The two simulation runs differ only with respect to inlet velocity magnitude ($\|\mathbf{u}_{in}\| = 40.5\,\text{m/s}$ for Run I and $\|\mathbf{u}_{in}\| = 1.5\,\text{m/s}$ for Run II), causing Run I to diverge at time step t_{112}, whereas Run II does not diverge during the simulated 1600 time steps.

4.3   Mesh Resolution Experiment

To gain more insight on the interpretation of residual fields, we investigate different simulation grid resolutions (19766 cells, 4738 cells, 986 cells, and 444 cells), with the same relative refinement around the obstacle as for the Kármán Run I and II. The basic setup is the same as described in Sect. 4.2, with $\|\mathbf{u}_{in}\| = 1.5\,\text{m/s}$. As can be seen from Fig. 9, reducing the resolution increases the overall residual field magnitude. However, at the lowest resolution, residual magnitude drops again. This seems to be related to the fact that this resolution does not exhibit vortex shedding anymore, i.e., it results in a quasi-stationary solution. The corresponding residual curves exhibit nice tight clusters for the highest resolution, whereas they exhibit a more irregular behavior for the medium resolution. Notice also that for larger cell sizes or higher inlet velocities (Fig. 4), the solver shows residual peaks behind the obstacle, which may be related to too large time step size with respect to the cell size. In contrast, Fig. 9 shows a rather uniform residual distribution, which indicates a well chosen ratio between cell size and inlet velocity. The simulation with the grid consisting of 19766 cells shows results similar to those of Kármán Run II, and is therefore not depicted.

4.4   Grid Refinement Experiment

In this last experiment, we want to investigate grid refinement based on residual fields. As discussed in Sect. 4.3, higher grid resolutions with too large time step sizes tend to result in larger residuals. This motivates the investigation of residual fields for grid refinement, and at the same time provides a better understanding

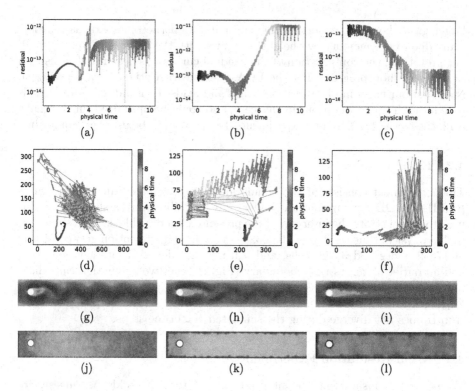

(a)   (b)   (c)

(d)   (e)   (f)

(g)   (h)   (i)

(j)   (k)   (l)

Fig. 9. Mesh Resolution Experiment, with varying mesh resolution: 4738 cells (left column), 896 cells (middle column), and 444 cells (right column). (a)–(c) Total residual plots. (d)–(f) Residual curves. (g)–(i) Velocity $\mathbf{u}(\mathbf{x}, t_{1600})$ (color map from Fig. 2(g)). (j)–(l) Maximum-aggregated velocity residual $\mathbf{r}_{\max}^{\mathcal{R}_\mathbf{u}}(\mathbf{x})$ (color map from Fig. 4). Residuals increase with decreasing mesh resolution, until a resolution is reached that does not exhibit vortex shedding, but nevertheless shows a drop in residual magnitude. Our residual curves, in contrast, show increasing irregularity from (d) to (e). (Color figure online)

Table 1. Performance measurements. Number of nodes (nodes) and cells (cells) of respective simulation grids (dataset), time spent for simulation without visualization part (sim. only), time used for computing maximum-aggregated residual field ($r_{\max}^{\mathcal{R}_\mathbf{u}}$), time spent for physical-time residual stack composition ($\mathbf{r}(\mathbf{u}(\mathbf{x}, t_j))$) and solver-iteration residual stack composition ($\mathbf{r}(\mathbf{u}(\mathbf{x}, t_j^k))$), followed by time spent for residual curve (RC) computation of physical time series (RC t_j), and solver iterations (RC t_j^k). All simulations perform 1600 physical time steps. (This is the reason why the Kármán Run I was excluded from the comparison).

dataset	nodes	cells	sim. only	$r_{\max}^{\mathcal{R}_\mathbf{u}}$	$\mathbf{r}(\mathbf{u}(\mathbf{x}, t_j))$	$\mathbf{r}(\mathbf{u}(\mathbf{x}, t_j^k))$	RC t_j	RC t_j^k
Section 4.3	2496	4738	1 h 07 m	<1 m	<1 m	10 m	37 s	8 s
Section 4.3	10142	19766	18 h 57 m	4 m	3 m	2 h 04 m	2 m 20 s	37 s
Kár. Run II	17552	34422	23 h 06 m	2 h 04 m	1 h 59 m	10 h 27 m	3 m 38 s	59 s

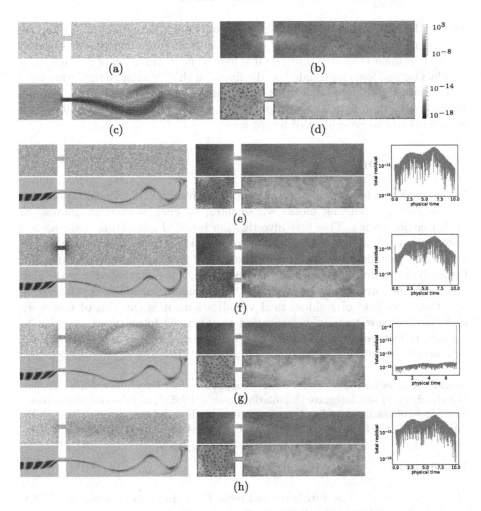

Fig. 10. Grid refinement experiment at $t_{4840} = 7.26\,$s. (a) Grid with approximately 10,000 cells, (b) respective divergence field $\nabla \cdot \mathbf{u}(\mathbf{x}, t_{4840})$, (c) velocity $\mathbf{u}(\mathbf{x}, t_{4840})$, and (d) maximum-aggregated velocity residual $\mathbf{r}_{\max}^{\mathcal{R}_\mathbf{u}}(\mathbf{x})$. (e)–(h) Include tracer $c(\mathbf{x}, t_{4840})$ (red/blue) instead of $\mathbf{u}(\mathbf{x}, t_{4840})$, and total residual plots (right). These grids all have about 20,000 cells, and are adapted (refined) (e) uniformly, (f) along the slit, (g) relative to divergence, and (h) relative to maximum-aggregated velocity residual $\mathbf{r}_{\max}^{\mathcal{R}_\mathbf{u}}(\mathbf{x})$. For color maps of c and $\mathbf{u}$, please refer to Fig. 2(f) and (g). (Color figure online)

of residual field behavior. Due to the rather uniform residual magnitude distribution in the Mesh Resolution Experiment, we choose a similar setup with uniform triangulation, however with a modified domain exhibiting a narrow passage (a slit), inlet velocity 0.25 m/s, with maximum velocity $\|\mathbf{u}_{\max}\| = 2.05$ m/s at the slit, and a corresponding time step of 0.0015 s. Figure 10 shows the results of this experiment. As one would expect, all residual fields for higher mesh resolution than the lowest resolution grid (Fig. 10(a)) show smaller residual magnitudes, whereas for similar mesh resolutions, the results differ less. Figure 10(e) and (f) show a rather non-uniform residual magnitude distribution, whereas divergence-based refinement (Fig. 10(g)) results in a more even distribution of residual magnitude. Our residual magnitude-based refinement (h) is similar to the divergence-based, but exhibits more uniform and overall slightly lower residual magnitude. Nevertheless, thorough investigation of the utility of residual fields for mesh refinement has to be subject of future work.

5   Conclusion

In this work, we have presented the concept of residual field visualization, and provided several building blocks whose interplay enables such an analysis in in-situ environments. This first investigation revealed interesting patterns and interrelations in the space-time and space-iteration structure of residual fields, which may provide a basis for future research of more advanced techniques for the analysis of solver behavior. On the other hand, it is clear that, due to the high complexity of solver processes, this first work cannot provide in-depth insights into the novel field of residual field visualization—it is the aim of this work to foster this new topic in visualization research. As future work, we plan to investigate feature extraction from residual fields, as well as more effective in-situ integration of our approach.

Acknowledgments. This work was supported by Forschungsallianz Baden-Württemberg, "Data-Integrated Simulation Science (DISS)", and the Heidelberg Graduate School of Mathematical and Computational Methods for the Sciences (HGS MathComp), founded by DFG grant GSC 220 in the German Universities Excellence Initiative.

References

1. Blatt, M., et al.: The distributed and unified numerics environment, version 2.4. Arch. Numer. Softw. **100**(4), 13–29 (2016)
2. Cabral, B., Leedom, L.C.: Imaging vector fields using line integral convolution. In: Proceedings of 20th Annual Conference on Computer Graphics and Interactive Techniques, pp. 263–270 (1993)
3. Dahlquist, G., Björck, Å.: Numerical Methods. Dover Books on Mathematics. Dover Publications, New York (2003)
4. Dahlquist, G.G.: A special stability problem for linear multistep methods. BIT Numer. Math. **3**(1), 27–43 (1963)
5. Haimes, R., Liu, E., Kirby, R.M., Nelson, B.: ElVis: a system for the accurate and interactive visualization of high-order finite element solutions. IEEE Trans. Vis. Comput. Graph. **18**, 2325–2334 (2012)
6. Hubbard, J., Schleicher, D., Sutherland, S.: How to find all roots of complex polynomials by Newton's method. Inventiones Mathematicae **146**(1), 1–33 (2001)
7. Karch, G.K., et al.: Visualization of piecewise linear interface calculation. In: Proceedings of IEEE Pacific Visualization Symposium (PacificVis), pp. 121–128 (2013)
8. Kress, J.: In situ visualization techniques for high performance computing. Technical report, University of Oregon (2017)

9. Schollmeyer, A., Froehlich, B.: Direct isosurface ray casting of NURBS-based iso-geometric analysis. IEEE Trans. Vis. Comput. Graph. **20**(9), 1227–1240 (2014)
10. Üffinger, M., Frey, S., Ertl, T.: Interactive high-quality visualization of higher-order finite elements. Comput. Graph. Forum **29**(2), 115–136 (2010)
11. Üffinger, M., Sadlo, F., Munz, C.D., Ertl, T.: Toward wall function consistent interpolation of flow fields. In: Short Paper Proceedings of EuroVis 2013, pp. 85–89 (2013)
12. Üffinger, M., Schweitzer, M.A., Sadlo, F., Ertl, T.: Direct visualization of particle-partition of unity data. In: Proceedings of International Workshop on Vision, Modeling and Visualization (VMV), pp. 255–262 (2011)
13. Usher, W., Wald, I., Knoll, A., Papka, M., Pascucci, V.: In situ exploration of particle simulations with CPU ray tracing. Supercomput. Front. Innov.: Int. J. **3**(4), 4–18 (2016)
14. Vetter, O.: Development and integration of an in-situ framework for flow visualization of large-scale, unsteady phenomena in ICON. Supercomput. Front. Innov.: Int. J. **4**(3), 55–67 (2017)

An In-Situ Visualization Approach for the K Computer Using Mesa 3D and KVS

Kengo Hayashi[1,2]([✉]), Naohisa Sakamoto[1,2][iD], Jorji Nonaka[2][iD],
Motohiko Matsuda[2][iD], and Fumiyoshi Shoji[2][iD]

[1] Kobe University, Kobe, Japan
171x219x@stu.kobe-u.ac.jp, naohisa.sakamoto@people.kobe-u.ac.jp
[2] RIKEN Center for Computational Science, Kobe, Japan

Abstract. Although K computer has been operational for more than five years, it is still ranked in the top 10 of the Top500 list, and in active use, especially in Japan. One of the peculiarity of this system is the use of SPARC64fx CPU, with no instruction set compatibility with other traditional CPU architecture, and the use of a two-staged parallel file system, where the necessary data is moved from the user accessible GFS (Global File System) to a faster LFS (Local File System) for enabling high performance I/O during the simulation run. Since the users have no access to the data during the simulation run, the tightly coupled (co-processing) in-situ visualization approach seems to be the most suitable approach for this HPC system. For the visualization purposes, the hardware developer (Fujitsu) did not provide or support the traditional Mesa 3D graphics library on their SPARC64fx CPU, and in exchange, it provided a non-OSS (Open Source Software) and non-OpenGL visualization library with Particle-Based Volume Rendering (PBVR) implementation, including an API for in-situ visualization. In order to provide a more traditional in-situ visualization alternative for the K computer users, we focused on the Mesa 3D graphics library, and on an OpenGL-based KVS (Kyoto Visualization System) library. We expect that this approach can also be useful on other SPARC64fx HPC environments because of the binary compatibility.

Keywords: Mesa3D graphics library · SPARC64fx CPU
KVS library · Particle-Based Volume Rendering (PBVR) · K computer

1 Introduction

The K computer [12] is a Japanese leading-edge supercomputer, which was ranked as the fastest machine in the Top500 list [23] when it was built in 2011. After almost six years in service operation, from September 2012, this supercomputer system is still ranked in the top 10 of this list, and has been used for running large-scale numerical simulations in various field of science and engineering.

© Springer Nature Switzerland AG 2018
R. Yokota et al. (Eds.): ISC 2018 Workshops, LNCS 11203, pp. 310–322, 2018.
https://doi.org/10.1007/978-3-030-02465-9_21

One of the peculiarity of this systems is the SPARC64fx CPU, which is a HPC-oriented variant of the SPARC family of processors, and is based on SPARC-V9 architecture processor developed by Fujitsu [10] (Fig. 1). The SPARC64 VIIIfx version was designed for the K computer, which was developed by Fujitsu, in collaboration with RIKEN, as a Japanese national project. After that, Fujitsu developed two generations of commercial supercomputers (PRIMEHPC FX) based on this processor architecture: the FX10 that uses the SPARC64 IXfx processors; and the FX100 based on SPARC64 Xfx processors. Although the next generation leading-edge Japanese supercomputer system, named temporarily as Post K computer, being developed as a national HPC project, will use different processor architecture, the SPARC64fx based supercomputers are still in active use, and running large-scale simulations in various fields of science and engineering.

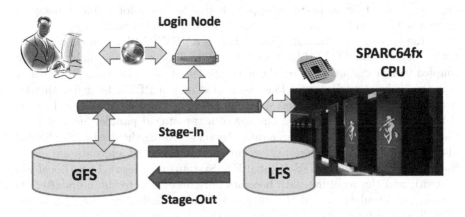

Fig. 1. A simplified view of the K computer environment and its usage.

It is widely recognized that the Mesa 3D graphics library [11] has become the de facto standard for the CPU-based execution of OpenGL functions. The Mesa 3D provides a variety of drivers, and the main drivers for the generic usage are: Legacy swrast; Gallium softpipe; and Gallium llvmpipe. From the list of HPC sites where the ParaView visualization application [8] has been installed, we can find the usage of Legacy swrast driver on the ANL Mira (IBM Blue Gene/Q), and the usage of Gallium llvmpipe driver on the ORNL Titan (Cray XK7) with AMD Opteron CPUs and NVIDIA Tesla K20 GPUs. It is worth noting that Intel provides its own driver, OpenSWR (swr) [17], which is highly optimized for the Intel x86 CPUs and Accelerators. However, for the K computer, Fujitsu did not provide the Mesa 3D graphics library to run on their SPARC64fx family of CPUs, and just provided a non-OpenGL Visualization Library [15] implementing Particle-Based Volume Rendering (PBVR).

The PBVR can be described as a projection based stochastic rendering method for semi-transparent volumetric objects. This rendering method has gradually matured over the years since its first appearance more than a decade ago [21]. Since then several improvements, including the handling of irregular volume datasets, and optimizations, including the use of GPU-based acceleration, have been proposed so far [18,19]. One of the main characteristics of the PBVR method is that, a given volumetric data is represented as a set of small and opaque particles, where the traditional degrees of transparencies used in the volume rendering, represented as alpha values, are converted as the density of particles inside a volumetric region. This means that higher degree of transparency will correspond to a lower density of particles and vice-versa. Since its uses an intermediate geometric objects for representing the densities inside a volumetric region, it becomes independent from the data format of the original data sets thus making easier the handling of irregular data sets. In addition, the use of tiny and opaque particles facilitates the handling of semi-transparency, since there is no need for the sorting, as required on the traditional alpha blending operation. This sorting-free approach makes easier for implementing the distributed or parallel processing version for large data visualization.

In the Fujitsu visualization library, there is a PBVR API, for integrating with both C/C++ and FORTRAN-based simulation codes, which enables tightly-coupled in-situ visualization on the K computer. It is worth noting that Kawamura et al. have worked on a loosely-coupled in-situ PBVR by generating the particle data on x86 CPU based supercomputer side and using the local PC for the interactive rendering [5,6]. The use of a two-staged parallel file system on the K computer (Fig. 1) imposes a difficulty on accessing the data while the simulation is running. The necessary executable code, library and data are moved from the user accessible GFS (Global File System) to a faster LFS (Local File System), and the resulting data becomes only accessible to the users after the finishing of simulation, and the output is written back from the LFS to the GFS. The simulation steering during run-time becomes difficult, and probably the most suitable in-situ visualization approach is the tightly coupled approach. In this work, we focused on the Mesa 3D and the Kyoto Visualization System (KVS) [20] for enabling tightly coupled in-situ visualization on the K computer, and in an effort to provide a more traditional alternative for the K computer users, and we expect that this approach can be useful for other SPARC64fx based HPC systems.

2 Related Work

OpenGL is widely recognized as the de facto standard for the 3D graphics API on a wide range of hardware systems, from embedded systems and hand-held devices to a leading-edge supercomputing systems. ParaView [7], developed and maintained by Kitware Inc., and VisIt [9], developed and maintained by LLNL (Lawrence Livermore National Laboratory), are probably two of the most well-known OSS for general purpose high performance visualization. They are based on the Visualization Tool Kit (VTK) [22], which has support for both distributed-memory and multithreaded parallel processing, and utilizes OpenGL for the graphics. OpenGL has continuously been updated to incorporate new features and to accompany the advances in the graphics hardware. OpenGL4 is the most recent version, which has been minorly updated from 2010. However, it is worth noting that the speed of incorporating these new features for the visualization purposes is not in the same pace. For instance, the VTK version 6 has used OpenGL2.1, released in 2006, and OpenGL3.2, released in 2009, was adopted from the VTK version 7.

High performance visualization on HPC systems relies on the Mesa 3D graphics library [11], which can be considered as the de facto standard approach for enabling software based rendering via OSMesa (Off-Screen Mesa) functionality. Different Mesa 3D graphics drivers have been used on different HPC systems [8], probably due to the different reasons. Thanks to these Mesa 3D graphics drivers, the VTK-based ParaView and VisIt becomes possible to be used for in-situ/in-transit Visualization via ParaView Catalyst [1] and VisIt-libsim [24] modules. For HPC systems with no support for the Mesa 3D, such as the SPARC64fx based supercomputers, the option is to use visualization applications, which do not use OpenGL API in their code. For instance, we can cite the Fujitsu Visualization Library [15], provided as the official visualization tool for the K computer users. Some Ray Tracing based applications are other alternatives, and we can verify some successful reports citing the LuxRender [2] and SURFACE (Scalable and Ubiquitous Rendering Framework for Advanced Computing Environments) [3].

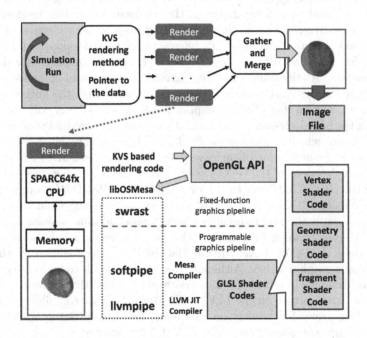

Fig. 2. Mesa 3D based tightly coupled in-situ visualization on the K computer.

Although Mesa 3D is not officially supported by the K computer hardware developers, some efforts have been done on utilizing some of the Mesa 3D graphics drivers on this supercomputing system [13]. One of the main impediments for building newer graphics drivers was the compiler version. The official Fujitsu compiler is based on GNU Compiler Collection (GCC) 4.4.7, and newer Mesa 3D drivers as well as the LLVM (for the Mesa 3D llvmpipe driver) require some C++11 functionalities, which are only supported from the GCC 4.8. Therefore, in-situ visualization with simulation codes, developed for using the official Fujitsu compiler, is restricted to use the Legacy swrast driver with no support for GLSL (OpenGL Shading Language) codes. Onishi et al. utilized the swrast driver from the Mesa version 9.2.5 for utilizing the Visit-libsim in their CFD simulation code [16]. In this work, we focused on the GCC 6.3.0, with MPI library support and was recently released for the K computer users, to build newer Mesa 3D graphics drivers. We also focused on the KVS, a general purpose visualization library, for enabling tightly coupled in-situ visualization on the K computer.

3   Mesa 3D on the K Computer

Usually, HPC operational sites have their hardware systems designed to meet their specific purposes, operated and maintained following their own policies and rules. Therefore, it is important to mention that the approach presented here may not be directly applicable on other HPC systems, and may require some adaptations. As shown in Fig. 2, except the hardware dependent Intel swr software graphics driver, there are three versions of drivers: Legacy swrast; Gallium softpipe; and Gallium llvmpipe. They have actually been developed and released in this order, and obviously the newer versions have more functionality than the initial versions. At the same time, the external libraries and compiler requirements for the newer version are proportionately higher than the initial versions. For instance, the Fujitsu official compiler for K computer was only capable of compiling the initial versions of the Mesa 3D graphics library, and also the swrast (Legacy) driver which implements only the fixed graphics pipeline.

To enable the utilization of the newer version of the Mesa 3D, we have tested with different versions of the GCC 6, and most of the results here were obtained by using the GCC 6.3.0, built to run directly on the SPARC64fx computational nodes. By using GCC 6, it becomes possible to build the Gallium softpipe, which implements the programmable graphics pipeline thus enabling the use of GLSL (OpenGL Shading Language) codes. In addition, it also become possible to build the LLVM (Low-Level Virtual Machine) compiler required for the Gallium llvmpipe graphics driver. Although it becomes possible to build the graphics driver, the llvmpipe graphics driver did not work because the relocation code for the SPARC architecture on the LLVM-JIT (Just-in-Time) compiler was simply missing. Our group has worked on this issue, and finally the llvmpipe graphics driver, from the Mesa 17.2.3 and LLVM 5.0.1, started working. There was another group effort trying to make the GCC 6.3.0 available for the K computer users, and since this approach included the MPI library support, we focused on this GCC version in this work.

Although we could successfully compile and run the Mesa 3D Gallium llvmpipe driver on the SPARC64fx CPU environment, we are aware that there will be a necessity to execute thorough performance measurements in order to verify if the obtained rendering performance is compatible with that obtained by traditional CPU architecture. Since Fujitsu official compiler for K computer was not able to compile the utilized version of the Mesa 3D library, it means that the available compiler optimizations on the Fujitsu compiler was not be applied, thus we also need to verify how it can affect in the performance of the generated llvmpipe driver. As one of the future works will be this detailed performance evaluation and analysis.

4   OpenGL-Based KVS Library

KVS [20] is a multi-platform OpenGL-based general purpose visualization library developed at Kyoto University, and currently maintained at Kobe University, and is publicly available via GitHub (https://github.com/naohisas/KVS). This library supports both distributed memory and multithreading parallel processing, and also an offscreen-based in-situ visualization API for both C/C++ and FORTRAN based simulation codes. It is worth noting that KVS also possesses the original implementation of the PBVR, which is being utilized for both in-situ [15] and in-transit [5,6] visualization on different HPC systems. In the proposed in-situ approach, the KVS is used not only for providing the PBVR-based visualization, but also for providing other traditional rendering techniques such as ray-casting, isosurface, and others. Since KVS utilizes GLSL-based functionalities in its code, it becomes crucial to utilize the Gallium llvmpipe graphics driver on the K computer.

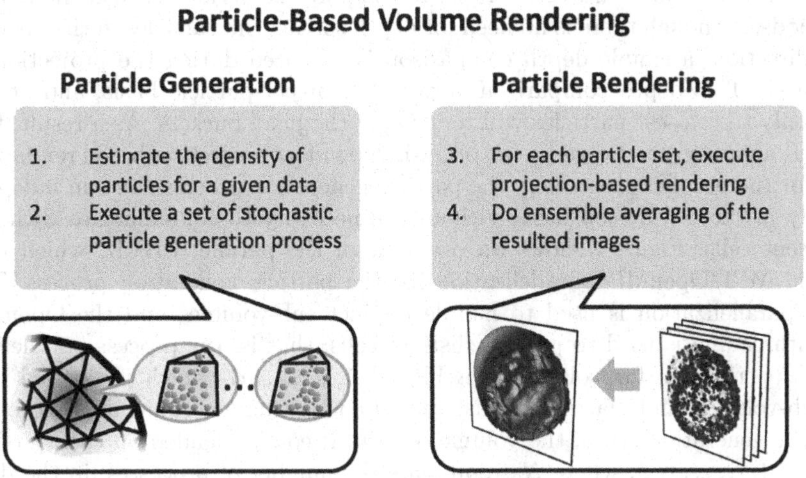

Fig. 3. An overview of the Particle-Based Volume Rendering method.

4.1   Particle Based Volume Rendering

PBVR can be defined as an object-space stochastic volume rendering approach, where the particle density within a given volume data is firstly estimated by taking into consideration the user-defined transfer function (Fig. 3). Independently to the data formats of the input volume data, it will then be represented as a set of small and opaque particles, and the particle generation is governed by the Eq. 1. The KVS framework supports particle generation from both structured and unstructured volume data formats, and in this equation: α represents the degree of transparency; r represents the radius of the particle; Δt represents the corresponding sampling size used by the traditional volume rendering [4]; and ρ represents the particle density, that is, the number of particles within a unit volume [19].

$$\rho = -\frac{log(1 - \alpha)}{\pi r^2 \Delta t} \tag{1}$$

After the particle generation stage, the particle rendering stage takes place (Fig. 3). Different PBVR implementations PBVR basically differs on that particle rendering stage. Fujitsu has implemented the "sub-pixel" based version where the pixels are subdivided in a user defined sub-pixel size. For instance, if sub-pixel size is set as three, each of the pixels will be subdivided into 3×3 sub-regions. Since this approach is high-memory consuming approach, we focused on the "repetition" method where a set of particles are generated in a loop and an ensemble averaging of the rendering results are executed for generating the final image. In addition, some GPU-based particle rendering implementations have also been proposed. Therefore, although these implementations are classified as PBVR methods, the computational cost for each of the approaches slightly differs and we should aware when trying to compare the performance of the PBVR methods. Although there is no need for depth sorting the particles in the viewing ray direction, a simple depth comparison is executed during the projection of particles. This depth comparison is executed in per-particle basis, and at the end only the closest particles will remains in the pixel buckets. As a result, this PBVR approach can be said as an order-independent projection-based rendering.

For the parallel processing, the particle generation process can run independently in the cell-by-cell basis without the necessity to communicate with the adjacent cells. Figure 4 shows an overview of the parallel PBVR, which uses hybrid MPI/OpenMP parallelization for the particle generation process. The MPI parallelization is used to handle distinct sub-volumes and the OpenMP multithreading is used to process distinct cells, that is, the process parallelization is performed for volume data $V_i(i = 1, 2, \ldots, m)$, which is divided into m sub-volumes and placed in a distributed computing environment. Before the particle generation stage, the volume data V_i is equally loaded on each process $P_j(j = 1, 2, \ldots, N_p)$, where N_p represents the number of processes, in the data loading stage. And the number of threads per process P_1 to P_{N_p} is the number of parallel instances of MPI. The coordinate information of the entire volumes and the physical quantity information are shared to all the processes in P_1 to P_{N_p} before the data loading stage. After that, each of the MPI processes will execute the projection-based rendering, and the generated sub-images are then gathered and composited, by using ensemble averaging, via an image compositing library named 234Compositor [14].

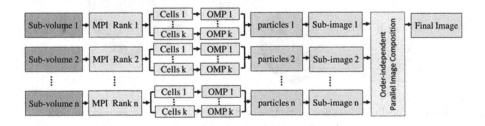

Fig. 4. Overview of the implemented parallel PBVR on the K computer.

4.2   Traditional Rendering Methods

As a general-purpose visualization library, KVS has implemented other traditional rendering methods such as isosurface extraction, contour slices, streamlines, and raycasting-based volume rendering. The aforementioned parallel PBVR framework serve as a basis for performing parallel rendering by substituting the PBVR rendering call from the simulation code to other KVS-based offscreen rendering APIs. Figure 5 shows an example of parallel isosurface extraction using 4 MPI processes, and its its depth-based image composition result. KVS is an open-source C++ library, and it provides offscreen rendering APIs for in-situ visualization for simulation codes written in C/C++ and FORTRAN. In the latter case, the traditional ISO C bindings are used. Figure 6 shows some examples of KVS rendering methods (external faces and isosurface) called from the same parallel FORTRAN code (mimicking a simulation code) using 8 nodes of the K computer.

5   Experimental Results

Considering that the objective is to provide a ready-to-use tightly-coupled in-situ visualization alternative for the K computer users, we focused on applying the officially available compilers and libraries on the K computer. Therefore, in addition to the K computer itself, we used the GCC 6.3.0 compiler, with MPI support (mpigcc, mpig++, and mpifrt), and the Mesa 3D llvmpipe driver, built from the Mesa 17.2.3 and LLVM 5.0.1, and by using the aforementioned GCC. In order to evaluate the correct execution of the GLSL-based offscreen rendering API on the K computer, we utilized a FORTRAN code, mimicking a simulation code, which generates a voxel-based volume data with a call to the KVS rendering API, and passing the size and the pointer for the volume data.

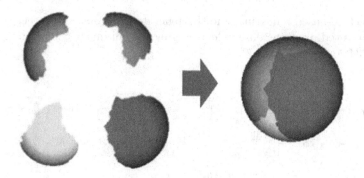

Fig. 5. Parallel isosurface extraction and its depth-based image composition.

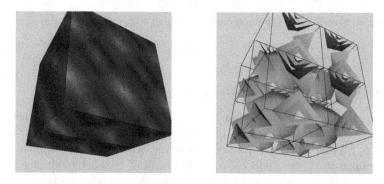

Fig. 6. Some KVS-based parallel rendering results on voxel data.

At the end of distributed image generation the 234Compositor is used for the final image compositing. Figure 6 shows three KVS rendering methods (external faces and isosurface) utilized in this evaluation using eight computational nodes (MPI processes).

In addition to this voxel-based volume data, we also utilized a irregular volume data composed of 18, 899, 767 prism cells. Although the KVS offscreen rendering API has still to be integrated to the simulation code, we evaluated the in-situ rendering API by mimicking the call from the simulation code. This code simulates the Magnus force acting on a rotating sphere placed in a uniform flow, and calculates the effect of rotation of a sphere around a uniform flow. Figure 7 shows some KVS-based parallel rendering results (PBVR, isosurface, slice plane) of this irregular volume data by using 32 computational nodes on the K computer. Figure 8 shows some of the obtained rendering times by using aforementioned KVS-based rendering methods.

The graph in the upper left side shows the rendering time for the utilized rendering methods (PBVR, isosurface, slice plane) by using 16 MPI processes and 8 OpenMP threads. We also plotted the obtained rendering time on a x86-based single-rack SGI UV300, named π-VizStudio running at Kobe University,

Fig. 7. Some KVS-based parallel rendering results of an irregular volume data.

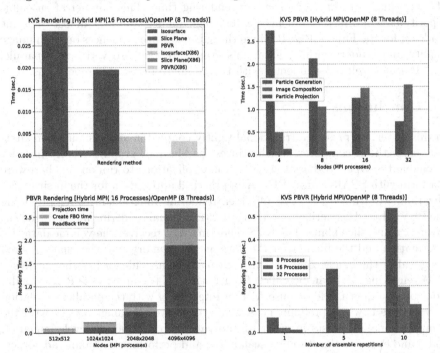

Fig. 8. KVS based rendering time on the K computer (with Mesa llvmpipe driver).

to compare the performance of Mesa llvmpipe driver running on different hardware architectures. In this initial performance measurements, we could observe that the performance on the K computer was around 5 times slower than that observed on x86 architecture system. We are aware that a more deep analysis and evaluation is needed for making a fair and solid comparison. The graph in the upper right side shows the scalability in the rendering performance of parallel PBVR using up to 32 computational nodes (256 CPU cores). From this figure, we could verify that the particle generation and projection scales as the increase in the number of MPI processes. However, the image composition part, which involves the image gathering and ensemble averaging, will probably be the bottleneck when running large-scale parallel PBVR jobs. As one of the future works, we are planning to evaluate other existing parallel image composition libraries.

The graph in the lower left side shows the image size dependency of the PBVR method. By using same set of the generated particles, we rendered using different image sizes ($512^2, 10242^2, 2048^2, 4096^2$), and we can verify that the rendering time becomes proportionally slow as the increase in the number of pixels in the rendered image. Finally, the graph in the lower right side shows the rendering time behavior when changing the number of ensemble repetitions. In the same way of the aforementioned number of pixels, we can confirm that the number of repetitions will directly affect the rendering time. This number of ensemble repetitions will directly influence in the image quality, and it is almost the same trade off for the Fujitsu PBVR where the sub-pixel size influences on both image quality and rendering time. From this graph, we can also verify that parallel PBVR scales well independently with the number of ensemble repetitions.

6 Conclusions

In this paper, we present a traditional tightly-coupled in-situ visualization alternative, for the K computer, which utilizes the Mesa 3D graphics library in order to enable the OpenGL-based visualization applications to run on this hardware platform with SPARC64fx CPUs. As a practical application for the in-situ visualization, we utilized the KVS offscreen rendering functionalities for providing the PBVR-based rendering as well as other traditional rendering methods such as isosurface and slice plane. The KVS rendering API receives the volume data size information and the pointer for the data on the memory, and the final rendered image, after the image composition, is then stored as a file for post-hoc analysis. This rendering API can be called from both C/C++ and FORTRAN simulation codes, and is a ready-to-use API for integrating with the parallel simulation codes. Since it was a preliminary evaluation, we are planning to work with the computational scientists in order to integrate with production-level simulation codes and evaluate the stability, scalability, and performance. Taking advantage of the binary compatibility among the SPARC64fx HPC systems, we expect that this in-situ visualization approach can be useful on other SPARC64fx based HPC systems (Fujitsu PRIMEHPC FX10 and FX100) still in active use especially in Japan. In addition, we expect to publicly release the necessary patches for making possible the use of Mesa 3D library on the SPARC CPU architecture after executing more detailed performance evaluations and stability testings. We are also interested in ameliorating the PBVR in the aspects of image quality, rendering performance, usability, and others. Therefore we will continue looking for any technique that can be helpful for achieving these goals.

Acknowledgement. Some of the results were obtained using the K computer at RIKEN Center for Computational Science (R-CCS) in Kobe, Japan. This work is partially supported by the "Joint Usage/Research Center for Interdisciplinary Large-scale

Information Infrastructures" in Japan (Project ID: jh180060-NAH), JSPS KAKENHI Grant Number JP17K00169 and Social Implementation Program on Climate Change Adaptation Technology (SI-CAT) from the Ministry of Education, Culture, Sports, Science and Technology (MEXT) in Japan.

References

1. Ayachit, U., et al.: ParaView catalyst: enabling in situ data analysis and visualization. In: Proceedings of In Situ Infrastructures for Enabling Extreme-Scale Analysis and Visualization, ISAV 2015 (2015)
2. FORUM8: HPCI Project ID (hp130034): Building of High Speed Rendering Environment by Using Photorealistic Rendering Engine. http://www.hpci-office.jp/output/hp130034/outcome.pdf
3. Fujita, M., Nonaka, J., Ono, K.: LSGL: large-scale graphics library for peta-scale computing environments. In: HPG 2014: High Performance Graphics 2014 (Poster) (2014)
4. Johnson, C., Hansen, C.: Visualization Handbook. Academic Press Inc., Orlando (2004)
5. Kawamura, T., Noda, T., Idomura, Y.: In-situ visual exploration of multivariate volume data based on particle based volume rendering. In: Proceedings of the 2nd Workshop on In Situ Infrastructures for Enabling Extreme-Scale Analysis and Visualization, ISAV 2016, pp. 18–22 (2016)
6. Kawamura, T., Noda, T., Idomura, Y.: Performance evaluation of runtime data exploration framework based on in-situ particle based volume rendering. Supercomput. Front. Innov. 4(3), 43–54 (2017)
7. Kitware Inc.: ParaView. http://www.paraview.org
8. Kitware Inc.: ParaView and Mesa3D. http://www.paraview.org/Wiki/ParaView_And_Mesa_3D
9. LLNL: VisIt. http://wci.llnl.gov/simulation/computer-codes/visit
10. Maruyama, T., Motokurumada, T., Morita, K., Aoki, N.: Past, present, and future of SPARC64 processors. Fujitsu Sci. Tech. J. 47(2), 130–135 (2011)
11. Mesa: Mesa 3D Graphics Library. http://www.mesa3d.org/
12. Miyazaki, H., Kusano, Y., Shinjou, N., Shoji, F., Yokokawa, M., Watanabe, T.: Overview of the K computer system. Fujitsu Sci. Tech. J. 48(3), 255–265 (2012)
13. Nonaka, J., et al.: A study on open source software for large-scale data visualization on SPARC64fx based HPC systems. In: Proceedings of the International Conference on High Performance Computing in Asia-Pacific Region, HPC Asia 2018, pp. 278–288. ACM, New York (2018)
14. Nonaka, J., Ono, K., Fujita, M.: 234Compositor: a flexible parallel image compositing framework for massively parallel visualization environments. Future Gener. Comput. Syst. 82, 647–655 (2018)
15. Ogasa, A., Maesaka, H., Sakamoto, K., Otagiri, S.: Visualization technology for the K computer. Fujitsu Sci. Tech. J. 48(3), 348–356 (2012)
16. Onishi, K., Jansson, N., Bale, R., Wang, W.H., Li, C.G., Tsubokura, M.: A deployment of HPC algorithm into pre/post-processing for industrial CFD on K-computer. In: The International Conference for High Performance Computing, Networking, Storage and Analysis (SC 2017) Poster (2017)
17. Rowley, T.: Software Rasterizer (SWR). Intel HPC Developers Conference at SC 2014

18. Sakamoto, N., Kawamura, T., Koyamada, K.: Improvement of particle-based volume rendering for visualizing irregular volume data sets. Comput. Graph. **34**(1), 34–42 (2010)
19. Sakamoto, N., Koyamada, K.: Stochastic approach for integrated rendering of volumes and semi-transparent surfaces. In: SC Companion: High Performance Computing, Networking Storage and Analysis (UltraVis2012), pp. 176–185 (2012)
20. Sakamoto, N., Koyamada, K.: KVS: a simple and effective framework for scientific visualization. J. Adv. Simul. Sci. Eng. **2**(1), 76–95 (2015)
21. Sakamoto, N., Nonaka, J., Koyamada, K., Tanaka, S.: Particle-based volume rendering. In: Proceedings of the IEEE Asia-Pacific Symposium on Visualization, pp. 129–132 (2007)
22. Schroeder, W., Martin, K., Lorensen, B.: The Visualization Toolkit: An Object-Oriented Approach to 3D Graphics. Kitware, Inc., New York (2006)
23. Top500: Top500 supercomputer sites. http://www.top500.org/
24. Whitlock, B., Favre, J.M., Meredith, J.S.: Parallel in situ coupling of simulation with a fully featured visualization system. In: Proceedings of the 11th Eurographics Conference on Parallel Graphics and Visualization, GPGV 2011, pp. 101–109 (2011)

4th International Workshop on Communication Architectures for HPC, Big Data, Deep Learning and Clouds at Extreme Scale (ExaComm 2018)

4th International Workshop on Communication Architectures for HPC, Big Data, Deep Learning and Clouds at Extreme Scale (ExaComm 2018)

Hari Subramoni and Dhabaleswar. K. Panda

Department of Computer Science and Engineering,
The Ohio State University, Columbus, OH
{subramoni.1,panda.2}@osu.edu

1 Introduction

Extreme Scale computing in HPC, Big Data, Deep Learning and Clouds are marked by multiple-levels of hierarchy and heterogeneity ranging from the compute units (many-core CPUs, GPUs, APUs etc) to storage devices (NVMe, NVMe over Fabrics etc) to the network interconnects (InfiniBand, High-Speed Ethernet, Omni-Path etc). Owing to the plethora of heterogeneous communication paths with different cost models expected to be present in extreme scale systems, data movement is seen as the soul of different challenges for exascale computing. On the other hand, advances in networking technologies such as NoCs (like NVLink), RDMA enabled networks and the likes are constantly pushing the envelope of research in the field of novel communication and computing architectures for extreme scale computing.

This workshop is targeted for various categories of people (Scientists, engineers, researchers, developers and students) working in the area of high performance communication and I/O, Big Data, Deep Learning, Clouds, networking, middleware, virtualization, quality of service, accelerators and applications related to exascale computing. Specific audience this workshop is aimed at include:

- Scientists, engineers, researchers and students working on the design and development of communication architectures for next-generation exascale systems including clusters, data centers, storage centers, deep learning, cloud computing and Big Data systems.
- Newcomers to the field of HPC and exascale computing who are interested in familiarizing themselves with programming models, accelerators, networking, and communication architectures.
- Developers of next generation networked computing architectures and middleware.

This workshop will help the attendees learn multiple aspects of modern high performance networking technologies. For scientists, engineers, and researchers from both academia and industry engaged in designing scalable communication architectures and protocols over high performance networks and their associate runtimes and middlewares, the workshop provides a forum for them to discuss and share their experience, expertise and expectation about the trends on high performance programming networks and middleware for exascale systems.

ExaComm 2018 focused on a range of areas, including but not limited to:

- Scalable communication protocols
- High performance networks
- Runtime/middleware designs
- Impact of high performance networks on Deep Learning/Machine Learning
- Impact of high performance networks on Big Data
- Novel hardware/software co-design
- High performance communication solutions for accelerator based computing
- Power-aware techniques and designs
- Performance evaluations
- Quality of Service (QoS)
- Resource virtualization and SR-IOV

2 Organization

The workshop had talks from experts in the field including an invited keynote talk, other invited talks. Apart from this, we also had refereed research papers and invited research papers.

Several rounds of Call for Papers (CFP) and Call for Participation were issued. The important deadlines were:

- Technical paper submission deadline 11:59 PM Anywhere on Earth Friday, April 27, 2018
- Author notification Friday, June 1, 2018
- Conference-ready deadline Friday, June 8, 2018

2.1 Program Committee

The workshop had a set of internationally recognized experts in the field of high-performance computing and networking to review the papers. Each research paper was taken through a comprehensive peer review process by the program committee. Papers were be evaluated along the metrics of (a) Quality of Presentation; (b) Novelty/Originality; (c) Relation to State of the Art; (d) Technical Strength; (e) Significance of Work; and (f) Relevance to Workshop. Each paper had atleast five reviews. We would like to express our sincere gratitude to all the PC members for fantastic effort in reviewing the research papers submitted to the workshop.

The list of PC members of ExaComm'18 are listed below.

- Taisuke Boku, University of Tsukuba, Japan
- Ron Brightwell, Sandia National Laboratories
- Hans Eberle, NVIDIA

- Brice Goglin, INRIA, France
- Dror Goldenberg, Mellanox Technologies
- R. Govindarajan, Indian Institute of Science, Bangalore, India
- Ryan Grant, Sandia National Laboratories
- Hai Jin, Huazhong University of Science and Technology, Wuhan, China
- Sven Karlsson, Technical University of Denmark, Lyngby, Denmark
- Takeshi Nanri, University of Kyushu, Japan
- Dimitrios Nikolopoulos, Queen's University of Belfast, Belfast, Northern Ireland, UK
- Antonio Pena, Barcelona Supercomputing Center, Barcelona, Spain
- Sebastien Rumley, Columbia University
- Smruti Ranjan Sarangi, Indian Institute of Technology, Delhi, India
- Martin Schulz, Technical University of Munich, Munich, Germany
- John M. Shalf, National Energy Research Scientific Computing Center/Lawrence
- Berkeley National Laboratory
- Tor Skeie, Simula Research Laboratory, Norway
- Sayantan Sur, Intel
- Xin Yuan, Florida State University
- Jidong Zhai, Tsinghua University, Beijing, China

3 Workshop Summary

Throughout the day, on average 30 participants attended the workshop. We had a good mix of talks from experts in the field of high-performance networking, programming models and tools. The various sessions had vigorous participation from the audience members. A short summary of the presentations is provided below. The slides of the presentations are available on the workshop's webpage: http://nowlab.cse.ohio-state.edu/exacomm/.

The keynote talk was delivered by Dr. Craig Stunkel, Principal Research Staff Member at IBM's T. J. Watson Research Center in Yorktown Heights, NY. Dr. Stunkel also serves as the Network Lead in the Data Centric Systems department, and for the upcoming CORAL systems to be delivered to both Oak Ridge National Lab and Lawrence Livermore National Lab. The keynote talk, entitled "Network challenges and directions for the exascale era" outlined the most significant challenges for building high-performance networks for exascale systems and discuss desirable network attributes for potential workloads. It covered recent network trends, and then examined several promising ideas and directions for addressing the exascale challenges and desirable attributes, particularly in the areas of technology, topologies, protocols, and support for offloaded remote transactions.

3.1 Invited Talks

The workshop had seven talks from internationally recognized experts in the filed of high-performance networking, programming models and tools. The details of the various invited talks are given below.

- Vanguard: Maturing the Arm Ecosystem for U.S. DOE/ASC Supercomputing, Kevin Pedretti, Principal Member of Technical Staff, Sandia National Laboratories
- InfiniBand In-Network Computing Technology and Roadmap, Dror Goldenberg, Vice President of Software Architecture, Mellanox Technologies
- Advanced Network Semantics for Converged HPC, Analytics and AI Workloads, Sayantan Sur, Software Engineer, Intel Corporation
- ABCI: AI Bridging Cloud Infrastructure for Scalable AI/Big Data, Hitoshi Sato, Senior Research Scientist, National Institute of Advanced Industrial Science and Technology (AIST), Japan
- DataFlow SuperComputing for BigData Analytics, Veljko Milutinovic, Academy of Europe
- Interconnects and topologies options open up thanks to co-packaged optics, Nicolas Dubé, Chief Strategist for HPC, Hewlett Packard Enterprise
- Delivering Scalable Communication Solutions for Diverse Workloads: The Cray Approach, Luiz DeRose, Senior Principal Engineer and Programming Environments Director, Cray

3.2 Research Papers

Doctoral students pursuing their studies presented two research papers at the workshop. The details of the research papers are given below.

- Supercomputer in a laptop: Distributed application and runtime development via architecture simulation, Samuel Knight, Joseph Kenny and, Jeremiah J. Wilke
- Comparing Control Flow and Data Flow for Tensor Calculus: Speed, Power, Complexity, and MTBF, Milos Kotlar, Veljko Milutinovic

3.3 Panel Discussion

The workshop had a panel discussion entitled "Performance Analysis and Instrumentation for Current and Future Extreme-Scale Networks". Ron Brightwell, R&D Manager, Scalable System Software, Sandia National Laboratories was the moderator for the panel. The panelists included:

- Luiz DeRose, Senior Principal Engineer and Programming Environments Director, Cray.
- Torsten Hoefler, Associate Professor, ETH Zürich.
- Bernd Mohr, Institute for Advanced Simulation (IAS), Jülich Supercomputing Centre (JSC).
- Sameer Shende, Director of the Performance Research Lab, NIC, University of Oregon.
- Anthony Skjellum, Professor, The University of Tennessee at Chattanooga.

Comparing Controlflow and Dataflow for Tensor Calculus: Speed, Power, Complexity, and MTBF

Milos Kotlar[1]([✉])[iD] and Veljko Milutinovic[2,3,4,5][iD]

[1] School of Electrical Engineering, University of Belgrade, Belgrade, Serbia
kotlarmilos@gmail.com
[2] Fellow of the IEEE, Washington DC, USA
[3] Academia Europaea, London, UK
[4] Department of Computer Science, University of Indiana,
Bloomington, IN, USA
[5] Mathematical Institute of the Serbian Academy of Arts and Sciences,
Belgrade, Serbia
vm@etf.rs

Abstract. This article introduces ten different tensor operations, their generalizations, as well as their implementations for a dataflow paradigm. Tensor operations could be utilized for addressing a number of big data problems in machine learning and computer vision, such as speech recognition, visual object recognition, data mining, deep learning, genomics, mind genomics, and applications in civil and geo engineering. As the big data applications are breaking the Exascale barrier, and also the Bronto scale barrier in a not so far future, the main challenge is finding a way to process such big quantities of data.

This article sheds light on various dataflow implementations of tensor operations, mostly those used in machine learning. The iterative nature of tensor operations and a large amount of data makes them situable for the dataflow paradigm. All the dataflow implementations are analyzed comparatively with the related control-flow implementations, for speedup, complexity, power savings, and MTBF. The core contribution of this paper is a table that compare the two paradigms for various data set sizes, and in various conditions of interest.

The results presented in this paper are made to be applicable both for the current dataflow paradigm implementations and for what we believe are the optimal future dataflow paradigm implementations, which we refer to as the Ultimate dataflow. This portability was made possible because the programming model of the current dataflow implementation is applicable also to the Ultimate dataflow. The major differences between the Ultimate dataflow and the current dataflow implementations are not in the programming model, but in the hardware structure and in the capabilities of the optimizing compiler. In order to show the differences between the Ultimate dataflow and the current dataflow implementations, and in order to show what to expect from the future dataflow paradigm implementations, this paper starts with an overview of Ultimate dataflow and its potentials.

© Springer Nature Switzerland AG 2018
R. Yokota et al. (Eds.): ISC 2018 Workshops, LNCS 11203, pp. 329–346, 2018.
https://doi.org/10.1007/978-3-030-02465-9_22

Keywords: Big data · Dataflow computing · Tensor calculus
Ultimate dataflow

1   Introduction to Ultimate Dataflow

Some recent public talks and university courses on Advances in dataflow were concentrating on the concept of Ultimate dataflow for big data, its potentials (up to 2000 in speed up, up to 200 in transistor count, up to 20 in power savings, and up to 2 in precision), and its essence. Consequently, this position paper covers the issues related to the potentials of the concept, using the programming model of Maxeler. The Maxeler dataflow approach is still far away from the ideal Ultimate dataflow, but does achieve considerable speedups over control-flow machines, and thus is of interest for the educational and research missions described here. What is good, however, about the Maxeler dataflow approach, is that its dataflow programming model is directly applicable to the case of Ultimate dataflow.

For precision, the ratio 2x was quoted, since the approach could benefit from approximate computing, due to its data format flexibility, as explained later.

For power, the ratio 20x was quoted, because control-flow machines like Intel operate on about 4 GHz and current FPGAs on about 200 MHz, which makes about 20x.

For transistor count, the ratio of 200x was quoted, for the following reason: If one looks up the Intel microprocessor floorplan, one finds out that only 0.5% of the area is for Arithmetic and Logic, making the 1/200x ratio.

For speedup, the frequently quoted numbers are: (a) 20x as the lowest number on Maxeler speedup in recent publications at prestigious journals, (b) 200x as the highest number ever reported by Maxeler, at a respectable publication, and (c) 2000x for the reason, that has nothing to do with existing dataflow implementations, but has a lot to do with Ultimate dataflow; (d) even 20000x could be hoped for some applications, as explained next.

In Ultimate dataflow, the speedup depends predominantly on the contribution of loops to the overall execution time:

- If loops contribute with more than 99.95% to the overall run time, then one can hope for a speedup of 2000x.
- If one looks up some of the applications on the list of current dataflow successes, one finds out that in many cases the contribution of loops was well over 99.995%, which is why the potentials of Ultimate dataflow could reach even 20000x.

The fact is that about 4000 students world wide have used the Maxeler MIS-ANU dataflow machine (https://maxeler.mi.sanu.ac.rs/), and that these students come from universities like: MIT, Harvard, Princeton, Yale, Columbia, NYU, Purdue, University of Indiana in Bloomington, University of Michigan in Ann Arbor, Ohio State, Georgia Tech, CMU, FIU, FAU, etc. (in the USA),

ETH, EPFL (in Switzerland), UNIWIE, TUWIEN (in Austria), Karlsruhe, Heidelberg (in Germany), Manchester, Bristol, Cambridge, Oxford (in England), and, of course, from the leading schools of Belgrade: ETF, MATF, FON, FFH.

The Ultimate dataflow, as a concept, is built on the following two premises (each one with 4 sub-premises):

1. *Compiler does the following:*
   (a) Separates effectively spatial and temporal data, to satisfy the requirements of the Nobel Laureate Ilya Prigogine, since that action lowers the entropy of a computer system, meaning that the rest of the compiler could do a much better optimization job (lower entropy brings more order and consequently better optimization opportunities).
   (b) Maps the execution graph in the way that makes sure that edges are of the minimal length, to be consistent with the observations of Nobel Laureate Richard Feynman.
   (c) Enables one to go to a lower precision, for what is not of ultimate importance, and consequently to save on resources, that could be reinvested into what is of ultimate importance, following the wisdom of Nobel Laureate Daniel Kahneman.
   (d) Enables one to trade between latency and precision, which, in latency-tolerant applications, brings more precision with less resources, and in latency-intolerant applications, brings less latency, in exchange for a lower precision, thus following the wisdom of Nobel Laureate Andre Geim.

Unfortunately, none of the dataflow compilers, as far as we know, does any of the above.

2. *Hardware consists of the following:*
   (a) Analog datapath of the honeycomb structure, to which one could effectively map the execution graphs corresponding to loops.
   (b) The DataPath clocked at a much lower frequency, and hopefully not clocked at all, if the analog path is not unacceptably long, so it is literally the voltage difference between input and output, that moves data thru the graph.
   (c) Digital memory is on the side of the DataPath, so that computing parameters could be kept non-volatile, and temporary results could be stored more effectively.
   (d) The I/O connecting the host and the dataflow is much faster.

Unfortunately, FPGAs offer none of the above today! Consequently, FPGA is today only the least bad solution on the road to the ultimate goal!

In conclusion, the benefits of the Ultimate dataflow approach will become fully achievable only once the semiconductor and the compiler technologies become capable of supporting the above specified two sets of requirements. References leading to the above conclusion are spreading four decades of the research of the author [14–16, 19, 26–31, 35–37].

2   Introduction to Tensor Calculus

During the last few years, big data has become key focus in almost any area of business or society. Data is growing faster than ever before, and by the year 2020, volume of big data will increase from 4.4 zettabytes to roughly 44 zettabytes. More data has been created in a past few years, than in the entire previous digital history. At the moment, less than 0.5% of all data is ever analysed [20,21]. The big analysis mostly involves machine learning algorithms, which extract important information from data and perform prediction and classification. Most of these algorithms are based on a tensor calculus.

The origin of the tensor calculus dates back to the beginning of the last century. The first well-known concept of tensor was introduced in Einstein's theory of relativity [9]. After that, tensors have been used in many fields such as physics, quantum mechanics, quantum chemistry, engineering, and more recently in the machine learning. Since Google has launched the TensorFlow library for machine learning based on tensor calculus, the artificial intelligence witnessed the meteoric rise [1,38]. Tensors are also used in natural language processing, for estimating parameters of latent variable models like Hidden Markov Model [2], in computer vision, for storing valuable data and correlations between [13], and in deep neural networks, for describing relations between neurons in a network [17].

The main challenge is finding a way to process such big quantities of data. Most of the existing approaches are dissipating enormous amount of electrical power, by solving big data problems. The amount of data will grow over the time, which requires the shift in the computing paradigm and the programming model [36]. Massive growth in the scale of data puts the control-flow paradigm out and brings a dataflow paradigm into the focus.

This paper presents ten different tensor operations on the dataflow architecture, of interest for machine learning algorithms. Proposed dataflow implementations offer superior energy efficiency acceleration, achieving significant speedup per watt and transistor count, compared against control-flow implementations. Ten tensor operations presented in this paper are widely used in machine learning algorithms, which are based on arithmetic operations, transformations, and factorizations [22,25].

Section 3 gives an overview of ten tensor operations and discusses state-of-the-art solutions that overcome big data problems. Section 4 explains the concept of the dataflow paradigm comparatively to the traditional control-flow paradigm. It also discusses advantages and disadvantages, and compares the two paradigms trough different aspects, such as speed, power dissipation, complexity, and MTBF. Section 5 presents implementations of ten dataflow tensor operations. Section 6 evaluates dataflow tensor operations performance, and compares them with the control-flow implementations. Section 7 concludes the paper, discusses achievements, and what are possible topics for further research.

3   Existing Solutions

This section gives an overview of ten tensor operations and discusses control-flow implementations. In the open literature exists a number of solutions that address tensor calculus, and most of them are based on the control-flow paradigm.

3.1   An Overview of Tensor Operations

Tensor operations could be divided in three main groups: (A) arithmetic group, (B) transformation group, and (C) factorization group. The arithmetic group includes basic arithmetic operations, such as tensor addition, tensor composition, transpose of a tensor, and divergence of a tensor field. The transformation group includes operations that compute inverse and invariants of a tensor. Transformation of a coordinate system does not affect attributes of a tensor. The factorization group includes operations that perform tensor decompositions, such as eigenvalues and eigenvectors, spectral decompositions, and operations for computing rank of a tensor.

Table 1 gives an overview of tensor operations with time complexities for state-of-the-art implementations. Since second-order tensors are of considerable use in machine learning, and most high-order tensor operations are NP-hard [12], this paper focuses only on second-order tensors.

Table 1. List of ten tensor operations with time complexities, divided in three main groups. Time complexities presented in this table are related only to algorithmic improvements.

Operation	Group	Optimal complexity
Tensor addition	*Arithmetic*	$O(n^2)$
Tensor transpose	*Arithmetic*	$O(n^2)$
Tensor composition	*Arithmetic*	$O(n^{2.373})$
Tensor inverse	*Transformation*	$O(n^3)$
Primary invariants	*Transformation*	$O(n^3)$
Principal invariants	*Transformation*	$O(n^3)$
Eigenvalues and eigenvectors	*Factorization*	$O((4/3)n^3 + n^2)$
Spectral decomposition	*Factorization*	$O(n^3)$
Divergence of a tensor field	*Arithmetic*	$O(n^3)$
Rank of a tensor	*Factorization*	$O(n^3)$

Time complexities presented in Table 1 are related only to algorithmic improvements. Possible improvements using different architectures are discussed later.

Tensor addition is a basic arithmetic operation with time complexity of $O(n^2)$. In open literature does not exist many improvements that could accelerate the operation. Most of improvements are based on the underlying hardware. For sparse tensors, where most elements are equal to zero, instead of keeping all data in a tensor, a map function could be used for storing only valuable elements, depending on a position [10].

Tensor transpose is an operator which flips a tensor over its diagonal with time complexity of $O(n^2)$. Beside time complexity, the operation may also differs in memory complexity. With decreasing the time complexity, the memory complexity could be increased. Many software libraries that support this operation avoid explicitly transposing a tensor in memory by simply accessing the same data in a different order [23].

Tensor composition is a wide-spreaded operation, uses in many areas of mathematics and engineering. The naive implementation has complexity $O(n^3)$, which is also known as schoolbook algorithm. The state-of-the-art algorithm for tensor multiplication is Coppersmith-Winograd algorithm [7] with time complexity of $O(n^{2.376})$. Despite its lower time complexity, it is rarely used in practice because of large constant factors in their running times that makes them impractic.

Tensor inverse is operation that is often used for solving linear equations in mathematic. It is also used in computer graphics, particularly in 3D graphics rendering and 3D simulations. In the open literature exists a number of methods that produce inverse of a tensor [18]. Gaussian elimination [4] is an algorithm that could be used for solving systems of linear equations and also for tensor inversion, with time complexity of $O(n^3)$. In numerical analysis and linear algebra, LU decomposition factors a tensor as the product of a lower triangular tensor and an upper triangular tensor. The LU decomposition can be viewed as the tensor form of Gaussian elimination.

Primary invariants in multilinear algebra are coefficients of the characteristic polynomial of a tensor. Invariants do not change with rotation of the coordinate system. In the open literature exists a number of decomposition algorithms, that could efficiently calculate invariants of a tensor, such as LU decomposition and QR factorization [41]. Principal invariants of a tensor is similar to primary invariants. For example, the first principal invariant, known as trace, is always the sum of the diagonal elements. The n-th principal invariant is determinant of a tensor.

Eigenvector of a linear transformation is a non-zero vector that does not change direction when a linear transformation is applied to it. One of the most important problems is designing efficient and stable algorithms for finding the eigenvalues and eigenvectors of a tensor. Well known algorithm for finding eigenvalues and eigenvectors is QR algorithm with complexity of $O(6n^3 + O(n^2))$.

Spectral decomposition, also known as eigendecomposition, is factorization of a tensor into a canonic form, in terms of eigenvalues and eigenvectors. There are a number of algorithms that could be used for computing spectral decomposition, such as singular value decomposition [11].

Divergence [6] is a tensor operator that produces a tensor field, giving the quantity of a tensor field's source at each point. In other words, the divergence represents the volume density of the outward flux of a tensor field from an infinitesimal volume around a given point. From the computational perspective, divergence and curl of a tensor field could be interpreted as tensor multiplication that, with time complexity of $O(n^2)$.

A common approach to finding the rank of a tensor is reducing it to the simpler form, generally row echelon form, by elementary row operations [24]. Algorithms such as Gaussian elimination, singular value decomposition, or QR decomposition could be used for transforming tensor in the echelon form. When applied to floating point computations on computers, basic Gaussian elimination can be unreliable, and a rank-revealing decomposition should be used instead.

3.2   An Overview of Underlying Hardware

Existing multi-core microprocessors, known as CPUs, exploit advantages of the control-flow constructs, like several levels of instruction and data caches, memory and I/O management, and branch and data predictors - all this in order to improve the performance of an algorithm. In essence, for big data problems, the described architecture does not satisfy the performance expectations.

In contrast to the multi-core microprocessors, the alternative approach for fast computing is many-core microprocessing, known as GPU. The GPU approach is better for big data streaming algorithms, such as tensor calculus. Tensor calculus could exploit architecture constructs like fast shared memories, and thus achieves a much better performance. The results presented in paper [8] show that the GPU implementations of sorting algorithms with use of shared memory is two times faster than implementations that use only device's global memory, and up to 7.5 times faster than the CPU implementation. While GPUs operate at lower frequencies, they typically have many times the number of cores, compared with conventional CPU and thus, GPUs can process far more data per second. For many years, the GPU stands for the state-of-the-art high performance computing systems. The main disadvantage of such an approach is large power dissipation. Due to the existance of a large number of transistors, power dissipation could be enormously high, especially for big data algorithms.

In the dataflow approach, compilation reaches a much lower level, in contrast to the control-flow approaches, all the way to the level of wires and gates. In addition to acceleration, the dataflow are powerful because they are adaptable and make it easy to implement changes by reusing an existing chip. Most emerging technologies are increasingly requiring processing power capabilities. In the open literature, there exists a number of the dataflow implementations of machine learning algorithms. Huang et al. [32] shows that FPGA outperforms the GPU when using pruned or compact data types versus full 32 bit floating point data, for deep neural networks. Using the FPGA architecture, neural networks are running faster then on GPUs on small (32x32) inputs, while consuming up to 20x less energy and power [5]. Nils Voss et al. discuss the high performance implementation of convolutional neural networks and compare the obtained performance against other implementations, showing that the proposed design reaches 2,450 GOPS when running VGG16 as a test case [39].

In last decade, the ASIC chips are mostly used for specific applications, such as cryptocurrency mining, where enormous computing power is needed. The ASIC is customized for a particular use, rather than intended for general-purpose use. Using the ASIC that is specially designed for an algorithm, it would definitely outperforms most of above-mentioned paradigms under conditions of interest. Three main advantages of the ASIC chips are: (A) smaller physical size, (AB) better speedup, and (C) less electric power to operate. Despite these advantages, the ASIC chip does not have flexibility to run a number of algorithms. The ASIC is hard to design and also very expensive and time consuming time if it need to be redesigned. The time of a manufacturing process can be up to 18 months [40].

Most of existing solutions of tensor operations in the open literature are based on the control-flow paradigm. This paper introduces ten tensor operations implemented on the dataflow paradigm. Due to the iterative nature of tensor operations, and a great amount of data, the dataflow approach is situable for tensor calculus. Tensor operations are fully tuned to the paradigm's concept, thus achieving better performance for orders of magnitude compared to the cutting edge control-flow implementations.

4   The Dataflow Approach

In the dataflow paradigm, data streams from memory into the engine where data is forwarded from one arithmetic unit to another. Dataflow engine (DFE) contains a number of basic arithmetic units, which are reconfigurable, in appropriate order. Each arithmetic unit can compute only one simple arithmetic operation that enables one to combine lots of cores in one engine, as shown in Fig. 1. The typical execution process is that the dataflow core units are configured before data arrives and then data actually flows through the pipeline of arithmetic units, all along to the output.

The control-flow presents *computing in time* because operations are computed at different moments in time in the same functional units. On the opposite, the dataflow presents *computing in space* because computations are placed dimensionally on a chip.

5   Tensor Operations on the Dataflow Architecture

The bottom-line of this paper is to present which operations are situable for the dataflow architecture under certain conditions, and to compare performance against the control-flow implementations. The dataflow based tensor operations are implemented in a way to exploit advantages of the dataflow paradigm. Optimization constructs that could be applied to the tensor operations include arithmetic changes, modifying input data choreography, utilizing internal pipelines,

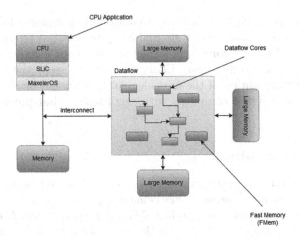

Fig. 1. Architecture of the dataflow engine.

utilizing on-chip memory, and low precision computations. Each tensor operation has several variants that exploit optimization constructs, to analyze how these constructs effect on the performance.

5.1 Tensor Addition

Tensor addition is an operation of adding two tensors, by adding the corresponding elements, as shown in Eq. 1.

$$e_i + e_j = \delta_{ij} \tag{1}$$

As 99% of the execution time is spent in loops, the entire algorithm could be migrated to the accelerator. In the naive implementation, the host program sends tensors in rowwise order to the DFE, and waits for the result. Controlflow loops are unrolled in the execution graph, which means that each element in a tensor has a separated pipeline that consists of only one arithmetic unit. Elements of tensors flow through pipelines and compute entire row of a new tensor simultaneously.

5.2 Tensor Transpose

Tensor transpose is an operator which flips a tensor over its diagonals. Symetric elements over diagonals in a tensor exchange their positions, as shown in Eq. 2.

$$[A^T]_{ij} = [A]_{ji} \tag{2}$$

Similar to the previous operation, transposing of a tensor can be done in the DFE. In the naive implementation, the host sends entire tensor to the DFE and waits for result. Elements in a tensor have its own pipelines placed in the transposed order, without any arithmetic units.

The second approach that utilizes stream offset is situable for DFEs that does not have enough resources for streaming big tensors or keeping them in the on-chip memory. In the second approach, the host sends elements of a tensor, instead of sending an entire tensor. Using the stream offsets, the DFE dynamically calculates the position of the next element that should be streamed to the output. The first result is computed with small latency but pipelines are fully utilized.

5.3   Tensor Composition

Tensor composition is a basic operation in linear algebra, and as such has numerous applications in many areas of mathematics, physics, and engineering. If A and B are tensors, their tensor product AB is a tensor, in which the elements across a row of A are multiplied with the elements down a column of B and summed to produce a new tensor T.

In the naive dataflow implementation, the DFE receives entire tensors and produces a new tensor simultaneously. Elements from the first tensor have separated pipelines, which is later combined with pipelines from the second tensor, as shown in Fig. 2.

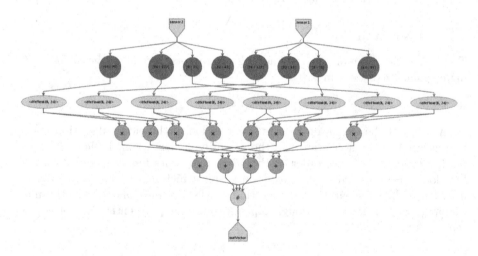

Fig. 2. A part of the execution graph for tensor composition with four pipelines.

5.4   Tensor Inverse

This subsection sheds light on following three factorization algorithms used for calculating inversion of a tensor: (A) Doolittle algorithm, (B) Crout decomposition, and (C) Cholesky decomposition. First two methods are variants of LU decomposition, with small arithmetic changes.

The LU decomposition refers to the factorization of a tensor, with proper row and column permutations, into two factors, a lower triangular tensor L and an upper triangular tensor U.

The Cholesky decomposition transforms tensor into product of a lower triangular tensor and its conjugate transpose. The Cholesky decomposition could be computed only for positive-definite matrix.

The dataflow implementations of above mentioned methods are based on the data streaming. In each iteration, the DFE receives entire tensor. The dataflow implementations could be divided in two phases: (A) LU/Cholesky decomposition and (B) computing the inverse of a tensor using result from the previous phase.

In the first phase, elements in a tensor has separated pipelines. These pipelines are created by unroling the control-flow loops during the compilation time. One pipeline is connected with other pipelines in order to use previously computed elements of a new decomposed tensor. A small latency exists before the first result is computed, due to depth of the execution graph. At the final stage of the execution graph, all elements are collected in new tensors, which present factorized tensor. Once when the first phase is done, a new tensor arrives at the beginning of the first phase, while the factorized tensor arrives at the beginning of the second phase, which includes solving a set of linear equations, which are performed in parallel.

5.5   Primary and Principal Invariants

The best approach for finding determinant of a tensor is an factorization method that can iterates fast. The dataflow implementation computes determinant as a scaling factor of the transformation described by the tensor. Algorithms from the previous section, such as LU decomposition, could be also used for calculating determinant of a tensor.

As indicated in the Cayley-Hamilton theorem, an invertible tensor with non-zero determinant, could thus be written as n-th order polynomial expression. The proposed dataflow implementation computes characteristic polynomial coefficients using factorization method called power iterations. The dataflow implementation exploits advantage of the off-chip memory. The data is streamed to the off-chip memory, which has a higher bandwidth than the link between the host and the DFE. The dataflow manager orchestrates data movements between DFE, off-chip memory, and the host. In each iteration, the algorithm computes a new eigenvalue and eigenvector, which are transferred to the off-chip memory. The algorithm is fully parallelized due to existance of separated pipelines for each element in a tensor.

5.6   Eigenvalues and Eigenvectors

Computing eigenvalues and eigenvectors is not a trivial problem. The power iteration algorithm from the previous subsection could be utilized for calculating eigenvalues and eigenvectors of a tensor. The proposed dataflow solution implements the QR decomposition using two different methods: (A) Gram-Schmidt method and (B) Householder method.

In the dataflow implementations, the DFE receives entire tensor where elements has parallel pipelines. The data dependency is acyclic, which means that internal pipelines are fully utilized without data buffering. In each iteration the new result is computed.

5.7 Spectral Decomposition

This subsection introduces the dataflow implementation of Jacobi eigen algorithm, that is also used for computing eigenvalues and eigenvectors. The Jacobi eigen algorithm is an iterative method that is based on rotations and could be applied only for real symmetric tensors.

Each Jacobi rotation can be done in n steps when the pivot element p is known. However the search for p requires inspection of all off-diagonal elements. The dataflow implementation streams data to the off-chip memory. In each iteration, data are retrieved from the off-chip memory, the rotations are computed, and data are streamed back to the memory. Once when an eigenvector is computed, the result is transferred from the off-chip memory the host.

5.8 Divergence of a Tensor Field

In essence, calculating the divergence could be represented as tensor-vector multiplication. The naive dataflow implementation uses data streaming between the host and the DFE. Such an approach is situable for a set of data that could not be stored in the on-chip memory, due its capacity. However, if a vectors could be stored in the on-chip memory, significant performance could be achieved, because a vector is retreived from the memory with a much higher access bandwidth. In each iteration new tensor is computed, by utilizing parallel internal pipelines.

5.9 Tensor Rank

The rank is equal to non-zero rows in the tensor echelon form. Gaussian elimination is an algorithm for solving systems of linear equations, and could be used for calculating rank of a tensor using echelon form. The process of row reduction makes use of elementary row operations. In the dataflow implementation, in memory row swapping are performed using hardware variables, which flow through pipelines. The implementation is fully parallelized by unrolling the control-flow loops. The performance depends on size of a tensor, where elements are processed in different pipelines.

6 Performance Evaluation

This section discuses performance of ten dataflow based tensor operations and compares them against control-flow implementations trough different aspects such as speed, power dissipation, complexity, and meantime between failure. The set of ten tensor operations analyzed in this paper are chosen in a way to cover all important algorithms used in machine learning, which have big data problems.

Dataflow tensor operations contain several variants, divided in the following groups:

- (N) Naive implementation - A naive implementation includes simple mapping of an algorithm to the accelerator.
- (A) Arithmetic changes - Arithmetic changes include changing basic arithmetic properties, which are association, distribution, and commutative. By changing and swapping these basic operations, performance could be improved significantly, since some operations are more situable for the dataflow accelerators than others.
- (IP) Input data choreography/Utilizing the pipelines - Input data choreography is an important method for performance optimization. Using such an approach, if the host streams data in a specific order, performance improvements may be achieved. Utilization of internal pipelines is often used when execution graph contains cyclic path. By utilizing the internal pipeline, latency is higher, but when first result is computed, every next result should be computed much faster.
- (M) Using on-chip/off-chip memory - On board memories could improve performance due to efficient memory access bandwidth.
- (F) Reducing number precision - By reducing number precision from the floating-point to the fixed-point number representation, performance could be drastically improved. An extreme case in which performance are drastically improved is based on the bit level number representation.

Next subsection discusses performance of dataflow based ten tensor operations, and how above mentioned optimization constructs effect on the performance.

6.1 Speedup

Table 2 shows speedup that is achieved for ten tensor operations using the dataflow paradigm for different data sets. Complex operations, such as tensor decompositions, are situable for big data and achieves significant performance compared against the conventional control-flow implementations. The dataflow tensor operations like addition and transpose, which have a low complexity, does not achieve significant performance.

Performance evaluation is based on the **speedup per watt and transistor count**, which means that the only fair comparison of the control-flow and the dataflow paradigm will be if both chips have the same number of transistors. Data presented in Table 2 are normalized in order to compare two paradigms using the same number of transistors.

Table 2. Execution speed for ten tensor operations per watt and transistor count in milliseconds. Results shown in the table are obtained for different data sets, depending on available resources on the dataflow accelerator. The dataflow accelerator MAX3 24 GB @ 75 MHz is compared with Intel(R) Xeon(R) CPU X5650 @ 2.67 GHz.

Operation	Data size	Control-flow	Dataflow	Speedup	Speedup transistor count
Tensor addition	256M	491 ms	1363 ms	0.36x	~4x
Tensor transpose	160M	203 ms	278 ms	0.73x	~7x
Tensor composition	16M	54 ms	78 ms	0.69x	~7x
Tensor inverse	16M	313 ms	57 ms	5.49x	~55x
Primary invariants	256M	732 ms	222 ms	3.29x	~33x
Principal invariants	2.5M	83261 ms	210 ms	396.38x	~3964x[a]
Eigenvalues and eigenvectors	16M	181 ms	76 ms	2.38x	~24x
Spectral decomposition	16M	173 ms	79 ms	2.19x	~22x
Divergence of a tensor field	16M	54 ms	63 ms	0.85x	~9x
Rank of a tensor	16M	64 ms	56 ms	1.14x	~11x

[a]The reasons for this outlier are currently being investigated.

6.2 Power Dissipation

Power dissipation depends on the clock frequency and number of transistors. The control-flow microprocessors are working on 4 GHz, while the dataflow accelerators are working on 200 MHz. Using the dataflow paradigm, power dissipation is more than 20x lower, compared to the conventional control-flow paradigm. Lower dissipation of the dataflow paradigm also comes from the fact that transistors dissipate during a shorter period of time since the applications get executed in a shorter period of time.

6.3 Complexity

Complexity of two paradigms is measured with number of transistors. For example, the control-flow microprocessor like GT200 Tesla or Intel Xeon has about 2,000,000,000 transistors, while the dataflow accelerators like Xilinx or Altera has roughly about 200,000,000 transistors. In other words, the dataflow paradigm could perform faster computation with 10x small number of transistors and with a smaller clock frequency. Figure 3 shows how transistor count has been changed in past 40 years [33]. Transistor counts still follow the exponential growth line, which goes up to 20 billion transistors. With the upcoming introduction of 10 nm process nodes [3], the exponential growth curve for transistor counts should continue for the next few years, and thus power dissipation should be also increased exponentially.

6.4 Mean Time Between Failures

The MTBF domain depends a lot on the transistor count, the power dissipation, and the presence of components prone to failure. If a microprocessor is working

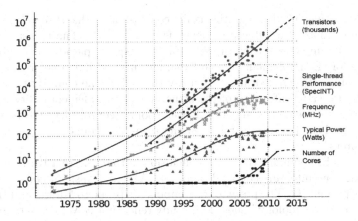

Fig. 3. 40 years of microprocessor trend data based on data by M. Horowitz, F. Labonte, O. Shacham, K. Olukotun, L. Hammond, and C. Batten.

on the higher clock frequency, the probability of fail is also higher. One of the hardest problems in high-performance computing is avoiding and recovering from failures. Clusters of accelerators require the simultaneous use of hundreds of thousands of processing, storage, and networking elements. With a large number of elements involved, element failure will be frequent. The extensive analysis of failures in the petascale computers is presented in paper [34].

7   Conclusion

This work analyses the issues in four different domains, and therefore, four sets of conclusions could be derived: for performance, power, complexity, and MTBF.

In the performance domain, the main conclusion is that the relative ratio of the five compared architectures depends a lot on the structure of the loops and data involved. The loop characteristics that favorize dataflow are: (A) An extremely high contribution of loops to the overall execution time, (B) An extremely high level of data reusability within the loops. The data characteristics that favorize dataflow are: (C) An extremely high data volume and (D) The streaming nature of data input.

In the power domain, the main conclusion is that the relative ratio of the five compared architectures depends a lot on the clock frequency and on the amount of resources that consume power. The dataflow paradigm is characterized with: (A) A slower clock, and (B) No von-Neumann resources known for a relatively high power dissipation due to a relatively high number of transistors needed for implementation, like instruction predictors, data predictors, caches, and memory management. Finally, (C) The lower dissipation of the dataflow paradigm also comes from the fact that transistors dissipate during a shorter period of time since the applications get executed in a shorter period of time. Also, (D) Architectures that are more uniform in their structure may be implementable with a lower voltage, meaning less dissipation.

In the complexity domain, the main conclusion is that the relative ratio of the five compared architectures depends a lot on: (A) The transistor count needed for the implementation of the paradigm. Again, paradigms needing less transistors for the implementation are characterized with a smaller complexity. Other factors, not included into this study that affect the complexity of implementation are: (B) Uniformity of the structure, (C) Implementability with the simple structure elements, and (D) Lower cooling complexity due to a lower power dissipation. This study relies on the transistor count data given by the manufacturers.

In the MTBF domain, the main conclusion is that the relative ratio of the five compared architectures depends a lot on: (A) The transistor count, (B) The power dissipation, (C) The presence of components prone to failure, and (D) The implementation technology issues. This study relies on the MTBF data given by the manufacturers.

Of course, all the above mentioned issues interact synergistically. If an approach is based on two or more paradigms working in symbiosis, the relative contributions coming from each involved paradigm have to be superimposed in a selected manner (differently for different applications, in accordance with how much an application spends time in a each and every paradigm involved). These aspects (synergy, symbiosis, superimposing, and selectivity) are the subjects of a followup research.

References

1. Abadi, M., et al.: TensorFlow: a system for large-scale machine learning. In: OSDI, vol. 16, pp. 265–283 (2016)
2. Anandkumar, A., Ge, R., Hsu, D., Kakade, S.M., Telgarsky, M.: Tensor decompositions for learning latent variable models. J. Mach. Learn. Res. **15**(1), 2773–2832 (2014)
3. Auth, C., et al.: A 10 nm high performance and low-power CMOS technology featuring 3rd generation FinFET transistors, Self-Aligned Quad Patterning, contact over active gate and cobalt local interconnects. In: 2017 IEEE International on Electron Devices Meeting (IEDM), p. 29-1. IEEE (2017)
4. Barndorff-Nielsen, O.E.: Processes of normal inverse Gaussian type. Finan. Stochast. **2**(1), 41–68 (1997)
5. Baskin, C., Liss, N., Mendelson, A., Zheltonozhskii, E.: Streaming architecture for large-scale quantized neural networks on an FPGA-based dataflow platform. arXiv preprint arXiv:1708.00052 (2017)
6. Brillouin, L.: Tensors in mechanics and elasficify (1964)
7. Coppersmith, D., Winograd, S.: Matrix multiplication via arithmetic progressions. In: Proceedings of the Nineteenth Annual ACM Symposium on Theory of Computing, p. 16. ACM (1987)
8. Dobravec, T., Bulic, P.: Comparing CPU and GPU implementations of a simple matrix multiplication algorithm. Int. J. Comput. Electr. Eng. **9**(2), 430–439 (2017)
9. Einstein, A.: Relativity: The Special and The General Theory. Princeton University Press, Princeton (2015)
10. Gilbert, J.R., Moler, C., Schreiber, R.: Sparse matrices in MATLAB: design and implementation. SIAM J. Matrix Anal. Appl. **13**(1), 333–356 (1992)

11. Golub, G.H., Reinsch, C.: Singular value decomposition and least squares solutions. Numerische Mathematik **14**(5), 403–420 (1970)
12. Hillar, C.J., Lim, L.H.: Most tensor problems are NP-hard. J. ACM (JACM) **60**(6), 45 (2013)
13. Hsu, D., Kakade, S.M., Zhang, T.: A spectral algorithm for learning hidden Markov models. J. Comput. Syst. Sci. **78**(5), 1460–1480 (2012)
14. Blagojevic, V., et al.: A systematic approach to generation of new ideas for PhD research in computing. In: Advances in Computers, vol. 104, pp. 1–19. Elsevier (2016)
15. Milutinovic, V., et al.: A new course on R&D project management in computer science and engineering: subjects taught, rationales behind, and lessons learned. In: Advances in Computers, vol. 106, pp. 1–19. Elsevier (2017)
16. Stojanovic, S., Bojic, D., Bojovic, M.: An overview of selected heterogeneous and reconfigurable architectures. In: Advances in Computers, vol. 96, pp. 1–45. Elsevier (2015)
17. Janzamin, M., Sedghi, H., Anandkumar, A.: Beating the perils of non-convexity: guaranteed training of neural networks using tensor methods. arXiv preprint arXiv:1506.08473 (2015)
18. Jennings, A., McKeown, J.J.: Matrix Computation. Wiley, Hoboken (1992)
19. Jovanović, Ž., Milutinović, V.: FPGA accelerator for floating-point matrix multiplication. IET Comput. Digit. Tech. **6**(4), 249–256 (2012)
20. Kaisler, S., Armour, F., Espinosa, J.A., Money, W.: Big data: issues and challenges moving forward. In: 2013 46th Hawaii International Conference on System Sciences (HICSS), pp. 995–1004. IEEE (2013)
21. Kanellos, M.: 152,000 smart devices every minute in 2025: IDC outlines the future of smart things. Forbes.com (2016)
22. Karatzoglou, A., Amatriain, X., Baltrunas, L., Oliver, N.: Multiverse recommendation: n-dimensional tensor factorization for context-aware collaborative filtering. In: Proceedings of the Fourth ACM Conference on Recommender systems, pp. 79–86. ACM (2010)
23. Lawson, C.L., Hanson, R.J., Kincaid, D.R., Krogh, F.T.: Basic linear algebra subprograms for FORTRAN usage. ACM Trans. Math. Softw. (TOMS) **5**(3), 308–323 (1979)
24. Meyer, C.D.: Matrix Analysis and Applied Linear Algebra, vol. 71. SIAM, Philadelphia (2000)
25. Miller, E., Ladenheim, S., Martin, C.: Higher order tensor operations and their applications. TCNJ J. Stud. Sch. **11**, 1–15 (2009)
26. Milutinovic, D., Milutinovic, V., Soucek, B.: The honeycomb architecture (1987)
27. Milutinovic, V., et al.: Splitting spatial and temporal localities for entropy minimiation. Tutorial of the IEEE ISCA (1995)
28. Milutinovic, V.: A comparison of suboptimal detection algorithms applied to the additive mix of orthogonal sinusoidal signals. IEEE Trans. Commun. **36**(5), 538–543 (1988)
29. Milutinovic, V., Kotlar, M., Stojanovic, M., Dundic, I., Trifunovic, N., Babovic, Z.: DataFlow Supercomputing Essentials. Springer, Cham (2017). https://doi.org/10.1007/978-3-319-66125-4
30. Milutinović, V., Salom, J., Trifunović, N., Giorgi, R.: Guide to DataFlow Supercomputing. Springer, Cham (2015). https://doi.org/10.1007/978-3-319-16229-4
31. Milutinovic, V., Salom, J., Veljovic, D., Korolija, N., Markovic, D., Petrovic, L.: DataFlow Supercomputing Essentials. Springer, Cham (2017). https://doi.org/10.1007/978-3-319-66128-5

32. Nurvitadhi, E., et al.: Can FPGAS beat GPUS in accelerating next-generation deep neural networks? In: Proceedings of the 2017 ACM/SIGDA International Symposium on Field-Programmable Gate Arrays, pp. 5–14. ACM (2017)
33. Rupp, K., et al.: Years of microprocessor trend data. http://www.karlrupp.net/wp-content/uploads/2015.06/40-years-processor-trend.png (40)
34. Schroeder, B., Gibson, G.A.: Understanding failures in petascale computers. J. Phys.: Conf. Ser. **78**, 012022 (2007)
35. Trifunovic, N., Milutinovic, V., et al.: The AppGallery.Maxeler.com for bigdata supercomputing. J. Big Data **3**(1), 1–9 (2016)
36. Trifunovic, N., Milutinovic, V., Salom, J., Kos, A.: Paradigm shift in big data SuperComputing: DataFlow vs. ControlFlow. J. Big Data **2**(1), 4 (2015)
37. Trobec, R., Vasiljevic, R., Tomasevic, M., Milutinovic, V., et al.: Interconnection networks for petacomputing. ACM Comput. Surv. **49**(1), 1–24 (2016)
38. Tuffley, D.: Google's release of TensorFlow could be a gamechanger in the future of AI (2015)
39. Voss, N., Bacis, M., Mencer, O., Gaydadjiev, G., Luk, W.: Convolutional neural networks on dataflow engines. In: 2017 IEEE International Conference on Computer Design (ICCD), pp. 435–438. IEEE (2017)
40. Wu, K.C., Tsai, Y.W.: Structured ASIC, evolution or revolution? In: Proceedings of the 2004 International Symposium on Physical Design, pp. 103–106. ACM (2004)
41. Ye, J., Li, Q.: A two-stage linear discriminant analysis via QR-decomposition. IEEE Trans. Pattern Anal. Mach. Intell. **27**(6), 929–941 (2005)

Supercomputer in a Laptop: Distributed Application and Runtime Development via Architecture Simulation

Samuel Knight[✉], Joseph P. Kenny, and Jeremiah J. Wilke

Sandia National Laboratories, 7011 East Ave, Livermore, CA, USA
sknigh@sandia.gov

Abstract. Architecture simulation can aid in predicting and understanding application performance, particularly for proposed hardware or large system designs that do not exist. In network design studies for high-performance computing, most simulators focus on the dominant message passing (MPI) model. Currently, many simulators build and maintain their own simulator-specific implementations of MPI. This approach has several drawbacks. Rather than reusing an existing MPI library, simulator developers must implement all semantics, collectives, and protocols. Additionally, alternative runtimes like GASNet cannot be simulated without again building a simulator-specific version. It would be far more sustainable and flexible to maintain lower-level layers like uGNI or IB-verbs and reuse the production runtime code. Directly building and running production communication runtimes inside a simulator poses technical challenges, however. We discuss these challenges and show how they are overcome via the macroscale components for the Structural Simulation Toolkit (SST), leveraging a basic source-to-source tool to automatically adapt production code for simulation. SST is able to encapsulate and virtualize thousands of MPI ranks in a single simulator process, providing a "supercomputer in a laptop" environment. We demonstrate the approach for the production GASNet runtime over uGNI running inside SST. We then discuss the capabilities enabled, including investigating performance with tunable delays, deterministic debugging of race conditions, and distributed debugging with serial debuggers.

1 Introduction

Architecture simulation can provide a flexible and low-cost tool for evaluating application performance on different platforms. This is especially useful for specialized or proposed hardware configurations that do not exist. In high-performance computing (HPC), simulation can also be critical for system-level design, exploring scales far exceeding those practical for test beds. In particular, discrete event simulators like the Structural Simulation Toolkit (SST) have been critical in evaluating future system designs [1].

The U.S. government retains certain licensing rights. This is a U.S. government work and certain licensing rights apply.

© Springer Nature Switzerland AG 2018
R. Yokota et al. (Eds.): ISC 2018 Workshops, LNCS 11203, pp. 347–359, 2018.
https://doi.org/10.1007/978-3-030-02465-9_23

In many cases, the main simulation focus is the design of interconnect hardware and management software: routing, flow control, or topology of the network switches or details of the network interface controller (NIC) [2]. An ideal goal for simulation is providing a "supercomputer in a laptop," simulating the traffic of thousands or millions of network endpoints on a single machine. Beyond hardware, communication runtimes managing network traffic are also critical to achieving high performance. The message-passing interface (MPI) is the dominant communication runtime in HPC applications, but other runtimes such as GASNet [3] and Portals [4] are also used to support applications (albeit indirectly through UPC++ with GASNet and as an MPI conduit with Portals). These communication runtimes abstract away the complexities of different hardware platforms and their respective low-level communication libraries, such as uGNI or IB-verbs, to provide portable APIs with well defined semantics. For large or proposed systems, simulation could then also be useful for *software design* of the communication runtime and other system libraries. Beyond hardware or software individually, simulation can also show tradeoffs of software implementation versus hardware support by providing tunable delays for different operations.

Simulation often requires the creation of simulator-implemented models, particularly for applications. In order to recreate application behavior within memory and time constraints on the node running the simulator, thousands of MPI processes cannot execute natively. Usually, traffic traces are extracted from MPI applications or applications are rewritten as lightweight motifs. These approaches hinder co-design as tuning of the parent application requires the trace or motif to be manually updated (or vice versa).

Communication runtimes involve thousands or even millions of lines of code. Maintaining a simulator-specific version of these libraries is extremely challenging. In MPI's case, however, this is the state-of-practice, with simulators providing their own MPI implementations. A far more sustainable and useful strategy would be simulating MPI applications by directly using, e.g., OpenMPI [5] or MPICH [6] as the MPI implementation. Consider the software stacks in Figs. 1 and 2. In Fig. 1, the simulator provides MPI bindings and captures MPI calls. The simulator must provide all MPI collectives, protocols, matching, types, and ordering semantics - replicating hundreds of thousands of lines of code found in other MPI implementations. In Fig. 2, the simulator instead provides low-level bindings of a layer such as IB-verbs, uGNI, or libfabrics. These layers, while still complex, are much simpler than higher-level communication runtimes since they only provide a message transfer layer with basic completion notifications. Under the design in Fig. 2, runtime code developed within the simulator can be moved directly to a real system.

While such an approach can be useful for MPI, it can also be applied to libraries like GASNet (Fig. 3). Given traces or models of Legion [7] or UPC++ [8] generating GASNet calls, a simulator could generate network traffic directly from the production GASNet runtime rather than needing to completely reimplement a simulator-specific library.

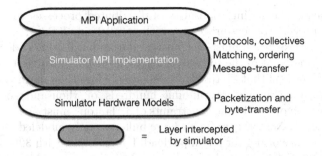

Fig. 1. Illustration of a possible software stack within the simulator for an MPI application. The simulator provides the entire MPI implementation.

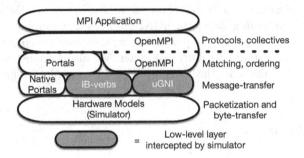

Fig. 2. Illustration of a possible software stack within the simulator for an MPI application. The sections highlighted in green are possible interception points within SST/-macro.

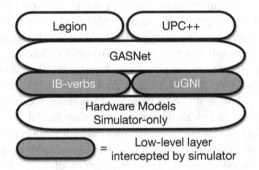

Fig. 3. Software stack for running GASNet applications within a simulator. The sections highlighted in green are possible interception points in SST/macro 8.0.

In this work, we discuss the significant technical challenges involved in adapting the "supercomputer in a laptop" approach to development of production communication runtimes. These challenges can be generally divided into:

- Encapsulation: Managing thousands of distributed processes within a single simulator process (or few processes, with parallel simulation).
- Interception: Execution must be transferred from production code to the simulator at some point in the software stack. This usually involves the simulator providing bindings that "intercept" messages before they reach the network.
- Skeletonization: Simulators running hundreds or thousands of processes within the memory and time constraints of a "laptop" must avoid large memory allocations. Network traffic for large buffers is only modeled and does not actually allocate or deliver a real payload. For example, with 32GB of system memory and 1000 simulated processes, each process must be "skeletonizable" to less than 30MB.

We show how these challenges are solved within the Structural Simulation Toolkit (SST) using the macroscale components (SST/macro). We demonstrate the approach by providing simulator uGNI bindings and running the full GASNet stack within the simulator. In particular, we show how this process is greatly simplified by a basic source-to-source compiler. We also demonstrate the use of arbitrary, tunable delays in the simulator for an example design study with GASNet.

2   Prior Work

Simulator endpoint models can be divided into offline (post-mortem) trace replay or online models that run either state machines or modified application code. Two of the most common trace formats in HPC are DUMPI and OTF2 (via Score-P [9]), which are variously supported in SST/macro [10], Tracer [11], and LogGOPSim [12]. The Ember module of SST supports "motifs" [1], lightweight state machine models for generating traffic. SMPI [13] and SST/macro support skeleton apps, which are regular MPI codes that link to the simulator and might be modified either through macros or source-to-source translation.

Hardware models vary in fidelity from highly-detailed flit-level models in BookSim [14], packet-level models in SST and CODES [15], message-level flow models in SMPI [13], and more basic message-level delay models in LogGOPSim. In this work, the focus is primarily on the endpoint model and communication runtime. In this regard, all components only interact with a message transfer layer (MTL) and are agnostic to the actual hardware models underneath.

Although we discuss simulation in the context of a single (serial) process on one node, architecture simulation can be parallelized. Parallel discrete event simulation (PDES) [16] can be a challenging problem. In many cases, PDES for architecture simulation is limited to tens, possibly hundreds, of nodes. Many scalability challenges for a single simulator node are therefore generally true even for simulators supporting PDES, such as SST and CODES. PDES can be either optimistic or conservative, with SST being conservative and CODES supporting an optimistic algorithm. Optimistic algorithms can create event ordering violations in virtual simulation time, which then require rollback to fix. Efficient rollback requires so-called "reverse handlers" to undo events rather than check-pointing and restoring from memory. Reverse handlers are generally feasible with traces or state machines. The online simulation approach that we describe, running real software stacks, is not compatible with reverse handlers and is unlikely to be useful with optimistic PDES.

3   Simulator Implementation

3.1   Encapsulation

The Structural Simulation Toolkit (SST) is a discrete event architecture simulator. In such simulations, "virtual" time advances by scheduling events at specific times and advancing the simulator clock as events are dequeued. Distributed processes in an MPI or GASNet job must become "virtual processes" that are managed by a single simulator process that maintains a consistent clock for events in each concurrent virtual process. One possibility is to spawn virtual processes as full kernel-level processes and send events via pipes or sockets. When thousands of virtual processes execute on a small number of physical cores, simulating concurrent execution requires context switching between processes. Rather than requiring the operating system to manage context switching for thousands of kernel processes, encapsulating each virtual process as a user-space thread within a unified simulator process is far more efficient.

While encapsulation greatly improves simulator performance, it introduces new challenges. Each virtualized process is required to have private:

- Heap memory
- Stack memory
- Global variables

Virtual processes can share the same heap without breaking the "illusion" of private heaps because they have no knowledge of memory that they do not privately allocate. Each virtual process still gets its own thread stack (as a user-space thread). Global variables, however, are much more challenging. Automatic refactoring of global variables is achieved via source-to-source transformation of the code using Clang [17]. Clang is only used as a preprocessing step and the generated code can be used with any compiler. Accesses to global variables are intercepted and redirected to thread-local storage (local to a user-space thread).

3.2   Interception and uGNI Bindings

Interception involves two steps. First, symbols such as `MPI_Send` are renamed to, e.g., `SSTMAC_MPI_Send` either through included macros or the source-to-source tool. Second, the simulator provides an `SSTMAC_MPI_Send` function implementing the correct functionality. This interception could occur at any layer, e.g. `GNI_PostRdma` or `ibv_post_send`. SST/macro provides basic versions of most MPI functions. Encapsulation and interception together allow for MPI *emulation*, running full MPI applications as if the simulator were a real MPI implementation. The application will run and produce equivalent results, albeit with all MPI ranks executed within a single simulator process.

The simulator stack underneath uGNI or IB-verbs is shown in Fig. 4. A "universal" message transfer layer (MTL) called SUMI (Simulator Unified Message Interface) provides the simulator implementation of completion queues and message delivery. SUMI is intended to support the functionality of all message layers including libfabrics, IB-verbs, and uGNI. For each library, SUMI therefore provides a superset of all needed features. All uGNI calls are easily mapped into SUMI calls. In total, the simulator uGNI implementation is 1000 lines. This is compared to the over 20,000 lines in the bare-bones SST/macro MPI implementation and hundreds of thousands of lines in, for example, OpenMPI. Implementation of an IB-verbs layer is in progress.

SUMI can pass messages to a packetizer, which then pushes traffic into a packet-based network simulator. The main SST network model is called Merlin. SST/macro provides a packet model called PISCES by default. Alternatively, SUMI can pass messages to a basic delay model (similar to LogGOPSim) without packetizing. A detailed discussion of these models is out of scope here.

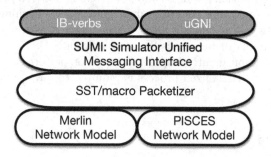

Fig. 4. Illustration SST/macro's simulated network and hardware topology stack. The IB-verbs and uGNI layers colored in green are new interception points. (Color figure online)

3.3   Skeletonization

Skeletonization is the most challenging step in implementing the "supercomputer in a laptop" approach. Here we discuss skeletonization of the communication runtime in the context of MPI traces, but the discussion also applies to motifs and other online models. Suppose we wish to replay a DUMPI or OTF2 trace directly through the real OpenMPI implementation. In the MPI trace, no memory is allocated and no buffers are available for the MPI calls. At best, the trace replay can pass a sentinel "null" value to, e.g., `MPI_Send`.

Null buffers are completely compatible with SUMI and the simulator implementations of uGNI and IB-verbs. These implementations check for null buffers, skipping certain operations for null payloads. Wherever OpenMPI touches or dereferences send buffers, special code refactoring is required to skip the operation and not segfault. Using the source-to-source tool, SST can automatically refactor calls to memcpy and memset. These calls instead are directed to sstmac_memcpy that checks for null buffers and simulates the compute delay.

The source-to-source tool provides numerous pragmas for indicating how code should be refactored for more complicated skeletonization. A common set of pragmas are delete_if, replace_if, and init_if that modify the code based on a given runtime condition.

```
#pragma sst init_if(sendBuffer == NULL, NULL)
void* tmpBuffer = malloc(...)
memcpy(tmpBuffer, sendBuffer, size);
```

The refactored code would be

```
void* tmpBuffer = sendBuffer == NULL ? NULL : malloc(...);
sstmac_memcpy(tmpBuffer, sendBuffer, size);
```

which removes the memory allocation when the buffer is null and calls sstmac_memcpy.

Another approach is a "data-centric" pragma that marks a variable as null and automatically removes all code touching the underlying memory.

```
#pragma sst null_variable
void* tmpBuffer = malloc(...);
...
```

"Nullness" of a variable propagates through assignments such as

```
void* x = tmpBuffer;
```

Data-centric pragmas can be useful for large code blocks that would otherwise require several pragmas. Inter-procedural analysis (IPA) of null variables creates complications, but other pragma hints are available to assist the compiler. Full discussion of the SST pragma language is beyond the scope of this work.

3.4 Overhead Pragma

Beyond skeletonization, the source-to-source tool can insert arbitrary delays for certain functions or operations. Time advances in the simulator *between* events as dequeued events advance the clock. Time spent during an event is not counted in the simulation time by default, including the code executed within MPI or GASNet (discussed more in Sect. 5.3). Pragmas can indicate to the source-to-source tool where and how to advance time. For example, given a software implementation, the performance benefits of hardware support could be tested:

```
#pragma sst overhead work_cost
DoSomeWork();
```

In the SST/macro parameter file, one can then specify, e.g.

```
work_cost = 3us
```

to simulate the application with a 3 microsecond delay. We consider an example use of this with GASNet in Sect. 4.2.

4   Example Results

4.1   Methodology

Simulations were performed with a development version of SST/macro 8.0 [18]. The source-to-source tool was built using the Clang libtooling interface in LLVM 5.0 [17]. GASNet simulations were based on v1.30, the master branch in the repository [19]. All simulations were performed on a MacBook Pro with 16GB of memory and a consumer Intel Core i7 processor.

4.2   GASNet Benchmark

As a basic illustration of the approach, we study the performance of a GAS-Net benchmark by varying overheads in an underlying uGNI layer. GASNet provides different message transfer mechanisms for short, medium, long, and asynchronous long messages. Medium messages send "eagerly" by first copying into a pre-allocated and pre-registered buffer. Long messages, however, must register (pin) memory first, but can be transferred in a zero-copy fashion. The benchmark is derived from `testcore2` in the GASNet test suite. In this case, we run a skeletonized version of GASNet that is compatible with null buffers. In total, five pragmas were added to the GASNet library to support skeletonization. In the pingpong benchmark, buffers are decorated with data-centric pragmas:

```
#pragma sst null_variable
uint32_t *localseg;
```

All dereferences are then elided. When passed as an argument to functions, a sentinel null value is passed instead. For example, the GASNet code

```
gasnet_AMRequestMedium0(peerproc, handler, localseg);
```

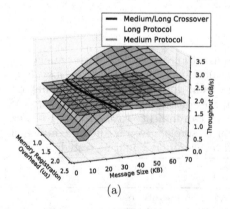
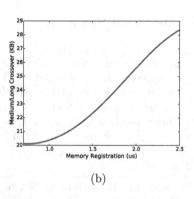

(a)   (b)

Fig. 5. Ping-pong benchmark for medium and long message protocols in GASNet for varying memory registration overheads. (a) 2D scan of throughput for different message sizes/registration overheads for medium and long protocols. (b) Crossover point for long message protocol achieving higher throughput as a function of memory registration overhead.

becomes

```
gasnet_AMRequestMedium0(peerproc, handler, nullptr);
```

For the study, an extra pragma creates a tunable delay within the simulator:

```
#pragma sst overhead gni_mem_register
       GNI_MemRegister(...);
```

To illustrate, we measure the effective throughput (GB/s) achieved for different message sizes and different memory registration overheads (Fig. 5). As memory registration overhead increases, it becomes more favorable to use the medium pathway despite the extra memory copies. Although this example is simple and highly synthetic, it illustrates the approach that could be applied for more complicated workloads.

4.3 Scaling of Skeletonized Runtime

Without skeletonization, at best only a few tens or possibly hundreds of virtual processes could be simulated on a single node. With skeletonization, ideally several thousand processes should be feasible. We examine the scaling of both wall clock time and memory usage of the skeletonized GASNet runtime running the `testcore2` benchmark. In Fig. 6, we run up to 4 K processes on a single laptop (see Methodology). The benchmark scatters active messages of increasing size up to 10KB to a fixed number of partners. When the active message is invoked on the receiving partner, an active message reply is returned. The total memory footprint remains under 10GB even up to 4 K processes. Much of this memory footprint is due to the all-to-all data structures maintained by GASNet in the default build, which could be significantly reduced by a dynamic connection setup. Charm++ [20], for example, supports a dynamic bootstrapping of uGNI endpoint connections only between endpoints that actually communicate. The

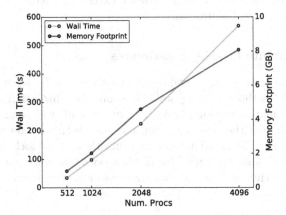

Fig. 6. Wall time and memory usage of the GASNet testcore2 benchmark up to 4 K skeletonized GASNet processes.

execution time of nearly 10 min for the largest benchmark is reasonable, but ideally should be reduced. SST/macro supports multi-threaded execution, but this has not been explored here.

5 Additional Features and Future Work

5.1 Deterministic Debugging of Distributed Race Conditions

The simulator executes dynamically, allowing runtimes to make adaptive decisions based on their simulated environment and runtime parameters. However, the simulator is still *deterministic*, executing exactly the same events in the same order if repeated (unless the application generates random numbers). Once a race-dependent bug is detected, SST/macro can repeat the event by retracing the same code with the same parameters. To generate different event orders on the same benchmark, various hardware parameters, such as the network bandwidth, can be parametrically "randomized" using seeds. Thousands of different event orderings can be generated by changing seeds. The race condition can be replayed on demand, provided the seed is known. While this overlaps somewhat with the ReMPI project [21], this approach allows for easy creation of thousands of different message order scenarios and debugging on a single node.

5.2 Deterministic, Controlled Environment for Performance Comparisons

Comparing software implementations, particularly MPI, is a notoriously challenging problem [22]. Numerous variables can impact performance, notably system noise. Beyond debugging or development, simulation can help analyze performance differences across platforms or between implementations. Simulation can isolate certain effects, revealing to what extent they contribute to performance differences on real platforms.

5.3 Host Compute Overhead Estimates

As discussed above, time only advances in the simulator between events. Thus runtime software, although using wall time on the physical node, does not advance virtual time in the simulator. The amount of wall time spent on the physical node running the simulator can, however, estimate the software overhead of the runtime. The simulator can measure these wall clock delays and use it to advance the simulation time. This method does introduce non-determinism since the compute time will not be exactly the same on each execution.

5.4 Valgrind and GDB

Valgrind and GDB can be used without the need for distributed debugging tools because SST/macro encapsulates thousands of processes as user-space threads within a single simulator process. Moreover, SST/macro provides callable functions that GDB and LLDB can use for jumping between user-space threads. At a given breakpoint, a debugger can inspect the states of any individual simulated process (such as an MPI rank). Work is currently underway to support conditional breakpoints for specific ranks.

5.5   Extending to OpenMPI and Infiniband

Efforts are underway to run the full OpenMPI software stack within the simulator. The OpenMPI + uGNI stack has been successfully built, but is missing certain wrapper libraries. OpenMPI expects a local daemon to spawn and manage the MPI process. While SST/macro already provides wrapper libraries for pthreads, std::threads, sockets, uGNI, and MPI, wrappers have not been implemented for intercepting fork and IPC calls. System calls, such as `fork()`, pass through to the physical operating system rather than creating another virtual process in the simulator. Efforts are underway to produce these wrappers. Additional work is underway on an IB-verbs (Infiniband) implementation and, eventually, libfabrics, which will function similarly to the existing uGNI layer.

6   Conclusion

Developing and testing communication libraries faces significant challenges, such as non-deterministic bugs. Tuning and developing libraries for future systems poses even more significant challenges. Architecture simulation has long used simulator-specific models to design hardware or understand application performance. Simulation, however, has not typically been used to evaluate and develop production system software like communication runtime libraries. In this work, we have presented an approach to support simulation of distributed runtime software within a single simulator process. We outlined the technical challenges overcome in extending the macroscale components of the Structural Simulation Toolkit (SST). This involved providing both a combination of libraries to intercept low-level communication calls (e.g. uGNI) and a source-to-source tool to automatically refactor code for the simulator.

Encapsulating thousands of distributed processes in a simulator creates numerous opportunities for debugging and performance evaluation. This includes deterministic debugging of race conditions, using serial debugging tools with distributed applications, and performing detailed design studies by easily tuning delay parameters for important operations. We have demonstrated initial success with GASNet, tuning overheads in an example design study. The approach is also shown to be scalable when using skeletonization, a process made semiautomatic through the source-to-source compiler. These initial results show the promise of our approach and will hopefully encourage wider adoption. Work is underway to extend the approach to support more production communication runtimes and more low-level communication layers.

Acknowledgment. This work was funded by Sandia National Laboratories, which is a multimission laboratory managed and operated by National Technology and Engineering Solutions of Sandia, LLC, a wholly owned subsidiary of Honeywell International, Inc., for the U.S. Department of Energy's (DOE) National Nuclear Security Administration (NNSA) under contract DE-NA-0003525. The views expressed in the article do not necessarily represent the views of the U.S. Department of Energy or the United States Government.

References

1. Groves, T., et al.: (SAI) Stalled, Active and Idle: characterizing power and performance of large-scale dragonfly networks. In: IEEE International Conference on Cluster Computing (CLUSTER) 2016, pp. 50–59 (2016)
2. Hoefler, T., et al.: sPIN: high-performance streaming processing in the network. In: SC 2017: International Conference for High Performance Computing, Networking, Storage and Analysis (2017)
3. Bonachea, D.: Gasnet specification, v1.1, Berkeley, CA, USA, Technical report (2002)
4. Barrett, B., et al.: The Portals 4.0.2 Network Programming Interface. Technical report SAND2014-19568
5. Graham, R., et al.: Open MPI: a high performance, flexible implementation of MPI point-to-point communications. Parallel Process. Lett. **17**(01), 79–88 (2007)
6. Gropp, W.: MPICH2: a new start for MPI implementations. In: Kranzlmüller, D., Volkert, J., Kacsuk, P., Dongarra, J. (eds.) EuroPVM/MPI 2002. LNCS, vol. 2474, pp. 7–7. Springer, Heidelberg (2002). https://doi.org/10.1007/3-540-45825-5_5
7. Bauer, M., Treichler, S., Slaughter, E., Aiken, A.: Legion: expressing locality and independence with logical regions. In: SC 2012: International Conference for High Performance Computing, Networking, Storage and Analysis, pp. 1–11 (2012)
8. Zheng, Y., et al.: UPC++: A PGAS extension for C++. In: International Parallel and Distributed Processing Symposium (2014)
9. Knüpfer, A., et al.: Score-P: A Joint Performance Measurement Run-Time Infrastructure for Periscope, Scalasca, TAU, and Vampir, pp. 79–91, January 2012
10. Wilke, J., Kenny, J.: SST/macro GitHub. https://github.com/sstsimulator/sst-macro (2016)
11. Jain, N., et al.: Evaluating HPC networks via simulation of parallel workloads. In: SC 2016: International Conference for High Performance Computing, Networking, Storage and Analysis, pp. 154–165 (2016)
12. Hoefler, T., Schneider, T., Lumsdaine, A.: LogGOPSim: simulating large-scale applications in the LogGOPS model. In: HPDC, pp. 597–604 (2010)
13. Degomme, A., Legrand, A., Markomanolis, G.S., Quinson, M., Stillwell, M., Suter, F.: Simulating MPI applications: the SMPI approach. IEEE Trans. Parallel Distrib. Syst. **28**, 2387–2400 (2017)
14. Jiang, N., et al.: A detailed and flexible cycle-accurate network-on-chip simulator. In: ISPASS, pp. 86–96 (2013)
15. Mubarak, M., Carothers, C.D., Ross, R.B., Carns, P.: A case study in using massively parallel simulation for extreme-scale torus network codesign. In: SIGSIM PADS (2014)
16. Fujimoto, R.M.: Parallel discrete event simulation. Commun. ACM **33**, 30–53 (1990)

17. Clang 5.0 Download (2018). http://releases.llvm.org/download.html
18. SST/macro GitHub Repository. https://github.com/sstsimulator/sst-macro
19. GASNet 1.30 website (2018). https://bitbucket.org/berkeleylab/gasnet
20. Kumar, S., Sun, S., Kale, L.V.: Acceleration of an asynchronous message driven programming paradigm on IBM blue Gene/Q. In: IPDPS (2013)
21. Sato, K., et al.: Clock delta compression for scalable order-replay of non-deterministic parallel applications. In: SC 2015: International Conference for High Performance Computing, Networking, Storage and Analysis, pp. 62:1–62:12 (2015)
22. Hunold, S., Carpen-Amarie, S., Träff, J.L.: Reproducible MPI micro-benchmarking isn't as easy as you think. In: EuroMPI/ASIA (2014)

International Workshop on OpenPOWER for HPC 2018 (IWOPH 2018)

International Workshop on OpenPOWER for HPC 2018 (IWOPH 2018)

Oscar Hernandez[1], M. Graham Lopez[1], Dirk Pleiter[2], and Jack Wells[1]

[1] Oak Ridge National Laboratory, TN 37831 Oak Ridge, Tennessee, USA
{oscar,lopezmg,wellsjc}@ornl.gov
[2] Forschungszentrum Jülich, JSC, 52425 Jülich, Germany
d.pleiter@fz-juelich.de

Abstract. The third edition of the International Workshop on OpenPOWER for HPC (IWOPH18) continued to establish itself as a forum for exchanging experience using technologies and architectures, which emerged from this new ecosystem. The goal was to bring together experts for applications and the different technologies as well as data centre professionals.

Keywords: OpenPOWER · High-performance computing · Big data · GPU acceleration · Programming models · Energy efficiency

Just about five years after being established, a very visible landmark in the field of HPC emerged from the OpenPOWER ecosystem with two supercomputers based on OpenPOWER technologies making it to position #1 and #3 of the Top500 list published during ISC 2018. These systems will not only be used for scientific computing applications, but also data analytics and AI workloads are expected to play an increasingly important role. The goal of this workshop was to provide a venue for a broader community for sharing experience, to further understand OpenPOWER technologies, and to discuss how they can be harnessed to address science and engineering challenges.

After a call for papers was published in January 2018, a total of 20 paper submissions had been received. The 23 members of the program committee, who came from academia, industry, and research laboratories, provided at least 3 reviews per paper. On the basis of their assessment and recommendations 9 papers have been accepted for this workshop.

The workshop took place on 28 June, 2018 co-located with the ISC conference in Frankfurt, Germany. The workshop was started with a welcome from the workshop organizers and a round of introduction involving all participants. Paper presentations were scheduled such that sufficient time for discussions was available, which participants indeed used for lively discussions. The workshop ended with a panel discussion focussing on future efforts for supporting developers in the context of OpenPOWER.

Several contributions focussed on scientific computing applications. E. Calore reported on the results of a project of Italian physicists and HPC experts who developed a new application for simulating strong interactions using the Lattice Quantum Chromodynamics (LQCD) approach [2]. The team used a recently deployed

OpenPOWER system installed by E4 at the Italian supercomputing centre CINECA. Also E. Berkowitz presented work done in the context of LQCD. He and his collaborators developed a tool called mpi_jm that allows execution of different parallel workloads within a larger allocation [1]. The tool aims on facilitating high-throughput computations of physical observables in LQCD. I. Sfiligoi, one of the authors of a different kind of simulation application, namely CGYRO, presented performance results for a variety of platforms [8]. CGYRO is an Eulerian gyrokinetic solver, which was designed and optimized for certain plasma simulations. The authors have ported the application to servers similar to those used for Summit. The focus of a contribution presented by O. Hernandez was on using different features of OpenMP 4.5 for application parallelisation on POWER CPUs [3]. The team worked on an efficient implementation of a mini-application version of DMRG++, an application used for investigating strongly correlated electron systems.

This year again several contributions had been submitted related to data intensive problems. Ting Wang analysed the network requirements to facilitate scaling of applications for sorting large datasets on several GPU-accelerated nodes [4]. On a single dual-socket POWER9 system with 4 V100 GPUs he and his collaborators could achieve a throughput of 28 GByte/s. Based on these performance results, network bandwidth requirements for a multi-node implementation were provided. G. Narayanasamy presented a scaling analysis for the widely used bio-informatics tool BWAKIT on two POWER8 sockets [5].

A final set of contributions addressed hardware architecture and system software topics. C. Pearson presented a systematic study of the data transport capabilities within a POWER8 server with GPUs attached through NVLink [6]. He an his collaborators did not only consider various data paths but also analysed how efficient different programming environments allow to exploit the hardware capabilities. V. Elisseev reported on porting the Global Extensible Open Power Manager (GEOPM) [7] to POWER. This software framework is now available for power profiling on scientific applications and is in the future planned to be used for power consumption optimisations. Finally, O. Hernandez presented results on his and his collaborators work on CAASCADE [9]. This tool allows to analyse application source code and extract calls to third-party libraries. This allows to automatise detection of important libraries and their use.

References

1. Berkowitz, E., Jansen, G., McElvain, K., Walker-Loud, A.: Job management with mpi_jm. In: Yokota, R., Weiland, M., Shalf, J., Alam, S. (eds.) ISC 2018 Workshops, LNCS, vol. 11203, pp. 432–439. Springer, Cham (2018)
2. Bonati, C., Calore, E., DElia, M., Mesiti, M., Negro, F., Schifano, S.F., Silvi, G., Raffaele, T.: Early experience on running OpenStaPLE on DAVIDE. In: Yokota, R., Weiland, M., Shalf, J., Alam, S. (eds.) ISC 2018 Workshops, LNCS, vol. 11203, pp. 387–401. Springer, Cham (2018)

3. Chatterjee, A., Alvarez, G., D'Azevedo, E., Elwasif, E.W., Oscar, H., Vivek, S.: Porting DMRG++ scientific application to OpenPOWER. In: Yokota, R., Weiland, M., Shalf, J., Alam, S. (eds.) ISC 2018 Workshops, LNCS, vol. 11203, pp. 418–431. Springer, Cham (2018)

4. Fossum, G.C., Wang, T., Hofstee, H.P.: A 64-GB sort at 28 GB/s on a 4-GPU POWER9 node for uniformly-distributed 16-Byte records with 8-Byte keys. In: Yokota, R., Weiland, M., Shalf, J., Alam, S. (eds.) ISC 2018 Workshops, LNCS, vol. 11203, pp. 373–386. Springer, Cham (2018)

5. Kathiresan, N., Al-Ali, R., Jithesh, P., Narayanasamy, G., Al-Ars, Z.: Porting and benchmarking of BWAKIT pipeline on OpenPOWER architecture. In: Yokota, R., Weiland, M., Shalf, J., Alam, S. (eds.) ISC 2018 Workshops, LNCS, vol. 11203, pp. 402–410. Springer, Cham (2018)

6. Pearson, C., Chung, I.H., Sura, Z., Hwu, W.M., Xiong, J.: NUMA-aware data-transfer measurements for Power/NVLink multi-GPU systems. In: Yokota, R., Weiland, M., Shalf, J., Alam, S. (eds.) ISC 2018 Workshops, LNCS, vol. 11203, pp. 448–454. Springer, Cham (2018)

7. Puzovic, M., Elisseev, V., Jordan, K.: Improving performance and energy efficiency on OpenPower systems using scalable hardware-software co-design. In: Yokota, R., Weiland, M., Shalf, J., Alam, S. (eds.) ISC 2018 Workshops, LNCS, vol. 11203, pp. 411–417. Springer, Cham (2018)

8. Sfiligoi, I., Candy, J., Kostuk, M.: CGYRO performance on Power9 CPUs and Volta GPUs. In: Yokota, R., Weiland, M., Shalf, J., Alam, S. (eds.) ISC 2018 Workshops, LNCS, vol. 11203, pp. 365–372. Springer, Cham (2018)

9. Zhao, J., Hernandez, O.R., Budiardja, R.D., Lopez, M.G., Sarkar, V., Wells, J.C.: Compile-time library call detection using CAASCADE and XALT. In: Yokota, R., Weiland, M., Shalf, J., Alam, S. (eds.) ISC 2018 Workshops, LNCS, vol. 11203, pp. 440–447. Springer, Cham (2018)

CGYRO Performance on Power9 CPUs and Volta GPUs

I. Sfiligoi[(⊠)], J. Candy, and M. Kostuk

General Atomics, San Diego, CA 92121, USA
{sfiligoii,candy,kostukm}@fusion.gat.com

Abstract. CGYRO, an Eulerian gyrokinetic solver designed and optimized for collisional, electromagnetic, multiscale fusion plasma simulation, has been ported and benchmarked on a Summit-like Power9-based system equipped with Volta GPUs. We present our experience porting the application and provide benchmark numbers obtained on the Power-based node and compare them with equivalent tests from several leadership class systems. The tested node provided the fastest single-node CGYRO runtimes we've measured to date.

Keywords: Power9 · Volta · CGYRO

1 Introduction

The Magnetic Fusion Energy Division of General Atomics (GA) purchased a set of Power9-equipped nodes in early 2018, configured to be as close as possible to the nodes that will be available at the upcoming OLCF Summit system [1]. We have been eagerly porting and benchmarking various software packages on the new hardware, the most prominent being CGYRO [2–5]. In this document we present our experience and compare the results with benchmarks obtained on other leadership class systems.

1.1 CGYRO: A Multiscale-Optimized Fusion Plasma Solver

CGYRO is an Eulerian gyrokinetic solver designed and optimized for collisional, electromagnetic, multiscale fusion plasma simulation. It is written in Fortran 2008 and was designed to be suitable for next-generation computational systems that require high levels of parallel concurrency. The implementation combines 15 years of algorithmic lessons learned from GYRO [6–9], together with an array distribution scheme and loop structure that targets modern multicore and accelerated (GPU) architectures. CGYRO was designed for operation on Petascale systems, and employs MPI to split the problem over a potentially very large number of compute processes. Moreover, the in-process parallelization scheme

Supported by General Atomics internal research and development funds.

R. Yokota et al. (Eds.): ISC 2018 Workshops, LNCS 11203, pp. 365–372, 2018.
https://doi.org/10.1007/978-3-030-02465-9_24

for most kernels employs cache-aligned data arrays, OpenMP parallelized loops and vectorization-friendly operations.

The CGYRO code can be logically split into three different kernels. The *streaming kernel*, hereafter referred to as str, the *nonlinear kernel*, hereafter referred to as nl, and the combination of *field* and *collisional* kernels, hereafter referred to as coll. It is worth noting that the nl kernel is implemented as a series of 2D Fast-Fourier (FFT) transforms. A large fraction of the computation is thus offloaded to external libraries. Moreover, two versions of the collisional kernel are provided. The high fidelity version of coll requires a large amount of memory, and is typically memory-throughput bound. The alternative is a simplified version which still provides reasonable simulation fidelity, is much cheaper, uses a fraction of the memory, and is typically FLOPS bound.

1.2 Porting CGYRO to GPUs

CGYRO was ported to the OLCF Titan [10] system several years ago. The approach taken was to port the most compute intense kernels to GPU, and leave the rest on the CPU. No attempt has been made to make MPI communication GPU-aware, so all relevant memory must be present on the CPU for all inter-process communication, even on the same node. The nl kernel is normally the dominant one. Due to the heavy reliance on FFT, it was relatively easy to port to GPU through the use of the cuFFT libraries, with the rest of the logic implemented using OpenACC. The second most time-consuming kernel is normally str. Since all of its logic is natively implemented, the most time consuming part was also ported to the GPU using OpenACC. A significant part of str was however left on the CPU due to several MPI communications needed inside the kernel which would have made CPU to GPU memory movements prohibitively expensive. No attempt was made to port coll to the GPU. The most accurate variant requires a large amount of memory (exceeding the amount provided by most GPUs). The simplified, fast version was instead considered cheap enough to not warrant the effort at that time.

1.3 Simulations Suitable for Benchmarking

CGYRO can be used for small-scale simulations of the plasma core, or for large-scale simulations required for accurately describing the pedestal region in a tokamak fusion reactor. For the purpose of this document, we restricted ourselves to simulations that would fit on the available hardware. This limited the tests to small-scale simulations only. We chose two configurations that would be most useful given the hardware limitations. The nl01 test case is representative of a plasma core simulation, and includes the full, high-fidelity coll kernel. The sh02 test case is similar, but has a finer compute mesh, a larger FFT size and uses the simplified, fast coll kernel.

2   Compiling and Running CGYRO on Power9

The Power9-equipped nodes were deployed in early 2018. The configuration was chosen to be as close as possible to the nodes that will be available on the upcoming OLCF Summit system. The delivered nodes are IBM AC922 servers, each with two 16-core 4-hyperthread IBM Power9 CPUs at 3.1 GHz and four NVIDIA Tesla V100 with NVLINK Volta GPUs. Each node has 512GB of CPU RAM and 4x16GB of GPU RAM. For the purpose of this work, we limited our tests to a single node, that we are calling `GAsummit`.

2.1   Porting CGYRO to Power9

CGYRO is written in standard Fortran 2008 and can be compiled with all major Fortran compilers. For GPU-enabled systems, the PGI Fortran compiler has always been used in the past, so we decided to use PGI on `GAsummit`. Installing and configuring PGI Fortran on `GAsummit` was simple and produced no major surprises. PGI provides both the base compiler, as well as CUDA, MPI and BLAS libraries out of the box. Easy to follow instructions for building FFTW are also provided. For building CGYRO we used the same recipe as on other GPU-based systems (e.g., OLCF Titan) and the build succeeded on the first try. The overall experience was very positive. The CGYRO version built was v16 [11].

It should be noted that we did not try out the gcc compiler suite, since CGYRO is typically not compiled with gcc on production systems and gcc has only rudimentary support for OpenACC. We did not have a license for the IBM xlf compiler, and its lack of support for OpenACC would have made the porting more difficult.

2.2   Evaluating the Effect of Hyperthreading

A Power9 CPU on `GAsummit` has 16 cores, and each core supports 4 hardware threads (i.e. *hyperthreads*), for a total of 128 logical cores on the node. To test the impact of hyperthreading, we compiled CGYRO for CPU only, and ran the `sh02` test case with one, two and four hardware threads per core. As can be seen from the data in Table 1, there is actually not much difference between the times for the three tests, although different kernels respond differently to hyperthreading; while the FFT-based `nl` seems to prefer more hardware threads, the other two kernels actually slow down at higher hyperthreading. We ran all further tests with two hardware threads per core.

2.3   The Impact of Volta GPUs on CGYRO Performance

On `GAsummit`, the bulk of the theoretical peak FLOPS comes from the four NVIDIA Tesla V100 cards. However, given that CGYRO is only partially ported to GPU, a significant part of the code is still bound to the performance of the

Table 1. Hyperthreading provides only minor benefit in wallclock time for the Power9 CPU-only CGYRO sh02 test case

Hyperthreads per core	str kernel	nl kernel	coll kernel	Total time
1	110s	563s	76s	817s
2	119s	452s	79s	746s
4	143s	437s	83s	771s

Table 2. The GPUs provide a significant reduction in wallclock time for CGYRO on GAsummit, but only on some kernels

sh02 test case	str kernel	nl kernel	coll kernel	Total time
2 CPUs + 4 GPUs	66s	53s	81s	274s
2 CPUs, no GPUs	119s	452s	79s	746s
nl01 test case	**str** kernel	**nl** kernel	**coll** kernel	Total time
2 CPUs + 4 GPUs	9s	6s	24s	50s
2 CPUs + 1 GPU	12s	13s	25s	70s
2 CPUs, no GPUs	13s	35s	24s	87s

CPU. We thus compiled the code with OpenACC enabled, and ran tests sh02 and nl01 with all four GPUs enabled. For the smaller nl01 test case, we also ran a test with only one GPU enabled; the larger case would not fit in the memory of a single GPU. Results can be found in Table 2. On the larger sh02 test case, we observed about a 3x speedup overall. The FFT-based nl kernel gets a remarkable 9x speedup and the str kernel gets a more modest 2x speedup. On the small nl01 case which uses the high-fidelity coll kernel, we get only a 75% improvement on overall times. After the respectable 6x speedup on nl, its fraction on the total runtime shrinks so much that most of the time now gets spent in the CPU-only coll kernel and the on-node communication libraries.

3   Comparing to Other Systems

CGYRO performance has been previously studied on several leadership systems, so we compare the performance of CGYRO on GAsummit against these other systems, both CPU-only and GPU-equipped ones. The leadership systems being tested are OLCF Titan, CSCS Piz Daint [12], NERSC Cori [13], and TACC Stampede2 [14]. The respective node hardware is described in Table 3. The KNL nodes on Cori are configured to use MCDRAM in cache memory mode.

3.1   CPU-Only Tests

The first set of tests was aimed at comparing the performance of the Power9 CPUs against other CPU-based systems. It should be noted that the binary on

Table 3. Summary description of the systems being tested

	CPUs	GPUs
GAsummit CPU	2x 16-core Power9	None
GAsummit GPU	2x 16-core Power9	4x V100 (Volta)
Piz Daint GPU	1x 12-core Xeon E5-2690 v3 (Haswell)	1x P100 (Pascal)
Titan GPU	1x 16-core Opteron 6274 (Interlagos)	1x K20x (Kepler)
Cori CPU	1x 68-core Xeon Phi 7250 (KNL)	None
Stampede2 CPU	2x 24-core Xeon Platinum 8160 (Skylake)	None

GAsummit was compiled with PGI Fortran with FFTW, while the binaries on Cori and Stampede2 were compiled with Intel Fortran, using the FFTW libraries on Cori and the FFT libraries inside the Intel MKL library on Stampede2. Results for sh02 and nl01 can be found in Table 4, with a statistical error of about 5%. Please note that the total wallclock time includes communication and I/O overhead, so kernel-only timing is also included for completeness.

Table 4. The Power9 CPUs compare favorably to Xeon Phi KNL in both CPU-only CGYRO test cases, but Xeon Skylake CPUs provide a shorter wallclock time.

sh02 test case	CPU type	str kernel	nl kernel	coll kernel	Total (kernels) time
GAsummit CPU	Power9	119s	453s	79s	746s (651s)
Cori CPU	Xeon Phi KNL	116s	415s	84s	666s (616s)
Stampede2 CPU	Xeon Skylake	90s	309s	47s	485s (445s)
nl01 test case	CPU type	str kernel	nl kernel	coll kernel	Total (kernels) time
GAsummit CPU	Power9	13s	35s	24s	87s (72s)
Cori CPU	Xeon Phi KNL	11s	38s	28s	83s (77s)
Stampede2 CPU	Xeon Skylake	8s	21s	14s	49s (42s)

The two Power9 CPUs in GAsummit seem to compare favorably against the single Xeon Phi KNL CPU on Cori nodes, for both the larger sh02 test case and the small nl01 test case. The best CGYRO performance, however, is observed on the two Xeon Skylake CPUs (Stampede2) which outperform the Power9 CPUs by 50% on the large sh02 test case and by 70% on the small nl01 test case.

3.2 Full Node Tests

In the second set of tests, benchmarks were run with the GPU-enabled CGYRO binaries. It should be noted that the sh02 test case was too large for many GPU-enabled systems, so multiple nodes had to be used. Since we could not provide single-node timings for all the systems, the node timings in Table 5 are chosen to approximately match the total times on GAsummit. For the nl01 test case, all tests were run on a single node on all systems, with results available in Table 6. In both cases, CPU-only systems are included for comparison, the statistical error is about 5%, and kernel-only timing is included.

On the larger sh02 test case, one GAsummit node is about as fast as 4 Pascal-equipped Piz Daint nodes, 8 Kepler-based Titan nodes, 3 KNL-based Cori nodes, or 2 Skylake-based Stampede2 nodes. The FFT-based nl kernel obviously benefits from the fast Volta GPUs, but the added CPU power due to the use of multiple nodes compensates in the other kernels. Furthermore, it should be noted that on Titan the inter-node communication costs are quite high, resulting in a need for more than 10 Titan nodes to match a single GAsummit node.

The smaller nl01 test case with its high-fidelity coll kernel spends a significant amount of time on the CPU, so having a fast CPU is as important as having fast GPUs. As such, a GAsummit node is about as fast as a Skylake-based Stampede2 node, 2x faster than a KNL-based Cori node, about 3x faster than a Pascal-equipped Piz Daint node, and about 6x faster than a Kepler-based Titan node.

Table 5. Several nodes from other leadership systems are needed to match one GAsummit node in the GPU-enabled CGYRO sh02 test case.

Number of nodes	str kernel	nl kernel	coll kernel	Total (kernels) time
1x GAsummit GPU	66s	53s	81s	274s (201s)
4x Piz Daint GPU	79s	60s	41s	271s (179s)
8x Titan GPU	66s	79s	42s	376s (187s)
2x Cori CPU	47s	204s	40s	339s (291s)
2x Stampede2 CPU	44s	150s	21s	241s (215s)

Table 6. Even with the CPU-heavy coll kernel, the GAsummit node is still delivering the lowest single node wallclock time for the GPU-enabled CGYRO nl01 test case.

Single node	str kernel	nl kernel	coll kernel	Total (kernels) time
GAsummit GPU	9s	6s	24s	50s (38s)
Piz Daint GPU	35s	26s	56s	133s (117s)
Titan GPU	71s	72s	106s	297s (249s)
Cori CPU	11s	38s	28s	83s (77s)
Stampede2 CPU	8s	21s	14s	49s (42s)

4   Summary

The Magnetic Fusion Energy division of General Atomics has acquired an OLCF Summit-like system (2x Power9 CPUs and 4x Volta GPUs) as part of its commitment to state of the art computing, and has used it to run benchmarks of the premier fusion plasma simulation code, CGYRO. CGYRO has logged millions of node hours on OLCF Titan and NERSC Cori, and has been benchmarked on many other systems, making possible real-world performance comparisons between different architectures.

Porting CGYRO to Power9 (using PGI Fortran) was straightforward and simple. As only the most computationally intensive kernels of CGYRO are currently written for GPUs, both individual CPU and whole node (CPU+GPU) performance was evaluated. The CPU-only results show that performance of CGYRO on dual Power9 CPUs is comparable to a single socket Xeon Phi (KNL), and also to Intel Skylake on a per-core basis, yet with less available cores per socket.

For whole node tests, including GPUs, the performance of a single Summit-like node is matched with that of 4 Piz Daint nodes or about 10 Titan nodes, making it the fastest single node we have ever tested. As the GPU portion of modern supercomputers is responsible for an increasing share of overall performance claims, these initial tests indicate the need for heavier reliance on GPU kernels for cutting-edge codes like CGYRO to maximize utilization. The early adoption of this new platform has motivated and made possible additional GPU development of CGYRO to this effect, in advance of Summit coming online.

References

1. Summit Homepage. https://www.olcf.ornl.gov/olcf-resources/compute-systems/summit/. Accessed 24 Apr 2018
2. Candy, J., Belli, E., Bravenec, R.: A high-accuracy Eulerian gyrokinetic solver for collisional plasmas. J. Comput. Phys. **324**, 73 (2016)
3. Belli, E., Candy, J.: Implications of advanced collision operators for gyrokinetic simulation. Plasma Phys. Control. Fusion **59**, 045005 (2017)
4. Candy, J., Belli, E.: Spectral treatment of gyrokinetic shear flow. J. Comput. Phys. **356**, 448 (2018)
5. Belli, E., Candy, J.: Impact of centrifugal drifts on ion turbulent transport. Phys. Plasmas **25**, 032301 (2018)
6. Candy, J., Waltz, R.: An Eulerian gyrokinetic-Maxwell solver. J. Comput. Phys. **186**, 545 (2003)
7. Candy, J., Waltz, R.: Anomalous transport in the DIII-D tokamak matched by supercomputer simulation. Phys. Rev. Lett. **91**, 045001–1 (2003)
8. Candy, J., Waltz, R., Dorland, W.: The local limit of global gyrokinetic simulations. Phys. Plasmas **11**, L25 (2004)
9. Candy, J., Belli, E.: GYRO technical guide. In: General Atomics Technical Report, vol. GA-A26818 (2010)
10. Titan Homepage. https://www.olcf.ornl.gov/olcf-resources/compute-systems/titan/. Accessed 24 Apr 2018

11. CGYRO Git repository. https://github.com/gafusion/gacode.Commit4f8940c3b09 d3558b149ff5662d7d0577904a1f6. Accessed 24 Apr 2018
12. Piz Daint Homepage. https://www.cscs.ch/computers/piz-daint/. Accessed 24 Apr 2018
13. Cori Homepage. http://www.nersc.gov/systems/cori/. Accessed 24 Apr 2018
14. Stampede2 Homepage. https://www.tacc.utexas.edu/systems/stampede2. Accessed 24 Apr 2018

A 64-GB Sort at 28 GB/s on a 4-GPU POWER9 Node for Uniformly-Distributed 16-Byte Records with 8-Byte Keys

Gordon C. Fossum[1], Ting Wang[2], and H. Peter Hofstee[1,3]($\boxtimes$)

[1] IBM Research, Austin, TX, USA
{fossum,hofstee}@us.ibm.com
[2] IBM Systems, Shanghai, China
wtingsh@cn.ibm.com
[3] TU Delft, Delft, Netherlands

Abstract. Govinderaju et al. [1] have shown that a hybrid CPU-GPU system is cost-performance effective at sorting large datasets on a single node, but thus far large clusters used on sorting benchmarks have been limited by network and storage performance, and such clusters have remained CPU-only. With network and storage bandwidths improving more rapidly than CPU throughput performance, the cost effectiveness of CPU-GPU clusters for large sorts should be re-examined. As a first step, we evaluate sort performance on a single GPU-accelerated node with initial and final data residing in system memory. Access to main memory is limited to two reads and two writes, while executing the partitioning and sort in GPU memory. On a dual-socket IBM POWER9 system with four NVlink-attached NVIDIA V100 GPUs a single-node sort of 64 GB 8-byte key, 8-byte value records completes in under 2.3 s corresponding to a sort rate of over 28 GB/s. On a small (4-node) cluster with the same amount of data per node, the cluster sort completes in under 4.5 s. Sort performance is enabled by high system memory bandwidth, managing system-memory NUMA affinities, high CPU-GPU bandwidth, an efficient GPU-based partitioner, and an optimized GPU sort implementation. A cluster version of the algorithm benefits from minimizing copy operations by using RDMA. Matching the throughput of an optimized partitioner for our system would require a 50-100 GB/s network, which is feasible with a dual-socket POWER9 system.

Keywords: Sorting · Hybrid · GPGPU

1 Introduction

This paper represents a first step in an investigation on sorting very large datasets, such as those used in the well-known "Terasort" benchmark and the HPC "BigSort" benchmark [2, 3], but to do so leveraging a high-bandwidth CPU-GPU hybrid system.

Govinderaju et al. [1] showed that a hybrid CPU-GPU system can deliver better cost-performance on this type of sort benchmark at the single node level, but, for cluster benchmarks of this type, CPU-based systems continue to dominate. This is because it has not been cost effective to equip a system with the network and storage that operates at the

© Springer Nature Switzerland AG 2018
R. Yokota et al. (Eds.): ISC 2018 Workshops, LNCS 11203, pp. 373–386, 2018.
https://doi.org/10.1007/978-3-030-02465-9_25

sorting bandwidth a CPU-GPU complex can handle. Over the last several years, however, network and storage bandwidth growth has outpaced throughput performance growth on the CPU [4], as well as DRAM bandwidth growth, and it is our belief that the most cost-effective cluster for sorting large volumes of data will soon be a cluster with hybrid nodes.

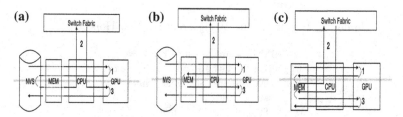

Fig. 1. a, b, c Dataflow for a large sort on an accelerated system. Phase 2 and 3 are pipelined. (1) Partition, (2) Shuffle, (3) Final sort. All lines represent the same bandwidth. (a) Data per node exceeds node memory. (b) Initial and final data in non-volatile storage (NVS), but per-node data fits in node memory. (c) Flow used in this paper.

An efficient large sort on a processing network generally consists of three phases: a first phase where the data is (sampled and) partitioned in parallel, a second communication or "shuffle" phase where the partitioned data is delivered to the target node so that all partitions with the same range end up on the same node, and a final phase where partitions with the same range are merged (or sorted together). No approaches that we are aware of start the third phase before the first phase is completed, but the second phase can be overlapped with either the first phase or with the final phase.

We consider three levels of memory in each node: local non-volatile storage (NVS) being the largest, local (DRAM) memory the next largest, and finally high-bandwidth memory (HBM) on the accelerator. When data per node exceeds the DRAM capacity NVS must be accessed four times as shown in Fig. 1a. Ideally such a sort would bypass DRAM altogether. A sort where initial and final data must be stored in NVS but data per node fits in DRAM is shown in Fig. 1b. This corresponds to an optimized dataflow for the Terasort "Indy" benchmark [3, 5]. With direct GPU access to NVS and to system memory across the network most accesses to DRAM can be avoided. A balanced system for this case has matched storage, memory, network, and accelerator bandwidth. Figure 2 depicts a notional such system based on POWER9 with a peak throughput of 100 GB/s. An upper bound on the sort performance of such a system is 50 GB/s (two phases at 100 GB/s each).

The experiments reported in this paper do not use GPUdirect communication, and initial and final data is stored in DRAM memory. This corresponds to the dataflow depicted in Fig. 1c. DRAM memory is accessed six times.

The current leader on sortbenchmark.org [5] with 100 Gb/s network and storage per node sorts 100 TB in about 100 s on 512 nodes, corresponding to about 2 GB/s per node. A "reasonable" next-generation system would take this to 200 Gb/s, and roughly double the per-node performance, but we claim a cost-effective hybrid system should target substantially more. We have pointed out that it is possible today to build a dual-socket POWER9 system with 100 GB/s peak throughput (Fig. 2). This system would

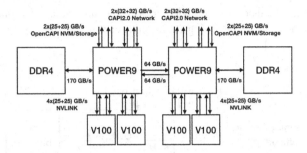

Fig. 2. Notional POWER9-based system with ~ 100 GB/s storage & network throughput. The limiting bandwidth would be the OpenCAPI NVM adapters (at 100 GB/s peak).

have four PCIe Gen4 or CAPI 2.0 200 Gb/s network adapters, four 25 GB/s Open-CAPI NVMe adapters, and up to four GPUs connected at 50 GB/s each as well as memory throughput exceeding 100 GB/s. Therefore, it is reasonable to ask if such a system could beat the current leader by an at least order of magnitude on per-node performance (i.e. greater than 20 GB/s) with a CPU-GPU hybrid system. The required sort rate significantly exceeds the sort rate of the fastest reported CPU-only sorts [10].

This paper presents work at a single node level and initial results on a small cluster to help demonstrate that this is indeed feasible. For this initial investigation, we read input data and produce final data in system memory. Early results of the clustered version of our algorithm show that with conventional networks (100 Gb/s for POWER8 and 200 Gb/s for POWER9) it is indeed network bandwidth-bound. Our work could also be used as an indication that for hybrid systems such as these we should re-think the conventional choices for network bandwidth per node.

.For our initial work, our focus is on randomly distributed data. We have chosen records with an 8-byte key and 8-byte payload. In practical situations, the key might represent a hash of the actual key and the payload may represent a pointer to the actual data. Eight bytes are sufficient to enumerate 256 Exabytes of 16-byte records. Stable sorts can be achieved (for example) by extending the key with a sequence number, and skewed datasets can be handled effectively by either sampling or performing a randomization step. Even at a large scale these can be handled at no less than half the speed of a dataset with randomly distributed data (our dataset is large enough so that random is essentially equivalent to uniformly distributed). Therefore, we feel that limiting our initial investigations to this dataset is meaningful.

The remainder of this paper is organized as follows. Section 2 provides an overview of two systems used in this study and estimates an upper bound on throughput. Section 3 provides a more detailed description of the sort algorithm. Section 4 reports measured performance. Section 5 details how the work could be extended.

2 System Attributes and Upper Bounds

In this section, we describe the two systems we have used for our studies at a high level and derive some upper bounds on the sort performance. We use peak bandwidths in our calculations, but we estimate only 2/3 of this is achievable due to control and other overheads. We first focus on single node performance, and we assume initial and final data is in main memory (representing future high-bandwidth storage).

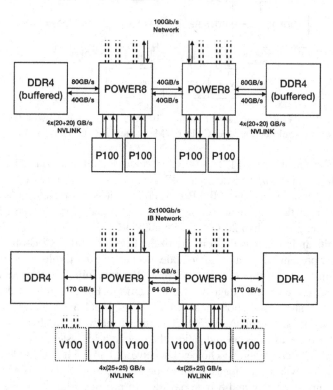

Fig. 3. High-level attributes of the "Minsky" and "Newell" systems used. Numbers shown represent peak bandwidths. For Minsky 38.4 GB/s is rounded to 40 GB/s.

We first consider the IBM POWER8 + NVIDIA P100–based "Minsky" system shown on top in Fig. 3. The Minsky system has an asymmetric memory interface, with the memory buffers providing 2×80 GB/s of read bandwidth and 2×40 GB/s of write bandwidth. NVLINK bandwidths for a 4GPU system are matched to the read bandwidth, but write bandwidth is limited to half the read bandwidth. Thus, even with 4 GPUs the partition and sort/merge stages are limited to the 50 GB/s effective write bandwidth, calling for a 400 Gb/s network, and an upper bound to overall sort throughput on Minsky is 25 GB/s. A clustered version using the pattern in Fig. 1c writes main memory twice limiting the second stage to 25 GB/s and overall estimated performance to about 18 GB/s. A 200 Gb/s (25 GB/s) network is required to achieve this.

For the IBM POWER9 + NVIDIA V100-based "Newell" system shown on the right aggregate (read + write) peak memory bandwidth at 340 GB/s is just below the aggregate NVLINK peak bandwidth at 400 GB/s. Assuming optimal placement of the data where each GPU reads from the memory attached to the same POWER9 processor that GPU is attached to, throughput of the first phase can reach 170 GB/s. The SMP bandwidth is sufficient as each node would write 42.5 GB/s locally and 42.5 GB/s across the SMP interconnect. In the second stage where we assume data is both read and written locally peak bandwidth is also limited to 170 GB/s. At effective bandwidths of 2/3 of peak, this puts an expected (NUMA best-case) upper bound of 57 GB/s (two phases at 113 GB/s, limited by main memory effective bandwidth) on the single-node sort performance of the Newell system. Cluster bandwidth without GPUdirect for the second stage is cut in half limiting overall theoretical sort throughput to about 38 GB/s requiring at least a 600 Gb/s network to match the 67 GB/s throughput of the second stage. With GPUdirect, a 1 Tb/s network (125 GB/s) would be needed to match the 113 GB/s throughput of the second stage.

We summarize our upper-bound estimates for Minsky and Newell to sort 64 GB in Tables 1 and 2 below.

Table 1. Bandwidth-limited upper bounds on performance for Minsky.

Minsky 64 GB	Read	Eff. Read BW	Write	Eff. Write BW
1 GPU	2.56 s	25 GB/s	2.56 s	25 GB/s
2 GPU	1.28 s	50 GB/s	2.56–1.28 s	25–50 GB/s[a]
4 GPU	0.64 s	100 GB/s	1.28 s	50 GB/s

[a]Provided memory is allocated on both nodes. If not memory write bandwidth drops to 25 GB/s.

Table 2. Bandwidth-limited upper bounds on performance for Newell.

Newell 64 GB	Read	Read BW	NUMA Write	NUMA Write BW	Local Write	Local Write
1 GPU	1.92 s	33 GB/s	1.92 s	33 GB/s	1.92 s	33 GB/s
2 GPU	0.96 s	67 GB/s	0.96 s	67 GB/s	0.96 s	67 GB/s
4 GPU	0.57 s	113 GB/s	0.80–0.57 s	80–113 GB/s[b]	0.57 s	113 GB/s

[b]Lowest bandwidth occurs when each pair of GPUs writes simultaneously to memory attached to the opposite CPU. Highest bandwidth occurs when half of the writes traverse the SMP.

3 Sorting Algorithm

This section provides a more detailed description of the GPU-based sorting algorithm. Because NUMA effects matter, the sort algorithm is most easily understood if one assumes each GPU with its supporting threads on the host (with the same NUMA affinity) to make up individual nodes, even though they may share a network adapter. In our case this means that we think of a single server with four GPUs as effectively four nodes.

Input data resides in contiguous memory with NUMA affinity for each GPU and similarly final output data must reside in contiguous memory ranges with NUMA affinity for each GPU. Additionally, memory buffers with NUMA affinity are allocated for each generated partition for each GPU. If the input does not need to be preserved this memory can be de-allocated at the start of the shuffle phase (after partitioning is complete) and before buffers with NUMA affinity are allocated to receive the shuffle data.

Our sort algorithm consists of three stages. In the first stage, data is split into fixed-range partitions that are small enough such that the size of a (single-node) partition multiplied by the number of nodes in a cluster can be sorted by a single GPU. In a second stage partitions are redistributed across the nodes such that each node receives all records within a contiguous key range. If there is just a single node then the second stage is skipped. In the third stage partitions with the same key range (from the different nodes) are read into the GPU, sorted and written back to main memory.

Sort performance is further optimized by organizing the final sort into overlapping waves [5], where each wave pipelines the transfer of partitions from host memory to the GPU, the sort within the GPU, and writing back sorted partitions to host memory. Optimizing performance in this manner places a further constraint on partition size, as the number of partitions must be at least the number of GPUs in the entire system times the number of waves.

During the shuffle phase partitions are sent to their destination nodes and partitions from the individual nodes with corresponding ranges are coalesced into larger partitions. By first communicating partition sizes an additional memory to memory copy operation to create a contiguous aggregated partition is avoided.

We choose to overlap the shuffle with the final sort rather than the initial partitioning phase, and to not start the shuffle until all data is locally partitioned. This makes it easier to extend the algorithm (in the future) to deal with skewed data distributions.

The GPU final sort pipelines reading data from host memory to GPU memory, sorting the data in GPU memory, and writing the data back to host memory. For the GPU-based final sort of a coalesced partition we use our version of a hybrid radix sort [6–8]. The algorithm first creates large numbers of buckets within GPU memory leveraging a parallel histogram operation followed by a parallel prefix sum to determine bucket boundaries, a parallel operation to place the data in the buckets, and finally a sort of many small buckets leveraging the large number of GPU threads. At the final stage, each bucket contains just a small number of elements so that a simple in-situ sort algorithm can be used (we use bubblesort because it is memory-efficient). If a stable sort is required an additional transformation is added upon loading the data that extends the keys with ordering information and replaces the value with a pointer to an array that stores the values. At the end of the partition sort the original records are reconstructed.

Our main point of reference is the recent Stehle and Jacobsen [8], which also provides a more comprehensive overview of prior art for this type of sort. Stehle and Jacobsen use a system with a single PCIe-attached NVIDIA "Pascal" GPU, similar to the GPUs used in our "Minsky" system where they are NVlink rather than PCIe attached. With a single GPU the 64 GB sort (uniform distribution in both cases, and 8B key, 8B value) takes about 11 s on our "Minsky" system and about 16 s in [8], likely primarily due to the difference in the GPU-CPU bandwidth, though different sort approaches are used. Our results scale to about 4 s for the same sort on the same system with 4 GPUs, and 2.26 s on the next-generation "Newell" system with four NVIDIA V100 GPUs. In contrast to [8], to limit main memory access to the minimum two reads and two writes, the CPU is not used in the sort, except to provide high-level control. We also compared our sort to the "Thrust" [9] and "CUB" libraries. Even when we arrange the data in two separate arrays for keys and values, respectively, our implementation outperforms these libraries by a factor of two (and by a significantly larger factor if the data is provided as one array of 16-byte records with 8-byte keys).

3.1 Partitioner Design

This section describes the design of the GPU-based partitioner. Our aim is to come as close as possible to the performance limits derived from main-memory read and write bandwidths. As mentioned before, we treat the system as effectively four virtual nodes, and input data has NUMA affinity with the GPU that partitions that set of input data.

The GPU-based partitioner works like the final sort, except that the contents within each bucket are not sorted, and the number of buckets is smaller. We provide more detail in Sect. 3.3. For uniformly distributed data we choose the number of partitions such that two constraints are met:

(1) The size of each (local) partition times the number of nodes must be small enough such that the entire coalesced partition can be sorted in the GPU (HBM) memory.
(2) The number of partitions should be large enough so that the total number of partitions is more than the total number of GPUs (across the cluster) times the number of desired waves. Our design uses eight such waves.

The output of the partitioner consists of a data structure containing the partitioned data in host memory, as well as the total number of partitions and an array with a pointer to each partition and a second array with the size of each partition.

3.2 Design of the Shuffle Phase

During the shuffle phase data is redistributed across the nodes. The most efficient way to do this is to deliver shuffled data for each partition directly to the GPU, however, not all systems support this option. When it is not supported it implies that we must receive the shuffle data into a buffer and incur an additional set of main-memory read and write operations.

The output of the shuffle phase is equivalent to the output of the partitioner: a data structure containing the partitioned data, as well as the total number of partitions, and an array with a pointer to each partition and a second array with the size of each partition.

3.3 Sorting a Single Partition

As described in the earlier sections, the sort of a single partition provides the GPU with a list of (variable-sized) sub-partitions to coalesce and sort. Sorting a single partition consists of the following steps:

1. Load:
   a. Load all data for a given sub-partition from the list of (NUMA-affinitized) host memory buffers into a contiguous array in GPU memory. This is achieved with a series of cudaMemcpyAsync calls.
2. Sort:
   a. In the first phase of the sort one GPU thread is run for each element of the input array.
      (1) If a stable sort is requested, the 8-byte value for each record is saved in a separate array and replaced with the sequence number (GPU thread ID). This approach can also readily be extended to allow our sorter to handle arbitrary size records.
      (2) A histogram is created by leveraging the atomic add operation in CUDA to increment counters corresponding to the high order bits of the active sort key.
   b. The next phase of the sort creates the buckets to be sorted. The number of buckets is chosen such that each bucket is expected to hold approximately 5-10 elements.
      (1) Using a parallel prefix sum an array of indices is calculated from the histogram denoting the start of each bucket. Calculating a second set of indices denoting the end of each bucket allows us to double the amount of concurrency in the next step and effectively doubles the number of buckets.
      (2) Based on the bit in the key following the key bits used to build the histogram either the bucket lower index is atomically read and incremented, or the upper index is atomically read and decremented, and the data is placed at the target index.
      (3) Each CUDA block works on a set of 128 buckets, bringing in the corresponding data to local memory for faster processing. Eight GPU threads are assigned to each bucket. Four of these work on the "first half" of the bucket, and four work on the "second half" of the bucket (the two halves having been created in the bucketize step above). Each thread concentrates on its 4-byte word of the 16-byte working record, to sort them in-place.
      (4) If the sort is not required to be stable, the sorted data is written back to the destination array. If, however, the sort is required to be stable, this sorted data (specifically the address of the original data stored in the working records) is used to copy the original data to the destination array.
3. Store:
   a. cudaMemcpyAsync is used to append the sorted chunks in each GPU to the previously sorted host-side data in their large output arrays.

3.4   Single-Node Sort

As mentioned previously, NUMA affinity must be carefully managed, and it is easiest to consider each GPU and associated CPU cores/threads to be separate "nodes". The algorithm works best if the input data set can be partitioned to have GPU NUMA affinity. We also set up monolithic host-side arrays (one per GPU) that will accumulate the sorted output from each sort call. These arrays are also carefully allocated to have proper NUMA affinity ("close" to the executing host core and to the associated GPU).

Internally, we create buffers to hold chunks of sort data that fit the GPU HBM memories as well as the associated histogram/bucket information on these data.

To run a single-node sort, we specify:

(1) The number of input records,
(2) A pointer to the input, (per GPU)
(3) The number of GPUs to be used,
(4) The starting location of the bits in the key to sort on,
(5) The number of partitions to use per GPU, (how many bits to sort on)
(6) The number of buckets to use.

We find that it is especially important to carefully choose how many buckets are to be used. If too many buckets are used then bucketizing, and especially the parallel prefix operation, can take too long. If the number of buckets is too small, then the final sort of the bucket may take too long and even has the potential to degrade performance if the records referenced by a set of buckets cannot fit into the GPU caches forcing the GPU to use its global memory directly.

To support the multi-threaded operations that implement each sort, we set up "stream" variables for use by CUDA, and state variables to keep track of the pipeline stage for each package. The user makes calls to do sorts in batches, such that each call sends a separate input structure of data for each GPU in the node. Every time a sort call is made, we spawn posix threads (three threads for each GPU), and each thread independently interacts with the GPUs using the stream synchronization feature in CUDA to keep the various operations from interfering with each other.

Internally these calls make use of a pipeline state machine. The first sort call will only execute the "copy-host-to-device" threads, the second call does a "copy-host-to-device" on the second batch of inputs, while simultaneously doing sort computations on the first batch. With the third call, steady state is reached, where batch N is read, batch N-1 is sorted, and batch N-2 is written back. Before returning from a sort call the state variables are updated to correctly point at the internal buffers in preparation for the next sort call. After the user has made all the sort calls, a "flush" call is made, which internally makes two more sort calls, to: (1) sort the last batch of input, and (2) write back the last two batches of output data. After all threads have ended, the host code prints a line of information to report this timing data.

Note that for proper memory affinity, we require that all the input data be channeled through the correct GPU. So, for example, if we have four GPUs, then all input shards whose active sort keys start with binary '00' must be fed to the first sort, '01' to the second sort, '10' to the third sort, and '11' to the fourth sort. Thus, the first sort call must contain the first input structures in each of the four quadrants of the eventual output.

3.5 Multi-node Sort

For the multi-node sort the partition phase and sort phase are the same as for the single node sort, but a shuffle phase is added, and parameters differ from the single-node case.

For the partitioner the k key bits specified by sort order designate the index of memory buffer that the record goes to. Then, these memory buffers are shuffled through the network such that all buffers with same index bits goes to the same node, and every node gets a roughly equal share of buffers. When network shuffle finishes partitions with similar key bits have been put together and sent to GPU in a single sort call. After all buffers are processed by GPU, the overall sort is done.

In multi-node sort, RDMA is used in network shuffle to avoid memory copy, and to reduce the CPU usage. Since RDMA device requires memory in the data transfer being registered, and the registration takes time, we estimate the maximum size of memory buffer, and do the registration before shuffle start. These registered memory buffers are then used by radix sort bucketizer to store its output.

4 Sort Performance

4.1 Single-Node Sort Performance

Table 3 reports single system measurements for Minsky and for convenience also repeats the estimated bounds based on bandwidth limitations.

Table 3. "Minsky" bandwidth-limited estimates and measured results.

64 GB Sort ("Minsky")	1 GPU	2 GPU	4 GPU
Local read (estimate)	2.56 s	1.28 s	0.64 s
Partitioner (measured)	2.7 s	1.3 s	0.68 s
NUMA write (estimate)	2.56 s	1.28–2.56 s	1.28 s
Partitioner write (measured)	2.3 s	2.2 s	1.8 s
Local (read-) Write (estimate)	2.56 s	1.28–2.56 s	1.28 s
Final sort (measured)	6.2 s	3.1 s	1.6 s
Total sort (measured)	11.2 s	6.6 s	4.0 s
Throughput (estimate)	12.5 GB/s	25 GB/s	25 GB/s
Throughput (measured)	5.7 GB/s	9.7 GB/s	16 GB/s

Our conclusion from these measurements is that Minsky single-node sort performance is bandwidth bound for 1st stage read, likely still affected by some details of NUMA behavior for the 1st stage write (esp. 2 GPU) and GPU-performance bound in the final stage. The 4 GPU version, that was most heavily tuned, achieves a reasonable fraction of our estimated bandwidth-limited bounds. The final stage sort operates at nearly 40 GB/s, which would justify a 400 Gb/s network (if GPUdirect could be used) (Table 3).

Table 4. "Newell" bandwidth-limited estimates and measured results for 64 GB sort.

64 GB Sort ("Newell")	1 GPU	2 GPU	4 GPU
Local read (estimate)	1.92 s	0.96 s	0.48 s
Partitioner (measured)	1.71 s	0.90 s	0.85 s
NUMA write (estimate)	1.92 s	0.96 s	0.57–0.80 s
Partitioner write (measured)	1.95 s	1.03 s	1.16 s
Local (read-) Write (estimate)	1.92 s	0.96 s	0.57 s
Final sort (measured)	3.42 s	1.79 s	0.91 s
Total sort (measured)	5.91 s	3.12 s	2.26 s
Throughput (estimate)	17 GB/s	33 GB/s	67 GB/s
Throughput (measured)	11 GB/s	17 GB/s	28 GB/s

For Newell in the first stage we are doing somewhat better than estimated for the 1 and 2 GPU case (but not exceeding peak NVlink bandwidth) indicating that there may have been some protocol improvements in addition to the NVlink frequency improvement.

Table 5 summarizes our estimated and measured single-node performance.

Table 5. Single node sort performance summary.

	Minsky (BW bound)	Minsky (measured)	Newell (BW bound)	Newell (measured)
1 GPU	8.3 GB/s	5.7 GB/s	17 GB/s	11 GB/s
2 GPU	16.6 GB/s	9.7 GB/s	33 GB/s	20 GB/s
4 GPU	25 GB/s	16 GB/s	67 GB/s	28 GB/s

4.2 Multi-node Sort Performance

Shuffle Performance

Because the Minsky system does not support GPUdirect, the shuffle operation adds an additional memory read and write operation (for the fraction of data that needs to be shuffled to a remote node). On a 4-node Minsky cluster with 100 Gb IB interconnect, without running any other phases of the sort, the shuffle of 48 GB of data takes 5.36 s, equivalent to 8.95 GB/s of network bandwidth. On a 4-node Newell the shuffle of 48 GB of data per node takes just under 3 s, or 16 GB/s (with a 200 Gb network).

Multi-node Sort Performance

A local partitioner on Minsky takes 1.19 s and the integrated pipelined shuffle and final sort on 4 nodes with 64 GB of data per node (256 GB total data) takes 6.94 s, about what we might hope to achieve with a 100 Gb network. Note that for the multi-node case our local partitioner writes its output to memory with the correct GPU affinity and therefore our partitioner is faster than in the single-node 4-GPU case.

With memory bandwidth and accelerator bandwidth and accelerator sort performance optimized, network bandwidth is the next bottleneck. The final sort phase for the Minsky system with 4 GPUs sorts 64 GB in 1.6 s or, equivalently, sorts at a bandwidth of nearly 40 GB/s. For the shuffle to keep up with this processing rate would require a 400 Gb/s network. Because the system has three PCIe Gen3 ×16 slots, it would be possible to configure a system with three adapters per node and come close.

Table 6. 4-node Newell cluster performance. 64 GB per node. 4 of 6 GPUs used.

#GPU_sort/node	Batch size	Sort	Partition	Shuffle/final sort
32	2 GB	4.578 s	0.767 s	3.774 s
64	1 GB	4.744 s	0.738 s	3.966 s
128	512 MB	4.764 s	0.731 s	3.993 s
256	256 MB	4.567 s	0.642 s	3.885 s
512	**128 MB**	**4.470 s**	0.644 s	3.787 s
1024	**64 MB**	**4.484 s**	0.676 s	3.769 s
2048	32 MB	4.527 s	0.763 s	3.724 s

Table 7. Pipelined final sort/shuffle vs. non-pipelined. Final sort batch size is 64 MB.

	Overall sort time	Shuffle/sort	Shuffle	Sort
pipelined	4.484 s	3.769 s		
non-pipelined	4.694 s		2.967 s	1.013 s

Tables 6 and 7 report measured results on a small (4-node) Newell cluster. The partitioner, which completes in about 0.65 s for 64 GB, achieves nearly 100 GB/s (we earlier estimated 113 GB/s as an upper bound). The final sort completes in just over a second, achieving a sort rate of about 64 GB/s. A stand-alone shuffle completes in under 3 s, or close to 16 GB/s (only 48 GB is shuffled). A pipelined integrated sort completes in under 2.3 s, achieving a sort rate greater than 28 GB/s. The pipelined version is slower than the shuffle by itself and succeeds only partially in overlapping the shuffle and final sort. We attribute this to limits on available memory bandwidth, as this version does not use GPUdirect. The overall sort performance is limited by the network. Matching the capabilities of the rest of the system would require three 200 Gb/s adapters. The Newell system can indeed support this, and we expect to configure a system accordingly in the near future.

5   Future Work

While we have come close to our estimated bandwidth-limited performance in the 4-GPU single node case, there is clearly additional work that could be done:

(1) As pointed out in the previous section, cluster sort results are network bandwidth limited, and it would be interesting to see to what extent performance can be improved by configuring more network adapters.

(2) Even for a sort that has its initial and final data in memory it should be possible to reduce the number of main memory accesses from six to four using GPUdirect communication.

(3) Improvements in NVMe bandwidth (per dollar) make it feasible to configure a system as shown in Fig. 2 and do a sort that would meet the sortbenchmark.org rules [2].

(4) Handling skewed distributions. We have tried to ensure our algorithm is organized to not make this too difficult. The partitioning is not overlapped with the network shuffle and final sort, making our approach easier to adapt to non-uniform distributions.

6 Summary and Conclusions

We have presented a sorting method and GPU-based algorithm to sort CPU host-memory-based data. On a 4-GPU POWER8 system performance reaches 16 GB/s, about 2/3 of a bandwidth-limited bound estimated at 25 GB/s. On the POWER9 Newell System with four NVIDIA V100 GPUs a 64 GB sort of uniformly distributed records with an 8-byte key and 8-byte value completes in under 2.3 s, a 28 GB/s sort rate. A single-node sort reads and writes main memory only twice, one read and one write each for the partitioning and final partition sort stages. The final partition sort achieves up to 40 GB/s with 4 GPUs on one node. These results are enabled by high-bandwidth memory, the high-bandwidth NVlink to the GPU, and by improved GPU-based sorting and partitioning algorithms. Similar per-node throughputs could likely be supported in a cluster, but would require a 400 Gb/s network, which is achievable on the POWER9 system. We therefore expect a hybrid CPU-GPU cluster to provide better cost-performance than current CPU-only clusters for sorting very large datasets. Using GPUdirect could justify using 800 Gb/s or even 1 Tb/s networks.

Acknowledgements. The authors would like to thank Mark Nutter for discussions early-on in the project. We thank Bruce D'Amora for his support and feedback, and we want to thank the anonymous reviewers of an earlier version of this paper for their extensive feedback that contributed to significant improvements in this version of the paper.

References

1. Govindaraju, N., Gray, J., Kumar, R., Manocha, D.: Gputerasort: high performance graphics co-processor sorting for large database management. In: SIGMOD (2006)
2. www.sortbenchmark.org
3. Parallel Integer Sort/BigSort. https://asc.llnl.gov/coral-2-benchmarks/
4. Kruger, F.: CPU Bandwidth, the Worrisome 2020 Trend, March 2016. https://blog.westerndigital.com/cpu-bandwidth-the-worrisome-2020-trend/. Accessed Feb 2018
5. Jiang, J., et al.: Tencent Sort. http://www.sortbenchmark.org/TencentSort2016.pdf. Accessed Dec 2017

6. Satish, N., Harris, M., Garland, M.: Designing efficient sorting algorithms for manycore gpus. In: IEEE International Symposium on Parallel and Distributed Processing, IPDPS 2009. IEEE, pp. 1–10 (2009)
7. Arkhipov, D.I., Wu, D., Li, K., Regan, A.C.: Sorting with GPUs: a survey. arXiv.org 1709.02520, September 2017. (www.arxiv.org/pdf/1709.02520)
8. Stehle, E., Jacobsen, H.-A.: A memory bandwidth-efficient hybrid radix sort on GPUs. In: Proceedings of the 2017 ACM International Conference on Management of Data, pp. 417–432, ACM, New York (2017)
9. Hoberock, J., Bell, N.: Thrust: A Parallel Template   Library (2016). https://thrust.github.io
10. Cho, M., Brand, D., Bordawekar, R., Finkler,   U., Kulandaisamy, V., Puri, R.: Paradis: an efficient parallel algorithm for in-place radix sort. In: PVLDB (2015)

Early Experience on Running OpenStaPLE on DAVIDE

Claudio Bonati[1], Enrico Calore[2(✉)], Massimo D'Elia[1], Michele Mesiti[3], Francesco Negro[4], Sebastiano Fabio Schifano[2], Giorgio Silvi[5], and Raffaele Tripiccione[2]

[1] Università di Pisa and INFN Sezione di Pisa, Pisa, Italy
claudio.bonati@df.unipi.it,massimo.delia@unipi.it
[2] Università degli Studi di Ferrara and INFN Sezione di Ferrara, Ferrara, Italy
{calore,schifano,tripiccione}@fe.infn.it
[3] Academy of Advanced Computing, Swansea University, Swansea, UK
michele.mesiti@swansea.ac.uk
[4] INFN Sezione di Pisa, Pisa, Italy
francesco.negro@pi.infn.it
[5] Jülich Supercomputing Centre, Jülich, Germany
g.silvi@fz-juelich.de

Abstract. In this contribution we measure the computing and energy performance of the recently developed DAVIDE HPC-cluster, a massively parallel machine based on IBM POWER CPUs and NVIDIA Pascal GPUs. We use as an application benchmark the OpenStaPLE Lattice QCD code, written using the OpenACC programming framework. Our code exploits the computing performance of GPUs through the use of OpenACC directives, and uses OpenMPI to manage the parallelism among several GPUs. We analyze the speed-up and the aggregate performance of the code, and try to identify possible bottlenecks that harm performances. Using the power monitor tools available on DAVIDE we also discuss some energy aspects pointing out the best trade-offs between time-to-solution and energy-to-solution.

Keywords: LQCD · OpenACC · POWER8 · NVLink

1 Introduction

Simulation based on Lattice QCD (LQCD) methods are an example of HPC grand challenge applications, with accuracy of results strongly depending on available computing resources [1,2]. This has led – starting from the mid '80s – to the development of massively parallel systems [3–8] specifically designed and optimized to fit the computing requirements of LQCD.

This approach has lost its effectiveness as general purpose high performance computing (HPC) processors started to be available on the market. Nowadays typical HPC systems include powerful nodes based on multi-core standard CPUs

© Springer Nature Switzerland AG 2018
R. Yokota et al. (Eds.): ISC 2018 Workshops, LNCS 11203, pp. 387–401, 2018.
https://doi.org/10.1007/978-3-030-02465-9_26

and on GPUs, sharing architecture features based on an increasing number of computing cores and levels of data vectorization.

On the software side, different programming languages are still necessary to develop applications for CPUs and GPUs. This poses significant code portability and maintainability issues. In this direction, high level programming frameworks have been recently developed, looking at code portability and eventually at performance portability across different architectures. The OpenACC [9] standard is one such framework, using a directive based programming model similar to OpenMP [10], specifically designed to support accelerator computing. OpenACC abstracts code functionalities to a descriptive level, leaving architecture-specific implementations to the compiler. Using this approach, the same source code can be run on different processors, such as CPUs and GPUs, as long as they are supported by the compiler, achieving an easy and good level of code portability. OpenACC is becoming increasingly popular in several computational communities and it is increasingly used in many stencil-based applications, mostly running on GPU, including Lattice Boltzmann Methods [11–13], and more recently also Lattice QCD [14,15].

In this paper we analyze the computing and energy performance of the *Open-ACC Staggered Parallel LatticeQCD Everywhere* (OpenStaPLE) application that we have recently developed [15,16], compiling with PGI 18.1 and running on the *Development for an Added Value Infrastructure Designed in Europe* [17] (DAVIDE) HPC cluster.

The remainder of this paper is organized as follow: the next section describes the OpenStaPLE application and Sect. 3 describes the architecture of the DAVIDE machine. Sect. 4 analyzes the computing and energy performance of the code running on the DAVIDE system, while Sect. 5 gives some concluding remarks.

2   OpenStaPLE

OpenStaPLE is an MPI + OpenACC implementation of a state-of-the-art Monte Carlo Lattice QCD Code for staggered fermions, recently used for production runs [18]. OpenStaPLE derives from an earlier version coded with CUDA [19], and ported to OpenACC to allow for code portability on multiple architectures [20]. Its first implementation, able to run only on single-accelerator systems, GPUs (NVIDIA and AMD) and CPUs, has been described in [15]. In this work we adopt the latest version of OpenStaPLE, described in [16], in which the physical data domain can be sliced along one dimension and parallelized on multiple computing nodes, and multiple processors (*e.g.* CPUs or GPUs), using MPI (Message Passing Interface).

As customary in lattice QCD simulations, space-time is discretized on a finite lattice of N_t, N_x, N_y, N_z sites and spacing a. The dynamical variables are the gauge fields $U_\mu(x)$, 3×3 unitary matrices associated to the link extending from point x in direction μ, their conjugate momenta $H_\mu(x)$ and the pseudofermions

$\varphi(x)$. All variables are Monte Carlo sampled according to the probability distribution function

$$P(U, H, \varphi) = exp\left(-\frac{1}{2}H^2 - S_g(U) - \varphi M(U)^{-1/4}\varphi\right) ; \qquad (1)$$

H^2 represents the sum of the traces of the squared momenta, and $S_g(U)$ is a sum of traces of path-ordered products along closed circuits of the U_μ matrices. The term involving the φ variables is the fermion part of the action, and $M(U)$ is the Dirac matrix; in our staggered discretization $M(U)$ connects only nearest neighbor sites on the lattice. It can be conveniently written as

$$M = m\,I + \begin{pmatrix} 0 & D_{oe} \\ D_{eo} & 0 \end{pmatrix} \qquad (2)$$

with m the fermion mass, I the identity matrix and D_{eo} and D_{oe} the out-of-diagonal blocks of the matrix, depending on the U and connecting even and odd sites on the lattice.

OpenStaPLE uses the Rational Hybrid Monte Carlo algorithm (RHMC) [21–23]. The fractional power of $M(U)$ is approximated by a rational function of $M(U)$ and the update is performed by a combination of Molecular Dynamics (MD) evolution of the gauge fields and accept/reject steps, like in the ordinary Hybrid Monte Carlo update [24,25].

Most simulation time goes in the computation of the forces acting on the gauge fields (for the MD evolution) and in the evaluation of the action at the end of the trajectory, which is needed for the final accept/reject step. These high level operations map onto just two basic classes of operations: products of $U_\mu(x)$ matrices along simple paths and solutions of linear equations of the following form:

$$(m^2\,I - D_{eo}D_{oe} + \sigma^{(i)})\varphi^{(i)} = b , \quad i \in \{1,\ldots,r\} ; \qquad (3)$$

where r is the order of the rational approximation used in the RHMC and $\sigma^{(i)}$ are the positions of the poles in the rational approximation. These equations are conveniently solved by the shift (also known as multi-mass) form of the Conjugate Gradient [26,27], whose basic building blocks are vector linear algebra operations (scalar products and sums) and the application of the matrices D_{oe} and D_{eo} to a vector.

In OpenStaPLE, domain decomposition is performed along one dimension, having each MPI process to manage a sub-lattice, surrounded by halos [16]. As the lattice is split along one dimension, each MPI process would need to communicate with its left and right neighbor in a ring fashion. The discretization adopted in OpenStaPLE consists of stout improved fermions and tree-level Symanzik improved gauge action [28,29]; in this setup for the application of the Dirac operator an halo thickness of 1 site is enough, while for the computation of the pure-gauge force term, a thickness of 2 sites is needed.

When running on GPUs all data structures are permanently allocated to GPU memory, drastically limiting the need for CPU-GPU data transfers. Data movements then only follow the GPU-to-GPU path and are controlled by MPI. Since MPI communications are asynchronous with respect to computations, a perfect overlap between communications and computations on the inner bulk of the lattice can be appreciated. On the other side communications and computations on the borders of the lattice can not overlap, but need to be performed serially, due to data dependencies.

As shown in [16], in general, OpenStaPLE shows a perfect *Strong Scaling* behavior of the Dirac operator – which drives the scaling behavior of the whole application – as long as the computations on the inner lattice require a longer execution time than the halos/borders exchange with neighboring processes.

The four nested loops of the D_{oe} and D_{eo} kernels (main parts of the Dirac operator) are annotated with OpenACC directives as shown in details in [16]. In particular we use the *collapse* clause to join together the two outer loops to increase the level of coarse parallelism, while we exploit the *tail* clause to perform blocking and increase data locality for the two inner loops. All kernel are executed in asynchronous mode using the *async* clause, allowing to overlap computations and communications.

3   The DAVIDE Cluster

DAVIDE is an energy efficient HPC cluster designed by E4 Computer Engineering for the European Prace Pre-Commercial Procurement (PCP) programme. This architecture is based on POWER8+ CPUs and NVIDIA Pascal GPUs. The first pilot system has been deployed in 2017 and is now part of the CINECA HPC computing resources.

The POWER8 architecture has been on the market since 2014; it has been used for HPC scientific applications [30], but only in late 2016 did IBM release the POWER8+ processor embedding NVLink 1.0 interfaces [31]. NVLink 1.0 uses the High-Speed Signaling interconnect developed by NVIDIA and operating up to 20 Gbps. Eight of these mono directional connections form a so called Sub-Link, and two Sub-Links – one for each direction – form a Link. A link has a bidirectional bandwidth of up to 40 GB/s and multiple Links can be combined to form Gangs. In POWER8+, IBM removed the A-Bus and PCI interfaces for SMP connections and replaced them with NVLink 1.0 interfaces, so inter-socket CPU-CPU are only supported by the X-Bus [32].

DAVIDE has 45 computing nodes, each with 2× POWER8+ CPUs and 4× NVIDIA Tesla P100 GPUs; nodes are connected by 2× Mellanox InfiniBand EDR 100 Gb/s network links, see Fig. 1. The POWER8+, has 4 NVLink connections with an aggregate maximum theoretical bidirectional bandwidth of 160 GB/s granting an high bandwidth between the CPUs and the NVIDIA GPUs directly connected, via NVLink, to it. It also features 4 memory buffer chips to interface between the POWER8+ processor and DDR4 memory through 4 different channels providing a bandwidth of 28.8 GB/s each. The buffer chips includes an L4 16MB cache to reduce the latency of local memory accesses. In DAVIDE, each NVIDIA P100 is connected to one CPU through 2× NVLink, thus each CPU is directly connected to two GPUs, as shown in Fig. 1, with a total bidirectional bandwidth of 80 GB/s for each of them. The two CPUs within each node are connected through the SMP X-Bus, providing a peak bidirectional bandwidth of 38.4 GB/s. This link is used to share the memory banks attached to each POWER8 and to maintain cache coherency. Two InfiniBand cards are connected respectively to the two processors through PCI Express lanes.

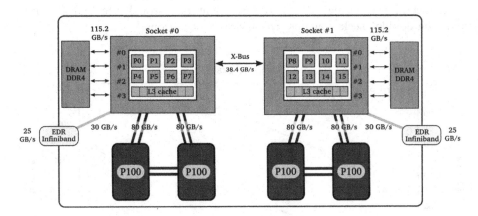

Fig. 1. Sketch of the main buses and links interconnecting the main computational and memory components of a DAVIDE compute node.

The architecture of DAVIDE tightly couples the two GPUs of each processor between themselves and to their host processor, but on the other side offers a looser connectivity between GPUs attached to different CPUs. This because it has been designed to meet the computing and data transfer requirements of data-analytics applications. From this point of view, see Fig. 1, a single DAVIDE node may be considered as made up of two distinct symmetrical units connected via the intra-node X-Bus offering a peak transfer bandwidth very close to that of the InfiniBand extra-node links.

4   Performance Analysis of OpenStaPLE

In this section we analyze the performance of the Dirac operator on DAVIDE, using two different lattice sizes, and compare with results we have measured on COKA [16], an earlier GPU-based cluster with a peak performance of $\approx$100 TFLOPs. In that cluster, each compute node hosts 2× Mellanox ConnectX-3 Single FDR 56 Gb/s Infiniband cards, 2× Intel Xeon E5-2630v3 CPUs and 8× NVIDA K80 dual-GPU boards (4 boards connected to each CPU socket). Each K80 board hosts 2× GK210 GPUs, so there are 16 independent CUDA devices for each compute node.

For both DAVIDE and COKA, communications between GPUs attached to the same CPU socket use the NVIDIA Peer-to-Peer technology, while GPUs on different nodes exploit GPUDirect feature implemented by NVIDIA and Mellanox drivers.

The lattice is assigned to several nodes, slicing one of the four lattice dimensions among different GPUs. We measure the execution time using an increasing number of GPUs, and analyze the aggregate computing and memory performance. For the aggregate computing performance of the Dirac operator we estimate ≈ 1560 double-precision floating-point operations per lattice site, measured experimentally accessing GPU hardware counters (through the PGI Profiler) and then double checked against theoretical expectations.

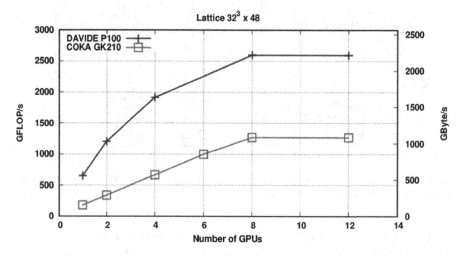

Fig. 2. Aggregate GFLOP/s and Bandwidth, showing the *Strong Scaling* behavior of the Dirac Operator implementation of OpenStaPLE, running respectively on the GK210 GPUs of COKA and on the P100 GPUs of DAVIDE. One COKA K80 board contains two GK210 GPUs.

In Fig. 2 we show the performance using a lattice size of $32^3 \times 48$. For both clusters the computing peak is achieved using 8 GPUs, but on DAVIDE the aggregate performance is approximately $2\times$ larger, that is a peak of approximately 2.6 TFlops. For both cases, running with more GPUs does not improve performance since execution time becomes dominated by communication time.

As the evaluation of the Dirac operator is memory-intensive, we expect that on a P100 GPU the performance should be approximately $3\times$ better compared to a GK210 GPU, since memory bandwidth is $3\times$ larger. This is true when running on a single GPU, but it reduces to $\approx 2.3\times$ when using 8 GPUs. This is also evident from Fig. 2 showing that the DAVIDE performance already departs from linearity when going from 2 to 4 and again from 4 to 8 GPUs. This is different from the COKA cluster where performance scales linearly up to 8 GPUs.

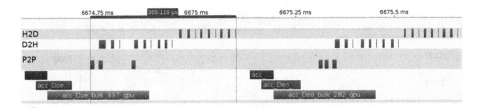

Fig. 3. NVIDIA Profiler View of the computing kernels and communications performed on one P100 GPU while computing one iteration of the Dirac operator. The $32^3 \times 48$ lattice has been divided across the 4 GPUs contained in one DAVIDE node. Purple-blue colored: execution of D_{eo} and D_{oe} on the borders of the lattice; turquoise colored: execution of D_{eo} and D_{oe} operations on the bulk of the lattice; gold colored: communication steps, as seen from the GPUs.

In Fig. 3 we profile the execution of the Dirac operator running on 4 P100 GPUs, using the NVIDIA profiler. As we see two distinct communication patterns occur:

1. the first two communications rows, marked as H2D (Host to Device) and D2H (Device to Host), trace data exchange between GPUs attached to different CPUs performed through the inter-socket communications X-Bus;
2. the third row, marked as P2P (Peer-to-Peer), traces communications between GPUs attached via NVLink.

As easily seen, communication of halo data does not overlap with the computation performed on the bulk (marked in turquoise), because communications via X-Bus are much slower. Conversely, on the COKA cluster, 8 GPUs – corresponding to 4 dual-GPU boards – are connected to the same processor, and communications between them occur through NVIDIA Peer-to-Peer memory transfers, without involving the CPU, and exploiting a large fraction of the PCIe bandwidth. Data exchange between 2 GPUs connected to different CPUs, for the lattice sizes shown in Figs. 2 and 3, has a measured bandwidth of ≈ 5 GB/s. This is more than 7× lower then the peak bandwidth of the X-Bus. Similar bandwidth issues in the inter-socket link have been reported for different architectures, such as in the Intel QPI bus, for the case of a linear algebra library [33] designed for deep-learning applications and meant to be highly scalable on GPU based clusters.

Scaling on more GPUs and nodes on DAVIDE is in principle possible using a larger lattice size, as long as communications are hidden by computation. For this reason we now consider a lattice size of $48^3 \times 96$, still of interest for physics simulations, and measure the Dirac operator performance. In this case, since the amount of memory available on P100 GPUs is 16 GB, we need at least 8 GPUs to host this lattice. As we see in Fig. 4 with 8 GPUs we measure a performance exactly 8 times larger than the one measured with just one GPU on the smaller lattice (see Fig. 2).

Adding more GPUs increases performance, but does not translate into linear speedup. This is again due to communication time becoming predominant with

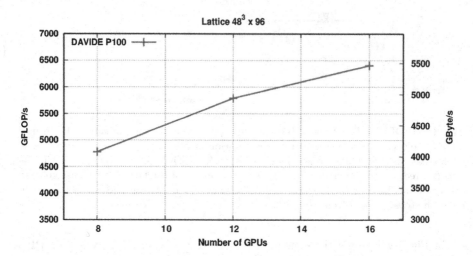

Fig. 4. Aggregate GFLOP/s and Bandwidth, showing the *Strong Scaling* behavior of the Dirac Operator implementation of OpenStaPLE, running the P100 GPUs of DAVIDE.

(a) GPU #0 communicating via InfiniBand (upper H2D and D2H) and via NVLink (lower left P2P).

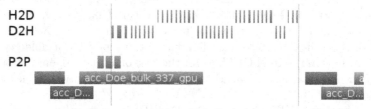

(b) GPU #2 communicating via X-Bus (upper H2D and D2H) and via NVLink (lower left P2P).

Fig. 5. NVIDIA Profiler View of the computing kernels and communications performed on two P100 GPUs while computing one iteration of the Dirac operator. The $48^3 \times 96$ lattice has been divided across the 16 GPUs contained in 4 DAVIDE nodes. In a the profiler view of a GPU communicating through NVLink with a local GPU and through InfiniBand with a remote GPU on another node. In b the profiler view of a GPU communicating through NVLink with a local GPU and through X-Bus with a local GPU connected to the remote socket.

respect to computation time, and can be clearly seen from the profiler view of Fig. 5. Here, we also see the differences in terms of bandwidth between the X-Bus and IB communications. For the X-Bus we measure ≈ 5 GB/s, while for the IB link we measure $\approx 6/8$ GB/s, with an high variability between different iterations.

To better understand the issues related to the X-Bus communications, we measure the bandwidth between MPI processes bound to two different CPUs. This is described in detail in the next Section.

4.1 Benchmarking of Interconnects

In this Section we use the OSU (Ohio State University) Micro-Benchmarks (version 5.4), performing data exchanges with different possible communication components available in OpenMPI (we have used OpenMPI version 1.10.7) to asses the performance of the different interconnect paths for GPU communications. In OpenMPI several components (*i.e.* plugins) provide processes with different communication means, *e.g.* across different network types, with different software protocols or through shared memory if available. In our benchmarks we take into account mainly four different components: the *sm* (Shared Memory) component, the *vader* (Shared Memory) component, the *smcuda* (Shared Memory for CUDA) component and the *openib* (Open InfiniBand) component. Two processes bound respectively to the different CPU sockets, when using *sm* or *vader* communicates through the X-Bus; the same is true when using *smcuda*, but in this case GPU memory buffers are exchanged; on the other side, when using *openib*, processes exchange data only through the external InfiniBand network.

In Fig. 6 we show the bandwidth for different communication paths and protocols, and for different buffer sizes. As we clearly see, the two MPI processes reach at most 6 GB/s when communicating through the X-Bus, while using InfiniBand they almost reach the maximum theoretical bandwidth of 12.5 GB/s. A possible explanation for this behavior is that the X-Bus bandwidth is shared with the cache coherency mechanism, thus only a fraction of the full bandwidth is available for MPI communications. Moreover, two processes may not be enough to completely saturate the available bandwidth. In fact, in Fig. 7 we show that using more than two processes and the default shared memory component (*i.e.* *vader*), the achievable aggregate uni-directional bandwidth through the X-Bus can be much higher, although still lower than the peak theoretical value of 38.4 GB/s.

In this case almost 20 GB/s of aggregate unidirectional bandwidth can be reached through the X-Bus, showing that multiple processes are needed to better exploit this link bandwidth. Unfortunately in many lattice based simulations, and in general, in any application needing to communicate using a ring-topology, just one pair of processes need to exchange data through the inter-socket link.

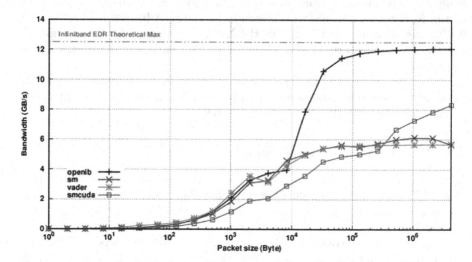

Fig. 6. Mono-directional bandwidth measured between 2 MPI processes binded respectively to the two different CPU sockets of DAVIDE for increasing packet size. Components *sm*, *vader* and *smcuda* exploit the X-Bus, while *openib* exploits the outer InfiniBand network. The maximum theoretical EDR InfiniBand bandwidth is also shown.

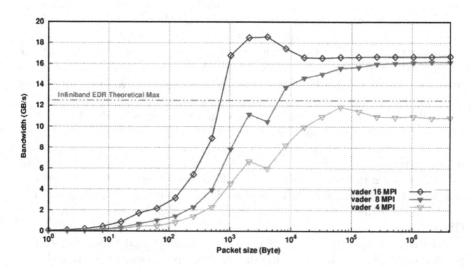

Fig. 7. Aggregate mono-directional bandwidth measured between MPI process pairs, binded respectively to the two different CPU sockets of DAVIDE, for increasing packet size. The *vader* component exploits the X-Bus. The maximum theoretical EDR InfiniBand bandwidth is also reported.

4.2   Energy Performance

DAVIDE has an innovative power monitoring system [34], integrated with the SLURM job scheduler. This allows users to query the system about power and energy related metrics of their jobs. The system actually samples the power drain of several components – CPUs, GPUs, PCIe lanes, etc. – with kHz resolution, saving power traces in a database. Users can query aggregate data, such as the average power drain of different hardware components during the execution of a job, and derive the corresponding energy consumption by the run integrating the average power drained over the job execution time.

Using this monitoring system, we have profiled the execution of the Dirac operator on a lattice of size $32^3 \times 48$. As a result of this we have found – for example – that running on one node with one GPU the total power drained is $\approx 680\,W$, of which $\approx 246\,W$ are drained by the GPUs (the one in use, plus the idle power consumption of the others). Conversely, running on 4 GPUs of one node, the power drained is $\approx 1150\,W$, corresponding to $1.7\times$ the power drained using only one GPU, of which $\approx 584\,W$ are accounted to the GPUs.

Power information can also be used to evaluate the best trade-off between the number of nodes to use for running an application and the energy necessary to operate such run. As an example, for a lattice of size $48^3 \times 96$, the computation of 10^5 applications of the Dirac operator on 3 nodes is approximately 7% more expensive compared to the energy necessary to run on just two nodes; this becomes 31% more expensive when running on 4 nodes. Consequently, running on 12 GPUs improves time-to-solution with a slight increase on energy-to-solution, compared to the case using just 8 GPUs. On the other hand, using 16 GPUs is not convenient from the energy-to-solution point of view, even if it still improves the computing performance.

This is because using 2 nodes, all 8 GPUs are fully busy for most of the execution time, and the average power drained by each of them is $\approx 157\,W$; while using 3 nodes, GPUs are idle for a portion of time (waiting for data exchanges), and their average power drain drops to $\approx 132\,W$. Moreover, using 4 nodes, the average power drain per GPU became $109\,W$, since they are idle for a larger amount of time, see Fig. 5.

In summary, a trade-off between the additional power drained due to the increasing number of GPUs adopted, and the reduction in the execution time can be found out. In fact, for example, comparing the runs with 2 and 3 nodes, the execution time decreases by $\approx 18\%$, balancing the increase of 20% of the power drained; while using 4 nodes, the execution time decreases by $\approx 26\%$, but the total power increases by 36%, rising up the energy-to-solution.

5   Conclusions and Future Prospects

In this contribution we have measured the performance of the recently developed DAVIDE machine using the OpenStaPLE Lattice QCD code written using the OpenACC programming framework.

We have successfully run our code on the P100 GPU boards of DAVIDE, and the performances measured on one GPU are 3× better compared to the performance we have measured on the NVIDIA GK210 – the previous generation of NVIDIA GPUs – perfectly in line with the corresponding technological improvement.

Running on several GPUs results are somewhat different. Using 4 GPUs of one node the speed-up is quite good (approximately 3×), while running on more nodes the performance quickly drops and does not improve anymore using more GPUs. In fact, for a better scaling of our code on this machine, we would need either to increase the size of bulk computation per GPU, or a faster inter-socket communication link. However, bulk computation is limited by the size of the lattice that can be stored within the P100 GPU memory, and the bandwidth of X-Bus can not be fully exploited. Of course, in this situation, we may also consider to further improve the code, making it possible to tile the lattice in more dimensions. This for sure helps to scale the communication time, but as we have seen in other applications [35], tiling the lattice domain in many dimensions implies several additional issues: (i) a significantly more complex code structure, (ii) the size of communication chunks become smaller reducing the effective sustained bandwidth [36] of communication links, and not all communications may be overlapped with computation. As result of this, a multi-dimensional tiling allows to scale the execution increasing the number of processing nodes, but is not obvious that aggregate performance will scale as well.

In summary the combination of POWER8+ plus P100 GPUs gives a high level of computing performance, but the interconnecting links between sockets and nodes of this system quickly become a bottleneck for our code when scaling to a large number of GPUs. However, we believe that this is not a problem specific to DAVIDE, or related just to POWER8 machines, but is a more general problem related to most HPC systems (*e.g.* we measure similar results also on Intel based machines using QPI inter-socket links). Having NVLink interconnections between GPUs attached to the different CPU sockets, would allow to avoid using the inter-socket link for GPU to GPU communications, granting a much higher bandwidth with lower latencies, which would for sure increase our code scalability.

Energy consumption is increasingly becoming a major issue in operating HPC parallel systems, and computing centers are considering to charge the users not only for the execution time, but also for the energy consumption of their jobs. In view of this, it is important to have tools that allow users to monitor the power drained by their jobs and to optimize them also in terms of energy-to-solution, and not only in terms of time-to-solution. In this direction, DAVIDE offers a very powerful monitoring system that allow users to monitor the power drained by several components of the machine during the run of the application.

In the future, we plan to better investigate the energy aspects, trying to develop effective programming methodologies to reduce the energy cost of a given computation. We also plan to add more general tiling options to the OpenStaPLE code and to measure the corresponding performance and scalability properties.

Acknowledgements. We thank CINECA and E4 Computer Engineering for granting access to the DAVIDE cluster and for their support. We thank Università degli Studi di Ferrara and INFN Ferrara for granting access to the COKA cluster. This work has been developed in the framework of the COKA and COSA projects of INFN.

References

1. Bernard, C., et al.: Panel discussion on the cost of dynamical quarksimulations. Nucl. Phys. B-Proc. Suppl.**106-107**(Suppl. C), 199–205 (2002). https://doi.org/10.1016/S0920-5632(01)01664-4
2. Bilardi, G., Pietracaprina, A., Pucci, G., Schifano, F., Tripiccione, R.: The potential of on-chip multiprocessing for QCD machines. In: Bader, D.A., Parashar, M., Sridhar, V., Prasanna, V.K. (eds.) HiPC 2005. LNCS, vol. 3769, pp. 386–397. Springer, Heidelberg (2005). https://doi.org/10.1007/11602569_41
3. Albanese, M., et al.: The ape computer: an array processor optimized for lattice gauge theory simulations. Comput. Phys. Commun. **45**, 345–353 (1987). https://doi.org/10.1016/0010-4655(87)90172-X
4. Boyle, P., et al.: Overview of the QCDSP and QCDOC computers. IBM J. Res. Dev. **49**(2.3), 351–365 (2005). https://doi.org/10.1147/rd.492.0351
5. Belletti, F., et al.: Computing for LQCD: Ape NEXT. Comput. Sci. Eng. **8**(1), 50–61 (2006). https://doi.org/10.1109/MCSE.2006.4
6. Adiga, N.R., et al.: An overview of the BlueGene/L Supercomputer. In: ACM/IEEE 2002 Conference on Supercomputing, pp. 60–60, November 2002. https://doi.org/10.1109/SC.2002.10017
7. Goldrian, G., et al.: QPACE: quantum chromodynamics parallel computing on the cell broadband engine. Comput. Sci. Eng. **10**(6), 46–54 (2008). https://doi.org/10.1109/MCSE.2008.153
8. Haring, R., et al.: The IBM Blue Gene/Q Compute Chip. IEEE Micro **32**(2), 48–60 (2012). https://doi.org/10.1109/MM.2011.108
9. OpenACC.org: OpenACC directives for accelerators. http://www.openacc-standard.org
10. OpenMP: The OpenMP API specification for parallel programming. http://www.openmp.org/
11. Blair, S., Albing, C., Grund, A., Jocksch, A.: Accelerating an MPI lattice boltzmann code using OpenACC. In: Proceedings of the Second Workshop on Accelerator Programming Using Directives, WACCPD 2015, pp. 3:1–3:9. ACM, New York (2015). https://doi.org/10.1145/2832105.2832111
12. Kraus, J., Schlottke, M., Adinetz, A., Pleiter, D.: Accelerating a C++ CFD code with OpenACC. In: 2014 First Workshop on Accelerator Programming using Directives (WACCPD), pp. 47–54 (2014). https://doi.org/10.1109/WACCPD.2014.11
13. Calore, E., Gabbana, A., Kraus, J., Schifano, S.F., Tripiccione, R.: Performance and portability of accelerated lattice Boltzmann applications with OpenACC. Concurr. Comput. Pract. Exp. **28**(12), 3485–3502 (2016). https://doi.org/10.1002/cpe.3862
14. Gupta, S., Majumdar, P.: Accelerating lattice QCD simulations with 2 flavours of staggered fermions on multiple GPUs using OpenACC - a first attempt arXiv:1710.09178, [hep-lat] (2017)
15. Bonati, C., et al.: Design and optimization of a portable LQCD Monte Carlo code using OpenACC. Int. J. Mod. Phys. C **28**(5) (2017). https://doi.org/10.1142/S0129183117500632

16. Bonati, C., et al.: Portable multi-node LQCD Monte Carlo simulations using OpenACC. Int. J. Mod. Phys. C **29**(1) (2018). https://doi.org/10.1142/S0129183118500109

17. Ahmad, W.A., et al.: Design of an energy aware petaflops class high performance cluster based on power architecture. In: 2017 IEEE International Parallel and Distributed Processing Symposium Workshops (IPDPSW), pp. 964–973, May 2017. https://doi.org/10.1109/IPDPSW.2017.22

18. Bonati, C., et al.: Roberge-Weiss endpoint and chiral symmetry restoration in $N_f = 2 + 1$. QCD arXiv:1807.02106, [hep-lat] (2018)

19. Bonati, C., Cossu, G., D'Elia, M., Incardona, P.: Qcd simulations with staggered fermions on gpus. Comput. Phys. Commun. **183**(4), 853–863 (2012). https://doi.org/10.1016/j.cpc.2011.12.011

20. Bonati, C., et al.: Development of scientific software for HPC architectures using OpenACC: the case of LQCD. In: The 2015 International Workshop on Software Engineering for High Performance Computing in Science (SE4HPCS), pp. 9–15. ICSE Companion Proceedings (2015). https://doi.org/10.1109/SE4HPCS.2015.9

21. Clark, M., Kennedy, A., Sroczynski, Z.: Exact 2+ 1 flavour RHMC simulations. arXiv hep-lat/0409133 (2004)

22. Clark, M., Kennedy, A.: Accelerating dynamical-fermion computations using the rational hybrid monte carlo algorithm with multiple pseudofermion fields. Phys. Rev. Lett. **98**(5), 051601 (2007)

23. Clark, M., Kennedy, A.: Accelerating staggered-fermion dynamics with the rational hybrid Monte Carlo algorithm. Phys. Rev. D **75**(1), 011502 (2007)

24. Duane, S., Kennedy, A.D., Pendleton, B.J., Roweth, D.: Hybrid Monte Carlo. Phys. Rev. D **195**(2), 216–222 (1987)

25. Kennedy, A.: Algorithms for dynamical fermions. arXiv hep-lat/0607038 (2006)

26. Jegerlehner, B.: Krylov space solvers for shifted linear systems. arXiv hep-lat/9612014 (1996)

27. Simoncini, V., Szyld, D.B.: Recent computational developments in krylov subspace methods for linear systems. Numer. Linear Algebr. Appl. **14**(1), 1–59 (2007)

28. Weisz, P.: Continuum limit improved lattice action for pure yang-mills theory (i). Nucl. Phys. B **212**(1), 1–17 (1983)

29. Curci, G., Menotti, P., Paffuti, G.: Symanzik's improved lagrangian for lattice gauge theory. Phys. Lett. B **130**(3–4), 205–208 (1983)

30. Adinetz, A.V., et al.: Performance evaluation of scientific applications on POWER8. In: Jarvis, S.A., Wright, S.A., Hammond, S.D. (eds.) PMBS 2014. LNCS, vol. 8966, pp. 24–45. Springer, Cham (2015). https://doi.org/10.1007/978-3-319-17248-4_2

31. Eshelman, E.: Comparing NVLink vs PCI-e with NVIDIA Tesla P100 GPUs onOpenPOWER servers, January 2017. https://www.microway.com/hpc-tech-tips/comparing-nvlink-vs-pci-e-nvidia-tesla-p100-gpus-openpower-servers/

32. Caldeira, A.B., Haug, V., Vetter, S.: IBM Power System S822LC for High Performance Computing Introduction and Technical Overview. IBM, October 2016

33. Eliuk, S., Upright, C., Skjellum, A.: dMath: Linear algebra for scaleoutGP-GPUs. In: 2016 IEEE 18th International Conference on High PerformanceComputing and Communications; IEEE 14th International Conference on SmartCity; IEEE 2nd International Conference on Data Science and Systems(HPCC/SmartCity/DSS), pp. 647–654, December 2016. https://doi.org/10.1109/HPCC-SmartCity-DSS.2016.0096

34. Beneventi, F., Bartolini, A., Cavazzoni, C., Benini, L.: Continuous learning of HPC infrastructure models using big data analytics and in-memory processing tools. In: Proceedings of the Conference on Design, Automation & Test in Europe, DATE 2017, pp. 1038–1043 (2017). https://doi.org/10.23919/DATE.2017.7927143
35. Calore, E., Marchi, D., Schifano, S.F., Tripiccione, R.: Optimizing communications in multi-GPU Lattice Boltzmann simulations. In: 2015 International Conference on High Performance Computing Simulation (HPCS), pp. 55–62, July 2015. https://doi.org/10.1109/HPCSim.2015.7237021
36. Calore, E., Gabbana, A., Kraus, J., Pellegrini, E., Schifano, S.F., Tripiccione, R.: Massively parallel lattice-Boltzmann codes on large GPU clusters. Parallel Comput. **58**, 1–24 (2016). https://doi.org/10.1016/j.parco.2016.08.005

Porting and Benchmarking of BWAKIT Pipeline on OpenPOWER Architecture

Nagarajan Kathiresan[1(✉)], Rashid Al-Ali[1], Puthen Jithesh[1],
Ganesan Narayanasamy[2], and Zaid Al-Ars[3]

[1] Biomedical Informatics, Research Division, Sidra Medicine, Doha, Qatar
{nkathiresan, ralali, pjithesh}@sidra.org
[2] OpenPOWER Leader in Education and Research, IBM India Ltd.,
Bangalore, India
ganesana@in.ibm.com
[3] Quantum and Computer Engineering, Delft University of Technology, Delft,
Netherlands
Z.Al-Ars@tudelft.nl

Abstract. Next Generation Sequencing (NGS) technology produces large volumes of genome data, which gets processed using various open source bioinformatics tools. The configuration and compilation of some bioinformatics tools (e.g. BWAKIT, root) is a challenging activity in its own right, not to mention the need to perform more elaborate porting activities for these applications on some architectures (e.g. IBM Power). The best practices of application porting should ensure (i) the semantics of the program or algorithm should not be changed, (ii) the output generated from the original source code and the modified source code (i.e., after porting) should be same even though the code is ported into different architectures and (iii) the output should be similar across different architectures after porting. Burrows-Wheeler Aligner (BWA) is the most popular genome mapping application used in the BWAKIT toolset. This BWAKIT provides pre-compiled binaries for x86_64 architecture and an end-to-end solution for genome mapping. In this paper, we show how to port various pre-built application binaries used in BWAKIT into OpenPOWER architecture and execute the BWAKIT pipeline successfully. Additionally, we demonstrate the validity of output results on OpenPOWER as well as present benchmarking results of BWAKIT applications that indicate the suitability of the highly multithreaded OpenPOWER architecture to execute these applications.

Keywords: BWAKIT · Genome mapping · Burrows-Wheeler Aligner
Parallelization · Scalability · Efficiency · POWER architecture

1 Introduction

The Burrows-Wheeler Aligner (BWA) [1] and Genome Analysis ToolKit (GATK) [2] are the two of the most widely used applications for next generation sequencing workflows. BWA is a popular genome alignment tool that contains three algorithms: BWA-backtrack, BWA-SW and BWA-MEM. These algorithms support (i) thread

© Springer Nature Switzerland AG 2018
R. Yokota et al. (Eds.): ISC 2018 Workshops, LNCS 11203, pp. 402–410, 2018.
https://doi.org/10.1007/978-3-030-02465-9_27

parallelization (ii) data-parallelization and (iii) data-parallel with concurrent execution [3]. The thread parallelization is controlled by the number of pthreads allocated by using -t #threads option. For the data-parallelization, the provided genome data is divided into small parts (called chunks) and distributed on a number of physical cores in the system using third-party tools (e.g. split) and execute multiple instance of BWA on every chunk of the genome data and merge the partial results in the same order of split data to get a final result [4]. Using the data-parallel approach with concurrent execution, the chunks of genome data are distributed to the available CPUs and execute the BWA on every chunk concurrently with number of "Cores per CPU" set to be the same as the available CPU threads. Finally, we merge the partial results in the same order of split data into the final result. In this paper, we will use the thread parallelization approach to run our experiments and measure the performance of the tools on a single server node.

2   BWAKIT Pipeline Implementation

DNA sequence mapping using BWAKIT has a couple of steps. First, the genome sequence data (stored in the form of FASTQ files) are mapped to a reference genome resulting into a file with the Sequence Alignment/Map (SAM) format or BAM (Binary version of SAM) format. Then, merging, sorting and marking the duplicates is carried out. BWAKIT provides an end-to-end pipeline solution for genome mapping using a set of predefined scripts. This BWAKIT pipeline scripts use 5 open-source applications: (i) SeqTK, (ii) Trimadap, (iii) BWA-MEM, (iv) Samblaster and (v) SAMtools that are executed one after the other in the fashion described in Fig. 1.

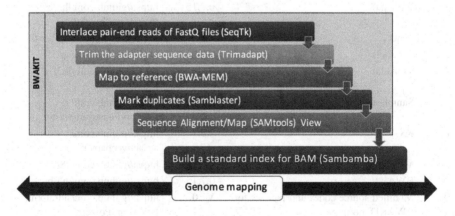

Fig. 1. BWAKIT pipeline

SAMtools is used for sequence alignment and mapping. Trimadap is used for trimming the adapter sequence from the FASTQ data. The latest version of the BWA algorithm is BWA-MEM, which provides fast and accurate alignment of genome sequence, supporting long-query and split-alignment. Samblaster helps in marking duplicates as removing duplicates is important to mitigate the effects of polymerase chain reaction (PCR) amplification, and reducing the number of reads to be processed during variant discovery.

In addition to the applications shown in Fig. 1, BWAKIT uses the following third-party libraries: K8 which is a Javascript shell library and Google V8 Javascript engine library. These libraries are linked during compilation of the BWAKIT source code, and are pre-requisite to execute the BWAKIT run-script. However, they are not part of the BWAKIT workflow steps.

In order to execute the BWAKIT pipeline on the OpenPOWER architecture, these open-source applications need to be ported appropriately.

BWAKIT provides a mapping script that can be executed as follows:

```
bwa.kit/run-bwamem -o out -H hs38DH.fa read1.fq \
read2.fq | sh
```

where, the run-bwamem is the bash script, which provides an end-to-end pipeline solution for genome mapping. Moreover, the various operations like merging, sorting and marking the duplicates described in Fig. 1 during the genome mapping are automated in the run-bwamem script.

In Table 1, we list the genome applications/tools needed for this BWAKIT porting on OpenPOWER architectures.

Table 1. Genome applications/tools to be ported

# No.	Genome application/tools	Version	Download link
1	BWAKIT	0.7.15	https://github.com/lh3/bwa/tree/master/bwakit
2.	Seqtk	1.2	https://github.com/lh3/seqtk
3.	Samtools	1.3	http://www.htslib.org
4.	Trimadap	0.1	https://github.com/lh3/trimadap
5.	Samblaster	0.1.23	https://github.com/GregoryFaust/samblaster
6.	K8	0.2.3-r67	https://github.com/attractivechaos/k8
7.	V8	3.14.5.9	https://github.com/v8/v8
8.	BWA	0.7.15	https://github.com/lh3/bwa
9.	Modified source codes and patches for BWAKIT porting	V1.0	https://github.com/sidratools/BWA_in_Power8

The source codes of the applications are downloaded from the above link and modified into OpenPOWER architecture standards. The step-by-step instructions are available in https://github.com/sidratools/BWA_in_Power8.

3 Experimental Benchmarking Setup

In this section we describe the experimental setup we used to benchmark our BWAKIT pipeline. First, we present the dataset used and then we describe the system architecture.

Dataset:

1. **Reference genome:** The Human genome reference build hs37d5.fa is used and can be downloaded from 1000 genome project:

   ```
   ftp://ftp.1000genomes.ebi.ac.uk/vol1/ftp/technical/reference/pha
   se2_reference_assembly_sequence/hs37d5.fa.gz
   ```

2. **Genome dataset for benchmarking:** The GCAT (Genome Comparison & Analytics Testing) provides benchmarking genomic datasets [6]. We used datasets (gcat set 041) that are 100–150 bp, paired-end and large INDELs. These datasets are used to validate and optimize the OpenPOWER system.

System Architecture:

The used system is the IBM 8247 is a Power Sy stemS824L. This server (8247-42L) supports two processor sockets, offering 20-core 3.42 GHz configurations in a 19-inch rack-mount, 4U (EIA units) drawer configuration. All the cores are active. The Power S824L server supports a maximum of 16 DDR3 CDIMM slots. Memory supported are 32 GB, and 64 GB and run at speeds of 1600 Mbps, allowing for a maximum system memory of 1024 GB. This IBM S824L server supports little endian OS Ubuntu 15.04 and Big endian with PowerVM installed for RHEL 6.6 and RHEL 7.1. However, for our benchmarking experiment, we used RHEL 7.1 (kernel 3.10.0) and compiler GNU 4.8.3. The complete summary of the benchmarked POWER system configuration is shown in Table 2.

Table 2. OpenPOWER system architecture details

Processor	0 - 159
CPU	POWER8E (raw), altivec supported
clock	2061.000000 MHz
Revision	2.1 (pvr 004b 0201)
Timebase	512000000
Platform	PowerNV
Model	8247-42L
Machine	PowerNV 8247-42L
Firmware	OPAL v3

4   Benchmarking Methodology

To generate BWA index for the reference human genome data.

```
time -p ~/bwa.kit/bwa index -p ~/ref/hs37d5.fa ~/ref/hs37d5.fa
```

To genome mapping using multi-Processors:

We provided the below sample script to run the BWA mapping on multiple processors. To execute the scalability of benchmarking experiment, the NO_CORES=<#> will be changed and the BWA mapping is executed on multi-processors.

```
export LC_ALL=en_US.UTF-8
export BWAKIT=/home/nkathiresan/bwa.kit
export NO_CORES=160
export prefix=gcat_set_041
export BAMDIR=/home/nkathiresan/test
mkdir -p ${BAMDIR}/${prefix}
export REF=/home/nkathiresan/ref/hs37d5.fa
export INDIR=/home/nkathiresan/input/gcat_set_041
#CMD="$BWAKIT/run-bwamem -t${NO_CORES} -R
\"@RG\tID:${prefix}\tLB:${prefix}\tSM:${prefix}\tPL:ILLUMINA\" -
aHds -o out $REF ${INDIR}/${prefix}_1.fastq
${INDIR}/${prefix}_2.fastq ; "
CMD="$BWAKIT/run-bwamem -t${NO_CORES} -R
\"@RG\tID:${prefix}\tLB:${prefix}\tSM:${prefix}\tPL:ILLUMINA\" -
${BAMDIR}/${prefix} $REF ${INDIR}/${prefix}_1.fastq.gz
${INDIR}/${prefix}_2.fastq.gz ; "
echo ${CMD} > runme.sh
chmod +x runme.sh
time -p ./runme.sh | sh ;
```

The POWER system provides the simultaneous multi-threading (SMT) option for better performance. The processor refers the execution unit and it's represented as "Core". We benchmarked the scalability numbers with Core = 1, 10 (Number of sockets = 1) and 20 (Number of sockets = 2). Additionally, the scalability benchmarking is extended to simultaneous multi-threading options (SMT = 2, 4 and 8), where Cores = 40 (SMT = 2 is enabled), Cores = 80 (SMT = 4 is enabled) and Cores = 160 (SMT = 8 is enabled) for BWA multi-threads experiments on logical cores of POWER system.

5   Performance Metrics Used for Benchmarking

In this section, we will present an evaluation of the performance of the ported algorithms, and show how they are particularly suited to benefit from the high number of threads available on OpenPOWER systems. The performance metrics used in this section are defined as follows [5].

Application execution time (Run time): The run time is defined as the time that elapses from the moment that an application execution on parallel computation starts to the moment that the last processor finishes execution. The execution times are classified into two:

Table 3. Execution time (E), Speedup (S) and Efficiency (E) for BWAKIT on OpenPOWER architecture

# Cores	Exec. time (in Min)	Speedup	Efficiency (in %)
1	134.99	1	100%
10	16.75	8	81%
20	9.35	14	72%
40	6.59	20	51%
80	5.37	25	31%
160	5.85	23	14%

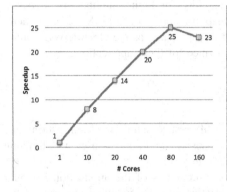 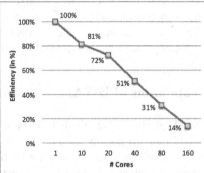

Fig. 2. BWAKIT speedup (left) and efficiency (right) on POWER architecture using the input dataset gcat set 041

1. Serial execution time (Ts) using 1 core (1 threaded)
2. Parallel execution time (Tp) using p number of cores (p-threads).

Speedup (S): The speedup is defined as the ratio of the serial execution time of the best sequential algorithm for solving a problem to the time taken by the parallel algorithm to solve the same problem on p processors.

$$S = \frac{T_s}{T_p}$$

Efficiency (E): The efficiency is defined as the ratio of speedup to the number of processors. Efficiency measures the fraction of time for which a processor is usefully utilized.

$$E = \frac{T_s}{p \, x \, T_p}$$

The BWAKIT execution time, speedup and efficiency are summarized in Table 3 and Fig. 2. We observed that the scalability is close to linear for smaller number of cores (Cores = 10 and Cores = 20), but continues to increase as a slower rate when increasing the number of cores (Cores = 80 and Cores = 160). This can be attributed to the fact that the system used has 20 physical cores, each of which providing an exceptionally high number 8 simultaneous multithreads, with a total number of threads of up to 160. For most high-performance computing applications, the speedup would normally flatten when the number of threads equal the number of physical cores, resulting in little performance advantage for more than 20 threads. However, BWA uses a large index data structure of the reference genome with a size of up to 6 GB, which does not fit in the cache of the processor. This index needs to be repeatedly accessed at various locations, with little special locality. This results in heavy cache miss penalty that causes many idle processor cycles, which in turn makes multi-threading exceptionally effective for this application. This behavior was also observed in the Intel architecture. This effective scalability for higher number of threads is exhibited by most bioinformatics genome mapping applications [7, 8, 12–14]. Therefore, systems providing a higher number of threads (such as the OpenPOWER architecture) can provide better scalability performance for these applications.

6   Validation of BWAKIT Results

BWAKIT produces the aligned BAM files after successful execution. During the BWAKIT pipeline porting, couple of source codes are modified and used with different APIs. The modified source codes are available in [10].

These modifications should not affect the semantics of the application behavior because of (i) the architecture specific instruction sets are included (ii) architecture specific vectorization (Example: IBM Power Vector Intrinsic Functions for vectorization of 128 bit [11]) is called during the execution. Hence, we verified the aligned

Table 4. Validation of aligned BAM generated on x86_64 and OpenPOWER architectures.

```
On x86_64                                    On Power8
Number of records read = 7963505             Number of records read = 7963505
Number of valid records = 7963505            Number of valid records = 7963505

TotalReads(e6)   7.96                         TotalReads(e6) 7.96
MappedReads(e6)  7.88                         MappedReads(e6)      7.88
PairedReads(e6)  7.96                         PairedReads(e6)      7.96
ProperPair(e6)   7.88                         ProperPair(e6) 7.88
DuplicateReads(e6)       0.00                 DuplicateReads(e6) 0.00
QCFailureReads(e6)       0.00                 QCFailureReads(e6) 0.00

MappingRate(%)   98.94                        MappingRate(%) 98.94
PairedReads(%)   100.00                       PairedReads(%) 100.00
ProperPair(%)    98.94                        ProperPair(%) 98.94
DupRate(%)       0.02                         DupRate(%)     0.00
QCFailRate(%)    0.00                         QCFailRate(%)  0.00

TotalBases(e6)   1194.53                      TotalBases(e6) 1194.53
BasesInMappedReads(e6)   1181.87             BasesInMappedReads(e6)      1181.87
Returning: 0 (SUCCESS)                        Returning: 0 (SUCCESS)
```

BAM files using BamUtil tools [9] across x86_64 and POWER architecture. The results show that the aligned BAM generated on the OpenPOWER architecture is the same as x86_64 architecture. The summary of BamUtil results is shown in Table 4.

7 Conclusion

The BWAKIT source code was successfully ported into the OpenPOWER architecture. During this application porting, architecture specific vector intrinisic functions and instruction sets are used. This architecture specific tunings are important to reproduce the same output of original source code versus the modified code. Also, the execution time of the application was shown to improve on the generic code. Further, the validation of aligned BAM generated on x86_64 and OpenPOWER architectures are compared and the results are observed to be the same. Performance measurements show that BWA scales effectively with the available number of physical cores, and continues to scale for a higher number of threads due to high idle processor time the application exhibits. This allows the application to effectively use the high number of threads the OpenPOWER architecture provides.

Acknowledgement. The authors gratefully acknowledge the access that was provided to OpenPOWER hardware at Forschungszentrum Jülich Supercomputing Center. Special thanks goes to Dr. Dirk Pleiter and Dr. Marcus Richter, Jülich Supercomputing Center, Germany. Also, the authors would like to thank Mr. Jaideep Bajwa, Mr. Michael Dawson, and Dr. Yinhe Cheng for helping on V8, K8 and trimadap source code modifications for POWER architecture.

References

1. Li, H., Durbin, R.: Fast and accurate short read alignment with burrows–wheeler transform. Bioinformatics **25**(14), 1754–1760 (2009)
2. Broad Institute. GATK best practices for the NGS Pipeline (2016). https://goo.gl/mjdmU2. Accessed 19 Jan 2016
3. Kathiresan, N., Temanni, R., Al-Ali, R.: Performance improvement of BWA MEM algorithm using data-parallel with concurrent parallelization. In: International Conference on Parallel, Distributed and Grid Computing (PDGC), pp. 406–411. IEEE (2014)
4. Al-Ali, R., Kathiresan, N., El Anbari, M., Schendel, E., Zaid, A.: Workflow optimization of performance and quality of service for bioinformatics application in high performance computing. J. Comput. Sci. **15**, 3–10 (2016)
5. Parallel Computing, Chapter 7 Performance and Scalability. https://www.cs.uky.edu/~jzhang/CS621/chapter7.pdf
6. Genome Comparison and analysis testing. standard genome data (2016). http://www.bioplanet.com/gcat. Accessed 19 Jan 2016
7. Kathiresan, N., Al-Ali, R.: Intelligent resource management system. U.S. Patent Application 15/194,052, filed December 28 2017 (2017)
8. Kathiresan, N., Temanni, R., Almabrazi, H., Syed, N., Jithesh, P.V., Al-Ali, R.: Accelerating next generation sequencing data analysis with system level optimizations. Sci. Rep. **7**(1), 9058 (2017)
9. BamUtil tools. https://github.com/statgen/bamUtil

10. BWAKIT porting source code. https://github.com/sidratools/BWA_in_Power8/tree/master/IBM
11. IBM Power Vector Intrinisic Functions version 1.0.4. https://github.com/vcflib/vcflib/blob/master/src/vec128int.h
12. Ahmed, N., Sima, V.M., Houtgast, E.J., Bertels, K.L.M., Al-Ars, Z.: Heterogeneous hardware/software acceleration of the BWA-MEM DNA alignment algorithm. In: International Conference on Computer Aided Design (ICCAD 2015) (2015)
13. Al-Ars, Z., Mushtaq, H.: Scalability potential of BWA DNA mapping algorithm on apache spark. In: International Symposium on Information Management and Big Data (SIMBig 2015) (2015)
14. Mushtaq, H., Al-Ars, H.: Cluster-based apache spark implementation of the GATK DNA analysis pipeline. In: IEEE Conference on Bioinformatics and Biomedicine (BIBM 2015) (2015)

Improving Performance and Energy Efficiency on OpenPower Systems Using Scalable Hardware-Software Co-design

Miloš Puzović[1], Vadim Elisseev[2]([✉]), Kirk Jordan[3], James Mcdonagh[2], Alexander Harrison[2], and Robert Sawko[2]

[1] The Hartree Centre, STFC Daresbury Laboratory, Sci-Tech Daresbury, Cheshire WA4 4AD, UK
milos.puzovic@stfc.ac.uk
[2] IBM Research, STFC Daresbury Laboratory, Sci-Tech Daresbury, Cheshire WA4 4AD, UK
vadim.v.elisseev@ibm.com,
{james.mcdonagh,alexander.harrison1,rsawko}@uk.ibm.com
[3] Data Centric Solutions, IBM T. J. Watson Research, 75 Binney Street, Cambridge, MA 02142, USA
kjordan@us.ibm.com

Abstract. Exascale level of High Performance Computing (HPC) implies performance under stringent power constraints. Achieving power consumption targets for HPC systems requires hardware-software co-design to manage static and dynamic power consumption. We present extensions to the open source Global Extensible Open Power Manager (GEOPM) framework, which allows for rapid prototyping of various power and performance optimization strategies for exascale workloads. We have ported GEOPM to OpenPower® architecture and have used our modifications to investigate performance and power consumption optimization strategies for real-world scientific applications.

Keywords: OpenPOWER · Energy efficiency
Performance optimization

1 Introduction

Upcoming High Performance Computing (HPC) systems are on the critical path towards delivering the highest level of performance for large scale applications. If contemporary technologies were used to build ever more powerful HPC systems, the power demand required by those systems would be unsustainable, as it would require hundreds of megawatts of power. Thus, current HPC systems must be built considering *energy efficiency* as one of the foremost design goals. In order to achieve a sustainable power draw, future HPC systems will have to feature a power efficiency of around 50 GFlops/Watt [1]. Such power efficiency

© Springer Nature Switzerland AG 2018
R. Yokota et al. (Eds.): ISC 2018 Workshops, LNCS 11203, pp. 411–417, 2018.
https://doi.org/10.1007/978-3-030-02465-9_28

levels require novel software/hardware co-design, with software guiding static and dynamic power management.

According to the Exasacle Computing Project, the most promising area for improving energy efficiency lies with applications optimizations [2]. Consequently, development of techniques and tools for energy consumption and performance optimizations of applications becomes very important [2,17,18]. Developers of such tools have to address a number of challenges such as dynamic behaviour of applications due to changing resources requirements, changing load on processors and accelerators over time, all of which lead to variable power consumption profiles. Additionally, tools have to be non intrusive, have minimum overhead, scalable, extensible and provide cross-architectural support.

One project, which tries to address the above challenges is Global Extensible Open Power Manager (GEOPM), an open source, scalable, plug-in extensible, runtime framework for energy management [7].

In this paper we present our ongoing work on porting GEOPM to Open-Power [10] architecture. We provide details of the port and discuss some preliminary results from using GEOPM with several scientific applications.

The rest of the paper is structured as follows: Sect. 2 provides details on porting GEOPM to OpenPower. Section 3 describes some preliminary results of using GEOPM with several real-world scientific applications. Finally, Sect. 4 presents conclusions and future directions of our work.

2   GEOPM on OpenPower

2.1   GEOPM Overview

GEOPM provides the following features: job level framework for in-band power management and optimization, on-the-fly monitoring of HW counters and application profiling, feedback-guided optimization of HW control knob settings, scalable via distributed tree-hierarchical design, extensible via plug-ins, supports MPI and OpenMP+MPI programming models. GEOPM features include automatic runtime job profiling, sampling of processor counters and correlating hardware activity to each OpenMP parallel region, automatic runtime rebalancing of power and performance among nodes to accelerate critical path nodes in MPI bulk-synchronous applications [7].

2.2   Measuring Power and Performance

GEOPM relies on system and hardware support for collecting performance and energy metrics. OpenPOWER architecture includes an On-Chip-Controller (OCC), which is responsible for Power/Thermal management [12]. The OCC reads total system power every 250 us and core temperature every 2 ms. There are two ways to obtain power and temperature information from the OCC [3]. The first one uses the Baseboard Management Controller(BMC) to communicate with the OCC and makes data available via Intelligent Platform Management Interface (IPMI) (in-band or out-of-band). In the second one, OCC is programmed to copy relevant sensors data from OCC SRAM to Main System memory at regular intervals. Sensors copied to main memory can be consumed via standard Linux interfaces like `perf`, `lm-sensors`, `sysfs`. The first method comes with typical latency of about 100 ms, while the second one with only 90 ns [3]. We used the second method, in-band sensors, to obtain power readings in GEOPM. We have built a firmware patch and an accompanying kernel module, which wrote sensors data to `/sys` file system [4]. We have used total system power as well as CPU and DRAM power metrics. Additionally, we have used `libpfm4` library [6] for collecting performance counters on CPUs and NVIDIA Management Library (NVML) [16] for collecting performance and energy metrics from GPUs.

2.3 Port

Figure 1 shows changes that we made to GEOPM. We have implemented two new classes: `OCCPlatform` and `PowerPlatformImp`. The `OCCPlatform` class is used to register OpenPower architecture with GEOPM runtime. In order to do this we detect at compile time that system used under GEOPM has OpenPower architecture and statically create an instance of the class when GEOPM starts. We have also added code to GEOPM to detect which variant of OpenPower architecture it is running on by reading special purpose register `0x11F` using instruction `mfspr`. Once the class `OCCPlatform` has been initialized it then uses `PowerPlatformImp` to obtain samples.

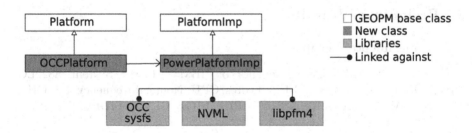

Fig. 1. Additional classes and libraries to support GEOPM on OpenPower

The `PowerPlatformImp` class uses three new library implementations to read data. The first library reads power consumption for cores and DRAM from OCC sensors using low latency in-band OCC sensors approach described above, which allowed us to obtain new sample every 30 ms. We have used this interval as a refresh rate. In addition to power consumption, this library also reads the frequency of each core from `sysfs`. The second library uses methods from NVML to obtain power consumption of each available GPU on the system. More specifically, it uses method `nvmlDeviceGetPowerUsage()`. The third and last library, reads performance counters using `perf_event`. This library obtains samples for number of instructions retired, number of cycles executed and memory

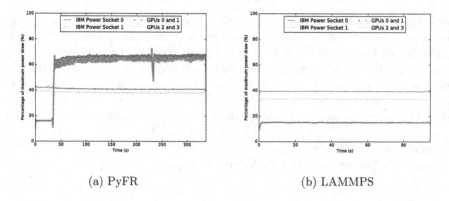

(a) PyFR   (b) LAMMPS

Fig. 2. Power consumption of CPUs and GPUs on a single node

load bandwidth (MLB) for processor. To find MLB we have used derived metrics, where we have summed data from remote (PM_DATA_FROM_RMEM) and local (PM_DATA_FROM_LMEM) memories multiplied by last level cache size and divided by wall clock time [14]. MLB metric helps to understand level of memory boundedness of an application.

The most recent implementation of GEOPM has introduced a new class IOGroup that acts as a plug-in for sampling different sensors. As a result, one of our next immediate steps, is to wrap three libraries into this new class.

3   Preliminary Results

3.1   Experimental Setup

We have conducted our experiments on IBM® Power System S822LC servers [13] (2 POWER8® CPU: 10 cores/CPU, Nominal frequency 4.23 GHz, 512 GB RAM, 4 NVIDIA Tesla P100 GPUs, 16 GB/GPU, NVIDIA NVLink).

3.2   Applications Profiles

We ran three different applications under GEOPM: Large-scale Atomic/ Molecular Massively Parallel Simulator (LAMMPS) [11], PyFR [5] and Livermore Unstructured Lagrangian Explicit Shock Hydrodynamics (LULESH) [8]. LAMMPS is a classical molecular dynamics code that can be used to model atoms. In our case we modelled all-atom rhodopsin protein that had 32,000 atoms for 10,000 steps. PyFR is a performance portable implementation for studying advection-diffusion type problems. Finally, LULESH is a mini-appl that solves the simple Sedov blast problem with analytic answers.

Figure 2 shows power consumption as percentage of maximum power per CPU and per GPU, when PyFR and LAMMPS are running on a single node. Both applications were launched with four MPI ranks with two ranks pinned to different cores on the first socket and other two ranks pinned to different cores on the second socket. All four GPUs are used by PyFR and LAMMPS, but from the Fig. 2, we can see that PyFR has higher GPU utilisation, which is reflected by power consumption. Furthermore, the GPU power consumption profile of PyFR is less steady, indicating that utilisation of GPUs is not as constant as in LAMMPS. Also, for both applications the first socket uses more power then the second socket and this is more noticeable in LAMMPS. The reason for such unbalance is the leakage current, which varies between chips due to defects in the manufacturing process. POWER8 firmware and hardware mitigates negative effects of these discrepancies by adjusting cores clock frequencies to maintain constant performance across sockets [12]. We plan to add frequency and current monitoring to GEOPM to be able to factor in effects of leakage into load balancing algorithms.

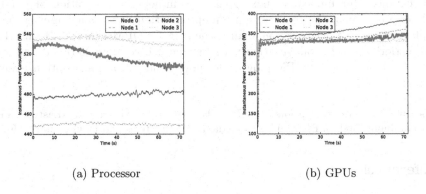

(a) Processor   (b) GPUs

Fig. 3. Power consumption when running LULESH across four nodes

Figure 3 shows power consumption when running LULESH across four nodes. Each node ran two MPI ranks, with each rank using a separate CPU socket and one GPU. This Figure illustrates that there is significant imbalance in power consumption between nodes. It is not so much the case between GPUs, but it is interesting to note that nodes with higher GPU power consumption also have lower CPU power consumption. This means that there is opportunity to distribute power between processor and GPUs to reduce execution wall clock time.

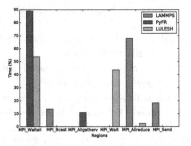

Fig. 4. Time spent in MPI regions

This is further illustrated by Fig. 4 that shows percentage of time spent in each MPI region out of wall clock time spent in MPI stack. For LULESH, the majority of MPI time is spent waiting in MPI_Wait. Therefore, there is potential to reduce waiting time by introducing more balanced execution across the nodes.

As described in next section this is active area of research that we are pursuing at the moment. Since time and energy spent in MPI regions for LULESH benchmark is around 5% of total execution we would expect to see noticeable savings, especially once the number of nodes for execution is increased since time spent in MPI regions will be increased. For comparison, in LAMMPS and PyFR time and energy spent in MPI regions is negligible (around 0.06%) as they are running on single nodes so any imbalance (such as one observed between sockets) is not noticeable.

4   Conclusions and Future Work

We have presented our on-going work on porting GEOPM framework onto Open-Power architecture. We have shown results of power profiling on some scientific applications. Our immediate next goals are: in-depth investigation of potential performance and power consumption optimizations for profiled applications, implementation of active power management in GEOPM using MSR-safe [15] and Variorium [9] in collaboration with Lawrence Livermore National Laboratory, development of GEOPM plug-ins for power and performance optimizations policies.

Acknowledgements. Authors would like to acknowledge J. Eastep and C. Cantalupo, Intel, S. Bhat and T. Rosedahl, IBM Systems and D. Graham, STFC.

References

1. Scientific Grand Challenges: Architectures and Technology for Extreme Scale Computing, San Diego, CA. U.S. Department of Energy, Office of Science, Washington, D.C., 8–10 December 2009
2. Ang, J.: The DOE exascale computing project: overview of relevant energy/power efforts. In: 8th Annual Workshop for Energy Efficient HPC Working Group at SC (2017)
3. Bhat, S.: Programming on-chip components to retrieve sensor data. In: Open-POWER Summit (2016)
4. Bhat, S.: Openpower based Inband OCC sensors (2017). https://github.com/shilpasri/-inband_sensors
5. Vermeire, B.C., et al.: On the utility of GPU accelerated high-order methods for unsteady flow simulations: a comparison with industry-standard tools. J. Comput. Phys. **334**, 497–521 (2017)
6. Eranian, S.: Perfmon2: a flexible performance monitoring interface for Linux. In: Proceedings of the Ottawa Linux Symposium (2006)
7. Eastep, J., et al.: Global extensible open power manager: a vehicle for HPC community collaboration on co-designed energy management solutions. In: ISC (2017)
8. Karlin, I., Keasler, J., Neely, R.: Lulesh 2.0 updates and changes. Technical report LLNL-TR-641973, August 2013
9. Labasan, S., et al.: Variorum: extensible framework for hardware monitoring and contol. In: E2SC at SC (2017)

10. OpenPower Foundation: Openpower technical resources. https://openpowerfoundation.org/technical/
11. Plimpton, S.: Fast parallel algorithms for short-range molecular dynamics. J. Comput. Phys. **117**, 1–19 (1995)
12. Rosedahl, T., et al.: Power/performance controlling techniques in OpenPOWER. In: ISC (2017)
13. IBM: IBM Power System S822LC (2018). https://www.ibm.com/us-en/marketplace/high-performance-computing
14. IBM: Parallel Performance Toolkit (2018). https://www.ibm.com/support/knowledgecenter/en/SSFK5S_2.3.0/com.ibm.cluster.pedev.v2r3.pedev100.doc/bl7ug_derivedmetricspower8.htm
15. LLNL: MSR-SAFE (2018). https://github.com/LLNL/msr-safe
16. NVIDIA: NVIDIA Management Library (2018). https://developer.nvidia.com/nvidia-management-library-nvml
17. READEX: READEX project (2017). https://www.readex.eu/
18. Ahmad, W., et al.: Design of an energy aware petaflops class high performance cluster based on power architecture. In: 2017 IEEE International Parallel and Distributed Processing Symposium Workshops, IPDPS Workshops 2017, Orlando/Buena Vista, FL, USA, 29 May–2 June 2017, pp. 964–973 (2017)

Porting DMRG++ Scientific Application to OpenPOWER

Arghya Chatterjee[1,3(✉)], Gonzalo Alvarez[2], Eduardo D'Azevedo[1],
Wael Elwasif[1], Oscar Hernandez[1], and Vivek Sarkar[3]

[1] Computer Science and Mathematics Division, Oak Ridge National Laboratory,
Oak Ridge, TN 37831, USA
{chatterjeea,dazevedoef,elwasif,oscar}@ornl.gov
[2] Computational Chemical and Material Sciences, Oak Ridge National Laboratory,
Oak Ridge, TN 38932, USA
alvarezcampg@ornl.gov
[3] School of Computer Science, Georgia Institute of Technology,
Atlanta, GA 30332, USA
{arghya,vsarkar}@gatech.edu

Abstract. With the rapidly changing microprocessor designs and architectural diversity (multi-cores, many-cores, accelerators) for the next generation HPC systems, scientific applications must adapt to the hardware, to exploit the different types of parallelism and resources available in the architecture. To get the benefit of all the in-node hardware threads, it is important to use a single programming model to map and coordinate the available work to the different heterogeneous execution units in the node (e.g., multi-core hardware threads (latency optimized), accelerators (bandwidth optimized), etc.).

Our goal is to show that we can manage the node complexity of these systems by using OpenMP for in-node parallelization by exploiting different "programming styles" supported by OpenMP 4.5 to program CPU cores and accelerators. Finding out the suitable programming-style (e.g., SPMD style, multi-level tasks, accelerator programming, nested parallelism, or a combination of these) using the latest features of OpenMP to maximize performance and achieve performance portability across heterogeneous and homogeneous systems is still an open research problem.

We developed a mini-application, Kronecker Product (KP), from the original DMRG++ application (*sparse matrix algebra*) computational

G. Alvarez—Author contribution consisted in explaining the DMRG algorithm and its implementation, and not in the OpenMP use and evaluation.

This manuscript has been co-authored by UT-Battelle, LLC, under contract DE-AC05-00OR22725 with the US Department of Energy (DOE). The US government retains and the publisher, by accepting the article for publication, acknowledges that the US government retains a nonexclusive, paid-up, irrevocable, worldwide license to publish or reproduce the published form of this manuscript, or allow others to do so, for US government purposes. DOE will provide public access to these results of federally sponsored research in accordance with the DOE (http://energy.gov/downloads/doe-public-access-plan).

© Springer Nature Switzerland AG 2018
R. Yokota et al. (Eds.): ISC 2018 Workshops, LNCS 11203, pp. 418–431, 2018.
https://doi.org/10.1007/978-3-030-02465-9_29

motif to experiment with different OpenMP programming styles on an OpenPOWER architecture and present their results in this paper.

Keywords: Power8 · OpenMP · OpenMP 4.5 · Nested parallelism Task parallelism · Data parallelism

1   Introduction

Our goal is to learn how to experiment with OpenMP for in-node parallelization incrementally by exploiting different "programming styles" supported by OpenMP 4.5 to program CPU cores and accelerators available in the OpenPOWER architecture. The heterogeneous architectures on these systems provide different types of parallelism, data locality and memory management, which is an added level of complexity when addressing an efficient use of an architecture. Mapping work efficiently onto the execution units (e.g. GPU, team of threads) while hiding data access latencies, data movement, synchronization points (e.g. across devices, etc.) requires asynchronous programming with multiple levels of parallelism and different "types" of parallelism. Expressing all of this, with a single programing model like OpenMP using a single programming style, is a challenge.

We explore ways to program the OpenPOWER architecture using an incremental approach where we can first express the different types of parallelism and map them first to the CPU cores and then to the accelerators. How to write performance portable code across multiple architectures (heterogeneous and homogeneous), is still an open research problem. A given solution of programming style may be specific to the application algorithm or computational motif. We first find ways to express multi-level parallelism using an OpenMP programming style while minimizing significant changes to the code and incrementally porting the application on-to accelerators.

To accomplish this, we have developed a mini-application, Kronecker Product (KP), from the original DMRG++ application (*sparse matrix algebra* computational motif, developed at ORNL). This is one of the key computational kernel in DMRG which computes the lowest eigenvector by evaluating the matrix-vector product of the Hamiltonian operator, in an iterative method such as the Lanczos algorithm. The new KP formulation can lead to an order of magnitude reduction in memory compared to storing the operators as sparse matrices in compressed sparse row storage. Exploiting the property of Kronecker product and with adaptive conversion from sparse to dense matrix computations can lead to significant speedups on large problems. This KP formulation has been implemented in DMRG++. Numerical experiments using DMRG++ show the new KP formulation can lead to 15X speedup in some cases.

Our mini-application uses different types of parallelism that can be implemented via different OpenMP 4.5 constructs to express multi-level parallelism and map it to multi-core threads. This work-in-progress paper primarily focuses on porting the DMRG++ mini-application to the Power-8 processors, is a first step towards expressing and mapping all the available parallelism, that we can later map to accelerators.

2   Motivation

The increasing complexity and power in modern day high performance computing platforms has resulted in an explosive growth in available hardware threads of execution to be exploited by application codes. It is expected that the upcoming Exascale platforms will provide O(1 Billion) hardware execution threads [5,8,9]. Efficient exploitation of this massive parallelism presents a major challenge for programming models and application codes. Historically, the "MPI+X" methodology has been adopted as the de-facto standard for large scale distributed application. In this model, inter-node message passing based on the MPI [3,11] standard providing the foundation for Multiple Program Multiple Data (MPMD) *top level* programming model, while a separate programming model is used to exploit on-node hardware parallelism. Recent trends in HPC node design have resulted in the increased adoption of *fat nodes* where each node exposes a significant number of hardware threads [7,10], organized around complex and deep memory hierarchies. Efficient execution on such architectures require application codes to expose a significant level of parallelism, while simultaneously avoiding synchronous programming styles that rely on global on-node barriers which introduce significant overheads.

Increased node parallelism and the need to support more irregular algorithms have driven the programming model community to explore options beyond single level parallel constructs (exemplified by a variant of **parallel for** loop and/or SIMD data-parallel vector operations). Hierarchical or nested parallelism has emerged as a major focus for modern programming model development. Mapping multi-level parallel algorithm onto hierarchical or nested programming model constructs enable a more *natural* representation of the underlying algorithm, alleviating the requirement to artificially transform the algorithm into another formulation that better matches single level parallel programming models. This however requires careful implementation and/or introduction of resource management and load balancing primitives into the underlying programming model that increases its complexity. Another challenge involves *heterogeneous hierarchy* where different nested levels implement different parallelism constructs (e.g. a higher level irregular task-parallel invoking lower level data-parallel operations).

In this paper, we outline our experience optimizing the core computational kernel of the DMRG++ application on Power8 platform using different permutations of hierarchical parallel constructs of the OpenMP 4.5 standard. We investigate the performance of a mini-application designed to faithfully represent the multi-level parallelism of the underlying patched matrix vector multiplication kernel. The work illustrates several challenges in using hierarchical parallelism in OpenMP under load imbalance conditions and issues with mixing task and data parallelism (particularly when leveraging external libraries).

3   Density Matrix Renormalization Group

3.1   The Application

The density matrix renormalization group (DMRG) is the preferred method to study low-dimensional strongly correlated electrons. It was developed to overcome the problems arising in the application of the Numerical Renormalization Group (NRG) to quantum lattice many-body system. Strongly correlated materials are a wide class of materials that show unusual - often technologically useful - electronic and magnetic properties, such as metal- insulator transitions or half-metalicity. The term "correlated" refers to the way electrons behave in these materials, which precludes relying on simple one-electron approximations.

We have used DMRG++ (developed at the Oak Ridge National Lab), a fully developed application that uses a *sparse matrix algebra* computational motif for the simulation of Hubbard-like models and spin systems [1]. In this work, we present insights into the acceleration of the DMRG++ algorithm by making use of the inherent Kronecker Product (KP) structure of the problem. The compact storage property of Kronecker Product allows us to write efficient algorithms to compute matrix-products [12]. For example, if matrices A and B are $n \times n$ matrices, then the Kronecker product $C = A \otimes B$ is $n^2 \times n^2$. Moreover, computing matrix vector product $vec(Y) = C * vec(X)$ takes $O(n^4)$ operations if matrix C were used explicitly, but can be evaluated as $Y = B * X * At$ that requires only $O(n^3)$ operations.

As we explore the opportunity to port the DMRG++ application to Open-POWER, a mini-application capturing the core algorithmic and computational structure of the application (Kronecker Product) will serve as the foundation for the exascale-ready implementation of DMRG++. One goal of DMRG++ is to compute the lowest eigenvalue λ (which is related to the "ground-state" energy of the system) and the eigenvector Ψ of the full Hamiltonian (H_{full}) with N sites

$$H_{\text{full}}\Psi = \lambda\Psi, \text{ or } \lambda = \text{minimize}_{v \neq 0} \frac{v' H_{\text{full}} v}{v'v} \tag{1}$$

where the unit norm vector attaining the minimum value of Rayleigh quotient λ is eigenvector Ψ. Because the full Hamiltonian matrix is conceptually a very large $4^N \times 4^N$ matrix, we can only approximate this within a limited subspace of M vectors. The DMRG++ algorithm is a systematic process to find this subspace of vectors that approximates well the lowest eigenvector. The algorithm partitions the sites on the 1D lattice into the left part (called "system") and the right part (called "environment").

The full Hamiltonian can then be written as Kronecker product of operators on left and right

$$H_{\text{full}} = H_L \otimes I_R + I_L \otimes H_R + \sum_{k=0}^{K} C_L^k \otimes C_R^k \tag{2}$$

where $H_L(H_R), I_L(I_R), C_L(C_R)$ are the Hamiltonian, identity, and interaction operators on the left (right).

By bringing DMRG++ to exascale, condensed matter theorists, will be able to solve problems such as correlated electron models of *ladder geometries* as opposed to just *chain geometries*, and *multi-orbital* models as opposed to just *one-orbital* models.

3.2 Baseline Performance Characteristics of the Application

The DMRG++ application[1] spends most of its computational time calculating the sparse matrix *Hamiltonian*. We profiled the existing implementation to identify the performance bottlenecks and use this as a baseline for comparison with the implementation of our novel algorithm. We modified the original Pthreads version of DMRG++ to use OpenMP to help us quantify load imbalances.

We used this version to measure the time spent in the parallel regions and on each individual task, in-order to quantify useful work versus time spent on synchronizations as a result of load imbalances, task creation, or parallel region creation overheads.

We observed that 80% of the time was spent on the OpenMP parallel region responsible for calculating the sparse matrix *Hamiltonian*, when using eight threads on a Bulldozer AMD Opteron processor (Titan node). As seen in Fig. 1 there is a significant load imbalance across the different phases, executed by the threads for the different instances of the parallel region. The application runs in phases, and due to the dynamic nature of the problem as the application progresses the Hamiltonian matrix grows in size, and the load imbalance problem gets worse over time.

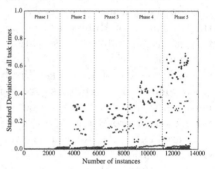

Fig. 1. Standard deviation of all execution times per parallel region instance over time. As the application progresses over time these points become more disperse. Execution uses 8 threads on a single TITAN node (8 blue dots per instance). (Color figure online)

These preliminary profiling results suggest that an asynchronous *task-based execution* model that leverages *multi-level parallelism* as exposed by the new algorithm for Kronecker Product (KP) using the latest OpenMP 4.5 constructs (see, Algorithm 1) is important to address the load imbalances by breaking down the computational workload into smaller and more uniform units of work.

---

[1] DMRG++ is used as a convergence algorithm to compute the lowest *eigenvector* by evaluating the matrix vector product of the Hamiltonian operator in an iterative method (Lanczos algorithm).

3.3 Hamiltonian Matrix

The key computational kernel in DMRG++ for computing the lowest eigenvector is the evaluation of matrix-vector product of the Hamiltonian matrix (H_{full}) in an iterative method such as the Lanczos algorithm. The Kronecker Product formulation expresses the Hamiltonian matrix as sum of smaller KP matrices.

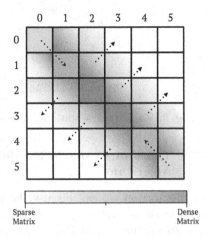

The H_{full} has a special property that it "conserves" quantum number such that H_{full} matrix can reordered (or permuted) to consist of diagonal blocks. Each diagonal block is associated with a particular $(M_\uparrow, M_\downarrow)$ quantum number.

Due to the special block diagonal structure of H_{full}, the eigen-decomposition of the full system can be obtained by separately computing the eigen-decomposition of each diagonal block. Moreover, the lowest eigen-pair will be attained at one of the diagonal

Fig. 2. Each cell is made up of smaller matrices with different sparsity/density. The arrows show how the sparsity/density, increases/decreases.

blocks. For many systems, the diagonal block associated with $(M_\uparrow = N/2, M_\downarrow = N/2)$ at "half-filling" is of special interest and commonly contains the lowest eigen-pair. The use of $(M_\uparrow = N/2, M_\downarrow = N/2)$ will be assumed in the rest of the paper and the corresponding diagonal block is called H_{target}.

The two-dimensional block diagonal Hamiltonian matrix is made up of smaller operators (matrices) that are of varying weights (density). This matrix is the primary workload for our Kronecker Product application. The sparsity/density of the matrix contributes to our data layout challenges that we must overcome and the types of parallelism we can use to exploit the underlying hardware. As shown in Fig. 2, the cells get denser as we traverse towards the center of the 2-D matrix, and the sparsity of the cell increases as we traverse away from the primary diagonal.

3.4 Pseudo Code: Apply Hamiltonian Target

In order to motivate this paper and show the need for multi-level parallelism, data- and task-level parallelism, in this section we summarize the algorithm (see Algorithm 1) that we use as our research vehicle. Figure 3 shows the structure of the data-layout and the computation to evaluate the Kronecker Product. We use this algorithm to show a use-case of a triple-nested loop that can benefit from using nested-parallelism or task-based parallelism without compromising the time-complexity due to the added synchronization overheads.

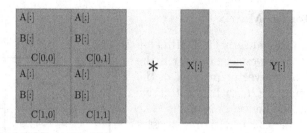

Fig. 3. Visual representation of the data layout and computation for Algorithm 1

3.5 Types of Available Parallelism in the Kronecker Product Algorithm

In this section we will discuss the potential of using two different parallelism techniques to exploit maximum benefits to the Kronecker Product algorithm (see Algorithm 1). Based on the growth aspect of the Hamiltonian matrix over time (as discussed in Sect. 3.2), the nature of the workload (as discussed in Sect. 3.3), and the dependencies between the cells in the Hamiltonian matrix, we believe, to gain the most out of the underlying hardware, we must use two different parallelism techniques in conjunction. We briefly discuss how each of these technique can benefit our algorithm.

- **Task Parallelism.** There exist no data dependencies between any of the adjacent cells in the two-dimensional Hamiltonian matrix. Each cell in the matrix can be viewed as an isolated task which computes the KP for that cell. As seen in Fig. 1, the work at each instance is sparse, to effectively use the underlying hardware threads, we must aggregate smaller workloads together. Since each task can be handled asynchronously, we can reduce the load-balancing challenges, there by reducing the sparsity of the work, per instance, of the Kronecker product.
- **Data Parallelism.** As seen in Fig. 2, the two-dimensional matrix is neither completely sparse nor dense. Just dividing the computation into a number tasks and allocating equal resources to each task will not be beneficial. Since each cell (or task) has a variable workload, we must use data parallelism with variable thread count (based on the work) in conjunction with task-parallelism.

The granularity of the amount of tasks to be created, and the variable thread count (resource allocation) per task, is of the prime importance and the key to getting maximum benefit of using machines with significant number of hardware threads on a single node.

Algorithm 1. Pseudo code to compute Kronecker multiplication

```
 1: procedure HTARGET(C[][], LPatch[], RPatch[], X[])
 2:     NPatches ← Size(C)
 3:     VSize ← PatchSize(LPatch, RPatch, NPatches)
 4:     for i ← 1, C.rows do
 5:         YI ← zeros(VSize[i])
 6:         for j ← 1, C.cols do
 7:             YIJ ← zeros(VSize[i])
 8:             ElemInC ← Size(C[i][j])
 9:             for k ← 1, ElemInC do
10:                 [MatA, MatB] ← GetMat(C[i][j], k)
11:                 YIJ[i] ← YIJ[i] + (MatA ⊗ MatB * X[])
12:             end for
13:             for l ← 1, VSize[i] do
14:                 YI[l] ← YI[l] + YIJ[l]
15:             end for
16:         end for
17:         for m ← 1, VSize[i] do
18:             Y[m] ← YI[m]
19:         end for
20:     end for
21:     return Y
22: end procedure
23:
24: procedure PatchSize(LPatch[], RPatch[], NPatches)
25:     for i ← 1, NPatches do
26:         LPatchRows ← LPatch[i]
27:         RPatchRows ← RPatch[i]
28:         VSize[i] ← LPatchRows * RPatchRows
29:     end for
30:     return VSize
31: end procedure
32:
33: procedure GETMAT(c, k)
34:     MatrixA ← c.A[k]
35:     MatrixB ← c.B[k]
36:     return MatrixA, MatrixB
37: end procedure
```

4   Problem Statement

OpenMP offers different ways to express multi-level parallelism and how this parallelism can be mapped to the architectures [2,4,6]. One of the approaches is to specify nested parallelism, which increases the number of threads available to the program, to exploit more parallelism, which can be used to break the amount of work to a hierarchy of teams of threads. The other approach is to decompose work into units of work that can be schedule to teams of threads.

Both approaches have pros and cons. Using OpenMP nested parallelism increases dynamically the number of threads available to an OpenMP program which is good for load balancing, but it comes at the cost of thread creation and data locality. Nested threads may be destroyed and re-created again. This is an expensive operation if the amount of work in the nested region is small compared to the thread creation overhead. It also affects data locality as different instances of the threads touches data, affecting implicit data placement.

Using tasking improves asynchronous execution, can more easily mapped to accelerators, and improves load balancing on the application. The challenge in using tasks is that OpenMP 4.5 does not support task reduction (which are being discussed to be included in OpenMP 5.0) on certain groups of tasks. Another challenge with the tasking approach is when tasks contain data parallel work (e.g. matrix multiplications) that maps better to OpenMP work-sharing directives (e.g. parallel loops). A given task may need different resources and this becomes a scheduling and nested parallelism challenge. Given these limitations in the OpenMP programming model, if we want to explore tasks, we have to use both tasks and nested parallelism to allow the synchronization among threads, to perform reductions among a group of threads.

5   Implementation and Experimental Evaluations

5.1   Experimental Setup

For our evaluation we used the OLCF's early access system, SummitDev, with each node running on a 2 10-core IBM POWER8 CPUs (IBM S822LC) with

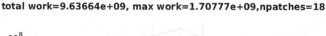

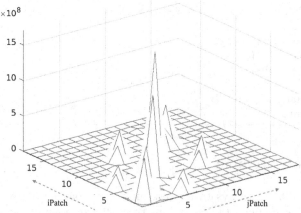

Fig. 4. Shows a three-dimensional line plot to show one of the workloads we have used for our evaluation, per cell in the Hamiltonian matrix (workload). x- and y- axes shows the matrix cells and the z-axis depicts the amount of work available per cell. One must note that the structure of the workload corresponds to the structure of the Hamiltonian matrix as discussed in Sect. 3.3.

each core supporting up-to 8 hardware threads with 256 GB DDR4 memory per node.

We tested our mini-application with different workloads, synthetically generated datasets that mimic the original structural complexity of the Hamiltonian Matrix. Figure 4 shows the distribution of work across the two dimensional matrix. The workload distribution stays the same for larger Hamiltonian matrices as well. For our evaluation purposes we have used only 20 threads (1 hardware thread per core) so that we don't oversubscribe. This setup yielded the best performance. We have used clang/clang++ compilers (version 4.0.0) for all our evaluations.

5.2 Pseudo Codes for Evaluation

For evaluation purposes we have used different parallelism styles with OpenMP constructs and IBM ESSL for the DGEMM operations in our Kronecker Product kernel (Algorithm 1). Some of the techniques used, are as follows:

Algorithm 2. Pseudo code for nested parallel work-sharing loops with OpenMP

1: **procedure** HTARGET(C[][], LPatch[], RPatch[], X[])
2:     $NPatches \leftarrow Size(C)$
3:     $VSize \leftarrow PatchSize(LPatch, RPatch, NPatches)$
4:     #pragma omp parallel num_threads(numZero)
5:                     proc_bind(levelZero)
6:     #pragma omp for schedule(dynamic,1)
7:     **for** $i \leftarrow 1, C.rows$ **do**
8:         #pragma omp parallel num_threads(numOne)
9:                         proc_bind(levelOne)
10:                         reduction(YI)
11:         #pragma omp for schedule(dynamic,1)
12:         **for** $j \leftarrow 1, C.cols$ **do**
13:             **for** $k \leftarrow 1, ElemInC$ **do**
14:                 $YIJ[i] \leftarrow YIJ[i] + (MatA \otimes MatB * X[])$
15:             **end for**
16:             **for** $l \leftarrow 1, VSize[i]$ **do**
17:                 $YI[l] \leftarrow YI[l] + YIJ[l]$
18:             **end for**
19:         **end for**
20:         **for** $m \leftarrow 1, VSize[i]$ **do**
21:             $Y[m] \leftarrow YI[m]$
22:         **end for**
23:     **end for**
24:     **return** Y
25: **end procedure**

5.2.1   Nested OpenMP Work-Sharing Loops (2 Levels)

Algorithm 2 shows the use of nested OpenMP work-sharing constructs in two levels. For the matrix multiplication we use the IBM ESSL (non-threaded) DGEMM kernel. For experimental evaluation we used up-to 20 hardware threads on a single node (using OMP_THREAD-_LIMIT set to 20) to account for, no over-subscription of threads, which might account for higher execution time. We have used OMP_PROC_BIND at each level of the parallel region to account for thread bindings. For all experimental results we have used *spread* for the outer region and *close* for the inner region.

5.2.2   Nested OpenMP Work-Sharing with Tasking

Algorithm 3 shows the use of the tasking constructs of OpenMP with the nested OpenMP parallel regions. Ideally, we would want to use nested tasks or OpenMP 4.5 taskloop construct to exploit the tasking model, but due to no current support of task-reductions, all reductions are being performed in the OpenMP par-

---

Algorithm 3. Pseudo code for tasking within OpenMP parallel regions

---

```
1: procedure HTARGET(C[][], LPatch[], RPatch[], X[])
2:     NPatches ← Size(C)
3:     VSize ← PatchSize(LPatch, RPatch, NPatches)
4:     #pragma omp parallel num_threads(numZero)
5:                          proc_bind(levelZero)
6:     for i ← 1, C.rows do
7:         #pragma omp single
8:         #pragma omp task
9:         YI ← zeros(VSize[i])
10:        #pragma omp parallel num_threads(numOne)
11:                             proc_bind(levelOne)
12:                             reduction(YI)
13:        for j ← 1, C.cols do
14:            #pragma omp single
15:            #pragma omp task
16:            for k ← 1, ElemInC do                        ▷ Data Parallel Loop
17:                YIJ[i] ← YIJ[i] + (MatA ⊗ MatB * X[])
18:            end for
19:        end for
20:        for l ← 1, VSize[i] do
21:            YI[l] ← YI[l] + YIJ[l]
22:        end for
23:        // End Parallel Region for j iteration
24:        for m ← 1, VSize[i] do
25:            Y[m] ← YI[m]
26:        end for
27:    end for
28:    return Y
29: end procedure
```

---

allel regions. Due to this restriction, and using OpenMP parallel regions with OpenMP tasks, we don't observe the complete benefits of using nested tasking. Future OpenMP constructs will support task-reductions and we plan to modify our code accordingly.

5.2.3 Threaded ESSL Without Any OpenMP Constructs

Algorithm 4 shows the use the IBM threaded ESSL version for computing the DGEMM operations. Since ESSL-smp with nested OpenMP is currently not supported (or undefined), we wrapped the DGEMM operation in a single OpenMP parallel region to control the thread count for the threaded ESSL. As seen in Fig. 4, since the work is not uniformly divided, calling a threaded ESSL for each cell in the Hamiltonian matrix creates a massive overhead. We do not observe any performance benefits of using the threaded ESSL version because it currently has no support for dynamically allocating the threads (number of threads used in the ESSL-smp must be defined using the OMP_NUM_THREADS environment variable during compile time).

5.3 Evaluation

Figure 5 shows the execution time of computing the Kronecker Product over the total number of OpenMP threads used in the calculation. The bar chart shows two bars, the blue bar corresponds to the version with nested OpenMP work-sharing loops (see pseudo code Algorithm 2), and the orange bar corresponds to

---

Algorithm 4. Pseudo code with BLAS (using multi-threaded IBM ESSL)

1: **procedure** HTARGET(C[][], LPatch[], RPatch[], X[])
2:     $NPatches \leftarrow Size(C)$
3:     $VSize \leftarrow PatchSize(LPatch, RPatch, NPatches)$
4:     #pragma omp parallel num_threads(numZero)
5:     **for** $i \leftarrow 1, C.rows$ **do**
6:         **for** $j \leftarrow 1, C.cols$ **do**
7:             **for** $k \leftarrow 1, ElemInC$ **do**   ▷ *Data Parallel Loop*
8:                 Using threaded ESSL (ESSL-smp)
9:                 $YIJ[i] \leftarrow$ DGEMM$(MatA, MatB, *X)$
10:            **end for**
11:        **end for**
12:        **for** $l \leftarrow 1, VSize[i]$ **do**
13:            *Custom reduction with accumulators*
14:            $YI[l] \leftarrow YI[l] + YIJ[l]$
15:        **end for**
16:        **for** $m \leftarrow 1, VSize[i]$ **do**
17:            $Y[m] \leftarrow YI[m]$
18:        **end for**
19:    **end for**
20:    **return** Y
21: **end procedure**

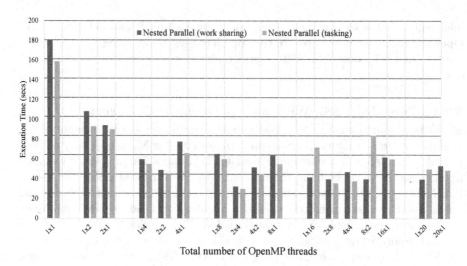

Fig. 5. Shows the execution time of computing the Kronecker product using two parallelism strategies as discussed in Sects. 5.2.1 and 5.2.2. The x-axis shows the total number of OpenMP threads used. Processor bindings for each execution is, spread for the outer region and close for the inner parallel region. Total number of threads in x-axis is shown by outer threads × inner threads. (Color figure online)

the version with nested OpenMP tasks (see pseudo code Algorithm 3). As discussed in the problem statement, challenges with using nested OpenMP tasks, is the lack of support of task-reductions across the group of threads. This forces us to use OpenMP Parallel regions to compute the reductions thereby accounting for added overhead, due to the creation/deletion of parallel regions. One might note that for most of the cases, nested parallel version gives us a better execution time than the tasking, although a pure tasking model (without nesting OpenMP tasks in parallel regions) with dynamic resource allocation would be the optimal strategy for applications like DMRG++ (dynamic data-structure with a high load imbalance across the workload). As discussed in Sect. 5.2.3, using the threaded version to compute the Kronecker product incurred a higher overhead than any of the other parallelism strategies, hence we are not providing any evaluation data-points for the threaded ESSL method.

Acknowledgment. This research used resources of the Oak Ridge Leadership Computing Facility at the Oak Ridge National Laboratory, which is supported by the Office of Science of the U.S. Department of Energy under Contract No. DE-AC05-00OR22725. Research sponsored by the Laboratory Directed Research and Development Program of Oak Ridge National Laboratory, managed by UT-Battelle, LLC, for the U.S. Department of Energy.

References

1. Alvarez, G.: The density matrix renormalization group for strongly correlated electron systems: a generic implementation. Comput. Phys. Commun. **180**, 1572–1578 (2009)
2. Ayguade, E., Martorell, X., Labarta, J., Gonzalez, M., Navarro, N.: Exploiting multiple levels of parallelism in OpenMP: a case study. In: Proceedings of the 1999 International Conference on Parallel Processing, pp. 172–180 (1999)
3. Barker, B.: Message passing interface (MPI). In: Workshop: High Performance Computing on Stampede, vol. 262 (2015)
4. Broquedis, F., Diakhaté, F., Thibault, S., Aumage, O., Namyst, R., Wacrenier, P.-A.: Scheduling dynamic OpenMP applications over multicore architectures. In: Eigenmann, R., de Supinski, B.R. (eds.) IWOMP 2008. LNCS, vol. 5004, pp. 170–180. Springer, Heidelberg (2008). https://doi.org/10.1007/978-3-540-79561-2_15
5. Department of Energy, Office of Science. ECP: Exascale Computing Project, addressing challenges, March 2017
6. Duran, A., Gonzàlez, M., Corbalán, J.: Automatic thread distribution for nested parallelism in OpenMP. In: Proceedings of the 19th Annual International Conference on Supercomputing, ICS 2005, pp. 121–130. ACM, New York (2005)
7. NERSC, Lawrence Berkley National Laboratory. CORI: Cray XC40, November 2017
8. NNSA, US Department of Energy: Office of Science. ECP: Exascale Computing Project, addressing challenges (2017)
9. Oak Ridge National Lab. Stepping up software for Exascale, May 2017
10. OLCF, Oak Ridge National Laboratory. Summit: Scale new heights. Discover new solutions, November 2017
11. OpenMPI developers. OpenMPI: Open Source High Performance Computing, May 2017
12. Van Loan, C.F.: The ubiquitous Kronecker product. J. Comput. Appl. Math. **123**, 85–100 (2000)

Job Management with mpi_jm

Evan Berkowitz[1]($\boxtimes$)(iD), Gustav Jansen[2](iD), Kenneth McElvain[3](iD),
and André Walker-Loud[4](iD)

[1] Institut für Kernphysik and Institute for Advanced Simulation, Forschungszentrum
Jülich, 52425 Jülich, Germany
e.berkowitz@fz-juelich.de
[2] National Center for Computational Sciences and Physics Division,
Oak Ridge National Laboratory, Oak Ridge, TN 37831, USA
jansengr@ornl.gov
[3] University of California, Berkeley, Berkeley, CA 94720, USA
kenmcelvain@berkeley.edu
[4] Lawrence Berkeley National Laboratory, Berkeley, CA 94720, USA
awalker-loud@lbl.gov

Abstract. Access to Leadership computing is required for HPC applications that require a large fraction of compute nodes for a single computation and also for use cases where the volume of smaller tasks can
only be completed in a competitive or reasonable time frame through
use of these Leadership computing facilities. In the latter case, a robust
and lightweight manager is ideal so that all these tasks can be computed in a machine-friendly way, notably with minimal use of mpirun
or equivalent to launch the executables (simple bundling of tasks can
over-tax the service nodes and crash the entire scheduler). Our library,
mpi_jm, can manage such allocations, provided access to the requisite
MPI functionality is provided. mpi_jm is fault-tolerant against a modest number of down or non-communicative nodes, can begin executing
work on smaller portions of a larger allocation before all nodes become
available for the allocation, can manage GPU-intensive and CPU-only
work independently and can overlay them peacefully on shared nodes. It
is easily incorporated into existing MPI-capable executables, which then
can run both independently and under mpi_jm management. It provides a
flexible Python interface, unlocking many high-level libraries, while also
tightly binding users' executables to hardware.

Keywords: Pilot systems · Job management · CORAL

1 Introduction

The enormous power of the CORAL supercomputers Summit and Sierra, Open-
POWER machines with nVIDIA GPUs, provides challenges for efficient use
[13,15]. Some applications may need to scale to an $\mathcal{O}(1)$ fraction of the whole
machine for a single run of an executable, while others may need a variety of

© Springer Nature Switzerland AG 2018
R. Yokota et al. (Eds.): ISC 2018 Workshops, LNCS 11203, pp. 432–439, 2018.
https://doi.org/10.1007/978-3-030-02465-9_30

executables excuting heterogenous tasks that require different computational resources. One example is lattice field theory, the numerical prescription for solving quantum field theories.

We typically wish to study quantum field theories in continuum spacetime; with lattice methods we discretize spacetime and extrapolate to take the continuum limit. Computations are typically done in spacetime boxes with periodic boundary conditions, while we are interested in extrapolating to the infinite-volume result. Finally, the computational physicist may adjust the input parameters to the theory, if the physical parameters are too computationally costly, and attempt to extrapolate or interpolate to the true parameters.

Each choice of discretization scale, volume size, and input parameters requires the generation of a stochastic ensemble of the spacetime configuration of the quantum field via importance sampling and 'measurements' on each configuration in the ensemble. The configurations are stored and can be reused when computing other observables.

Computing a single observable on a single configuration generally consists of two parts, *solves* for quark propagators and *tensor contractions*, building quantities out of one or more quark propagator.

Solving for a propagator means solving the *Dirac matrix*. In the case of QCD, the theory of quarks and gluons, the Dirac matrix is a discretization-dependent (typically nearest-neighbor) stencil operator whose linear size is the number of spacetime points in the configuration. Each entry in that matrix is a 12×12 matrix which describes how quantities should be parallel transported around the lattice[1]. Solving this linear system is often accomplished with numerical acceleration; the community library for nVIDIA GPUs is QUDA [4,12].

The tensor contraction step may also be accelerated. However, in practice, the tensor contractions require substantially less numerical effort than propagator solves, and are largely site-parallel, and so it makes sense to perform them on CPU resources while the GPUs focus on solves.

So, in one research project one may expect to run solves and contractions on a variety of different lattices spacings, with different sizes, and different input parameters. The time to complete a tensor contraction step depends only on the number of lattice sites, while time-to-solution for a quark propagator can depend on all three variables. For each ensemble, one hopes to take thousands to millions of measurements.

Modern lattice QCD calculations are performed on lattices of dimension $(48 - 96)^3 \times (48 - 128) \sim 2^2 4$ sites. On CORAL resources, solves on large lattices can be performed with just a few nodes (meaning 8 or 16 or 32, but certainly not 1024). Thus, it is unlikely that LQCD can effectively use a large fraction of a CORAL machine without the ability to finely manage a large allocation, running different problems instances and problem sizes simultaneously, independently executing tensor contractions from propagator solves, and creating new work as work is completed, intelligently back-filling an allocation to ensure very little time is wasted idling. Executing contractions on the CPUs while the GPUs solve for

---

[1] $12 = (4$ fermionic spin degrees of freedom$) \times (3$ fermionic *color* degrees of freedom$)$.

propagators effectively amortizes the cost of the contractions, yielding a large effective savings.

We developed METAQ [8, 9], a suite of bash scripts that sits between the batch scheduler and the user. Tasks are described by scripts that, much like a job script for a batch scheduler, describes the needed resources and the anticipated amount of wall-clock time needed to complete the task. In the job script submitted to the batch scheduler the user describes to METAQ the available resources, and which are then consumed by as many tasks as can peacefully coexist in the allocation. We have used METAQ in the production of a variety of LQCD results [6, 7, 10, 11, 14].

Separating the description of work from the description of the job itself has a number of benefits: multiple collaborators may all submit tasks that can be accomplished by a single job, and the waiting tasks may be adjusted or entirely changed between the submission of the job script and the tasks' execution, even while the job is running. Additionally, tasks launched by METAQ are robust, in the sense that the tasks are independent: if one fails the others continue happily and the relinquished resources may be dedicated to a new task.

However, METAQ has serious shortcomings. First, it requires the user to honestly and accurately describe the needed resources—if the user makes an error, the available resources may be oversubscribed, yielding a performance hit. Second, the ability to separately assign work to the GPUs and CPUs depends on administrative policy—amortization of the CPU work may not be possible. Third, the tasks themselves aren't flexible, in that if a task could run in two different configurations with acceptable performance, there is no natural way to METAQ of these different possibilities. Fourth, each task executes a separate mpirun (or batch-scheduler equivalent), putting a lot of stress on the service nodes of the machine, a serious concern for CORAL-scale machines.

Finally METAQ has no tight integration with or knowledge of the actual hardware in a machine. As resources are dedicated and freed by tasks, a suboptimal group of nodes may be set to a task—if they are far apart in terms of communication, for example—reducing performance.

The success of METAQ in production, and the drawbacks just mentioned, motivated us to develop mpi_jm, a C library that overcomes these drawbacks at minimal cost.

2   mpi_jm

The MPI specification [2] includes a mechanism by which a parent process can spawn a child process that receives its own MPI_COMM_WORLD: MPI_Comm_spawn. After disconnecting the parent-child intercommunicator, the parent survives a child's MPI_Abort, thereby making the parent robust against its children's problems. It is around this structure mpi_jm is built.

The mpi_jm model consists of a master, a scheduler, and workers. The master jm_master is launched on every node, and is responsible for launching and monitoring jobs, and reporting information to the scheduler. The scheduler jm_sched is a single process that tracks the available resources, manages a queue of computational tasks, distributes those tasks to nodes, and collect status. The workers are the user applications that will execute the computational work, linked against a library libjm_worker.

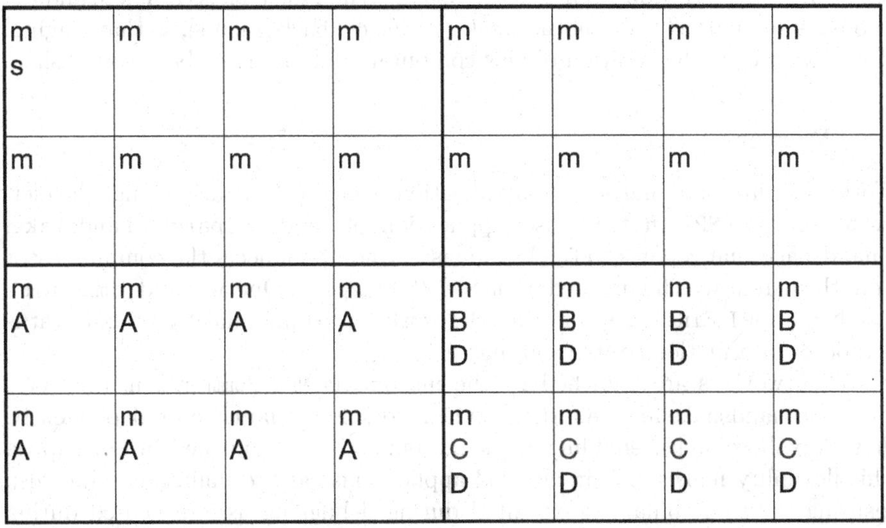

m s	m	m	m	m	m	m	m
m	m	m	m	m	m	m	m
m A	m A	m A	m A	m B D	m B D	m B D	m B D
m A	m A	m A	m A	m C D	m C D	m C D	m C D

Fig. 1. An example 32-node layout, with four blocks of eight nodes. Every node launches jm_master (m), one jm_sched (s) is spawned, and workers of different sizes (A, B, C, D) and requiring different resources are launched. In this case, worker A consumes all the resources in a block, while B, C, and D can peacefully coexist in a block. Perhaps D requires GPUs but only a few CPU cores, while B and C are CPU-intensive but do not need GPUs.

2.1   Masters

jm_master is launched across the entire allocation with mpirun (or equivalent), with one MPI task per node, as depicted in Fig. 1. Each jm_master also reports its location in the system hierarchy, so that they may be organized into blocks with fast communication, avoiding resource fragmentation across the communication fabric.

Workers can only be assigned resources inside a single block. Each block gets a sub-communicator, through which the masters coordinate and launch workers.

2.2   The Scheduler

Just one instance of the scheduler is started, via MPI_Comm_spawn (on the upper-left node in Fig. 1). It loads configuration information about the machine and assigns the masters to blocks with good communication performance.

After initialization, jm_sched begins to collect computational tasks, constructing a queue of work. Each task might know a variety of hardware resources that it can run on efficiently.

The scheduler matches work with available resources, performs a task-specific callback, dispatches them to the relevant block subcommunicator's rank-0 process, which starts the job via MPI_Comm_spawn. When the task is complete and the resources are marked free, another task-specific callback is made, so that logging, clean-up, or even the creation of new computational tasks can be accomplished.

2.3   Workers

Workers require minimal source modification. One must include a single header, jm.h. After the MPI_Init of a user application, one adds jm_parent_handshake, a handshake that reports to the local master and disconnects the communicator from the parent which launched it via MPI_Comm_spawn. One also adds jm_finish just before MPI_Finalize, allowing the worker to communicate its exit status and other information to its local master.

When workers are launched by the master via MPI_Comm_spawn, they perform said handshake and reporting. When workers are launched independently, they skip those steps, enabling the same binary to be launched in both ways. This flexibility makes mpi_jm-enabled applications easy to maintain, while also ensuring the same binary is executed during debugging as is executed during production.

Only if the worker crashes between launching and the disconnect of the intercommunicator can a problem in a worker (such as a call to MPI_Abort) bring down the whole job. Most executables perform only minimal work (such as simple initialization, reading of input files, etc.) between launching and the MPI initialization, providing very little opportunity for this to become an issue.

2.4   Issues and Dependencies

As it happens, many MPI implementations do not currently respect the specification, and the MPI_Comm_spawn parent may abort if its child aborts, even after disconnection.[2]

The SpectrumMPI installed on the CORAL systems[3] do not yet support MPI_Comm_spawn, and other MPI libraries are not as highly optimized for these systems, yielding a ∼20% performance hit in our initial tests. We hope to have MPI_Comm_spawn incorporated in the acceptance regimen for Summit at Oak Ridge. Further investigation has shown that SpectrumMPI inherited a problem from OpenMPI that keeps MPI_Comm_spawn from completely disconnecting, keeping the resilience against individual task failure from succeeding. In our latest

---

[2] Bug reports are in the works, and we are exploring alternate architecture using other aspects of the MPI specification.

[3] (as of the beginning of August, 2018).

tests using MVAPICH 2.3 we seem to achieve only a 1% slowdown when compared to the native SpectrumMPI and a correct adherence to the MPI standard.

mpi_jm also depends on a python installation, as will be discussed in the next section.

3   Individual Tasks and the Python Interface

The scheduler contains a python interpreter and exposes an interface to the work queue. In python, one simply creates a new job object that is naturally in an unstaged state. The user provides information about the work, such as which executable to use, what environment to provide, what parameters to provide, the required resouces and wallclock time, a priority flag, and what callbacks to execute before launching the task and after its completion. Then, the user queues the job, at which point jm_sched may deploy it to a block for execution.

We expect to provide a METAQ-like set of routines, where the user can describe their work in yaml[5] files. However, because the description of work is accomplished via python, many more advanced methods are possible. For example, to create work one may access databases, other pilot programs (for example, [3]), or can create work in other tasks' callbacks. It is easy to imagine unlocking computational steps as prerequisite tasks are accomplished.

4   Initial Performance

We were fortunate to receive some early time on Sierra, the CORAL machine at LLNL, where we tested mpi_jm. We integrated mpi_jm into QMP [1], the communications layer of the lattice USQCD community libraries, and successfully overlayed a GPU-capable executable performing linear solves and a CPU-only executable performing tensor contractions.

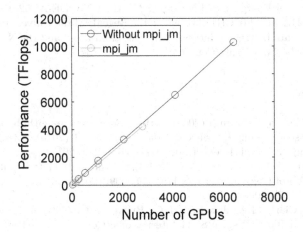

Fig. 2. Sustained performance as one scales GPU-hungry lattice QCD tasks with the available allocation.

We found that for our examples of interest, a $48^3 \times 64$ lattice, the linear solves were best accomplished by four nodes (16 GPUs), while the scaling of the tensor contractions is essentially perfect. In Fig. 2 we show the analog to weak scaling—the scaling as we increase the number of examples (the problem size) with the number of nodes. We quote only the performance of the GPU tasks, and find no performance reduction when executing both GPU and CPU tasks.

We encountered unexpected problems when launching on a very large number of nodes (`mpirun` encountered some limitations that we now known can be cured with particular command-line arguments). However, up to that limit, we found identical scaling with just the naively-expected scaling. The performance corresponds to a sustained $\sim 20\%$ of peak possible performance, and we expect to be able to scale to arbitrary allocation size while still relying on only a single invocation of `mpirun` (or equivalent).

Acknowledgements. We are indebted to the Livermore Computing Center for access to Sierra and help getting set up there. In particular, our contacts John Gyllenhal and Adam Bertsch were very helpful and responsive, and other early users were very cooperative and collaborative, keeping us appraised of the state of the machine, difficulties they encountered, and workarounds. In particular, Jim Glosli, Tomas Oppelstrup, and especially Tom Scogland were very generous with their time and concern. At the Oak Ridge Leadership Computing Facility, Jack Wells provided excellent help, advice, and encouragement.

An award of computer time was provided by the Innovative and Novel Computational Impact on Theory and Experiment (INCITE) program to CalLat (2016) as well as the Lawrence Livermore National Laboratory (LLNL) Multiprogrammatic and Institutional Computing program through a Tier 1 Grand Challenge award. This research used the NVIDIA GPU-accelerated Titan and Summit supercomputers at the Oak Ridge Leadership Computing Facility at the Oak Ridge National Laboratory, which is supported by the Office of Science of the U.S. Department of Energy under Contract No. DE-AC05-00OR22725, and the NVIDIA GPU-accelerated Surface, Ray, and Sierra supercomputers LLNL. This work was performed under the auspices of the U.S. Department of Energy by LLNL under Contract No. DE-AC52-07NA27344 and under contract DE-AC02-05CH11231, which the Regents of the University of California manage and operate Lawrence Berkeley National Laboratory and the National Energy Research Scientific Computing Center.

References

1. `QMP` (QCD Message Passing) (2004). http://usqcd-software.github.io/qmp/
2. `MPI`: A message-passing interface standard, version 3.1 (2015). http://mpi-forum.org/docs/mpi-3.1/mpi31-report.pdf. Accessed 14 Feb 2017
3. Ayyar, V., Hackett, D.C., Jay, W.I., Neil, E.T.: Automated lattice data generation. In: EPJ Web of Conferences, vol. 175, p. 09009. (2018). https://doi.org/10.1051/epjconf/201817509009
4. Babich, R., Clark, M.A., Joo, B., Shi, G., Brower, R.C., Gottlieb, S.: Scaling lattice QCD beyond 100 GPUs. In: SC11 International Conference for High Performance Computing, Networking, Storage and Analysis Seattle, Washington, 12–18 November 2011 (2011). http://inspirehep.net/record/927455/files/arXiv:1109.2935.pdf

5. Ben-Kiki, O., Evans, C., döt Net, I.: YAML Ain't Markup Language (YAML^{TM}) Version 1.2 (2001–2009). http://www.yaml.org/spec/1.2/spec.html
6. Berkowitz, E., et al.: An accurate calculation of the nucleon axial charge with lattice QCD (2017)
7. Berkowitz, E., et al.: Möbius Domain-Wall fermions on gradient-flowed dynamical HISQ ensembles. Phys. Rev. D **96**(5), 054513 (2017). https://doi.org/10.1103/PhysRevD.96.054513
8. Berkowitz, E.: METAQ: Bundle Supercomputing Tasks (2017). https://github.com/evanberkowitz/metaq
9. Berkowitz, E., Jansen, G.R., McElvain, K., Walker-Loud, A.: Job Management and Task Bundling. In: EPJ Web of Conferences, vol. 175, p. 09007 (2018). https://doi.org/10.1051/epjconf/201817509007
10. Chang, C., et al.: Nucleon axial coupling from Lattice QCD. In: 35th International Symposium on Lattice Field Theory (Lattice 2017) Granada, Spain, 18–24 June 2017 (2017). http://inspirehep.net/record/1631340/files/arXiv:1710.06523.pdf
11. Chang, C., Nicholson, A., et al.: A percent-level determination of the nucleon axial coupling from quantum chromodynamics. Nature **558**, 91 (2018). https://doi.org/10.1038/s41586-018-0161-8. arXiv:1805.12130
12. Clark, M.A., Babich, R., Barros, K., Brower, R.C., Rebbi, C.: Solving lattice QCD systems of equations using mixed precision solvers on GPUs. Comput. Phys. Commun. **181**, 1517–1528 (2010). https://doi.org/10.1016/j.cpc.2010.05.002
13. Lawrence Livermore National Laboratory: Sierra https://hpc.llnl.gov/hardware/platforms/sierra
14. Nicholson, A., et al.: Neutrinoless double beta decay from lattice QCD. PoS LATTICE2016, 017 (2016)
15. Oak Ridge Leadership Computing Facility: Summit https://www.olcf.ornl.gov/olcf-resources/compute-systems/summit/

Compile-Time Library Call Detection Using CAASCADE and XALT

Jisheng Zhao[2], Oscar R. Hernandez[1(✉)], Reuben D. Budiardja[1],
M. Graham Lopez[1], Vivek Sarkar[2], and Jack C. Wells[1]

[1] Oak Ridge National Laboratory, Oak Ridge, TN 37831, USA
{oscar,reubendb,lopezmg,wellsjc}@ornl.gov
[2] Georgia Tech, Atlanta, GA, USA
{jisheng,vsarkar}@gatech.edu

Abstract. CAASCADE — *C*ompiler-*A*ssisted *A*pplication *S*ource *C*ode *A*nalysis and *D*atabas*E*—is a tool that summarizes the use of parallel programming language features in application source code using compiler technology. This paper discusses the library detection capability within CAASCADE to find information about the usage of scientific libraries within the source code. The information that CAASCADE collects provides insights into the usage of library calls in an applications. CAASCADE can classify the APIs by scientific libraries (e.g. LAPACK, BLAS, FFTW, etc). It can also detect the context in which a library API is being invoked, for example within a serial or multi-threaded region. To collect this information, CAASCADE uses compiler plugins that summarize procedural information and uses Apache Spark to do inter-procedural analysis to reconstruct call chains. In addition to this, we also integrated CAASCADE to work with XALT to collect library information based on linkage and modules installed on a system.

Keywords: HPC scientific libraries · Source code analysis · Libraries usage in applications

1 Introduction

As we move towards exascale computing, one of the most important components of next-generation programming environments are libraries. Hence, understanding which are the most important libraries for a given application portfolio

© Springer Nature Switzerland AG 2018
R. Yokota et al. (Eds.): ISC 2018 Workshops, LNCS 11203, pp. 440–447, 2018.
https://doi.org/10.1007/978-3-030-02465-9_31

and how they are being used in those applications is critical for preparing for these upcoming HPC environments. One key component is identifying third-party libraries that are required by an application but are developed as a separate effort apart from the application. Typically, these are developed by the open source community and/or vendors, and include high-performance numerical libraries such as BLAS, LAPACK, PETSc, FFTW, etc., communication libraries such as MPI or SHMEM, and I/O and data management libraries like HDF5, ADIOS, and NetCDF. Currently, there is no robust and automated way to gather detailed information about usage of these libraries in production HPC applications. By using compiler-based analysis to parse the application, and by summarizing accurate information about actual usage of programming languages and parallelization methods, the CAASCADE project can help HPC practitioners and system architects understand where in the application the libraries calls are being invoked and the broader context of these invocations. Examining the actual function calls from the source code elucidates specific usage of features from third-party libraries. And when combined with tools that gather link-time information such as XALT [1], information about the implementation of these calls can be derived, such as the source of the implementation (e.g. ACML, Intel MKL, Cray LibSci, LAPACK), version of the library, and where in the system they are installed.

2   CAASCADE Overview

CAASCADE implements a mechanism for gathering information directly from application source code that is compiled and linked using a production HPC software stack, and a mechanism for storing this information into a database. For maximum accuracy and flexibility, CAASCADE gathers its information from the intermediate representations (IR) of production compilers such as the GNU Compiler Collection (GCC)[3]. Most information is gathered from the compiler at the highest level of IR representation that is closest to the source code. Once collected from the compiler, statistics and detailed source code characteristics are assembled at link time and stored in a back-end database in order to most generally support further analysis. This approach requires no intervention from the application developers and is non-intrusive to the application itself (performance, optimization, or functional, since it does not change anything in the final executable and does not alter the way it is being created). Turning on/off the collection is controlled by loading/unloading a module installed on the system.

3   Library Detection

CAASCADE relies on local procedural summarizations and inter-procedural analysis to detect the library usage of an application. Currently, the local procedure summarization is done via compiler plugins and the inter-procedural analysis via an Apache Spark [2] component that was designed to detect library usage.

---

[3] https://gcc.gnu.org/.

3.1   Compiler Plugins

CAASCADE implements compiler plugins to summarize programming model and language usage information in application source codes. A detailed description of what it collects can be found here [3]. The compiler plugins currently support Fortran and C++ and they can detect where in a source code a call site appears and the context the call occurs: for example using the compiler plugins, we can detect where a call site occurs in a subroutine and source line information, if it appears inside a multi-threaded region (e.g. OpenMP or OpenACC), a loop nest, or both. We also have the ability to detect if call sites are indirect calls where pointer or runtime analysis is needed to disambiguate the call graph information. This is the case for C++ and virtual methods, which are difficult to detect at compile time. The compiler plugins dump the information using JSON format to store the call site and context information.

3.2   Classification of the Libraries Calls

Our analysis leverages XALT function detection [4] capability to delineate if a call site detected by CAASCADE is part of the application or if it is an external function/subroutine provided by a library installed on the system. XALT accomplishes this by having a stored knowledge of all the libraries provided by the system software stack that may be linked by an application. During link time, a behind-the-scenes, separate link process is launched where all object files that are part of libraries provided by the system software stack are removed. The resulting link failure forces the linker (typically GNU's ld) to show unresolved symbols, revealing the external function calls needed by the application.

Having the list of these library functions, we can cross-reference with CAASCADE data from its call-chain detection feature to do analysis such as aggregating number of calls, and marking if the calls are from inside a loop-nest or OpenMP/OpenACC parallel regions directives. Since XALT also has knowledge of which library an object file belongs to (typically organized by *modulefile*), we can also map which library an external function call belongs to.

3.3   Call Graph Analysis for Library Detection

In addition to the library classification capability performed via XALT, we build the program call graph from the information extracted by our compiler plugins and identify the library call sites via analyzing this call graph. This is important to detect "third-party" libraries that we were not able to detect via our initial classification. For example, we may not get information for those libraries that the user independently built in user space.

We give here some more details about how we employ this two-phase analysis: feature collection followed by off-line program analysis to capture additional characteristics of the library usage in the program using the program call graph. The feature collection phase uses compiler plugins to collect application source code usage features, and the program analysis phase further resolves the program information that can not be identified during the feature collection phase. For call graph construction, the feature collector identifies the call sites that contains the position of the function invocation and the information related to the target function of the call. There are two reasons that the target functions cannot be resolved directly: 1. The polymorphism resulting from virtual function calls; 2. The pointer aliasing resulting from function pointer invocations. To identify the target functions, we implement the call graph builder in the program analysis phase.

To handle polymorphism, the call graph builder applies rapid type analysis (RTA) [5] to identify the type set T_V of the virtual function calls' receiver, then works out all possible target functions based on T_V. For the pointer alias case, we currently match all global functions to the function pointer invocation sites.

Our call graph contains both the traditional caller to callee connection and the meta-information for invocations in parallel regions. The meta-information indicates if the call site C is inside an OpenMP or OpenACC parallel region, and if so, all of C's target functions and their descendants are marked as *potentially invoked from a parallel region*. Based on the call graph information, we build the library usage analysis that identifies the library calls and their usages (i.e. if the library call is invoked within an OpenMP or OpenACC parallel region). A function F is a library function if F satisfies a set of simple constraints:

- F does not have function body;
- F is not an interface function in C++ or Fortran;
- F is not a pure virtual function in C++.

To identify if a library function F was called from an OpenMP or OpenACC parallel region, we can simply check if F is potentially invoked from a parallel region based on the meta-information from the call graph.

Considering the increasing data volume from collected program features and the pressure on the off-line program analysis, we implemented our program analyzer within Apache Spark [2] which is a scalable data processing framework that is designed to run on distributed parallel systems.

4   Experiments and Results

In this section we present the library detection results of two applications: QMC-PACK and NUCCOR. Both of these codes were compiled on Summit [6], a Department of Energy parallel supercomputer at the Oak Ridge National Laboratory (ORNL), in which each node has two Power 9 CPUs and six Volta V100 GPUs, using the CAASCADE plugins for GCC 6.2. The application compiled successfully and their information was sent to the CAASCADE database, which we used for the call graph analysis via Spark and for all queries based on XALT library symbol information.

QMCPACK: QMCPACK is an electronic-structure application for materials and chemical sciences written in C++. Information on some of the source code characteristics of QMCPACK from CAASCADE 's feature detection can be found in [7]. When running our inter-procedural analysis via Spark, we were able to detect 1684 library calls (excluding C++ operators and intrinsics). Of these, 3.5 percent were called inside the dynamic extent of an OpenMP parallel region. 32 percent of the libraries are called within a loopnest. When we ran our experiment with CAASCADE and XALT, we were able to detect 52 library calls that belong to scientific libraries and I/O, based on libraries installed on the system. Figure 1 shows the libraries detected by XALT and their number of call sites as computed by CAASCADE for QMCPACK. We can classify these libraries as belonging to LAPACK (red), FFTW (green) and HDF5 (blue). When we combined the XALT information with Spark, we are able to detect that of these scientific libraries, dgemm is invoked inside the dynamic extent of OpenMP parallel regions in two call sites (out of 10 call sites in the code). Our Spark analysis was not able to resolve the FFTW call sites within the overall call graph of the application. This is part of the analysis limitation of the static call graph. One way to improve this is to perform pointer analysis or disambiguation of indirect calls using runtime information to fully build a complete program call graph.

NUCCOR: NUCCOR is a nuclear-structure application for nuclear sciences that predicts the structure and reactions of atomic nuclei to study fundamental interactions in the universe that are difficult to observe in the laboratory. NUCCOR is written in Fortran 2003. Figure 2 shows that we were able to detect 45 library calls that belong to LAPACK (Red) and HDF5 (Blue) using XALT and CAASCADE.

5   Related Work

Program comprehension understanding is an important technique that helps identify the program behaviors, including performance bottlenecks, privilege vulnerabilities, and so on. The common approach is to use *static analysis* that works at the control-flow or data-flow level of intermediate representations and identifies software structure via software dependence graph (SDG)-like data structures [8]. There has been a number of static analysis tools and compiler plugins built for this purpose.

Software reuse offers the hope that software construction can be made easier by systematic reuse of well-engineered components. In practice, reusing well-tuned libraries has proven to be a robust way to improve productivity for building large-scale software systems and reducing defects. The correct usage of the library requires that users obey the program specifications. There have been several works that automatically identify the program specification via probabilistic models [9] and machine learning approaches [10].

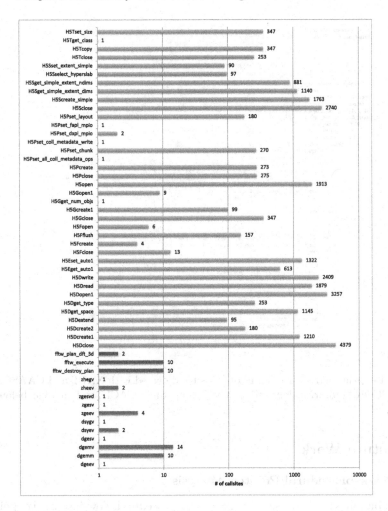

Fig. 1. Libraries and their number of call sites detected with XALT and CAASCADE in QMCPACK. Libraries depicted in red belong to LAPACK, in green belong to FFTW, and in blue belong to HDF5.

Most current work focuses on the analysis of the sequential program. In our work, we focus on studying the library usage in high-performance computing applications that heavily employ parallelism on multiple, hierarchical levels. The library APIs invoked from parallel-code regions may imply some differentials in relation to the specification for sequential execution. Our work aims to study the libraries used in the HPC domain and to identify correct specifications that helps improve the quality and productivity of HPC application development and library design.

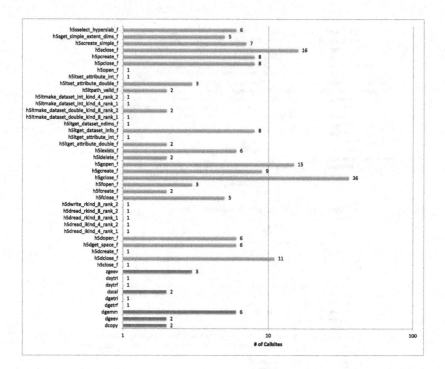

Fig. 2. Libraries and their number of call sites detected with XALT and CAASCADE in NUCCOR. Libraries depicted in red belong to LAPACK and in blue belong to HDF5.

6   Future Work

6.1   Inter-procedural Pointer Analysis

We are building an Andersen [11]-like, inter-procedural, flow-insensitive, pointer analysis in Spark. This analysis is based on data-log computation. This will enable us to reduce some over-approximations in the current analysis, for example, provide more accurate analysis for the call targets for C++ virtual function call chains.

6.2   Linkage Information

We are currently working to connect the library detection functionality of CAASCADE with the XALT data. This will provide additional information about the library implementation: the provider and version available on the HPC system. For example, LAPACK libraries are provided by different vendors such as ESSL (IBM), ACML (AMD), etc.

Acknowledgment. This material is based upon work supported by the U.S. Department of Energy, Office of Science, Office of Advanced Scientific Computing Research, under contract number DE-AC05-00OR22725. This research used resources of the Oak Ridge Leadership Computing Facility at the Oak Ridge National Laboratory, which is supported by the Office of Science of the U.S. Department of Energy under Contract No. DE-AC05-00OR22725. This project is sponsored by the Laboratory Directed Research and Development (LDRD) Program of Oak Ridge National Laboratory, managed by UT-Battelle, LLC, for the U.S. Department of Energy via the LDRD project 8277: "Understanding HPC Applications for Evidence-based Co-design".

References

1. Budiardja, R., Fahey, M., McLay, R., Don, P.M., Hadri, B., James, D.: Community use of XALT in its first year in production. In: Proceedings of the Second International Workshop on HPC User Support Tools, HUST 2015, pp. 4:1–4:10. ACM, New York (2015)

2. Zaharia, M., et al.: Apache spark: a unified engine for big data processing. Commun. ACM **59**(11), 56–65 (2016)

3. Lopez, M.G., Hernandez, O., Budiardja, R.D., Wells, J.: Caascade: a system for static analysis of HPC software portfolios. In: Proceedings of 6TH Workshop on Extreme-Scale Programming Tools (2018). (to be published)

4. Budiardja, R.D., Agrawal, K., Fahey, M., McLay, R., James, D.: Library function tracking with XALT. In: Proceedings of the XSEDE 2016 Conference on Diversity, Big Data, and Science at Scale, XSEDE 2016, pp. 30:1–30:7. ACM, New York (2016)

5. Bacon, D.F., Sweeney, P.F.: Fast static analysis of c++ virtual function calls. In: Proceedings of the 11th ACM SIGPLAN Conference on Object-oriented Programming, Systems, Languages, and Applications, OOPSLA 1996, pp. 324–341. ACM, New York (1996)

6. Summit   Supercomputer.   https://www.olcf.ornl.gov/olcf-resources/compute-systems/summit/

7. Budiardja, R.D., Lopez, M.G., Zhao, J., Hernandez, O., Sarkar, V., Wells, J.: Using CAASCADE and CrayPAT for analysis of HPC applications. In: Proceedings of Cray User Group (2018) (to be published)

8. Horwitz, S., Reps, T., Binkley, D.: Interprocedural slicing using dependence graphs. In: Proceedings of the ACM SIGPLAN 1988 Conference on Programming Language Design and Implementation, PLDI 1988, pp. 35–46. ACM, New York (1988)

9. Ammons, G., Bodík, R., Larus, J.R.: Mining specifications. In: Proceedings of the 29th ACM SIGPLAN-SIGACT Symposium on Principles of Programming Languages, POPL 2002, pp. 4–16. ACM, New York (2002)

10. Murali, V., Chaudhuri, S., Jermaine, C.: Bayesian specification learning for finding API usage errors. In: Proceedings of the 2017 11th Joint Meeting on Foundations of Software Engineering, ESEC/FSE 2017, pp. 151–162. ACM, New York (2017)

11. Andersen, L.O.: Program analysis and specialization for the c programming language. Technical report (1994)

NUMA-Aware Data-Transfer Measurements for Power/NVLink Multi-GPU Systems

Carl Pearson[1](✉), I-Hsin Chung[2](✉), Zehra Sura[2](✉), Wen-Mei Hwu[1](✉),
and Jinjun Xiong[2](✉)

[1] University of Illinois Urbana-Champaign, Urbana, IL 61801, USA
{pearson, w-hwu}@illinois.edu
[2] IBM Thomas J. Watson Research Center, Yorktown Heights, NY 10598, USA
{ihchung, zsura, jinjun}@us.ibm.com

Abstract. High-performance computing increasingly relies on heterogeneous systems with specialized hardware accelerators to improve application performance. For example, NVIDIA's CUDA programming system and general-purpose GPUs have emerged as a widespread accelerator in HPC systems. This trend has exacerbated challenges of data placement as accelerators often have fast local memories to fuel their computational demands, but slower interconnects to feed those memories. Crucially, real-world data-transfer performance is strongly influenced not just by the underlying hardware, but by the capabilities of the programming systems. Understanding how application performance is affected by the logical communication exposed through abstractions, as well as the underlying system topology, is crucial for developing high-performance applications and architectures. This report presents initial data-transfer microbenchmark results from two POWER-based systems obtained during work towards developing an automated system performance characterization tool.

Keywords: CUDA · NVLink · Unified Memory · GPGPU
Benchmark

1 Introduction

With the end of Dennard scaling, computer architects have sought to satisfy the demand for increasing performance by providing specialized hardware

This work is supported by IBM-ILLINOIS Center for Cognitive Computing Systems Research (C3SR) - a research collaboration as part of the IBM Cognitive Horizon Network. This work was supported by the Center for Applications Driving Architectures (ADA), one of six centers of JUMP, a Semiconductor Research Corporation program co-sponsored by DARPA. This research is part of the Blue Waters sustained-petascale computing project, which is supported by the National Science Foundation award OCI-0725070 and the state of Illinois. Blue Waters is a joint effort of the University of Illinois at Urbana-Champaign and its National Center for Supercomputing Applications.

© Springer Nature Switzerland AG 2018
R. Yokota et al. (Eds.): ISC 2018 Workshops, LNCS 11203, pp. 448–454, 2018.
https://doi.org/10.1007/978-3-030-02465-9_32

accelerators tuned to computation with particular characteristics. Perhaps the most successful example of this trend is the widespread adoption of graphics processing units (GPUs) for more general data-parallel compute tasks. Figure 1 shows two such systems with two CPUs and four GPUs; an IBM S822LC for High Performance Computing [4], and an IBM AC922 [3].

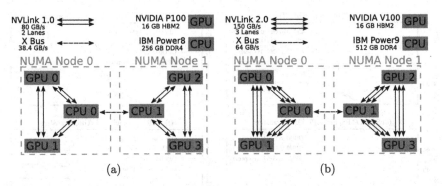

Fig. 1. Summary of the examined systems. (a) shows S822LC, a POWER8-based system with NVLink 1.0 running nvcc 9.1.85, CUDA driver 390.31, linux kernel 4.4.0-96. (b) shows AC922, a POWER9-based system with NVLink 2.0 running nvcc 9.2.88, CUDA Driver 396.26, linux kernel 4.14.0-49.

The enormous compute capability of GPUs demands high-bandwidth access to data to "feed the beast." The GPUs have high-bandwidth memories (732 GB/s and 900 GB/s on P100 and V100 respectively) to help provide this data, but relatively slow interconnects. A consequence of this architecture is that moving data into accelerator memory to support high-performance execution is a first-order design consideration for any accelerated application. This must be managed by either the application developer explicitly, or by the programming system. In either case, understanding the communication capabilities exposed by the system is foundational to building high-performance applications.

The application does not interface directly with the hardware, but through software abstractions such as the Linux Non-Uniform Memory Access [1] (NUMA) system or the NVIDIA Compute Unified Device Architecture [2] (CUDA) programming system. These software abstractions expose a set of logical communication capabilities on top of the hardware. As this report demonstrates, these capabilities are substantially affected by the underlying hardware, but have distinct performance profiles in their own right. This report describes some initial results obtained while developing an automated approach for understanding how applications use these systems and the capabilities the systems provide.

The rest of this report is organized as follows: Sect. 2 reports initial measurements of data transfer using cudaMemcpy. Section 3 reports initial measurements of data transfer bandwidth using CUDA managed memory. Section 4 discusses future work and concludes.

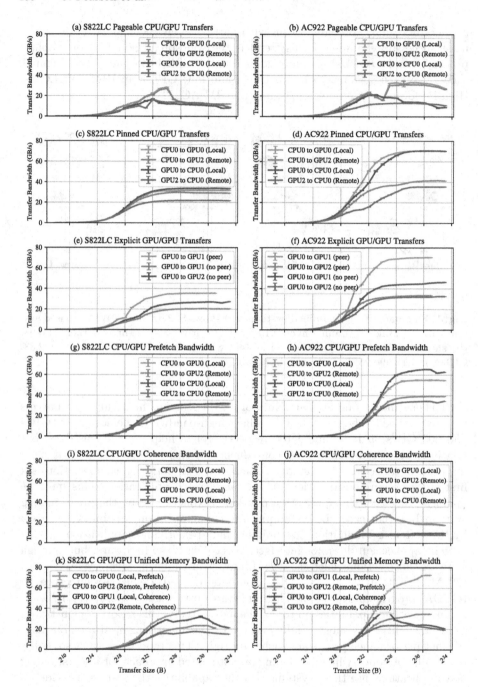

Fig. 2. Measured transfer bandwidths for explicit and unified-memory transfers for S822LC and AC922. Transfer bandwidth vs. transfer size is shown. Each measurement point is the average of at least five iterations, repeated five times. Error bars show the standard deviation of the five average measures.

2   Explicit Data Transfer

The microbenchmark results presented in this report are available at `microbench` [7], a set of microbenchmarks developed using Google's Benchmark support library [5].

Explicit CPU-GPU transfers are caused by the `cudaMemcpy` family of functions being invoked on one pointer to a host allocation and one pointer to a device allocation. The host allocation may be pageable (created by `malloc` or `new`), or pinned (created by `cudaMallocHost` or `cudaHostAlloc`). The device allocation is created by `cudaMalloc`. Algorithm 1 demonstrates a Google Benchmark loop for CUDA operations. The explicit transfers are all asynchronous `cudaMemcpAsync` operations. In the setup phase of the benchmark, a source and destination allocation are created on the host and device. Execution is pinned to the correct host and device through `libnuma` [1,8] and/or `cudaSetDevice` APIs, respectively. For CUDA operations that are asynchronous with respect to the host, CUDA events are used to accurately measure the operation time without measuring other system overhead. For synchronous operations, the operating system wall time is used to measure the operation. In the *teardown* phase, resources are freed.

Algorithm 1. Measuring transfer time of *bytes* between *src* and *dst* for asynchronous and synchronous CUDA operations using Google Benchmark support library.

```
 1: function ASYNC_BANDWIDTH(dst, src, bytes)
 2:     ...                                              ▷ benchmark setup
 3:     for state do                                     ▷ Google Benchmark loop
 4:         cudaEventRecord(start)
 5:         asynchronousTransfer(dst, src, bytes)        ▷ timed asynchronous operation
 6:         cudaEventRecord(stop)
 7:         millis ← cudaEventElapsedTime(start, stop)
 8:         state.SetIterationTime(millis/1000)          ▷ record time
 9:     end for
10:                                                      ▷ benchmark teardown
11: end function

12: function SYNC_BANDWIDTH(dst, src, bytes)
13:     ...                                              ▷ benchmark setup
14:     for state do                                     ▷ Google Benchmark loop
15:         state.PauseTiming()
16:         ...                                          ▷ per-iteration setup
17:         state.ResumeTiming()
18:         synchronousTransfer(dst, src, bytes)         ▷ timed synchronous operation
19:     end for
20:     ...                                              ▷ benchmark teardown
21: end function
```

Figures 2a–f shows measured transfer rates. The NVLink 2.0 bandwidth of 150GB/s on AC922 compared to the 80 GB/s NVLink 1.0 bandwidth on S822LC is reflected in higher transfer rates on AC922 in most cases. This is especially evident in pinned local transfers or local GPU-GPU transfers. In the GPU-GPU transfers, peer access refers to whether the GPUs are configured to support direct DMA between GPUs. Without peer access, a GPU-to-GPU transfer is implemented with a GPU-to-CPU transfer followed by a CPU-to-GPU transfer, effectively halving the bandwidth observed by the application. On S822LC, remote GPUs do not support peer access (Fig. 2e). Underscoring the performance complexities in these systems are the direction- and affinity-dependent performance seen in almost all CPU/GPU transfers involving pageable and pinned allocations. There is also a strong affinity effect in GPU-GPU transfers when peer access is enabled.

3   Unified Memory

CUDA Unified Memory allows allocations to be transparently referenced by the CPUs and GPUs [6]. Instead of the programmer explicitly moving data, the CUDA system is responsible for ensuring accessed data is present on the correct device. On both these systems, the unified memory allocations operate at page granularity. A "coherence" or "demand" migration occurs when an accessing device does not have the page in its local memory, and that page must be moved from the currently owning device. A "prefetch" migration occurs when pages are bulk-migrated to a device ahead of their use.

Algorithm 1 shows the asynchronous and synchronous measurements used for unified memory benchmarks. In the *setup* phase, a single unified memory allocation is created, which is accessible from any device. `cudaMemPrefetchAsync` is used to move the allocation's backing pages to the source or destination device in the *per-iteration setup* phase. The timed operation is `cudaMemPrefetchAsync` to generate prefetch transfers, or CPU/GPU kernels to generate demand transfers.

Figures 2g–l show example results for CPU/GPU and GPU/GPU transfers, for both prefetch and demand migrations. Prefetch bandwidth is capable of achieving nearly the same performance as pinned memory transfers; demand migration bandwidth is substantially lower for large transfers. The GPU-to-CPU demand transfer rate is limited by the rate that a single CPU thread can generate loads. Prefetch transfers exhibit some performance variation based on device affinity and direction of transfer. Coherence overhead limits CPU/GPU demand transfer bandwidth and these transfers do not show strong correlation with device affinity.

3.1   Page Fault Latency

Unified memory page fault latency is estimated by constructing a linked list in managed memory, forcing it to be migrated to the source device, and executing a single-threaded CPU or GPU kernel on the destination device to traverse it.

The stride between linked-list elements is large enough to avoid the effects of prefetching. Each access to the list incurs a page fault. The incremental change in function execution time as the number of strides increases is therefore an approximate measure of the page fault latency. Table 1 summarizes the estimated page fault latencies. There is no substantial difference in page fault latencies for different CPUs in the same system, so values for faults involving CPU0 are shown. AC922 is slower than S822LC in all categories.

Table 1. Measured page-fault latencies.

Page Fault	Latency (μs)	
Type	S822LC	AC922
CPU $\rightarrow$ GPU	14.9	24.1
CPU $\leftarrow$ GPU	13.6	27.4
GPU0 $\leftrightarrow$ GPU1 (local)	25.5	38.0
GPU0 $\leftrightarrow$ GPU2 (remote)	28.8	41.5

4   Conclusion

This report presents initial results of a system interconnect characterization effort. Other relevant transfer bandwidths under investigation include CPU-to-CPU, CUDA remote mappings, system atomics, GPU-direct I/O and network data transfers, and more detailed characterizations of the communication methods discussed in this report. A basis set of these algorithms will be used to create a microbenchmark suite. This suite could be leveraged to sanity-check system configuration during firmware development and help eliminate performance bottlenecks caused by incorrect parameters or implementation heuristics.

Furthermore, the NUMA and CUDA libraries present a logical abstraction of the system communication. To create accurate performance models, a relationship between the logical communication paths and underlying hardware should be established. This work will be expanded to enumerate the underlying hardware through the operating system, and observe traffic on that hardware to establish the logical-to-physical mapping. Tying the underlying hardware to the observed bandwidths allows the appropriate performance models to be automatically generated. Those models may then be utilized to create NUMA and multi-GPU topology-aware communication runtimes and allocators. Those models may also be used for architecture studies to understand the high-level architectural tradeoffs for affecting application performance.

References

1. NUMA(3) Linux Programmer's Manual (August 2007)
2. Cuda c programming guide (Nov 2017)
3. Caldeira, A.B.: Ibm power system ac922 introduction and technical overview. IBM Redbooks (2018)
4. Caldeira, A.B., Haug, V., Vetter, S.: Ibm power system 822lc for high performance computing introduction and technical overview. IBM Redbooks (2016)
5. Google: Benchmark. https://github.com/google/benchmark (2018)
6. Harris, M.: Unified memory in cuda 6 (2013), https://devblogs.nvidia.com/parallelforall/unified-memory-in-cuda-6/
7. Pearson, C., Dakkak, A., Li, C.: microbench. https://github.com/rai-project/microbench (2018)
8. Wickman, C., Lameter, C., Schermerhorn, L.: numactl v2.0.11. https://github.com/numactl/numactl (2015)

IXPUG Workshop: Many-Core Computing on Intel Processors: Applications, Performance and Best-Practice Solutions

IXPUG Workshop: Many-Core Computing on Intel Processors: Applications, Performance and Best-Practice Solutions

Thomas Steinke[1], Simon J. Pennycook[2], Estela Suarez[3], and David E. Martin[4]

[1] Zuse Institute Berlin (ZIB), Takustr. 7, D-14195 Berlin, Germany
steinke@zib.de
[2] Intel Corporation, Santa Clara, USA
[3] Jülich Supercomputing Centre (JSC) - Forschungszentrum
Jülich GmbH, Jülich, Germany
[4] Argonne National Laboratory, Argonne, USA

Abstract. IXPUG has extended its scope to cover all aspects of HPC systems, and this is reflected in the agenda of this year's IXPUG Workshop. The selected presentations covered traditional HPC workloads and their optimization on Intel Xeon and Xeon Phi platforms as well as experience reports of applying machine learning methods. An update in the area of programming models were given with the presentation of the new features in OpenMP 5. Approaches to achieve portable performance were outlined in the two invited talks.

Keywords: Many-core computing · Application optimization ·
Machine learning · Scalability · Intel Xeon · Intel Xeon Phi

1 IXPUG in an Evolving World - The New IXPUG

Intel technologies are ubiquitous in the HPC landscape. Processors are by far not the only important ingredient of modern HPC systems, and maximizing performance often requires that attention be paid to the system as a whole. Therefore, **IXPUG** - formerly known as the *Intel Xeon Phi User's Group* - has extended its scope to cover *all* aspects of HPC systems and, accordingly, has been renamed to **Intel eXtreme Performance User's Group**.

This is reflected in the technology that Intel provides for other significant system components, in addition to processors: Intel® Omni-Path Fabric and FPGA devices, for example. The Intel processor roadmap is evolving, and the most recent Intel® Xeon® processors are very similar in many ways to Intel® Xeon Phi™ processors. Both feature AVX-512 SIMD units, a 2D mesh to connect cores, and even a similar number of cores (in a two socket system). The only significant difference to date is the availability of on-package high-bandwidth memory. Due to these similarities, the key techniques and best practices for optimizing performance have proven not to be unique to one processor design.

1.1 What You Should Know About IXPUG

The Intel eXtreme Performance User's Group (IXPUG) is an independent users group whose mission is to provide a forum for the free exchange of information that enhances the usability and efficiency of scientific and technical applications running on large High Performance Computing (HPC) systems using data processing devices, network, or storage and other system-critical technologies developed by Intel. IXPUG is administered by representatives of member sites that operate large Intel-based HPC systems.

IXPUG holds meetings and other activities as determined by its members to further its mission. Participation in IXPUG meetings and other activities is open to anyone interested in using Intel technology for HPC systems - today Xeon and Xeon Phi processors, the Omni-Path interconnect, heterogeneous configurations including FPGAs - for large-scale scientific or technical computing. Current participants include staff from member sites, users of member sites' facilities, Intel staff, and others with an interest in using the Intel processor offerings for scientific computing on large HPC systems.

A Steering Committee (see Sect. 1.3) manages the overall direction of IXPUG, planning meetings and activities and working with members and sponsors to determine the most effective way to serve the HPC community.

IXPUG provides an effective conduit for application developers to interact directly with Intel engineers and other experts. As part of its community activities, IXPUG regularly organizes workshops and BoFs at the main supercomputing conferences, plus longer self-hosted user meetings distributed over the year and world-wide geography.

The IXPUG Workshop at ISC'18 is already the fourth of a workshop series initiated at ISC 2015, which have been very positively taken up by the community. Slides and training materials presented at IXPUG events are accessible through the group website [1].

IXPUG workshops cover topics in application performance and scalability challenges at all levels - from single processors to moderately-scaled clusters, up to large HPC configurations with many e.g. Xeon Phi devices. The next IXPUG event is the *2018 IXPUG US Annual Meeting*, which is jointly organized by Sandia National Laboratories, Los Alamos National Laboratory and Intel, and will take place at Intel Corporation in Hillsboro (Orgeon), USA, in September 25–28, 2018.

Further information can be found under http://www.ixpug.org/events.

1.2 Working Groups and Discussion Forum

The IXPUG working group sessions have adapted over the past year to include an ongoing webinar series, covering a wide range of topics including: new and upcoming features of Intel tools; high productivity languages; and cutting-edge research results. Recordings of these sessions and additional information can be found at https://www.ixpug.org/working-groups.

At last year's workshop, the IXPUG website introduced an online discussion forum for users to ask questions, share experience and get support from the rest of the community. Usage of this forum has not seen the level of adoption that was expected, and at this year's workshop it was suggested that the forum be retired in favour of a more modern alternative.

1.3 The IXPUG Steering Committee

The IXPUG Steering Committee oversees the development of IXPUG and guides the organization of IXPUG events, workshops, and working group meetings. The following list covers a wide range of Intel-based supercomputing institutions and geographic areas:

- Fabio Affinito, CINECA, Italy
- Taisuke Boku, University of Tsukuba, Japan
- Richard Gerber, NERSC - National Energy Research Scientific Computing Center/LBL - Lawrence Berkeley National Laboratory, USA
- Clay Hughes, Sandia National Laboratory, USA
- David Keyes, KAUST - King Abdullah University of Science & Technology, Saudi Arabia
- James Lin, Shanghai Jiao Tong University, China
- Kent Milfeld, Texas Advanced Computing Center, USA
- Hai Ah Nam, Los Alamos National Laboratory, USA
- John Pennycook, Intel Corporation, USA
- Thomas Steinke, Zuse Institute Berlin, Germany
- Vit Vondrak, VSB - Technical University of Ostrava, Czech Republic

The steering board is chaired by a leadership board. Its current members are:

- **President:** David Martin, Argonne National Laboratory, USA
- **Vice-President:** Estela Suarez, Jülich Supercomputing Center, Forschungszentrum Jülich GmbH, Germany
- **Secretary:** Melyssa Fratkin, Texas Advanced Computing Center, The University of Texas at Austin, USA

2 Workshop Overview

The full day workshop *Many-core Computing on Intel Processors: Applications, Performance and Best-Practice Solutions* indicates already in its title that we wanted to extend the scope beyond Xeon Phi topics.

The workshop brought together over 40 software developers and technology experts of a world-wide community to share challenges, experiences and best-practice methods for the optimization of HPC and Machine Learning workloads on Intel Xeon Scalable Processors and Intel Xeon Phi Processors.

Each of the morning and afternoon sessions started with a keynote presentation. Mark Seagler presented Intel's view on how HPC is impacting the digital economic transformation today and in the new future. Michel Klemm, CEO of OpenMP, gave a glimpse on the new OpenMP 5.0 features including the support of heterogeneous node configurations.

The two invited talks of the workshop were dedicated to portabability without sacrifying performance. Simon Hammond from Sandia Lab dived into the recent history of the Kokkos programming framework and presented how the code developer can benefit from using Kokkos with SIMD support. Matthias Noack from the Zuse Institute Berlin talked about his approaches to achieve portable performance on homogeneous and heterogeneous node configurations, and to enable scalability over a wide range of computer architectures - from laptop to supercomputer - to solve the Hierarchical Equations of Motion.

The submitted talks covered optimization and scalability topics in real-world high-performance computing and machine learning applications, e.g. data layouts and code restructuring for efficient SIMD operation, utilization of new AVX-512 instructions, work distribution and thread management.

From various sites an update of their recent system installations or future plans were given in sort presentations.

Finally, the workshop ended with sharing various thoughts among the attendees about "Quo vadis IXPUG?". Aspects related to, for example, the reach-out towards other HPC-related Intel technology communities, the means of communication, and the format of annual and regional workshops were brought up for discussion.

3 Call for Papers

The call for papers to the ISC'18 IXPUG Workshop opened on March 7, 2018.

IXPUG welcomed paper submissions on innovative work from users of Intel Xeon and Xeon Phi technology in academia, industry and government labs, describing original discoveries and experiences that will promote and prescribe efficient use of manycore and multicore systems. Authors were requested to submit papers not published in or being in preparation for other conferences, workshops or journals.

Topics of interest are (but not limited to):

- sharing techniques in vectorization, memory, communications, thread and process management
- multi-node application experiences
- programming models
- algorithms and methods
- software environment and tools
- benchmarking and profiling tools
- visualization development

For the workshop, the high-quality submissions were selected, with the best three ending in this ISC'18 Workshop Proceedings volume.

4 Workshop Agenda

Time	Title	Authors (Speaker*)
09:00	IXPUG Welcome	Thomas Steinke (ZIB)
09:15	KEYNOTE: HPC's Impact on the Digital Economy Transformation	Mark Seager (Intel)
10:00	CSB_Coo sparse matrix vector performance on Intel Xeon and Xeon Phi architectures	Brandon Cook, Charlene Yang, Thorsten Kurth* and Jack Deslippe (LBL)
10:30	Lessons Learned from Optimizing Kernels for Algebraic Multigrid Solvers in Lattice QCD	Balint Joo (Jefferson Lab) and Thorsten Kurth* (LBL)
11:00	Break	
11:30	INVITED TALK: Mapping SIMD into Kokkos	Simon Hammond (Sandia)
12:00	Distributed Training of Generative Adversarial Network	Sofia Vallecorsa* (CERN), Federico Carminati (CERN), Gulrukh Khattak (CERN), Damian Podareanu (SURFSARA), Valeriu Codreanu (SURFSARA), Vikram Saletore (Intel) and Hans Pabst (Intel)
12:30	MxNet and BigDL at AWS	Presentation by Amazon
12:45	Performance optimization for modern many-core architectures using PSYclone embedded-DSL	Sergi Siso*, Rupert Ford and Andrew Porter (STFC)
13:00	Lunch	
14:00	KEYNOTE: OpenMP API Version 5.0: A Story about Threads, Tasks, and Devices	Michael Klemm (CEO OpenMP)
15:00	Optimised Data Decomposition for Reduced Communication Costs	Manos Farsarakis* and Adrian Jackson (Univ. Edinburgh)
15:15	Site Updates:	
	IPCC Asian activity	Taisuke Boku (University of Tsukuba)
	TACC Science Stories	John Cazes (TACC)
	JSC Site Update	Bernd Mohr (Jülich Supercomputing Centre)
	KNL/OPA based KISTI 5th Supercomputer	Oh-Kyoung Kwon (KISTI South Korea)
	Recent Progress of Big Data Reseach in IPCC China	Shun Xu (Chinese Academy of Sciences)
	SSCC: Siberian supercomputer center for applied scientific computing	Igor Chernykh (Siberian Supercomputer Center)
16:00	Break	
16:30	INVITED TALK: DM-HEOM: A Portable and Scalable Solver-Framework for the Hierarchical Equations of Motion	Matthias Noack (ZIB)
17:00	Open Discussion: *Quo Vadis IXPUG?*	Thomas Steinke (ZIB)
17:55	Closing	Thomas Steinke (ZIB)

5 Program Committee

Taisuke Boku	University of Tsukuba
Doug Doerfler	Lawrence Berkeley National Lab (LBL)
Clayton Hughes	Sandia National Laboratories
Doug Jacobsen	Intel Corporation
Michael Klemm	Intel Corporation
David E. Martin	Argonne National Laboratory
Hai Ah Nam	Los Alamos National Laboratory
Simon J. Pennycook	Intel Corporation
Thomas Steinke	Zuse Institute Berlin (ZIB)
Estela Suarez	Jülich Supercomputing Centre (JSC)
Zhengji Zhao	Lawrence Berkeley National Lab (LBL)

6 Workshop Organizers

David E. Martin	Argonne National Laboratory (ANL)
Simon J. Pennycook	Intel Corporation
Thomas Steinke	Zuse Institute Berlin (ZIB)
Estela Suarez	Jülich Supercomputing Centre (JSC)

7 Reference

1. IXPUG: The Intel eXtreme Performance User's Group. http://www.ixpug.org

Sparse CSB_Coo Matrix-Vector and Matrix-Matrix Performance on Intel Xeon Architectures

Brandon Cook$^{(\boxtimes)}$, Charlene Yang , Thorsten Kurth , and Jack Deslippe

Lawrence Berkeley National Laboratory, Berkeley, CA 94720, USA
{bgcook,cjyang,tkurth,jrdeslippe}@lbl.gov

Abstract. The CSB_Coo sparse matrix format is especially useful in situations such as eigenvalue problems where efficient SPMV and transposed SPMV_T operations are required. One strategy to increase the arithmetic intensity of large scale parallel solvers is to use a blocked eigensolver such LOBPCG and to operate on blocks of vectors to achieve greater performance. However, this solution is not always practical as MPI communication may be higher leading to inefficiencies or the increased memory usage of dense vectors may be impractical. Additionally the Lanczos algorithm is well tested in production and may be preferred in some situations. On modern architectures vectorization is key for obtaining good performance. In this paper we show the performance optimization and benefits of vectorization with AVX-512 Conflict Detection (CD) instructions in the case of a standard SPMV operation on a single vector. We also present a modified version of the CSB_Coo format which allows more efficient vector operations. We compare and analyze performance on Haswell, Xeon Phi (KNL and KNM) and Intel Xeon Scalable processors (Skylake).

Keywords: SPMV · SPMM · Performance · AVX-512 · Vectorization

1 Introduction

Sparse matrix - dense vector linear algebra is important in a number of contexts, particularly in the solution of sparse eigenvalue/eigenvector problems. Sparse solvers typically are using iterative methods where the matrix is applied to the vectors repeatedly. These methods could operate on a single vector as in the well known Lanczos method [5] or in the case LOBPCG (Locally optimal block preconditioned conjugate gradient) could operate on blocks of vectors at once [4]. In both cases the key kernel is either a SPMM or SPMV operation. The SPMM case has been previously studied [3] for the Xeon Phi architecture. As expected an optimal choice of vector block size leads to significant performance improvements.

© Springer Nature Switzerland AG 2018
R. Yokota et al. (Eds.): ISC 2018 Workshops, LNCS 11203, pp. 463–471, 2018.
https://doi.org/10.1007/978-3-030-02465-9_33

However, using a blocked method can often come with some tradeoffs: increased memory usage and algorithmic complexity. Therefore an analysis of the single dense vector (SPMV) is also desired for modern architectures.

Intel introduced the AVX-512 instruction set with the Xeon Phi architecture. This instruction set comes with many new instructions and features including masking, compress and expand, conflict detection, 512 bit registers, rounding control, gather-scatter support, and more. Of particular interest for CSB_Coo operations are the conflict detection instructions which enabled otherwise non-safe vectorization of histogram type operations.

In this paper we investigate the performance of SPMM and SPMV operations on HSW, SKX, KNL and KNM. In Sect. 5 we focus on the SPMV operations.

2   System Architecture

Haswell and KNL nodes are on Cori at NERSC, a Cray XC40. The KNM and SKX nodes are at the University of Oregon's performance research laboratory (for details see Table 1).

Table 1. Architectures

CPU	Model	Cores	Vector length (bits)	Clock speed (GHz)
KNL	Xeon Phi 7250	68	512	1.40
KNM	Xeon Phi 7295	72	512	1.50
HSW	Xeon E5-2698 v3	16	256	2.30
SKX	Xeon Gold 6140	18	512	2.30

3   Methodology

All codes were compiled with Intel C++ compiler version 18.0.2 20180210 with -std=c++11 -O3 -qopenmp and the -xARCH flag set appropriately. The OS was CLE6up04 on the NERSC Cray systems (HSW, KNL) at the time of the tests. The University of Oregon systems (SKX, KNM) were running CentOS 7.5.

For dual socket systems we restricted threads to a single socket. The KNM system was booted into flat mode and the KNL runs were done with cache mode.

Timings were done with 100 iterations of the main kernel. At least one warmup iteration is always performed and not included in the timings. FLOPS are computed manually. All FLOPS in this work are single precision.

Listing 1.1. CSB_Coo data structure

```
struct Block {
  int iblk ,jblk ;  // base coordinates of the block
  std :: vector<short> i , j ;
  std :: vector<float> value ;
};
```

3.1 CSB_Coo

The CSB_Coo sparse matrix format was introduced to provide an efficient format for multicore architectures [1]. It is particularly suited to cases where both the matrix vector and matrix transpose vector operations are both required to be efficient. For example: in the case of sparse eigensolvers the MFDn configuration interaction code for nuclear structure calculations [2,6–8]. The main idea of the format is to store only the non-zero blocks of the matrix and within each block to use the Coo format. This has the advantage of similarly efficient access to the transpose by simply swapping the block indices. In C++11 the block data structure, using structures of arrays, is shown in listing 1.1.

4 SPMM

In some cases it is possible to use a block method such as LOBPCG. In that case best performance is realized by applying the matrix to a block of vectors at a time.

4.1 Vectorization

Unfortunately STL containers are difficult to align for vectorization. Generally one has to write a custom allocator. To achieve alignment and vectorization the data structure was modified from 1.1 to 1.3 and alignments were done with the _mm_malloc() routines with 64 byte alignment.

It was necessary to remove the computation of indices from the inner most loop of 1.2 to 1.4 in order to get the compiler to generate vector code.

For the vectorization tests the square sparse matrix has dimensions $n = 4e\text{-}6$ with 25000 non-zero blocks with dimension $K = 4000$ each with 16000 non-zero elements for a total of 4e-8 non-zero elements. The matrix elements and indices occupy 3.2 GB (64 bits per element) and the dense vectors occupy 16 MB each.

Figure 1a shows the performance benefit of increasing the number of dense vectors that are simultaneously operated on by the sparse matrix. In the naive case of simply increasing the number of vectors performance is increased by 3-4X with diminishing returns. On KNL the peak performance without vectorization is approximately 38 GFLOPS. After nrhs $>=$ 30 the performance of both KNL and KNM drops. In the case of KNL performance drops to the same as HSW with approximately 30–35 GFLOPS. Due to the memory overhead, diminishing returns and algorithmic details of block solvers nrhs $>$ 16 are less common.

Listing 1.2. CSB_Coo SPMM

```
void kernel_omp(Block ** __restrict__ H,
                float * __restrict__ X,
                float * __restrict__ Y,
                int N, int m, int B)
{
#pragma omp parallel for schedule(dynamic,1) shared(N,m,H)
  for (int I=0; I<N; I++)
    {
      for (int J=0; J<N; J++)
        {
          Block &h = H[I][J];
          const int nelem = h.value.size();
          if ( nelem != 0)
            {
              for (int k=0; k<nelem; k++)
                {
                  for (int rhs=0; rhs<m; rhs++)
                    {
                      const int ii = I*B + h.i[k] + rhs;
                      const int jj = J*B + h.j[k] + rhs;
                      Y[ii] += h.value[k] * X[jj];
                    }
                }
            }
        }
    }
}
```

Listing 1.3. CSB_Coo data structure

```
struct Block {
  int iblk, jblk; // base coord of the block
  int nnz=0;
  short *i, *j;
  float *value;
};
```

The diminishing returns are explained by a simple model considering 2 flops (1 multiply and 1 add) and 12 bytes of reads and writes for each vector and 8 bytes for each non-zero matrix element (value and indices) which is reused:

$$AI(nrhs) = \frac{2 * nrhs \text{ flops}}{8 + 12 * nrhs \text{ bytes}} \quad (1)$$

For small values of nrhs big gains in reuse are possible, but in the limit of large nrhs approaches an AI of $1/6$.

Figure 1b shows the increase in performance due to vectorization. On Haswell vectorization and data alignment results in a 2-3X increase in performance.

Listing 1.4. CSB_Coo vectorized aligned SPMM

```
if ( nelem != 0)
  {
    __assume_aligned(h.i, 64);
    __assume_aligned(h.j, 64);
    for (int k=0; k<nelem; k++)
      {
        const int ii = I*B + h.i[k];
        const int jj = J*B + h.j[k];
        __assume_aligned(h.value, 64);
        __assume_aligned(X, 64);
        __assume_aligned(Y, 64);
        for (int rhs=0; rhs<m; rhs++)
          {
            Y[ii+rhs] += h.value[k] * X[jj+rhs];
          }
      }
  }
```

On Haswell and Skylake the performance shows clear peaks at multiples of vector length. When operating on blocks of vectors which are not a multiple of the vector length Skylake and Xeon Phi show better performance characteristics due to masking instructions and registers. Interestingly the Intel compiler does not generate AVX-512 code by default for Skylake for this code. Enabling the `-qopt-zmm-usage=high` option shows increased performance only in some cases and also results in a more significant performance drop at large numbers of vectors. On KNL and KNM vectorization is critical for achieving good performance. In the scalar case Skylake had similar performance, but when executing the vectorized kernels KNL and KNM show an advantage. Vectorization and multiple right hand sides result in up to 5X increases in performance over the non-vector code. The changes made in the SPMM kernel, 1.2 to 1.4, actually *decrease* the performance in the case of nrhs = 1.

5 SPMV

Operating on multiple dense vectors at once may not always be possible or desirable. It can increase memory usage or require a complete rewrite of a solver (e.g. Lanczos to LOBPCG).

5.1 Thread Scaling

Figures 2a and b show the thread scalability of the SPMV operation on KNL and Skylake, respectively. The matrix has dimensions $n = 4e\text{-}6$ with 5000 non-zero blocks with dimension $K = 4000$ each with 16000 non-zero elements for a

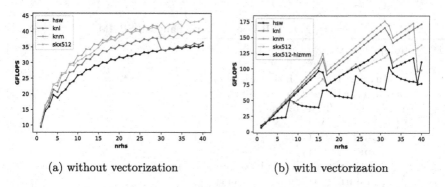

(a) without vectorization   (b) with vectorization

Fig. 1. SPMM single precision performance for different numbers of right hand side as implemented in 1.2. The matrix has dimensions $n = 4e\text{-}6$ with 25000 non-zero blocks with dimension $K = 4000$ each with 16000 non-zero elements for a total of 4e-8 non-zero elements.

total of 8e-7 non-zero elements. In the case of Skylake the threads are bound to a single socket. Despite the much larger core count the thread scalability on KNL is better than on Skylake. The better thread scaling on the KNL is due to the problem fitting entirely within MCDRAM vs spilling out of L3 on HSW/SKX with a total footprint of ∼672 MB. The thread scaling performance also depends on the non-zero block size. In general not all blocks will have the same number of non-zero elements and therefore dynamic scheduling of work to threads is required which causes appreciable overhead when the number of non-zero elements per block is small. It should also be noted that KNL is much more sensitive to data alignment than Skylake.

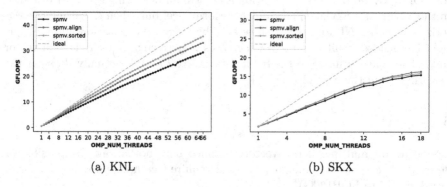

(a) KNL   (b) SKX

Fig. 2. SPMV thread scaling performance on KNL and SKX. The matrix has dimensions $n = 4e\text{-}6$ with 5000 non-zero blocks with dimension $K = 4000$ each with 16000 non-zero elements for a total of 8e-7 non-zero elements.

Listing 1.5. CSB_Coo data structure

```
struct Block {
  int iblk,jblk; // base coordinates of the block
  int nnz=0; // total non-zero elements
  int nnz_conflict=0;
  short *i, *j; // no conflicts in blocks of VLEN
  float *value;
  short *ic, *jc; // potentially conflicting
  float *valuec;
};
```

5.2 AVX-512 CD Instructions

Even with `-qopt-zmm-usage=high -xSKYLAKE-AVX512` the Intel C++ compiler does not generate collision detection instructions. The opt report indicates that it correctly identifies the "histogram" operation, but it chooses to not generate the instructions.

On KNL and KNM the conflict detection (CD) instructions enable efficient vectorization of the inner most loop. This loop is 4-5X faster than the SPMM case with nrhs = 1 due to the vectorization enabled by the CD instructions. Careful alignment of the data was found to be especially important on KNL and KNM when using these instructions, resulting in 10–15% better performance.

5.3 Manually Removing the Conflicts

However, while the CD instructions enable efficient vectorization on KNL and KNM the instructions come with some additional overhead. Since the SPMV kernel will be executed many thousands of times as one of the main kernels of a solver it is worth investigating other means to improve the performance further.

One method is to manually remove potential conflicts in blocks of VLEN from the Coo blocks during the initialization phase. Depending on the sparsity and block dimensions it may not be possible to remove all conflicts. To enable this sorting we modify the basic block data structure from 1.3 to 1.5.

The removal of conflicts can be done on-the-fly by maintaining a set of the last VLEN indices that were processed during the initialization phase. When each new matrix element is generated if it is not in the set then it is added to no-conflicts bucket and otherwise put in the conflict bucket. Once the size of the set reaches VLEN the contents are cleared. While other methods to remove conflicts are possible this method was found to be efficient at removing most conflicts from the Coo blocks.

In order to gain an advantage from this the compiler must also not generate CD instructions when they are no longer required. This is done by iterating over the bucket with no conflicts (i,j,values) and the bucket with potential conflicts separately. In the former case `#pragma ivdep` is added to avoid generation of AVX-512 CD instructions.

Figure 3 shows SPMV performance for a range of matrix sparsities and architectures. On KNL and KNM the addition of this sorting step improved the SPMV performance of this kernel by an additional 5–10%. While there is some overhead added to the initialization phase this cost easily amortized by better performance of a kernel which is executed many thousands of times. On HSW and SKX these changes have a minimal (1–3%) impact on performance due to the additional overheads and lack of CD instructions.

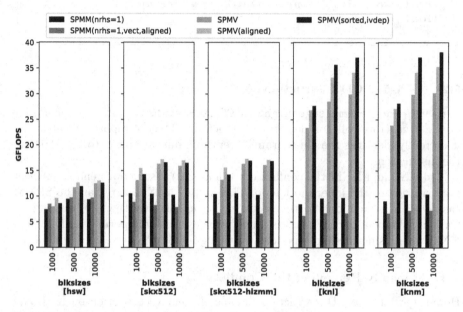

Fig. 3. Performance of SPMM and SPMV kernels with different optimizations for various CPU architectures

6   Conclusions

In conclusion we studied the vectorization of SPMM and SPMV kernels with a CSB_Coo sparse matrix on a range of Intel Xeon architectures. As expected, we found that vectorization was important for achieving good performance on all architectures, but KNL and KNM were especially reliant on vectorization for realizing good performance. We identified some potential pitfalls with utilizing the vectorized SPMM kernel in the case of a single dense vector. In particular we highlight the role of the AVX-512 conflict detection instructions on platforms which support them. We found they were beneficial on the phi platforms, but that the compiler avoided generating them for the SKX architecture. Additionally we introduced a method to avoid conflicts manually in the initialization phase to obtain additional speedups by avoiding the conflict detection instructions and only using gather/scatter operations.

Acknowledgments. This work used resources provided by the Performance Research Laboratory at the University of Oregon. This research used resources of the National Energy Research Scientific Computing Center (NERSC), a DOE Office of Science User Facility supported by the Office of Science of the U.S. Department of Energy under Contract No. DE-AC02-05CH11231.

References

1. Aktulga, H.M., Buluç, A., Williams, S., Yang, C.: Optimizing sparse matrix-multiple vectors multiplication for nuclear configuration interaction calculations. In: 2014 IEEE 28th International Parallel and Distributed Processing Symposium, pp. 1213–1222. IEEE (2014)
2. Binder, S., Calci, A., Epelbaum, E., Furnstahl, R.J., Golak, J., Hebeler, K., Kamada, H., Krebs, H., Langhammer, J., Liebig, S., Maris, P., Meißner, U.G., Minossi, D., Nogga, A., Potter, H., Roth, R., Skiniński, R., Topolnicki, K., Vary, J.P., Witała, H.: Few-nucleon systems with state-of-the-art chiral nucleon-nucleon forces. Phys. Rev. C **93**(4), 044002 (2016). https://doi.org/10.1103/PhysRevC.93.044002
3. Cook, B., Maris, P., Shao, M., Wichmann, N., Wagner, M., OâĂŹNeill, J., Phung, T., Bansal, G.: High performance optimizations for nuclear physics code MFDn on KNL. In: Taufer, M., Mohr, B., Kunkel, J.M. (eds.) ISC High Performance 2016. LNCS, vol. 9945, pp. 366–377. Springer, Cham (2016). https://doi.org/10.1007/978-3-319-46079-6_26
4. Knyazev, A.V.: Toward the optimal preconditioned eigensolver: locally optimal block preconditioned conjugate gradient method. SIAM J. Sci. Comput. **23**(2), 517–541 (2001)
5. Lanczos, C.: An iteration method for the solution of the eigenvalue problem of linear differential and integral operators. J. Res. Natl Bur. Std. **45**, 255–282 (1950)
6. Maris, P., Caprio, M.A., Vary, J.P.: Emergence of rotational bands in ab initio no-core configuration interaction calculations of the Be isotopes. Phys. Rev. C **91**(1), Article no. 014310 (2015). https://doi.org/10.1103/PhysRevC.91.014310
7. Maris, P., Vary, J.P., Navratil, P., Ormand, W.E., Nam, H., Dean, D.J.: Origin of the anomalous long lifetime of ^{14}C. Phys. Rev. Lett. **106**(20), Article no. 202502 (2011). https://doi.org/10.1103/PhysRevLett.106.202502
8. Maris, P., Vary, J.P., Gandolfi, S., Carlson, J., Pieper, S.C.: Properties of trapped neutrons interacting with realistic nuclear Hamiltonians. Phys. Rev. C **87**(5), 054318 (2013). https://doi.org/10.1103/PhysRevC.87.054318

Lessons Learned from Optimizing Kernels for Adaptive Aggregation Multi-grid Solvers in Lattice QCD

Bálint Joó[1] and Thorsten Kurth[2](✉)

[1] Thomas Jefferson National Accelerator Facility, Newport News, VA, USA
bjoo@jlab.org
[2] National Energy Research Scientific Computing Center, Berkeley, CA, USA
TKurth@lbl.gov

Abstract. In recent years, adaptive aggregation multi-grid (AAMG) methods have become the gold standard for solving the Dirac equation in Lattice QCD (LQCD) using Wilson-Clover fermions. These methods are able to overcome the critical slowing down as quark masses approach their physical values and are thus the go-to method for performing Lattice QCD calculations at realistic physical parameters. In this paper we discuss the optimization of a specific building block for implementing AAMG for Wilson-Clover fermions from LQCD, known as the coarse restrictor operator, on contemporary Intel processors featuring large SIMD widths and high thread counts. We will discuss in detail the efficient use of OpenMP and Intel vector intrinsics in our attempts to exploit fine grained parallelism on the coarsest levels. We present performance optimizations and discuss the ramifications for implementing a full AAMG stack on Intel Xeon Phi Knights Landing and Skylake processors.

1 Introduction

Quantum Chromodynamics (QCD) is the theory of the nuclear force and strong interaction. It is responsible for binding quarks into protons and neutrons through the exchange of gluons. Further, residual strong force interactions are responsible for binding protons and neutrons into nuclei which make up atoms and, ultimately, most of the visible matter in the universe. In the discretized formulation of QCD called Lattice QCD (LQCD) [11,17,19], 4-dimensional space-time is discretized onto a 4-dimensional, regular, hypercubic lattice. LQCD itself is a fully renormalizable quantum field theory, which is amenable to numerical solution. As such LQCD calculations can be used to study the non-perturbative low energy regime of QCD.

Most of the computational cycles in typical LQCD calculations are spent on solving the lattice Dirac equation, $D\psi = \chi$ which is a large sparse system of linear equations. The linear operator D is known as the Dirac Operator and encodes how quarks and gluons interact. For quark masses close to the physical values

© Springer Nature Switzerland AG 2018
R. Yokota et al. (Eds.): ISC 2018 Workshops, LNCS 11203, pp. 472–486, 2018.
https://doi.org/10.1007/978-3-030-02465-9_34

of the light quark masses, the condition number of D grows large and the Dirac Equation becomes computationally expensive to solve, a phenomenon referred to as *critical slowing down* of the solver. A recent development in the field of Lattice QCD have been the development of multi-grid preconditioned solvers [2,5,8,12,18] and related methods [16] which solve the problem of critical slowing down with the quark mass for the Sheikholeslami-Wohlert [20] formulation of quarks (colloquially referred to as Wilson-Clover or just Clover quarks). The application of multi-grid to other fermion formulations is in progress, but is still very much an open research area (e.g. cf. [4,6,10,23]). Efficiently implemented multi-grid algorithms such as the one in the QUDA library for GPUs [7,9] provide an order of magnitude speedup in the solution of the Dirac Equation for Clover fermions over the Conjugate Gradients (CG) [13] and Stabilized Bi-Conjugate Gradients (BiCGStab) [21] solvers in standard use. Colloquially, the multi-grid approach is to produce successive corrections to an approximate solution, such that the correction reduces short wavelength contributions to the error on a fine grid, and those due to longer wavelengths are reduced on a succession of coarser grids. The operation of projecting a vector onto a coarser level from a finer level is known as restriction, and the operator which performs the restriction is known as the *restrictor*. Conversely, moving from a coarse level to a finer level is known as *prolongation*. Multi-grid solvers are also more stable in terms of solver iterations and tend to provide better quality solutions than CG and BiCGStab, as mulit-grid works on minimizing the error of the solution, rather than the residual.

In this paper we focus on optimizing the restrictor operator with vector intrinsics and OpenMP. As such the full description of multi-grid algorithms is beyond our scope and we refer the reader to many refernces outlined earlier. We also do not claim originality for vectorizing the restrictor, many issues were also considered in [14] although our vectorized layout is slightly different. Rather, as the restriction operation exhibits a variety of levels of parallelism it is a natural laboratory to study approaches to expressing these forms of parallelism in OpenMP, especially in the latency sensitive strong scaling limit, where on GPU architectures the exploitation of fine grained parallelism was necessary for efficient utilization of the compute resources and high performance [9].

Our paper is organized as follows: In Sect. 2 we describe the implementation strategies for the restrictor including our vectorization approach and the approaches we have investigated for parallelization with OpenMP. In Sect. 3 we discuss our numerical results, and finally in Sect. 4 we draw our conclusions.

2 Restrictor Definition and Implementation

We implemented the restrictor in the prototype *mg_proto* code [15]. This is a work-in progress prototype code which implements a basic Wilson-Clover aggregation multi-grid, and is functional, though not yet well optimized. Concretely, we will consider optimizing the restriction from one coarse level to the next, such as one would have in a 3 or more level solver. It is at this point where strong scaling problems are most challenging due to there being very few lattice sites on the coarsest level. Since the multi-grid is typically used as a preconditioner we consider only a single precision implementation.

In order to move from a lattice on one grid level to another, the finer lattice is split into N_B hypercubic blocks, each of which will utimately correspond to a single site on the coarse grid. One then also generates N_{vec} near null-space vectors $v^{a,i}(x)$ of the linear operator D_c on our current grid level (on the finest level this is just the Dirac operator D, whereas on coarser levels D_c are successive coarsenings of D). There are several ways to generate $v^{a,i}$, we refer the reader to the literature cited earlier. In our notation a will index the $2N_{fine}$ complex components of $v^{a,i}(x)$ on every (fine)site x while i labels the vectors: $i \in \{0, ..., N_{vec} - 1\}$. We will refer to the first N_{fine} components of $v^{a,i}(x)$ as the "upper" and the second set as the "lower" components respectively.

The application of the restrictor operator $R\psi$ is a matrix vector multiplication. The matrix R has the structure shown in Fig. 1a. For each block of the fine lattice, R has $2N_{vec}$ rows. These will correspond the upper and lower color components on the restricted coarse vector. The columns of the matrix come from the $2N_{fine}$ components of each of the N_{inner} sites within each block. Blocks are non-overlapping and contain equal numbers of sites, hence each fine site appears only once in each block. In particular the submatrix $V_U^H(x)$ for a (fine) site x is the hermitian conjugate of the matrix $V_U(x) = [v_U^0(x)|v_U^1(x)| \ldots |v_U^{N_{vec}-1}(x)]$ where the $v_U^i(x)$ are the upper components of the null space vectors on fine site x. $V_L^H(x)$ is similarly constructed using the lower components of the vectors.

To apply the restrictor we therefore need to perform 2 independent matrix vector operations at each inner site for the upper and lower rows of the result respectively. Each row of the result can be computed independently. The parallelism over the rows of the result can be expressed using SIMD parallelism on Intel Xeon Phi Knights Landing (KNL) and Intel Xeon Server Skylake (SKX) processors. One needs to pick the correct component from the right hand side, broadcast it to a SIMD vector and then it can be multiplied simultaneously by the appropriate column of the matrix and accumulated as shown in Fig. 1b. We use single precision AVX512 intrinsics, hence we store 8 complex numbers in a 512-bit wide SIMD vector laid out in the natural way:

$$v_{SIMD} = \{Re_0|Im_0|Re_1|Im_1|...|Re_7|Im_7\} \tag{1}$$

A Complex-FMA where a single component from the RHS vector is multiplied with a SIMD vector of complex numbers from the column of the matrix can be implemented as shown Appendix A. With this in place, evaluating the 2 block matrix vector products by rows is straightforward (also in Appendix A). In order for all this to work we choose both N_{vec} and N_{fine} to be multiples of 8, so our vectors are always 'full' and, as long as the data for the first site is 64-byte aligned, the data of all the other sites will be aligned as well.

Finally we must express parallelism over sites and blocks. In a serial implementation this is easily done, the naive loop ordering is shown in Fig. 2. We also show that parallelizing over the blocks is straightforward and is a matter of adding a single OpenMP parallel-for pragma.

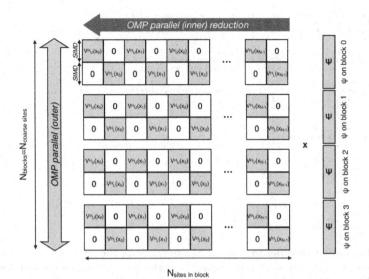

(a) A schematic of the restriction operator. A description is given in the main text. We also show the opportunities for parallelism (SIMD over the number of vectors, threading over the blocks and possible threading over the the sites within the blocks which involves a reduction. In the implementation the zero sub-blocks are not stored)

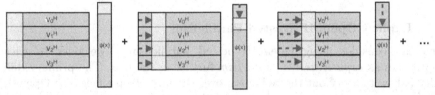

(b) SIMD-ization of the Matrix Vector Multiply by accumulating columns . Two of these are needed to apply the block diagonal matrices V_U^H and V_L^H at each site

Fig. 1. Overview of thread- and SIMD-parallelism in the coarse restrictor kernel.

Parallelization over the inner loop (lines 17–26) of Fig. 2 can be performed in several ways:

2.1   No Inner Parallelism or Parallelism Using Atomics

One may choose to not parallelize over this loop at all. If there are a sufficient number of output sites (e.g. one per thread) this is a perfectly fine choice to make. However, in the strong scaling limit (e.g. the output has only a 2^4 blocks) the total of number of threads is limited to only 16. On a system like KNL with over 64 cores and 4 threads per core, this can at best utilize only a quarter of the number of the cores running at 1 thread per core.

Alternatively one could, in principle, consider parallelizing over both the outer and inner loops simultaneously by using atomics, similar to histogramming.

```
1   #pragma omp parallel for collapse(2) schedule(static)
2   for(int block_cb = 0; block_cb < n_checkerboard; ++block_cb) {
3       for(int block_cbsite=0; block_cbsite < num_coarse_cbsites; block_cbsite++) {
4           int block_idx = block_cbsite + num_coarse_cbsites*block_cb;
5
6           const Block& block = _blocklist[block_idx];
7           auto block_sitelist = block.getCBSiteList();
8           auto num_sites_in_block = block_sitelist.size();
9
10          // One result per block: zero it before entering inner region
11          float* coarse_site_spinor = out.GetSiteDataPtr(block_cb,block_cbsite);
12          for(int i=0; i < n_floats; ++i) {
13              coarse_site_spinor[i] =0;
14          }
15
16          // Inner parallel region
17          for( IndexType fine_site_idx = 0;
18               fine_site_idx < static_cast<IndexType>(num_sites_in_block); ++fine_site_idx) {
19
20              // compute site result here...
21
22              for(int i=0; i < n_floats; ++i) {
23                  coarse_site_spinor[i] += ...; // accumulate site result
24              }
25
26          } // fine_site_index
27      } // block_cbsite
28  } // block_cb
```

Fig. 2. The basic loop order to evaluate the restriction. The outer two loops loop over all the blocks. The loop over `fine_site_idx` performs the summation over the inner sites making up the block.

However, we did not pursue this method as in our case it would ideally require atomic adds of AVX512 vectors which we were unsure how to achieve.

2.2   Explicit OpenMP Nested Parallelism

One can consider using OpenMP nested parallelism – we refer to these approaches as *explicit nested parallelism* further in the text. The primary difficulty is how to carry out the reduction over the inner loop efficiently: OpenMP offers two approaches: *array reductions* and *custom reductions*.

Implementing array reductions is straightforward in terms of OpenMP notation. We show the decorated loop in Fig. 3 – all that is needed is to add appropriate array notation on the reduction variable.

```
1   // Inner parallel region
2   #pragma omp parallel for reduction(+: coarse_site_spinor[:4*num_coarse_color])
3   for( IndexType fine_site_idx = 0;
4        fine_site_idx    < static_cast<IndexType>(num_sites_in_block);
5        fine_site_idx ++ ) {
6
7       // Private result
8       float site_accum[4*num_coarse_color] __attribute__((aligned(64)));
9
10      // compute site result here...
11
12      // Accumulate (reduce)
13  #pragma omp simd simdlen(16) safelen(16) aligned(coarse_site_spinor,site_accum:64)
14      for(int i=0; i < n_floats; ++i) {
15          coarse_site_spinor[i] += site_accum[i]; // acimmulate site result
16      }
17  } // fine_site_index
```

Fig. 3. Array sum version of inner loop

One issue with the array sum is that for C/C++ it is a very recent OpenMP 4.5 feature and is not universally well implemented. Our version of the Intel 17

compiler produced a syntax error. We managed to compile it with GCC and
Clang-6.0, however using GCC we encountered run-time errors as private arrays
were not appropriately aligned. We could make things work by removing the
SIMD decoration from the accumulating loops.

2.3   OpenMP Custom Reductions

One way to try and get around compiler issues and to ensure that summations
in the reduction are vectorized was to use OpenMP custom reductions. A simple
way is to define a class which can hold our partial results. The only thing to
beware of is that this must have a default constructor so that OpenMP can create
private copies as it needs. Our custom type and its accumulation operation are
defined inside the reduction class as in Fig. 4.

```
1   template<int N> class SIMDArray {
2    public:
3     SIMDArray() { /* Zeros itself on instantiation , code not shown */ }
4
5     float array[N] __attribute__((aligned(64)));
6
7     inline void operator+=(const SIMDArray<N>& addme) {
8       for(int i = 0; i < N; i+=16) {
9         __m512 out = _mm512_load_ps(&array[i]);
10        __m512 in  = _mm512_load_ps(&addme.array[i]);
11        out = _mm512_add_ps(out,in);
12        _mm512_store_ps(&array[i],out);
13      }}
14  };
```

Fig. 4. The custom type used in our custom reduction approach

Once the custom type was ready, we could implement the custom reduction
as shown in Fig. 5

```
1   // Declare the custom reduction
2   #pragma omp declare reduction(customAdd:SIMDArray<n_floats>:omp_out += omp_in)
3
4   // Use the custom reduction
5   #pragma omp parallel for reduction(customAdd:block_sum) schedule(static) \
6                                       num_threads(_r_threads_per_block)
7   for( IndexType fine_site_idx = 0;
8        fine_site_idx < static_cast<IndexType>(num_sites_in_block);
9        fine_site_idx ++ ) {
10
11     // Site local copy
12     SIMDArray<n_floats> site_accum;;
13     {
14       // ... matvec multiply into site_accum.array
15     }
16     block_sum += site_accum;   // custom reduction via operator+=()
17  }
18  // copy out block_sum.array to coarse_site_spinor , code not shown
```

Fig. 5. The custom reduction using SIMDArray from Fig. 4

2.4   Manual Fake-Out of Nested Parallelism

Finally one can consider using a manually implemented version of nested parallelism, where OpenMP functions with a single level of parallelism and the programmer deals with the multiple levels of parallelism by splitting the thread index manually into outer (block) and inner (fine site) indices. We will refer to this as *manual nesting* from here on. In this case one must allocate resources for the partial sums of the threads and worry about mapping the loops over the threads. The code for this is sketched in Figs. 6 and 7 which show the partial result computation and reduction over threads respectively. We implemented two reduction approaches: in Fig. 7 we show a single thread looping and reducing the partial results, to which we refer as *serial reduction*. We have also tried to have a *single thread per block* sum the results of the blocks. The code for this is a straightforward modification of Fig. 7 which we relegate to Appendix B. We refer to this as *parallel reduction* to distinguish it from the *serial version*.

```
1        // Threads can accumulate in here
2        float site_accum[ n_floats*_n_threads] __attribute__((aligned(64)));
3
4        // number of outer threads
5        int r_block_threads = _n_threads / _r_threads_per_block;
6
7        // number of steps in outer loop
8        int n_steps = _n_blocks / r_block_threads;
9        if ( _n_blocks % r_block_threads != 0  ) n_steps++; // Round steps to ceiling
10
11        // Travers outer blocks in steps
12        for(int step = 0; step < n_steps; ++step) {
13            // Do each step with a parallel region
14 #pragma omp parallel shared(site_accum, r_block_threads)
15        {
16            // Setup inner and outer indices
17        int tid = omp_get_thread_num();
18            int block_tid = tid / _r_threads_per_block;
19        int site_tid =  tid % _r_threads_per_block;
20
21            // Each thread zeroes site_accum_buffer
22 #pragma omp simd simdlen(16) safelen(16) aligned(site_accum:64)
23            for(int i=0; i < n_floats; ++i) {
24                site_accum[i+n_floats*(site_tid + _r_threads_per_block*block_tid)]= 0;
25            }
26
27            // Only enter the site loop if block_idx is sensible
28        if( block_idx < _n_blocks ) {
29
30                // ... identify block sitelistes etc.
31
32                // Compute thread partial results
33                for( IndexType fine_site_idx = site_tid;
34                    fine_site_idx < static_cast<IndexType>(num_sites_in_block);
35                    fine_site_idx += _r_threads_per_block ) {
36
37                    // Matrix vector product accumulation in here ...
38
39                } // fine site index
40            } // if block_idx
41        } // parallel region -- implied barrier
42
43            // Reduce results somehow
44        } // n_step
```

Fig. 6. Faking nested parallelism by manual thread indexing. The serial reduction step at the end is shown in Fig. 7

```
 1        // Reduce via single thread
 2        for(int block_tid = 0; block_tid < r_block_threads; block_tid++) {
 3          int block_idx = step*r_block_threads + block_tid;
 4          if( block_idx < _n_blocks ) {
 5            int block_cb = block_idx /num_coarse_cbsites;
 6            int block_cbsite = block_idx % num_coarse_cbsites;
 7
 8            float* coarse_site_spinor = out.GetSiteDataPtr(block_cb,block_cbsite);
 9
10 #pragma simd safelen(16) simdlen(16) aligned(coarse_site_spinor:64)
11            for(int colorspin=0; colorspin < n_floats; ++colorspin) {
12              coarse_site_spinor[colorspin]=0;
13            }
14
15            // Sum the results of all the threads
16            for(int s=0; s < _r_threads_per_block; ++s) {
17              int soffset =n_floats*(s  + _r_threads_per_block*block_tid);
18
19 #pragma simd safelen(16) simdlen(16) aligned(coarse_site_spinor , site_accum:64)
20              for(int colorspin=0; colorspin <  n_floats; ++colorspin) {
21                coarse_site_spinor[colorspin] += site_accum[colorspin+soffset];
22              } //colorspin
23            } // s
24          } // if block_idx < _n_blocks
25        } // block tid loop
26      } // n_step (surrounding loop)
```

Fig. 7. Serial reduction in the manual nesting approach (end of Fig. 6)

3   Performance Results

3.1   Experimental Setup

For our experiments we used the NERSC Cori system [1], comprised of 9688 nodes featuring Intel Xeon Phi 7250 (KNL) CPUs and 96 GB of DDR and 16 GB of high-bandwidth on-package memory, and another system, a single node comprised of two Intel Xeon Gold 6140 (SKX) CPUs with 192 GB DDR memory. Both CPUs support the relevant parts of the AVX-512 instruction set for our code. For compiling the USQCD software stack and our restrictor test code we used the Intel Compiler v17.0.3 on Cori and v17.0.5 on the Skylake machine. For the GNU compiler tests we used gcc v6.3.0. For thread affinity and other OpenMP runtime settings we use the runtime independent environment variables. Specifically, we set OMP_NESTED to true or false depending on whether we are measuring our kernel with explicit nested parallelism or the two with manual nesting. Furthermore, in order to ensure compatibility with the GNU OpenMP runtime, we had to set OMP_DYNAMIC to true when nesting was enabled. Since we never have more than two levels of nested parallelism, we set OMP_MAX_ACTIVE_LEVELS to 2. For the manually nested kernels we set OMP_PROC_BIND to spread and for the explicitly nested kernel to either spread,spread or spread,close[1]. The variable OMP_PLACES was always set to threads. Finally, we set the number of outer and inner threads, i.e. othreads,ithreads for the explicitly nested kernels by setting OMP_NUM_THREADS to that value. For the manually nested kernels we set that variable to their product and specified the decomposition by passing the number of inner threads via a command line argument of the test code. We ran different fine grid input volumes with $4^4, 4^3 \times 8, 4^2 \times 8^2$ and 4×8^3 sites. We ran the tests on a single KNL

---

[1] due to a bug in the libgomp runtime, we replaced spread by true to achieve correct binding for the GCC compiler tests.

node, and on a single socket on the Skylake system where we forced binding to
NUMA node 0 using `numactl -N 0`. The block size was always set to $2^4 = 16$
sites and we performed 500 iterations for each measurement.

3.2 Performance Results

We performed a thread scaling study on KNL and SKX for the manually nested
kernel with serial and parallel reduction. The number of threads was increased
from 16 to 256 in powers of two on KNL and from 16 to 32 on SKX. The number
of inner threads was varied from one (which corresponds to flat parallelism) to
16 in powers of two on both platforms. Since the block size was 16 sites we do
not expect that deploying more than a single thread per inner site will improve
performance. The results are displayed in Fig. 8. As one would expect, when the
opportunity for parallelism increases (bigger volumes) more threads win over
fewer threads and flat parallelism is preferred. For the smaller volumes, manually
nested parallelism performs slightly better and 2 or 4 inner threads are preferred
on KNL. On SKX, flat parallelism is preferred for all observed problem sizes and
concurrencies. On KNL, the parallel reduction can only improve performance on
the biggest volume whereas on the smaller, latency dominated volumes, the serial
reduction performs better. Especially the manually nested kernels which exploit
a lot of parallelism perform better than the explicitly nested kernels. In case of
the latter, only flat parallelism performs really well. When we try to run more
than 1 thread per block, performance drops precipitously.

On SKX, the difference between serial and parallel reduction is not as significant but the data favor the serial reduction for the observed problem sizes. The
best performing kernel here was the explicitly nested kernel with custom reduction *but in flat parallelism mode*. For both architectures, the manually nested
kernels perform much better when more than one inner thread is used, showing that the OpenMP nested parallelism has a substantially higher overheads
than the manually nested versions. We tried to use the `KMP_HOT_TEAMS` on a
development node and while it helped a small amount the results were still not
competitive with nesting. As it is not part of the OpenMP standard we do not
include those results here.

Figure 9 shows the best observed timings on KNL for various volumes with
$N_{fine} = 24$ and $N_{vec} = 32$. Here, the best performance result for each of our
three kernels is shown along with the thread concurrency used to achieved the
performance result.

The plot shows again that the parallel reduction needs bigger volumes. The
explicitly nested variant with custom OpenMP reduction shows the worst performance in almost all cases but is actually not far off from the other two kernels.
Again for explicit nesting flat parallelism is always preferred, in which case neither nested OpenMP nor the custom reduction are really needed.

Note that in a realistic multi-grid application involving multiple levels, various different coarse grid sizes are used and each may favor a different combination
of outer and inner thread parallelism, serial or parallel reductions. In order to

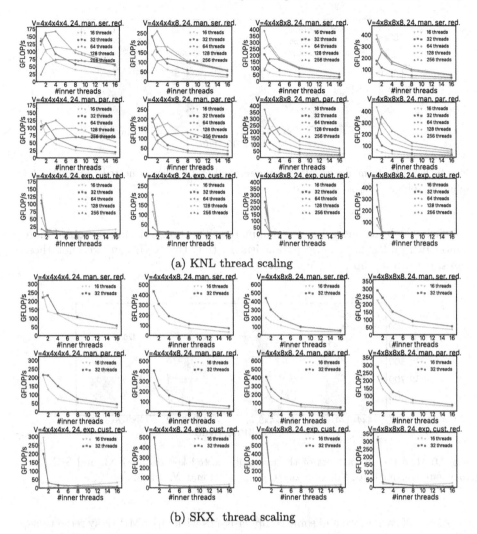

(a) KNL thread scaling

(b) SKX thread scaling

Fig. 8. Thread scaling on (a) KNL and (b) SKX for different volumes and $N_{vec} = 24$. Different colors correspond to changing the total threads from 16 to 256 in powers of 2 for KNL and for 16 and 32 on SKX. The x-axis corresponds to the number of inner threads. The number of outer threads is given by number of total threads divided by the number of inner threads. The different rows correspond to, from top to bottom: manual nesting with serial reduction, same with parallel reduction, explicit nesting with custom reduction.

implement this efficiently, some degree of auto-tuning might be required in order to ensure optimal performance for the whole multi-grid kernel stack.

We also compared the restrictor kernel performance on KNL and SKX for the best performing variant of the manually nested kernel and thread concurrency. Figure 10 shows that Skylake performs up to 1.97x faster on the smaller

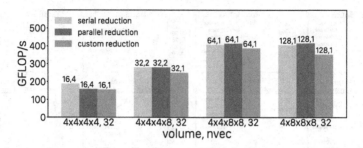

Fig. 9. KNL Performance results for the manual and explicitly nested restrictions for different volumes, $N_{fine} = 24$ and $N_{vec} = 32$.

volumes which are more latency dominated. The bigger volumes require more bandwidth and expose more parallelism so that the KNL can excel for these cases, performing up to 1.85x faster.

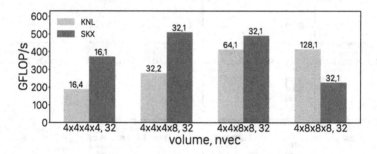

Fig. 10. The fastest variants of the manually nested kernels for KNL and SKX and their outer/inner thread distributions, $N_{fine} = 24$ and $N_{vec} = 32$.

As noted earlier, we had some compiler issues with OpenMP array reductions, which ultimately necessitated encoding the reduction using a custom reduction. The latter worked well on all the compilers we tried. Our results comparing performance for compilation with the Intel and GNU compilers for KNL are displayed in Fig. 11. We can see that the performance for the GCC compiled kernels are at least more than 30% lower than those from the Intel compiler, in extreme cases the Intel compiler generates even 2.14x faster code. Since most of the code is written in intrinsics and thus should be compiler independent, the difference can be most likely explained by differences in the OpenMP runtime.

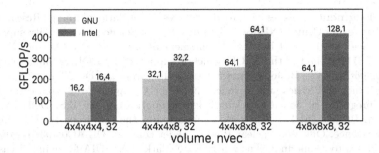

Fig. 11. Comparison between GCC and Intel compiler on KNL for the fastest variant of the manually nested kernels and thread concurrencies, $N_{vec} = 32$.

4   Conclusions and Outlook

We have presented results for numerical experiments with the coarse grid restrictor kernel from mg_proto AAMG code for LQCD with Clover fermions. Our results indicate that while explicit OpenMP nested parallelism with custom reductions allows the expression of fine grained parallelism in a straightforward way, the actual resulting performance was very poor if the number of threads in the nested level was increased beyond 1. Competitive performance was obtained with the same code when nested parallelism settings were set to being essentially flat. However, in that scenario one does not need go to the bother of defining the custom reductions. We have also found issues with compiler support for array-reductions in some cases.

By dealing with nested parallelism manually, in some cases it was possible to gainfully employ more than one thread per block. In this case for the smaller (more latency sensitive) fine lattices, the serial reduction was faster than the parallel one indicating that overheads of joining/launching threads is non negligible. The natural conclusion would be to enlarge the threaded regions in a more MPI-like mode, to avoid fork-join and implied barrier overheads, but to express these naturally would need features such as group based reductions or barriers (akin to barriers or reductions over MPI sub-communicators) which are currently not part of OpenMP.

For our smallest volume, with the fewest number of near-null vectors in the restrictor, latency optimized processors such as Skylake show superior performance whereas massively parallel processors such as KNL excel for bigger problems. Therefore, hybrid architectures which have both latency and bandwidth-optimized parts may well be beneficial for such algorithms.

Finally, our results indicate that in order to guarantee best performance across different levels of the multi-grid solver as well as across different platforms, it is mandatory to implement some kind of auto-tuning similar to the one utilized in the QUDA library [3, 7] and the QDP-JIT implementation of QDP++ [22].

With the lessons learned here, we will continue to further optimize our multi-grid code implementation and look forward to presenting more results in future publications.

Acknowledgment. This research used resources of the National Energy Research Scientific Computing Center (NERSC), a DOE Office of Science User Facility supported by the Office of Science of the U.S. Department of Energy under Contract No. DE-AC02-05CH11231, and of the ALCF, which is supported by DOE/SC under contract DE-AC02-06CH11357. B. Joo acknowledges funding from the DOE Office Of Science, Offices of Nuclear Physics and Advanced Scientific Computing Research through the SciDAC program. B. Joo also acknowledges support from the U.S. DOE Exascale Computing Project (ECP). This work is supported by the U.S. Department of Energy, Office of Science, Office of Nuclear Physics under contract DE-AC05-06OR23177. B. Joo would like to thank and acknowledge Kate Clark of NVIDIA for many discussions about expressing and mapping parallelism in multi-grid solver components in a variety of programming models and hardware and her helpful comments after a reading of this manuscript, as well as Christian Trott of Sandia Labs for discussions about nested parallelism in OpenMP. This work used resources provided by the Performance Research Laboratory at the University of Oregon. We would especially like to thank Sameer Shende and Rob Yelle for their professional support of the Performance Research Laboratory computers and their timely response to our requests.

Appendix A - AVX512 SIMD Routines

We show below the code for the complex matrix vector multiplication, where a SIMD length column in_v is multiplied by complex scalar whose first element is being pointed to by in_s. The resulting vector is accumulated onto out_v.

```
1   inline
2   void CMadd(float *out_v, float *in_v, float *in_s)
3   {
4       // Load broadcast scalar complex in_s
5       __m512 in2_re = _mm512_set1_ps( in_s[0]);
6       __m512 in2_im = _mm512_set1_ps( in_s[1]);
7
8       // Load input and result.
9       __m512 ivec = _mm512_load_ps(in_v);
10      __m512 ovec = _mm512_load_ps(out_v);
11
12      // Permute input to shuffle re<->im lanes
13      __m512 v_perm = _mm512_shuffle_ps(ivec,ivec,0xb1);
14
15      // Carry out complex FMA with two fmaddsub instructions
16      __m512 tmp = _mm512_fmaddsub_ps(v_perm,in2_im,ovec);
17      ovec = _mm512_fmaddsub_ps(ivec,in2_re,tmp);
18
19      // Store results
20      _mm512_store_ps(out_v,vec);
21
22  }
```

Once a routine such as CMadd available the 2 block diagonal matrices for a given site can be applied with code like below. Here we assume that the final output has been initialized (either to zero, or it has already some inner site's worth of data in it) outside this routine.

```
1   // fine data points to input vector for inner site
2   const CBSite& fine_cbsite = block_sitelist[fine_site_idx];
3   const float *fine_data  = fine_in.GetSiteDataPtr(fine_cbsite.cb,
4       fine_cbsite.site);
5
6   const int coffset = 2*num_coarse_color;
7   const int foffset = 2*num_fine_color;
8   // site_accum points to an array to accumulte the site results
9   for(int color=0; color < num_fine_color; ++color) {
10      // Index into v
11      float* v= const float* v = ((*this).indexPtr(block_idx,
12          fine_site_idx,color));
13
14      // Upper chirality
```

```
15    for(int i=0; i < 2*num_coarse_color; i+=16 ) {
16        Cmadd(&site_accum[i],&v[i],&fine_data[2*color]);
17    }
18
19    // Lower chirality
20    for(int i=0; i < 2*num_coarse_color; i+=16 ) {
21        Cmadd(&site_accum[i+coffset],&v[i+coffset],
22            &fine_data[2*color+foffset]);
23    }
24 }
```

Appendix B - Parallel Reduction for Manual Nesting

The code for the *parallel reduction* (parallel over blocks, with 1 site per block) is listed below. We note that rather than closing the preceding region and re-opening it as below, we could have attempted to keep one parallel regions and used `#pragma omp barrier` to ensure all results were written before summing. However, ideally the barrier would need to be only in a group of threads within a block whereas the OpenMP barrier would synchronize all active threads in the workgroup. Given that some may be idle, this could lead to much more messy code.

```
1    #pragma omp parallel shared(site_accum,r_block_threads)
2    {
3        int tid = omp_get_thread_num();
4        int block_tid = tid / _r_threads_per_block;
5        int site_tid =  tid % _r_threads_per_block;
6
7        int block_idx = step*r_block_threads + block_tid;
8
9        if( block_idx < _n_blocks ) {
10
11           int block_cb = block_idx /num_coarse_cbsites;
12           int block_cbsite = block_idx % num_coarse_cbsites;
13           float* coarse_site_spinor = out.GetSiteDataPtr(block_cb,block_cbsite);
14
15           // Only 1 thread per block (with site_tid == 0) sums
16           if( site_tid == 0 ) {
17    #pragma simd safelen(16) simdlen(16) aligned(coarse_site_spinor:64)
18               for(int colorspin=0; colorspin < n_floats; ++colorspin) {
19                   coarse_site_spinor[colorspin]=0;
20               }
21
22               for(int s=0; s < _r_threads_per_block; ++s) {
23
24                   int soffset =n_floats*(s + _r_threads_per_block*block_tid);
25
26    #pragma simd safelen(16) simdlen(16) aligned(coarse_site_spinor, site_accum:64)
27                   for(int colorspin=0; colorspin < n_floats; ++colorspin) {
28                       coarse_site_spinor[colorspin] += site_accum[colorspin+soffset];
29                   } // colorspin
30               } // s
31           } //site_tid == 0
32       } // block_idx < n_blocks
33    } // parallel region implied barrier
```

References

1. NERSC Cori Website. https://www.nersc.gov/users/computational-systems/cori/
2. Babich, R., Brannick, J., Brower, R., Clark, M., Manteuffel, T., et al.: Adaptive multigrid algorithm for the lattice Wilson-Dirac operator. Phys. Rev. Lett. **105**, 201602 (2010)
3. Babich, R., Clark, M.A., Joo, B., Shi, G., Brower, R.C., Gottlieb, S.: Scaling lattice QCD beyond 100 GPUs. In: SC 2011 International Conference for High Performance Computing, Networking, Storage and Analysis Seattle, Washington, 12–18 November 2011 (2011). http://inspirehep.net/record/927455/files/arXiv:1109.2935.pdf

4. Boyle, P.A.: Hierarchically deflated conjugate gradient (2014)
5. Brannick, J., Brower, R.C., Clark, M.A., Osborn, J.C., Rebbi, C.: Adaptive multi-grid algorithm for lattice QCD. Phys. Rev. Lett. **100**, 041601 (2008)
6. Brower, R.C., Weinberg, E., Clark, M.A., Strelchenko, A.: Phys. Rev. D **97**, 114513 (2018). https://journals.aps.org/prd/abstract/10.1103/PhysRevD.97.114513
7. Clark, M.A., Babich, R., Barros, K., Brower, R.C., Rebbi, C.: Solving Lattice QCD systems of equations using mixed precision solvers on GPUs. Comput. Phys. Commun. **181**, 1517–1528 (2010)
8. Clark, M.A., Brower, R., Cheng, M.: Hierarchical algorithms on heterogeneous architectures: adaptive multigrid solvers for LQCD on GPUs. In: Proceedings of the 2014 GPU Technology Conference (2014)
9. Clark, M.A., Joó, B., Strelchenko, A., Cheng, M., Gambhir, A., Brower, R.: Accelerating lattice QCD multigrid on GPUs using fine-grained parallelization. In: ACM/IEEE International Conference on High Performance Computing, Networking, Storage and Analysis, Salt Lake City, Utah (2016)
10. Cohen, S.D., Brower, R.C., Clark, M.A., Osborn, J.C.: Multigrid algorithms for domain-wall fermions. In: PoS LATTICE 2011, 030 (2011)
11. Creutz, M.: Quarks, Gluons and Lattices. Cambridge Monographs on Mathematical Physics, 169 p. Cambridge University Press, Cambridge (1983)
12. Frommer, A., Kahl, K., Krieg, S., Leder, B., Rottmann, M.: Adaptive aggregation based domain decomposition multigrid for the lattice wilson dirac operator. SIAM J. Sci. Comput. **36**, A1581–A1608 (2014)
13. Hestenes, M.R., Stiefel, E.: Methods of conjugate gradients for solving linear systems. J. Res. Natl. Bur. Stand. **49**(6), 409–436 (1952)
14. Heybrock, S., Rottmann, M., Georg, P., Wettig, T.: Adaptive algebraic multigrid on SIMD architectures. In: PoS LATTICE 2015, 036 (2016)
15. Joó, B.: `mg_proto` github repository. https://github.com/jeffersonlab/mg_proto.git
16. Luscher, M.: Deflation acceleration of lattice QCD simulations. JHEP **12**, 011 (2007)
17. Montvay, I., Munster, G.: Quantum Fields on a Lattice. Cambridge Monographs on Mathematical Physics, 491 p. Cambridge University Press, Cambridge (1994)
18. Osborn, J., Babich, R., Brannick, J., Brower, R., Clark, M., et al.: Multigrid solver for clover fermions. In: PoS LATTICE 2010, 037 (2010)
19. Rothe, H.J.: Lattice Gauge Theories: An Introduction. World Scientific Lecture Notes in Physics, vol. 74, pp. 1–605 (2005)
20. Sheikholeslami, B., Wohlert, R.: Improved continuum limit lattice action for QCD with wilson fermions. Nucl. Phys. B **259**, 572 (1985)
21. van der Vorst, H.A.: Bi-CGSTAB: a fast and smoothly converging variant of Bi-CG for the solution of nonsymmetric linear systems. SIAM J. Sci. Stat. Comput. **13**(2), 631–644 (1992)
22. Winter, F.T., Clark, M.A., Edwards, R.G., Joó, B.: A framework for lattice QCD calculations on GPUs. In: Proceedings of the 2014 IEEE 28th International Parallel and Distributed Processing Symposium, IPDPS 2014, pp. 1073–1082. IEEE Computer Society, Washington, DC, USA (2014). http://dx.doi.org/10.1109/IPDPS.2014.112
23. Yamaguchi, A., Boyle, P.: Hierarchically deflated conjugate residual. In: PoS LATTICE 2016, 374 (2016)

Distributed Training of Generative Adversarial Networks for Fast Detector Simulation

Sofia Vallecorsa[1]([✉]), Federico Carminati[1], Gulrukh Khattak[1],
Damian Podareanu[2], Valeriu Codreanu[2], Vikram Saletore[3], and Hans Pabst[4]

[1] CERN, Geneva, Switzerland
sofia.vallecorsa@cern.ch
[2] SURFsara, Amsterdam, Netherlands
[3] Intel, Santa Clara, USA
[4] Intel, Zurich, Switzerland

Abstract. The simulation of the interaction of particles in High Energy Physics detectors is a computing intensive task. Since some level of approximation is acceptable, it is possible to implement *fast simulation* simplified models that have the advantage of being less computationally intensive. Here we present a fast simulation based on Generative Adversarial Networks (GANs). The model is constructed from a generative network describing the detector response and a discriminative network, trained in adversarial manner. The adversarial training process is compute-intensive and the application of a distributed approach becomes particularly important. We present scaling results of a data-parallel approach to distribute GANs training across multiple nodes on TACC's Stampede2. The efficiency achieved was above 94% when going from 1 to 128 Xeon Scalable Processor nodes. We report on the accuracy of the generated samples and on the scaling of time-to-solution. We demonstrate how HPC installations could be utilized to globally optimize this kind of models leading to quicker research cycles and experimentation, thanks to their large computation power and excellent connectivity.

Keywords: High performance computing
High energy physics simulations · Deep Neural Networks
Generative Adversarial Networks · Detector simulation
High energy physics · Radiation transport · Intel Xeon Phi · Intel Xeon

1 Introduction

High Energy Physics (HEP) simulations rely on detailed Monte Carlo evaluations requiring complex and time-consuming computations. Experiments at the Large Hadron Collider (LHC) devote today a large fraction (50%) of their worldwide distributed computing power (WLCG, the LHC Grid [1]) to simulation tasks. In 10 years from now, with the next High Luminosity LHC phase, the need for simulated data is expected to increase by a factor of 100 [2].

© Springer Nature Switzerland AG 2018
R. Yokota et al. (Eds.): ISC 2018 Workshops, LNCS 11203, pp. 487–503, 2018.
https://doi.org/10.1007/978-3-030-02465-9_35

Several initiatives are on-going to modernize Monte Carlo simulation software and make it better suited to leverage the latest hardware advancement. [3,4] The HEP community is exploring alternative strategies to reduce the amount of data that needs to be simulated or trade some accuracy in order to reduce computation time (*fast simulation*) [5].

This article describes a new fast simulation algorithm based on Deep Learning methods, typically used in the field of image recognition: Generative Adversarial Networks (GANs) [6]. These techniques seem well suited to replace Monte Carlo since it is straightforward to use them to produce realistic samples. From the computing perspective, once the model is trained, the inference step is orders of magnitude faster than traditional Monte Carlo simulation. In this work, we describe how we can use GANs to simulate the response of detectors such as highly segmented calorimeters, whose Monte Carlo-based simulation is particularly time-consuming. This study represents the initial step of a wider plan aimed at providing a generic detector simulation tool based on Deep Learning, fully configurable for different detector use cases. Our final goal is to prove that, by using meta-optimization and hyper-parameters scans, it is possible to tune the network architectures to simulate different detectors.

In this perspective, an efficient training process becomes essential and the accent should therefore be on optimizing the computing resources needed to train the networks, studying parallelization on clusters and cross-platform development. Technological trends seem to be bringing the Deep Learning (and AI) and HPC worlds closer together with impressive development in terms of performance capabilities related to storage, networks and computing architectures. It seems only natural to see an equivalent effort spent on the development of HPC friendly Deep Neural Networks (DNN).

After a brief review on previous related work, we introduce our 3D convolution GANs models and describe how we validate physics results. We then discuss the implementation of a distributed approach together with some preliminary results on scaling. We will then conclude with a brief outlook on our plans for future development.

2   Previous Work

Machine Learning techniques have been applied to different tasks within the HEP community for quite many years already [7,8]. One example is the search for the Higgs boson employing Artificial Neural Networks [9]. Recently, the advances on Deep Learning and its application to many domains, have generated a renewed interest for possible applications in HEP [10,11].

GANs are among the most interesting Deep Neural Network recently developed. They implement the idea of adversarial training as introduced by Goodfellow in [6]. In spite of being relatively recent, GANs have inspired research in many fields and several variations and applications exist [12–14]. Since HEP detectors can be regarded as cameras that take pictures of the decay products of particles colliding in modern accelerators, such as the Large Hadron Collider, researchers have been experimenting with GANs for generating images belonging to particularly complicated distributions. LAGAN, for example, or Location Aware GAN used locally connected layers to generate images corresponding to transverse section of a jet of particles traversing a simplified calorimeter detector [15]. Soon after, CaloGAN extended LAGAN results to a more realistic example, inspired by the ATLAS electromagnetic calorimeter [16].

As Deep Learning models increase in complexity, model size and training time, the role played by distributed training becomes of primary importance. Several different algorithms have been developed in recent years. Generally, these algorithms work by splitting the training load across multiple concurrent processes, either threads on a single machine or jobs spread across separate nodes [17].

Two main approaches exist to distribute the training workload: model parallelism and data parallelism. Model parallelism distributes the training across the model dimension, by having multiple processes train distinct parts of the model, whereas data parallelism employs a distribution of the dataset, each process training the whole model, but on different parts of the data. Out of the two methods, data parallelism is the most popular, being easier to implement. The DL frameworks employ two main methods to maintain the model consistent across all processes, based on where the neural network parameters are stored: parallel (also called replicated) and parameter server. In the parallel case, all nodes maintain a local copy of the weights (a local *replica* of the model), whereas in the parameter server mode, the nodes are assigned separate roles: workers (nodes that run training) and parameter servers (nodes that store the parameters of the model). In both cases, nodes need to exchange data (gradients) to keep the model consistent. With parallel training, nodes need to apply the global (averaged) gradient, an operation that is equivalent to calling a classical reduce operation (e.g. implemented in MPI via `MPI_Allreduce` [18]) to get the average gradient across all nodes. In the parameter server approach, workers send the gradient data to the parameter server nodes that hold the global state of the model, and then read the current state (model parameters) before moving on the next training step. Typically, the size of the data that is sent across the network is considerably large, directly relating to the size of the neural networks in terms of number of parameters (weights and biases).

Existing Deep Learning tools and frameworks implement the communication layer with sockets or MPI. TensorFlow's distributed layer [19] uses by default gRPC [20] for the data transfers between workers and parameter servers, while also providing the alternative of using MPI or Remote Direct Memory Access (RDMA) (but still following the parameter server approach). For the purely parallel mode, MPI is undoubtedly the most popular choice for the communication layer. The different existing libraries implement various communication patterns in order to allow for better scalability: the MaTEx project [21] using `MPI_Allreduce`; a more scalable communication pattern was proposed by Baidu via the ring allreduce [22] where workers are organized as a ring and data is exchanged only between neighbors; based on the ring allreduce pattern, Uber developed their own communication library that uses NVIDIA's Collective Communication Libraries (NCCL and NCCL2), called Horovod [23].

Distributed training of GANs is a new research subject. We believe our work to be one of the first detailed contributions in this direction.

3   Three-Dimensional GANs for Calorimeter Simulation

Calorimeters are important components of HEP detectors. They are intended to measure the energy of particles traversing their dense material. Calorimeters are segmented in a large number of cells. By recording the energy deposited in each cell, it is possible to reconstruct the energy pattern produced by showers of secondary particles inside the detector volume (commonly "energy shower"). These showers can be treated as 3-dimensional images, interpreting each cell as a pixel in an image and the amount of deposited energy per cell as the pixel grey-scale intensity.

3.1   Calorimeter Data

The dataset for the present work was simulated using Geant4 [24]. As described in [25], this dataset is produced in the context of the current design studies of the Linear Collider Detector (LCD) for the Compact Linear Collider (CLIC) [26]. The LCD electromagnetic calorimeter (ECAL) is a sampling calorimeter consisting of 25 layers of tungsten absorbers with silicon sensors between them. It consists of a regular grid of 3D cells of 5.1 mm^3. Individual electrons are shot into the central part of the detector, in a region with regular sensor geometry and orthogonally to the calorimeter surface. Each entry in the dataset represents the energy depositions in individual calorimeter cells produced by one incoming electron (called "events"). These "events" are stored as $25 \times 25 \times 25$ cell slices of the electromagnetic calorimeter in 3D arrays (*ECAL arrays*) and they are stored in compressed HDF5 files. The present work trains on $200,000$ electrons with energies ranging from 10 to 510 GeV (Fig. 1).

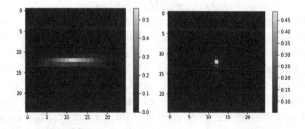

Fig. 1. (right) Longitudinal section of a single electron energy shower. (left) Corresponding transverse section.

3.2   Networks Architecture

Our 3DGAN model is based on three-dimensional convolutions to capture the whole shower development along the three space dimensions. As shown in Fig. 2, the generator and discriminator networks contain, respectively, three and four 3-dimensional convolution layers. Details about the networks architectures can be found in [27].

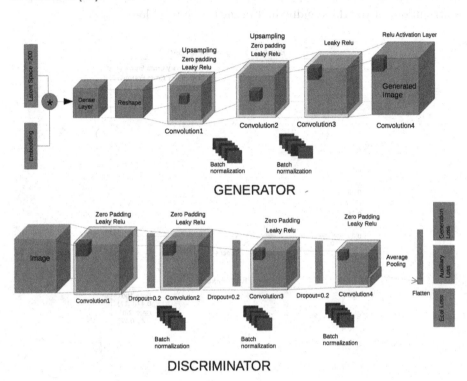

Fig. 2. The 3D GAN architecture

The generator uses as input a vector of random numbers (the latent vector) generated according to normal distributions, and outputs $25 \times 25 \times 25$ images corresponding to the ECAL energy shower.

The discriminator takes as input the generated image. Its structure is very similar to the generator. In addition, a set of three dense layers maps the flattened discriminator network response to three different outputs.

Loosely following the strategy of auxiliary classifier GANs [14], indicating that the introduction of labels provides faster convergence and stability, we assign to the discriminator two additional regression tasks: an estimation of the incoming particle energy (E_p) and of the total energy measured by the calorimeter (E_{cal}), corresponding to the sum of all the energy depositions in the cells of the image.

The adversarial training uses a loss function based on the probability of the discriminator correctly differentiating between real and fake images. In our case we use a binary cross entropy function Fig. 3. The generator in turn uses the inverse of the discriminator loss as the cost to minimize. The absolute mean percentage error is used to calculate the loss terms corresponding to the additional regression tasks performed by the discriminator: the incoming particle energy and total energy deposited in the detector. Weights are employed to balance the contributions of the three individual terms to the total loss.

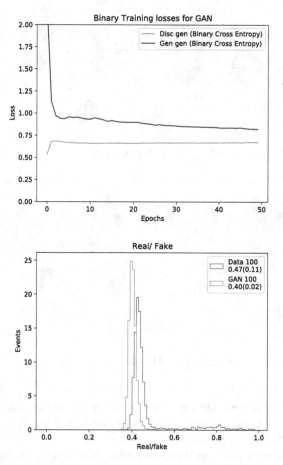

Fig. 3. (top) Binary cross-entropy loss function for the generator and discriminator networks. (bottom) The discriminator real/fake probability for a real image (in blue) and a generated one (orange). The optimal result should peak around 0.5 showing that the discriminator can no longer distinguish the generated images from the original ones. (Color figure online)

The RMSProp [28] optimizer is used, with a learning rate of 10^{-3}. The architecture is implemented using Keras [29] with Tensorflow [30] as a backend.

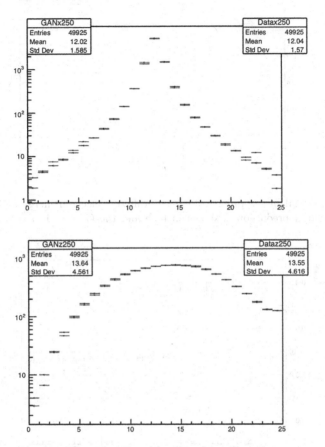

Fig. 4. Transverse energy profile along x (top) and longitudinal energy profile along z (bottom) for 250 GeV electrons. Geant4 prediction is shown in blue and the GANs's in red. Units are GeV. (Color figure online)

3.3   Physics Validation

We used the proposed 3DGAN to reproduce energy showers deposited in the detector by electrons with energies sampled from a uniform spectrum between 10 and 500 GeV. To fully validate GANs results in terms of physics we compare to standard Monte Carlo simulation based on Geant4. We have studied both low level variables describing the calorimeter energy response, i.e. the single cell energy distributions, and more complicated features such as average profiles of the energy showers along the three calorimeter axes Fig. 4. The z axis

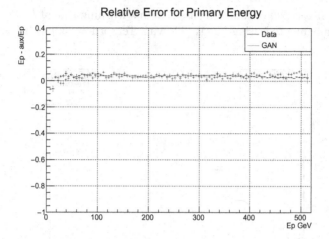

Fig. 5. Longitudinal energy profiles along z for different electron energies (50, 100, 400, 500 GeV). Geant4 prediction is shown in blue and the GANs's in red. (Color figure online)

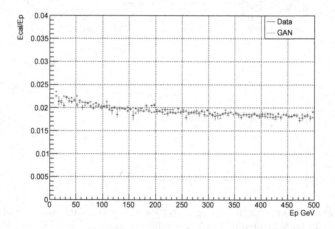

Fig. 6. Calorimeter sampling fraction as a function of the incoming electron energy as predicted by Geant4 simulation (in blue) and GANs (in red) (Color figure online)

is chosen along the direction of the incoming electron, while x and y are on the transverse plane, perpendicular to z. These profiles, usually called the energy "shower shapes", are relevant quantities for identifying, for example, the type (electron, photon, pion, etc.) of the particle that generated them. Figure 7 shows the shower profile along the x and z axes for 300 GeV electrons: the distributions in x and y are quite similar so only the x profile is presented. The GANs prediction (red) is compared to the corresponding Geant4 simulation (blue). Figure 5 shows the performance of the auxiliary regression task on the primary particle energy assigned to the discriminator. It shows the excellent performance achieved by the discriminator network across the whole energy spectrum and shows the network correctly identifies the main shower images features. Similar agreement can be seen in Fig. 6: it represents the calorimeter response in terms of deposited energy (calorimeter sampling fraction). The network performance over this large energy range is remarkably good considered that no effort was made to optimize the network architecture for different energy values. Convolutional layers are sensitive to the spatial shape of the energy showers, which changes according to the primary particle energy, while the architecture parameters were optimized to reproduce at best particles with energies around the central region of the spectrum. In the same way the network is capable of correctly reproduce energy showers produced by different particles, such as pions. Pions are hadronic particles that tend to deposit a smaller amount of energy with respect to electrons in an electromagnetic calorimeter such as the ECAL. Figure 5 represent the network response for pions with energies between 10 and 500 GeV. Once again it is remarkable the agreement with Geant4 simulation although the network and training hyper-parameters were optimized on electrons.

3.4 Computing Performance and Training Time

Once trained, the GANs simulation tool is a relatively lightweight application: a few MB are enough to describe the layers configuration for the two networks and the inference step is orders of magnitude faster than a standard Monte Carlo. We have run a test on an Intel Xeon 8180 processor (codenamed "Skylake") measuring the time it takes to generate one electromagnetic shower for our benchmark detector. We obtained 17 s/shower using Geant4 and 4 ms/shower using our trained GANs model, yielding a speedup factor larger than 2500. Using dedicated hardware, such as GPGPUs, the generation time reduces further (we choose not to quote comparison results since the Geant4 application cannot run on GPGPUs).

Unfortunately, training performance is not as good in terms of time. As mentioned above, the core structure of our generator and discriminator models is based on four 3-dimensional convolutional layers, so the models are not very deep, compared to other existing convolutional networks. Even so, our generator network sums up to more than 1M parameters when a relatively small latent space is chosen (latent space dimension = 200). Moreover, the adversarial training itself, relying on continuous feedback between the discriminator network and the generator network is particularly time-consuming. In fact, we do train each network twice following a process that is sketched in Fig. 8. The two-steps discriminator training helps to insure fast convergence of the network. It has become frequent practice while training GANs to build separate batches of real and fake images [31]. This results in a relatively large computing time: training the 3DGAN on 200,000 electrons for 30 epochs takes about 1 day on a NVidia GTX-1080 card. While this does not represent, per se, a critically long amount of time, it critically impacts any attempt to run large hyper-parameter scans or implement meta-optimization algorithms, which are key to our model generalization effort (optimizing the network architecture for the type of detector that is

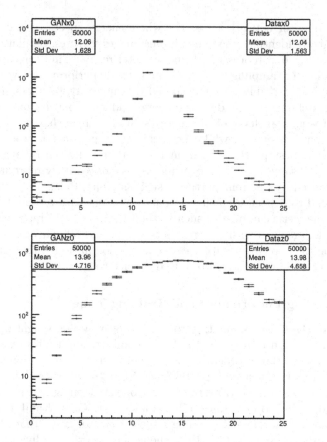

Fig. 7. Transverse energy profile along x (top) and longitudinal energy profile along z (bottom) for pions. Geant4 prediction is shown in blue and the GANs's in red. Units are GeV. (Color figure online)

being simulated). Moreover, the simulation of more realistic detectors and more complicated physics processes could increase the complexity of the networks and the subsequent training time.

4   Distributed Training

Training of large neural networks on large datasets is a computationally intensive task, taking a substantial amount of time, from several hours to days or even weeks. Parallelizing the training workload is thus critical and key to obtaining meaningful results in a timely manner.

In this work, we focus on distributing the training of the 3DGAN via data parallelism and *synchronous* and RMSprop optimization. This optimizer divides the learning rate for a weight by a running average of the magnitudes of recent

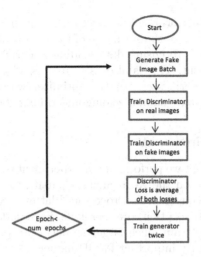

Fig. 8. 3DGAN training process

gradients for that weight. Moreover, we use more than one worker per node to maximize the hardware efficiency as described in the sections below.

4.1 Distributing the Training of the 3DGAN with Keras/Tensorflow and Horovod

Training 3D convolutional networks is an even more time-consuming task compared to their traditional 2D counterpart, therefore training these generative models can take weeks. To speed up this research cycle, we leverage the power of modern supercomputers to decrease the time necessary for training these models.

Due to the more controllable nature of *synchronous* stochastic gradient descent and relatively limited straggling effects, we chose a synchronous instead of an asynchronous approach for the 3D GANs optimization. Also, due to the limited communication pressure imposed by our 3D GANs architecture, we chose to use a data parallel approach.

As deep learning framework we have chosen Keras for its simplicity in use and high productivity. As for Keras's backend we have used Tensorflow. Tensorflow was configured and compiled with MKL-DNN support, so that its ops can be well mapped on CPU-based HW. The binaries were built with architecture specific flags (AVX512 FMA) and XLA support. The distribution framework that is used for aggregating Tensorflow tensors on CPUs based systems is Horovod, that internally uses an MPI-based all-reduce primitive to implement the essential allreduce operations performed on gradients in the backward pass. Depending on the cluster topology, MPI_AllReduce collectives are optimized for shared-memory communication within a single node and interconnection fabric across multiple nodes.

Adding Horovod support to a single-device Keras/Tensorflow training program is trivial, the only changes needed are initializing the library, broadcasting the initial weights, and performing all-reduce on the gradients, obtained by wrapping the Tensorflow/Keras optimizer inside of the HorovodDistributedOptimizer class. Another concern is to ensure data loading is performed properly for the data parallel environment. This is also as simple as adapting existing code to consider the Horovod world size. For the optimizer we compared Adam with RMSprop, resulting in quite similar scaling and timings behavior for both.

4.2   Execution Environment

As execution environment we performed our experiments on TACC's Stampede2 system[1], predominantly on the Xeon Skylake partition. This partition is composed of dual-socket Xeon Scalable Processors Platinum 8160 CPUs, each with 24 cores for a total of 48 execution cores per node. Each node also features 192 GB of RAM, allowing us to train much larger models than possible on commodity GPUs. This is particularly important for 3D models.

To increase the efficiency, we schedule 2, 4, or 8 MPI processes on each node, with each process utilizing 24, 12, or 6 cores respectively. We also carefully set the *inter_op_parallelism_threads* and *intra_op_parallelism_threads* for these hybrid configurations. This is effectively handled by Horovod, leading to intra-node distributed training, the aggregation operation being performed in shared-memory. Results comparing these execution modes are presented in the section below.

We did not notice severe bottlenecks due to communication when scaling to 64 nodes and 256 workers on the current GANs architecture.

Since dwelling into the distributed training revealed performance implications of having a multiple of 16 number of filters, we re-checked the efficiency of the algorithm for a single node with various combinations of underlying libraries. The comparison in timings between Eigen and MKL-DNN and the importance of number of filters can be found in Fig. 9. For this test we are using Eigen commit cc79f86b2ace23b92b0760ca798595a0c84fcbad, MKL version 0.14, MKL-DNN commit a29d8487a63afca3d5b8c5bbdbb473cf8ccc6e51, and Tensorflow v1.9.

The results show a performance improvement when using Tensorflow in combination with MKL-DNN and four workers per node compared to just Tensorflow and Eigen. This difference comes from a large number of reorder ops. MKL needs the tensors in an internal data format that is suitable for vectorization, which is different from the TensorFlow format. MKL Reorders happen when a certain op (layer) is not supported in MKL-DNN and so the tensors have to converted between TF and MKL. The fewer the reorder ops, the better the performance. We could also observe that the forward pass has fewer reorders compared to backward pass. When the number of output channels is not a multiple of 16, MKL-DNN uses GEMM-based convolution (from Eigen) which is slower compared to native JIT-based convolution. Both GEMM and native JIT-

---

[1] https://www.tacc.utexas.edu/.

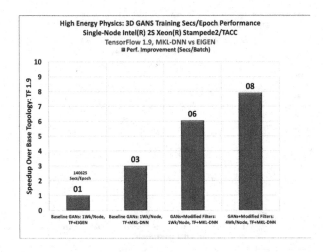

Fig. 9. Comparison of Eigen with MKL-DNN for Tensorflow

based convolutions use AVX512 instructions, but GEMM case has additional data transformation overheads.

In order to efficiently use the multi-core CPUs in Tensorflow, we ensured that the *inter_op_parallelism_threads* and *intra_op_parallelism_threads* parallelism flags are correctly passed to the underlying Tensorflow session. Tensorflow makes use of two separate thread pools, one that controls the parallelism for operations that can be parallelized internally, such as matrix-matrix multiplications (*intra_op_parallelism_threads*), and one that controls the parallelism for independent nodes in the Tensorflow graph (*inter_op_parallelism_threads*).

4.3   Scaling Results

When performing scale-out experiments, there are two components to keep in focus: the scaling efficiency and the machine efficiency. Empirical evidence lead us to determine that the highest machine efficiency can be obtained if each node hosts four workers. This is the setup used for most of the results. To illustrate this point, we can present the one node - one worker setup compared to the one node - four workers. The time per batch in the first case is 16.5 s and in the second is it is 12.8 s.

In SubSect. 4.4 we will discuss the impact of large batches on the final accuracy, while in this subsection we are concerned with weak scaling results. This means that the problem size (workload) assigned to each processing element stays constant and additional elements are used to solve a larger total problem. We will present here a weak scaling case with a starting batch size of 8. The efficiency going from one node to 128 nodes is above 94%. In future experiments we will re-implement our solution in Tensorflow directly and check the framework implications on scaling. Figure 10 shows this behavior for our application.

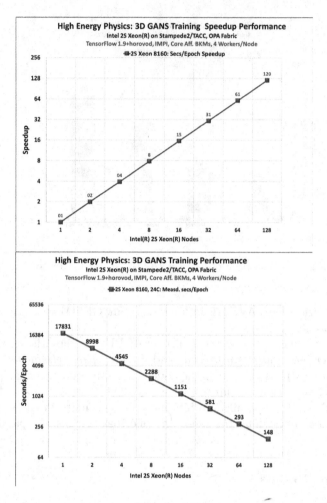

Fig. 10. Training and speedup performance going from 1 node to 128 nodes

4.4   Validation at Scale

At larger scales, the effective batch size (the amount of data that is globally used during one stochastic step) can have a negative impact on accuracy. The degradation of accuracy results while scaling training over a large number of processes is a known issue and several studies are proposing strategies to regularize the SGD multi-process evolution in order to recover most of the single process accuracy [32–36].

Therefore, we have studied the consistency of parallel training results in terms of several physics quantities. Figure 11, for example, shows the calorimeter sampling fraction E_{cal}/E_p (E_{cal} being the deposited energy and E_p the energy of the incoming particle) as a function of E_p. It compares the result of scalar training to multi-process training.

While the overall performance stays stable and the different training configurations manage to reproduce very well the energy dependency, as we increase the batch size, the performance clearly degrades at the two edges of the energy spectrum. Those two cases generate energy shower images that can look very different than the images belonging to the center of the energy spectrum (with the maximum of the energy distribution that shifts along the z axis). This could suggest that the parallel training reduces the capability of the network to generalize to cases that look "different" than the standard one. In fact, as previously mentioned, our network architecture was originally optimized for 100–200 GeV energy showers. This area corresponds exactly to the part of the spectrum were the multi-process curves seem to agree better and results stay consistent.

At the time of this writing, we only applied warmup (techniques established by Goyal et al. 2017) and scaling of initial learning rate (according to Horovod best practices) to stabilize the training procedure. Further studies are currently on-going in order to better understand the origin of this accuracy loss and implement other possible solutions, including SGD with momentum correction and exploration of capsule-based network architectures.

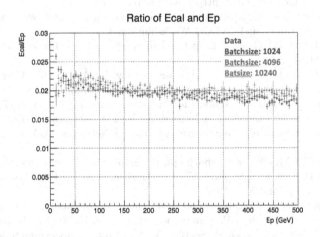

Fig. 11. Calorimeter sampling fraction as a function of the incoming electron energy for batch sizes up to 10240

Figure 11 shows a pronounced degradation above a global batch size of 4096 so we have capped our scaling experiments to this value.

5   Conclusions and Future Goals

Monte Carlo production has been so far a major fraction of WLCG computing workload and the High Luminosity LHC experiments needs will increase by orders of magnitude, in the next ten years. In this context, generative models relying on the possibility to treat detector response as images, seem natural candidates to speedup simulation. Generative Adversarial Networks require relatively small amounts of data to train and are the subject of many ongoing studies. Their performance as imaging tools for calorimeter simulation is very promising, and from a computing resources perspective, the gain in the time needed to generate a shower is huge. We have presented an application of 3D convolutional GANs to the simulation of high-granularity detectors, typically foreseen for the next generation accelerators. We have successfully generated images of shower energy deposition in three dimensions, including energy-related information. A detailed validation of the physics results based on the comparison to state-of-the-art Monte Carlo simulation software shows very good results. We plan to work on the generalization of our model to the simulation of different detectors and therefore implementing large hyper-parameter scans to optimize the network architecture to the specific detector to simulate. We have also presented the first results on distributed GANs training.

References

1. The WorldWide LHC Grid. http://wlcg.web.cern.ch
2. Bird, I.: Workshop introduction, context of the workshop: Half-way through run2; preparing for run3, run4, WLCG Workshop (2016)
3. Amadio, G., et al.: Geantv: from CPU to accelerators. J. Phys.: Conf. Ser. **762**, 012019 (2016)
4. Gheata, A., et al.: GeantV apha-release preview. In: ACAT 2017 Conference Proceedings to be Published in Journal of Physics: Conference Series
5. Vallecorsa, S.: Generative models for fast simulation. In: ACAT 2017 Conference Proceedings to be Published in Journal of Physics: Conference Series
6. Goodfellow, I.J., et al.: Generative Adversarial Networks, ArXiv e-prints, June 2014
7. Vannerem, P., Mueller, K., Schoelkopf, B., Smola, A., Soldner-Rembold, S.: Classifying LEP Data with Support Vector Algorithms, ArXiv High Energy Physics - Experiment e-prints, May 1999
8. Bock, R.K., et al.: Methods for multidimensional event classification: a case study using images from a cherenkov gamma-ray telescope. In: Nuclear Instruments and Methods in Physics Research Section A: Accelerators, Spectrometers, Detectors and Associated Equipment, vol. 516, no. 2, pp. 511–528 (2004)
9. Whiteson, S., Whiteson, D.: Machine learning for event selection in high energy physics. Eng. Appl. Artif. Intell. **22**(8), 1203–1217 (2009)
10. Vitek, A., Stachon, M., Krmer, P., Snel, V.: Towards the modeling of atomic and molecular clusters energy by support vector regression. In: 2013 5th International Conference on Intelligent Networking and Collaborative Systems, pp. 121–126, September 2013
11. Gligorov, V.V., Williams, M.: Efficient, reliable and fast high-level triggering using a bonsai boosted decision tree. J. Instrum. **8**(02), P02013 (2013)
12. Goodfellow, I.J.: On distinguishability criteria for estimating generative models, ArXiv e-prints, December 2014
13. Radford, A., Metz, L., Chintala, S.: Unsupervised representation learning with deep convolutional generative adversarial networks, CoRR, vol. abs/1511.06434 (2015)

14. Odena, A., Olah, C., Shlens, J.: Conditional Image Synthesis With Auxiliary Classifier GANs, ArXiv e-prints, October 2016
15. de Oliveira, L., Paganini, M., Nachman, B.: Learning particle physics by example: location-aware generative adversarial networks for physics synthesis, arXiv preprint arXiv:1701.05927 (2017)
16. Paganini, M., de Oliveira, L., Nachman, B.: Calogan: simulating 3D high energy particle showers in multi-layer electromagnetic calorimeters with generative adversarial networks, arXiv preprint arXiv:1705.02355 (2017)
17. Spiropulu, M., Anderson, D., Vlimant, J.: A MPI-based Python Framework for Distributed Training with Keras. arXiv:1712.05878 [cs.DC]
18. open MPI Team, "Message Passing Interface"
19. Abadi, M., et al.: TensorFlow: a system for large-scale machine learning. In: Proceedings of the 12th USENIX Conference on Operating Systems Design and Implementation OSDI 2016, pp. 265–283, Berkeley, CA, USA. USENIX Association (2016)
20. Google Inc., "GRPC: A high performance, open-source universal RPC framework"
21. Machine learning toolkit for extreme scale (matex). https://github.com/matex-org/matex
22. Baidu allreduce. https://github.com/baidu-research/baidu-allreduce
23. Horovod: distributed training framework for tensorflow. https://github.com/uber/horovod
24. CERN, Geant4, July 2017. Accessed 31 July 2017
25. Carminati, F., et al.: Calorimetry with deep learning: particle classification, energy regression, and simulation for high-energy physics. In: NIPS (2017)
26. The CLIC collaboration, "Conceptual Design Report"
27. Vallecorsa, S., Carminati, F., Khattak, G., et al.: Three dimensional generative adversarial networks for fast simulation. In: ACAT 2017 Conference Proceedings to be Published in Journal of Physics: Conference Series
28. Hinton, G., Srivastava, N., Swersky, K.: Lecture 6a overview of minibatch gradi-ent descent (2012)
29. Chollet, F., et al.: Keras (2015). https://github.com/keras-team/keras
30. Abadi, M., et al.: TensorFlow: large-scale machine learning on heterogeneous systems (2015). Software available from, www.tensorflow.org
31. Chintala, S., et al.: How to Train a GAN? Tips and tricks to make GANs work
32. Keskar, N.S., et al.: On large-batch training for deep learning: Generalization gap and sharp minima
33. Chaudhari, P., et al.: Entropy-SGD: Biasing gradient descent into wide valleys
34. Dinh, L., et al.: Sharp minima can generalize for deep nets
35. Huang, G.: Snapshot ensembles: Train 1, get M for free
36. Krizhevsky, A.: One weird trick for parallelizing convolutional neural networks, CoRR, vol. abs/1404.5997 (2014)

Workshop on Sustainable Ultrascale Computing Systems

Workshop on Sustainable Ultrascale Computing Systems

Jesus Carretero

University Carlos III of Madrid, Madrid, Spain
jesus.carretero@uc3m.es

Abstract. Sustainable Ultrascale Computing Systems. (UCS) are envisioned as large-scale complex systems joining parallel and distributed computing systems, maybe located at multiple sites that cooperate to provide solutions to the users, that will be two to three orders of magnitude larger that today s systems. The topics of the workshop were open from runtimes and middlewares to applications in UCS. The workshop program included 2 keynote speakers, 1 discussion panel and presentation of research papers.

Keywords: Ultrascale systems · Programmability · Scheduling · Performance · High-Performance applications

1 Introduction

Sustainable Ultrascale Computing Systems. (UCS) are envisioned as large-scale complex systems joining parallel and distributed computing systems, maybe located at multiple sites that cooperate to provide solutions to the users, that will be two to three orders of magnitude larger that today s systems. Sustainability is understood not only in terms of energy, but also related to programmability, usability, and maintenance to facilitate the adoption of UCS. The workshop was aimed to present major results of the COST Action IC1305, ?Network from Sustainable Ultrascale Computing Systems (NESUS)?. Ultrascale computing systems, included the Research Roadmap proposed, but it was also open for external speakers proposing realistic solutions addressing major challenges of building sustainable ultrascale computing systems, as well as developing collaborative activities among the involved research groups to target cross-layer design issues to offer a unified view of ultrascale platforms.

The topics of the workshop were open from runtimes and middlewares to applications. More specifically, contributions covering new programming paradigms and techniques to increase productivity, scalability, and reliability of parallel and distributed programming suitable for UCS; Adaptive runtimes and malleable applications that can adapt their resource usage at runtime; New approaches of continuous running in the presence of failures, such as resilient schedulers; reactive and proactive error

---

[1] This work has been partially supported through grant TIN2016-79637-P "Towards unification of HPC and Big Data Paradigms" from the Spanish Ministry of Economy and Competitiveness, the COST Action IC1305 "Network for Sustainable Ultrascale Computing Platforms" (NESUS).

handling; and monitoring and assessment of failures; Sustainable data management proposals for addressing the predicted exponential growth of digital information. synergistic approaches for the whole data life cycle in parallel and distributed systems; New proposal to enhance the Input/Output (I/O) stack, including advanced predictive and adaptive data management and techniques to improve data locality; Energy efficiency of ultrascale systems, including novel metrics for energy monitoring, profiling and modeling in ultrascale components and applications, energy-aware resource management; And, finally, aspects related to applications, such as high-level algorithms, services amenable to UCS, redesign and reprogramming techniques for applications to efficiently exploit ultrascale platforms, and energy-aware algorithms.

2 Workshop Program Committee

The member of the organizing Program Committee is listed below:

Workshop Chair

Jesus Carretero   University Carlos III of Madrid, Spain

Program Committee

Carlos Jaime Barrios   Universidad Industrial de Santander, Colombia
Angelos Bilas   ICS FORTH, Greece
Harold Castro   Universidad de los Andes, Colombia
F. Javier García-Blas   University Carlos III of Madrid, Spain
J. Daniel Garcia   University Carlos III of Madrid, Spain
Alexey Lastoveysky   University College, Dublin, Ireland
Laurent Lefevre   Ecole Normale Superiour Lyon, France
Svetozar Margenov   Bulgarian Academy of Science, Bulgaria
Radu Prodan   Alpen-Adria University of Klagenfurt, Austria
Gudula Ruenger   Technical University Chemnitz, Germany
Leonel Sousa   INESC, Lisbon, Portugal
Xavier Vigoroux   ATOS-BULL, France
Vladimir Voevodin   Lomonosov Moscow State University, Russia
Zhiyi Huang   University of Otago, New Zealand

3 Workshop Summary

The workshop was a very interesting full day meeting including two keynote speakers, two paper presentation papers and, to conclude, a discussion panel.

The first keynote speaker was Prof. Rosa Badía, from Barcelona Supercomputing Center (Spain), who talked about the **programmability-performance trade-offs with a task-based approach**, as task-based programming models have proven to be a good alternative to traditional programming models for HPC. The talk presented an overview of PyCOMPSs, a pioneer approach on task-based programming in Python that enables simple sequential codes to be executed in distributed computing platforms, and showed how it offers a good trade-off between programmability and performance in HPC. Our second speaker was Prof. Thomas Ludwig, from DKRZ (Germany), that showed the importance of **reproducibility in Computer Science and Climate Science in the Era of Exascale Systems** to compare the results of experiments in silico and, even, confronting them with computer simulations. The talk presented different levels of concern: reproducing third party code, reproducing our own results with a modified computer infrastructure, and finally achieving a bitwise reproduction of a single program run. The talk discussed several of these critical issues and concentrated on aspects of programming and hardware issues that are connected to reproducibility of findings in science.

The first paper presentation session included several interested contributions related to algorithms, runtime systems and scalability. Prof. Vladimir Voevodin, from Lomonosov MSU (Russia) presented the AlgoWiki project, a structured way to define algorithms, and its usage to compare any supercomputers on any algorithms. Prof. Radu Prodan, from Klagenfurt University (Austria), presented an algorithm and techniques for multi-objective large-scale workflow scheduling on clouds. Prof. Alexey Lastovetsky, from University College Dublin (Ireland) showed how pre-multicore methods and algorithms perform in multicore era, presenting trade-offs that limits scalability. Md. Silvina Caino, from University Carlos III of Madrid (Spain), presented a proposal of an architecture for scaling Spark in HPC systems.

Our second paper presentation session included was devoted to models and applications deployment. Ms. Estefania Serrano, form University Carlos III of Madrid (Spain), presented, together with Prof. Leonel Sousa, from INESC-D (Portugal), a cache-aware roofline model and it usage for medical imaging optimization. Dr. Carlos Jaime Barrios, from Universidad Industrial de Santander (Colombia) showed a proposal to advance towards an efficient software model supporting UltrasScale applications. Dr. Jose Luis Gonzalez-Compean, from CINVESTAV (Mexico), presented an architecture to make large-scale application composition by using containerized building blocks. Finally, Prof. Nina Popova, from Lomonosov MSU (Russia), presented the approach used at Moscow State University for Ultrascale Computing education, based primarily on practice.

The workshop was closed with a panel about the **Landscape of Sustainable Ultrascale/Exascale Computing Systems in the EU programs**, chaired by Prof. Jesus Carretero, from University Carlos III of Madrid (Spain), and including four speakers: Dr. Xavier Vigoroux, from Bull/Atos (France), Dr. Marcin Ostasz, from ETP4HPC, Dr. Tomi Ilijas, from ARCTURC (Slovenia), and Prof. Thomas, from University of Innsbruck (Austria). The members of the panel talked about the industry situation, how to make the path toward next generation of HOC computers, and the need to make bigger investment on new hardware and software to push the leadership of Europe in this area.

Acknowledgments. I would not like to finish this preface without showing my gratitude to the workshops organizers, the ISC team, the Program Committee, and the speakers for their cooperation and participation in the workshop. This activity would have not been possible without their help. Thank you.

Cache-Aware Roofline Model and Medical Image Processing Optimizations in GPUs

Estefania Serrano[1(✉)], Aleksandar Ilic[2], Leonel Sousa[2], Javier Garcia-Blas[1], and Jesus Carretero[1]

[1] University Carlos III of Madrid, Madrid, Spain
esserran@inf.uc3m.es
[2] INESC-ID, Instituto Superior Tecnico, University of Lisbon, Lisbon, Portugal

Abstract. When optimizing or porting applications to new architectures, a preliminary characterization is necessary to exploit the maximum computing power of the employed devices. Profiling tools are available for numerous architectures and programming models, making it easier to spot possible bottlenecks. However, for a better interpretation of the collected results, current profilers rely on insightful performance models. In this paper, we describe the Cache Aware Roofline Model (CARM) and tools for its generation to enable the performance characterization of GPU architectures and workloads. We use CARM to characterize two kernels that are part of a 3D iterative reconstruction application for Computed Tomography (CT). These two kernels take most of the execution time of the whole method, being therefore suitable for a deeper analysis. By exploring the model and the methodology proposed, the overall performance of the kernels has been improved up to two times compared to the previous implementations.

Keywords: Medical image · Computed Tomography · CARM · GPU Reconstruction

1 Introduction

Performance optimization and parallelization of scientific applications represent an important research topic for computer scientists. The impact of applying hardware-specific optimizations in certain methods and algorithms can provide the difference between obtaining the results in near real-time or consuming hours or even days.

This work has been partially supported through grant TIN2016-79637-P "Towards unification of HPC and Big Data Paradigms" from the Spanish Ministry of Economy and Competitiveness, the COST Action IC1305 "Network for Sustainable Ultrascale Computing Platforms" (NESUS), grant FPU14/03875 from the Spanish Ministry of Education and by the Portuguese national funds through FCT under the projects UID/CEC/50021/2013 and LISBOA-01-0145-FEDER-031901 (PTDC/CCI-COM/31901/2017).

R. Yokota et al. (Eds.): ISC 2018 Workshops, LNCS 11203, pp. 509–526, 2018.
https://doi.org/10.1007/978-3-030-02465-9_36

A precise characterization of the target application is needed for optimizing or porting applications to new architectures. Profiling tools are available for numerous architectures and programming models, making it easier to spot possible sources of execution bottlenecks in the application code. However, to perform a deeper performance analysis, collected hardware metrics are typically used together with novel and insightful performance models. An example of these performance models are roofline models [1,2], which have been used for several years to assess performance of applications for different architectures, by considering their hardware limitations. Different roofline models have been developed considering a diverse set of hardware characteristics such as memory bandwidth and hierarchy, theoretical computational performance limits etc. These models are usually based on two main metrics: performance (in Flops/s) and arithmetic intensity (Flops/Byte) [2]. Additionally, a set of roofline models focused on other parameters (e.g., power and energy consumption) have recently appeared [3]. Some of these models have been already included in well-known profiling tools, such as Intel Advisor [4,5].

One of the main contributions of this work lies in the application of Cache-aware Roofline Model (CARM) to a medical image processing algorithm as the use case. In this work, we discuss the benefits of CARM for GPU applications, by exploring the huge optimization space of GPU-based kernels. Specifically, we have carried out the characterization of two kernels that are part of an iterative reconstruction solution for medical image processing in Computed Tomography (CT). The analyzed kernels take most of the execution time of the whole method, being therefore suitable for a deeper analysis.

The rest of the paper is structured as follows. In Sect. 2, a brief description of CARM and the rationale behind reconstruction algorithms for CT medical image processing is provided. Section 3 describes the methods employed in this study including the tools developed and the algorithms evaluated. In Sect. 4, the experiments made to assess our proposal, and their results are shown. Section 5 discusses other solutions proposed in the literature, while Sect. 6 presents major conclusions and future research lines of our work.

2   Background

In this section, we provide a brief description of the CARM fundamentals and the rationale behind reconstruction algorithms for CT medical image processing.

2.1   CARM: Cache-Aware Roofline Model

The original roofline model [1], developed for traditional shared memory architectures, focuses on the data traffic occurring at a single level of memory hierarchy to construct the model. For example, one can consider only the peak DRAM bandwidth and compute the operational intensity based on the bytes transferred between the DRAM and Last Level Cache (LLC). As a consequence, the original roofline model gave the first insight into an easy differentiation between memory-bound and compute-bound regions that could be identified easily with this model.

In contrast, the CARM [2] considers the complete memory hierarchy (caches and DRAM) within a single model, thus increasing the number of regions to classify an application. Hence, this approach provides a different perspective when characterizing the applications, by including several other fundamental micro-architecture aspects besides the processing speed and the DRAM bandwidth. In Fig. 1, we depict the CARM as presented by the Intel Advisor tool [4]. Lines in different colors represent the different regions that can be generated from the model depending on the roof lines. It includes the peak bandwidth of all the caches present in the memory hierarchy, as well as the different computational roofs, which represent the upper-bound capability of the computational units of a given processor.

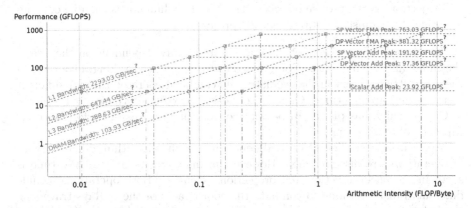

Fig. 1. Example of CARM as depicted by Intel Advisor. Bandwidth for the three cache levels and DRAM are shown, as well as the peak compute performance for Single Precision (SP) vector fused multiply-add (FMA), Double Precision (DP) Vector FMA, SP Vector Add, DP Vector Add and Scalar Add. (Color figure online)

Furthermore, the CARM has been recently extended to characterize other features of the architecture and application, such as energy efficiency and power consumption [3]. Additionally, this model was also applied to NVidia GPUs with the objective of creating a GPU CARM [6], which provided coherent results with respect to other tools in terms of application and architecture characterization. With this model, it is possible to extend the typical compute or memory bound characterization to a larger amount of intermediate classification regions thanks to the inclusion of the different GPU memory hierarchy levels and components (caches, shared and global memory etc.).

2.2 Reconstruction Algorithms in Medical Imaging

The medical imaging field is closely related to scientific computing and high performance models. Many of the techniques used in medical imaging require of a reconstruction process, which, in some cases, can be computationally expensive. This is the case of MRI reconstruction or CT reconstruction.

Although analytical methods for CT reconstruction exist since many years ago (e.g., filtered backprojection as in the case of FDK algorithm [7]), iterative reconstruction algorithms are a very widespread approach due to the utilization of novel dose reduction techniques. This type of algorithms are computationally more intensive than traditional algorithms and require a higher amount of resources, such as memory and CPU, as shown in previous works [8]. The increased computational load comes from the iterative repetition of the following two main operators or *kernels*:

- Backprojection: represents the main operator of most reconstruction algorithms, either traditional or iterative. It transforms the initially acquired data (2D projections) into a 3D volume.
- Projection: is the inverse operator. From a 3D volume, it is capable of simulating the acquisition of different 2D projections.

In terms of complexity both operators are mainly dependent on the size of the input and output data. Computation can be reduced taking advantage of the symmetries present in the geometry and can be accelerated through different methods and architectures. One of the most successful alternative is the usage of GPUs, which has proven to be very convenient in terms of performance for this type of applications.

Apart from these operators, and depending on the algorithm, different types of operations are also included. However, in many cases, most of the time is spent in the backprojection and projection execution. Both operations include different transformations to compute the coordinates of the X-Rays traversing the volume. In general, an integral of the values included in the line formed between the X-Ray source and the detector is computed for every unit included in the output data, voxels in the case of the backprojection and pixels for the projection.

Ideal arrangement between projection and backprojection is shown in Fig. 2. Irregular movements of the detector and source can be applied to simulate possible misalignments and they must be considered in the reconstruction process. These misalignments introduce additional computation in the kernels. Additionally, the interpolation function used in order to compute the values must also be considered. In this work, we will focus on a voxel-driven backprojector and a ray-driven projector with support for misalignments in the form of displacements of the detector (shifts) and rotations (tilt, roll and skew).

3 Characterization and Profiling Method

In this section we describe the methods employed in this study, including the tools developed and the algorithms evaluated. We will focus on the application of the CARM on GPUs [6]. The differences in the construction of the model for a CPU and for GPU mainly reside in the memory hierarchy used inside the

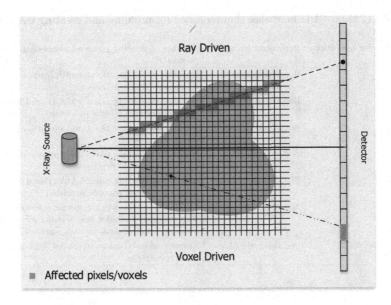

Fig. 2. Ideal geometry for a given angle between X-Ray source and detector.

GPUs. The number of cache levels is smaller, as well as the types of operations that can be performed. Therefore the number of roofs obtained varies, but their meaning is nearly identical, being able to identify the different bottlenecks in the explored kernels.

3.1   CARM-Based Profiling Tool for GPU Applications

We have developed an auxiliary tool for the automatization of the data model recollection and the generation of their corresponding GPU CARM visualization for their interpretation.

Performance information is obtained through hardware counters present in different NVidia architectures by using NVProf (NVidia profiler) tool. The counters are mainly chosen following their relation with CARM in terms of performance (operations) or memory accesses (memory instructions). Detailed information of each counter and their meaning can be found in Table 1.

By relying on these counters we can obtain the two main factors that influence the CARM: arithmetic intensity and performance. To compute the performance of the kernel, we collected the total amount of floating point operations (either in double or single precision) using the following equations:

$$fp_{sp} = flop\_count_{sp}\_add + flop\_count_{sp}\_mul + \\ +2*(flop\_count_{sp}\_fma) + flop\_count_{sp}\_special \quad (1)$$

Table 1. Main GPU hardware counters used for profiling and creating CARM.

Floating point operations	flop_count_sp_add	Number of floating point add operations (single precision)
	flop_count_sp_mul	Number of floating point multiplication operation (single precision)
	flop_count_sp_fma	Number of floating point FMA (Fused Multiply Add) operations (single precision)
	flop_count_dp_add	Number of floating point add operations (double precision)
	flop_count_dp_mul	Number of floating point multiplication operation (double precision)
	flop_count_dp_fma	Number of floating point FMA (Fused Multiply Add) operations (double precision)
	flop_count_sp_special	Number of floating point special operations. This category includes operations such as: fast division, cosines, sines or root squares
Memory operations	inst_compute_ld_st	Number of instructions executed with load and store operations

$$fp_{dp} = flop\_count_{dp}\_add + flop\_count_{dp}\_mul +$$
$$+2 * (flop\_count_{dp}\_fma) \quad (2)$$

where FMA instructions ($flop\_count_{sp}\_fma$) are multiplied by two since it represents the execution of two operations, multiplication and addition, in a single step. We also obtained the execution time of the kernel and the number of both load and store instructions (inst_compute_ld_st) to calculate the performance, using Eq. 3, and the arithmetic intensity, as shown in Eq. 4.

$$perf_{sp} = \frac{fp_{sp}}{ex\_time} \quad (3)$$

$$ai_{sp} = \frac{fp_{sp}}{inst\_compute\_ld\_st * 4} \quad (4)$$

3.2   Kernels for Medical Image Processing in CT

In a previous work, we introduced and examined FUX-Sim [9], a simulation/reconstruction framework for X-Ray medical imaging. When analyzing the different components of FUX-Sim, the most time consuming layer was the Kernel layer. This layer contained the implementation of both backprojection and projection algorithms. Both of them are present in all possible configurations of the framework and take part in advanced iterative reconstruction algorithms. Thus, any possible optimization that can be applied effectively reduces the overall execution time of many functionalities of FUX-Sim.

For both kernels, in standard baseline versions, output data are stored in global memory while volume and projection data for input are stored in a CUDA array, bound to 3D or 2D textures. This texture-based implementation has proven to be much more efficient than the implementations based on global memory due to the caching and spatial arrangement of textures in memory and the hardware-based interpolation that is provided by the texture units. Geometric data are stored in constant memory, thus providing fast access to all threads.

Backprojection. An outline of the operations included in the backprojection kernel is shown in Pseudocode 1. From the two types of interpolation modes that are available in the framework, we will focus on the ray-driven method. This interpolation is commonly used and represents a higher priority for kernel optimization. The computational complexity of this kernel is therefore defined as $O(u\_vol\_size \times v\_vol\_size \times z\_vol\_size \times projections)$.

Algorithm 1. Voxel Driven Backprojection.

1: **procedure** BACKPROJECTION$((projections, tilt, skew, shifts...))$
2:   **for** $u \leftarrow u\_vol\_size$ **do**
3:     **for** $z \leftarrow z\_vol\_size$ **do**
4:       *Compute centered u and z coordinates in volume*
5:       **for** $\theta \leftarrow projections$ **do**
6:         **for** $v \leftarrow v\_vol\_size$ **do**
7:           Compute centered v coordinates in volume
8:           Compute real SO and DDO distances
9:           *Compute u and v rotated coordinates for θ angle*
10:          Compute magnification factor
11:          *Obtain ideal x and y coordinates*
12:          **if** shift **then**
13:            *Apply x- and/or y-shift to (x, y) coordinates*
14:          **end if**
15:          **if** tilt OR roll **then**
16:            *Apply tilt or roll to (x, y) coordinates*
17:          **end if**
18:          **if** skew **then**
19:            *Apply skew to (x, y) coordinates*
20:          **end if**
21:          **Update weighted value**
22:          $value \leftarrow Bilinearinterpolationofprojections(\theta, x, y)$
23:          $volume(u, v, z) \leftarrow volume(u, v, z) + value$
24:        **end for**
25:      **end for**
26:    **end for**
27: **end for**
28: **return** $volume$
29: **end procedure**

The operations carried out in this kernel can be divided in three regions:

- Rotation of the volume and magnification. The rotated coordinates of the volume in axis u and v are computed for the selected angle. Magnification in z is also computed. In these operations several computations for equivalences between real measurements (mm) and voxel and pixel sizes are calculated.
- Computation of misalignments with respect to the ideal geometry. These operations are executed for every projection coordinates that is computed. Control instructions are dominant in this region of the algorithm.
- Memory accesses and computation of the final value. The value on the selected coordinates is obtained from memory with their corresponding bilinear interpolation. Depending on the configuration of the kernel, this bilinear interpolation can be executed using hardware or software functions.

Furthermore, in all these regions special mathematical functions are also included (*sin*, *cos*, *tan*, *sqrt*, etc). These functions consist of several floating point operations that can be optimized by the compiler at compilation time. Starting from this initial pseudocode, different configurations of the kernel were created taking into account optimizations over the three regions of the code.

The configurations designed for this kernel are the following:

std (Standard baseline): This configuration represents the initial implementation of the algorithm without any modification or profiling input. The algorithm is unchanged with respect to the one presented in the pseudocode. This standard version does not establish a maximum number of registers and is compiled with the $--use\_fast\_math$ flag.

opt (Branch optimized): This configuration modifies the computation of the geometrical distortion computation (tilt and roll). The main modification consists on reducing the computation of the misalignments, pre-computing the sign of the final coordinates before the actual branch appears. Therefore, we reduce the number of branches by two and generate only one computation independently of the direction of the tilt parameter.

mreg32 (Maximum number of registers 32): With this configuration, we limit the number of registers per thread to 32[1]. The number of register per thread depends on the number of variables present in the system and it is limited. A high number of registers per thread can decrease the occupancy of the device and the performance.

nofm (Disabling fast-math): A version that eliminates the use of *fast-math* operations (special operations for division, cos, sin...). This specially affects to the computation of misalignments and rotated indexes.

gm (Change texture memory fetching by global memory): In this version the projection data is stored in standard global memory and the interpolation functions are implemented as _device_ functions.

---

[1] Using the compilation flag $-maxrregcount=32$.

Projection. The pseudocode for the algorithm implemented in the kernel is shown in Pseudocode 2. Thread parallelization in the GPU is based on x and y coordinates of the resultant projection, executing a kernel for each angle. This approach effectively reduces the memory requirements being capable of only storing one projection at a time, one of the main differences with the backprojection kernel.

Algorithm 2. Ray Driven projection.

1: **procedure** PROJECTION()($volume, tilt, skew, shifts...$)
2: **for** $\theta \leftarrow projections$ **do**
3:   **for** $x \leftarrow x\_proj\_size$ **do**
4:    **for** $y \leftarrow y\_proj\_size$ **do**
5:     *Compute centered x coordinate in projection*
6:     *Compute centered y coordinate in projection*
7:     **if** skew **then**
8:      *Apply skew to (x,y) coordinates*
9:     **end if**
10:     **if** tilt OR roll **then**
11:      *Apply tilt or roll to (x,y) coordinates*
12:     **end if**
13:     **if** shift **then**
14:      *Apply x- and/or y-shift to (x,y) coordinates*
15:     **end if**
16:     **for** $v \leftarrow v\_vol\_size$ **do**
17:      Compute centered v coordinate
18:      *Compute (u,v) rotated coordinates for θ angle*
19:      **Compute $(u1,v)$ and $(u2,v)$ rotated coordinates for θ angle**
20:      Compute real SO and DDO distances
21:      Compute inverse magnification factor: $InvMag$
22:      *Obtain ideal u coordinate: $InvMag \cdot u_{rot}$*
23:      *Obtain ideal z coordinate: $InvMag \cdot z$*
24:      **Update weighted value**
25:      $value \leftarrow Trilinear interpolation of volume(u,v,z)$
26:      $projection(\theta, x, y) \leftarrow value$
27:     **end for**
28:    **end for**
29:   **end for**
30: **end for**
31: **return** $projection$
32: **end procedure**

Similarly to the backprojection, the projection can also be divided in three regions:

- Rotation of the volume and inverse magnification. The rotated coordinates of the volume in axis u and v are computed for the selected angle. The inverse magnification in z is also computed. In these operations, multiple computations for equivalences between real measurements (mm) and voxel and pixel sizes are calculated.
- Computation of misalignments with respect to the ideal geometry. These misalignments are computed over the projection coordinates, which are the initial coordinates of the GPU threads. Therefore, these additional computations that in the backprojection are computed for every coordinate in the depth axis v, in projection are computed once for all v coordinates. It also contains a large quantity of control instructions.
- Memory access and computation of the final value. The final value is retrieved from memory with the computed coordinates of the volume. At this point a trilinear interpolation function is employed for non ideal coordinates.

The configurations implemented for this kernel are the following:

- **std** (Standard baseline): This configuration represents the initial implementation of the algorithm without any modification or profiling input. The algorithm followed is unchanged with respect to the one presented in Pseudocode 2. This standard version does not establish a maximum number of registers and is compiled with the *–use_fast_math flag*.
- **opt** (Branch optimized): This configuration modifies the computation of the geometrical misalignments computation (tilt and roll). The main modification consists on reducing the computation of the misalignments, pre-computing the sign of the final coordinates before the actual branch appears. Therefore, we reduce the number of branches by two and generate only one computation independently of the sign. This configuration effectively reduce the number of control instructions executed by the kernel.
- **reg** (Manually unroll v loop to increase register usage): The v loop is unrolled with a factor of 2 in order to increase the register usage and the texture locality. This optimization also implies an increase in the number of registers employed in the kernel.
- **mreg32** (Maximum number of registers 32): With this configuration we limit the number of registers per thread to 32 with the compilation flag – *maxrregcount=32*. In this kernel, standard versions do not surpass the maximum number of registers available per block, however, this configuration can be useful combined with others, such as, reg, which increase the number of registers per thread and can reduce the effective occupancy.
- **nofm** (Disabling fast-math): A version that does not use fast-math operations (special operations for division, cos, sin...). This affects specially to the computation of misalignments and rotated indexes.
- **gm** (Change texture memory fetching by global memory): In this version the volume data is stored in standard global memory and the interpolation functions are implemented as *__device__ functions*.

4   Experimental Results

We have evaluated both kernels with the different configurations explained in the previous sections. We employed two different families of GPUs, whose specifications are described in Table 2. In all cases we used CUDA 8.0 and NVidia Profiler version 8.0 to compile and obtain the main counters from the hardware. All experiments were executed 10 times and here we show the median execution time.

We evaluated all configurations by combining 2D block configurations from 8 to 128 threads per dimension. We executed the algorithms over two studies datasets with different sizes: 512^2 projection size and 512^3 volume size; and 1024^2 projection size and 1024^3 volume size. In the case of the GTX 980, only the first image was obtained due to memory constraints.

Table 2. Specifications of the GPUs employed in the evaluation.

Specification	GTX 980	Tesla K40c
Architecture	Maxwell (GM204)	Kepler (GK110B)
Clock speed (GHz)	1.126	0.745
Cores	2,048	2,880
Theoretical performance (TFlops)	4.5	4.29
SMs	16	15
Global memory (GBytes)	4	12
Internal memory bandwidth (GB/s)	224	288
L2 Cache size (KB)	2,048	1,536
Texture units	128	240
Texture cache	✗	✓
Compute capability	5.2	3.5

Hardware counters are collected to later characterize the kernel in terms of performance (GFlops/s) and Arithmetic Intensity (Flops/Byte). For this purpose, we gather multiple metrics, all described in Table 1, in order to obtain the number of floating point operations executed in both single and double precision inside the kernel. We finally construct the model based on this information.

4.1   High-End GPU Evaluation

We started with a thorough evaluation on a NVidia Tesla K40. In Fig. 3, we plot the execution times for multiple configurations for projection and backprojection kernels. For each configuration the execution time from the block size combination with the best performance was taken. For the backprojection kernel, the configuration that gave best results was the *opt* version. The reduction of the

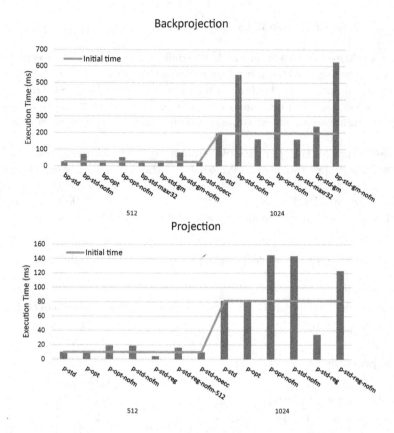

Fig. 3. Execution time for different configurations with their best block sizes. Results are shown for the backprojection (top) and the projection (down)

computation on the internal branches of the algorithm helps to reduce the time spent in this part of the algorithm that, since it is inside the internal loop of the kernel, is executed v times per thread. For the projection kernel the same behavior is not expected. The branches for the computation of the geometrical distortions are not inside the internal kernel, thus reducing its impact over the overall execution time. In this case, the best configuration is the *reg* configuration. This configuration increases the number of registers used inside the kernel, reducing the effect of register spilling and increasing the performance.

After applying the Equations described in Sect. 3, we obtained the characterization of the application inside the CARM of Tesla K40. The models obtained are shown in Fig. 4. Both of them are obtained with the data acquired from the configurations executed with the block sizes leading to the best performance. None of the kernels are in the compute-bound region, although p-std-reg is near. The kernels with different size do not significantly differ in their characterization in the model, although in some cases only slightly better performance was obtained when executing kernels with the larger data set.

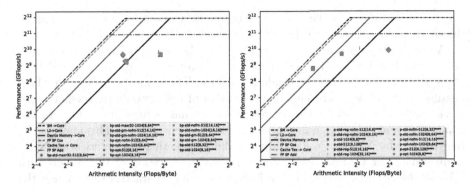

Fig. 4. CARM for NVidia Tesla K40 GPU for all configurations with the thread block dimensions that lead to best performance in backprojection (left), and projection (right).

We compare the results obtained using the GPU CARM with the characterizations obtained from the NVidia Profiler. In Table 3, we summarize the different characterizations obtained for both kernels in some of the configurations, experimenting with the best and worst block dimensions. We found discrepancies between both tools with differences between compute-bound and memory-bound characterizations when the block dimension is altered.

NVidia classifies kernels taking into account the time spent in different types of instructions (compute instructions vs load/store instructions). However, CARMs do not take into account this mix of instructions, focusing on the performance of the whole kernel execution as well as the arithmetic intensity. Therefore, when employing a GPU CARM only, performance can be modified if the block dimensions are changed causing a vertical movement in the plot. For

Table 3. Table with the characterizations obtained for different configurations of the kernels in the Tesla K40c with the GPU CARM and with the NVidia profiler.

Name	Characterization best block size	Characterization worst block size	Characterization CARM
bp-std	compute bound	Instruction and memory latency	memory bandwidth
bp-opt	compute bound	Instruction and memory latency	memory bandwidth
bp-std-nofm	compute bound	compute bound	compute bound
bp-opt-nofm	compute bound	compute bound	compute bound
bp-std-mreg32	compute bound	Instruction and memory latency	compute bound
bp-std-gm	compute bound	Instruction and memory latency	compute bound
p-std	memory bandwidth	memory bandwidth	memory bandwidth (L2)
p-opt	memory bandwidth	memory bandwidth	memory bandwidth (L2)
p-opt-nofm	Instruction and memory latency	Instruction and memory latency	memory bandwidth
p-std-nofm	Instruction and memory latency	Instruction and memory latency	memory bandwidth
p-std-gm	compute bound	Instruction and memory latency	memory bandwidth
p-std-gm-nofm	compute bound	Instruction and memory latency	memory bandwidth
p-reg	Instruction and memory latency	Instruction and memory latency	memory bandwidth
p-reg-nofm	compute bound	Instruction and memory latency	memory bandwidth

NVidia, this also affects the time spent on memory operations, which can affect the characterization of the kernel.

Additionally, roofs are computed based on the maximum performance that can be reached by the GPU, that is with the maximum occupancy and level of parallelism that is possible inside the device. Therefore, for kernels in which possible trade-offs exists (occupancy vs number of registers/shared memory size) these roofs do not necessarily represent the actual performance limits of the application and can change the characterization of the kernels. This may also be the reason why NVidia Profiler provides different kernel characterization when compared to the CARM. This affects the characterization of the kernels with different block sizes and configurations since these characteristics change the occupancy ratio of the GPU.

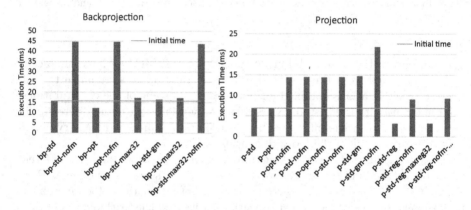

Fig. 5. Execution time for different configurations with their best block sizes. Results are shown for the backprojection (left) and the projection (right)

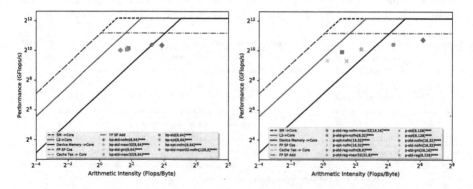

Fig. 6. CARM for GTX980 GPU for all configurations with the block sizes that lead to best performance in backprojection (left), and projection (right).

4.2 Commodity GPU Evaluation

With the aim of studying if the results obtained with the High-Profile GPU are also applicable to other GPUs using other architectures, we have replicated the evaluation on an NVidia GTX980. Total execution times are coherent with what has been obtained from the Tesla K40. In this case, only the small study of 512^3 volume dimension was evaluated due to the memory limitation of this device.

Speedups obtained for *bp-opt* and *p-reg* are significant (as we can see in Fig. 5), obtaining a speedup of 1.28× for backprojection and 2.22× for projection. The worst execution time is still reached with the *nofm* versions of the different kernels. The penalization is larger for the backprojection kernel in which the *nofm* version can be 3× slower.

Representation of the different configurations in the CARM are less clustered than in the case of the Tesla option and are closer to the compute-bound region (see Fig. 6). Both models (Tesla K40 CARM and GTX980 CARM) are very similar in terms of how the configurations are ordered, although in general they obtain a higher performance and arithmetic intensity. GTX 980, although with a newer architecture, is directed towards the commodity hardware segment, meanwhile Tesla products are specific for HPC. The small study is capable of obtaining better advantage of the hardware, occupying in a better way the computation units.

5 Related Work

To be able to optimize and implement complex algorithms in different architectures it is necessary to understand how the algorithm is behaving and what problems must be overcome. For this purpose, different tools and methodologies have appeared to assist to the programmers about their applications.

Monitoring and tracing tools have been developed in order to better characterize applications and algorithms executed over different hardware. One of the first tools that are used when characterizing scientific applications is *perf* [10], mainly used for obtaining information of the execution of an application at both kernel and user levels. This includes access to information provided by the hardware counters if support for the Performance API (PAPI) [11] is available. In the case of accelerators one of the most well-known tools is NVProf [12] created by NVidia to obtain information from the execution of kernels on their devices.

Using the information provided by these profilers, it is possible to characterize applications to assist in the optimization process [13,14] or to obtain the maximum performance provided by the hardware [15,16]. Those problems are addressed through the usage of performance models that can provide an aid into understanding the limits of the hardware and the bottlenecks present in the characterized application. The main difficulty of these performance models is to achieve generality, since they are defined for specific architectures and normally can not be generalized, as device-specific models are more accurate than those applicable to different architectures [17]. This is the reason why multiple performance models for different devices have been made available in the last years.

One of the most important performance models for shared memory architectures is the Roofline Model [1,2], which represents a visual tool for detecting the performance roof of the microprocessor architecture. This model has been translated successfully to GPU accelerators, as shown in [6,18]. Another similar example if the Quadrant-Split visual performance model [19] used by Konstantinidis et al. to predict the performance of different kernels in NVidia GPUs. Even roofline models with Dynamic voltage and frequency scaling (DVFS) applied to GPUs [3,6,20] have been created.

An important feature for creating performance models is the knowledge of the architecture. In many cases some of the key characteristics of the hardware are not explicitly described by the vendor, thus making the optimization of the applications difficult. Efforts have been done in this line of research for NVidia GPUs in different works [6,21,22] obtaining information about the different cache levels and their internal organization.

6   Conclusions

Although some benchmark applications have been already characterized with the GPU CARM, in this work we have presented a real-world application and the effects of characterizing it in terms of assisting in the process of optimization to obtain better execution times. More specifically, we have presented a full characterization of two medical image processing kernels: backprojection and projection. These kernels, highly used in modern reconstruction algorithms, present certain characteristics that make them suitable for an extensive characterization.

Both of them have been implemented in multiple versions and analyzed in several architectures, including GPUs. Implementations have included different optimization levels to increase their performance, based on the data obtained from the NVidia profiler and the constructed CARM. One example is the usage of texture mechanisms or cache optimizations. With respect to our baseline implementation we have been able to obtain a speedup of $2\times$ for the projection kernel and $1.25\times$ for the backprojection kernel.

The next step will consist on the construction of application specific roofs enabling a more accurate characterization of the kernels in order to further explore their optimization space. Additionally, the effects of the optimization techniques employed in this work can also be studied in other type of architectures in which CARM is also available.

References

1. Williams, S., Waterman, A., Patterson, D.: Roofline: an insightful visual performance model for multicore architectures. Commun. ACM **52**(4), 65–76 (2009)
2. Ilic, A., Pratas, F., Sousa, L.: Cache-aware Roofline model: upgrading the loft. IEEE Comput. Archit. Lett. **13**(1), 21–24 (2014)
3. Ilic, A., Pratas, F., Sousa, L.: Beyond the roofline: cache-aware power and energy-efficiency modeling for multi-cores. IEEE Trans. Comput. **66**(1), 52–58 (2017)
4. Shinsel, A.: Intel Advisor Roofline (2017). https://software.intel.com/en-us/articles/intel-advisor-roofline. Accessed 02 Mar 2017
5. Marques, D., et al.: Performance analysis with cache-aware roofline model in intel advisor. In: 2017 International Conference on High Performance Computing and Simulation (HPCS), pp. 898–907. IEEE (2017)
6. Lopes, A., Pratas, F., Sousa, L., Ilic, A.: Exploring GPU performance, power and energy-efficiency bounds with Cache-aware Roofline Modeling. In: 2017 IEEE International Symposium on Performance Analysis of Systems and Software (ISPASS), pp. 259–268. IEEE (2017)
7. Feldkamp, L., Davis, L., Kress, J.: Practical cone-beam algorithm. JOSA A **1**(6), 612–619 (1984)
8. de Molina, C., Serrano, E., Garcia-Blas, J., Carretero, J., Desco, M., Abella, M.: Gpu-accelerated iterative reconstruction for limited-data tomography in CBCT systems. BMC Bioinform. **19**(1), 171 (2018)
9. Abella, M., et al.: FUX-Sim: implementation of a fast universal simulation/reconstruction framework for X-ray systems. PLOS ONE **12**(7), 1–22 (2017)
10. Weaver, V.M.: Linux perf_event features and overhead. In: The 2nd International Workshop on Performance Analysis of Workload Optimized Systems, FastPath, vol. 13 (2013)
11. Dongarra, J., et al.: Performance application programming interface
12. NVidia, "NVidia Profiler." http://docs.nvidia.com/cuda/profiler-users-guide/index.html
13. Kim, K.-H., Kim, K., Park, Q.-H.: Performance analysis and optimization of three-dimensional FDTD on GPU using roofline model. Comput. Phys. Commun. **182**(6), 1201–1207 (2011)
14. Carvalho, P., Drummond, L.M.A., Bentes, C., Clua, E., Cataldo, E., Marzulo, L.A.J.: Analysis and characterization of GPU benchmarks for kernel concurrency efficiency. In: Mocskos, E., Nesmachnow, S. (eds.) CARLA 2017. CCIS, vol. 796, pp. 71–86. Springer, Cham (2018). https://doi.org/10.1007/978-3-319-73353-1_5
15. Ryoo, J.H., Quirem, S.J., Lebeane, M., Panda, R., Song, S., John, L.K.: GPGPU benchmark suites: how well do they sample the performance spectrum? In: 2015 44th International Conference on Parallel Processing (ICPP), pp. 320–329. IEEE (2015)
16. Che, S., Skadron, K.: BenchFriend: correlating the performance of GPU benchmarks. Int. J. High Perform. Comput. Appl. **28**(2), 238–250 (2014)
17. Lopez-Novoa, U., Mendiburu, A., Miguel-Alonso, J.: A survey of performance modeling and simulation techniques for accelerator-based computing. IEEE Trans. Parallel Distrib. Syst. **26**(1), 272–281 (2015)
18. Jia, H., Zhang, Y., Long, G., Xu, J., Yan, S., Li, Y.: GPURoofline: a model for guiding performance optimizations on GPUs. In: Kaklamanis, C., Papatheodorou, T., Spirakis, P.G. (eds.) Euro-Par 2012. LNCS, vol. 7484, pp. 920–932. Springer, Heidelberg (2012). https://doi.org/10.1007/978-3-642-32820-6_90

19. Konstantinidis, E., Cotronis, Y.: A practical performance model for compute and memory bound GPU kernels. In: 2015 23rd Euromicro International Conference on Parallel, Distributed and Network-Based Processing (PDP), pp. 651–658. IEEE (2015)
20. Nugteren, C., van den Braak, G.-J., Corporaal, H.: Roofline-aware DVFS for GPUs. In: Proceedings of International Workshop on Adaptive Self-tuning Computing Systems, p. 8. ACM (2014)
21. Wong, H., Papadopoulou, M.-M., Sadooghi-Alvandi, M., Moshovos, A.: Demystifying GPU microarchitecture through microbenchmarking. In: 2010 IEEE International Symposium on Performance Analysis of Systems and Software (ISPASS), pp. 235–246. IEEE (2010)
22. Mei, X., Chu, X.: Dissecting GPU memory hierarchy through microbenchmarking. IEEE Trans. Parallel Distrib. Syst. 28(1), 72–86 (2017)

How Pre-multicore Methods and Algorithms Perform in Multicore Era

Alexey Lastovetsky[1(✉)], Muhammad Fahad[1], Hamidreza Khaleghzadeh[1],
Semyon Khokhriakov[1], Ravi Reddy[1], Arsalan Shahid[1], Lukasz Szustak[2],
and Roman Wyrzykowski[2]

[1] School of Computer Science, University College Dublin, Belfield, Dublin 4, Ireland
`alexey.lastovetsky@ucd.ie`
[2] Czestochowa University of Technology, Czestochowa, Poland

Abstract. Many classical methods and algorithms developed when single-core CPUs dominated the parallel computing landscape, are still widely used in the changed multicore world. Two prominent examples are load balancing, which has been one of the main techniques for minimization of the computation time of parallel applications since the beginning of parallel computing, and model-based power/energy measurement techniques using performance events. In this paper, we show that in the multicore era, load balancing is no longer synonymous to optimization and present recent methods and algorithms for optimization of parallel applications for performance and energy on modern HPC platforms, which do not rely on load balancing and often return imbalanced but optimal solutions.

We also show that some fundamental assumptions about performance events, which have to be true for the model-based power/energy measurement tools to be accurate, are increasingly difficult to satisfy as the number of CPU cores increases. Therefore, energy-aware computing methods relying on these tools will be increasingly difficult to verify.

Keywords: Multicore platforms · Load balancing
Power and energy modeling · Performance monitoring counters

1 Introduction

Multicore CPUs and accelerators have become the standard building blocks of computing systems at all levels from supercomputers to mobile and embedded devices. At the same time, fundamentals of the dominant methods and algorithms currently used for performance and energy optimization of these systems were developed in the time when single-core CPUs dominated the computing landscape.

Two prominent examples are load balancing, which has been one of the main techniques for minimization of the computation time of parallel applications since the beginning of parallel computing, and model-based power/energy

© Springer Nature Switzerland AG 2018
R. Yokota et al. (Eds.): ISC 2018 Workshops, LNCS 11203, pp. 527–539, 2018.
https://doi.org/10.1007/978-3-030-02465-9_37

measurement techniques using performance events as model parameters. In this paper, we demonstrate that in the multicore era, load balancing is no longer synonymous to optimization. We also outline recent methods and algorithms for optimization of parallel applications for performance and energy on modern computing platforms, which do not rely on load balancing and often return imbalanced but optimal solutions.

We also show that some fundamental assumptions about performance events, which have to be true for the model-based power/energy measurement tools to be accurate, are increasingly difficult to satisfy as the number of CPU cores increases. Therefore, energy-aware computing methods relying on these tools will be increasingly difficult to verify.

The paper is organized as follows. Section 2 explains limitations of load balancing for performance and energy optimization of applications on multicore-based computing platforms. It also presents recent optimization methods and algorithms, returning optimal but typically unbalanced solutions. Section 3 discusses the accuracy of the popular methods for power and energy measurements of multicore processors in the light of recently discovered irregularities of some fundamental building blocks of these methods. Section 4 concludes the paper.

2   How Much Performance and Energy You Can Lose Through Load Balancing on Multicore Platforms

In this section, we formulate conditions that allow load balancing algorithms to minimize the execution time and the energy consumption of parallel applications. We then show that while these conditions are satisfied for single-core based platforms, they do not hold for multicore-based ones. We outline new workload distribution algorithms that address this problem. We also demonstrate the extent of performance and energy losses due to the use of load-balanced but not optimal application configurations.

2.1   When Does Load Balancing Work?

Load balancing algorithms can be classified as static or dynamic. Static algorithms (for example, those based on data partitioning) [1–6] require a priori information about the parallel application and platform. Dynamic algorithms (such as task scheduling and work stealing) [7–9] balance the load by moving fine-grained tasks between processors during the calculation. Dynamic algorithms do not require a priori information about execution but may incur significant communication overhead due to data migration.

The intuition behind the assumption that balancing the application improves its performance is the following: a balanced application does not waste processor cycles on waiting at points of synchronization and data exchange, maximizing this way the utilization of the processors and minimizing the computation time.

Let us analyze this assumption following [10]. Consider an application, the computational performance of which can be modeled by speed functions. Namely, let p parallel processors be used to execute the application and $s_i(x)$ be the speed of execution of the workload of size x by processor i. Here the speed can be measured in floating point operations per second or any other fix-sized computation units per unit time. The size of workload can be characterized by the problem size (for example, the number of cells in the computational domain or the matrix size) or just by the number of equal-sized computational units. The speed $s_i(x)$ is calculated as $\frac{x}{t_i(x)}$, where $t_i(x)$ is the execution time of the workload of size x on processor i. Using these definitions, it was proved [10] that in order to guarantee that the balanced configuration of the application will execute the workload of size n faster than any unbalanced configuration, the speed functions $s_i(x)$ should satisfy the condition:

$$\forall \Delta x > 0: \frac{s_i(x)}{x} \geq \frac{s_i(x + \Delta x)}{x + \Delta x} \tag{1}$$

Geometrically, it is illustrated in Fig. 1. The angle $\alpha(x)$ between the straight line, connecting the point $(0,0)$ and the point $(x, s(x))$ on the speed curve, and the x-axis will be inversely proportional to the execution time of the workload of size x by the processor. Indeed, the cotangent of this angle is directly proportional to the ratio $\frac{x}{s(x)}$ representing the execution time of the workload x. Therefore, larger angles correspond to shorter execution times. Condition 1 means that the increase of the workload, x, will never result in the decrease of the execution time, or equivalently in the increase of the angle $\alpha(x)$: $\forall \Delta x > 0: \alpha(x) \geq \alpha(x + \Delta x)$. Figure 1 illustrates the situation when load balancing will minimize the time of parallel execution of the application. For simplicity, assume that all our p processors are identical, characterized by the speed function in Fig. 1. Equal distribution of the total workload, w, allocating each processor workload $x = \frac{w}{p}$, will result in the execution time characterized by $\alpha(x)$. Any workload redistribution would lead to one of the processors executing larger workload $x + \Delta x$. As in general the parallel execution time is characterized by $\min_i \alpha(x_i)$, where x_i is the workload allocated to i-th processor, then $\min_i \alpha(x_i) \leq \alpha(x + \Delta x) \leq \alpha(x)$. This means that the load-balanced equal distribution will minimize the parallel execution time of any workload.

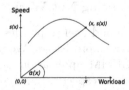

Fig. 1. Speed function suitable for minimization of computation time through load balancing. Angle $\alpha(x)$ represents the computation time: the greater the angle, the shorter the computation time.

The main body of the load balancing algorithms designed for performance optimization explicitly or implicitly assume that the speed of processor does not depend on the size of workload [1, 2, 11–14]. In other words, the speed functions $s_i(x)$ are assumed to be positive constants, in which case Condition 1 is trivially satisfied. More advanced algorithms are based on functional performance models (FPMs), which represent the speed of processor by a continuous function of the problem size [15, 16]. However, the shape of the function is not arbitrary but has to satisfy the following assumption [4]: Along each of the problem size variables, either the function is monotonically decreasing, or there exists point x such that

- On the interval $[0, x]$, the function is
  - monotonically increasing,
  - concave, and
  - any straight line coming through the origin of the coordinate system intersects the graph of the function in no more than one point.
- On the interval $[x, \infty)$, the function is monotonically decreasing.

These restrictions on the shape of speed functions guarantee that the efficient load balancing algorithms, proposed in [17–22], will always return a unique solution, minimizing the computation time. At the same time, it is easy to show that the restrictions imposed on FPMs will make them comfortably satisfy Condition 1.

Thus, the state-of-the-art load balancing algorithms designed for optimization of the computational performance of parallel applications assume that their performance profiles satisfy Condition 1.

Adding energy to the picture, let $E_i(x)$ be the energy consumed by processor i during the execution of workload of size x. In the case of p identical processors characterized by the same energy function $E(x)$, the equal distribution of the workload will always minimize the energy consumption if $\frac{dE(x)}{dx} \geq 0$ and $\frac{d^2 E(x)}{dx^2} \geq 0$. If $E(x)$ is linear, that is, $\frac{d^2 E(x)}{dx^2} = 0$, then any distribution of the workload w will result in the same energy consumption, $E(x_1) + \ldots + E(x_p) = (p-1) \times E(0) + E(x_1 + \ldots + x_p) = (p-1) \times E(0) + E(w)$. If $E(x)$ is strictly convex, that is, $\frac{d^2 E(x)}{dx^2} > 0$, then any uneven distribution will consume more energy than the equal load-balanced one, which is evident from Fig. 2.

2.2 When Does Load Balancing Not Work?

The conditions on performance and energy profiles formulated in Sect. 2.1 are comfortably satisfied for single-core processors. We illustrate this using the execution of the OpenBLAS DGEMM application on a single core of an Intel Haswell server. Figures 3a and b respectively show the shapes of the experimentally built speed and dynamic energy functions. The application multiplies two square matrices of size $n \times n$ (problem size is equal to n^2). In these experiments, the *numactl* tool is used to bind the application to one core. The dynamic energy consumptions are obtained using Watts Up Pro power meter.

However, if we run the same application on all 24 cores of the multicore CPU of the Haswell server executing 24 threads, the picture will drastically change as shown in Fig. 4. The performance and energy profiles are no longer smooth and

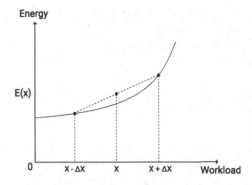

Fig. 2. Convex energy function suitable for minimization of energy consumption through equal distribution of the workload between identical processors. It is evident that for any x, $E(x) < \frac{E(x-\Delta x)+E(x+\Delta x)}{2}$, and hence, $E(x) + E(x) < E(x - \Delta x) + E(x + \Delta x)$.

deviate significantly from the shapes observed before. Even more spectacular variations in speed and energy can be seen in Fig. 5 for the FFTW application [23] performing a 2D FFT of size $n \times n$ (the problem size being n^2). The variations in energy reach a maximum of 125%, and the average variation in speed is 60%. It is important to note that these variations are not noise but an inherent trait of applications executing on multicore servers with resource contention and NUMA. It is evident that equal distribution of the workload between identical processors with such performance and energy profiles will no longer guarantee minimization of execution time or energy consumption. More generally, traditional methods and algorithms used for optimization of performance and/or energy of parallel applications will not work for modern multicore-based platforms.

2.3 New Methods and Algorithms for Performance and Energy Optimization on Multicore-Based Platforms

The challenges for performance and energy optimization of parallel applications on multicore-based platforms explained in Sect. 2.2 have been addressed over last 2 years in few publications. In [24], the problems of optimal workload distribution between identical processors for performance and dynamic energy consumptions were formulated and solved. Performance optimization problem (**POPT**) was formulated as follows:

- Given a discrete speed/performance function $s(x)$ of a processor
- Obtain partitioning, $d = \{x_1, \cdots, x_p\}$, of workload of size n using p identical processors so as to: $minimize \ \max_{i=1}^{p}(\frac{x_i}{s(x_i)}) \quad s.t. \quad \sum_{i=1}^{p} x_i = n$.

An exact algorithm solving this problem, **POPTA**, of complexity $O(m^2 \times p^2)$, where m is the cardinality of the discrete speed function $s(x)$, was proposed. The average and maximum performance improvements of POPTA over the equal

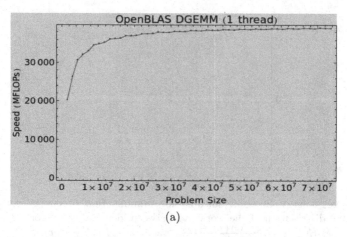

(a)

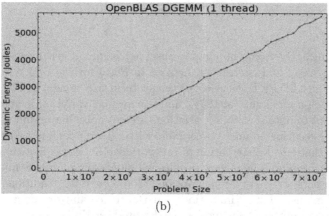

(b)

Fig. 3. (a) Speed function of OpenBLAS DGEMM application executed on a single core on the Intel Haswell server. (b) Dynamic energy consumption of OpenBLAS DGEMM application executed on a single core on the Intel Haswell server.

distribution solution were $(13\%, 71\%)$ for DGEMM and $(40\%, 95\%)$ for FFTW on a cluster of Haswell workstations.

Energy optimization problem (**EOPT**) was formulated as follows:

- Given a discrete dynamic energy function $e(x)$ of a processor
- Obtain partitioning, $d = \{x_1, \cdots, x_p\}$, of workload of size n using p identical processors so as to: $minimize \sum_{i=1}^{p} e(x_i)$ $s.t$ $\sum_{i=1}^{p} x_i = n$.

An exact algorithm solving the energy optimization problem, **EOPTA**, of complexity $O(m^2 \times p^2)$, where m is the cardinality of the discrete energy function $e(x)$, was designed. The average and maximum energy improvements of EOPTA over the equal distribution solution were $(18\%, 71\%)$ for DGEMM and $(22\%, 127\%)$ for FFTW.

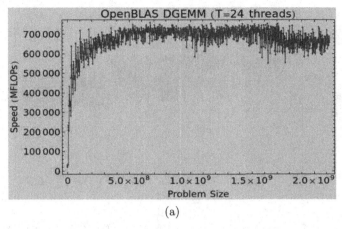

(a)

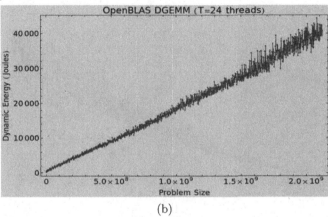

(b)

Fig. 4. (a) Speed function of OpenBLAS DGEMM executing 24 threads on the Intel Haswell server. (b) Function of dynamic energy consumption against problem size for OpenBLAS DGEMM executing 24 threads on the Intel Haswell server.

It was observed that optimization for performance only also reduced the energy consumption: $(12\%, 68\%)$ for DGEMM and $(22\%, 55\%)$ for FFTW. At the same time, optimization for energy only significantly degraded the performance: by 95–100% for both DGEMM and FFTW.

In order to better understand the interplay between optimization for performance and energy, a bi-objective optimization problem was studied in [25]. It was mathematically formulated as follows. Consider a workload of size n to be executed using p available identical processors. The performance of a processor executing a problem size x is given by $s(x)$, and the dynamic energy consumption of the execution of a problem size x by a processor is given by $e(x)$. Then the bi-objective optimization problem for minimization of execution time and minimization of total dynamic energy of computations during the execution of the workload is as follows:

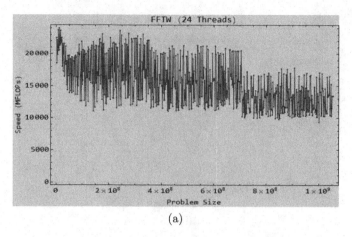

(a)

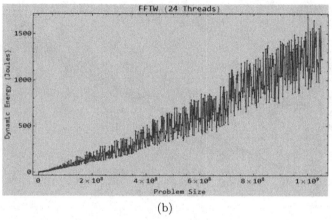

(b)

Fig. 5. (a) Speed function of FFTW executing 24 threads on the Intel Haswell server. (b) Function of dynamic energy consumption against problem size for FFTW executing 24 threads on the Intel Haswell server.

$$\mathbf{BOPPE}(n, p, s, e, q) :$$

$$minimize \quad \{\max_{i=1}^{q} \frac{x_i}{s(x_i)}, \sum_{i=1}^{q} e(x_i)\}$$

$$\text{Subject to} \quad x_1 + x_2 + ... + x_q = n$$

$$x_i \geq 0 \qquad i = 1, ..., q$$

$$x_i \leq n \qquad i = 1, ..., q$$

$$1 \leq q \leq p$$

$$\text{where} \quad p, q, n, x_i \in \mathbb{Z}_{>0},$$

$$s(x), e(x) \in \mathbb{R}_{>0}$$

The output of a solution method solving *BOPPE* is a set of Pareto-optimal solutions represented by workload distributions. It is important to note that the optimal number of processors (q) that are selected in a Pareto-optimal solution satisfies the constraint, $1 \le q \le p$.

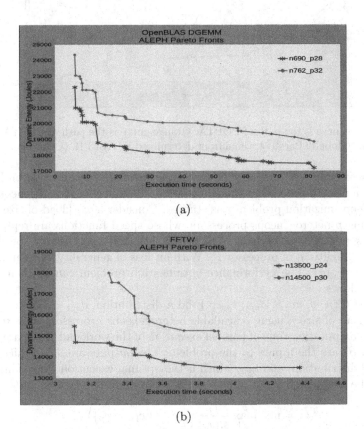

(a)

(b)

Fig. 6. Globally Pareto-optimal set of solutions with maximum sizes determined by *ALEPH* for OpenBLAS DGEMM and FFTW applications. Each curve shown as nX_pY represents results for data-parallel application workload size given by n (in multiples of granularity) and number of available processors, p.

A global optimization algorithm solving BOPPE (**ALEPH**) of complexity $O(m^2 \times p^2)$, where m is the cardinality of discrete functions $s(x)$ and $e(x)$, was designed. Figure 6 demonstrates solutions returned by ALEPH for DGEMM and FFTW for different problem sizes and numbers of processors. The interplay between single-objective optimizations for performance and energy can be visually studied using POPTA and EOPTA trajectories in the objective space together with the Pareto optimal front as shown in Fig. 7. This visual model can serve as a guidance for the choice of optimization method for performance and energy.

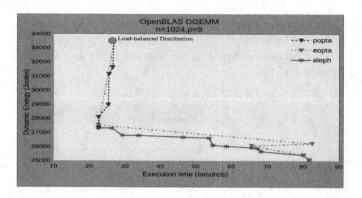

Fig. 7. Blue curve is the path of POPTA. Orange curve is the path of EOPTA. Green curve is the Globally Pareto-optimal front determined by ALEPH. (Color figure online)

The next step was done in [26], where performance optimization on heterogeneous multicore processors was addressed. The following heterogeneous performance optimization problem was studied. Consider a workload of size n executed using p heterogeneous processors, whose speed functions are represented by $S = \{s_1(x), ..., s_p(x)\}$ where $s_i(x)$, $i \in \{1, 2, \cdots, p\}$, is a discrete speed function of cardinality m of processor P_i. Without loss of generality, one can assume $x \in \{1, 2, \cdots, m\}$. The performance optimization problem can be then formulated as follows:

HPOPT$(n, p, m, S, d_{opt}, t_{opt})$: Find a distribution, $d_{opt} = \{w_1, ..., w_p\}$, of the workload of size n using p available heterogeneous processors so as to minimize the computation time of parallel execution of the workload. The parameters (n, p, m, S) are the inputs to the problem. The outputs are d_{opt}, which is the workload distribution, and t_{opt}, which is the optimal execution time. This problem can be formulated as an integer nonlinear programming problem (INLP):

$$t_{opt} = \min_d \max_{i=1}^{p} \frac{x_i}{s_i(x_i)} \quad (d = \{x_1, ..., x_p\})$$

$$\text{Subject to:} \quad x_1 + x_2 + ... + x_p = n$$
$$0 \leq x_i \leq m, \qquad i = 1, ..., p \tag{2}$$
$$\text{where} \quad p, m, n \in \mathbb{Z}_{>0} \quad \text{and} \quad x_i \in \mathbb{Z}_{\geq 0} \quad \text{and}$$
$$s_i(x) \in \mathbb{R}_{>0}$$

The objective function in the formulated minimization problem is a function of workload distribution d, $d = \{x_1, ..., x_p\}$, of a given workload n between the p processors. For each given d, it returns the time of its parallel execution, which is calculated as the time taken by the longest running processor to execute its workload. Any distribution that minimizes this function is considered optimal as its execution time of workload n by the p processors cannot be improved. An algorithm, **HPOPTA**, of complexity $O(m^3 \times p^3)$, solving the HPOPT optimization problem was proposed [26]. Its efficiency was demonstrated using DGEMM and 2D–FFT on a heterogeneous cluster of hybrid servers, integrating Intel multicore Haswell CPUs, Nvidia GPUs, and Intel Xeon Phi co-processors. Significant average and multifold maximum speedups were achieved for both applications against best load-balanced solutions.

3 PMC-Based Power and Energy Modelling in Multicore Era

Efficient methods for performance optimization of parallel applications require accurate measurements of the execution time at all levels of the application, from individual threads to processes to the whole program, from data movements between memory levels to point-to-point and collective communications between processes. Similarly, efficient methods for energy optimization also require accurate measurements of the energy consumption at all levels of the parallel application. The energy consumption of the whole application, running on a server or a data center, can be accurately measured using power meters. Measuring the energy consumption by application components at a thread level is a wide open problem. At the same time, some approaches have been developed for power and energy measurements at the level of processes running on individual processors. The mainstream approach is to employ models predicting power/energy consumption using performance monitoring counters (PMCs). The PMC-based models are predominantly linear [27].

Modern hardware processors provide a large set of PMCs. Determination of the best subset of PMCs for energy predictive modeling is a non-trivial task given the fact that all the PMCs can not be determined using a single application run. Several techniques have been devised to address this challenge. While some techniques are based on statistical methodology, some use expert advice to pick a subset (that may not necessarily be obtained in one application run) that, in experts' opinion, are significant contributors to energy consumption. While a significant number of PMC-based models have been proposed [27], there is still no model, the predictive accuracy of which would be sufficiently high. The best verifiable average prediction error of average dynamic power by such models for a Intel Haswell platform is in the range of 90–100% [27].

One of the causes of this inaccuracy has been recently discovered [28]. It was found that many popular PMCs, widely used in predictive models, are not *additive*. The property of additivity is based on the simple and intuitive observation that the energy consumed by a serial execution of two applications should be equal to the sum of energies consumed by individual applications. This observations is just a manifestation of the fundamental energy conservation law, and it was validated by extensive experimentation [28]. One consequence of this observation is that any PMC parameter in a linear power/energy predictive model should be additive, that is, the value of this parameter for a serial execution of two applications should be equal to the sum of its values for individual applications. The study found many popular PMCs non-additive, some reaching up to 200% deviation from additivity. We conducted a simple experiment and found that just by removing highly non-additive PMCs from the model, we can significantly improve its predictive power. We also found that the number of non-additive PMCs increases with the increase of the number of cores used to run applications, with very few non-additive PMCs in the case of single core.

4 Conclusion

In this paper, we have demonstrated that transition from single-core to multicore-based platforms makes many traditional methods for performance and energy optimization of parallel applications inefficient, and requires development of new methods and algorithms.

Acknowledgement. This publication has emanated from research conducted with the financial support of Science Foundation Ireland (SFI) under Grant Number 14/IA/2474. This work is partially supported by EU under the COST Program Action IC1305: Network for Sustainable Ultrascale Computing (NESUS).

References

1. Fatica, M.: Accelerating Linpack with CUDA on heterogenous clusters. In: GPGPU-2, pp. 46–51. ACM (2009). https://doi.org/10.1145/1513895.1513901
2. Yang, C., Wang, F., Du, Y., et al.: Adaptive optimization for petascale heterogeneous CPU/GPU computing. In: Cluster 2010, pp. 19–28 (2010)
3. Ogata, Y., Endo, T., Maruyama, N., Matsuoka, S.: An efficient, model-based CPU-GPU heterogeneous FFT library. In: IPDPS 2008, pp. 1–10 (2008)
4. Lastovetsky, A., Reddy, R.: Data partitioning with a functional performance model of heterogeneous processors. Int. J. High Perform. Comput. Appl. **21**(1), 76–90 (2007)
5. Rojek, K., Wyrzykowski, R.: Parallelization of 3D MPDATA algorithm using many graphics processors. In: Malyshkin, V. (ed.) PaCT 2015. LNCS, vol. 9251, pp. 445–457. Springer, Cham (2015). https://doi.org/10.1007/978-3-319-21909-7_43
6. Zhong, Z., Rychkov, V., Lastovetsky, A.: Data partitioning on multicore and multi-GPU platforms using functional performance models. IEEE Trans. Comput. **64**(9), 2506–2518 (2015)
7. Linderman, M.D., Collins, J.D., Wang, H., et al.: Merge: a programming model for heterogeneous multi-core systems. SIGPLAN Not. **43**, 287–296 (2008)
8. Augonnet, C., Thibault, S., Namyst, R.: Automatic calibration of performance models on heterogeneous multicore architectures. In: Lin, H.-X., et al. (eds.) Euro-Par 2009. LNCS, vol. 6043, pp. 56–65. Springer, Heidelberg (2010). https://doi.org/10.1007/978-3-642-14122-5_9
9. Quintana-Ortí, G., Igual, F.D., Quintana-Ortí, E.S., van de Geijn, R.A.: Solving dense linear systems on platforms with multiple hardware accelerators. SIGPLAN Not. **44**, 121–130 (2009)
10. Lastovetsky, A., Szustak, L., Wyrzykowski, R.: Model-based optimization of EULAG kernel on Intel Xeon Phi through load imbalancing. IEEE Trans. Parallel Distrib. Syst. **28**(3), 787–797 (2017)
11. Luk, C.K., Hong, S., Kim, H.: Qilin: exploiting parallelism on heterogeneous multiprocessors with adaptive mapping. In: MICRO-42, pp. 45–55 (2009)
12. Cierniak, M., Zaki, M., Li, W.: Compile-time scheduling algorithms for heterogeneous network of workstations. Comput. J. **40**, 356–372 (1997)

13. Kalinov, A., Lastovetsky, A.: Heterogeneous distribution of computations solving linear algebra problems on networks of heterogeneous computers. J. Parallel Distrib. Comput. **61**(4), 520–535 (2001)
14. Martínez, J., Garzón, E., Plaza, A., García, I.: Automatic tuning of iterative computation on heterogeneous multiprocessors with ADITHE. J. Supercomput. **58**(2), 151–159 (2011)
15. Lastovetsky, A., Twamley, J.: Towards a realistic performance model for networks of heterogeneous computers. In: Ng, M.K., Doncescu, A., Yang, L.T., Leng, T. (eds.) High Performance Computational Science and Engineering. ITIFIP, vol. 172, pp. 39–57. Springer, Boston, MA (2005). https://doi.org/10.1007/0-387-24049-7_3
16. Lastovetsky, A., Reddy, R.: Data partitioning with a realistic performance model of networks of heterogeneous computers. In: Proceedings of the 18th International Parallel and Distributed Processing Symposium (IPDPS 2004). IEEE Computer Society, Santa Fe (2004)
17. Ilic, A., Pratas, F., Trancoso, P., Sousa, L.: High-performance computing on heterogeneous systems: database queries on CPU and GPU. In: High Performance Scientific Computing with Special Emphasis on Current Capabilities and Future Perspectives. IOS Press, Amsterdam (2011)
18. Colaço, J., Matoga, A., Ilic, A., Roma, N., Tomás, P., Chaves, R.: Transparent application acceleration by intelligent scheduling of shared library calls on heterogeneous systems. In: Wyrzykowski, R., Dongarra, J., Karczewski, K., Waśniewski, J. (eds.) PPAM 2013, part I. LNCS, vol. 8384, pp. 693–703. Springer, Heidelberg (2014). https://doi.org/10.1007/978-3-642-55224-3_65
19. Lastovetsky, A., Reddy, R.: Data distribution for dense factorization on computers with memory heterogeneity. Parallel Comput. **33**(12), 757–779 (2007)
20. Clarke, D., Lastovetsky, A., Rychkov, V.: Dynamic load balancing of parallel computational iterative routines on highly heterogeneous HPC platforms. Parallel Process. Lett. **21**(02), 195–217 (2011)
21. AlOnazi, A., Keyes, D., Lastovetsky, A., Rychkov, V.: Design and Optimization of OpenFOAM-based CFD Applications for Hybrid and Heterogeneous HPC Platforms. arXiv preprint arXiv:1505.07630 (2015)
22. Clarke, D., Lastovetsky, A., Rychkov, V.: Column-based matrix partitioning for parallel matrix multiplication on heterogeneous processors based on functional performance models. In: Alexander, M., et al. (eds.) Euro-Par 2011. LNCS, vol. 7155, pp. 450–459. Springer, Heidelberg (2012). https://doi.org/10.1007/978-3-642-29737-3_50
23. FFTW: Fastest Fourier Transform in the West (2018). http://www.fftw.org/
24. Lastovetsky, A., Reddy, R.: New model-based methods and algorithms for performance and energy optimization of data parallel applications on homogeneous multicore clusters. IEEE Trans. Parallel Distrib. Syst. **28**, 1119–1133 (2017)
25. Reddy, R., Lastovetsky, A.: Bi-objective optimization of data-parallel applications on homogeneous multicore clusters for performance and energy. IEEE Trans. Comput. **67**, 160–177 (2018)
26. Khaleghzadeh, H., Reddy, R., Lastovetsky, A.: A novel data-partitioning algorithm for performance optimization of data-parallel applications on heterogeneous HPC platforms. IEEE Trans. Parallel Distrib. Syst. **29**, 2176–2190 (2018)
27. O'Brien, K., Petri, I., Reddy, R., Lastovetsky, A., Sakellariou, R.: A survey of power and energy predictive models in HPC systems and applications. ACM Comput. Surv. **50**, 37 (2017)
28. Shahid, A., Fahad, M., Manumachu, R.R., Lastovetsky, A.: Additivity: a selection criterion for performance events for reliable energy predictive modeling. Supercomput. Front. Innov. **4**, 50–65 (2017)

Approximate and Transprecision Computing on Emerging Technologies (ATCET 2018)

Approximate and Transprecision Computing on Emerging Technologies (ATCET 2018)

Costas Bekas[1], Luca Benini[2], A. Cristiano I. Malossi[1],
Dimitrios S. Nikolopoulos[3], and Enrique S. Quintana-Ortí[4]

[1] IBM Research – Zurich, Switzerland
[2] Department of Information Technology and Electrical
Engineering, ETH Zurich, Switzerland
[3] School of Electronics, Electrical Engineering and
Computer Science, Queen's University, Belfast, UK
[4] Dpto. de Ingeniería y Ciencia de Computadores,
Universidad Jaume I, Spain

1 Preface

Guaranteed numerical precision of each elementary step in a complex computation has been the mainstay of traditional computing systems for many years. This era is at its twilight: to overcome the "power wall" in Exascale systems, a shift from traditional computing paradigms is now mandatory.

In the last 10 years, the demand for new computing strategies driven by energy-efficiency has grown exponentially. Flops-per-Watt (and, thus, per-Euro) has become de-facto a driving model in hardware design. Results in this direction have been significant, leveraging first multi-core parallelism and then recently moving toward heterogeneous architectures (e.g., multicore CPU coupled with GP-GPUs). However, these evolutions will not be sufficient in the long term. To maintain an exponential increase in computational efficiency, we will need to rely either on an unlikely breakthrough discovery in hardware technology, or on a fundamental change in computing paradigms.

Approximate computing [1–3] is a viable method for building more efficient, scalable and sustainable systems. However, it also places formidable challenges across the entire computing software and hardware stack. Addressing these challenges requires balanced expertise in mathematics, algorithms, software, architecture design and emerging computing platforms. The intention of the ATCET Workshop, organized by some of the partners of the EU H2020 OPRECOMP project,[1] was to bring together experts across these areas to present the latest findings and discuss future opportunities for approximate computing.

The ATCET Workshop investigated the theoretical and practical understanding of the energy efficiency boost obtainable when accuracy requirements on data being processed, stored and communicated can be lifted for intermediate calculations. The

---

[1] http://oprecomp.eu.

target applications ranged from Big Data Analytic and Deep Learning, up to classical scientific computing simulations in HPC environments.

In more detail, the workshop covered the following areas:

- Approximate and transprecision computing: from the physical limits to the architecture and circuit design; from the algorithm design to the error analysis; from innovative technology to real applications.
- Programming abstractions: from structured and disciplined approximation in computation, communication and data transfers, to quality control and techniques to recover from over-approximation.
- Computing platforms: from tiny low-power devices for IoT applications, up to classical HPC systems embedding imprecise massively parallel accelerator.
- Applications: examples from data analytics, machine learning, deep learning, and scientific computing, where uncompromised quality with scalable order-of-magnitude time- and energy-to-solution reduction is reachable relying on approximation for a significant amount of calculations.

The ATCET Workshop included the following selection of papers:

1. "Impact of approximate memory data allocation on a H.264 software video encoder", by G. Stazi, L. Adani, A. Mastrandrea, M. Olivieri and F. Menichelli.
2. "Residual replacement in mixed-precision iterative refinement for sparse linear systems", by H. Anzt, G. Flegar, V. Novakovic, E. S. Quintana-Orti and A. Tomas.
3. "Training deep neural networks with low precision input data: A hurricane prediction case study", by A. N. Kahira, L. A. B. Gomez and R. M. Badia.
4. "A transparent view on approximate computing methods for tuning applications", by M. Bromberger.
5. "Exploring the effects of code optimizations on CPU frequency margins", by K. Parasyris, N. Bellas, C. Antonopoulos and S. Lalis.

The topics covered by these works offer a good cross section of current challenges on Approximate and Transprecision Computing.

Acknowledgements. The organization of the ATCET Workshop at ISC 2018 was sponsored by the EU H2020 project 732631 OPRECOMP.

References

1. Mittal, S.: A survey of techniques for approximate computing. ACM Comput. Surv. **48**(4), 62:1–62:33 (2016). https://doi.org/10.1145/2893356, http://doi.acm.org/10.1145/2893356
2. Palem, K.V.: Inexactness and a future of computing. Phil. Trans. R. Soc. London A: Math. Phys. Eng. Sci. **372**(2018) (2014). https://doi.org/10.1098/rsta.2013.0281, http://rsta.royalsocietypublishing.org/content/372/2018/20130281
3. Xu, Q., Mytkowicz, T., Sung Kim, N.: Approximate computing: a survey. IEEE Design Test **33**, 8–22 (2015). https://doi.org/10.1109/MDAT.2015.2505723

Impact of Approximate Memory Data Allocation on a H.264 Software Video Encoder

Giulia Stazi(iD), Lorenzo Adani, Antonio Mastrandrea(iD), Mauro Olivieri(iD), and Francesco Menichelli(✉)(iD)

Department of Information Engineering, Electronics and Telecommunications (DIET), Sapienza University of Rome, Rome, Italy
{stazi,mastrandrea,olivieri,menichelli}@diet.uniroma1.it
adani.1342114@studenti.uniroma1.it

Abstract. This paper describes the analysis, in terms of tolerance to errors on data, of a H.264 software video encoder; proposes a strategy to select data structures for approximate memory allocation and reports the impact on output video quality. Applications that tolerate errors on their data structures are known as ETA (Error Tolerant Applications) and have an important part in pushing interest on approximate computing research. We centered our study on H.264 video encoding, a video compression format developed for use in high definition systems, and today one of the most widespread video compression standard, used for broadcast, consumer and mobile applications. While data fault resilience of H.264 has already been studied considering unwanted and random faults due to unreliable hardware platforms, an analysis, considering controlled hardware faults and the corresponding energy quality tradeoff, has never been proposed.

1 Introduction

Reducing power consumption in digital architectures gained a prominent role in research since almost two decades, especially when technology shrinking of physical devices started to rise important design issues due to increased power density. The problem has been further amplified by application requirements demanding increasingly amounts of processing power and memory size (e.g. high definition multimedia, high speed communication, big data applications).

The contribution of this work is to propose a strategy for selecting error tolerant data structures and to study the impact of faults on the quality of the H.264 video stream. The results, as a case study, allow to find the relationship between video output quality and hardware fault rate, which is the final metric to guide the relaxation of hardware design constraints to save power (energy quality tradeoff [3]).

© Springer Nature Switzerland AG 2018
R. Yokota et al. (Eds.): ISC 2018 Workshops, LNCS 11203, pp. 545–553, 2018.
https://doi.org/10.1007/978-3-030-02465-9_38

1.1 Approximate Memory

In modern digital systems memory represents a significant contribution to system power consumption. Approximate memories are memory circuits where cells are subject to hardware errors (bit flips) with controlled probability. From a conceptual point of view they are not different from standard memories (which are also affected by errors), but, in approximate memories, errors are allowed by design and are non-negligible for the software application. The presence of errors is the result, in general, of design implementations introduced to significantly reduce power consumption [2,6,11]. Different design strategies can be actively used in order to introduce approximation, depending on memory technology. Specifically for eDRAM/DRAMs, the refresh operation degrades performance and wastes energy; for example, when the system is in standby mode, it can reach up to 50% of total power consumption [5].

In exact DRAMs refresh time interval is set according to the worst case access-statistics of the most leaky cells. Commercial DRAM modules, for example, have a worst case retention time of 64ms determined by the leakiest cells in the entire array [11]. High refresh rate, which guarantees a storage without errors at the expense of power consumption, may not be necessary, especially considering low occurrence probability of the worst case.

In [15] the authors propose to abandon worst case design paradigm, showing the benefits that can be achieved by relaxing the refresh time interval at the expense of increasing error rates. In particular, tests on 8 chips of GC-eDRAMS show that, admitting an error rate of 10^{-3} and relaxing refresh rate from 11ms (worst case retention time) to 24 ms, 55% of energy can be saved; while an error rate of 10^{-2} guarantees energy savings up to 75%. These experimental results are just an example of the potential benefits that approximate memories can achieve, depending on memory technologies and approximation levels that the target applications can tolerate.

2 OS Managed Approximate Memory and AppropinQuo Emulator

In this section we briefly describe our previous work regarding the introduction of approximate memory support in Linux kernel and the development of a hardware emulator, AppropinQuo, for platforms containing approximate memory.

Linux kernel support for approximate memory [14] allows the OS to distinguish between exact memory banks and approximate memory banks. Approximate memory management has been integrated in the kernel memory management, relying on the internal concept of *physical zone*. In this way, the Linux kernel is aware of exact memory and approximate memory physical pages, managing them as a whole for the common part (e.g. optimization algorithms, page reuse) but distinguishing them in terms of allocation requests and page pools management.

AppropinQuo [7] is a platform emulator that supports approximate memory models (along with normal exact memory) and allows the execution of the operating system and applications while injecting faults at run time. The fault injection mechanism has different levels of insertion, tunable at byte level and at segment level, as well as configurable error rates and error injection models. In particular, faults are based on models designed to reproduce the effects on memory cells of circuital and architectural techniques for approximate memories (e.g. errors on cells can be introduced by access operations or can occur randomly, even if the cell is not accessed).

3   H.264 Video Encoding

H.264, or MPEG-4 AVC, is a video compression format developed for use in high definition systems. Because of its widespread use and computational requirements, advanced platforms for its efficient implementation in terms of cost, power, quality, have been proposed. Research has been conducted on processing units and memory subsystems [1].

Data fault resilience of H.264 algorithm has already been studied [12,13], however the approaches consider unwanted and random faults due to unreliable hardware platforms. These faults, manifested as spurious bit flips, can be characterized in terms of statistical probability, but cannot be controlled at data level. In our work, faults are intentionally allowed on selected data structures and with controlled and higher probability than the former works.

The x264 encoder is a free software library and application for encoding video streams into H.264 [8]. We characterized heap memory usage for different video resolutions and encoding options. Heap memory is commonly used by applications for dynamic allocation of large memory buffers during data processing, which, for the x264 encoder and in general for ETAs, are good candidates for approximate memory storage.

We expected larger memory requirements for higher resolution video, but also for different encoding options. Encoding options in x264 set a tradeoff between encoding speed and output quality (considering the same bitrate) and are another source of increasing memory requirements. For practical use these options are grouped in presets ranging from high speed/low quality (*ultrafast* preset) to extremely low speed/high quality (*slow* preset).

Table 1 reports memory usage for different input video resolutions and encoding options, showing the expected dependency on them. Peak heap represents memory peak allocation, while useful heap is the actual memory used for application data; the difference being memory consumed by allocation size rounding and administrative byte associated with each allocation. We note that not all heap can be allocated in approximate memory, since part of its data, typically called *critical data*, are not tolerant to errors. A strategy for selecting candidates for approximate memory allocations is then required, and it is described in the following section.

Table 1. Heap memory usage

Video resolution	x264 option (preset)	Peak heap [MB]	Peak usefulheap [MB]
176 × 144	Medium	15.6	15.4
704 × 576	Veryfast	57.2	49.6
1920 × 1080	Ultrafast	90.1	77.8
1920 × 1080	Superfast	216.0	192.1
1920 × 1080	Veryfast	269.0	238.6

3.1   Approximate Memory Data Allocation for the x264 Encoder

In order to select candidate data structures for approximate memory allocation, we analyzed the x264 memory usage traces during execution (memory profiling). We traced all functions called to allocate heap memory and then determined which data are not critical for program execution. The profiling has been performed using the Valgrind debug and profiling suite [10]; in particular, the heap profiler tool called Massif. In Fig. 1 we report an extract (peak memory sample) of Massif output for the encoding of a 1920 × 1080 resolution video and *veryfast* option setting. The following analysis is valid for other preset options and resolutions since, apart from absolute memory usage, relative percentages remain similar.

```
88.69% (250,198,526B) (heap allocation functions)
malloc/new/new[], --alloc-fns, etc.
->88.03% (248,347,652B): x264_malloc
| ->70.33% (198,419,648B): x264_frame_new
| | ->70.33% (198,419,648B): x264_frame_pop_unused
| | ->41.92% (118,246,016B): x264_encoder_encode
| | | ->41.92% (118,246,016B):encode_frame
| | | ->41.92% (118,246,016B): main
| | ->12.18% (34,360,128B): x264_encoder_open_152
| | ->12.18% (34,360,128B): x264_encoder_encode
| | ->04.06% (11,453,376B): x264_encoder_encode
| ->08.82% (24,883,200B):x264_encoder_open_152
| ->04.47% (12,603,136B):
x264_macroblock_cache_allocate
| ->04.41% (12,441,668B): x264_encoder_open_152
```

Fig. 1. Memory allocation profiling: Massif output

From the profiling reported we deduce that the total amount of *useful heap* memory is about 239 MB. The largest part of heap memory allocation is indeed handled by function *x264_malloc*, which covers about 88.03% of total allocated heap memory. The function *x264_frame_new*, which in turn calls *x264_malloc*, covers 70.33% of heap allocations.

The next step involved the analysis of source code in order to identify the actual data allocated by these functions. By this analysis we discovered that the first one, *x264_malloc*, is too generic, handling also allocation of critical data structures. We could classify as critical in x264, for example, data regarding encoder behavior, frames analysis, color space bits depth setting and encoding bitrate control. These data are critical because they are responsible of program control flow, which cannot be altered randomly by faults without completely compromising the encoding algorithm. The analysis of the function *x264_frame_new* revealed that this routine is used to create and allocate frames for encoding or decoding the video, in the form of *frame structures*. For each of these frames, x264 allocates a heap space large enough to contain the whole picture buffer and other information, depending on encoder options. In particular the *frame structure*, among others, stores data concerning frame encoding options, colors space information, buffers for frame pixels, motion vector buffers and rate control; some of this information is involved in the encoding control flow and must be still kept exact. Conversely, buffers for frame pixels are optimal candidates for approximate memory, because introducing errors in them does not alter program execution flow. Further analysis showed that image pixels are grouped into three different buffers, containing the pixel values for each color component, each 1-byte large (8-bit per pixel). This data representation analysis is important for the optimization of approximate memory techniques, as will be discussed in the following section.

4   Results

The approximated x264 encoder was compiled and executed in the Appropin-Quo emulator, running Linux kernel version 4.3 with support for approximate memory management and built for the x86 architecture.

Input test files were selected from the Xiph.org Video Test Media (derf's collection) [9]. Given the large number of choices available, we selected videos in raw format (no compression applied), color and characterized by moving and still parts. A list of them is present in Table 2.

Table 2. Test videos from derf's collection

Name	Resolution	Length [frames]
ducks_take_off	1080p	500
dinner	1080p	950
crowd_run	1080p	500
blue_sky	1080p	217

Tests were executed configuring the approximate memory model in Appropin-Quo for DRAM memories using slower refresh rate [5,11], considering different fault rates and bit-level error masking (looseness level). The range of fault rates was chosen according to a refresh rate increase ranging from 8x (256 ms) up to 400x (25 s), while bit-level error masking allows to take into account more advanced approximate techniques that distinguish between bit weights (the quality of the user experience in multimedia application is mainly defined by the most significant bits [4]).

Results are provided in terms of user perceived video quality, comparing original and coded frames. In particular, as quality metric, we used peak signal-to-noise ratio (PSNR), defined as the ratio between the maximum pixel value and rms of corrupting noise that affects the fidelity of its representation.

All tests were executed with the x264 *veryfast* preset option, since this setting provides a good balance between encoding processing time and quality.

In order to produce reference values, we first run the original x264 encoder, with buffers allocated in exact memory. The average results are a global PSNR of 29.696 dB and an output bitrate of 17537 kbps. We note that the global PSNR value on output videos for exact compression should be considered an upper bound to evaluate x264 with the present settings.

4.1   Output with Approximate Memory and Energy Saving Considerations

Table 3 shows the results of the same encoding using approximate memory. Global PSNR values are reported for each fault rate/looseness mask combination. According to AppropinQuo simulation parameters [7], looseness mask is a 32-bit configurable mask (constant for the whole memory array) that is applied to every 32-bit location in memory in order to allow selective fault protection at bit level (i.e. the MSBs); considering that pixel values stored by approximated buffers have 8-bit size and are packed on 32-bit locations by the compiler (see Sect. 3.1), we set the looseness mask as repetitions of an 8-bit submask.

Table 3. Video output PSNR [dB]

Looseness mask	Fault rate [$errors/(bit \times s)$]		
	10^{-2}	10^{-3}	10^{-4}
0x3F3F3F3F	19.97	25.18	28.84
0x1F1F1F1F	24.47	28.01	29.43
0x0F0F0F0F	27.35	29.13	29.59
0x07070707	28.96	29.52	29.63
0x03030303	29.47	29.61	29.64
0x01010101	29.61	29.64	29.64

We note that for a fault rate of 10^{-3} *errors*/($bit \times s$) and a looseness mask set to 0x0F0F0F0F (i.e. error allowed on the four LSBs of each byte), PSNR is 29.13 dB, or about 0.5 dB under the exact case, confirming good tolerance to errors. The table shows also that, with the same fault rate, all masks more protective than 0x0F0F0F0F (i.e 0x07...07, 0x03...03, 0x01...01) produce very close outputs, but would result in larger energy consumption (since they imply a larger portion of exact bits). Figure 2 shows the visible effects, for 0x0F0F0F0F and 0x3F3F3F3F bit masks, on a portion of a frame.

Fig. 2. Extract from HD frame: exact (left), 0x0F0F0F0F mask (center), 0x3F3F3F3F mask (right), fault rate 10^{-3} $errors/(bit \times s)$

Simulations with fault rate set to 10^{-2} $errors/(bit \times s)$ illustrate that the 0x0F0F0F0F mask produces a PSNR value about 2 dB under the exact case, resulting in more visible effects of corruption on the output. Figure 3 plots output PSNR for an extended fault rate range.

Actual energy saving, related to the application of our test cases, can be extracted assuming as reference the results showed in [11]. Refresh power depends on refresh rate, if we assume a 10^{-3} error rate, a 60x increase in refresh period can be allowed. A looseness mask set to 0x0F0F0F0F means that half the cells must be exact while the other can be approximate memory cells. In our tests, data structures selected to be allocated in approximate memory are about 60% of total data, resulting in a system where, globally, about 30% are approximate memory cells while 70% are exact memory cells.

According to this partition, and considering only refresh power, we can expect a normalized refresh power in the range of 0.3–0.5 [11] with respect to the original exact implementation.

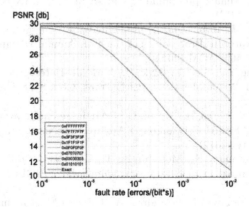

Fig. 3. Video Output PSNR graph [dB]

5   Conclusion

In this work we presented the analysis of the x264 video encoder and the impact of using approximate memory for storing its error tolerant data structures. We started by profiling memory usage and finding a strategy for selecting error tolerant data buffers. We then run the modified application on AppropinQuo emulator, for several combination of fault rates (derived from actual refresh rate reduction strategies) and fault masking at bit level (looseness level).

Results show the importance of exploring the relation between these parameters and output quality. For example, leaving some of the MSBs exact demonstrated to be an effective way of allowing error probabilities up to 100x higher with the same output quality and a refresh period increase in the order of 60x.

Since leaving exact a portion of memory cells reduces global energy savings, this knowledge is also fundamental in order to drive research on hardware techniques specifically tailored to the application, revealing the tradeoff between designing more aggressive approximate circuits and the number of bit cells that must be kept exact.

Future works can consider better allocation strategies and more advanced DRAM architectures for embedded systems, as DRAMs chips with integrated ECC units. Another important aspect is a more accurate quantification of power savings, which could be obtained by integrating a power consumption model in the approximate DRAM memory model.

References

1. Asma, B.H., Jarray, N., Abdelkrim, Z.: Low-power hardware design of binary arithmetic encoder in H. 264. Int. J. Adv. Comput. Sci. Appl. **8**(7), 412–416 (2017)
2. Esmaeilzadeh, H., Sampson, A., Ceze, L., Burger, D.: Architecture support for disciplined approximate programming. In: ACM SIGPLAN Notices, vol. 47, pp. 301–312. ACM (2012)
3. Huang, J., Lach, J., Robins, G.: A methodology for energy-quality tradeoff using imprecise hardware. In: Proceedings of the 49th Annual Design Automation Conference, pp. 504–509. ACM (2012)
4. Kwon, J., Chang, I.J., Lee, I., Park, H., Park, J.: Heterogeneous sram cell sizing for low-power H. 264 applications. IEEE Trans. Circ. Syst. I Regul. Pap. **59**(10), 2275–2284 (2012)
5. Liu, J., Jaiyen, B., Veras, R., Mutlu, O.: RAIDR: retention-aware intelligent dram refresh. In: ACM SIGARCH Computer Architecture News, vol. 40, pp. 1–12. IEEE Computer Society (2012)
6. Liu, S., Pattabiraman, K., Moscibroda, T., Zorn, B.G.: Flikker: saving DRAM refresh-power through critical data partitioning. ACM SIGPLAN Not. **47**(4), 213–224 (2012)
7. Menichelli, F., Stazi, G., Mastrandrea, A., Olivieri, M.: An emulator for approximate memory platforms based on QEmu. In: De Gloria, A. (ed.) ApplePies 2016. LNEE, vol. 429, pp. 153–159. Springer, Cham (2018). https://doi.org/10.1007/978-3-319-55071-8_20
8. Merritt, L., Vanam, R.: x264: A High Performance H. 264/avc Encoder (2006). http://neuron2.net/library/avc/overview_x264_v8_5.pdf

9. Montgomery, C., et al.: Xiph.org Video Test Media (Derf's Collection), The xiph Open Source Community (1994). https://media.xiph.org/video/derf
10. Nethercote, N., Seward, J.: Valgrind: a framework for heavyweight dynamic binary instrumentation. In: ACM Sigplan Notices, vol. 42, pp. 89–100. ACM (2007)
11. Raha, A., Sutar, S., Jayakumar, H., Raghunathan, V.: Quality configurable approximate DRAM. IEEE Trans. Comput. **66**(7), 1172–1187 (2017)
12. Rehman, S., Shafique, M., Kriebel, F., Henkel, J.: ReVC: computationally reliable video coding on unreliable hardware platforms: a case study on error-tolerant H. 264/AVC CAVLC entropy coding. In: 2011 18th IEEE International Conference on Image Processing (ICIP), pp. 397–400. IEEE (2011)
13. Shafique, M., et al.: Application-guided power-efficient fault tolerance for H. 264 context adaptive variable length coding. IEEE Trans. Comput. **66**(4), 560–574 (2017)
14. Stazi, G., Menichelli, F., Mastrandrea, A., Olivieri, M.: Introducing approximate memory support in Linux Kernel. In: 2017 13th Conference on Ph. D. Research in Microelectronics and Electronics (PRIME), pp. 97–100. IEEE (2017)
15. Teman, A., Karakonstantis, G., Giterman, R., Meinerzhagen, P., Burg, A.: Energy versus data integrity trade-offs in embedded high-density logic compatible dynamic memories. In: Proceedings of the 2015 Design, Automation & Test in Europe Conference & Exhibition, pp. 489–494. EDA Consortium (2015)

Residual Replacement in Mixed-Precision Iterative Refinement for Sparse Linear Systems

Hartwig Anzt[1], Goran Flegar[2], Vedran Novaković[2],
Enrique S. Quintana-Ortí[2], and Andrés E. Tomás[2(⊠)]

[1] Karlsruhe Institute of Technology, Karlsruhe, Germany
hartwig.anzt@kit.edu
[2] Dpto. de Ingeniería y Ciencia de Computadores, Universidad Jaume I,
12071 Castellón, Spain
{flegar,novakoni,quintana,tomasan}@uji.es

Abstract. We investigate the solution of sparse linear systems via iterative methods based on Krylov subspaces. Concretely, we combine the use of extended precision in the outer iterative refinement with a reduced precision in the inner Conjugate Gradient solver. This method is additionally enhanced with different residual replacement strategies that aim to avoid the pitfalls due to the divergence between the actual residual and the recurrence formula for this parameter computed during the iteration. Our experiments using a significant part of the SuiteSparse Matrix Collection illustrate the potential benefits of this technique from the point of view, for example, of energy and performance.

Keywords: Sparse linear systems · Krylov solvers
Iterative refinement · Mixed precision · Residual replacement
Performance and energy modelling

1 Introduction

Consider the linear system $A\hat{x} = \hat{b}$, where $A \in \mathbb{R}^{n \times n}$, $\hat{b} \in \mathbb{R}^n$ is the right-hand side vector, and $\hat{x} \in \mathbb{R}^n$ is the sought-after solution. In this context, iterative refinement is a well-known technique to improve the accuracy of an initial approximation $\hat{x}_0 \in \mathbb{R}^n$ to the actual solution of the system [4]. On recent computer architectures, iterative refinement is often combined with mixed precision arithmetic in order to compose a faster solver [1,2]. Concretely, *mixed-precision iterative refinement* (MPIR) enfolds an inner solver that comprises most of the arithmetic operations and performs all computations in reduced precision, with a refinement step that works in extended precision. The MPIR framework can be thus formulated as follows:

for $k := 0, 1, 2, \ldots$

$$r := \hat{b} - A\hat{x}_k \quad \text{Residual calculation (extended precision)}$$
$$\text{Solve } Ay = r \text{ for } y \quad \text{Inner solver} \qquad \text{(reduced precision)}$$
$$\hat{x}_{k+1} := \hat{x}_k + y \quad \text{Solution update} \qquad \text{(extended precision)}$$

© Springer Nature Switzerland AG 2018
R. Yokota et al. (Eds.): ISC 2018 Workshops, LNCS 11203, pp. 554–561, 2018.
https://doi.org/10.1007/978-3-030-02465-9_39

Roughly speaking, if the machine precision in extended arithmetic is u_e, and the conditioning of the problem satisfies $u_e \kappa(A) \leq 1$, iterative refinement eventually produces a solution that is correct to full extended precision [4].

In a practical implementation, the reduced and extended precisions in MPIR respectively boil down to the standard IEEE 754 single and double precisions supported by hardware. From the performance point of view, the principle MPIR exploits is that, on one hand, for a compute-bound inner solver, single precision arithmetic is (at least) twice faster than its double precision counterpart on current architectures. On the other hand, for a memory-bound inner solver, the use of single precision datatypes involves transferring half the amount of data (bits) than double precision.

In this paper we introduce a specialized version of MPIR applied to sparse linear systems when the inner solver is a Krylov-based method such as the Conjugate Gradient (CG), GMRES, BiCGStab, etc. [5]. In more detail, our work makes the following contributions:

- We combine MPIR with an inner solver that is also an iterative method, in particular a Krylov method enhanced with residual replacement (RR) strategies to avoid the unnecessary computations due to undetected stagnation of the "true" residual [7]. While the positive effects of RR have been known for some time, this is the first time this type of techniques are applied in the context of an inner solver that operates in reduced precision, inside an outer framework for iterative refinement.
- We assess the benefits of the new MPIR algorithms from the point of view of volume of data transfer, using a theoretical cost model that can accommodate both performance and energy consumption, and a set of test problems from the SuiteSparse matrix collection [3]. Here, we emphasize that the solution of sparse linear systems via iterative methods in general results in a memory-bound algorithm where the key to attaining high performance lies in reducing the amount of data transferred between the memory and the floating-point units.

2   Residual Replacement for Krylov Methods

In this section we briefly review the CG method, as a representative example of many other Krylov subspace-based solvers for sparse linear systems, and the rationale behind the residual replacement strategies evaluated in our work.

2.1   Preconditioned Conjugate Gradient (PCG)

Let us rewrite the inner linear system solver as $Ay = r \equiv Ax = b$, and consider that its coefficient matrix A is symmetric and positive definite (s.p.d.). For this particular type of systems, the algorithm in Fig. 1 illustrates (a simplified version of) the PCG method, equipped with a generic preconditioner M. Starting from an initial approximation x_0 to the solution, the algorithm produces a sequence of vectors $x_1, x_2, \ldots$ that, under mild circumstances, gradually approach the solution of the system [5]. From the mathematical point of view, the preconditioner improves the condition number of the matrix $M^{-1}A$, which causes the PCG solver to converge in a moderate number of steps [5]. The convergence is monitored via the implicit recurrence for the residual $r_{j+1} := r_j - \rho_j w_j$, which in exact arithmetic satisfies $r_{j+1} := r_j - \rho_j w_j = b - Ax_{j+1}$.

$r_0 := b - Ax_0$, $z_0 := M^{-1}r_0$, $d_0 := z_0$, $\beta_0 := r_0^T z_0$,	Initializations
$\tau_0 := \parallel r_0 \parallel_2$, $j := 0$	
while $(\tau_j > \tau_{\max})$	**Iterative PCG solve**
$\quad w_j := Ad_j$	SPMV
$\quad \rho_j := \beta_j / d_j^T w_j$	DOT product
$\quad x_{j+1} := x_j + \rho_j d_j$	AXPY
$\quad r_{j+1} := r_j - \rho_j w_j$	AXPY
$\quad z_{j+1} := M^{-1} r_{j+1}$	Preconditioning
$\quad \beta_{j+1} := r_{j+1}^T z_{j+1}$	DOT product
$\quad \alpha_j := \beta_{j+1}/\beta_j$	
$\quad d_{j+1} := z_{j+1} + \alpha_j d_j$	AXPY-like
$\quad \tau_{j+1} := \parallel r_{j+1} \parallel_2$	2-norm
$\quad j := j + 1$	
endwhile	

Fig. 1. Algorithmic formulation of the PCG method for the solution of the linear system $Ax = b$, with initial approximation to the solution x_0 and preconditioner M. $\tau_{\max}$ is an upper bound on the relative residual for the computed approximation to the solution.

The most complex and challenging operations in the PCG method are the computation of the preconditioner M; its application as in $z_{j+1} := M^{-1}r_{j+1}$; and the sparse matrix-vector product (SPMV) $w_j := Ad_j$. The remaining computations involve basic linear algebra operations such as the DOT (or inner) product, AXPY-like updates, and the calculation of a vector 2-norm (equivalent to a DOT product).

2.2   Residual Replacement

A well-known problem for Krylov methods, such as PCG, is that a long iteration process can result in a non-negligible deviation between the (computed) recurrence residual $r_{j+1}^{rec} := r_j - \rho_j w_j$ and the true residual $r_{j+1}^{true} = b - Ax_{j+1}$ [7]. Concretely, when all arithmetic of the (inner) PCG solver is performed in a certain (reduced) precision (u_r), the iteration can yield a sequence for r_j^{rec} that converges to a level that is much smaller than that precision. Unfortunately, the sequence for r_j^{true} can stagnate at a much higher level, meaning that a significant part of the work was wasted.

Periodic RR. A simple solution to the discrepancy problem is to replace the recurrence residual by the true residual periodically during the iteration. However, doing it without the proper care, at random iteration steps, can deteriorate the convergence rate of the process, as briefly hinted next.

Van der Vorst and Ye's (VY) Strategy for RR. To avoid the problems with a periodic RR, Van der Vorst and Ye proposed to monitor the divergence between the two residuals, via some recurrence error bounds, in order to decide when to trigger a *residual replacement* [7]. Concretely, given an initial solution $z := x_0$, their variant of the PCG method enhanced with residual replacement initially applies PCG to the linear system $Ax = b$, with a starting guess $\tilde{x}_0 = 0$, to produce a sequence of solution vectors denoted as $\tilde{x}_1, \tilde{x}_2, \ldots$. Now, let us define

$$d_0 = d_{init} := u_r(||r_0|| + N||A||||x_0||),$$
$$d_{j+1} := d_j + u_r(||r_j|| + N||A||||\tilde{x}_j||), \quad j = 0, 1, 2, \ldots,$$

where N is the maximal number of nonzero entries per row of A. Then, at iteration j, VY's test monitors whether the following three conditions hold:

$$d_j \leq \epsilon ||r_j||, \qquad d_{j+1} > \epsilon ||r_{j+1}||, \qquad d_{j+1} \geq 1.1 \, d_{init};$$

and, if that is the case, realizes the replacement as follows:

$$z := z + \tilde{x}_{j+1}, \quad \tilde{x}_{j+1} := 0,$$
$$r_{j+1} := b - Ax, \quad d_{init} := u_r(||r_{j+1}|| + N||A||||z||).$$

The PCG method is then applied again, with the new starting solution $\tilde{x}_{j+1}$, yielding $\tilde{x}_{j+2}, \tilde{x}_{j+3}, \ldots$ so that, upon convergence of the global procedure, it produces the sought-after solution of the linear system $Ax = b$ in z.

Explicit Residual Deviation (ERD) Test for RR. For an MPIR solver, an alternative to the previous two RR schemes consists in explicitly computing the true residual (in reduced precision) at periodic steps, $t, 2t, 3t, \ldots$, while checking for deviations with the recurrence residual, e.g. as $||r_{k+1}^{true}||_2 / ||r_{k+1}^{rec}||_2$, with k denoting an integer multiple of t. If the gap between the two residuals exceeds a threshold τ, the inner CG solver is then stopped, and a new iteration of refinement is started at the outer iteration. This technique aims to detect the stagnation of the inner PCG iteration at an early stage, at the cost of a potentially expensive computation of the actual residual. Obviously, the overhead introduced by the computation of the true residual depends on how often this operation is actually performed; i.e., on the periodicity of the test.

3 Evaluation

3.1 Cost Model

We next quantify the advantage of the MPIR implementations over a conventional (or plain) PCG solver using double precision arithmetic. For this purpose, we propose a cost model that can be instantiated to capture both time and energy consumption. This model builds upon the following premises:

- After each particular operation of the method (e.g., AXPY, SPMV, DOT, etc.), no data remains in the cache so that the next operation has to reload any data it requires. This is reasonable if the data does not fit in the cache (and no attempt is done to pipeline the sequence of operations).
- In the cost model, we ignore the arithmetic operations and consider the data transfers from (main) memory only. For a memory-bound algorithm, such as PCG (and variants), this is fair for the following reasons:
  - In the case of execution time, provided the arithmetic operations are optimized (e.g., via vectorization), the cost corresponds to the memory accesses as the computations can be overlapped with the communication.
  - In terms of energy consumption, the accesses to main memory are at least one order of magnitude more expensive than the arithmetic. As this gap is expected to increase in future systems [6], we can neglect the energy costs due to arithmetic.
- The time and energy costs of memory accesses are linearly dependent on the bit length of the data. Therefore, we will set the cost of accessing a single bit of data, either as part of a read or a write, as 1 cost-unit (cu).
- We will consider a problem of size n, with a sparse matrix that comprises n_z nonzero elements and is stored in CSR format. This specific data layout is chosen because of it flexibility [5]. Furthermore, we will consider a plain Jacobi preconditioner (i.e., $M = \text{diag}(A)$), because of the simplicity of its application.

Under these premises, the cost of a single SPMV, in a customized-precision that employs xx bits (fpxx), is

$$\mathcal{C}_{\text{SPMV}}(\text{xx}) = \underbrace{(n + 2n_z) \cdot \text{fpxx}}_{\text{Vector, matrix entries}} + \underbrace{(n + n_z) \cdot \text{int32}}_{\text{indices}} \quad \text{cus} \qquad (1)$$

(i.e., cost-units in terms of bit-transfers). Similarly, the costs of the vector operations AXPY, DOT and NORM (on vectors of length n, with entries of datatype fpxx) are respectively $3n \cdot \text{fpxx}$, $2n \cdot \text{fpxx}$ and $n \cdot \text{fpxx}$ cus. Therefore, the cost of a plain implementation of the PCG method, which also operates in fpxx, is then

$$\mathcal{C}_{\text{PCG}}^{\text{iter}}(\text{xx}) = \underbrace{14n \cdot \text{fpxx}}_{\text{vector ops.}} + \mathcal{C}_{\text{SPMV}}(\text{xx}) + \underbrace{3n \cdot \text{fpxx}}_{\text{preconditioner appl.}} \quad \text{cus} \qquad (2)$$

per iteration.

The formula in (2) offers the cost of the PCG method when operating in the standard IEEE 754 single and double precisions, by simply replacing fpxx with either 32 or 64 bits (fp32 or fp64, respectively). These two cases respectively capture the costs of the single-precision inner solver (without RR) leveraged inside MPIR and the plain double-precision PCG solver (without iterative refinement).

In our case, we are interested in assessing the cost of MPIR, with a single-precision inner PCG solver that possibly integrates RR, and the outer solver operating in double-precision. For example, with the VY strategy for RR, the total cost of such solver is

$$\mathcal{C}^{\mathrm{VY}}_{\mathrm{MPIR}}(32,64) = \underbrace{\mathcal{C}^{\mathrm{iter}}_{\mathrm{PCG}}(32) \cdot \#\mathrm{IS}}_{\text{Plain inner PCG solver}} + \underbrace{n \cdot \mathsf{fp32} \cdot \#\mathrm{IS}}_{\text{Replacement condition test}}$$

$$+ \underbrace{(4n \cdot \mathsf{fp32} + \mathcal{C}_{\mathrm{SPMV}}(32)) \cdot \#\mathrm{RR}}_{\text{RRs in inner PCG solver}} \qquad (3)$$

$$+ \underbrace{(6n \cdot \mathsf{fp64} + n \cdot \mathsf{fp32} + \mathcal{C}_{\mathrm{SPMV}}(64)) \cdot \#\mathrm{RS}}_{\text{Refinement steps}} \text{ cus.}$$

In this last expression, #IS stands for the total number of iterations of the inner solver; #RR is the total number of residual replacements; and #RS is the total number of iterative refinement steps (outer iteration). How Eq. (3) simplifies when no RR is in-place is straight-forward.

The cost of the MPIR method with the ERD strategy depends on how often the true residual is computed. When applied with periodicity t (in the number of iterations), the test is performed around $\#\mathrm{IS}/t$ times. To derive the cost of this strategy, we first remind that the true residual can be computed in single precision as well. Now, the explicitly computation of the actual residual $r^{true}_{j+1} :=$ $b - Ax_{j+1}$ requires an SPMV followed by a subtraction of two vectors; and finally the norm of this difference has to be computed. The cost is essentially the same as that of a single RR in VY's approach, and therefore the total cost of the solver with ERD for RR becomes

$$\mathcal{C}^{\mathrm{ERD}}_{\mathrm{MPIR}}(32,64) = \underbrace{\mathcal{C}^{\mathrm{iter}}_{\mathrm{PCG}}(32) \cdot \#\mathrm{IS}}_{\text{Plain inner PCG solver}} + \underbrace{(4n \cdot \mathsf{fp32} + \mathcal{C}_{\mathrm{SPMV}}(32)) \cdot \#\mathrm{IS}/t}_{\text{Residual tests in inner PCG solver}}$$

$$+ \underbrace{(6n \cdot \mathsf{fp64} + n \cdot \mathsf{fp32} + \mathcal{C}_{\mathrm{SPMV}}(64)) \cdot \#\mathrm{RS}}_{\text{Refinement steps}} \text{ cus.} \qquad (4)$$

In summary, VY's RR strategy incurs a detection overhead at each iteration (replacement condition test) and pays a correction cost in case the test determines a RR is due. The EDR alternative reduces the detection overhead by testing the replacement condition with a "sparse" periodicity, at the cost of potentially wasting a significant number of iterations. Also, the cost of correction in VY's RR matches the cost of detection in EDR's case; in other words, correction adds no cost to that of detection in EDR's scheme.

3.2   Cost Analysis

Setup. For the tests in this subsection, the sought-after solution $\hat{x}$ (of the target linear system $A\hat{x} = \hat{b}$) and the initial solution $\hat{x}_0$ are both set to vectors with random entries uniformly distributed in $(0,1)$; and the right-hand side vector is computed as $\hat{b} := A\hat{x}$. Moreover, we employ a subset of 123 s.p.d. matrices from the SuiteSparse Matrix Collection [3], for which a plain implementation of the

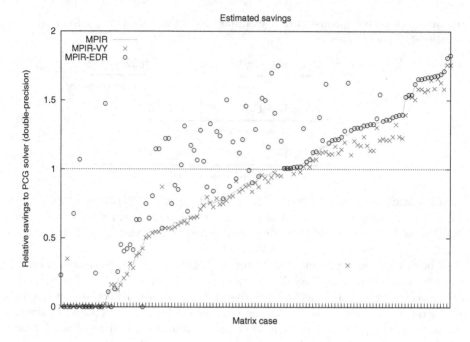

Fig. 2. Estimated savings of the three variants of MPIR over the plain PCG solver operating in double-precision.

CG method can solve the linear system, using double precision, with an absolute residual below 10^{-7} in less than 10^5 iterations. In addition, we removed problems involving diagonal coefficient matrices and the problems of size less than 200. All arithmetic is performed in double precision but, for the MPIR variants, the matrices A and M^{-1} and vectors w, d, x, r used in the CG inner solver are stored in single precision.

Cost Evaluation. Figure 2 shows the relative cost of three different variants of CG with MPIR compared with that of the plain CG method in double precision. These three variants correspond to MPIR (without RR), MPIR with VY's RR, and MPIR with EDR RR. Each position in the x–axis corresponds to the same matrix, sorted form left to right by the cost savings of MPIR (solid line). The savings for (MPIR-)VY and (MPIR-)EDR are denoted by crosses and circles respectively. For VY, the RR parameter is set to $\epsilon = \sqrt{u}$, the infinity norm is used for $\|A\|$, and N is set to the number of non-zeros of the matrix. For EDR, the checking periodicity t was set to 100 iterations with a threshold $\tau = 10$. In both cases the maximum number of iterative refinement steps was set to 10. In the plot a value of 0 in the y-coordinate indicates a variant that did not converge for that particular matrix.

Figure 2 show that VY has generally worse energy consumption than MPIR without RR, with tangible savings in only two cases due to the extra cost of computing the RR test at each iteration. Compared with this, the cost of the EDR test is small (due to the relaxed periodicity) though still avoiding the costly stagnations, yielding substantial savings for a large number of cases. Furthermore, the cost of the EDR variant never exceeds that of MPIR without RR, except in two pathological cases. VY only converges in one case for which the MPIR without RR does not, while EDR is able to converge in five cases. However, it does not converge in two cases where the other variants attain the target threshold on the absolute residual.

4 Concluding Remarks

We have proposed specialized versions of MPIR for the solution of sparse linear systems, with the CG method as inner solver, combined with two strategies for residual replacement that prevent a waste of computations due to the stagnation of the "true" residual. Our cost analysis, using a significant fraction of test problems from the SuiteSparse matrix collection, shows that at least one of this variants produces a significant reduction of the data transfers. This observation can potentially result in relevant performance improvement and energy savings with respect to a plain solver that operates in double precision.

Acknowledgements. This research was partially sponsored by the EU H2020 project 732631 OPRECOMP and the CICYT project TIN2017-82972-R of the MINECO and FEDER.

References

1. Barrachina, S., Castillo, M., Igual, F.D., Mayo, R., Quintana-Ortí, E.S., Quintana-Ortí, G.: Exploiting the capabilities of modern GPUs for dense matrix computations. Conc. Comput. Pract. Experience **21**(18), 2457–2477 (2009). https://doi.org/10.1002/cpe.1472
2. Buttari, A., Dongarra, J.J., Langou, J., Langou, J., Luszcek, P., Kurzak, J.: Mixed precision iterative refinement techniques for the solution of dense linear systems. Int. J. High Perform. Comput. Appl. **21**(4), 457–486 (2007). https://doi.org/10.1177/1094342007084026
3. Davis, T.A., Hu, Y.: The University of Florida sparse matrix collection. ACM Trans. Math. Softw. **38**(1), 1–25 (2011). https://doi.org/10.1145/2049662.2049663
4. Golub, G.H., Loan, C.F.V.: Matrix Computations, 3rd edn. The Johns Hopkins University Press, Baltimore (1996)
5. Saad, Y.: Iterative Methods for Sparse Linear Systems, 3rd edn. Society for Industrial and Applied Mathematics, Philadelphia (2003)
6. Shalf, J.: The evolution of programming models in response to energy efficiency constraints. Slides Presented at Oklahoma Supercomputing Symposium 2013, October 2013. http://www.oscer.ou.edu/Symposium2013/oksupercompsymp2013_talk_shalf_20131002.pdf
7. van der Vorst, H.A., Ye, Q.: Residual replacement strategies for Krylov subspace iterative methods for the convergence of true residuals. SIAM J. Sci. Comput. **22**(3), 835–852 (2000). https://doi.org/10.1137/S1064827599353865

Training Deep Neural Networks with Low Precision Input Data: A Hurricane Prediction Case Study

Albert Kahira[1,2], Leonardo Bautista Gomez[1(✉)], and Rosa M. Badia[1,3]

[1] Barcelona Supercomputing Center, Barcelona, Spain
{albert.kahira,leonardo.bautista,rosa.m.badia}@bsc.es
[2] Universitat Politècnica de Catalunya, Barcelona, Spain
[3] Spanish National Research Council (CSIC), Madrid, Spain

Abstract. Training deep neural networks requires huge amounts of data. The next generation of intelligent systems will generate and utilise massive amounts of data which will be transferred along machine learning workflows. We study the effect of reducing the precision of this data at early stages of the workflow (i.e. input) on both prediction accuracy and learning behaviour of deep neural networks. We show that high precision data can be transformed to low precision before feeding it to a neural network model with insignificant depreciation in accuracy. As such, a high precision representation of input data is not entirely necessary for some applications. The findings of this study pave way for the application of deep learning in areas where acquiring high precision data is difficult due to both memory and computational power constraints. We further use a hurricane prediction case study where we predict the monthly number of hurricanes on the Atlantic Ocean using deep neural networks. We train a deep neural network model that predicts the number of hurricanes, first, by using high precision input data and then by using low precision data. This leads to only a drop in prediction accuracy of less than 2%.

Keywords: Deep neural network · Low precision
Hurricane prediction

1 Introduction

The number and spectrum of Machine Learning (ML) applications has increased tremendously in the last decade and this trend is likely to continue. ML now powers major industries such as self-driving cars, recommendation systems, computer vision and natural language processing. In particular, Deep Neural Networks (DNN) have become a model of choice and achieved superior accuracy than traditional models in areas such as computer vision. This is in part attributed to new advanced computing devices such as graphics processing unit (GPU) and most recently tensor processing unit (TPU) that can significantly

© Springer Nature Switzerland AG 2018
R. Yokota et al. (Eds.): ISC 2018 Workshops, LNCS 11203, pp. 562–569, 2018.
https://doi.org/10.1007/978-3-030-02465-9_40

brought down the training time of advanced learning algorithms. More importantly, this tremendous increase in ML applications, especially DNN, can be attributed to availability of big data. ML algorithms have the ability to identify complex relationships in data and generate meaningful insights that would otherwise be impossible or not computationally feasible using traditional statistical approaches. However, big data comes with several challenges.

First, big data requires large amount of storage and companies like Google own hundreds of data centres that occupy hectares of land and consume massive amounts of electricity. Furthermore, intelligent systems continuously generate data that needs to be processed in real time. Some of these intelligent devices are limited in both storage and computing power. Moreover, this data flows through a workflow that is subject to different constraints at different points. For instance, even the state of the art GPUs have limited memory and ML models must put the memory size into consideration. On the other hand, data transmission is an expensive process and data collected away from the processing unit must be carefully transformed to facilitate efficient transportation.

The main challenge in training DNNs is dealing with limited main memory and on chip memory. Main memory stores input data, weights of neurons, activations and feature maps. As neural networks become deeper and more complex, novel approaches such as distributed training have been proposed [3]. However, this comes with programming complexity and overheads such as data transfer and synchronization. Another approach that has the potential to significantly improve training DNNs is approximate computing. Existing computer architectures have focused on accuracy and reliability as major design constraints. However, in ML applications, the key idea is to extract meaningful information from vast amounts of data to some acceptable degree of accuracy. There is a need therefore, to rethink the architectures of the next generation intelligent systems taking into account the challenges posed by big data and the nature of the output expected.

Approximate computing proposes making a trade off in accuracy for better performance or energy consumption. Research has shown that ML applications are posed to significantly benefit from approximate computing. However, in applying approximate computing, there is need to look at the entire workflow. As we shall show later, previous work has focused on specific layers of workflow. However, a combination of approximate computing techniques at different layers of the workflow has compounded benefits [1]. Using reduced precision allows us to fit bigger batch sizes and even more layers. In fact, machine learning libraries such as Tensorflow offer the user the option to train the network with half precision in order to reduce memory requirements and gain on speed.

Whereas a lot of work has been done on training neural networks with low precision, not much has been done on using low precision data to train neural networks, yet input data also takes up space in the memory and is an important part of the workflow. In this study, we focus on the initial layers of the workflow i.e input. We show that we can significantly reduce the precision of input data used in training DNNs with little or no effect on the accuracy and overall performance of the algorithm. A combination of our proposal and existing low precision training schemes could therefore provide multiple benefits.

This study has two major contributions. First it introduces Machine Learning to hurricane prediction. We show that, given several weather variables, we can predict the number of hurricanes in a given month using deep neural networks. Second, this study shows that we can reduce the precision of input data with minimum change in accuracy and learning behaviour. This makes it possible to transmit and store data in lower precision for some variables such as sea surface temperatures. Furthermore, limited data precision opens a wide range of applications for deep neural networks such as wireless sensor networks and underwater sensors networks. These networks are faced with the challenge of low computing power due to battery constraints.

The remainder of this paper is divided into 4 sections. Section 2 gives some background information and related work, Sect. 3 presents the case study and describes all the performed experiments. In Sect. 4 we discuss the results and, finally, Sect. 5 concludes the paper.

2   Background and Related Work

The next generation of intelligent applications and devices will be data-centric, generating and using massive amounts of data. Research has shown that simple models coupled with a lot of data overperform more elaborate models based on less data [6] and often, big data leads to more accurate results [7]. This has led to the emergence of devices and applications that generate huge amounts of data. For instance, weather satellites generate Terabytes of data every day, which helps climate scientists to predict future extreme weather events. Future self-driving cars may generate nearly 1 Terabyte of data every hour [4]. Internet of things (IoT), social networks and search engines will also contribute to this tremendous growth in data. The challenge faced by computing in the wake of big data has attracted the interest of researchers in approximate computing.

Training neural networks with low precision is a well researched topic [2,5]. This is motivated by limited memory in computing units in comparison to large datasets and the need for new low power and inexpensive computing devices. Vanhoucke et al. [10] showed that approximate computing techniques can dramatically enhance the performance of neural network-based systems with no cost in accuracy. Shafique et al. [9] discussed the opportunities and challenges for approximate computing in machine learning and its contribution to energy efficient architectures. Recently, Wu et al. [11] proposed training and inference with integers. Their proposal, WAGE, limits weights, activations gradients, and errors to low-bit-width integers in both training and inference.

Previous attempts to use DNN in climate study have been very promising. Liu et al. [7] used deep neural networks to detect extreme climate in weather datasets. In the study, they implemented Convolutional Neural Networks (CNN) to detect climate patterns and achieved a high classification accuracy. Furthermore, their work showed that deep neural networks could identify complex patterns in data which are critical in climate change study and policy making.

Zhang et al. [12] also used Long Term Short Term memory (LSTM) networks to predict sea surface temperatures. Other studies such as [8] and [13] have also implemented several ML techniques for climate study.

3   Hurricane Prediction Case Study

The Atlantic hurricane season runs from June 1st to November causing massive destruction and loss of life. In 2017, 17 named storms hit the Atlantic Ocean, some making a landfall and causing destruction worth an estimated $316 million and at least 464 fatalities. Meteorologists, by studying previous weather data, predict the expected number of hurricanes in the season. These predictions help authorities prepare for disasters and over the years, better predictions have minimized loss of life and property. However, these predictions rely on human expertise and are often complex due to the thousands of parameters involved and the chaotic nature of weather.

We propose and implement a ML model based on a DNN to predict the number of hurricanes in the hurricane season. We train the model with more than 100 years of climate data and test it with 5 years. Our results show that we can achieve an accuracy of 72% in predicting the number of hurricanes in a month given the average sea surface temperatures of the previous month. To the best of our knowledge, this is the first attempt to predict the number of hurricanes in the hurricane season using DNN.

3.1   Deep Learning for Hurricane Prediction

Monthly averages of 6 weather variables (sea surface temperature, mean sea level pressure, sea ice cover, 2 m pressure, U wind speed and V wind speed) from 1901 to 2010 are provided by the earth science department of Barcelona Supercomputing Center. Domain expertise shows that these are the main determinants of the nature and intensity of hurricane season. The total number of named storms for each month in the years 1901 to 2010 is also provided and is used as the label for our regression model.

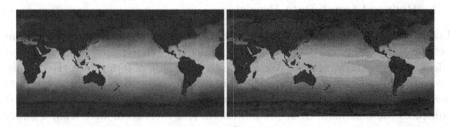

Fig. 1. Left: Sea surface temperature in full precision. Right: Sea surface temperature in 4 bit precision

We design a deep learning model with 6 convolutional layers and 4 fully connected layers. CNNs are chosen because of the grid nature of the data. The 2-dimensional grid has the following dimensions: 160 × 320; and therefore the input the layer has the shape (160, 320, 6), where 6 is the number of channels. There is a Max Pooling after every 2 convolutional layers and a Dropout layer after every fully connected layer. The Convolutional layers have 6 channels, which are the 6 weather variables. Previous research works in climate [7] showed that important climate events are often large in geographical size and few of them occur simultaneously; therefore we use few filters with large kernel sizes. Furthermore unlike ImageNET where millions of training samples are available, hurricane data is limited to approximately 100 years. For these reasons, very deep neural networks would lead to over-fitting. We train the network with 50 epochs and a batch size of 8. The small batch size is because of the large size of our data and a higher batch size almost always runs out memory.

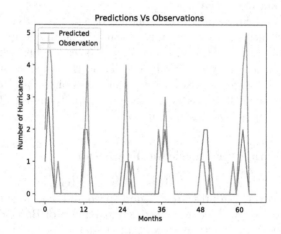

Fig. 2. Prediction using 6 channels

3.2   Reduced Input Data Precision

In the second set of experiments, we use just one channel (i.e. sea surface temperature). Domain expertise shows that sea surface temperature has the biggest effect on hurricane formation. We reduce the precision of input data. To do this, we transform sea surface temperature from Kelvin values (between 268.57202 and 308.71265) to integer values between 0 and 15. Our transformation function first subtracts the maximum from the minimum, and then normalizes from a larger distribution to a coarser one (4-bits). Figure 1 shows the difference between high precision input and low precision input. A clear distinction between the two images is visible. Whereas the image on the left presents high definition colours with hot sea surface temperatures clearly visible, the image on the right is just a rough representation of the sea surface temperatures. We run 100 epochs for both the low precision input and the high precision.

4   Results and Discussion

We first present and discuss the results of predicting the number of hurricanes using deep learning followed by the results of reducing precision in input data. Figure 2 shows the results of predicting the number of hurricanes by combining all the channels. In this case, the model attains an accuracy of 72% for testing data. It is also clear that the model follows the expected hurricane season pattern where the months of September, October and November have the highest hurricane activity and months such as January, February and March having almost no hurricane activity.

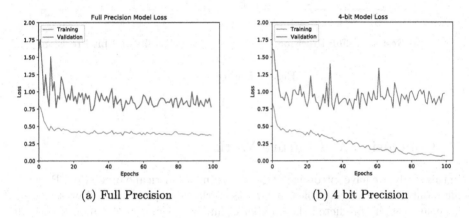

(a) Full Precision   (b) 4 bit Precision

Fig. 3. A comparison of training losses

Figure 3 shows the *loss* of both 4 bit input and full precision input over 100 epochs. Loss is one of the major metrics used to evaluate the performance of a deep learning model. The objective is to minimize the loss function over a number of epochs. In the 4 bit input, the loss decreases up to around 10 epochs before stabilizing and then going further down. This is an indication that after a certain number of epochs, the model begins to over-fit as the validation loss does not change. On the other hand, the full precision does not over fit and there is no significant change in loss after 20 epochs. As mentioned earlier, climate patterns are often few and large and this explains why the model completely learns with just a few epochs (i.e. 20).

Figure 4 shows the testing results after training with both 4 bit precision and full precision. It is important to note that both training are conducted with only one channel i.e sea surface temperature (sst). Even though using multiple channels provides more data to the model, these results show that sst is sufficient to get an acceptable prediction of hurricanes. There is a negligible difference in prediction accuracy when using one channel (sst) and using all channels. The results also show that the observations and predictions are very similar in both cases following the hurricane season patterns mentioned before. Accuracy for the 4 bit model ranged between 69% and 72% for several runs.

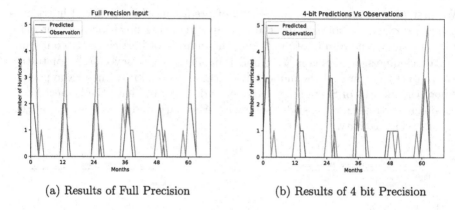

(a) Results of Full Precision   (b) Results of 4 bit Precision

Fig. 4. Testing results

5   Conclusion and Future Work

In this study, we have introduced Deep Learning to hurricane prediction. By feeding monthly weather variables such as sea surface temperature and pressure, we have successfully predicted the number of hurricanes in the next month with an accuracy of 72% using deep neural networks. Furthermore, we have successfully shown that we can reduce the precision of input data from 32 bit floating to 4 bit fixed representation with little effect on the accuracy of prediction. Even though the model could over-fit with reduced precision data, there are well laid out methods and techniques such as early stopping to prevent the model from over-fitting. Reducing the precision of input data shows that such data can be transferred in its reduced form from the point of creation and feed directly to a machine learning workflow. This study shows that Deep Learning can be applied in areas where data precision is limited due to different constraints. Future work shall include multiple instances of precision reduction at different layers to study of possible benefits of such implementations.

Acknowledgment. The authors would like to thank Dr. Alicia Sanchez, Dr. Louis-Philippe Caron and Dr. Dario Garcia for the many helpful discussions and providing data for this research work.

This project has received funding from the European Union's Horizon 2020 research and innovation programme under the Marie Skłodowska-Curie grant agreement No. 713673.

Albert Kahira has received financial support through the "la Caixa" INPhINIT Fellowship Grant for Doctoral studies at Spanish Research Centres of Excellence, "la Caixa" Banking Foundation, Barcelona, Spain."

This work is partly supported by the Spanish Government through Programa Severo Ochoa (SEV-2015-0493), by the Spanish Ministry of Science and Technology through TIN2015-65316 project, by the Generalitat de Catalunya under contracts 2014-SGR-1051 and 2014-SGR-1272.

References

1. Agrawal, A., et al.: Approximate computing: challenges and opportunities. In: IEEE International Conference on Rebooting Computing (ICRC), pp. 1–8. IEEE (2016)
2. Courbariaux, M., Bengio, Y., David, J.: Low precision arithmetic for deep learning. CoRR, abs/1412.7024 4 (2014)
3. Dean, J., et al.: Large scale distributed deep networks. In: Advances in Neural Information Processing Systems, pp. 1223–1231 (2012)
4. Grzywaczewski, A.: Training AI for self-driving vehicles: the challenge of scale. Tech. rep. NVIDIA corporation (2017). https://devblogs.nvidia.com/parallelforall/training-self-driving-vehicles-challenge-scale
5. Gupta, S., Agrawal, A., Gopalakrishnan, K., Narayanan, P.: Deep learning with limited numerical precision. In: International Conference on Machine Learning, pp. 1737–1746 (2015)
6. Halevy, A., Norvig, P., Pereira, F.: The unreasonable effectiveness of data. IEEE Intell. Syst. **24**(2), 8–12 (2009)
7. Liu, Y., et al.: Application of deep convolutional neural networks for detecting extreme weather in climate datasets. arXiv preprint arXiv:1605.01156 (2016)
8. Richman, M.B., Leslie, L.M., Ramsay, H.A., Klotzbach, P.J.: Reducing tropical cyclone prediction errors using machine learning approaches. Procedia Comput. Sci. **114**, 314–323 (2017)
9. Shafique, M., et al.: Adaptive and energy-efficient architectures for machine learning: challenges, opportunities, and research roadmap. In: 2017 IEEE Computer Society Annual Symposium on VLSI (ISVLSI), pp. 627–632. IEEE (2017)
10. Vanhoucke, V., Senior, A., Mao, M.Z.: Improving the speed of neural networks on CPUs. In: Proceedings of Deep Learning and Unsupervised Feature Learning NIPS Workshop, vol. 1, p. 4. Citeseer (2011)
11. Wu, S., Li, G., Chen, F., Shi, L.: Training and inference with integers in deep neural networks. arXiv preprint arXiv:1802.04680 (2018)
12. Zhang, W., Han, L., Sun, J., Guo, H., Dai, J.: Application of multi-channel 3D-cube successive convolution network for convective storm nowcasting. arXiv preprint arXiv:1702.04517 (2017)
13. Zhao, M., Held, I.M., Vecchi, G.A.: Retrospective forecasts of the hurricane season using a global atmospheric model assuming persistence of sst anomalies. Mon. Weather Rev. **138**(10), 3858–3868 (2010)

A Transparent View on Approximate Computing Methods for Tuning Applications

Michael Bromberger$^{(\boxtimes)}$ (iD) and Wolfgang Karl

Karlsruhe Institute of Technology, Kaiserstr. 12, 76131 Karlsruhe, Germany
{bromberger,karl}@kit.edu

Abstract. Approximation-tolerant applications give a system designer the possibility to improve traditional design values by slightly decreasing the quality of result. Approximate computing methods introduced for various system layers present the right tools to exploit this potential. However, finding a suitable tuning for a set of methods during design or run time according to the constraints and the system state is tough. Therefore, this paper presents an approach that leads to a transparent view on different approximation methods. This transparent and abstract view can be exploited by tuning approaches to find suitable parameter settings for the current purpose. Furthermore, the presented approach takes multiple objectives and conventional methods, which influence traditional design values, into account. Besides this novel representation approach, this paper introduces a first tuning approach exploiting the presented approach.

Keywords: Approximate computing · Tuning · Abstraction

1 Introduction

Modern used applications ranging from image processing to Recognition, Mining, and Synthesis have a significant tolerance against approximation, which can be exploited to reduce the required energy consumption or to improve the performance [4]. Even algorithms from scientific computing such as the Jacobi method have such a potential [3]. Approximate computing (AC) methods provide the right way to exploit this existing potential.

Problem Statement. However, the tuning of several AC methods integrated into a single application poses a huge challenge for system designers. The task is to find a suitable parameter setting for all involved methods in order to comply with constraints and to find (near) optimal values for the unrestricted objectives. For instance, considering an image application, where the method loop perforation [10], which skips certain iterations in between, and precision scaling are applied. Then, the perforation rate and the scaling are tuned in order to meet a quality of result (QoR) constraint. Having an energy budget or a firm

© Springer Nature Switzerland AG 2018
R. Yokota et al. (Eds.): ISC 2018 Workshops, LNCS 11203, pp. 570–578, 2018.
https://doi.org/10.1007/978-3-030-02465-9_41

real-time deadline, the challenge is to find a setting, which maximizes the QoR under such a restriction.

State-of-the-Art. A naïve way to find an optimal tuning is to apply an exhaustive parameter search. This approach is often not feasible due to its high computational effort. Therefore, researchers have introduced greedy-based methods to find a (near) optimal tuning according to a QoR constraint [1,7,9]. While these approaches significantly reduce the effort, changing the constraints or integrating further AC methods require a re-execution of the tuning method.

The aforementioned approaches solve the so-called forward problem, which determines the QoR loss for a specific parameter setting and thus several settings has to be considered to find the desired one. By using the inverse problem [11], which uses the constraints as input, we get a suitable parameter setting directly and hence drastically reduce the effort. But the existing approach for solving the inverse problem requires to learn models describing the QoR and performance behavior and to solve a resulting optimization problem. This method still has to consider various knob settings internally by using the learned models.

Additionally, all existing tuning approaches do not take multiple objectives into account, which is a desired aspect. They also do not integrate conventional methods, which can trade off performance for energy or vice versa.

Novel Approach. The concern of this paper is to introduce a transparent and abstract view on the influence of a set of AC methods on different design values for an approximation-tolerant application. The transparent view hides the actual meaning of the different parameters associated to the AC methods and thus reduces the complexity for a tuning. This also avoids to solve an optimization problem and to consider different knob settings for the tuning.

To realize the transparent view, we exploit so-called performance profiles (PPs), which are traditionally used in the domain of anytime algorithms [12]. A PP correlates the QoR with a required budget that has to be spent in a way that it presents the (near) Pareto-optimal front of parameter settings. Hence, each point on this front specifies a setting, where only a single value, QoR or budget, can be higher for other settings. The execution time, the energy consumption, or multiple objectives using a energy delay product metric can be used as budget. The presented approach considers conventional methods such as dynamic voltage and frequency scaling, while building a PP.

A tuning approach exploits a PP representation to solve the inverse problem directly. Since each point on the PP is associated with a certain parameter setting, a simple tuning approach selects a setting by either restricting the QoR or the budget for the PP.

Contributions. To sum up, this paper includes the following novel contributions:

- Introducing PPs as transparent view on a set of AC methods integrated into an application
- Considering multiple objectives for tuning AC Methods
- Allowing the consideration of conventional methods for tuning approximation-tolerant applications
- Design of a simple tuning approach.

2 Exploit Performance Profiles as Transparent View on Approximate Computing Methods

The proposed approach of exploiting PPs to have a transparent view on the resulting QoR allows us to cover existing approximation techniques, for instance, loop perforation. We categorize the generation of PPs for existing approximation methods into two different categories.

The first category is applicable for applications, where we can directly state a budget and after the budget is consumed, a results is returned. This is possible, for instance, in case the application is realized as contract algorithm. A certain setting of the internal AC methods changes the shape of the PP and thus different settings lead to different PPs. To generate the different PPs, representative input data is used. The challenge is now to find the best combined PP of all methods, which represents the PP of the application. This is achieved by the merger approach [12]. The best segment of all PPs in a certain interval is used for the combined PP. The corresponding parameter setting is attached to each segment.

Figure 1a shows this concept according to an illustrative example. Assuming that we have three AC hardware parameter values. Parameter value *AC-HW 2* applies a more aggressive internal approximation and therefore has a better QoR improvement but cannot reach the highest QoR at the end. Using parameter setting *AC-HW 0* leads to the correct solution but offers a worser QoR for lower budgets. Creating a merger for the different PPs, we get a PP that offers the best QoR for each budget.

The second category is useful for applications, where we cannot control the budget directly and thus we consider them as black boxes. The reason is that these methods are not made in a way that they provide a result in between the execution. Such applications can be called tunable applications [11], where the parameters of the AC methods are part of the applications parameters. Therefore, we suggest to build a model that describes the behavior of the parameters as a PP. Executing the application using a set of representative data and a certain knob setting leads to a point in the QoR versus budget space. For example, having two AC methods applied to an application, then different settings (a_i, b_i) result in various points as shown in Fig. 1b. In accordance with a Pareto-optimal front, we can identify these points for that a single objective has the best value compared to all other points, see Fig. 1b.

Generating the PP for a list of p settings is straightforward. Firstly, the list is sorted in ascending order regarding the required budget. Points that have the same budget value are sorted in descending order according to the QoR value. Then, the first point in the list is added to the PP. Further points are only added if the QoR value is larger compared to the one of the previous added point.

3 How to Consider Multiple Objectives?

A huge challenge in AC is to deal with multiple objectives such as the conflicting objectives, QoR, execution time, and energy consumption. Finding good settings

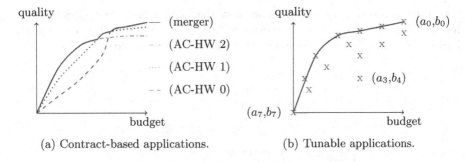

Fig. 1. A PP provides a transparent view on the QoR behavior.

in that space is difficult. Therefore, our approach is to reduce two objectives to a single one, which again allows us to represent the QoR behavior as PP. This is achieved by using the concept of energy delay product metrics (ED^nP) [6] coming from the domain of low power design, where E represents the consumed energy and D the execution time of the application. The value n states that it is tolerable to spend n percent more energy for an one percent reduction in execution time. Hence, n is a factor how high is the emphasis on the performance over the energy consumption. By measuring the value for the execution time and the energy consumption, we can easily combine them using any ED^nP metric, use this metric as budget and generate a PP for it. This makes it possible to constraint the ED^nP value and the energy consumption or execution time separately.

4   Taking Conventional Methods into Account

Computer systems provide different technical opportunities, which influence the execution behavior of an application and can even be controlled by an application, for instance, dynamic voltage and frequency scaling (DVFS). Moreover, modern CPUs are often multi-core architectures and therefore an application can exploit several cores. Increasing the frequency of a core or exploiting more cores can lead to reaching a certain QoR earlier in terms of execution time but impacts the energy consumption. However, the potential of such conventional methods is not exploited in the context of tuning approaches in the domain of AC for approximation-tolerant applications. Therefore, we exploit the presented transparent representation to model the behavior of these methods in the context of AC. We generate a PP for each setting of a conventional method. Following the principle of a Pareto-optimal front, all resulting PPs are combined into a single PP by employing the concept of a merger.

5   Exploiting PPs for System Tuning

Having realized a 2D convolution as a contract algorithm, we generate PPs for different budget metrics and use these representations to tune the application even during run time. Figure 2 shows how the budget metric changes the tuning decision. We note that the x-axis is scaled between 0 and 1 for each PP individually and therefore a direct comparison is not possible.

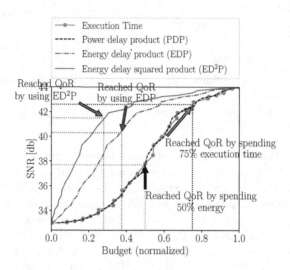

Fig. 2. Showing different PPs for the 2D convolution for varying budget metrics. This leads to a multiple objective consideration. It is important to emphasize, that each curve has a different meaning of the budget (x-axis) as stated by the label.

Let us consider that our objective is to spent not more than 75% of execution time, while maximizing the QoR. Then, we select the setting attached to the PP point, which reaches a SNR of roughly 43 db. Having an objective that we want to spent up to 50% of energy, we select the setting with a QoR of roughly 38 db.

Considering both objectives to the same time and thus finding a good compromise poses a significant challenge. Multiple objectives are mostly not considered by tuning approaches in the AC domain. Our proposed approach deals with this challenge by using a PP generated by an ED^nP metric. For instance, the restricted EDP for the given constraints is $50\% * 75\% = 37.5\%$ and hence the best achievable QoR is roughly 40 db according to the PP. Putting more emphasis on the performance objective, the ED^2P can be used. This results in a budget of $50\% * 75\% * 75\% = 28.125\%$ and the best achievable QoR is roughly 41.5 db. This clearly shows that the willingness of spending more time as done by using the ED^2P metric reduces the influence of considering the energy objective.

Considering Conventional Methods for the Tuning. To show how conventional methods can be tuned together with AC methods, we select the parallelization degree (number of used cores, T) and the frequency of a core. Integrating these methods to the contract-based 2D convolution application, we generate several PPs, see Fig. 3. Depending on the used budget metric, a certain PP outperforms the other ones and therefore the entire PP of this setting also poses the merger.

In this case, each PP has a certain fixed setting for the conventional methods. In case of the execution time, the best configuration is the one using four cores and the highest frequency for all cores (3.2 GHz). The configuration with four hardware threads and 2.2 GHz core frequency is the best configuration for the multiple objective case based on the EDP.

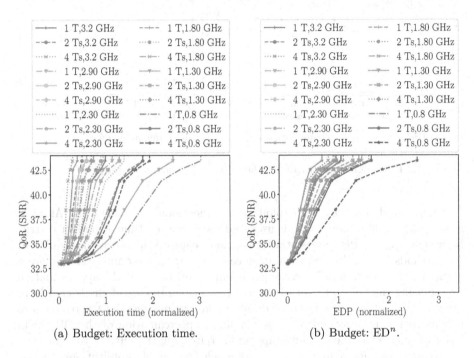

(a) Budget: Execution time.

(b) Budget: ED^n.

Fig. 3. Considering conventional methods for the contract-based 2D convolution.

PPs as General Behavior Description of Approximation Methods. Next, we discuss the generation of PPs for different existing AC methods according to the two different categories presented in Sect. 2. We show this according to the Richardson-Lucy deconvolution algorithm for the first category. The Richardson-Lucy deconvolution, especially, the internal 2D convolutions tolerates small approximations of floating-point operations. Therefore, we consider two different possibilities to approximate these operations. The first one is an AC hardware method that reduces the data that has to be transferred from a floating-point unit to the memory by using a conversion scheme [2]. The second method considers approximate main memories based on DRAM [8]. For the following test, we make a pessimistic assumption that each operation inside the 2D convolution requires an access to the approximate main memory. We note that approximate main memory will not influence the PP regarding the execution time but leads to a significant reduction of the power required for refresh.

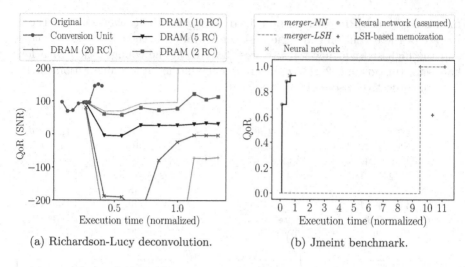

(a) Richardson-Lucy deconvolution.   (b) Jmeint benchmark.

Fig. 4. Generated PPs for the different application categories.

Figure 4a shows the PPs exploiting the mentioned AC methods. As QoR metric, the signal to noise ratio is used and the execution time as budget metric. As we can see, the PP representation is able to capture the behavior of different AC methods. Thus, this representation easily allows us to compare the different methods. Moreover, building a merger is important to adapt the approximation degree using the PP representation during run time. In case of the Richardson-Lucy deconvolution, the CU-based design builds the merger. But the results also reveals that it is beneficial to exploit a slight approximation of the DRAM in order to reduce the energy consumption for refreshing the DRAM content.

To show the applicability of our approach for tunable applications, we use a neural network-based approximation and fuzzy memoization. The PP of such a method consists of few points in the QoR budget space. The neural network based approach relies on a hardware support to infer the network in order to achieve an acceleration [5]. In the absence of such an accelerator, we use publicly available results and assume further configurations. Results are presented for a jmeint benchmark, see Fig. 4b. The results for fuzzy memoization are based on a LSH-based memoization method. As we can see, the LSH-based method achieves reasonable QoRs for different configurations, however, the performance it to low to be beneficial. During the generation of a merger, useless settings are filtered out as seen for fuzzy memoization. The merger for black box models present a step function, where each segment represents a parameter setting.

6   Conclusion

Our work introduces an innovative way how to provide a transparent view on the behavior of AC methods integrated into an approximation-tolerant application. The representation based on performance profiles is directly usable to tune the applications according to different constraints during design or runtime. This approach deals with multiple objectives. This is an important aspect for tuning AC-based methods. This novel approach allows for conventional methods for a tuning of applications. Our work presents the first step to decouple AC methods from tuning approaches that control these methods. So far, we do not take the variance of the QoR for different inputs into account. Therefore, in the future, we research how to integrate input awareness into our approach.

References

1. Baek, W., Chilimbi, T.M.: Green: a framework for supporting energy-conscious programming using controlled approximation. In: ACM SIGPLAN Notices, vol. 45, pp. 198–209. ACM (2010)
2. Bromberger, M., Heuveline, V., Karl, W.: Reducing energy consumption of data transfers using runtime data type conversion. In: Hannig, F., Cardoso, J.M.P., Pionteck, T., Fey, D., Schröder-Preikschat, W., Teich, J. (eds.) ARCS 2016. LNCS, vol. 9637, pp. 239–250. Springer, Cham (2016). https://doi.org/10.1007/978-3-319-30695-7_18
3. Bromberger, M., Hoffmann, M., Rehrmann, R.: Do iterative solvers benefit from approximate computing? An evaluation study considering orthogonal approximation methods. In: Berekovic, M., Buchty, R., Hamann, H., Koch, D., Pionteck, T. (eds.) ARCS 2018. LNCS, vol. 10793, pp. 297–310. Springer, Cham (2018). https://doi.org/10.1007/978-3-319-77610-1_22
4. Chippa, V., Chakradhar, S., Roy, K., Raghunathan, A.: Analysis and characterization of inherent application resilience for approximate computing. In: DAC 13: Proceedings of the 50th Annual Design Automation Conference, pp. 113:1–113:9. ACM, New York (2013)
5. Esmaeilzadeh, H., Sampson, A., Ceze, L., Burger, D.: Neural acceleration for general-purpose approximate programs. In: Proceedings of the 2012 45th Annual IEEE/ACM International Symposium on Microarchitecture, MICRO-45, pp. 449–460. IEEE Computer Society, Washington, DC (2012)
6. Gonzalez, R., Horowitz, M.: Energy dissipation in general purpose microprocessors. IEEE J. Solid State Circ. 31(9), 1277–1284 (1996)
7. Laurenzano, M.A., Hill, P., Samadi, M., Mahlke, S., Mars, J., Tang, L.: Input responsiveness: using canary inputs to dynamically steer approximation. ACM SIGPLAN Not. 51(6), 161–176 (2016)
8. Liu, S., Pattabiraman, K., Moscibroda, T., Zorn, B.G.: Flikker: saving dram refresh-power through critical data partitioning. In: Proceedings of the Sixteenth International Conference on Architectural Support for Programming Languages and Operating Systems, ASPLOS XVI, pp. 213–224. ACM, New York (2011). https://doi.org/10.1145/1950365.1950391
9. Samadi, M., Lee, J., Jamshidi, D.A., Hormati, A., Mahlke, S.: Sage: self-tuning approximation for graphics engines. In: Proceedings of the 46th Annual IEEE/ACM International Symposium on Microarchitecture, pp. 13–24. ACM (2013)
10. Sidiroglou-Douskos, S., Misailovic, S., Hoffmann, H., Rinard, M.: Managing performance vs. accuracy trade-offs with loop perforation. In: ESEC/FSE, pp. 124–134. ACM (2011)

11. Sui, X., Lenharth, A., Fussell, D.S., Pingali, K.: Proactive control of approximate programs. SIGOPS Oper. Syst. Rev. **50**(2), 607–621 (2016). https://doi.org/10. 1145/2954680.2872402
12. Zilberstein, S.: Operational Rationality through Compilation of Anytime Algorithms. Ph.D. thesis, University of California at Berkeley (1993)

Exploring the Effects of Code Optimizations on CPU Frequency Margins

Konstantinos Parasyris[✉], Nikolaos Bellas, Christos D. Antonopoulos, and Spyros Lalis

University of Thessaly, Glavani 37, 38221 Volos, Greece
{koparasy,nbellas,cda,lalis}@uth.gr

Abstract. Chip manufactures introduce redundancy at various levels of CPU design to guarantee correct operation even for worst-case combinations of non-idealities in process variation and system operation conditions. This redundancy is implemented partly in the form of voltage/frequency margins. However, for a wide range of real-world execution scenarios, these margins are excessive and translate to increased power and energy consumption. Among the various factors that affect the degree to which these margins are actually needed to avoid errors during program execution, the impact of compiler and source code optimizations has not been explored yet. In this work, we study the effect of such optimizations on the frequency margins and the energy efficiency of applications in the ARM Cortex-A53 processor.

Keywords: Energy efficiency · Compiler optimizations
Frequency margins

1 Introduction

As predicted by Moore's Law, the scalability of semiconductor manufacturing process has been the driving force behind the increase in the capabilities of computer systems. However, scaling into lower nanometer geometries has led to variability of transistor characteristics, resulting into increased failure rates in modern CPUs. Conventional techniques for providing reliable execution include extra provisioning in logic and memory circuits in the form of increased voltage margins and reduced operating frequencies (so-called guardbands), as well as special error correction circuitry. But all these techniques consume more power, thus are not very attractive in light of the ambitious goal to reach exascale performance with constrained power budgets [4]. More specifically, guardbanding may increase power dissipation in the order of 35% [6]. Yet most of the time these guardbands are excessive and translate to unnecessary overhead, as the worst-case combinations that were considered at design time may appear only rarely or even not at all during the life cycle of a given CPU part.

© Springer Nature Switzerland AG 2018
R. Yokota et al. (Eds.): ISC 2018 Workshops, LNCS 11203, pp. 579–587, 2018.
https://doi.org/10.1007/978-3-030-02465-9_42

Many factors affect the CPU margins during application execution, including the application's characteristics, the libraries used by it, the CPU microarchitecture and the environmental conditions (e.g., temperature) [10,11]. Among these factors, compiler and source code optimizations have not been investigated so far. It is important to analyze the impact of such optimizations though, given that these are common practice when trying to improve application performance.

The contributions of this work are the following: (i) we study the effect of common compiler optimizations on the energy efficiency and the frequency margins of four ARM Cortex-A53 processor parts; (ii) we examine the effect of memory access pattern optimizations on the energy efficiency and the frequency margins; (iii) we inspect the interaction of *SIMD* instructions on the energy efficiency and the frequency margins.

We perform bare metal executions to isolate the effect of the optimizations from the system software stack (OS). Our results show that the ARM Cortex A-53 has on average frequency margins equal to 14% of the nominal frequency. The maximum energy gain due to these frequency margins is 12%. Regarding the effect of compiler optimizations, the least optimized versions of the application typically exhibit wider margins. On the other hand, source code optimizations can increase the frequency margins, up to 4% of the nominal frequency.

The remainder of this paper is organized as follows. Section 2 presents the hardware setup and our methodology. Section 3 shows our experimental results when studying the effect of compiler optimizations. Section 4 presents the effect of source code optimizations. Section 5 presents the related work. Section 6 concludes our study.

2   Methodology

We perform our experiments on four raspberry PI 3b platforms. Each PI has a 4 core ARM Cortex A-53 in-order processor running at a nominal frequency of 1200 MHz, with a nominal supply voltage of 1.2 V. Cores feature a 64 KB L1 data cache and a 64 KB L1 instruction cache, a 512 KB L2 Cache and 1 GB LPDDR2 RAM (900 MHz). The power consumption of the entire platform is measured using an external data acquisition USB device [9]. To accurately capture the behavior of the different applications and optimizations without the interference of the system software stack (which can introduce significant non-determinism), we use a bare metal environment, called Circle [12].

To quantify the frequency margins of each CPU part, we identify the maximum frequency that can be reached while still achieving correct execution (f_{max}). This is done, for each application benchmark, using a binary search algorithm, which determines f_{max} within a range $[low, high]$. Initially, we set $low = 1200$ MHz and $high = 1500$ MHz, and set f_{max} equal to the middle of the interval (1350 MHz). Noticeably, although we increase the frequency, we do not increase the supply voltage. During the execution of the application, we detect any hardware traps raised (e.g., due to the execution of an illegal instruction) and infinite loops (if the execution takes much longer than the time required to run the application at the nominal frequency). If the application runs successfully, the produced output is compared against the correct golden output in order to detect any Silent Data Corruptions (SDCs).

To account for any non-deterministic behavior during execution, we run the application 1024 times for each tested frequency, which provides a confidence level of 99% and an error margin of 2%. If all runs complete successfully, the region $[low, f_{max}]$ is marked as safe, the low bound is increased to $low = f_{max}$, and f_{max} is adjusted accordingly (to the middle of the interval). Else, if erroneous behavior is detected, we mark the region $[f_{max}, high]$ as unsafe, and the high bound is decreased to $high = f_{max}$. The algorithm terminates when the interval width becomes less than 5 mV. No human intervention is needed, since we reboot after a CPU Crash using an external hardware watchdog.

3   Compiler Optimizations Analysis

In this work we use the *gcc 4.9.3* compiler. While modern compilers provide users with specific options to optimize their code, individual optimizations are usually grouped in higher-level options, such as O0, O1, O2, O3, Os. Our study only considers these options.

We use several applications/kernels taken from various benchmark suites [5, 7,13]. In this study, we analyze Sobel, DCT, Inversek2j, Blackscholes, Swaptions, Fluidanimate, Sjeng and Libquantum. Sobel is a 2D filter for edge detection in images. Discrete Cosine transform (DCT) is a module of the JPEG compression and decompression algorithm. Inversek2j is a robotics benchmarks that calculates the angles of a 2-joint arm using the kinematic equation. Blackshcoles implements a mathematical model for a market of derivatives, which calculates the buying and selling of assets to as to reduce the financial risk. Fluidanimate applies the smoothed particle hydrodynamics method to compute the movement of fluid in consecutive time steps. Swaptions uses the Heath-Jarow-Morton framework to price a portofolio of swaptions. Sjeng is a chess-player application that finds the next move via a combination of alpha-beta and priority proof-number tree searches. Finally, Libquantum simulates a quantum computer.

Compiler optimizations aim at improving performance, we first analyze the effects of the different optimization levels (O0, O1, O2, O3, Os) on the execution time and energy consumption of our benchmark applications. Increasing the optimization level augments the previous set of optimizations with additional ones. In the case of Os, the compiler uses most, but not all, of the O2 optimizations, together with some extra optimizations that decrease the size of the executable.

Figure 1 shows the normalized energy consumption and execution time of the different compiler optimization levels with respect to O0. As expected, the higher the compiler effort the greater the performance and the energy gain. DCT presents the higher speedup when using the O3 optimizations. On the other hand, Inversek2j shows almost no speedup when compiled with increasing

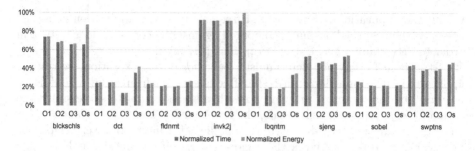

Fig. 1. Execution time and energy consumption of the application benchmarks for the different compiler optimization levels, relative to O0.

optimization levels. This is because it extensively uses trigonometric functions that are included in an already optimized version of the standard C library. According to our measurements, the different optimization levels do not impact CPU power consumption in a significant way, except of the case of Os level, which in some applications (blackscholes, DCT, inversek2j) increases the power consumption. This is due to the instruction selection performed on this optimization level as well as that alignment and function inlining is not performed. In any case typically, the larger energy gains that are achieved when using higher optimization levels are mainly due to the reduced execution times.

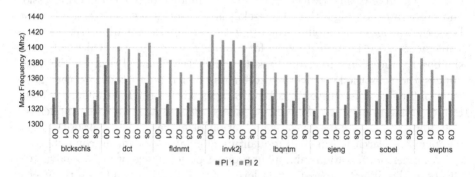

Fig. 2. Maximum frequency at which the application benchmarks run correctly for each compiler optimization level, on two of the raspberry PIs.

Figure 2 illustrates the experimentally identified f_{max} for the different optimizations levels, on two of the raspberry PIs; the results for the other two PIs are similar, and are not shown here for brevity. The exploitable extra frequency ranges from 9% to 19% of the nominal CPU frequency (1200 MHz). The highest frequency at which all applications can be executed reliably, is equal to 1309, 1356, 1346, 1356 MHz for the four raspberry PIs, corresponding to a CPU part-specific *static* frequency margin of 109, 156, 146, 156 MHz, respectively. The workload-specific dynamic frequency margin for the four raspberry PIs is equal to $75, 69, 69, 69\,\mathrm{MHz}$ respectively

Different optimization levels impact the dynamic frequency margin and can increase or decrease f_{max} by up to $32\,\mathrm{MHz}$ for a given application. Interestingly, O0 has a wider margin than higher optimization levels for the same application, in 62.5% of the configurations (combinations of different CPU parts and different applications). Despite the increased f_{max} of O0, the decrease in the execution time due to the extra frequency margin is relatively small, resulting in lower energy gains compared to higher optimization levels. Thus, using higher optimization levels is more beneficial not only in terms of performance but also in terms of energy gains, even though these have smaller frequency margins than O0. When comparing the remaining optimization levels (O1, O2, O3, Os) there is no dominant optimization level in terms of frequency margins. On the other hand, in 80% of the total cases $O3$ is the most energy efficient optimization level.

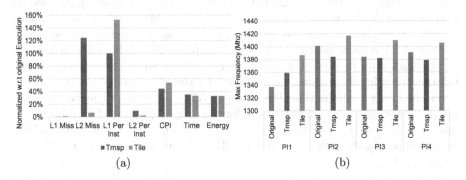

Fig. 3. (a) Performance metrics and energy consumption of the transposed and tiled MM versions, with respect to the original implementation. (b) Maximum frequency for all raspberry PIs and all MM implementations.

4   Source Code Transformations

Developers very often try to reduce the execution time of their applications by employing more efficient algorithms, optimizing memory accesses, reducing the number of instructions, or using special instructions for parallel processing and vectorization. In this study, we optimize a Matrix Multiplication (MM) kernel by using more efficient memory access patterns as well as Single Instructions Multiple Data (SIMD) instructions. In both cases we observe the effects of the optimizations on the energy efficiency, the execution time and the frequency margins of the different benchmark versions.

4.1   Memory Access Pattern Optimizations

The matrix multiplication (MM) kernel performs multiplication between two floating point matrices ($C = A * B$). We consider three different implementations/versions. The so-called original version accesses the first matrix (A) in a row-wise fashion and the second matrix (B) in a column wise fashion. The second implementation, performs a multiplication with the transposed B^T matrix, which is allocated on a new 2D-array. Finally, the third version uses a tiled version of the matrix multiplication. The size of the tile is equal to the cache line size (64 bytes).

Figure 3a presents the performance metrics and energy consumption of the transposed and tiled MM versions, normalized to the original implementation. As expected, both optimized versions have significantly lower L1-cache misses. They also demonstrate a significantly decreased CPI, which directly translates to performance and energy gains.

Figure 3b presents the maximum frequency of the different MM versions. In contrast to the compiler optimization analysis, where the non-optimized versions exhibit larger frequency margins, the memory access optimizations present mixed results. On the one hand, in all raspberry PIs, the largest margins are found for the tiled MM version, which in one of the raspberry PIs (PI1) yields an increase on the maximum frequency of up to 50 MHz compared to the original version. On the other hand, in three out of four PIs, the transposed MM version has lower frequency margins than the original. Also, the extra frequency margins result on average to an additional performance gain of 2.5%. We also observe margin variations across different parts, this difference can reach up to 63 MHz when comparing the original version of PI1 with the same version on PI2.

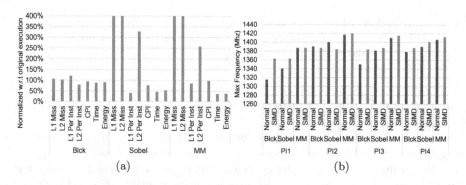

Fig. 4. (a) Normalized performance metrics and energy consumption of the three benchmarks, with respect to the implementations without SIMD instructions. (b) Maximum frequency for all raspberry PIs and benchmarks.

4.2 SIMD Optimizations

We use SIMD instructions to optimize the execution time and energy efficiency of Blackscholes, Sobel and tiled MM. Figure 4a presents the performance metrics and energy consumption, relative to the normal versions of the benchmarks without SIMD instructions. Figure 4b shows the frequency margins of the benchmarks for the four raspberry PIs.

As can be seen, when using SIMD instructions the execution time of Sobel and MM is decreased to 36% and 46% of the normal versions, respectively. This speedup is mirrored to energy gains since the power consumption does not increase significantly when using SIMD instructions. Blackscholes does not show any reduced execution time because many math functions used by that benchmark do not have a SIMD equivalent function. In PI1 the SIMD version of the blackscholes benchmark greatly increase the frequency margin by 44 MHz. This increase in frequency provides an extra performance gain of 3.5% on top of the performance gain obtained by the SIMD instructions. In general, the use of SIMD instructions actually increases the maximum frequency by *1*% on average.

5 Related Work

In [1] the authors explore the effects of compiler optimization on the vulnerability of HPC parallel applications in the presence of radiation-induced soft errors which effect the Static Random Access Memory. Their work focus on what happens when errors occur, in our case we identify the maximum frequency in which timing errors do not occur for different optimization.

Many research approaches have emerged in the last few years that relax conservative guardbands to improve energy efficiency. Prior work focusing on commercially available chips include [2,3,8,10,11,14]. In particular in [10] the authors present an automated system-level analysis on multi-core CPUs based on the ARMv8 64-bit architecture when pushed to operate in scaled voltage conditions. Due to the manifestation of SDCs before system crashes, the authors propose a severity function that can predict safe, SDC-free undervolt levels for each core of the processor. Based on this function and the corresponding core V_{min} resulted from the offline characterization, they produce a linear regression model that tries to predict the safe V_{min} of a core for any workload. The same authors present a study for two commercial x86-64 microprocessors [11]. The heuristics presented in [2,3] that dynamically reduce voltage margins while always preserving safe operation, are based on the error correction ECC hardware built on modern processors such as the server-class Intel Itanium 9560. The rate of ECC correctable errors is used as an indicator on how to adjust the V_{dd} voltage. Authors in [14] exploit the large margins available when only one core in a server-class 8-core Power7+ processor is utilized, turning under-utilized margin into power and performance benefits. A study of the voltage margins on several Kepler and Fermi GPUs is presented in [8]. They show that high energy efficiency can be achieved by shaving conservative guardbands in modern GPUs. In our work we focus on the frequency margins in contrast to these works which focus on the voltage margins. To the best of our knowledge we are the first that study the effect of optimizations to the margins of the system.

6   Conclusions

The impact of compiler optimizations on applications performance have been widely studied in the past. However, as we approach the exascale era, it can be worthwhile to understand the new trade-offs between application energy consumption and safety margins. Our study on four raspberry PIs equipped with an ARM Cortex A53 processor reveal wide frequency margins, up to 18% of the nominal operating frequency, as well as considerable margins variations across different CPU parts. Interestingly, typically non-optimized compiler code demonstrates wider margins than the optimized one. Moreover, memory optimizations which greatly increase the performance of an application also increase the width of the frequency margins. Finally, using SIMD instructions usually increases the frequency margins by a factor of 1%.

References

1. Ashraf, R.A., Gioiosa, R., Kestor, G., DeMara, R.F.: Exploring the effect of compiler optimizations on the reliability of HPC applications. In: Processing on the International Parallel and Distributed Processing Symposium Workshops (IPDPSW), pp. 1274–1283 (2017)
2. Bacha, A., Teodorescu, R.: Using ECC feedback to guide voltage speculation in low-voltage processors. In: Proceedings of 47th Annual IEEE/ACM International Symposium on Microarchitecture (MICRO), pp. 306–318, December 2014. https://doi.org/10.1109/MICRO.2014.54
3. Bacha, A., Teodorescu, R.: Dynamic reduction of voltage margins by leveraging on-chip ECC in itanium II processors. SIGARCH Comput. Archit. News **41**(3), 297–307 (2013). https://doi.org/10.1145/2508148.2485948
4. Bergman, K., Borkar, S., Campbell, D., Carlson, W., Dally, W., et al.: Exascale computing study: technology challenges in achieving exascale systems. Technical report, DARPA IPT (2008)
5. Bienia, C., Kumar, S., Singh, J.P., Li, K.: The PARSEC benchmark suite: characterization and architectural implications. In: Proceedings of the 17th International Conference on Parallel Architectures and Compilation Techniques (PACT), pp. 72–81. ACM (2008)
6. Das, S., et al.: A self-tuning DVS processor using delay-error detection and correction. IEEE J. Solid State Circuits **41**(4), 792–804 (2006)
7. Henning, J.L.: SPEC CPU2006 benchmark descriptions. SIGARCH Comput. Archit. News **34**(4), 1–17 (2006). https://doi.org/10.1145/1186736.1186737. ISSN 0163-5964
8. Leng, J., Buyuktosunoglu, A., Bertran, R., Bose, P., Reddi, V.J.: Safe limits on voltage reduction efficiency in GPUs: a direct measurement approach. In: Proceedings of the 48th Annual IEEE/ACM International Symposium on Microarchitecture (MICRO), pp. 294–307 (2015). https://doi.org/10.1145/2830772.2830811
9. Measurement Computing: USB 205 Data Acquisition USB Device

10. Papadimitriou, G., Kaliorakis, M., Chatzidimitriou, A., Gizopoulos, D., Lawthers, P., Das, S.: Harnessing voltage margins for energy efficiency in multicore CPUs. In: Proceedings of the 50th Annual IEEE/ACM International Symposium on Microarchitecture (MICRO), pp. 503–516 (2017)
11. Papadimitriou, G., Kaliorakis, M., Chatzidimitriou, A., Magdalinos, C., Gizopoulos, D.: Voltage margins identification on commercial x86-64 multi-core microprocessors. In: Proceedings of the 23rd International Symposium on On-Line Testing and Robust System Design (IOLTS), pp. 51–56 (2017). https://doi.org/10.1109/IOLTS.2017.8046198
12. rsta2: Circle: a c++ bare metal programming environment for the Raspberry Pi. https://github.com/rsta2/circle
13. Yazdanbakhsh, A., Mahajan, D., Lotfi-Kamran, P., Esmaeilzadeh, H.: AXBENCH: a multi-platform benchmark suite for approximate computing. IEEE Des. Test **34**, 60–68 (2016)
14. Zu, Y., Lefurgy, C.R., Leng, J., Halpern, M., Floyd, M.S., Reddi, V.J.: Adaptive guardband scheduling to improve system-level efficiency of the POWER7. In: Proceedings of the 48th Annual IEEE/ACM International Symposium on Microarchitecture (MICRO), pp. 308–321 (2015)

First Workshop on the Convergence of Large-Scale Simulation and Artificial Intelligence

Taking Gradients Through Experiments: LSTMs and Memory Proximal Policy Optimization for Black-Box Quantum Control

Moritz August[1(✉)] and José Miguel Hernández-Lobato[2]

[1] Department of Informatics, Technical University of Munich, 85748 Garching, Germany
august@in.tum.de
[2] Computational and Biological Learning Lab, University of Cambridge, Cambridge CB2 1PZ, UK
jmh233@cam.ac.uk

Abstract. In this work we introduce a general method to solve quantum control tasks as an interesting reinforcement learning problem not yet discussed in the machine learning community. We analyze the structure of the reinforcement learning problems typically arising in quantum physics and argue that agents parameterized by long short-term memory (LSTM) networks trained via stochastic policy gradients yield a versatile method to solving them. In this context we introduce a variant of the proximal policy optimization (PPO) algorithm called the memory proximal policy optimization (MPPO) which is based on the previous analysis. We argue that our method can by design be easily combined with numerical simulations as well as real experiments providing the reward signal. We demonstrate how the method can incorporate physical domain knowledge and present results of numerical experiments showing that it achieves state-of-the-art performance for several learning tasks in quantum control with discrete and continuous control parameters.

Keywords: Reinforcement learning · Quantum control
Numerical simulation

1 Introduction

As a result of collaborative efforts by academia and industry, machine learning (ML) has in recent years led to advancements in several fields of application ranging from natural language and image processing over chemistry to medicine. In addition to this, reinforcement learning (RL) has recently made great progress in achieving super-human performance in challenging problems like Go or Chess [22,23] with only small amounts of prior knowledge which was widely believed to be out of reach for the near future. Consequentially, RL is nowadays thought

© Springer Nature Switzerland AG 2018
R. Yokota et al. (Eds.): ISC 2018 Workshops, LNCS 11203, pp. 591–613, 2018.
https://doi.org/10.1007/978-3-030-02465-9_43

to hold promise for applications such as robotics or molecular drug design. This success naturally raises the question of what other areas of application might benefit from employing machine learning.

Quantum mechanics and especially quantum computing is of special interest to the machine learning community as it can not only profit from applications of state-of-the-art ML methods but is also likely to have an impact on the way ML is done in the future [2]. This bidirectional influence sets it apart from most other applications and is a strong incentive to investigate possible uses of machine learning in the field despite the comparably steep learning curve.

One challenging and important task in the context of quantum physics is the control of quantum systems over time to implement the transition between an initial and a defined target physical state by finding good settings for a set of control parameters [14]. This problem lies at the heart of quantum computation as performing any kind of operation on quantum bits (qubits) amounts to implementing a controlled time evolution with high accuracy in the face of noise effects induced by the environment. Apart from the relevance to quantum computation, the analysis and understanding of the properties of quantum control problems also is an interesting research problem in its own right. However, for a given physical system as implemented in a real experiment it is in general not possible to express all influence factors and dependencies of particles in mathematical form to perform an analytical analysis or gradient-based optimization of the control variables. Furthermore, a numerically exact simulation of the time evolution is only possible for small physical systems due to the exponential growth of the Hilbert space in the number of particles. Already for medium-sized systems, the time evolution can at best be approximated by tensor network techniques [19]. The available approximation methods however can not yet be combined with, e.g., gradient-based optimization approaches in practice. Analytical analyses and optimization algorithms requiring gradients are thus in general limited to small systems with relatively simple mathematical expressions.

Physicists have for some time been proposing automated solutions for these problems [1,3,11,15,26] that are able to find good control parameter settings while being as agnostic as possible about the details of the problem in question. Unfortunately though, these approaches are in general based on tailored solutions that do not necessarily generalize to other problems as they, e.g., only consider discrete variables when the underlying problem is actually continuous and are not always very sample efficient.

In this work we improve over the status quo by introducing a control method based on recurrent neural networks (RNNs) and policy gradient reinforcement learning that is generic enough to tackle every kind of quantum control problem while simultaneously allowing for the incorporation of physical domain knowledge. By taking a black-box approach towards the quantum dynamics, it allows for the computation of the reward signal by either a numerical simulation, approximately or exact, or by a real-life experiment. More precisely, we present an improved version of the recently introduced proximal policy optimization (PPO) algorithm [21] and use it to train Long Short-Term Memory

(LSTM) [8] networks to find stochastic policies obtaining high rewards in quantum control tasks. We furthermore show how physical domain knowledge can be incorporated to obtain state-of-the-art results for two recently addressed control scenarios [1,3], the protection of a one-qubit quantum memory connected to a multi-qubit environment and the transition of multi-particle systems between ground states. While our method is based on an analysis of the reinforcement learning problem underlying quantum control, it can also be applied to other RL problems with the same structure. Our contribution hence is threefold in that we firstly introduce the general method, secondly demonstrate how to successfully apply it to quantum control problems and thirdly, by doing so, try to stimulate a more intense exchange of ideas between quantum physics to the broader machine learning community to facilitate mutual benefit.

The rest of this work is structured as follows: in Sect. 2, we provide a very brief introduction to quantum control, followed by a discussion and analysis in Sect. 3 of the reinforcement learning problem posed by quantum control. Building on the analysis, we present the method in Sect. 4 and subsequently introduce two concrete quantum control problems in Sects. 5.1 and 5.2 respectively. We then present numerical results obtained by our method in these problems and compare them to those of existing solutions in Sect. 6. Finally, we conclude with a discussion of the work in Sect. 7.

2   Quantum Control

The time evolution of a physical system in quantum mechanics is described by the Schrödinger equation

$$ih\frac{\delta}{\delta t}\left|\psi(t)\right\rangle = H\left|\psi(t)\right\rangle \tag{1}$$

where H is the Hamiltonian, a complex Hermitian Matrix describing the energy of the physical system, and h is Planck's constant [6]. Hereby, $\left|\psi\right\rangle$ is the Dirac notation for a physical state which for finite dimensional systems as we treat here corresponds to a complex column vector of the same dimensionality as the Hamiltonian's. The conjugate transpose of a vector $\left|\psi\right\rangle$ then is denoted as $\left\langle\psi\right|$ such that $\langle\psi,\psi\rangle$ denotes the inner and $\left|\psi\right\rangle\left\langle\psi\right|$ the outer product. The Schrödinger equation yields the unitary quantum time evolution

$$\left|\psi(t)\right\rangle = e^{-itH/h}\left|\psi(0)\right\rangle. \tag{2}$$

In a discretized time setting with time steps Δt the evolution for a total time T can thus be written as

$$\left|\psi(T)\right\rangle = e^{-i\Delta t H/h^L}\left|\psi(0)\right\rangle \tag{3}$$

where we define $L = T/\Delta t$. In quantum control we now assume to be able to control the time evolution by application of so-called control Hamiltonians $H_1, \cdots, H_C$, which yields the controlled time evolution

$$\left|\psi(T)\right\rangle = e^{-i\Delta t \sum_{i=1}^{C} c_{iL}H_i/h} \ldots e^{-i\Delta t \sum_{i=1}^{C} c_{i1}H_i/h}\left|\psi(0)\right\rangle \tag{4}$$

where the c_{it} are time-dependent scaling constants for the control Hamiltonians. This formulation however assumes that we have full control over the system which due to various kinds of noise or environmental effects will not be the case. Hence we introduce a noise or drift Hamiltonian H_0, which we here assume to be time independent and of constant strength, and obtain the final formulation

$$|\psi(T)\rangle = e^{-i\Delta t(H_0 + \sum_{i=1}^C c_{iL} H_i)} \ldots e^{-i\Delta t(H_0 + \sum_{i=1}^C c_{i1} H_i)} |\psi(0)\rangle \qquad (5)$$

where we set $h = 1$ for convenience.

Now that we have a well-defined notion of our control problem, we need to state the actual goal that we aim to achieve. Generally, starting from an initial state $|\psi(0)\rangle$ or the corresponding density operator $\rho(0) = |\psi(0)\rangle \langle \psi(0)|$ we would like to obtain an evolution to target state $|\psi^*\rangle$ or $\rho^* = |\psi^*\rangle \langle \psi^*|$. Hence we need to define some similarity measure between the state we actually obtain after evolving for time T and our ideal result. The easiest way of doing this is simply to compute the overlap between these states by

$$S(\psi^*, \psi(T)) = \langle \psi^*, \psi(T) \rangle, \qquad (6)$$

or for instance its squared norm to guarantee a real-valued result, and

$$S(\rho^*, \rho(T)) = \mathsf{Tr} \rho^{*\dagger} \rho(T) \qquad (7)$$

respectively for Hermitian operators [9].

Equipped with this metric, we can formally define the problem we would like to solve as

$$\max_{\{c_{it}\}} S(\rho^*, \rho(T, \{c_{it}\})). \qquad (8)$$

This formulation is broad enough to capture every problem from synthesizing certain quantum gates over evolving from one eigenstate of a Hamiltonian to another to storing the initial state in a quantum memory setting.

3   Reinforcement Learning: Why and What?

As we have seen above, solving quantum control problems amounts to determining an optimal or at least good sequence of principly continuous variables that describe the influence we exert on the system at each discrete time step. If a rigorous mathematical description of the evolution dynamics is available and small system sizes are of interest, there exist methods like GRAPE [9] or CRAB [4,7] to obtain good solutions. However, the gap between theory and experiment also does not close in quantum mechanics and hence it is reasonable to assume that the actual dynamics of a real experiment will slightly differ from the mathematical model due to various noise effects induced by the environment. As can for instance also be observed in robotics, these slight differences between theory/simulation and real world implementation might still have a significant impact on the optimization problem to be solved. Additionally, it is clear that in general it is neither an interesting nor feasible task to derive a proper mathematical model for the effect of every influence factor in a real experiment [3]. These challenges are in addition only made harder by considering larger system sizes due to an increase in possible interactions and the necessity to approximate the exact analytical objects describing the systems and their dynamics.

This shows that it is worthwhile to investigate ways of optimizing such a control problem from a black box perspective in the sense that we are agnostic about the actual time evolution dynamics of the system and can only observe the final results generated by a chosen set of parameters. This final result can then be obtained by the most accurate numerical simulation available or even directly from a real experimental setup. In fact, in the absence of a mathematical model it is a reasonable assumption to only be able to obtain information after the end of an experiment. This is due to the fact that in quantum mechanics a measurement during an experiment would in general cause the wave function to collapse and hence destroy the experiment without any way of determining what the final outcome would have been. Hence the task we would like to solve is to find a controller or at least find a good sequence of control parameters based on the outcomes of trial runs of a given experiment or its simulation. In quantum control terminology, this corresponds to a closed-loop control setting.

While one viable route to solving this problem would be to use classical evolutionary or hill-climbing algorithms or more advanced black-box methods such as Bayesian optimization, another interesting option is to fit a generative probabilistic model from which we can efficiently sample good sequences. This approach has two advantages. Firstly, we can iteratively update the model by fitting it to additional data we might acquire after the initial fitting phase. Doing so allows it to improve over previous results or make it adapt to changing conditions, e.g. a change of the noise Hamiltonian after some time. This is in contrast to pure optimization methods which would have to start from scratch for every problem. Secondly, by examining the distribution over the sequence space the model has learned and inspecting the best sampled control sequences, it might be possible to gain a better understanding of the underlying dynamics of a system.

It is clear that the sequences of control parameters in a quantum control problem should not be treated as i.i.d. as a given choice of parameters c_t at time t potentially depends on all previous choices $c_1, \cdots, c_{t-1}$ and thus we have a conditional distribution $p(c_t|c_1, \cdots, c_{t-1})$. This kind of distribution can successfully be learned by modern RNN variants, such as LSTM or Gated Recurrent Unit [5] (GRU) networks. This can for instance be seen in natural language processing (NLP) problems, which feature similar structure and where RNNs have led to breakthrough results in recent years. Note that, with this modelling decision, we still capture the full multivariate distribution $p(c_1, \cdots, c_T)$ as by the factorization rule of probabilities it holds that

$$p(c_1, \cdots, c_T) = \prod_{t=1}^{T} p(c_t | c_1, \cdots, c_{t-1}). \qquad (9)$$

Having decided on the class of models to employ, we are left with the question of how to fit them. This is non-trivial as we obviously can not hope to be able to obtain gradients of real-world experiments or some black-box simulation and also can not assume to have any a priori data available. Hence, we must 'query' the physical setup to obtain tuples of sequences and results. Thereby we would naturally like to be as sample efficient as possible and hence have to find an intelligent way to draw samples from the experiment and learn from them.

In a recent attempt to address this problem, an evolutionary-style algorithm for training LSTMs was introduced [1] that iteratively generates better data and fits the models to that data, then uses sampling from these models instead of the usual mutation operations to generate new sequences. While the algorithm was able to find better sequences than known in theory for the considered control problem of quantum memory, it was only demonstrated for a discretized version of the problem and there is room for improvement with respect to the efficient use of sampleded sequences.

A more direct solution to this black-box optimization problem would however be if we were able to simply approximate the gradient of the error function with respect to the parameters of our model from the sampled data. Being able to obtain an approximate gradient would allow us to optimize our model in a gradient descent fashion and thus to leverage existing optimization methods mainly used in supervised learning. Indeed, this is a typical RL scenario which is commonly referred to as *policy gradient* learning. In the following, we will thus show how to solve the optimization task at hand by perceiving the problem of black-box quantum control as an RL problem and tackling it with a state-of-the-art policy gradient algorithm. To this end, we start by analyzing the particular reinforcement learning problem posed by black-box quantum control.

As we only receive a result or measurement, from now on also referred to as reward, after having chosen a complete sequence of control parameters, we can perceive the sequence $c = (c_1, \cdots, c_T)$ as a single action of the RL agent for which it receives a reward $R(c)$. This approach most clearly reflects the envisioned closed-loop control scenario explained above. Modelling the sequences and their respective results in this way then implies that our Markov decision process (MDP) takes the form of a bi-partite graph consisting of a single initial state s_0 on the left and multiple final states s_c on the right that are reached deterministically after exactly one action c. The set of states S of this MDP is thus given by $S = s_0 \cup \{s_c\}_c$ while the set of actions A corresponds to the set of all sequences c and the transition probabilities are defined as $P(s_0, c, s_c) = 1$. The reward $R(c)$ of an action c is determined by the associated value of the error function as defined in Sect. 2. We assume here that two different sequences always lead to different final states of the system, which is the most challenging conceivable case as equivalence classes in the sequence space would effectively reduce the size of the search space. This particular structure then implies that the value function simplifies to

$$V(s_0) = \max_c R(c) = R(c^{opt}) \qquad (10)$$

where c^{opt} is the optimal sequence and the Q-function

$$Q(s_0, c) = R(c) \qquad (11)$$

is in fact independent of the state and equal to the reward function $R(c)$ as each action c is associated with exactly one final state. Additionally, the number of actions $|A|$ and hence final states x_c is *at least* exponential in the number of possible values of control parameters per time step t and generally infinite. This learning setting can be perceived as a *multi-armed bandit* [17] problem but constitutes a special case as firstly we assume to be only able to perform one action, i.e. generate one sequence, before receiving the total reward and secondly the actions are not atomic but rather exhibit a structure we exploit for learning.

It is true that one could derive a different formulation of the problem by considering the c_t to be individual actions and using the discounted reward of the complete sequence as reward signal at time t. This approach however puts more emphasis on optimal local behavior of the agent when our goal clearly is to optimize the global performance, i.e. to generate the best possible complete sequences of control parameters as opposed to the best parameters at a given time step. Furthermore, it is not necessarily true that the dynamics in quantum physics are well-structured in the sense that an optimal sequence up to time t will yield the optimal one at the final time T when extended optimally. However, for the RL setting introduced above to be solvable, the compositional structure of the actions c is in fact of critical importance as we will discuss now.

In principle, the RL problem amounts to learning to choose the best out of up to infinitely many possible actions which in general clearly is unsolvable for every algorithm. So, why can we hope to achieve something with an algorithm learning from trials in the introduced problem setting? The main reason for this is in fact that we know that the actions the agent takes are not atomic but concatenations of multiple choices which have a physical meaning. Nature as we perceive it seems to be governed by simple underlying rules (or complex rules that are at least approximated very well by simple ones) which allows us to capture them with mathematical expressions. This in turn implies that there is much structure to be found in Nature and hence it is reasonable to assume that likewise the desirable actions in our learning problem share certain patterns which can be discovered. More precisely, we conjecture that solving the particular problems we are tackling in this work requires less abstract conceptual inference, which would still be out of reach for todays machine learning models, and more recognition of patterns in large sets of trials, i.e. control sequences, and hence in fact lends itself to treatment via machine learning and especially contemporary RNN models. Some empirical evidence for the validity of this conjecture has recently been provided for the problem of quantum memory [1] and for a problem related to quantum control, the design of quantum experiments [11].

4   The Learning Algorithm

Having discussed the modelling of the control sequences and the RL problem, we will now introduce the actual learning algorithm we employ. As we have seen above, we can not perform direct optimization of $R(c)$ as we cannot access $\nabla R(c)$. However, it has long been known that it is possible to approximate $\nabla_\Theta \mathbf{E}_c[R(c)]$ since

$$\nabla_\Theta \mathbf{E}_c[R(c)] = \mathbf{E}_c[\nabla \ln p_\Theta(c)R(c)] \tag{12}$$

where $\mathbf{E}_c$ is the expectation over the sequence space and $p_\Theta(c)$ is the stochastic policy of the agent parameterized by the weight vector Θ, which in this work corresponds to an LSTM. This insight is known as the likelihood ratio or REINFORCE [27] trick and constitutes the basis of the policy gradient approach to reinforcement learning.

From the physics point of view, the trick allows us to approximate the gradient of the expected outcome of a given experiment with respect to the parameters of our stochastic controller and perform gradient-based optimization while being agnostic about the mechanisms behind the experiment, i.e. model-free. In a sense we thus have a way of taking a gradient through an experiment without the necessity to mathematically model every variable of influence and their interplay. This of course also holds true when the experiment is replaced by a numerical simulation as for instance a tensor network algorithm to simulate the time evolution.

From a different perspective, this approach simply corresponds to maximizing the likelihood of sequences that are weighted by their results, such that the agent has a higher incentive to maximize the likelihood of good sequences. The approach can be refined by replacing the weighting by the pure reward $R(c)$ with an approximation of the advantage $A(s,c) = Q(s,c) - V(s)$. This has been shown to improve the convergence significantly and especially for continuous control problems, policy gradient methods outperform Q-learning algorithms [21].

Despite such improvements, policy gradient approaches still suffer from slow convergence or catastrophically large updates, which has led to the development of improvements such as trust region policy optimization [20] (TRPO). These methods however make use of second-order information such as inverses of the Hessian or Fisher information matrix and hence are very difficult to apply in large parameter spaces which are common in the deep learning regime. The underlying idea of such improvements thereby is limiting the magnitude of updates to Θ by imposing constraints on the difference between p_Θ and $p_{\Theta_{new}}$ in order to prevent catastrophic jumps out of optima and achieve a better convergence behavior.

In an effort to strike a balance between ease of application and leveraging the insights behind TRPO, recently a novel policy gradient scheme called proximal policy optimization [21] (PPO) was introduced. One main novelty hereby lies in the introduced loss, which is for a general RL scenario given by

$$L^{CLIP}(\Theta) = \mathbf{E}_t[\min(r_t(\Theta)A_t, \mathrm{clip}(r_t(\Theta), 1-\epsilon, 1+\epsilon)A_t)] \tag{13}$$

where $\mathbf{E}_t$ and A_t are the expectation over time steps and the advantage at time t respectively, which both need to be approximated. The term r_t is defined as the ratio of likelihoods

$$r_t(\Theta) = \frac{p_\Theta(c_t|s_t)}{p_{\Theta_{old}}(c_t|s_t)} \tag{14}$$

of actions c_t in states s_t in our notation and we define $\text{clip}(a, b, c)$ to be equal to $\min(\max(a, b), c)$. The distribution $p_\Theta(c_t|s_t)$ is a stochastic policy depending on parameters Θ. Note that this generic formulation assumes multiple actions c_t per episode and thus does not yet apply to the learning scenario discussed here.

The objective function poses a lower bound on the improvement induced by an update and hence establishes a trust region around Θ_{old}. The hyperparameter ϵ controls the maximal improvement and thus the size of the trust region.

Now, the basic algorithm is defined as follows:

1. Obtain new set of trajectories, i.e. sequences, C, by sequentially sampling from $p_\Theta(c_t|s_t)$.
2. Optimize L^{CLIP} over C for K iterations.
3. Set $\Theta_{old} = \Theta$.
4. Repeat until convergence.

Note that there exists a straight-forward generalization to the case of multiple agents but as we can not reasonably assume in our application to have access to multiple identical experiments, we only consider the case of one agent here. The algorithm was shown to achieve state-of-the-art performance for several discrete and continuous control tasks, which makes it ideally suited for the problems tackled in this work. However, we will now introduce a few improvements tailored to our specific reinforcement learning problem as defined in the previous section which we will for the sake of brevity from now on refer to as memory proximal policy optimization (MPPO).

Since in our problem we only consider episodes consisting of one action c, the objective becomes

$$L_1^{CLIP}(\Theta) = \mathbf{E}_c[\min(r(\Theta)A, \text{clip}(r(\Theta), 1 - \epsilon, 1 + \epsilon)A)] \tag{15}$$

with

$$r(\Theta, c) = \frac{p_\Theta(c)}{p_{\Theta_{old}}(c)} \tag{16}$$

and $p_\Theta(c)$ being parameterized by an LSTM, as discussed above. A again denotes the advantage function. We have omitted the dependence on c in L_1 for the sake of clarity. Since we know that in our problem setting it holds that $Q(c, s) = R(c)$, the advantage function becomes

$$A(c) = R(c) - V(c). \tag{17}$$

It is worth noting that this implies that in our scenario there is no need to approximate the Q-function as we can access it directly. In fact approximating the Q-function and hence $R(c)$ would be equivalent to solving the optimization problem as we could use the approximator to optimize over its input space to find good sequences. The quality of the approximation of $A(c)$ consequentially only depends on the approximation of $V(c)$. While there exist many sophisticated ways of approximating the value function [12,21] in our case the optimal approximation is given by

$$\hat{V}(c) = R(c^*) \tag{18}$$

where c^* is the best sequence we have encountered so far. Since we do not know the best sequence and its corresponding reward (at best we know an upper bound), the reward of the best sequence found so far is the closest approximation we can make. The optimal approximation of the advantage $A(c)$ hence is given by

$$\hat{A}(c) = R(c) - R(c^*). \tag{19}$$

Since we need to store c^* to compute the advantage approximation and are generally interested in keeping the best solution, it is a natural idea to equip the agent with a memory M of the best sequences found so far. We can then formulate a memory-enhanced version of the PPO algorithm:

1. Obtain new set of trajectories, i.e. sequences, C, by sampling from $p_\Theta(c)$.
2. Update the memory of best sequences M
3. Optimize L_1^{CLIP} over $C \cup M$ for K iterations.
4. Set $\Theta_{old} = \Theta$.
5. Repeat until convergence.

The memory sequences are treated as newly sampled sequences such that their weighting as defined in Eq. 16 always is performed with respect to the current values of Θ_{old} and Θ. This ensures compatibility with the policy gradient framework while the access to the best actions discovered so far leads to a better convergence behavior as we will see later. Note that, under the previously introduced assumption, the best sequences share common structural properties. Maximizing the expected reward over all sequences $\mathbf{E}_c[R(c)]$ is thus equivalent to maximizing the expected reward over the sequences in the memory $\mathbf{E}_{c \in M}[R(c)]$ which ensures relevance and stability of the updates computed over M. This memory scheme furthermore is different from experience replay in Q-learning [13] as only the best sequences are kept and reintroduced to the agent. The relation between $|C|$ and $|M|$ thereby is a new hyperparameter of the algorithm affecting the exploration-exploitation dynamics of the learning process. The larger $|M|$ is relative to $|C|$, the more greedily the agent will learn to reproduce the sequences in the memory. In contrast to this, the smaller $|M|$ gets in relation to $|C|$, the more the updates computed in each iteration will be dominated by the newly sampled sequences and thus induce a less greedy learning behavior.

Another factor that has a significant impact on the exploration behavior is the value of the scaling or variance parameter of the probability distributions employed in continuous control tasks, such as for instance the standard deviation σ of the univariate normal distribution or the covariance matrix Σ in the multivariate case. It is clear that a large variance induces more exploration while a small variance corresponds to a more exploitation-oriented behavior. Over the course of training an agent to find a good policy it is hence reasonable to start with a larger variance and reduce it during the optimization until it reaches a defined minimal value. However, while the agent usually learns to predict the mean of the given distribution, the variance parameter is currently often treated as fixed or follows a predefined decay schedule which does not account for the randomness in the training process. Utilizing the sequence memory, we propose an improvement by introducing a dynamical adaptation scheme for the variance parameters depending on the improvement of the memory M. More concretely, we propose to maintain a window W_i of the relative improvements of the average rewards in memory

$$W_i = \left[\frac{\overline{R(M_{i-l+1})} - \overline{R(M_{i-l})}}{\overline{R(M_{i-l})}}, \cdots, \frac{\overline{(M_i)} - \overline{R(M_{i-1})}}{\overline{R(M_{i-1})}} \right] \tag{20}$$

where $\overline{R(M_i)}$ denotes the average reward over the memory in iteration i of the optimization and l is the window length. At every l-th step in the optimization, we then compute a change parameter

$$\alpha_t = 1 + \frac{\overline{W_{t-l}} - \overline{W_t}}{\overline{W_{t-l}}} \tag{21}$$

with $\overline{W_t}$ being the window average and scale (possibly clipped) the variance parameters by it. Note that we assume here monotonic improvement of M and $R \in [0, 1]$. This scheme thus poses a dynamic adaptation of the variance parameters based on second-order information of the improvement of the average reward of M. It follows the intuition that if the improvement slows down, a decrease of the variance gives the agent more control over the sampled actions and allows for a more exploitation-oriented behavior. On the other side, when the improvement accelerates, it appears reasonable to prevent too greedy a behavior by increasing the uncertainty in the predicted actions. The same scheme can furthermore also be applied to parameters such as ϵ, which plays a similar role to the variance.

In conclusion, extending the PPO training with a memory of the best perceived actions prevents good solutions of the control problem to be lost, gives the agent access to the best available advantage estimate, improves convergence and allows to dynamically scale the variance parameters of respective distributions from which actions are sampled. While we introduce this variant of the PPO algorithm for our specific application, we believe that it would generalize to other applications of reinforcement learning yielding similar MDPs.

5 Applying the Method

In this section, we will now introduce two quantum control scenarios that were recently explored via machine learning [1,3]. We show how one can apply our method to tackle some interesting learning tasks arising in these control settings by leveraging physical domain knowledge.

5.1 Quantum Memory

One particular instance of a quantum control problem is the problem of storing the state of a qubit, i.e. a two-level system used in quantum computation. This is, next to quantum error correction, a very relevant problem in quantum computation. Here we assume that our qubit is embedded in some environment, called the bath, such that the complete system lives in the Hilbert space

$$\mathcal{H} = \mathcal{H}_S \otimes \mathcal{H}_B$$

with the subscripts S and B denoting the space of the system and bath respectively. If we let this system evolve freely, decoherence effects will over time destroy the state of the qubit. Hence the question is how we can intervene to prevent the loss of the state in the presence of the environment or, for computer scientific purposes, the noise where we assume to have control over the qubit only. From a quantum computing perspective, we would like to implement a gate that performs the identity function over a finite time interval.

Qubit states are commonly represented as points on the Bloch sphere [14] and the effect of the environment on the qubit can in this picture be perceived as some rotation that drives the qubit away from its original position. To counter this problem we must hence determine a good rotation at each time step such that we negate the effect of the environment. So, our goal is to dynamically decouple the qubit from its bath by performing these rotations. The rotation of a qubit is defined as

$$R_n(\alpha) = e^{-i\frac{\alpha}{2}n\sigma}$$

with n being a unit vector specifying the rotation axis, α denoting the rotation angle and σ the 'vector' of the stacked Pauli matrices $\sigma_{\{x,y,z\}}$ [18]. Thus our controlled time evolution operator per time step t becomes

$$U(n_t, \alpha_t) = e^{-i\Delta t(H_0 + \frac{\alpha_t}{2\Delta t}n_t\sigma \otimes I_B)},$$

expressing that we only apply the rotation to the qubit, but not the bath. The noise Hamiltonian H_0 here reflects the effect of the bath on the qubit and I_B simply denotes the identity of size of the dimensionality of $\mathcal{H}_B$ such that the Kronecker product yields a matrix of equal size to H_0.

One possible metric to quantify how well we were able to preserve the qubit's state is

$$D(U, I) = \sqrt{1 - \frac{1}{d_S d_B}\|\mathsf{Tr}_S(U)\|_{\mathsf{Tr}}}$$

with U denoting the total evolution operator, I the identity and Tr_S is the partial trace over the system [16]. $\|U\|_{\mathsf{Tr}} = \mathsf{Tr}\sqrt{U^\dagger U}$ is the trace or nuclear norm. This distance measure is minimized by the ideal case $U = I_S \otimes U_B$ with an arbitrary unitary U_B acting on the bath. Thus, the problem we would like to solve is a special instance of quantum control and can be formulated as

$$\min_{\{(n_t, \alpha_t)\}} D(U(\{(n_t, \alpha_t)\}, I).$$

Having introduced the quantum memory scenario, we now turn to a description of possible reinforcement learning tasks in this context. We present three different formulations of the setting which we will in the following refer to as the discrete, semi-continuous and continuous case. These formulations differ in the parametrization of the rotation $R_n(\alpha)$ that is to be performed at each time step.

Discrete case. It is known from analytical derivations that the Pauli matrices $\sigma_{\{0,x,y,z\}}$ give rise to optimal sequences under certain ideal conditions [24,25], where at each time step exactly one of the rotations $R_{\{0,x,y,z\}} = e^{-i\frac{\pi}{2}\sigma_{\{0,x,y,z\}}}$ is performed. σ_0 hereby denotes the identity. Hence, in the simplest formulation we can define the problem as choosing one of the four Pauli matrices at each time step. This formulation then leads to a sequence space S of size $|S| = 4^T$ being exponential in the sequence length T. This is the formulation which was also used in recent work on quantum memory [1].

Semi-continuous case. While the class of sequences introduced above is provably ideal under certain conditions, one might be interested in allowing the agent more freedom to facilitate its adaption to more adverse conditions. This can in a first step be achieved by allowing the agent full control over the rotation angle while keeping the discrete formulation for the rotation axis. That means that at each time step, the agent will have to choose a rotation axis from $\sigma_{\{0,x,y,z\}}$ as before, but now must also predict the rotation angle $\alpha \in [0, 2\pi]$. As α can take infinitely many values, this formulation of the problem now yields a sequence space S of infinite size, making it much harder from a reinforcement learning perspective. To lighten this burden we can make use of the fact that we know that in principle a rotation around π is ideal. Thus, we will interpret the output of the agent as the deviation from π $\Delta\alpha \in [-\pi, \pi]$. This should facilitate learning progress even in the early training phase.

Continuous case. Finally, we can of course also allow the agent full control over both the rotation angle and axis. This formulation of the problem requires the agent to predict a unit vector $n \in \mathbb{R}^3$ and a corresponding rotation angle α for each time step. It is clear that without any prior knowledge it will be very difficult for the agent to identify the 'right corner' of this infinite sequence space. We hence propose to again leverage the knowledge about Pauli rotations being a good standard choice by having the agent predict a Pauli rotation together with the deviation in n and α. While for α we have already seen how this can be easily achieved, n requires slightly more insight. As is customary in quantum physics, every state of a two-dimensional particle $|\psi\rangle$ can be represented by choosing two angles $\theta \in [0, \pi]$ and $\phi \in [0, 2\pi]$, yielding the three-dimensional real unit Bloch vector

$$b = \begin{pmatrix} \sin\theta\cos\phi \\ \sin\theta\sin\phi \\ \cos\theta \end{pmatrix}.$$

We can hence use this formulation to parameterize n by θ and ϕ. It is easy to see that the Pauli rotations correspond to the unit vectors that equal a one-hot encoding of the Pauli matrices such that we obtain the following identities

$$\theta_x = \theta_y = \phi_y = \frac{\pi}{2} \text{ and}$$
$$\phi_x = \phi_z = \theta_z = 0$$

with periodicity in π. We can now leverage this knowledge by translating the Pauli rotation axis chosen by the agent into its Bloch expression and requiring it to predict the deviations $\Delta\theta$ and $\Delta\phi$. In this way the agent has access to the full axis space. As with the rotation angle, this formulation has the effect that the agent starts learning from a reasonable baseline.

5.2   Ground State Transitions

Another scenario that was recently addressed in an anlysis of the characteristics of the optimization problem behind controlling systems out of equilibrium [3] is the transition between ground states of different Hamiltonians. The considered class of Hamiltonians was thereby defined to be the class of Ising Hamiltonians given by

$$H(J, g, h) = J \sum_{i=1}^{L-1} I^{\otimes i-1} \otimes \sigma_x \otimes \sigma_x \otimes I^{\otimes L-(i+1)}$$
$$+ g \sum_{i=1}^{L} I^{\otimes i-1} \otimes \sigma_z \otimes I^{\otimes L-i}$$
$$+ h \sum_{i=1}^{L} I^{\otimes i-1} \otimes \sigma_x \otimes I^{\otimes L-i}$$

where the $\sigma_{\{x,y,z\}}$ again denote the Pauli matrices and L specifies the number of particles. In this setting we furthermore set $J = g = -1$, leaving h as the only free parameter specifying the strength of the magnetic field represented by σ_x. From a mathematical perspective, the ground state $|E_{min}(h)\rangle$ of a given Hamiltonian $H(h)$ is then defined as the eigenvector of $H(h)$ corresponding to its lowest eigenvalue.

In the considered scenario we now choose the initial and target states to be $|\psi_i\rangle = |E_{min}(h_i)\rangle$ and $|\psi^*\rangle = |E_{min}(h^*)\rangle$ respectively where $h_i \neq h^*$ are particular choices of h. The controlled time evolution operator is then simply defined to be the one generated by $H(h)$ as given by

$$U(h_t) = e^{-i\Delta t/h H(h_t)}$$

where we assume h_t to be time dependent. The closeness between the state resulting from the controlled time evolution $|\psi(T)\rangle$ and the target state $|\psi^*\rangle$ is measured by their squared overlap

$$S_2(\psi^*, \psi(T)) = |\langle \psi^*, \psi(T) \rangle|^2,$$

similar to what was shown in Sect. 2. We thus obtain the optimization problem formulation

$$\max_{\{h_t\}} S_2(\psi^*, \psi(\{h_t\}))$$

representing the quantum control optimization problem.

Next, we will introduce some RL tasks arising in this control scenario. Similarly to the the taxonomy introduced above, we will thereby distinguish between a discrete, a continuous and a constrained case. These cases correspond to different domains of possible values for the time dependent field strengths h_t. All of them however have in common that we assume a maximal magnitude h_{max} of the field strength such that $h_t \in [-h_{max}, h_{max}]$ holds. This is simply done to reflect the fact that in real experiments infinite field strengths are impossible to achieve.

Discrete case. Knowing that the potentially continuous domain of our control parameter h_t is upper and lower bounded by $\pm h_{max}$, we can apply Pontryagin's principle to limit ourselves to actions $s_t \in \{-h_{max}, h_{max}\}$. We thus obtain a reinforcement learning problem where at each point in time the agent has to make a binary decision. While this is arguably the easiest conceivable scenario, the sequence space still is of size $|S| = 2^T$.

Continuous case. Although we know from theory that optimal sequences will comprise only extremal values of the control parameter h_t, it is still interesting to examine if the agent is able to discover this rule by itself. In this case we hence allow the agent to freely choose $h_t \in [-h_{max}, h_{max}]$ which again presents us with a sequence space of infinite size. Following our reasoning from the continuous quantum memory case, we cast the problem as learning the deviation $\Delta h \in [0, h_{max}]$ from $\pm h_{max}$. Hence, for each time t the agent must predict the deviation Δh and decide to which of the two extremal values the deviation should be applied. This formulation clearly allows the agent to predict any value in $[-h_{max}, h_{max}]$.

Constrained case. In the continuous case as defined above, we know that the agent should ideally learn to predict deviations of 0 to achieve sequences with extremal values of h_t. We can thus try to make the problem more challenging by imposing an upper bound $B < T|h_{max}|$ on $\sum_t |h_t|$, representing an upper limit of the total field strength. Imposing such a bound is not an artificial problem as it could for instance be used to model energy constraints in real experiments. This constraint can easily be realized by defining the reward of a sequence s to be

$$R(s) = \begin{cases} S_2(\psi^*, \psi(s)) \text{ if } \sum_t |h_t| \leq B \\ 0 \text{ else.} \end{cases}$$

This constraint requires the agent to learn how to distribute a global budget over a given sequence where it can maximally allocate an absolute field strength of $|h_{max}|$ to each action s_t. As it is not clear which values are optimal in principle for a given bound B, instead of a deviation we here let the agent directly predict the field strength h_t.

Table 1. The best values of $D(U, I)$ found by or method for the discrete, semi-continuous and continuous quantum memory learning tasks together with baseline results. The reference values were taken from [1] and computed with the corresponding algorithm for $T = 0.512$ and $\Delta t = 0.002$. Lower values are better.

	$\Delta t = 0.002$		$\Delta t = 0.004$	
$T =$	0.064	0.512	0.256	0.512
Ref.	$7 \cdot 10^{-5}$	$2 \cdot 10^{-4}$	$4 \cdot 10^{-4}$	$8 \cdot 10^{-4}$
Disc.	$7 \cdot 10^{-5}$	$2 \cdot 10^{-4}$	$4 \cdot 10^{-4}$	$8 \cdot 10^{-4}$
Semi-Cont.	$6 \cdot 10^{-5}$	$2 \cdot 10^{-4}$	$4 \cdot 10^{-4}$	$8 \cdot 10^{-4}$
Cont.	$6 \cdot 10^{-5}$	$2 \cdot 10^{-4}$	$4 \cdot 10^{-4}$	$7 \cdot 10^{-4}$

6 Results

In this section we will now present numerical results for the two application scenarios presented above to illustrate the validity of our method and the usefulness of the MPPO algorithm. As we did not have at our disposal real physical experiments implementing these scenarios, the results presented in the following are based numerical simulations.

6.1 Quantum Memory

For the quantum memory scenario, we investigate the performance of our algorithm for different lengths of the discrete time step, total evolution times and across the three formulations of the problem described above. More concretely, we explore the method's behavior for a discrete time evolution with $\Delta t \in \{0.002, 0.004\}$, $T \in \{0.064, 0.256, 0.512, 1.024\}$ and a physical system consisting of one memory qubit coupled to a bath of four qubits with up to three-body interactions to allow for a comparison with the baseline results [1]. We refer the interested reader to this article for a more precise description of the physical setup. While we ultimately would like to optimize $D(U(c), I)$ as defined above, we used $1 - D(U(c), I)$ as a reward signal to obtain an $R(c) \in [0, 1]$. We furthermore shifted the reward such that a uniformly random policy obtains zero reward on average.

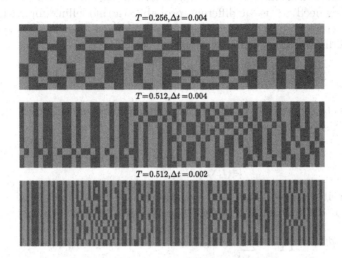

Fig. 1. The best 10 sequences found for the discrete learning problem with varying parameters of T and Δt. It is clearly visible how the best sequences for each setting share common structural properties and also exhibit recurring patterns making them amenable to machine learning models.

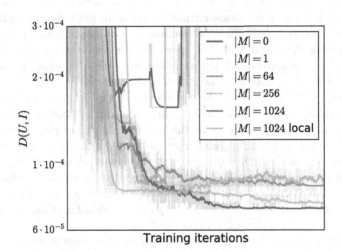

Fig. 2. A comparison of the convergence behavior of the best results sampled per iteration for different sizes of the memory, no memory and a memory with the L^{CLIP} loss applied to the individual c_t for $T = 0.064$ and $\Delta t = 0.002$. The convergence becomes more stable with larger memory and updates based on the entire sequences lead to convergence to better sequences.

As the three learning tasks introduced for this scenario differ in their action domains, we need to use a different probabilistic modelling for each setting. For the discrete case, we simply model each element c_t of a sequence c by a categorical distribution such that we have

$$p(c) = \prod_t Cat(c_t \in \{I, X, Y, Z\} | \{p_{I,t}, p_{X,t}, p_{Y,t}, p_{Z,t}\})$$

for a complete sequence c. In the semi-continuous case we employ a mixture-of-Gaussians distribution which yields

$$p(c) = \prod_t \sum_{i \in \{I,X,Y,Z\}} p_{i,t} \mathcal{N}(c_t = \Delta\alpha | \mu_{i,t}, \sigma_t).$$

This can easily be generalized to the continuous case via a multivariate mixture-of-Gaussians distribution with diagonal covariance matrix such that we obtain

$$p(c) = \prod_t \sum_{i \in \{I,X,Y,Z\}} p_{i,t} \mathcal{N}(c_t = \{\Delta\alpha, \Delta\theta, \Delta\phi\} | \boldsymbol{\mu}_{i,t}, \sigma_t I).$$

Note that we have omitted here the dependence on the weights Θ for the sake of brevity. As discussed in Sect. 3, we use an LSTM to parameterize these probability densities. More concretely, we use a two-layer LSTM and use its output as input to a softmax layer to predict the $p_{i,t}$. From this output state and the relevant parts of the output from the previous time step we also predict the μ_i for $\Delta\alpha$ in the semi-continuous case and analogously for $\Delta\theta$ and $\Delta\phi$ in the continuous case. For every deviation output we train an individual output unit for each discrete rotation. For the semi-continuous and continuous tasks, we scale the standard deviation σ_t and PPO parameter ϵ over the course of the optimization using our introduced adaption scheme with a window size of 10 and optimize the loss function with the Adam optimizer [10].

The scores $D(U(c), I)$ of the best sequences found in our numerical experiments are listed in Table 1. They clearly show that our method is able to achieve the same or slightly better results as the baseline algorithm from [1] for all considered settings and learning tasks. For the semi-continuous case, we observe that for the setting involving the shortest sequences slightly better sequences than in the discrete case can be found. For longer sequences the performance is on par with the discrete sequences. The same in principle holds for the continuous case with the exception of the results for $T = 0.512$ and $\Delta t = 0.004$ being slightly better then for the other two cases.

Overall we can conclude that our method finds sequences several orders of magnitude better than those a random policy generates, which are generally in the interval $[0.1, 0.5]$, showing that in all cases LSTMs trained by the MPPO algorithm seem to perform quite well. We can also see that the discrete sequences pose a strong baseline that is hard to beat even with a fully continuous approach and in fact we observed the predicted deviations to converge to very small values. The results furthermore support the conjecture that good sequences share common structure and local patterns that can be learned which is also illustrated in Fig. 1. Here, the best 10 sequences found during the training process in the discrete case for three different settings are shown, illustrating the high degree of structure that the best sequences exhibit. The structural similarities become more apparent with growing sequence length. Interestingly, in all cases the best sequences only make use of two of the four Pauli rotations and less surprisingly never use the identity 'rotation'.

In Fig. 2 we show the effect of different sizes of the memory M on the convergence of the best sequences in the discrete case for otherwise constant optimization parameters. As can be seen, when not using a memory or only storing the best sequence, the optimization diverges. For larger sizes of the memory, the algorithm converges to better and better sequences, arriving at the best sequence found for this setting with a memory of 1024 sequences. We also plot the convergence of our method for the case when the actions are considered to be the individual control parameters c_t at each time step and not the complete sequences c. In this case, we set the size of the memory to $|M| = 1024$ and use the discounted reward of the complete sequence $R(c)$ as reward for the individual times t. While this approach also performs well, learning to choose the best parameters per time step does not seem to yield quite as good results as learning to generate the best complete sequence. This might indicate that the learning problem is indeed not well-structured in the sense discussed above.

6.2   Ground State Transition

In the ground state transition setting, we evaluate our method for times $T \in \{0.5, 1, 3\}$ with $\Delta t = 0.05$ and an initial $h_i = -2$, target $h^* = 2$ as well as $|h_{max} = 4|$ to achieve comparability with the baseline results [3]. For the discrete and continuous case, we consider systems of size $L = 1$ and $L = 5$ and $B \in \{20, 30, 40, 50, 60, 100, 120, 140\}$ with $L = 1$ for the constrained case. Since the overlap S_2 as defined above already lies in the interval $[0, 1]$, we used it directly as reward function, again shifting it such that a uniformly random policy achieved zero reward.

The probabilistic modelling of the sequences is similar to the quantum memory case in that we use a categorical distribution for the discrete case and a mixture-of-Gaussians for both the continuous and constrained tasks. Thereby, we model the probability density of the deviations Δh_t in the continuous case and the predicted absolute value of h_t in the constrained case. The distributions are parameterized in the same way as above, namely by a two layer LSTM form whose output state both the discrete probabilities and the means for both discrete cases as predicted. The optimization is conducted as in the quantum memory scenario.

The results of our numerical experiments are listed in Table 2. As shown, our method was able to replicate the baseline results from [3] both for the discrete and the continuous formulation of the problem for a system size of $L = 1$ and also performs well for larger systems of $L = 5$ with both versions yielding generally the same results. We indeed found the continuous version to converge to predicting zero deviation as it was expected to. For the constrained case we can

Table 2. The best values of S_2 obtained by our method for the discrete, continuous and constrained ground state transition learning problems with reference values taken from [3]. Higher values are better.

	$T = 0.5$	$T = 1$	$T = 3$
Ref. $(L = 1)$	0.331	0.576	1
Disc. $(L = 1)$	0.331	0.576	1
Cont. $(L = 1)$	0.331	0.576	1
Disc. $(L = 5)$	0.57	0.767	1
Cont. $(L = 5)$	0.57	0.768	1
Const. $(B = 20)$	0.313	–	–
Const. $(B = 30)$	0.322	–	–
Const. $(B = 40)$	–	0.572	–
Const. $(B = 50)$	–	0.577	–
Const. $(B = 60)$	–	0.577	–
Const. $(B = 120)$	–	–	1
Const. $(B = 140)$	–	–	1
Const. $(B = 160)$	–	–	1

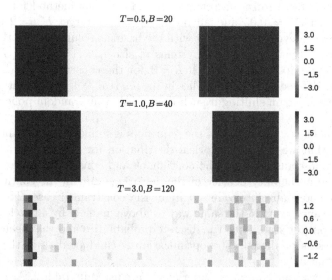

Fig. 3. The 10 best sequences found for different values of T and a maximal field strength B amounting to half of the maximally possible. While the best sequences for $T = 0.5$ and $T = 1.0$ are very similar und andfield strength, the best sequences for $T = 3.0$ use much smaller pulses.

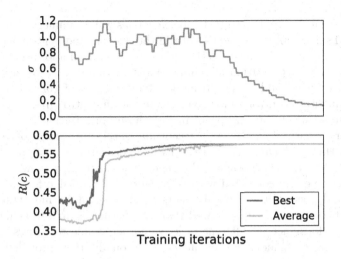

Fig. 4. The convergence the best and average reward per iteration together with the dynamically adapted σ for the constrained scenario with $T = 1.0$ and $B = 60$

see that our method converges to sequences whose performance is surprisingly close to the baseline results even when allowed to use only half of the maximal absolute field strength. For $T = 3.0$ the imposed constraints in fact seem to have no negative effect as apparently already sequences with a very small total field strength suffice to achieve perfect overlap. This is also illustrated by Fig. 3 which shows the best 10 sequences found during the training process for $T \in \{0.5, 1.0, 3.0\}$ and B set to half the maximal total field strength. While for the smaller two total times the sequences are very similar and always make use of the maximal field strength or apply no pulse at all, for $T = 3.0$ only the general scheme of applying positive pulses first, then doing nothing and finally applying negative pulses persists. The individual pulses that are applied are very weak and entire sequence typically only amounts to a total absolute strength of ~ 6. This phenomenon is likely caused by the fact that the optimization problem in this case becomes significantly easier for longer times [3]. In Fig. 4 we display the convergence of the best and average results sampled per iteration together with the dynamic schedule for sigma during the optimization. It can be seen that σ is dynamically increased when the convergence slows down, decreased when it speeds up and finally converges to a stable value as the optimization converges as well. In other scenarios we also observed our adaption scheme to perform similarly to a decayed annealing schedule.

7   Conclusion and Future Work

In this work we have introduced a general and versatile method to solve quantum control problems. The method is agnostic about the dynamics of the physical systems in question and based on state-of-the-art ML tools. As a consequence of this, it can easily be applied to real experiments as well as numerical simulations thereof and solve control problems both in the discrete and continuous domain.

We have given a brief introduction to quantum control and discussed different aspects of the application of reinforcement learning to it. We have argued that LSTMs are a good choice to model the sequences of control parameters arising in quantum control and shown how quantum control gives rise to a particular reinforcement learning problem for whose optimization policy gradient methods are a natural choice. As a recent and successful variant of policy gradient algorithms, we have adapted the PPO algorithm for our application and introduced the MPPO algorithm. We then went on to show how our general method can be easily combined with physical prior knowledge for two example scenarios and presented numerical results for a range of learning tasks arising in this context. These results showed that our method is able to achieve state-of-the-art performance in different tasks while being able to address problems of discrete and continuous control alike. Additionally, they provided evidence for the hypotheses that machine learning can successfully be employed for the automated optimization of parameters in experiments.

Finally, interesting directions of future work would be to apply the method to a real experiment and evaluate its performance there as well as to develop a set of benchmark problems in quantum control to compare the different already existing algorithms on neutral grounds. It would also be interesting to investigate which other problems of relevance yield reinforcement learning problems similarly structured to the formulation presented in this work. As this work constitutes one of the very first attempts at leveraging state-of-the-art ML techniques for quantum control, there naturally exists a plethora of other viable approaches that might prove highly useful but have not been evaluated thus far.

References

1. August, M., Ni, X.: Using recurrent neural networks to optimize dynamical decoupling for quantum memory. Phys. Rev. A **95**(1), 012335 (2017)
2. Biamonte, J., Wittek, P., Pancotti, N., Rebentrost, P., Wiebe, N., Lloyd, S.: Quantum machine learning. Nature **549**(7671), 195–202 (2017)
3. Bukov, M., Day, A.G., Sels, D., Weinberg, P., Polkovnikov, A., Mehta, P.: Machine learning meets quantum state preparation. the phase diagram of quantum control. arXiv preprint arXiv:1705.00565 (2017)
4. Caneva, T., Calarco, T., Montangero, S.: Chopped random-basis quantum optimization. Phys. Rev. A **84**(2), 022326 (2011)
5. Cho, K., et al.: Learning phrase representations using RNN encoder-decoder for statistical machine translation. arXiv preprint arXiv:1406.1078 (2014)
6. Cohen, C., Tannoudji, B.D., Laloë, F.: Quantum Mechanics, vol. i and ii. Hermann and Wiley, Paris and Hoboken (1977)
7. Doria, P., Calarco, T., Montangero, S.: Optimal control technique for many-body quantum dynamics. Phys. Rev. Lett. **106**, 190501 (2011). https://doi.org/10.1103/PhysRevLett.106.190501
8. Hochreiter, S., Schmidhuber, J.: Long short-term memory. Neural Comput. **9**(8), 1735–1780 (1997)

9. Khaneja, N., Reiss, T., Kehlet, C., Schulte-Herbrüggen, T., Glaser, S.J.: Optimal control of coupled spin dynamics: design of nmr pulse sequences by gradient ascent algorithms. J. Magn. Reson. **172**(2), 296–305 (2005)

10. Kingma, D.P., Ba, J.: Adam: A method for stochastic optimization. arXiv preprint arXiv:1412.6980 (2014)

11. Melnikov, A.A., et al.: Active learning machine learns to create new quantum experiments. In: Proceedings of the National Academy of Sciences, p. 201714936 (2018)

12. Mnih, V., et al.: Asynchronous methods for deep reinforcement learning. In: International Conference on Machine Learning, pp. 1928–1937 (2016)

13. Mnih, V., et al.: Human-level control through deep reinforcement learning. Nature **518**(7540), 529 (2015)

14. Nielsen, M.A., Chuang, I.: Quantum computation and quantum information (2002)

15. Palittapongarnpim, P., Wittek, P., Zahedinejad, E., Vedaie, S., Sanders, B.C.: Learning in quantum control: high-dimensional global optimization for noisy quantum dynamics. Neurocomputing **268**, 116–126 (2017)

16. Quiroz, G., Lidar, D.A.: Optimized dynamical decoupling via genetic algorithms. Phys. Rev. A **88**, 052306 (2013). https://doi.org/10.1103/PhysRevA.88.052306

17. Robbins, H.: Some aspects of the sequential design of experiments. In: Lai, T.L., Siegmund, D. (eds.) Herbert Robbins Selected Papers, pp. 169–177. Springer, Newyork (1985)

18. Sakurai, J.J., Commins, E.D.: Modern Quantum Mechanics, Revised edn. AAPT, College Park (1995)

19. Schollwöck, U.: The density-matrix renormalization group in the age of matrix product states. Ann. Phys. **326**(1), 96–192 (2011)

20. Schulman, J., Levine, S., Abbeel, P., Jordan, M., Moritz, P.: Trust region policy optimization. In: International Conference on Machine Learning, pp. 1889–1897 (2015)

21. Schulman, J., Wolski, F., Dhariwal, P., Radford, A., Klimov, O.: Proximal policy optimization algorithms. arXiv preprint arXiv:1707.06347 (2017)

22. Silver, D., et al.: Mastering chess and Shogi by self-play with a general reinforcement learning algorithm. arXiv preprint arXiv:1712.01815 (2017)

23. Silver, D., et al.: Mastering the game of Go without human knowledge. Nature **550**(7676), 354–359 (2017)

24. Souza, A.M., Álvarez, G.A., Suter, D.: Robust dynamical decoupling for quantum computing and quantum memory. Phys. Rev. Lett. **106**, 240501 (2011). https://doi.org/10.1103/PhysRevLett.106.240501

25. Viola, L., Knill, E., Lloyd, S.: Dynamical decoupling of open quantum systems. Phys. Rev. Lett. **82**, 2417–2421 (1999). https://doi.org/10.1103/PhysRevLett.82.2417

26. Wigley, P.B., et al.: Fast machine-learning online optimization of ultra-cold-atom experiments. Sci. Rep. **6**, 25890 (2016)

27. Williams, R.J.: Simple statistical gradient-following algorithms for connectionist reinforcement learning. In: Sutton, R.S. (ed.) Reinforcement Learning. SECS, vol. 173, pp. 5–32. Springer, Boston (1992). https://doi.org/10.1007/978-1-4615-3618-5_2

Towards Prediction of Turbulent Flows at High Reynolds Numbers Using High Performance Computing Data and Deep Learning

Mathis Bode[1] , Michael Gauding[2](✉) , Jens Henrik Göbbert[3] ,
Baohao Liao[1] , Jenia Jitsev[3] , and Heinz Pitsch[1]

[1] Institute for Combustion Technology, RWTH Aachen University,
Templergraben 64, 52062 Aachen, Germany
{m.bode,h.pitsch}@itv.rwth-aachen.de
[2] CORIA – CNRS UMR 6614, Saint Etienne du Rouvray, France
michael.gauding@coria.fr
[3] Jülich Supercomputing Centre, FZ Jülich,
Wilhelm-Johnen-Straße, 52425 Jülich, Germany
{j.goebbert,j.jitsev}@fz-juelich.de

Abstract. In this paper, deep learning (DL) methods are evaluated in the context of turbulent flows. Various generative adversarial networks (GANs) are discussed with respect to their suitability for understanding and modeling turbulence. Wasserstein GANs (WGANs) are then chosen to generate small-scale turbulence. Highly resolved direct numerical simulation (DNS) turbulent data is used for training the WGANs and the effect of network parameters, such as learning rate and loss function, is studied. Qualitatively good agreement between DNS input data and generated turbulent structures is shown. A quantitative statistical assessment of the predicted turbulent fields is performed.

Keywords: Turbulence · High Reynolds number · Deep learning
Wasserstein generative adversarial networks
Direct numerical simulation

1 Introduction

The turbulent motion of fluid flows is a complex, strongly non-linear, multi-scale phenomenon, which poses some of the most difficult and fundamental problems in classical physics. Turbulent flows are characterized by random spatio-temporal fluctuations over a wide range of scales. The general challenge of turbulence research is to predict the statistics of these fluctuating velocity and scalar fields. A precise prediction of these statistical properties of turbulence would be of practical importance for a wide field of applications ranging from geophysics to combustion science.

© Springer Nature Switzerland AG 2018
R. Yokota et al. (Eds.): ISC 2018 Workshops, LNCS 11203, pp. 614–623, 2018.
https://doi.org/10.1007/978-3-030-02465-9_44

Research in the field of turbulence has mostly focused on a statistical description in the sense of Kolmogorov's scaling theory. The theory proposed by Kolmogorov [10,11] (known as K41 in literature) hypothesizes that for sufficiently large Reynolds numbers, small-scale motions are statistically independent from the large scales. While the large scales depend on the boundary or initial conditions, the smallest scales should be statistically universal and feature certain symmetries that are recovered in a statistical sense. Following Kolmogorov's theory, the small scales can be uniquely described by simple parameters, such as the kinematic viscosity ν of the fluid and the mean dissipation rate $\langle \varepsilon \rangle$ (angular brackets denote ensemble-averaging). If the notion of small-scale universality was strictly valid, then there would be realistic hope for a statistical theory for turbulent flows. However, numerous experimental and numerical studies have reported a substantial deviation from Kolmogorov's classical K41 prediction [3,15], which is mostly due to internal intermittency. The consequence of internal intermittency is the break-down of small-scale universality, which dramatically complicates theoretical approaches from first principles.

In this work, a novel research route based on the method of deep learning (DL) is used to approach the challenge of turbulence modeling. In recent years, DL was improved substantially and has proven to be useful in a large variety of different fields, ranging from computer science to life science. However, to the knowledge of the authors, the application of DL to predict statistical behavior of small-scale turbulence is still new and many related issues are still unsolved. As described and despite its stochastic nature, turbulence exhibits certain coherent structures and statistical symmetries that are traceable by deep learning techniques. While analytical solutions exist for low-order correlation functions, for higher orders there is no such tractable solution available so far. Therefore, DL techniques are a promising approach to predict statistics of small-scale turbulence and an attempt to predict structures of turbulence is given here. Several DL networks from literature are tested by training them with high-fidelity direct numerical simulation (DNS) data of turbulence. The predicted turbulence data is evaluated by qualitative and quantitative comparisons with the original data and the statistics of the original data, respectively. As one challenge in the application of DL is to find optimal network architectures and hyperparameters, several combinations were evaluated for this work.

The remainder of this paper is organized as follows. In Sect. 2, future chances and challenges of DL in the context of turbulence are summarized. Then, the used DNS data base is described in Sect. 3. Section 4 presents results in terms of predicted turbulent structures and discusses the sensitivity of the results with respect to network parameters, such as learning rate and loss function. The paper finishes with conclusions in Sect. 5.

2   Deep Learning and Turbulence

The Reynolds number is the most important parameter for characterizing turbulent flows. It can be defined as the ratio of the size of the large vortices to the size of the smallest vorticies and can be understood as a measure for the scale separation [13]. Thus, it also plays a central role in any attempt to model turbulence accurately and must be considered in the DL network. As the application of DL for predicting turbulence is new, the following steps need to be taken on the way to find a turbulence model based on DL:

1. **A posteriori analysis with fixed Reynolds number:** The ability of certain network types to predict statistics of turbulence needs to be evaluated. Therefore, the Reynolds number should be fixed and unsupervised learning can be performed. The accuracy of the trained DL networks can be evaluated by comparison with the original data and corresponding statistics. The ability to predict statistics for a given Reynolds number is essential for an improved understanding of universality and intermittency as well as for the development of models.

2. **A posteriori analysis with flexible Reynolds numbers:** As a next step, DL should be used with flexible Reynolds numbers. A combination of unsupervised and supervised DL can be employed to improve the understanding of the universality of turbulence. For example, it will be interesting to see whether a DL network, which was trained within a certain range of Reynolds numbers, is able to also predict turbulent structures for higher Reynolds numbers correctly.

3. **A priori analysis:** Also, DL can be used to identify characteristic structures of the turbulent dissipation field by a pattern recognition technique. Relevant quantities under consideration should be the moments of the dissipation M_n, the kinetic energy, and two-point correlation functions or structure functions of the velocity field.

4. **Modeling of small-scale turbulence:** For many fields in turbulence research, small-scale quantities are not known, either due to modeling of the small scales in numerical approaches or due to lack of resolution in experimental techniques. For reduced order models of turbulence, it is required to be able to predict statistics of the dissipation without knowing the actual dissipation field. The goal is to develop a DL network that is able to predict statistics of the fine-scale motion by knowing the exact velocity field from DNS or a coarse-grained velocity field only. The reliability of the neural network can be statistically evaluated against data from DNS, keeping in mind that neural networks can fail under certain conditions.

3   DNS Data Base

The application of DL is only possible if a sufficiently large and accurate data base exists. In recent years, a comprehensive data base of DNSs has been created based on some of the world's largest turbulence simulations [4–6,12] using high performance computing (HPC). The data base contains different flow setups, such as forced homogeneous isotropic turbulence as well as free shear flows, and the data sets are freely available from the corresponding author upon request. DNS solves the governing equations of turbulence (namely the Navier-Stokes equations) numerically for all relevant scales, without relying on any turbulence models. Due to internal intermittency, turbulent flows reveal a hierarchy of viscous cut-off scales [2] and the computation of higher-order statistics of small-scale quantities requires a spatial resolution that may be finer than the Kolmogorov length scale. DNS has become an indispensable tool in the field of turbulence research as it provides accurate access to three-dimensional (3-D) fields under controlled conditions.

Characteristic properties of the DNSs are listed in Table 1. N denotes the number of grid points, Re_λ is the Reynolds number based on the Taylor microscale, κ_{max} is the largest resolved wave-number, η is the Kolmogorov length scale, $\langle \varepsilon \rangle$ is the mean energy dissipation. M denotes the number of statistically independent boxes being available.

Table 1. Characteristic parameters of the DNS data base. The DNS data base is used to train and test the neural network.

	S	R0	R1	R2	R3	R4	R5	R6
N	$1024 \times 512 \times 512$	512^3	1024^3	1024^3	2048^3	2048^3	4096^3	4096^3
Re_λ	≈ 50	88	119	184	215	331	529	754
ν	-	0.01	0.0055	0.0025	0.0019	0.0010	0.00048	0.00027
$\kappa_{max}\eta$	>2.5	3.93	4.99	2.93	4.41	2.53	2.95	1.60
M	1	189	62	61	10	10	10	11

Training of the DL is performed based on a passive scalar ϕ which is transported by an advection-diffusion equation. The passive scalar represents the dynamical motion of turbulence and its prediction by DL is of fundamental relevance for the modeling of turbulence. Figure 1 displays a visualization of the instantaneous scalar ϕ and the scalar dissipation rate χ for case R5. The scalar dissipation rate is defined as

$$\chi = 2D \left(\nabla \phi \right)^2 \tag{1}$$

and signifies the destruction of scalar fluctuations due to molecular diffusivity D. The scalar field reveals distinct coherent regions of roughly constant scalar values. The size of these regions is of the order of the scalar integral length scale and they are separated by sharp highly convoluted boundaries. At these boundaries, the scalar dissipation rate attains large values. As a consequence, the scalar dissipation rate is characterized by filamented structures representing a high level of intermittency.

4   Results

A first step towards the development of universal turbulent models based on DL is to study the ability of networks to generate small-scale turbulent structures. For that, slice-wise training of certain DL networks with the DNS data at fixed Reynolds number was performed. More precisely, the 3-D scalar fields ϕ of the DNS data are cut into 2-D slices, which are statistically similar. The distance

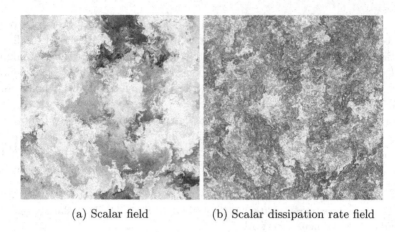

(a) Scalar field   (b) Scalar dissipation rate field

Fig. 1. Visualization of the instantaneous fields of the scalar ϕ and the scalar dissipation rate χ for case R5.

between two adjacent slices is chosen large enough to ensure that structures are uncorrelated. The 2-D slices are used as input for the training of the network, which is able to reproduce these structures as output in the end. For this reproduction of turbulent structures, 100 random values following a normal Gaussian distribution with zero-mean and a standard deviation, which is linearly mapped between 0 and 1 by the local Reynolds number, are considered as input data. The implementation was done using Keras/TensorFlow/Horovod and the training was performed on JURECA, a supercomputer at JSC, FZ Jülich featuring two NVIDIA Tesla K80 GPUs with a dual-GPU design on each used computing node.

More precisely, for this work, generative adversarial networks (GAN) [7], which use an adversarial game between generator and discriminator to optimize the network, were evaluated regarding their suitability to generate small-scale turbulence. Furthermore, Wasserstein GANs (WGANs) [1] featuring advantages in terms of stability and good interpretability of the learning curve as well as u-net [14], consisting of a contracting path to capture context and a symmetric expanding path that enables precise localization, were tried.

A visualization of one arbitrary input slice cut from the DNS data and one arbitrary output slice predicted by the DL networks for case S is shown in Fig. 2. The WGAN gives the best results and is able to reproduce coherent motions and small-scale structures, which are characteristic for fluid turbulence. GAN and u-net have problems especially to reproduce regions without any fluctuations and always feature some noise. Due to these results, the WGAN was tested in more detail and quantitative results based on statistics in the original and predicted data are presented in the following.

As briefly mentioned in the beginning, one main challenge in the context of DL is to find suitable network architectures and hyperparameters resulting in an accurate solution. For the considered turbulence, a WGAN made of four layers for the discriminator and three layers for the generator gave good results. Each discriminator-layer contained a convolution (Conv2D, kernel_size = 3, striding = 2 or 1), an activation (LeakyReLU, alpha = 0.2), and a dropout (Dropout). Partly,

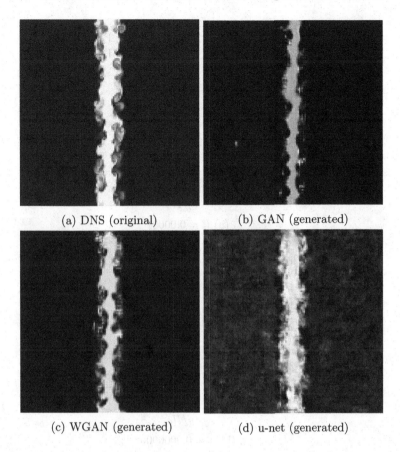

(a) DNS (original)   (b) GAN (generated)

(c) WGAN (generated)   (d) u-net (generated)

Fig. 2. Comparison of an arbitrary DNS data slice of the passive scalar ϕ and comparison with data generated by various DL networks.

zero-padding (ZeroPadding), batch normalization (BatchNormalization, momentum $= 0.8$), and flattening (Flatten) were employed. Each generator-layer used a convolution (Conv2D, kernel_size $= 4$) and batch normalization (BatchNormalization(momentum $= 0.8$) in combination with either tanh- or relu-activation.

A more rigorous quantitative analysis of the generated small-scale turbulence is shown in Figs. 3 and 4. It gives the resulting normalized mean $(\langle\phi\rangle^*)$ and variance profile $(\langle\phi'^2\rangle^*)$ of the scalar for different learning rates l_r as function of the non-dimensional cross-stream direction y/H_0. The maximum values are normalized to 1, H_0 is the initial jet width, and the asterisk indicates a normalized quantity. Furthermore, the scalar fluctuation is defined as $\phi' = \phi - \langle\phi\rangle$. It can be seen that the network is able to generate structures with the correct statistical properties as long as a proper learning rate is chosen. A too small value for the learning rate leads to non-converged results, while a too high value gives noise.

Finally, the DL approach is evaluated by means of two-point statistics. Turbulence is a non-local, multi-scale problem that is characterized by a transfer of

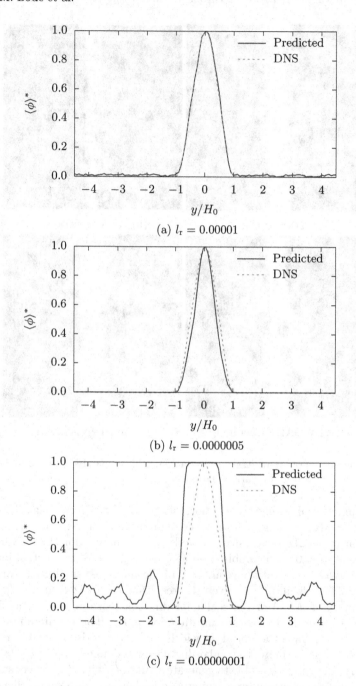

(a) $l_{\mathrm{r}} = 0.00001$

(b) $l_{\mathrm{r}} = 0.0000005$

(c) $l_{\mathrm{r}} = 0.00000001$

Fig. 3. Comparison of the normalized scalar mean profile $\langle\phi\rangle^*$ for case S for different learning rates l_{r} plotted as function of the non-dimensional cross-stream direction y/H_0.

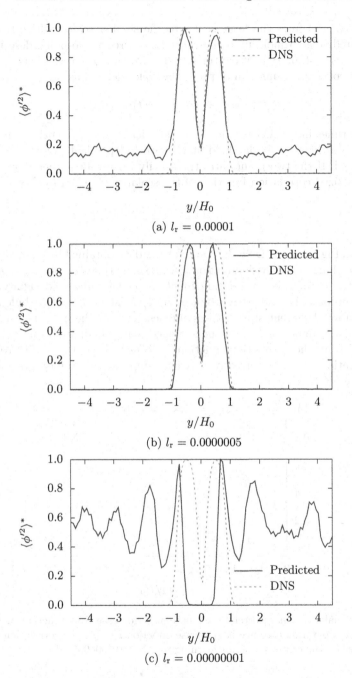

(a) $l_r = 0.00001$

(b) $l_r = 0.0000005$

(c) $l_r = 0.00000001$

Fig. 4. Comparison of the normalized scalar variance $\langle \phi'^2 \rangle^*$ for case S for different learning rates l_r as function of the non-dimensional cross-stream direction y/H_0.

turbulent energy from the large scales to the smaller scales, where the energy is dissipated due to molecular viscosity. Therefore, a two-point description of turbulence is customary as it captures both local and non-local phenomena. The two-point correlation function of the scalar field, defined as

$$f_\phi(\underline{r}; \underline{x}, t) = \langle \phi'(\underline{x} + \underline{r}; t)\phi'(\underline{x}; t) \rangle \tag{2}$$

with underlines indicating vectors, is a statistical quantity of prime importance and measures how the scalar field at the two independent points $\underline{x} + \underline{r}$ and $\underline{x}$ is correlated. If the two points are statistically independent then $f(\underline{r}; \underline{x}, t) = 0$. The normalized correlation function of the scalar field, given by

$$f_\phi^*(\underline{r}; \underline{x}, t) = \frac{\langle \phi'(\underline{x} + \underline{r}; t)\phi'(\underline{x}; t) \rangle}{\langle \phi'^2 \rangle}, \tag{3}$$

is shown in Fig. 5 for the DNS data and for the data obtained by DL evaluated at the center-plane in spanwise direction z for a single timestep. A good agreement between the normalized correlation functions can be observed signifying that the DL approach is able to reproduce the local structure of turbulence with high accuracy. Different statistical quantities, such as the integral length scale l_t, the scalar variance $\langle \phi'^2 \rangle$, and the averaged scalar dissipation rate $\langle \chi \rangle$, can be computed from the correlation function. In other words, the ability to predict the correlation function correctly is a first step towards building a model for turbulence (cf. [9]).

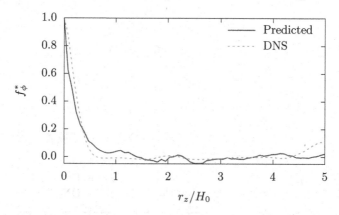

Fig. 5. Normalized scalar correlation function f_ϕ^* for case S as function of the non-dimensional separation distance in spanwise direction r_z/H_0. The correlation function is computed at the center-plane for learning rate $l_r = 0.0000005$.

5   Conclusions

In this work, DL is applied to turbulent fields obtained from DNS. The effect of various network and training parameters, such as learning rate and loss function, are discussed. Using WGANs, it was possible to generate small-scale turbulence which features the same structures as observed in DNS data. A comparison of the statistics evaluated on the original and predicted data showed promising agreement. This is an important first step towards the prediction of turbulent flows at various Reynolds numbers. As a next step, the ability of the trained network to generate turbulent structures for various given Reynolds numbers will be evaluated.

Acknowledgment. The authors gratefully acknowledge the computing time granted for the project JHPC55 by the JARA-HPC Vergabegremium and provided on the JARA-HPC Partition part of the supercomputer JURECA at Forschungszentrum Jülich. Also, the computing time granted for the projects HFG00/HFG02 on the super-computer JUQUEEN [8] at Forschungszentrum Jülich is acknowledged. MG acknowledges financial support by Labex EMC3, under the grant VAVIDEN.

References

1. Arjovsky, M., Chintala, S., Bottou, L.: Wasserstein GAN. arXiv:1701.07875v3 (2017)
2. Boschung, J., Hennig, F., Gauding, M., Pitsch, H., Peters, N.: Generalised higher-order kolmogorov scales. J. Fluid Mech. **794**, 233–251 (2016)
3. Frisch, U.: Turbulence - The Legacy of A.N. Kolmogorov. Cambridge University Press, Cambridge (1995)
4. Gauding, M., Danaila, L., Varea, E.: High-order structure functions for passive scalar fed by a mean gradient. Int. J. Heat Fluid Flow **67**, 86–93 (2017)
5. Gauding, M., Goebbert, J.H., Hasse, C., Peters, N.: Line segments in homogeneous scalar turbulence. Phys. Fluids **27**(9), 095102 (2015)
6. Gauding, M., Wick, A., Peters, N., Pitsch, H.: Generalized scale-by-scale energy budget equations for large-eddy simulations of scalar turbulence at various Schmidt numbers. J. Turbul. **15**, 857–882 (2013)
7. Goodfellow, I.J., et al.: Generative adversarial networks. arXiv:1406.2661 (2014)
8. Jülich Supercomputing Centre: JUQUEEN: IBM Blue Gene/Q supercomputer system at the Jülich supercomputing centre. J. Large-Scale Res. Facil. **1** (2015)
9. von Karman, T., Howarth, L.: On the statistical theory of isotropic turbulence. Proc. R. Soc. Lond. A: Math. Phys. Eng. Sci. **164**(917), 192–215 (1938)
10. Kolmogorov, A.N.: Dissipation of energy in locally isotropic turbulence. Dokl. Akad. Nauk SSSR **32**, 16–18 (1941)
11. Kolmogorov, A.N.: The local structure of turbulence in incompressible viscous fluid for very large Reynolds numbers. Dokl. Akad. Nauk SSSR **30**, 299–303 (1941)
12. Peters, N., Boschung, J., Gauding, M., Goebbert, J.H., Hill, R.J., Pitsch, H.: Higher-order dissipation in the theory of homogeneous isotropic turbulence. J. Fluid Mech. **803**, 250–274 (2016)
13. Pope, S.B.: Turbulent Flows. Cambridge University Press, Cambridge (2000)
14. Ronneberger, O., Fischer, P., Brox, T.: U-Net: convolutional networks for biomedical image segmentation. arXiv:1505.04597 (2015)
15. Sreenivasan, K.R.: The passive scalar spectrum and the Obukhov-Corrsin constant. Phys. Fluids **8**, 189 (1996)

Third Workshop for Open Source Supercomputing (OpenSuCo 2018)

Using a Graph Visualization Tool for Parallel Program Dynamic Visualization and Communication Analysis

Denise Stringhini$^{(\boxtimes)}$, Pedro Spoljaric Gomes, and Alvaro Fazenda

Universidade Federal de Sao Paulo, Sao Paulo, Brazil
dstringhini@unifesp.br

Abstract. Parallel program visualization and performance analysis tools have a high cost of development. As a consequence, there are many of these tools that are proprietary what makes difficult their adoption by the general community. This work introduces the use of general purpose open software for visualization and characterization of parallel programs. In particular, the use of an open graph visualization tool is presented as a case study for the dynamic communication characterization of a NAS parallel benchmark. The results show that a general purpose open graph tool could be used to analyze some important aspects related to the communication of parallel message passing programs.

1 Introduction

Parallel performance analysis tools have an important role guiding programmers to tune parallel programs in order to identify performance bottlenecks and potential improvement spots. Performance analysis allows the study of communication of processes and threads in different levels of hierarchy, memory contention, communication time and volume, among other aspects introduced by parallelism. These analysis are usually supported by trace file generators and visualization tools. Trace files contain the log of different types of events, along with their timestamps and types. They usually also record related information such as which entity generated the event or if it is a communication event, a memory access or a processor counter, among others. Trace files are usually huge, easily reaching some gigabytes of data [1]. Such information overload requires tools to facilitate the organization and interpretation of data. These tools usually relies on some kind of visual and statistical support.

Parallel program visualization enables to display program behavior at different levels of detail. The performance data obtained from a parallel program execution can be analyzed with a collection of different performance views. Besides, the statistical characterization of communication patterns of parallel programs has been used to better understand the behavior of such programs as well as to predict performance of large scale applications. A proper understanding of communication behavior of parallel applications may support the design of better

© Springer Nature Switzerland AG 2018
R. Yokota et al. (Eds.): ISC 2018 Workshops, LNCS 11203, pp. 627–636, 2018.
https://doi.org/10.1007/978-3-030-02465-9_45

communication subsystems as well as to help application developers to maximize their application performance on a target architecture [2]. Usually, the methodology to characterize communication patterns resides in to dynamically record communication events and statistically analyze and organize those data post-mortem. The characterization data are commonly presented through bar graphs or tables. An example of the characterization of communication patterns to improve the performance of MPI [3] programs could be found in [4].

The present work introduces the use of general purpose open software for visualization and characterization of parallel programs. As in [5], we also claim that this approach avoids the high costs of building totally new visualization systems. This work exposes the potential of the technique while we continue to develop more specific ways to apply it to parallel systems by exploring different types of information and temporal behavior. In our first attempt to use a general purpose open tool for visualization and analysis of parallel programs, we chose to work with a graph visualization tool called Gephi [6]. Along with Gephi, we adopted EZTrace [7] to generate the trace information used to build the programs' graphs.

Modeling parallel programs as graphs allows the analysis of different communication attributes and helps to characterize the communication patterns of parallel applications. The characterization usually explores three attributes of communication: spatial distribution, volume of data and average number of messages. Another interesting feature, highlighted in this work, is the dynamic post-mortem visualization of the communication recorded during the parallel program execution. After extract temporal information from the trace file it is possible to create graph dynamic visualizations. Enabling these step-by-step visualizations help to identify the global dynamic behavior of the communication patterns during the execution.

In order to expose the potential of the technique, this work presents a visual characterization of a NAS Parallel Benchmark. While in a previous work [8] we focused on some complex networks metrics, the present work highlights the potentials of dynamic visualization.

2   Related Work

Parallel program visualization enables to display program behavior at different levels of detail. Usually, the performance data obtained from a parallel program execution and recorded in a trace file can be analyzed with a collection of different performance views.

An example of such kind of tool is the Vampir performance analysis tool [9]. Vampir is a parallel program visualization tool that provides a framework for program analysis, which enables developers to display program behavior at any level of detail. Performance data obtained from a parallel program execution can be analyzed with a collection of different performance views. Vampir has a complete tool chain that allows a detailed performance analysis, but this comes with a price, since it is necessary to purchase a license to use it without time limits.

There are some recent interesting work on parallel visualization of message passing processes. Most of them are concerned with visualization of future exascale applications like the ones presented in [10] and [11]. The present work uses a graph platform capable of visualize thousands of nodes, what makes it also suitable for visualization of exascale applications.

The circular hierarchies presented in [10] is another way to evaluate parallel programs and could be related to Vampir as another potential view. The technique allows the visualization of large scale parallel programs as the visualization shows communication patterns and allows developers to correlate those with arbitrary performance metrics. This work is related to the present one in the sense that it allows the visualization of large parallel programs along with communication patterns. Nevertheless, it is a specific view focused only in MPI parallel programs while this paper stands for the use of general purpose and open source software tools, where the cost and effort to build it could be aimed to different areas. Further, the possibility of customize general purpose existent tools is also an advantageous pursued feature, since could grant the development of some desirable components intended for express parallelism.

Other recent effort in building a specific parallel program visualization tool is the CommGramm [11]. The tool generates a curve similar to an electrocardiogram to represent the dynamics of communication patterns over time. The curve represents the amount of variance corresponding to the degree of changes of communication patterns: a flat section means that the communication pattern is constant, while a highly wavy section indicates that communication pattern is changing greatly. The tool could help to identify the points of massive message exchange during the execution of a parallel program. Whereas it is a specific tool for analyze parallel programs, its main inspiration comes from a medical analysis tool, which is consistent to this work in the sense that uses an existing type of analysis for another purpose.

We also highlight the work presented in [5] considering the use of an existing tool to analyze and visualize parallel programs. The authors describe how to use a scientific visualization tool to evaluate MPI calls in a parallel program. They view such an approach that can leverage existing systems as paramount. Further, their findings demonstrate that linking these systems together can be done in a straightforward way, requiring only modest effort and yielding significant benefit. The present work has the same vision although it uses a completely different approach for visualization.

There exists some powerful open source tools like Paraver [12]. It is a traditional performance visualization and analysis tool based on traces that can be used to analyze any information that is expressed on its input trace format [13]. Although such tools are very powerful, they require a huge effort to develop and they are specific to parallel program performance analysis. The present work is an attempt to explore existing and general purpose open source tools with minimum effort providing different approaches for performance analysis. The general purpose tools could be used to complement the traditional analysis.

3 Methodology

The proposed methodology is presented in two phases: graph building and graph visualization. In the graph building phase first the communication data are collected from a trace file generator. Then the graph is built in a textual format considering the communicating nodes and some communication attributes. In the graph visualization phase, the communication graph is loaded into a graph visualization tool that allows different layouts, the use of filters to visualize subgraphs as well as the access to interesting complex networks metrics. The tools used in this work are EZTrace [7] as the trace file generator and the *Gephi* graph visualization tool [6] to visualize and analyze the communication graph. The methodology is detailed in the rest of this section.

3.1 Graph Building

Graphs become increasingly important in modeling complicated structures, such as circuits, images, chemical compounds, protein structures, biological networks, social networks, the Web, workflows, and XML documents. Among the various kinds of graph patterns, frequent substructures are the very basic patterns that can be discovered in a collection of graphs. They are useful for characterizing graph sets, discriminating different groups of graphs, classifying and clustering graphs, building graph indexes, and facilitating similarity search in graph databases [14]. The research in graph mining and graph visualization is producing a large collection of techniques and tools which could be useful in a variety of research areas. This section explains how a parallel message passing program can be modeled as a graph of communicating processes.

A graph G, is a pair of sets (V, E), where V is a finite set of vertices and E is a set of edges, each edge connecting a pair of vertices. In directed graphs (digraphs), each edge has a direction, self-loops are allowed. In undirected graphs, each edge is an unordered pair of vertices, thus the adjacency is symmetric. In weighted graphs, each edge has an associated weight, which is a value assigned to the edge.

A large parallel program consists of hundreds or thousands of distributed processes. These processes could be naturally modeled as the vertices of a graph. In order to execute a parallel algorithm the processes have to exchange messages, which creates connections or links between pairs of processes. These communication operations could be modeled as the edges of a graph. The number or the volume of messages exchanged could be assigned to the edges as their weight. Considering these characteristics it is straightforward to think in a parallel program as a graph whose attributes could characterize its communication patterns.

The methodology and tools used in this work are described bellow.

3.2 Data Collection

Different trace file generators could be used in order to extract information about the execution of a parallel program. Besides, there are some ways to instrument a program in order to generate data about specific events. This works' approach adopt EZTrace [7], a generic framework for performance analysis. It uses a two phase mechanism based on plugins for tracing applications. It allows to select the type of events as well as the target library. For example, in this work only MPI events were selected and recorded.

EZTrace also supports the conversion of the generated trace files to a more readable format called Pajé [15], also used in this work. We developed a *trace to graph converter* to read Pajé trace information and generate a textual representation for the communication graph. Among the data collected from the Pajé file are the processing nodes, the communication events between them (the edges), and the timestamp of each communication event. In addition to provide an execution trace file, EZTrace also produces a statistic file used in this work to collect some communication attributes, like the time spent in MPI communication routines.

3.3   Graph Textual Representation

Several graph formats could be used for textual representation: GEXF, GDF, GML, GraphML, CSV, among others [16]. In this work the GEXF format was used since it is XML based, being more flexible and providing more features than the others. GEXF (Graph Exchange XML Format) is a language for describing complex networks structures, their associated data and dynamics. The latter feature is the main reason GEXF was chosen, since it permits the dynamic visualization of graphs in Gephi.

The overall process could be visualized in Fig. 1.

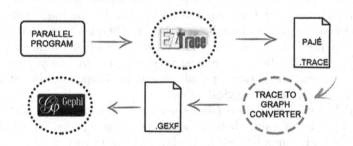

Fig. 1. Overall process to graph visualization

3.4   Graph Visualization and Analysis

Gephi is an open source network exploration and manipulation software. Developed modules can import, visualize, spatialize, filter, manipulate and export all types of networks.

Layout algorithms set the graph shape which is the most essential operation. Graphs are usually laid out with "force-based" algorithms. They follow a simple principle: linked nodes attract each other and non-linked nodes are pushed apart. The Gephi tutorial, which could be found in [16], summarizes the layout choices, for example: OpenOrd (emphasis in divisions), ForceAtlas, Yifan Hu, Fruchterman-Reingold (emphasis in complementarities), and others. The Yifan Hu layout [17], for example, has good results for large undirected graphs and could provide good visualizations for parallel programs as will be presented in this paper.

4   Case Study: NAS Parallel Benchmark

This section presents the methodology application and some results on characterizing parallel programs through graph visualization and complex networks metrics. The NAS parallel benchmarks [18] were chosen for its large use for testing the capabilities of parallel computers and parallelization tools. As the benchmarks are usually already optimized for better performance, the goal is not to search for optimization spots. Instead, the intention is to highlight some of their main characteristics through dynamic graph visualization and analysis.

4.1   Algorithm Topology

The graph representation of a parallel program could create a visual signature based on its logical topology. This is more effective with algorithms that presents some level of regularity in its communication patterns.

The NAS Parallel Benchmarks (NPB) [18] are well-known problems for testing the capabilities of parallel computers and parallelization tools. They exhibit mostly fine-grain exploitable parallelism and are almost all iterative, requiring multiple data exchanges between processes within each iteration. The Scalar Penta-diagonal (SP) solve a discretized version of the unsteady, compressible Navier-Stokes equations in three spatial dimensions. It operates on a structured discretization mesh that is a logical cube.

The SP-MZ implementation follows a stencil communication pattern with exchange of boundary values between zones taking place after each time step. Solution values at points one mesh spacing away from each vertical zone face are copied to the coincident boundary points of the neighboring zone [18]. The problem is periodic in the two horizontal directions (x and y), so donor point values at the extreme sides of the mesh system are copied to boundary points at the opposite ends of the system. This property characterizes a toroidal system and was captured by Yifan Hu [17] graph layout algorithm as demonstrated in Fig. 2.

Figure 2 presents the SP-MZ complete toroidal topology. The layout algorithm was able to capture the communication pattern and draw a figure that represents all point-to-point communications that happened during the execution. Additionally it is possible to observe that the nodes have different sizes

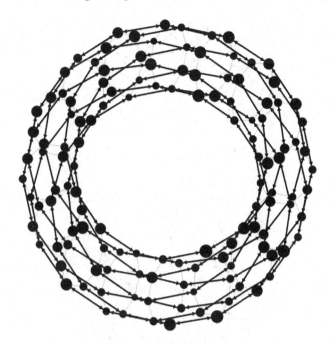

Fig. 2. SP-MZ with 128 processes

as they were configured to reflect the time spent in receive MPI routines. Also, the edges have different thickness, representing different volumes of messages exchanged between nodes. Unfortunately, given the limitations of size and scale, the little rings that connects the nodes are almost imperceptible. Nevertheless, these features illustrate how attributes could be used to transmit some useful information through visualization.

The topology provides a visual signature that is helpful to analyze algorithms where the communication pattern is fixed, like meshes, rings, centralized architectures, among others. In [8] the SP-MZ was confronted with BT-MZ, which presents a more irregular topology.

4.2   Dynamic Communication Behavior

Figure 3 presents three selected snapshots of the SP-MZ post-mortem execution. These snapshots were chosen to highlight some specific moments of the total execution, since the visualizations reproduces all communication events recorded from the trace file. From the top, the first one indicates a moment of local processing, since there are no communication edges. The second denotes a communication phase where processes are organized in sixteen groups of eight processes each and where the communication adopts a local ring pattern. The third presents a different moment where these groups exchange messages with

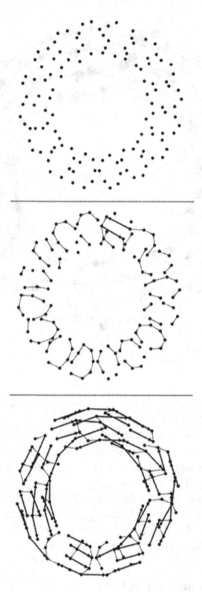

Fig. 3. Some dynamic phases of SP-MZ with 128 processes

neighbor groups. During the execution, it was possible to observe the repetition or the periodicity of these phases in regular intervals.

This case study shows the potential of using an existing graph visualization tool for parallel program analysis and characterization. The benefits include the visualization of communications phases that could help in the understanding of program behavior. This could lead to the identification of some possible bottlenecks or points of failure, since Gephi provides a timeline that allows to identify longer phases. It is possible, for example, to identify patterns were the program execution spends more time, indicating potential points of performance improvement.

5 Conclusion

This paper presented an effort to use a general purpose graph visualization tool as a parallel program analysis tool. A simple converter was built to create graphs from trace files. The graph generated from the SP-MZ NAS parallel benchmark was loaded to Gephi which made possible the post-mortem visualization of its execution in terms of communication. It was possible to identify visually at least three different communication phases as well as the complete topology pattern. Future short term work includes to demonstrate with more details how to use the graph visualization to improve communication in real applications. Besides visualization, as future work we intend to explore the automatic detection of such patterns in order to better measure the time spent in each of them. Future work also includes the exploration of other features of graph visualization and complex networks in order to better characterize parallel applications communication and performance.

References

1. Lee, C.W., Mendes, C.L., Kalé, L.V.: Towards scalable performance analysis and visualization through data reduction. In: 2008 IEEE International Symposium on Parallel and Distributed Processing, pp. 1–8 (2008)
2. Zamani, R., Afsahi, A.: Communication characteristics of message-passing scientific and engineering applications. In: Zheng, S.Q. (ed.) Proceedings of IASTED PDCS, Phoenix, AZ, USA, pp. 644–649. IASTED/ACTA Press, November 2005
3. Snir, M., Otto, S., Huss-Lederman, S., Walker, D., Dongarra, J.: The MPI Core. MPI-The Complete Reference, vol. 1, 2nd edn. MIT Press, Cambridge (1998)
4. Mercier, G., Clet-Ortega, J.: Towards an efficient process placement policy for MPI applications in multicore environments. In: Ropo, M., Westerholm, J., Dongarra, J. (eds.) EuroPVM/MPI 2009. LNCS, vol. 5759, pp. 104–115. Springer, Heidelberg (2009). https://doi.org/10.1007/978-3-642-03770-2_17
5. Huck, K.A., Potter, K., Jacobsen, D.W., Childs, H., Malony, A.D.: Linking performance data into scientific visualization tools. In: Proceedings of the First Workshop on Visual Performance Analysis, ser. VPA 2014, Piscataway, NJ, USA, pp. 50–57. IEEE Press (2014)
6. Bastian, M., Heymann, S., Jacomy, M.: Gephi: an open source software for exploring and manipulating networks. In: Proceedings of International AAAI Conference on Weblogs and Social Media, San Jose, CA, USA, May 2009
7. Trahay, F., Rué, F., Faverge, M., Ishikawa, Y., Namyst, R., Dongarra, J.: EZTrace: a generic framework for performance analysis. In: Proceedings of CCGRID. IEEE, Newport Beach, May 2011
8. Stringhini, D., Fazenda, A.: Characterizing communication patterns of parallel programs through graph visualization and analysis. In: Hunold, S., et al. (eds.) Euro-Par 2015. LNCS, vol. 9523, pp. 565–576. Springer, Cham (2015). https://doi.org/10.1007/978-3-319-27308-2_46

9. Knüpfer, A., et al.: The vampir performance analysis tool-set. In: Resch, M., Keller, R., Himmler, V., Krammer, B., Schulz, A. (eds.) Parallel Tools Workshop, pp. 139–155. Springer, Heidelberg (2008). https://doi.org/10.1007/978-3-540-68564-7_9

10. Schmitt, F., Dietrich, R., Kuß, R., Doleschal, J., Knüpfer, A.: Visualization of performance data for MPI applications using circular hierarchies. In: Proceedings of the First Workshop on Visual Performance Analysis, VPA 2014, New Orleans, Louisiana, USA, pp. 1–8, 16–21 November 2014. https://doi.org/10.1109/VPA. 2014.5

11. Wu, J., Zeng, J., Yu, H., Kenny, J.P.: Commgram: A new visual analytics tool for large communication trace data. In: Proceedings of the First Workshop on Visual Performance Analysis, VPA 2014. Piscataway, NJ, USA, pp. 28–35. IEEE Press (2014). https://doi.org/10.1109/VPA.2014.8

12. Pillet, V., Labarta, J., Cortes, T., Girona, S.: PARAVER: A tool to visualize and analyze parallel code. In: Proceedings of WoTUG-18: Transputer and Occam Developments, vol. 44, no. 1, pp. 17–31. IOS Press (1995)

13. PARAVER: a flexible performance analysis tool. https://tools.bsc.es/paraver

14. Han, J., Kamber, M.: Data Mining: Concepts and Techniques. Morgan Kaufmann Publishers Inc., San Francisco (2000)

15. de Kergommeaux, J.C., de Oliveira Stein, B.: Pajé: an extensible environment for visualizing multi-threaded programs executions. In: Bode, A., Ludwig, T., Karl, W., Wismüller, R. (eds.) Euro-Par 2000. LNCS, vol. 1900, pp. 133–140. Springer, Heidelberg (2000). https://doi.org/10.1007/3-540-44520-X_17. http://dl.acm.org/citation.cfm?id=646665.699423

16. The Gephi website. http://www.gephi.org/

17. Hu, Y.F.: Efficient and high quality force-directed graph drawing. Mathematica J. 10(1), 37–71 (2005)

18. Baily, D., et al.: The NAS parallel benchmarks. RNR-94-007.pdf, March 1994. http://www.nas.nasa.gov/assets/pdf/techreports/1994/

Offloading C++17 Parallel STL on System Shared Virtual Memory Platforms

Pekka Jääskeläinen[1,2(✉)] ⓘ, John Glossner[4,5], Martin Jambor[3],
Aleksi Tervo[1] ⓘ, and Matti Rintala[1]

[1] Tampere University of Technology, Tampere, Finland
pekka.jaaskelainen@tut.fi
[2] Parmance, Tampere, Finland
[3] SUSE, Prague, Czech Republic
[4] University of Science and Technology, Beijing, China
[5] Optimum Semiconductor Technologies, Tarrytown, NY, USA
http://parmance.com

Abstract. *Shared virtual memory* simplifies heterogeneous platform programming by enabling sharing of memory address pointers between heterogeneous devices in the platform. The most advanced implementations present a coherent view of memory to the programmer over the whole virtual address space of the process. From the point of view of data accesses, this *System SVM (SSVM)* enables the same programming paradigm in heterogeneous platforms as found in homogeneous platforms. C++ revision 17 adds its first features for explicit parallelism through its "Parallel Standard Template Library" (PSTL). This paper discusses the technical issues in offloading PSTL on heterogeneous platforms supporting SSVM and presents a working GCC-based proof-of-concept implementation. Initial benchmarking of the implementation on an AMD Carrizo platform shows speedups from *1.28X* to *12.78X* in comparison to host-only sequential STL execution.

Keywords: SVM · Offloading · C++17 · Parallel STL · HSA · GCC
Heterogeneous platforms

1 Introduction

Heterogeneous computing is known for its potential in improving power efficiency in high performance and embedded computing [2,13]. However, utilizing heterogeneous platforms to accelerate general purpose applications is still hindered by programming difficulties. In comparison to parallel programming on homogeneous multicore CPUs, heterogeneous platforms, due to their distributed memory systems and multiple different *instruction set architectures (ISA)*, present

R. Yokota et al. (Eds.): ISC 2018 Workshops, LNCS 11203, pp. 637–647, 2018.
https://doi.org/10.1007/978-3-030-02465-9_46

additional challenges to the programmer including manual management of data transfers, explicit launching of kernels, and multiple dissimilar programming tools. It is evident that the programmer's productivity in terms of engineering time required to implement an optimized algorithm is related to the programmer's skill level in programming languages and tools. Therefore, to extend the utility of heterogeneous platforms, it is beneficial to avoid domain and platform specific tools and provide programming models familiar to a large number of existing programmers.

C++ is a popular general purpose programming language that is widely used, especially in high performance computing, system programming and the embedded world. In C++ revision 17, the language includes its first features for explicit parallelism referred to as the *Parallel Standard Template Library (PSTL)* [9]. While the PSTL is a welcome step towards utilizing parallel platforms programmed in C++ efficiently, C++17 does not yet provide a complete solution for additional issues in heterogeneous platforms such as non-uniform address spaces or explicit data transfers. The question of how much support C++ should actually provide, or whether direct heterogeneous platform support should be included in the standard, is still an active topic within the C++ standards committee.

Compute platform vendors have approached simplifying the programming of heterogeneous platforms by providing a *shared virtual memory (SVM)* that enables pointer sharing between the heterogeneous devices in the platform, but the degree of SVM support provided by the commercial platforms varies. However, the most advanced SVM implementations are now able to present a coherent programmer view over the whole virtual memory address space of the process. In these implementations, the complete virtual memory of the process is visible and coherent to all devices in the platform without explicit API calls. In this paper we refer to this level of SVM support as *system SVM or SSVM*. From the data access point of view, SSVM bridges the gap between heterogeneous and homogeneous platforms.

This paper discusses the remaining implementation challenges in heterogeneous automatic parallelization (i.e. offloading) of C++17 PSTL on SSVM heterogeneous platforms. The discussion is backed with a proof-of-concept GCC-based implementation[1] and its evaluation results on a commercial platform with SSVM capabilities.

The rest of the paper is organized as follows. Section 2 provides an overview of related technologies. Section 3 describes the C++17 standard and outlines its limitations and challenges in heterogeneous offloading. Section 4 reviews the concept of SVM in relation to C++. Section 5 describes a proof-of-concept (PoC) implementation on GCC, with initial benchmark results presented in Sect. 6, finally, conclusions are presented in Sect. 7.

---

[1] The implementation is being upstreamed to the GCC project. It will be published before the workshop takes place.

2   Related Work

Features for supporting different degrees of SVM have appeared in various **lower level heterogeneous platform programming APIs** in the past few years. The *Open Computing Language (OpenCL)* standard from Khronos added an SVM API in OpenCL version 2.0 [12]. It defines multiple degrees of sharing and synchronization so that a conformant platform can be implemented. The optional *Fine-Grained System SVM* enables referring to any host memory without the need to allocate shared data objects using OpenCL-specific APIs and ensures data synchronization at atomic operation execution points. Thus, it fulfills the requirements of the "SSVM feature set" referred to in this paper. Khronos also specifies an intermediate language called SPIR-V [11], which together with fine grained system SVM provides an alternative implementation path for the platform abstraction components in the described proof-of-concept.

Heterogeneous System Architecture (HSA) [5] is a language neutral standard targeting heterogeneous systems. HSA specifies a coherent shared flat virtual memory as a core feature. Its "Full Profile" is similar to the *Fine-Grained System SVM* of OpenCL 2.0, allowing coherent sharing of data anywhere in the process address space. For the PoC described in this paper we used the HSA Runtime [7] as a heterogeneous platform middleware. The HSA Full Profile is ideal for this use primarily because its SSVM is designed to work seamlessly with the C++ memory model. There is also a wide selection of open source components that implement the different parts of the specifications, which can be used with the GCC toolchain. For example, its intermediate language HSAIL [6] has both frontend and backend support in the upstream GCC project.

NVIDIA is also moving in the direction of providing SSVM level capabilities. NVIDIA architectures since *Pascal* provide an advanced *unified memory* that provides SSVM level coherency and system-wide atomic operations [3,14]. A coherent view between the CPU and GPUs is implemented via on-demand virtual memory page migration. The first patch set (referred to as *heterogeneous memory management or HMM*) that provides support for this and various other types of SSVM implementations was upstreamed to the Linux kernel in version 4.14.

As PSTL is a recent addition to the C++ standard, there are only a few **open source implementations** of it available. Intel has published a PSTL implementation which is being upstreamed to libstdc++ of GCC [8]. It is implemented on top of the OpenMP 4's SIMD pragma and a parallel programming framework developed by Intel called *Threading Building Blocks (TBB)*. TBB supports only homogeneous multicore CPUs, and offloading to heterogenous devices is not implemented.

SYCL ParallelSTL [15] implements PSTL on top of SYCL [10]. SYCL is a Khronos heterogeneous programming model for the C++ language. To the best of our knowledge, there is currently no open source implementation of SYCL available that can offload PSTL to heterogeneous devices. We also consider the HSA Runtime a more suitable implementation component for PSTL as it is tailored for middleware purposes and doesn't define its own higher level programming model which could just complicate the implementation in this case.

The closest related implementation to the proposed one is *HCC* [1], a heterogeneous compiler collection from AMD. Its earlier versions worked on top of a standard HSA Runtime and HSAIL, but it has now moved to direct to ISA compilation, making the device interfacing and the binaries the compiler produces less portable to other HSA platforms.

3   Heterogeneous Offloading of Parallel STL

Section 28.4. Parallel Algorithms of the C++17 standard is often referred to as "Parallel STL" or abbreviated as "PSTL". It describes an additional *execution policy* argument in the standard template library's algorithm API. Execution policies enable the programmer to declare that the algorithm library call, along with any user-defined functionality the call uses, is safe to execute in parallel. The user-defined functionality is collectively referred to as *element access functions (EAF)* in the standard [9].

The following execution policies are supported: *sequenced_policy (seq)* forces serial execution of the EAFs in the calling thread of execution without interleaving, *parallel_policy (par)* promises parallelization safety of EAFs to multiple independent threads of execution, but does not guarantee "interleaving safety" *within* a single thread, and *parallel_unsequenced_policy (par_unseq)* additionally communicates interleaving safety in a single thread, e.g. by using SIMD instructions.

The parallelism related parts of C++17 focus on forward progress guarantees and their implications to parallelization safety on homogeneous processors. Execution on heterogeneous platforms, however, presents an additional consideration due to the different ISAs: The EAFs involved in the PSTL calls might rely on the target's (the host CPU's) properties, and assume the target specifics are uniform across all functions in the program. Thus, even if the user declares the strongest parallelization safety of *par_unseq*, which guarantees "vectorization safety", it is unclear if it is safe to offload to a device with a different ISA than in the host. Unsafe ISA features include different or undefined endianness, memory access alignment, and floating point rounding modes. However, an instruction-set abstraction layer such as HSAIL, which makes these attributes explicit, removes these ambiguities.

However, while it *might* be standard conformant to offload also *par_unseq* policy algorithm launches, offloading computation outside the host processor usually introduces additional invocation, synchronization and data transfer delays. Therefore, in the PoC presented in this paper, we added a new experimental execution policy we call *parallel_offload_policy* or *par_offload*. Using this policy, the programmer can declare the EAFs "heterogeneous offload" or "multiple-ISA" safe. *Par_offload* also implies *par_unseq* level SIMD-parallelization safety. An example code that calls the PSTL *transform* algorithm with this policy is shown in Fig. 1.

```
std::transform(std::experimental::execution::par_offload,
               pixel_data.begin(), pixel_data.end(),
               pixel_data.begin(),
               [](char c) -> char {
                 return c * 16;
               });
```

Fig. 1. Example of offloading *transform* with the function to execute for each element defined as a lambda expression.

4 System Shared Virtual Memory and C++17

The C++ memory model defines that data can be passed to other threads by pointers to objects in memory locations with unique addresses, thus implying a uniform address space. The pointers do not include the size of the pointed object. When considering heterogeneous offloading of PSTL, it is important to notice that the EAFs passed to PSTL algorithms are normal C/C++ functions, C++ function objects or "lambdas" which can refer to *any* data in the process. The accessed data is not limited to the containers handled by the launched algorithm. The EAFs can access arbitrary data allocated in any section of the process.

Having a unified coherent flat address space across all the processors in the heterogeneous platform, removes the major complexity of object access analysis that needs to track and wrap all the data accesses done by the EAFs, including their sizes. When reflecting against the C++ standard's memory model and the parallel algorithm requirements, a minimal feature set of a platform memory model that can semantically support PSTL algorithm offloading has the following properties:

– It presents a *flat process-wide address space* with unique physical locations identified by the pointer's address.
– All its locations can be *shared by default*. Data sharing between threads of execution does not need to be defined explicitly by the programmer.
– Shared locations can be updated with *atomic operations* without data races.

We rely on this SVM feature set in the described PoC and refer to it as SSVM (*system shared virtual memory*).

5 Proof of Concept Implementation

In order to identify the remaining challenges in heterogeneous offloading of C++17 PSTL when SSVM-level platform support is provided, we implemented a *proof-of-concept (PoC)* on top of GCC [4], the HSA runtime, and HSAIL.

We first describe an example of how an offloaded PSTL algorithm implementation looks like as an "HSA kernel". Figure 2 presents a templated kernel implementation of the HSA-offloaded parts of the PSTL algorithm *transform*.

```
template<typename ElementType, typename ResultType,
         typename FuncRetType, typename FuncArgType>
static void __attribute__((hsa_kernel))
__transform_array (void *args) {

    size_t i = __builtin_hsa_workitemflatabsid ();

    ResultType *d_first = *((ResultType**)args + 0);
    ElementType *first1 = *((ElementType**)args + 1);

    d_first[i] =
        _FUNC_PLACEHOLDER <FuncRetType, FuncArgType> (first1[i]);
}
```

Fig. 2. Templated HSA kernel implementation of *transform* with an indirect call specialization placeholder.

Transform executes a user-defined function for all elements in an input container, writing the result to a corresponding position in an output container.

As can be seen in the example, a new function attribute type *hsa_kernel* is added for marking function definitions as offloaded functions that can be launched from the host side. Other new attributes (not visible in the example) include *hsa_function* for functions that are compiled only to HSAIL and *hsa_universal* for functions which are compiled both to host native functions and HSAIL (later referred to as "universal functions").

Functions marked with the *hsa_kernel* attribute are *single program multiple data (SPMD)* style definitions called *kernels*. SPMD here means that the function defines what a single "work-item" (WI) does. The host runtime call (not visible in the example code) that launches the kernel defines the number of parallel work-items. In the case of *transform*, the host side launches the kernel with as many work-items as there are elements in the input container. The WI that executes the kernel function acquires its ID (location in the container) with a built-in call, reads the start location of the destination and the inputs from its argument data, and finally calls the user defined function.

Further technical details are discussed in the following subsections.

5.1   Binary Exchange Format

One of the issues in heterogeneous offloading is the program binary format. By the definition of *heterogeneous* computing, the potential target devices for the offloaded functions are diverse. Thus, the question of *binary portability* becomes an interesting one; even if storing a native binary for the host program, a portable heterogeneous binary format should preferably store an *intermediate language (IL)* or a virtual-ISA format for the offloaded kernels that can at finalization time be efficiently compiled to the final ISA. The time instant when to compile the IL to the real ISA can be delayed up until the program run time to enable maximum portability.

GCC's offload infrastructure uses an ELF-based "fat binary format", that, in addition to the ISA-targeted binary of the host program, can store different ILs, including HSAIL (which is used in the PoC), for the offloaded kernels. There is also an index for mapping the host-ISA and the IL versions of the included functions.

In the case of C++17, which doesn't support explicit marking of EAFs that might get offloaded, the compiler needs to somehow decide which functions should be compiled to the IL versions in the fat binary. Because the default assumption is that any function can be theoretically referred to in the EAFs, a full program link time call graph analysis starting from the PSTL algorithm calls would be needed to track all the possible functions recursively to collect the possible callees. For this first PoC, we decided to simplify this part and mark all functions as universal functions, without tracking whether they are potentially passed to PSTL algorithm calls or not. The bloat of the fat binaries produced by the duplication of functions is considered a lower priority problem.

It should be noted, however, that EAFs with certain unsupported features (such as exception handling or system calls) are dropped from the list of included IL functions based on the feasibility of their offloading. There are no inherent technical reasons to not support these features in EAF offloading and despite these omissions, the PoC is able to compile a large number of practical cases with the possibility to transparently extend the supported set in the future.

5.2   Indirect Calls and IL Specialization

While relying on SSVM takes care of pointers to data, the problem of multiple different ISAs and different disjoint *instruction* address spaces remain. Each targeted device can have its own ISA and therefore needs a separate program image in order to execute the offloaded EAFs. This means that there are potentially multiple copies of a function translated to the various ISAs in the heterogeneous platform simultaneously resident in the heterogeneous memory system. Furthermore, the targeted devices can have their own address spaces (ranges) for storing the functions; the flat host process address space can be assumed to contain only the bits for the host ISA versions of the functions. There is thus no uniform address range that can be used to uniquely identify a function's ISA binary. This complicates handling function pointers whose values can be treated as data in C/C++. While the sole efficient implementation of "universal function pointers" is an open problem, an additional consideration is the inefficiency of indirect calls in typical accelerator devices, thus they should be avoided for performance reasons whenever possible. Unfortunately, inheritance and virtual functions of C++ tend to increase their need.

In the PoC, indirect calls to the UEFs are supported via IL specialization. The PoC exploits the fact that the IL is compiled to the target ISA at runtime and at that point the called function is known. Thus, it is possible to "specialize" the IL version of the algorithm implementation at launch time by converting the indirect call to a direct one. The specialization idea is visible in the *transform* example of Fig. 2. It calls *_FUNC_PLACEHOLDER*, which is a function declaration annotated with a fourth new attribute type *hsa_placeholder*. The placeholder is replaced by the concrete target function definition when the algorithm is launched and the used function is known. As this happens before the kernel is compiled to the targeted ISA, the specialization avoids indirect calls that launch the EAF inside the offloaded kernel, leading to enhanced optimization opportunities.

6   Evaluation

The PoC was integrated with the latest GCC development code base and benchmarked on an AMD Carrizo desktop PC. AMD Carrizo is a heterogeneous notebook range SoC that supports end user programmable SSVM across the CPU and the GPU via its HSA Full Profile support.

For evaluating the performance of the implementation, we created a benchmark set that exercises various PSTL algorithms that heavily call UEFs. The benchmarks were executed on an Ubuntu 16.04 based Linux system with minimal other system activity. The PoC (referred to as *par_offload*) was compared to the *seq* and *par_unseq* execution policies implemented by the latest version of the CPU-only PSTL contributed by Intel [8].

Each of the benchmarks was executed 10 times in a row, with the best runtime recorded. The input data for the benchmarks is reinitialized for each run in the CPU side to avoid the effect of data being migrated only in the first run to the GPU caches, which would give unrealistically optimistic results for the later runs. Thus, the measured run time includes the transfer of input data blocks from the main memory or the CPU's cache to the GPU's local cache. Reading them back for verification or further processing is not included.

The benchmark descriptions and the measured wall clock runtimes are listed in Table 1. Figure 3 illustrates the relative execution times normalized to Intel PSTL's sequential run time.

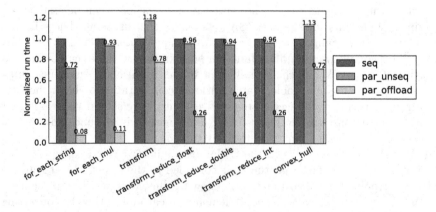

Fig. 3. Wall clock execution times, normalized to Intel PSTL seq execution policy.

Table 1. The benchmarks and their runtimes. Wall clock time (μs) reported for Intel PSTL when launched with the **seq**uential execution policy. Other runtimes given as relative speedups in comparison to it.

	seq	par_unseq	par_offload
for_each_string			
Convert a 100MB std::string to upper case	208303	1.39X	12.78X
for_each_mul			
Multiply 100MB of char data with a constant	156641	1.07X	9.48X
transform			
Gamma correct a 800 × 600 image	13800	0.85X	1.28X
transform_reduce_float			
Dot product of 100M element float vectors	1121486	1.05X	3.87X
transform_reduce_double			
Dot product of 100M element double vectors	2300442	1.06X	2.29X
transform_reduce_int			
Dot product of 100M element int vectors	1109145	1.04X	3.83X
convex_hull			
Convex hull from Intel PSTL examples	922030	0.89X	1.40X

The best **12.78X** speedup was received for *for_each_string*. The upper case conversion routine contains a bit of branching inside the EAF as it checks for the character ranges to avoid converting non-alphabetic characters, thus likely autovectorizes badly for *seq* and *par_unseq*, and executes more efficiently on the SIMT GPU. The 800 × 600 image in the *transform* gamma correction benchmark was added to serve as an example of offloading computation with relatively small input data to process. This case gets the most modest speedup of **1.28X**. The dot product cases received close to **4X** speedups with about half the performance for the double precision arithmetics as is expected.

The most apparent performance benefit of the single threaded *seq* policy is its possibility to compile the algorithm implementation together with the surrounding code at the call site. After template specialization and inlining the algorithm calls to the call site, autovectorization and other optimizations can be performed efficiently due to having more context information for the input and output iterators. In contrast, the *par_offload* policy requires a kernel dispatch call that isolates the algorithm implementation from its call site. The *par_unseq* policy suffers for the same reason due to its need to isolate the parallelized functionality to thread functions. Also, for the record, Intel's PSTL parallelizes much more efficiently on an Intel CPU due to TBB likely being better optimized for their own CPUs. We recorded *par_unseq* parallelization speedups up to 2.7X on a 4 HW thread Core i7 CPU.

7 Conclusions

SSVM is a key enabler for simplifying programming of heterogeneous platforms using traditional uniform address space languages such as C++. In this paper we discussed the remaining obstacles in seamless heterogeneous offloading of parallel standard template library algorithms introduced in the C++ revision 17 standard. With SSVM support in the platform, we identified efficient platform wide support for "universal function pointers" as a remaining key issue.

As a proof of concept, we presented technical details of a working heterogeneous offloading PSTL implementation implemented using GCC, the HSA runtime and the HSA Intermediate Language. Initial evaluation on an AMD Carrizo SoC in comparison to a sequential implementation running in the host CPU showed speedups from *1.28X* to *12.78X*.

For future work, we identified various further performance optimizations the PoC could benefit from. Utilizing HMM and the GCC's NVPTX backend to expand the set of supported platforms to new discrete GPUs from NVIDIA is also a very interesting future direction.

Acknowledgements. The authors would like to thank Academy of Finland (decision 297548) and the HSA Foundation for financially supporting the writing of this publication.

References

1. AMD: HCC : an open source C++ compiler for heterogeneous devices, 17 April 2018. https://github.com/RadeonOpenCompute/hcc
2. Chung, E.S., Milder, P.A., Hoe, J.C., Mai, K.: Single-chip heterogeneous computing: does the future include custom logic, FPGAs, and GPGPUs? In: Proceedings of 43rd Annual IEEE/ACM International Symposium on Microarchitecture (MICRO '43) (2010)
3. Foley, D., Danskin, J.: Ultra-performance pascal GPU and NVLink interconnect. IEEE Micro **37**(2), 7–17 (2017)
4. Free Software Foundation Inc.: GCC, the GNU compiler collection, 17 April 2018. https://gcc.gnu.org/
5. HSA Foundation: HSA Platform System Architecture Specification v1.0, January 2015
6. HSA Foundation: HSA Programmer Reference Manual Specification v1.01, July 2015
7. HSA Foundation: HSA Runtime Specification v1.0, January 2015
8. Intel: Parallel STL, implementation available in github, 17 April 2018. https://github.com/intel/parallelstl/
9. ISO/IEC: 14882:2017 Programming languages – C++, December 2017
10. Khronos: SYCL™ Specification v1.2.1, December 2017
11. Khronos: SPIR-V Specification v1.3 Revision 1, March 2018
12. Khronos Group: OpenCL Specification v2.0, July 2015

13. Nathuji, R., Isci, C., Gorbatov, E.: Exploiting platform heterogeneity for power efficient data centers. In: Fourth International Conference on Autonomic Computing (ICAC 2007), June 2007
14. NVIDIA: CUDA C Programming Guide v9.1, March 2018
15. Various authors: SYCL Parallel STL, implementation available in github, 17 April 2018. https://github.com/KhronosGroup/SyclParallelSTL

First Workshop on Interactive
High-Performance Computing

First Workshop on Interactive High-Performance Computing

Peter Messmer[1], Mike Ringenburg[2], John Stone[3],
Albert Reuther[4], and Sadaf Alam[5]

[1] NVIDIA Switzerland, Europaallee 39, 8004 Zurich, Switzerland
pmessmer@nvidia.com
[2] Cray Inc, 901 Fifth Ave, Suite 1000, Seattle, WA 98164, USA
[3] Beckman Institute for Advanced Science and Technology,
University of Illinois at Urbana-Champaign, 405 N Mathews Ave,
Urbana, IL 61801, USA
[4] MIT Lincoln Laboratory, 244 Wood St, Lexington, MA 02421, USA
[5] CSCS Swiss National Supercomputing Center, Via Trevano 131,
6900 Lugano, Switzerland

Abstract. Interactive exploration and analysis of large data sets, inter-active preparation and debugging of large-scale scientific simulations, in-situ visuali-zation, and application steering are compelling scenarios for exploratory science, design optimizations, and signal processing. However, a range of technical, organizational and sociological challenges must be overcome to make these interactive workflows mainstream in HPC centers: What simulation scenarios or problem domains can benefit most from interactivity? How can we simplify the toolchain? What center policies are needed to support highly interactive workflows? The goal of this workshop was to bring together domain scientists, tool developers, and HPC center administrators to identify the scientific impact and technical challenges of highly interactive access to HPC resources. In this preface paper, we describe the organization of the workshop, give some highlights of the presentations and the resulting discussion, as well as demonstrate the need for similar future events.

Keywords: Interactive Supercomputing · In-situ visualization and steering · On-demand computing

1 Introduction

Interactive exploration and analysis of large data sets, interactive preparation and debugging of large-scale scientific simulations, in-situ visualization, and application steering are compelling scenarios for exploratory science, design optimizations, and signal processing. However, a range of technical, organizational and sociological challenges must be overcome to make these interactive workflows mainstream in HPC centers: What simulation scenarios or problem domains can benefit most from interactivity? How can we simplify the toolchain? What center policies are needed to support highly interactive workflows? The goal of this workshop was to bring together domain scientists, tool developers, and HPC center administrators to identify the scientific impact and technical challenges of highly interactive access to HPC resources.

After two successful Birds-of-a-Feather session at SC15 and SC17 it became apparent that there should be a more structured form of forum, allowing for presentations and papers.

2 Organization of the Workshop

The workshop content was built on two tracks:

- Use cases highlighting the benefit of interactive HPC for specific computational science domains
- Experiences from HPC centers with interactive use cases

    The important deadlines for the workshop were:

- Call for papers sent out in early April 2018, including an announcement on the hpc-announce mailing list on April 19.
- Abstract submission May 31, 2018, with author notification shortly after
- Workshop was held on June 28, 2018
- Camera ready paper deadline July 29, 2018

2.1 Program Committee

Peter Messmer, NVIDIA Switzerland   Albert Reuther, MIT Lincoln Lab
Mike Ringenburg, Cray Inc   Sadaf Alam, CSCS Switzerland
John Stone, University of Illinois at
    Urbana-Champaign

2.2 Summary of the Submissions

We were pleased by the quality of the submissions. In the few months between the notification of acceptance of the workshop and the submission deadline, we had eight high quality submissions, and we chose all eight for presentations. At least three of the presentations will be submitted as full papers to be included in the ISC proceedings.

Several other organizations intended to submit, but, due to travel costs and scheduling conflicts, ended up not being able to attend. However, several of them still submitted summary slides for the conclusion of the workshop, and they have expressed their intention of attending future workshops in interactive HPC.

3 Workshop Summary

The workshop at ISC was scheduled in the largest room to accommodate workshops at the Frankfurt Messe Marriott, and it was scheduled in the afternoon of the last day of ISC 2018. Despite this scheduling, so many people came at the beginning of the workshop session, hotel staff had to add many more chairs to accommodate attendees. We started with 35 attendees, which grew to 42 attendees at the middle of the 4-hour workshop. A number of attendees apologetically left to catch flights, and we finished the workshop with 25 attendees.

The workshop presentations covered a diversity of application domains, workflows, infrastructures and technologies, and practical experience. The types of interactive HPC activities described in the presentations ranged from graphics-intensive HPC visualization and interactive CAD, to high performance physical modeling tasks, to lab notebook-driven computational campaigns, and to the application of interactive HPC to clinical medicine scenarios that posed challenges both in terms of computa-tional capability and interactivity guarantees. The technologies supporting these workloads ranged from hardware-optimized algorithms for GPUs and many-core CPUs, to interactive Jupyter notebooks that combine interactivity with powerful scripting, graphics, and reproducibility, to methods for exploiting high performance storage and emerging technologies such as persistent memory DIMMs to facilitate unprecedented interactive access to massive datasets that were previously inaccessible in a truly interactive setting. The presentations included discussions of contemporary challenges to scientific productivity that can be directly addressed by increased interactivity, and the kinds of obstacles to interactive computing that are posed by existing software systems, computing policies, and HPC system productivity metrics employed by HPC centers and/or their funding agencies. Several presentations included discussions of the kinds of computing and storage resources that were required to facilitate interactive workflows that met the needs of the community served, leading to post-presentation discussions on generalizations of some of these observations.

The discussions during and between presentations were lively and spanned many topics including metrics; managing and conveying the impact of interactive HPC to upper management, psychology of scarcity regarding resource scheduling; accommodating both large parallel jobs and interactive exploration jobs, and licensing of various high productivity software frameworks. Some of the more technical discussions centered on the practical impacts of low-level implementation details of key layers of HPC software stacks to encourage or inhibit interactivity related capabilities. It was noted that techniques for supporting interactivity such as on-demand job launching and on-the-fly resource resizing, and suspension and resumption of long-running batch jobs all depend on details of the behavior of key HPC software components such as MPI or parallel runtime components, e.g., when processes are suspended or resumed, and/or when processes are migrated. Many of the participants in the discussions pointed out examples of combinations of HPC libraries and system software that could be used to support different kinds of interactivity on existing HPC platforms within the limits set by institutional policies. Finally, the discussions included many interesting comparisons between conventional HPC environments and approaches found in the cloud and other non-HPC environments, and how the increasing adoption of some cloud software and machine learning stacks within HPC environments might help address their limitations with respect to technical underpinnings that facilitate interactivity. The workshop concluded with a summary of other HPC centers that were not represented in the presentations. These included Harvard University, the U.S. Department of Defense High Performance Computing Modernization Office centers, and others.

In conclusion, this workshop brought a great deal of momentum and interested participants together. It certainly achieved its goal of bringing together domain scientists, tool developers, and HPC center administrators to identify the scientific impact and technical challenges of highly interactive access to HPC resources. The interesting presentations, rich discussions, and enthusiastic attendees all indicate that further workshops will have the interest and attendance to make them quite worthwhile.

Lessons Learned from a Decade of Providing Interactive, On-Demand High Performance Computing to Scientists and Engineers

Julia Mullen[1], Albert Reuther[1]([⊠]) [ID], William Arcand[1], Bill Bergeron[1],
David Bestor[1], Chansup Byun[1], Vijay Gadepally[1,2] [ID], Michael Houle[1],
Matthew Hubbell[1], Michael Jones[1], Anna Klein[1],
Peter Michaleas[1], Lauren Milechin[2] [ID], Andrew Prout[1] [ID], Antonio Rosa[1],
Siddharth Samsi[1], Charles Yee[1], and Jeremy Kepner[1,2] [ID]

[1] MIT Lincoln Laboratory, 244 Wood Street, Lexington, MA 02420, USA
{jsm,reuther,warchand,bbergeron,david.bestor,cbyun,vijayg,michael.houle,
mhubbell,michael.jones,anna.klein,pmichaleas,lauren.milechin,aprout,
antonio.rosa,sid,yee,kepner}@LL.mit.edu
[2] Massachusetts Institute of Technology,
77 Massachusetts Avenue, Cambridge, MA 02139, USA
lauren.milechin@mit.edu

Abstract. For decades, the use of HPC systems was limited to those in the physical sciences who had mastered their domain in conjunction with a deep understanding of HPC architectures and algorithms. During these same decades, consumer computing device advances produced tablets and smartphones that allow millions of children to interactively develop and share code projects across the globe. As the HPC community faces the challenges associated with guiding researchers from disciplines using high productivity interactive tools to effective use of HPC systems, it seems appropriate to revisit the assumptions surrounding the necessary skills required for access to large computational systems. For over a decade, MIT Lincoln Laboratory has been supporting interactive, on-demand high performance computing by seamlessly integrating familiar high productivity tools to provide users with an increased number of design turns, rapid prototyping capability, and faster time to insight. In this paper, we discuss the lessons learned while supporting interactive, on-demand high performance computing from the perspectives of the users and the team supporting the users and the system. Building on these lessons, we present an overview of current needs and the technical solutions we are building to lower the barrier to entry for new users from the humanities, social, and biological sciences.

This material is based upon work supported by the Assistant Secretary of Defense for Research and Engineering under Air Force Contract No. FA8721-05-C-0002 and/or FA8702-15-D-0001. Any opinions, findings, conclusions or recommendations expressed in this material are those of the author(s) and do not necessarily reflect the views of the Assistant Secretary of Defense for Research and Engineering.

© Springer Nature Switzerland AG 2018
R. Yokota et al. (Eds.): ISC 2018 Workshops, LNCS 11203, pp. 655–668, 2018.
https://doi.org/10.1007/978-3-030-02465-9_47

Keywords: HPC abstractions · Interactive On-demand HPC

1   Introduction

Traditionally supercomputers and high performance computing (HPC) were the domain of experts with deep understanding of their scientific discipline, computer architecture and software. For virtually the entire history of HPC, the standard path to developing the skills necessary for supercomputer usage included graduate programs in the physical sciences and engineering. These research programs, with applications requiring massive computational effort, prepared students who had the time, inclination and mandate from their advisors to learn how to program and exploit the computational power of supercomputers. Many of these graduates went on to research positions at centers, research laboratories, and universities where they trained the next generation of HPC researchers thereby growing the HPC community and reinforcing the notion of a single path to HPC.

This single learning path may have been appropriate when computational approaches to science, engineering and design were in their infancy, but today computational approaches to problem solving have become commonplace, used by researchers from engineering and the physical sciences and more recently by members of the medical and social sciences and the humanities. While many engineering and science disciplines have long included computing in their undergraduate and graduate programs, such academic preparation is minimal to nonexistent for many of the disciplines that have recently adopted computational solution strategies. For these research communities the single path to HPC is a significant deterrent. Furthermore, industry relies on the use of HPC systems to stay globally competitive [26] but the majority of the industrial workforce has little or no HPC experience. Developing HPC experience among this portion of the workforce calls for new learning paths designed for mid-career professionals.

This friction between the steep requirements of a single pathway to HPC use and the need for high productivity HPC systems is not new. As few as 15 years ago, prior to the development of MathWorks' Parallel MATLAB® product and the parallel versions of standard engineering design tools, *e.g.*, Fluent, Ansys, NASTRAN, etc., the science and engineering community faced the same divide: a small number of researchers became expert HPC users while the vast majority of scientists and engineers used interactive, high productivity tools on their desktop systems, upgrading hardware when greater performance was required or available. However, as processor clock rates stagnated and hardware improvements because modestly incremental, hardware upgrades no longer delivered large gains. From this experience of the breaking down of Moore's Law, many have begun to realize that HPC is required.

It is easy to understand the limits of this single learning path for the broad community of scientists and engineers who faced increasingly complicated applications but no clear path to merging the productivity of interactive tools with the performance of compute clusters and supercomputers. For these researchers the traditional path to greater performance required building the software frameworks in a compiled language, learning to create batch scripts, and becoming accustomed to the software testing and development delays associated with batch systems. For many, the costs associated with these changes in terms of both time and distraction were perceived to be greater than the reward. For them, another approach was necessary.

At MIT Lincoln Laboratory a standard prototyping process for analysts includes developing, testing and debugging in MATLAB® to speed up the design and prototyping phase before passing the engineering code to a team of expert real time coders. The real time team is responsible for converting the MATLAB® to C or C^{++} code and tuning it for the target architecture [15]. This division of labor is ideal for certain situations, such as very large, well funded projects, but is not generally feasible for smaller companies and teams. For smaller, time critical projects, a merger of high productivity and high performance is essential.

For almost 15 years the Lincoln Laboratory Supercomputing Center (LLSC, formerly the Lincoln Laboratory Grid (LLGrid) team) at MIT Lincoln Laboratory has provided interactive on-demand cluster computing resources to over 1,000 researchers at the Laboratory [1]. As part of the LLSC mission to deliver new and innovative technologies and methods, we have developed and built the MIT SuperCloud [21] to enabling scientists and engineers to quickly ramp up the pace of their research and rapid prototyping by leveraging big compute and big data storage assets. The SuperCloud is a fusion of the four large computing ecosystems: supercomputing, enterprise computing, big data and traditional databases into a coherent, unified platform. The MIT SuperCloud has spurred the development of a number of cross-ecosystem innovations in high performance databases [3,13]; database management [19]; data protection [14]; database federation [6,11]; data analytics [12]; dynamic virtual machines [8,23] and system monitoring [7].

In general, interactive, on-demand supercomputing is very useful for a variety of research, engineering, and prototyping activities including algorithm development, data analysis, machine learning training, application steering, and visualization. Over the past 15 years, the common Laboratory use cases encompass many of these activities and have included algorithm development for sensor signal processing; development of multiple program, multiple data (MPMD) real time signal processing systems; high throughput computing for aircraft collision avoidance system testing; biomedical analytics to develop medical support techniques for personnel in remote areas; and prototyping capabilities for a range of systems. Unlike traditional HPC applications, most of these capabilities involve prototyping efforts for multi-year, but not multi-decade, mission-driven programs making it even more important that researchers are able to use familiar interactive tools and achieve a greater number of design cycles per day. To enable an interactive high performance development environment, our team turned the traditional HPC paradigm on its head. Rather than providing a batch system, training in MPI, and assistance porting serial code to a supercomputer, we developed the tools and training to bring HPC capabilities to the researchers' desktops and laptops. As common use cases and staff computational preparation change, we routinely update our tools so that we can provide relevant interactive research computing environments. From our initial experience, standing up an interactive on-demand cluster computing resource through our current support of machine learning, data analytics and user portals, we have focused on creating multiple paths to HPC usage. In this paper, we present and discuss the lessons we have learned and how they apply to the larger HPC ecosystem.

The paper is organized as follows, we present the high-level lessons that we have learned in Sect. 2. In Sect. 3 we dive deeper into the lessons we have learned about provisioning an appropriate system, creating a software abstraction layer and providing the training required to support interactive HPC. Section 4 considers standard HPC metrics and the reframing necessary to create metrics that capture the value of interactive HPC for smaller centers, universities, and industry. We close with a summary.

2   Lessons Learned

The key elements required to provide interactive on-demand HPC to a user base spanning neophytes to experts can be summed by four high level ideas. These four key elements are: broadening the definition of interactive within the HPC community; expanding the HPC ecosystem; re-architect the HPC system, where by system we include system architecture, software stack, and user support; and reframing the success metrics. Two of these key elements, the idea related to broadening the definition of interactive within the HPC community and the related idea of expanding the HPC community are philosophical in nature and are described within this section. The remaining elements are primarily structural and require a fuller description. These elements, the manner in which we re-architect the HPC system and reframing the success metric are described in this section and detailed in Sects. 3 and 4, respectively.

2.1   Broadening the Definition of Interactive HPC

First and foremost, we recognize that there is a large middle ground of users who want computational environments that balance performance and usability. In practice this translates to redefining the term "interactive High Performance Computing". Virtually every center sets aside a partition of compute cores for debugging and interactive use during normal working hours. Generally, these interactive partitions provide access to a command shell where a user can build, submit and track a compute job without having to interface through a batch scheduler or specifically request resources. For an expert HPC user familiar with the Linux command line and batch processing workflows, this partition provides a reasonable way to debug compiled code and scripts, including submission scripts, on a small scale prior to launching production level jobs. However, for the researcher who is familiar with a modern Integrated Development Environment (IDE), such a workflow is convoluted, confusing and opaque. A first step in supporting the work of a more general researcher base is to recognize the extensive use and value of IDEs and develop ways to bring them into the HPC environment. When the LLGrid project started, there were no widespread software tools that connected the IDE at a desktop to more robust compute resources. Over the past decade or so, pMatlab [1], StarP [5] and MATLAB® Distributed Compute Server (MDCS) have filled this void for researchers using MATLAB® while other commercial software products have created versions of their products that run seamlessly on parallel or high throughput systems but present the user with a familiar front end (e.g., Julia, Python, Mathematica, Fluent, NASTRAN, Anysys, and FEKO). For these applications and users, interactive assumes that there is a desktop or browser user interface, and the user will be able to simply hit the return key and the job will launch and run immediately. This is interactive and on-demand, matching the interactive desktop experience but with greater memory, compute and network resources. Starting from this broader definition of interactive HPC it is much easier to design the appropriate architecture and develop the necessary middleware tools to expand the HPC user community.

2.2   Re-architecting for Interactive HPC

At its essence, creating an interactive on-demand HPC environment means bridging the gap between standard HPC architectures and the user's desktop experience. An interactive on-demand system, like any HPC system is built with login nodes, a scheduler, compute nodes, a shared central file system and a network. The particular hardware selection and configuration—i.e., the amount of RAM, number of cores, network technology and topology, etc.—is a tradeoff between cost and the requirements of a set of common user applications. While the testing confirms that the applications will run, providing a compute system is not enough to attract users from beyond the expert user base trained through the graduate student pathway. To increase adoption from a broader segment of the scientific, engineering, business, social science and humanities domains as well as the mid-career professionals in industry we need to provide an HPC framework that is approachable and reliable. The components of such a framework include the compute system mentioned above along with an OS and the necessary systems tools, which we will call the system, and a layer of software, or middleware, between the system and user applications, which we will call the software. This middleware layer is where the technical challenges of supporting broader computing communities arise and where HPC expertise is essential to creating tools to lower the barrier to entry. Section 3 details the effective solution we have developed and particular lessons we have learned through their deployment.

2.3   Reframing the Metrics of Success

Virtually all HPC centers report the percentage of system utilization as their metric of success. This choice of metrics often leads to queuing systems and user behavior designed to feed the system with the type of jobs that yield high utilization. However, these utilization-based queuing practices are often at odds with rapid prototyping of algorithms and simulations, exploration of large datasets and real time steering of complicated multi-physics simulations [22]. Job queuing systems are configured to accumulate and maintain a backlog of large and small jobs so that as soon as an executing job completes, one or more jobs can replace it and execute. This encourages user behavior that includes submitting a multitude of jobs with many different parameters thus accumulating even more jobs in the queue backlog. Section 4 revisits work for DARPA's High Productivity Computing System program where a productivity metric was developed as part of a larger analysis of HPC Return On Investment for a broad range of applications and research domains.

2.4   Expanding the HPC Ecosystem

There will always be a place for large, batch processing systems that provide expert users the resources to attain the best performance for a given application or analytic. The case that we make here is not that all systems need to be interactive, but rather that we need to expand our vision of what an HPC ecosystem includes and how it supports research, design and prototyping at all levels. Across a spectrum of applications and centers, the weight given to performance versus productivity will and should vary based on the user applications to incorporate the computing regimes illustrated in Fig. 1. This approach means that as we reach out to new communities familiar with IDEs and workflows that incorporate research portals we need to rethink our presumed prerequisites. The community has put significant effort into teaching new users the basics of Linux and the command line interface and the gritty details of batch scheduler systems and MPI [24,27]—effort that reinforces the belief that new user communities must adopt our workflows and tools. These efforts are attempts at building shortcuts or mid-career bootcamps toward our single educational path to HPC. Re-evaluating our assumptions of what an HPC ecosystem includes offers the opportunity for HPC experts to apply Design Thinking [25] to the design of new paths to HPC usage for communities who require not just performance but a balance of productivity and performance. The first step in Design Thinking is to capture and understand the user perspective, goals and workflow; starting with this step increases the likelihood that tools and training will lead to additional pathways to HPC.

3   Architecture Requirements for Interactive HPC

As the community begins capturing the needs of these communities with an eye toward expanding the number of pathways to HPC resources, it is important to remember how we addressed a similar challenge: bringing an analyst and research community to using high productivity languages and interactive tools into the parallel and distributed computing environment. In the early 2000s, MIT Lincoln Laboratory staff were seeing steady increases in the fidelity and capability of sensors, leading to increasingly sophisticated sensor signal and image processing algorithms [1]. The level of complexity, combined with the sharp increase

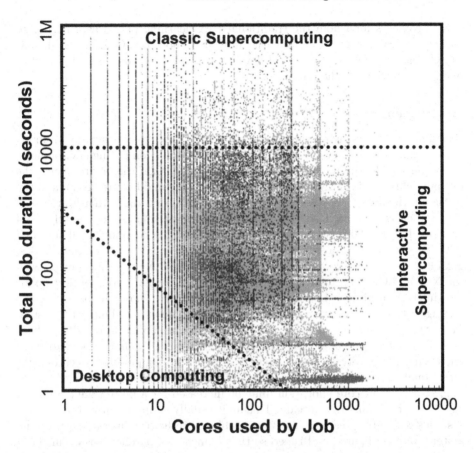

Fig. 1. A notional view of research computing regimes. The Desktop Computing region involves jobs that execute in less than five minutes, often for exploration and debugging. The Classic Supercomputing jobs are those that run for over three hours. Finally, the Interactive Supercomputing jobs run for between five minutes and three hours and are usually jobs that involve rapid turnarounds for insight.

in data to be processed and the end of Moore's Law [4] meant that desktop workstations were no longer able to provide adequate computational power. To advance their work, researchers and analysts had access to compute clusters, but these generally required relinquishing the interactive environment and converting application software written in high productivity languages to compiled languages. For many, the performance gain associated with compiled parallel code did not override the ease of use and rapid prototyping capabilities of interactive languages, especially for mission driven projects focused on design and algorithm prototypes.

In 2003, as grid computing was emerging, the question was, can systems carefully configured for high productivity and rapid prototyping fill the gap between slower desktops and big HPC systems and support the growing needs of analysts and researchers for whom the traditional HPC learning path was a barrier to entry? To evaluate this question, the Lincoln Laboratory Grid (LLGrid, now LLSC) was created to explore and develop interactive, on-demand high performance computing for the Laboratory.

3.1 System

Bringing a systems engineering approach to the challenge of designing an interactive, high productivity, on-demand high performance computing environment, we began by identifying the three subsystems that form the environment: the compute cluster; the software stack (particularly the middleware layer); and the development of user consultation and support unit. In terms of hardware selection and design, our HPC system was similar to most small to moderately-sized systems. In 2003–2005, we built our first clusters using commodity-off-the-shelf (COTS) system components including dual-socket, single-core compute nodes, gigabit Ethernet interconnects, a shared central RAID file system exported with the NFS and CIFS protocol standards, and the University of Wisconsin Condor scheduler. As is always the case, these components were chosen by balancing the cost against user application requirements. What differentiated our HPC system from others was not the choice of components, but the configuration of the scheduler. To provide on-demand computing services meant rethinking the traditional partition configurations: each user was limited to running jobs up to a core-count limit equaling approximately one eighth of the total cores available. They could request that their core allocation limit be increased for a finite time period via email to our administration team. This limit usually assured that a subset of the system's compute cores were always available. Also the scheduler and central file system were configured and tuned so that launches of parallel jobs occurred in less than 20 s on hundreds of cores, thereby providing the interactivity with job launches that users were used to on their desktop IDEs [22].

In subsequent clusters that we have built, we have used similar components as technology has progressed eventually including multicore (up to 64 core) compute nodes. Our latest systems have 10-gigabit Ethernet connections with a 1024-port non-blocking central core switch, along with a gigabit out-of-band management network. And the central file system has thousands of disk drives, many levels of redundancy, and can read and write tens of gigabytes of data per second. But hardware has not been the only place for improvements. Over the years, sensor and processing capabilities continued to increase, driving interest in using the compute system for data analysis applications. To accommodate the requirements (memory, storage, tools) of these applications, our traditional HPC system was extended to include High Performance Databases such as Accumulo and SciDB [3]. The databases are dynamically run on a set of compute nodes, creating a unified compute platform for the users as depicted in Figure 2. Researcher access to start, stop and monitor these databases was integrated into the system via a web-based portal, and software tools were created to easily connect databases and user applications. As the user application space expanded to include machine learning and medical science applications from users without traditional computing experience, the unified platform was extended to include portal interfaces [18] to support web applications, particularly ones that integrate into sensor processing and scientific computing workflows. As we extend the unified platform into these new capabilities, we will further develop and adapt all of our technical and support efforts to effectively enable users.

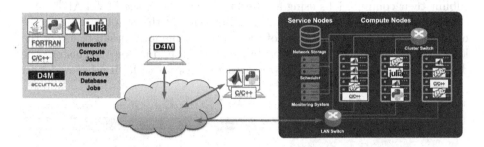

Fig. 2. The unified SuperCloud architecture and compute platform.

3.2   Software

Providing hardware is not enough, particularly for researchers whose academic training did not include HPC topics or exposure. Engaging new HPC users requires filling the gap between interactive high productivity programming and the high performance compute hardware. This middleware layer is crucial to the success of mainstream interactive HPC. In 2003, when roughly 85% of computational engineering and science was accomplished using MATLAB®, there was not only no communication library for the language but there was no plan to create a communication library [16]. If research analysts using MATLAB® were going to take advantage of a distributed cluster, they needed middleware to enable the parallel capability. As a first step, Dr. Jeremy Kepner created MatlabMPI, [9] a communication layer that used the file system as a communication fabric and leveraged the save and load functions in MATLAB® to execute send and receive commands. The choice of communication fabric was a design decision to retain MATLAB®'s platform agnostic feature and support the range of desktop systems in use at MIT Lincoln Laboratory and the broader science and engineering community. While MatlabMPI enabled parallel MATLAB applications, it had the same drawback as MPI, in that the programmer needed to spend significant effort to manage the communication. To separate the parallel programming details from the application programming concerns, Lincoln Laboratory created pMatlab [2,10]. pMatlab implemented Partitioned Global Address Spaces (PGAS) constructs so that the research programmer could design the application on the global level but use pMatlab constructs to distribute the data structures, manage the local-global mapping and communication.

The pMatlab library provided a high productivity ease-of-use approach to writing distributed computing applications, but it did not address the challenges of batch schedulers and job submission on shared cluster resources. The scheduler and job submission challenge was addressed by Dr. Albert Reuther through gridMatlab [20], a set of tools, written in MATLAB®, that provides the glue between the researcher's desktop and the compute cluster. Researchers submit their compute jobs using an overloaded version of the MATLAB® eval command that accepts three arguments: the name of the script to be run, the number of cores and the location of the cores, *i.e.* the local desktop; use of the local desktop along with the cluster; or as a background job on the cluster. The default is to assign node 0 to the researcher's desktop with all other nodes on

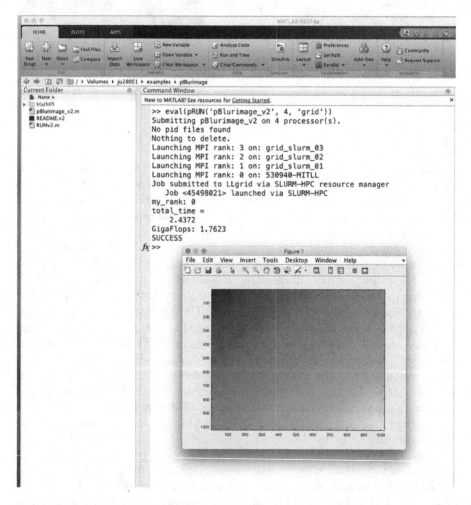

Fig. 3. Running a pMatlab job on four processors. The resulting image is gathered to Node 0, the desktop, for display.

the cluster. One benefit of this setting is that results are aggregated to node 0 local desktop and can easily be post-processed on the researcher desktop. This provides the user with a familiar interface for job launches versus traditional command line tools. Figure 3 illustrates the launch of a simple example on four processors. The reserved word 'grid' indicates that the job will be run with 3 processors on the cluster and one on the local desktop, as seen in the echo of each launch command. The job is submitted to the scheduler and when complete the results are written to the local MATLAB® command window. At no time in the process does the researcher log into the cluster; all of the development work and job submission is done from the Integrated Development Environment (IDE) on the user's desktop or laptop. When the job completes, or fails, the researcher has immediate feedback and can quickly modify the application and resubmit, offering a seamless prototyping environment.

This approach to developing middleware is key to HPC adoption by a broader range of research disciplines and should be a focus of the HPC experts. The philosophy behind pMatlab and gridMatlab is that HPC experts can create tools to abstract the tricky parallel details that can sidetrack beginner or intermediate HPC programmer progress thus lowering the barrier to entry for new users. In keeping with this philosophy, new tools for abstraction and ease of use were created to support new data analysis and machine learning applications.

3.3 Supporting Users

Building an effective tool does not guarantee adoption and what seems easy to the expert many not be intuitive to a novice or intermediate. To insure adoption, the LLSC team took a novel approach to on-boarding new HPC users by providing targeted individual tutorials to each new user. The tutorial included a general introduction to high performance and parallel computing, a careful walk through the process of building a parallel parameter sweep application from a serial code and a discussion of parallelization strategies for the user application. Over the years we have gathered much of this educational content and created a MOOC course that runs on the HPC system and provides the user with course examples to run on the HPC system thus building understanding of both general HPC concepts and the specifics of applications on our system [17].

More recently we have begun developing our examples within Jupyter notebooks because they provide a method to create sections that explain the concepts and tasks interleaved with sections where students can edit and run code. Consistent with our other tools and services (e.g., pMatlab and databases), the Jupyter notebook compute engines are run on compute nodes of our HPC system so that the educational examples are running directly on the system allowing users the opportunity to test and explore HPC strategies. All the while, the graphical interface of the Jupyter notebooks are executing in the browser of the user's desktop or laptop computer [18].

4 Metrics

After covering all of these system and user support topics, we now return to discussing metrics. Using the proper metrics is very valuable for determining whether an organization is getting the most out of their HPC investments. This leads to better leadership understanding of the value of HPC for the organization and encourages each organization to manage towards those goals that most benefit the organization.

As we briefly discussed in Sect. 2.3, managing toward maximum system utilization is directly at odds with enabling interactive, on-demand HPC. The DARPA High Productivity Computing Systems (HPCS) program brought this discrepancy to full light, and it was on through this program that a new method to measure the return on investment (ROI) was developed [26]. The ROI calculation places the benefit in the numerator and sums all of the costs in the denominator. Each organization can determine what the benefits for their use cases are, and they can compile all of the costs for the denominator. Examples of benefits at various organizations are presented in [26]. At Lincoln Laboratory, we chose to measure the benefit as the sum of all the time saved by users on a system by running parallel jobs over running single-process jobs. We enumerated the cost of enabling HPC at Lincoln to be the sum of the time to parallelize each code set, the time to train users, the time to launch jobs, the time to administrate the system, and the system cost. Details of our analysis can be found in [26] and [22]. We were pleased to find that the time saved often help us achieve organizational ROI of 2x to 10x (or more) – clearly, a very beneficial values for our Laboratory. Some of this can be attributed to very efficient system administration workflows and low launching and development overhead. However, a large part of the benefit is due the broad utilization across the entire Laboratory and the value it has brought to each of the users.

5 Summary and Future Work

In summary, the challenges to deploying interactive on-demand HPC environments are both technical and institutional. The technical challenges involve developing middleware at the correct level of abstraction to lower the slope of the learning curve for new users and provide a path to increased productivity. The human challenges center on the development of a community of practice that appreciates the importance of balancing performance and productivity, a re-evaluation of the assumptions surrounding the metrics of success and the creation of educational materials aimed at building new pathways to HPC expertise. Together these changes advance a new approach for provisioning HPC environments. The strategies presented here are general and easily adapted for any center where productivity and the rapid prototyping and testing of algorithms and analytics are key concerns. The challenge going forward is to recognize emerging needs from both new users and new domains and create the appropriate middleware and educational materials. While we started by abstracting the parallel and scheduling details of launching parallel MATLAB® in the early 2000's, we have since added HPC databases for analytics and Jupyter notebooks to abstract the command line concerns and launch details for new languages such as Julia, Python and R. As the user community and their applications change, we will continue to evaluate their preferred tools, languages and environments against the demands of the HPC system to uncover areas where abstractions, system efficiencies and education can yield both productivity and performance.

References

1. Bliss, N., Bond, R., Kepner, J., Kim, H., Reuther, A.: Interactive grid computing at Lincoln laboratory. MIT Lincoln Lab. J. **16**, 165–216 (2006)
2. Bliss, N.T., Kepner, J., Kim, H., Reuther, A.: pMATLAB: parallel MATLAB library for signal processing applications. In: 2007 IEEE International Conference on Acoustics, Speech and Signal Processing - ICASSP 2007, vol. 4, pp. IV-1189–IV-1192, April 2007. https://doi.org/10.1109/ICASSP.2007.367288
3. Byun, C., et al.: Driving big data with big compute. In: 2012 IEEE Conference on High Performance Extreme Computing HPEC, pp. 1–6, September 2012. https://doi.org/10.1109/HPEC.2012.6408678
4. Denning, P.J., Lewis, T.G.: Exponential laws of computing growth. Commun. ACM **60**(1), 54–65 (2016). https://doi.org/10.1145/2976758
5. Edelman, A.: The Star-P high performance computing platform. In: 2007 IEEE International Conference on Acoustics, Speech and Signal Processing - ICASSP 2007, vol. 4, pp. IV-1197-IV-1200, April 2007. https://doi.org/10.1109/ICASSP.2007.367290
6. Gadepally, V., et al.: D4M: bringing associative arrays to database engines. In: 2015 IEEE High Performance Extreme Computing Conference (HPEC), pp. 1–6, September 2015. https://doi.org/10.1109/HPEC.2015.7322472
7. Hubbell, M., et al.: Big data strategies for data center infrastructure management using a 3D gaming platform. In: 2015 IEEE High Performance Extreme Computing Conference (HPEC), pp. 1–6, September 2015. https://doi.org/10.1109/HPEC.2015.7322471
8. Jones, M., et al.: Scalability of VM provisioning systems. In: 2016 IEEE High Performance Extreme Computing Conference, HPEC 2016 (2016). https://doi.org/10.1109/HPEC.2016.7761629
9. Kepner, J.: MatlabMPI. J. Parallel Distrib. Comput. **64**(8), 997–1005 (2004). https://doi.org/10.1016/j.jpdc.2004.03.018
10. Kepner, J.: Parallel MATLAB for Multicore and Multinode Computers. Society for Industrial and Applied Mathematics, New York (2009). https://doi.org/10.1137/1.9780898718126
11. Kepner, J., et al.: D4M 2.0 schema: a general purpose high performance schema for the Accumulo database. In: 2013 IEEE High Performance Extreme Computing Conference (HPEC), pp. 1–6, September 2013. https://doi.org/10.1109/HPEC.2013.6670318
12. Kepner, J., et al.: Dynamic distributed dimensional data model (D4M) database and computation system. In: 2012 IEEE International Conference on Acoustics, Speech and Signal Processing (ICASSP), pp. 5349–5352, March 2012. https://doi.org/10.1109/ICASSP.2012.6289129

13. Kepner, J., et al.: Achieving 100,000,000 database inserts per second using Accumulo and D4M. In: 2014 IEEE High Performance Extreme Computing Conference (HPEC), pp. 1–6, September 2014. https://doi.org/10.1109/HPEC.2014.7040945
14. Kepner, J., et al.: Computing on masked data: a high performance method for improving big data veracity. In: 2014 IEEE High Performance Extreme Computing Conference (HPEC), pp. 1–6, September 2014. https://doi.org/10.1109/HPEC.2014.7040946
15. Lebak, J., Kepner, J., Hoffmann, H., Rutledge, E.: Parallel VSIPL++: an open standard software library for high-performance parallel signal processing. Proc. IEEE **93**(2), 313–330 (2005). https://doi.org/10.1109/JPROC.2004.840303
16. Moler, C.: Why there isn't a parallel MATLAB. MATLAB News and Notes, p. 12 (1995, Spring). https://www.mathworks.com/company/newsletters/articles/why-there-isnt-a-parallel-matlab.html
17. Mullen, J., Byun, C., Gadepally, V., Samsi, S., Reuther, A., Kepner, J.: Learning by doing, high performance computing education in the MOOC era. J. Parallel Distrib. Comput. **105**, 105–115 (2017). https://doi.org/10.1016/j.jpdc.2017.01.015
18. Prout, A., et al.: MIT SuperCloud portal workspace: enabling HPC web application deployment. In: 2017 IEEE High Performance Extreme Computing Conference (HPEC), pp. 1–6, September 2017. https://doi.org/10.1109/HPEC.2017.8091097
19. Prout, A., et al.: Enabling on-demand database computing with MIT SuperCloud database management system. In: 2015 IEEE High Performance Extreme Computing Conference (HPEC), pp. 1–6, September 2015. https://doi.org/10.1109/HPEC.2015.7322482
20. Reuther, A., et al.: Technology requirements for supporting on-demand interactive grid computing. In: Proceedings of the Department of Defense High Performance Computing Modernization Office (HPCMO) Users Group Conference (UGC) 2005. IEEE, Nashville, June 2005. https://doi.org/10.1109/DODUGC.2005.65
21. Reuther, A., et al.: LLSuperCloud: sharing HPC systems for diverse rapid prototyping. In: 2013 IEEE High Performance Extreme Computing Conference (HPEC), pp. 1–6, September 2013. https://doi.org/10.1109/HPEC.2013.6670329
22. Reuther, A., Kepner, J., MCcabe, A., Mullen, J., Bliss, N.T., Kim, H.: Technical challenges of supporting interactive HPC. In: Department of Defense - Proceedings of the HPCMP Users Group Conference 2007; High Performance Computing Modernization Program: A Bridge to Future Defense, DoD HPCMP UGC, pp. 403–409 (2007). https://doi.org/10.1109/HPCMP-UGC.2007.72
23. Reuther, A., Michaleas, P., Prout, A., Kepner, J.: HPC-VMs: virtual machines in high performance computing systems. In: 2012 IEEE Conference on High Performance Extreme Computing, HPEC 2012 (2012). https://doi.org/10.1109/HPEC.2012.6408668
24. Software carpentry. https://software-carpentry.org/
25. Design thinking bootcamp. https://dschool.stanford.edu/resources/the-bootcamp-bootleg
26. Tichenor, S., Reuther, A.: Making the business case for high performance computing: a benefit-cost analysis methodology. CTWatch Q. **2**(4A), 2–8 (2006)
27. Wilson, G.: Software carpentry: getting scientists to write better code by making them more productive. Comput. Sci. Eng. **8**(6), 66–69 (2006). https://doi.org/10.1109/MCSE.2006.122

Enabling Interactive Supercomputing at JSC Lessons Learned

Jens Henrik Göbbert[1]([✉]), Tim Kreuzer[1], Alice Grosch[1],
Andreas Lintermann[2,3], and Morris Riedel[1]

[1] Jülich Supercomputing Centre, Forschungszentrum Jülich GmbH, Jülich, Germany
{j.goebbert,t.kreuzer,a.grosch,m.riedel}@fz-juelich.de
[2] Institute of Aerodynamics and Chair of Fluid Mechanics,
RWTH Aachen University, Aachen, Germany
a.lintermann@aia.rwth-aachen.de
[3] Jülich Aachen Research Alliance (JARA) - High Performance Computing,
RWTH Aachen University, Aachen, Germany
http://www.fz-juelich.de/jsc, http://www.aia.rwth-aachen.de,
https://www.jara.org

Abstract. Research and analysis of large amounts of data from scientific simulations, in-situ visualization, and application control are convincing scenarios for interactive supercomputing. The open-source software Jupyter (or JupyterLab) is a tool that has already been used successfully in many scientific disciplines. With its open and flexible web-based design, Jupyter is ideal for combining a wide variety of workflows and programming methods in a single interface. The multi-user capability of Jupyter via JuypterHub excels it for scientific applications at supercomputing centers. It combines the workspace that is local to the user and the corresponding workspace on the HPC systems. In order to meet the requirements for more interactivity in supercomputing and to open up new possibilities in HPC, a simple and direct web access for starting and connecting to login or compute nodes with Jupyter or JupyterLab at Jülich Supercomputing Centre (JSC) is presented. To corroborate the flexibility of the new method, the motivation, applications, details and challenges of enabling interactive supercomputing, as well as goals and prospective future work will be discussed.

Keywords: Interactive supercomputing
High Performance Computing · Jupyter

1 Introduction

Extracting new scientific knowledge from large amounts of data is of crucial importance for science. However, scientific progress will only be achieved if the data obtained can be processed into meaningful results. But nowadays, researchers are increasingly confronted with an explosion in the volume of data.

© Springer Nature Switzerland AG 2018
R. Yokota et al. (Eds.): ISC 2018 Workshops, LNCS 11203, pp. 669–677, 2018.
https://doi.org/10.1007/978-3-030-02465-9_48

With the rapidly increasing computing power of supercomputers, huge amounts of data are generated in a short time that by far exceed the capacity typically available to scientists on their local computers. Moving such data from super-computing centers to local hardware is impractical if not impossible. As the size of simulations increases, post-processing becomes a bottleneck on the way to the desired scientific findings. Data analysis and visualization functions have therefore been shifted to the supercomputing centers.

High Performance Computing (HPC) systems are usually used by a large number of users simultaneously. The computer resources are accessed using asynchronous batch scheduling. However, scientific knowledge often only arises through interactive and iterative data analysis by "human in the loop" processes. These different application modes of supercomputers seem to be contrary to each other. Bridging those modes via interactive HPC with the method presented in this work closes the gap between explorative data analysis and pure HPC. It hence leads to an efficient workflow that can easily be integrated between data production and data analysis.

2   Background Jupyter

Jupyter[1] is a browser-based interactive computing environment that allows to combine code execution, math, plots and rich text and media into single documents called Jupyter Notebooks. Jupyter is the result of the IPython project[2], which is an extended interactive Python shell with additional functions. Initially IPython has been developed as a pure terminal application. It has been extended by graphical user interfaces and finally by a Web Application Framework. The concept of a human-readable notebook document is developed as a uniform interface.

Notebooks are intended for the creation of reproducible computer narratives. It combines analysis descriptions, executable source code and results, and is based on a series of open standards for interactive computing. These open standards can be used to develop specific applications for embedded interactive computing. Using these notebook documents, entire workflows and reproducible findings can easily be shared among researchers. At the same time, the notebooks can also be converted into other formats such as HTML or LaTeX. To run executable scripts in a notebook, it can be connected to one or more of Jupyter compute kernel instances. These kernels exist for different programming languages, i.e., Jupyter is by no means limited to Python.

With JupyterLab[3], the Web Application Framework has recently been revised and extended significantly. The developers of JupyterLab aim at offering a web interface with a high degree of integration between notebooks, documents,

---

[1] https://jupyter.org.
[2] https://ipython.org.
[3] https://jupyterlab.readthedocs.io.

and activities. It now represents an advanced interactive development environment for working with notebooks, code and data, and offers full support for Jupyter notebooks. JupyterLab also provides the user with text editors, terminals, data file viewers, and other specific components side by side with Jupyter notebooks in a tabular workspace.

On local machines, the user usually starts Jupyter from the command line and uses a web browser on the same system to access the software interface. However, if Jupyter is started on a multi-user system, it requires in the best case an intermediate layer, which enables shared usage of a computer system via Jupyter. This task can be performed by JupyterHub[4], which is a web application that enables a multi-user hub for spawning, managing, and proxying multiple instances of single-user Jupyter notebook servers.

At JSC a JupyterHub is operated in a virtual machine as a gateway to the compute clusters. Users authenticate via JupyterHub in a central identity management with their JSC web access credentials.

3   Jupyter Integration at JSC

Starting Jupyter on the HPC systems of JSC solely via a web frontend requires three basic steps. In the first step, the user must authenticate successfully. Subsequently, the system must determine how and where the Jupyter Notebook Server should be started. In the final step, the defined job must be executed on the HPC system via the user's account and the new Jupyter Notebook Server must be connected to the users web browser through the hub. These three steps of login, configuration, and startup are outlined in Fig. 1 and are described in detail for JSC's configuration in the following.

First, the user visits the Jupyter@JSC website[5] and clicks on the login button (Fig. 1 - step 1). The user is redirected to the Unity IdM[6] - Identity management and authentication platform, asking for the Web LDAP user credentials and checking them by Web LDAP (Fig. 1 - step 2). Upon successful authentication, Unity IdM asks the LDAP for additional user information. This information is compared to the local Unity IdM database. If a suitable account is present, the user is logged from Unity IdM's point of view and a cookie with an OAuth-state is created in the browser. If no suitable account is found, the user is offered to create one provided that the terms of use, data protection declaration, and declaration of consent are accepted. The user is redirected back to JupyterHub with the appropriate authorization code for the OAuth-state (Fig. 1 - step 3) and logged in. JupyterHub subsequently queries the missing user information from Unity IdM (Fig. 1 - step 4).

Various compute clusters are available at JSC. These clusters are usually divided into login and compute nodes and in different partitions with different access restrictions. In addition, a user can have multiple user accounts to access

---

[4] https://jupyterhub.readthedocs.io.

[5] https://jupyter-jsc.fz-juelich.de.

[6] https://www.unity-idm.eu.

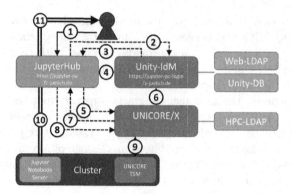

Fig. 1. Illustration of the interaction of JupyterHub, Unity IdM, UNICORE/X, and the compute cluster when starting a new Jupyter Notebook Server via the Jupyter Portal at JSC. Steps 1–4 show the login process, steps 5–7 the configuration process and steps 8–11 the starting process.

HPC computing resources. Therefore, the user chooses the appropriated user account and computing resources after successful login. This step is performed in the server configuration, which follows a successful login.

For this purpose, the service UNICORE/X[7] [1,6] with the valid OAuth-token is first asked which user accounts exist for the user (Fig. 1 - step 5). UNICORE/X asks Unity-IdM if this OAuth-token is known and requests parts of the user information of the Unity IdM account (Fig. 1 - step 6). This information is compared to the HPC-LDAP data and the corresponding user accounts on the HPC systems are determined. The response is forwarded to JupyterHub and presented to the user for selection (Fig. 1 - step 7).

In the name of the selected user account, UNICORE/X starts a Jupyter Notebook Server via its service UNICORE/TSM running on the cluster as soon as the user initiates the start of Jupyter (Fig. 1 - steps 8, 9). Finally, the URL of the Jupyter Notebook Server is returned to JupyterHub (Fig. 1 - step 10) and from there the website is transmitted to the user's browser (Fig. 1 - step 11).

4   Use Case: Rhinodiagnost

Rhinodiagnost[8] is a project in which partners from industry and research prepare personalized medicine in rhinology in order to offer practicing physicians new extended possibilities for functional diagnostics [3]. That is, JSC cooperates with the Institute of Aerodynamics and Chair of Fluid Mechanics (AIA), RWTH Aachen University, within the Jülich Aachen Research Alliance - High Performance Computing (JARA-HPC), and Sutter Medizintechnik GmbH, Med Contact GmbH, and Angewandte Informationstechnikgesellschaft mbH in this

---

[7] https://www.unicore.eu/.

[8] https://www.rhinodiagnost.eu/.

project. Rhinodiagnost will increase the surgical success rate by validating treatment therapies a priori to medical interventions. One of the goals of this project is to use simulations running on HPC systems to support surgeons in finding optimal procedures for the individual patient. This requires high-resolution flow simulations based on patient-specific anatomically correct geometries. In more detail, highly resolved lattice-Boltzmann simulations are preformed with the simulation framework Zonal Flow Solver [4,5] (ZFS), developed at AIA. These simulations necessitate computing resources that can only be provided by HPC centers such as JSC (Fig. 2).

Fig. 2. Exemplary visualization of particle dynamics in the upper human respiratory tract. The calculations employed the simulation framework ZFS developed by the Rhinodiagnost project partner AIA, RWTH Aachen University.

Simulations are, however, only a part of the whole processing pipeling that is necessary to allow for interactive supercomputing in medical context. Therefore, they need to be embedded in existing treatment processes to become a new way to support physicians in developing patient-specific treatment strategies through HPC results. Obviously, it is important to adapt HPC and the numerical methods to the requirements of the physician and not vice-versa. The amount of data generated by high-resolution simulations can hardly leave the data center due to its immense size and must therefore be evaluated on site. Furthermore, the physician should be allowed to modify the geometry for a virtual operation at simulation runtime ("in-situ computational steering") or for a subsequent simulation.

The main task of Forschungszentrum Jülich is to develop software components that provide physicians with interactive and targeted access to HPC and the analysis of simulation data on HPC systems. The software must offer an extensible interface from which simulations can be managed and flexibly evaluated. It is essential to make novel developments of visualization and analysis methods accessible to industry as fast as possible. Reimplementation of working solutions in another software environment must therefore be largely avoided. In JSC's view, Jupyter is a key component in achieving this goal.

5   Use Case: Deep Learning

The turbulent motion of fluid flows is a complex, highly non-linear, multi-scale phenomenon that raises some of the most difficult and fundamental problems of classical physics. Turbulent flows are characterized by random spatial-temporal fluctuations of their velocity and scalar fields. The general challenge of turbulence research is to predict the statistics of such fluctuations. An accurate prediction is of practical importance for a wide range of applications in engineering and natural sciences. A novel approach to this is the use of Deep Learning (DL) for this research.

In recent years, DL has improved considerably and has proven useful in a wide range of sciences, from computer science to life sciences. Despite its stochastic nature, turbulence has certain coherent structures and statistical symmetries that can be tracked over time by DL techniques, i.e., using DL is a promising approach for predicting the smallest statistics of turbulence.

On the one hand, research in this field requires the classical HPC approach in order to calculate sufficiently meaningful and high-resolution simulations with many time steps as a data basis for DL algorithms. On the other hand, the development of DL networks is a highly interactive work. Interactive supercomputing successfully combines these two requirements.

With the software psOpen [2], direct numerical simulations were performed on the HPC systems at JSC to generate the necessary reference data for the learning and test phase of the DL network with high accuracy. The DL strategy itself is based on Wasserstein Generative Adversarial Networks (wGANs) with the software Keras[9]/TensorFlow[10], which are very suitable for small-scale turbulences due to their stability and interpretability of the learning curve. In the first step, however, the development of universal turbulent models based on DL means defining and testing a wide variety of networks. To the best of the authors knowledge, a fully automatic method for this is not known. DL is therefore a classic case of "human-in-the-loop" processes in HPC.

The possibility of obtaining a large additional gain for HPC experts via the Jupyter software without discernible restrictions has proven itself. Above all, because the software landscape in DL can largely be controlled and interconnected via Python. The development of a sustainable network for a specific application case is always an iterative process in which various configurations have to be tested.

---

[9] https://keras.io.

[10] https://www.tensorflow.org.

6   Lessons Learned

Solutions have been found and lessons have been learned while establishing an interactive web access via Jupyter to the HPC systems at JSC. This includes first and foremost the secure authentication of the user via a separate identity management system to which the user of JupyterHub is forwarded. It is obvious, as for other web services of JSC, to use the already present and reliable open-source software Unity IdM. The combination with JupyterHub proved surprisingly simple using the well-known OAuth2 protocol.

The Unity IdM installation maintains its own user database for the Jupyter web service at JSC and uses the central web LDAP for web services at JSC to check user credentials. A direct comparison with the HPC-LDAP is technically possible, but not practical for the following reasons. Separating the web service accounts from the HPC accounts allows to better combine the different web services at JSC. Furthermore, computer systems can be supported that are not accessible via the central HPC-LDAP and which implement web-compatible authentication methods more easily. This solution lets the user decide to activate the web service for interactive HPC and to accesses the corresponding HPC account via a web frontend. Independent of that, access to other web services at JSC is maintained even if no HPC account exists. A 1:1 account mapping of Web-LDAP and HPC-LDAP (currently, status 07/2018) would not be possible anyway, since multiple HPC accounts for different HPC systems can belong to a single user. Therefore, no direct assignment is possible.

The new possibility to access the HPC systems via the web service Jupyter@JSC requires new solutions not only on the technical but also on the legal side. Consent, Terms of Use, and Privacy Policy must be developed and presented to the user during the registration process so that they can be accepted. Furthermore, it is required that a user can unregister from the Jupyter@JSC web service just as simple as register. The separate holding of user data in the Unity DB and checking the credentials using the Web LDAP allow a simple deletion of user-specific data in the Unity DB.

The integration of 3D-visualization methods in Jupyter notebooks is promising, however not yet suitable for more complex requirements and large-scale simulation data. A complete replacement for full software packages such as ParaView[11] or VisIt[12] is still a long way off. JSC therefore supports the porting of visualization functionalities in Jupyter plugins. In the meantime, better integration of remote desktop solutions could close the gap.

A diverse HPC software landscape is provided at JSC by means of a software module concept. Different software packages can be installed on the system without introducing dependency conflicts. However, this also allows a large number of possible combinations of software packages, which cannot all be loaded simultaneously under Jupyter. On the basis of the Jupyter kernel the user can load special software combinations. At present, this requires a deeper understanding

---

[11] https://www.paraview.org.
[12] https://wci.llnl.gov/simulation/computer-codes/visit.

of the Jupyter kernel. Since for non-experts this is a big hurdle, the software available via web frontend is currently limited.

Independent of the great possibilities to make HPC interactively accessible, the implementation phase showed new functionalities developed at JSC to be easily deployable to the user communities via the web-based Jupyter/JupyterLab. Solutions for individual users can quickly be distributed or referred to by a large user group. Instead of describing solutions only on web pages, they can be executed directly and thus integrated more quickly into existing workflows. In particular, the constant change of the user base on HPC systems in the scientific field requires that workflows can be passed on completely, correctly, and at the same time in an easy way to new researchers. That's why interactive HPC brings advantages for the entire HPC community far beyond the direct area of application.

7   Outlook

The first steps for interactive supercomputing at JSC have successfully been taken using the web service Jupyter. The implementations cover only a small part of the possibilities of interactive supercomputing, but from JSC's point of view the most important ones are already provided. In close cooperation with the users of the HPC systems the implementations are refined. The project is mainly driven by interactive visualization and collaborative work in HPC environments. In principle, JSC considers further web services accessible from Jupyter important. Here the integration of web based remote desktops are first possible candidates.

8   Conclusion

It was shown how interactive HPC is deployed to user of the HPC systems at JSC by means of Jupyter via JupyterHub. This requires a good integration into the existing services of JSC, especially the multi-layer authentication from a web service account to the HPC-LDAP accounts, not ignoring Consent, Terms of Use, and Privacy Policy. The integration of 3D-visualization methods in Jupyter notebooks is promising, however not yet suitable for more complex requirements and large-scale simulation data. How to support the almost infinite large number of combinations of software packages, especially for non-expert users, needs to be worked on. Containers are definitely a possible solution here. In general, on the basis of two use cases it was shown that interactive HPC is not only useful but also necessary to advanced research in new scientific disciplines and industry.

Acknowledgement. This work is supported by the Rhinodiagnost project funded by the Zentrale Innovationsprogramm Mittelstand (ZIM) of the Federal Ministry of Economical Affairs and Energy (BMWi) and the InHPC-DE project as part of the SiVeGCS project to promote closer technical integration of the three GCS HPC centers in Stuttgart (HLRS), Jülich (JSC) and Munich (LRZ).

References

1. Benedyczak, K., Schuller, B., Petrova-ElSayed, M., Rybicki, J., Grunzke, R.: UNI-CORE 7 - middleware services for distributed and federated computing. In: 2016 International Conference on High Performance Computing and Simulation, Innsbruck, Austria, 18 July 2016–22 July 2016, pp. 613–620. IEEE (2016). https://doi.org/10.1109/HPCSim.2016.7568392. http://juser.fz-juelich.de/record/820611

2. Goebbert, J.H., Gauding, M., Ansorge, C., Hentschel, B., Kuhlen, T., Pitsch, H.: Direct numerical simulation of fluid turbulence at extreme scale with psOpen. Adv. Parallel Comput. **27**, 777–785 (2016). https://doi.org/10.3233/978-1-61499-621-7-777

3. Lintermann, A., Göbbert, J.H., Vogt, K., Koch, W., Hetzel, A.: Rhinodiagnost: morphological and functional precision diagnostics of nasal cavities. Innov. Supercomput. Deutschl. **15**(2), 106–109 (2017). http://juser.fz-juelich.de/record/840544

4. Lintermann, A., Meinke, M., Schröder, W.: Fluid mechanics based classification of the respiratory efficiency of several nasal cavities. Comput. Biol. Med. **43**(11), 1833–1852 (2013). https://doi.org/10.1016/j.compbiomed.2013.09.003

5. Lintermann, A., Schröder, W.: A hierarchical numerical journey through the nasal cavity: from nose-like models to real anatomies. Flow Turbul. Combust. **101**, 1–28 (2017). https://doi.org/10.1007/s10494-017-9876-0

6. Petrova-ElSayed, M., Benedyczak, K., Rutkowski, A., Schuller, B.: Federated computing on the web: the UNICORE portal. In: Proceedings of the 2016 39th International Convention on Information and Communication Technology, Electronics and Microelectronics, Opatija, Croatia, 30 May 2016–3 June 2016, pp. 190–195. IEEE (2016). ISBN 978-953-233-086-1. https://doi.org/10.1109/MIPRO.2016.7522133. http://juser.fz-juelich.de/record/820398

Interactive Distributed Deep Learning with Jupyter Notebooks

Steve Farrell[1], Aaron Vose[2], Oliver Evans[3], Matthew Henderson[3],
Shreyas Cholia[3], Fernando Pérez[3], Wahid Bhimji[1(✉)], Shane Canon[1],
Rollin Thomas[1], and Prabhat[1]

[1] NERSC, Berkeley, CA, USA
{sfarrell,wbhimji}@lbl.gov
[2] Cray Inc., Seattle, WA, USA
avose@cray.com
[3] Lawrence Berkeley National Laboratory, Berkeley, CA, USA
scholia@lbl.gov

Abstract. Deep learning researchers are increasingly using Jupyter notebooks to implement interactive, reproducible workflows with embedded visualization, steering and documentation. Such solutions are typically deployed on small-scale (e.g. single server) computing systems. However, as the sizes and complexities of datasets and associated neural network models increase, high-performance distributed systems become important for training and evaluating models in a feasible amount of time. In this paper we describe our vision for Jupyter notebook solutions to deploy deep learning workloads onto high-performance computing systems. We demonstrate the effectiveness of notebooks for distributed training and hyper-parameter optimization of deep neural networks with efficient, scalable backends.

Keywords: Jupyter · Deep learning · Distributed training
Hyperparameter optimization · High-performance computing
Genetic algorithms

1 Introduction

Deep learning (DL) [14], the sub-field of machine learning which uses multi-layer neural networks (NNs) to solve complex tasks with data, has gained a great deal of popularity in recent years in part due to the availability of large datasets and increasingly powerful computing resources. Meanwhile, Jupyter [13] notebooks enable code, graphical results, and rich documentation to be combined into an interactive computational narrative, and have become the de facto standard for data science collaboration, development and pedagogy. Notebook-based DL workflows are widely used but typically deployed on small-scale computing systems (e.g. single server), but as the sizes and complexities of datasets and associated neural network models increase, distributed computing systems become

R. Yokota et al. (Eds.): ISC 2018 Workshops, LNCS 11203, pp. 678–687, 2018.
https://doi.org/10.1007/978-3-030-02465-9_49

essential for generating the best results in a reasonable time. In particular, models that are slow to train can benefit from distributed data-parallel training, and model-selection tasks can be accelerated with distributed hyper-parameter optimization (HPO). The development of scalable notebook-based DL workflows for high performance computing (HPC) systems will therefore be highly valuable to the DL and science communities and will enable new kinds of human-in-the-loop interactivity and monitoring in DL-based research.

In this paper we demonstrate several distributed notebook-based deep learning workflows on HPC systems, interfacing to the Cori supercomputer at NERSC. In Sect. 2, we describe our architecture to effectively use these HPC resources via Jupyter, taking into account the hardware and policy restrictions that are common with other large HPC machines. We then present our notebook-based approaches, including scaling results for distributed training in Sect. 3 and for distributed HPO in Sect. 4.

We take advantage of and build on features available in the Jupyter and Python ecosystem including JupyterHub, IPyWidgets, IPython "magic" commands, Dask, and IPyParallel which provide us with tools to interact with the backend tasks directly through a visual interface. This allows us to close the interactivity loop so that operating real-time, entirely within the notebook, we can allocate nodes on the Cori supercomputer; configure, monitor, tune and steer deep learning training runs; and perform further analysis on the outputs of models. As well as human interaction we couple this infrastructure with a powerful automated hyper-parameter framework incorporating genetic algorithms and population-based training as described in Sect. 4.3. Example notebooks and recipes for running these at NERSC are provided at the links in Sect. 6.

We demonstrate these methods with a science use-case and dataset from High Energy Physics which applies convolutional neural networks (CNNs) to classify images formed from Large Hadron Collider events, and is described in detail in [8]. We find that we can improve on state-of-the-art results by using distributed HPC resources to improve model parameters.

2   System Architecture

In order to achieve the aims of this project, we extended the Jupyter infrastructure at NERSC [1] to be able to execute distributed training on the Cori supercomputer [2]: a Cray XC40 with 2388 Intel Haswell and 9688 Intel Xeon Phi Knight's Landing compute nodes. The overall architecture is shown in Fig. 1. The components of this are described in more detail below.

The JupyterHub installation at NERSC [1] provides a multi-user gateway through which individual users can authenticate and spawn a private notebook server on the Cori login nodes to launch notebooks. Each notebook is associated with a Jupyter kernel, a wrapper around the Python process that executes user code. Currently these kernels run on the login node itself, a configuration that is widely used at NERSC, sufficient for small workloads and allows access to the Cori file-systems and for submitting scripts to the Cori batch-queues.

However, here we further use the HPC batch queue system to allocate dedicated compute nodes for executing long-running and resource-demanding tasks such as DL training from the notebook. To this end, we use two distributed execution frameworks, IPyParallel [3] and Dask Distributed [11,16], which facilitate the use of remote compute resources from the notebook. In both frameworks, a central Controller handles scheduling and communication with a number of execution Engines that are instantiated by the user. In our execution model (Fig. 1), the Controller and Engines run from the compute nodes after a batch allocation has been provided. To minimize boilerplate, we have created an IPython "magic" command[1] (an IPython-specific command beginning with %) which allocates HPC resources and deploys the IPyParallel cluster with a one-line command from the notebook.

As a further extension, the ability to individually stop and start tasks is supported through Kale [4], an extension to the Jupyter ecosystem for interactive HPC. Kale wraps each task with a worker process that provides full control of the task as well as resource usage monitoring for the task and participating compute node.

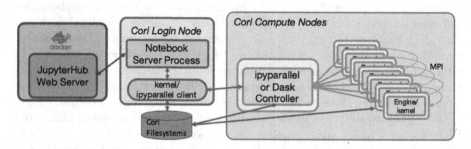

Fig. 1. Diagram of the distributed workload system. A user launches a notebook process via JupyterHub. They obtain an allocation of compute nodes on the batch system and launch the cluster processes (e.g. IPyParallel controller and worker engines) via a SLURM script or our `%ipcluster` magic within the Jupyter notebook. They then connect to the cluster via the notebook; launch the NN training tasks to the batch system and continue to monitor and interacts with those tasks. The notebook to cluster coordination occurs in communication with the controller node, however large-scale distributed training can avoid this bottleneck via the native MPI interface of, for example horovod (Sect. 3).

In order to create an interactive feedback loop to visualize results that the user can interact with, we make use of built-in Jupyter widgets (iPyWidgets [5]) along with third party Jupyter widgets qgrid [6] (Quantopian) and bqplot [7] (Bloomberg). Model results presented by the widgets are communicated asynchronously through the parallel controller (Dask or iPyParallel) in the Jupyter

---

[1] https://github.com/sparticlesteve/cori-intml-examples/blob/master/ipcluster_magics.py.

Kernel. We poll the kernel for these results through a background thread, updating the table in real-time as they come in, and rendering plots for the currently selected model.

3 Distributed Training

Slow training of NNs due to large datasets and complex models can inhibit DL research productivity. Distributed training techniques can speed up model learning by exploiting parallelism at the data and model levels. For example, in synchronous data-parallel training, batches of data are distributed across worker nodes along with copies of the model. Each worker processes its local batch of data and computes gradients. The gradients are then accumulated across workers to compute a global optimization step and all the models are updated synchronously. Tools like Uber's Horovod [17] and the Cray PE ML Plugin [15] provide the synchronization mechanism via MPI communication for efficiently scaling to large numbers of workers.

To implement distributed training in notebooks, we use the IPyParallel cluster with MPI-enabled worker engines. Once the cluster client is connected in the notebook, a user can mark individual cells for parallel execution using the %%px IPython magic command. Results from the model can be retrieved in the main notebook process for further analysis.

We used the Cori system to demonstrate the scalability of this approach with notebooks. We implemented a Horovod and Keras [9] distributed training implementation of the LHC CNN use-case and scaled up to 180 worker nodes both using the Jupyter notebook with IPyParallel infrastructure as well as a pure "batch" submission from python scripts. The training throughput, plotted in Fig. 2, shows that the notebook infrastructure introduces no noticeable overhead relative to distributed training with batch scripts.

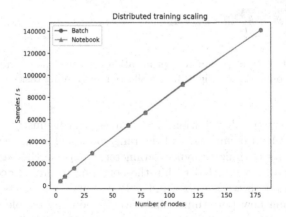

Fig. 2. Scaling of distributed training with and without the notebook infrastructure. No overhead from IPyParallel is observed up to 180 nodes on Cori.

4   Distributed Hyper-parameter Optimization

Hyper-parameter optimization (HPO) helps solve the problem of model selection for non-trained parameters such as hidden layer size, dropout probability and learning rate. HPO algorithms generally involve training models at various points in this parameter space and evaluating a metric such as model accuracy on a validation dataset. Depending on the choice of algorithm, many such tasks may be run in parallel on a distributed system.

We have developed several examples for distributed HPO with Jupyter notebooks. The first (Sect. 4.1) uses random search with independent tasks training in parallel on IPyParallel engines with load balancing. The second (Sect. 4.2) extends this with live, interactive widgets. The third (Sect. 4.3) is an advanced HPO example using population-based training via Dask scheduling.

4.1   Random Search HPO Notebook

We implemented a random search of hundreds of configurations of convolution and fully-connected layers, learning rate and dropout for the LHC CNN use case using Keras [9] in a Jupyter notebook and ran this using a 100 node allocation on the Cori system which was able to complete all experiments in under an hour.

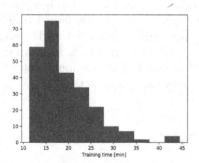 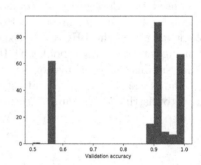

Fig. 3. Distributed hyper-parameter optimization distributions of training time [left] and best validation accuracy [right] for a collection of training tasks.

Figure 3 shows the distribution of run-times, which illustrates the value of using automatic load-balancing, and the range of model accuracies, which illustrates the need for optimizing hyper-parameters to obtain the best results. Further analysis can be conducted within the notebook to probe incoming results: for example Fig. 4 shows the loss and a ROC curve for the best performing model illustrating how performing this optimization can enable obtain similar performance results as previous analyses with a substantially smaller dataset.

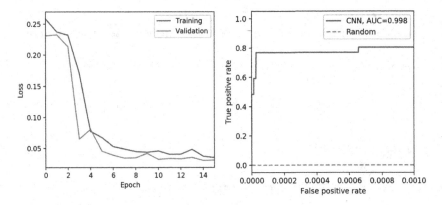

Fig. 4. Loss (left) and weighted ROC curve (right) of the best model found in hyper-parameter optimization. The achieved results are competitive with those presented in [8] while using less than 20% of the original dataset.

4.2 HPO with Interactive Widgets

We use Jupyter's interactive widget ecosystem as described in Sect. 2 to provide a graphical interface for controlling and monitoring training runs in human-in-the-loop hyper-parameter optimization, as shown in Fig. 5. Individual points in the hyper-parameter space can be specified in the notebook and Keras is used to construct and train the DL model with remote execution provided by IPyParallel. The qgrid widget provides a dynamic table interface for displaying the latest results and bqplot widgets provide live plotting of the full results. These tools are clickable and interactive, allowing us to switch between results or send messages back to the python kernel for further processing. This allows for dynamic task control and job steering. Based on the live results of individual training runs, the user can decide which areas of the parameter spaces are worth exploring further, and which areas are not likely to produce viable models, all before training is complete. Poorly performing runs can be prematurely canceled and replaced with runs from more hopeful regions of the hyper-parameter space.

4.3 Advanced HPO

As a more advanced example, we consider a variant of population-based training (PBT), which combines gradient-based approaches such as stochastic gradient descent (SGD) with a genetic algorithm (GA) to optimize both parameters (i.e., weights and biases) and hyper-parameters simultaneously [12]. By running a genetic algorithm synchronized with NN training such that each generation in the GA corresponds to some fixed number of SGD epochs, the GA applied to the HPs can be extended to optimize the model parameters.

At the end of each generation, each member of a population of neural networks is evaluated on a validation set to produce a fitness score based on the NN's accuracy. These fitness scores are then used to determine the probability of

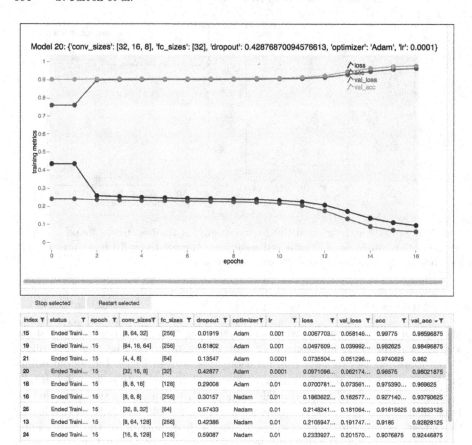

Fig. 5. Screenshot of interactive Jupyter widget for HPO. Each row in the table shows a parameter set which has been submitted to the batch system. Loss and accuracy values in the table update live as the training progresses. Clicking on a row plots live metrics for the associated run.

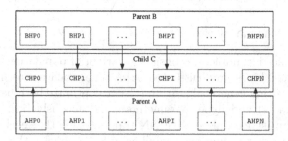

Fig. 6. Crossover combines hyperparameters from parents to create those of a child.

reproduction, where the most fit NNs are more likely to reproduce. Over multiple generations, the population of NNs evolves toward a good set of hyperparameters and parameters. The PBT variant in this work utilizes reproduction with pairs of NNs, where two sets of hyperparameters are mixed via crossover, depicted in Fig. 6, to create a child. The use of a GA with sexual reproduction and crossover provides for faster adaptation than simpler asexual reproduction [10].

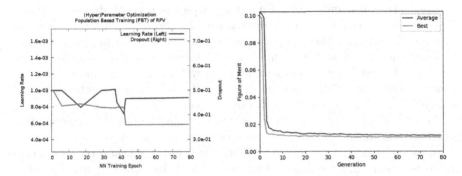

Fig. 7. Hyperparameter schedule discovered via HPO with PBT on the LHC CNN (left) as well as the average and best figure of merit in the population (right).

Figure 7 shows a hyperparameter schedule found through the application of HPO with PBT to the LHC CNN neural network (left) along with the average figure of merit and the FoM of the most-fit population member in each generation during the HPO process (right). This training schedule shows improvement can be attained through the application of a slightly decreasing learning rate as well as decreasing dropout. As can be seen in the figure of merit plot on the right (lower is better), the population of NNs quickly plateaus after only a few epochs, entering a phase which likely benefits from the different training regime introduced at that point by the discovered training schedule.

While automated approaches like PBT take a lot of the repetitive work out of HPO, they can achieve even better results when guided by humans. Specifically, the HPO process can be fine-tuned for specific NN and dataset combinations by adjusting details of the HPO search process such as the mutation rate and crossover rate of a GA. The image on the right of Fig. 7 is taken from a live plot produced in a Jupyter notebook which updates in real time during the HPO search. If the human in the loop sees that the automated HPO search is not performing well, details such as the mutation rate or search starting point can be quickly changed. Interactive and automated HPO can be combined to achieve better results than would be possible using either approach alone.

5 Conclusions

We have demonstrated that Jupyter notebooks can be a powerful interface for deploying distributed deep learning workflows on HPC systems. By framing modern DL frameworks on large computational resources in an interactive context, we achieve a human-in-the-loop system which enables rapid development of NN models through expert guidance of automated training.

We demonstrate several examples of this, all driven entirely from Jupyter notebooks, including distributed training of a single model across multiple compute nodes; distributed HPO of individual models where tasks are load-balanced across nodes; the use of widgets and plots within the notebook for steering and visualizing the runs; and more advanced hyper-parameter optimization methods. All these can be run within large interactive allocations on the Cori supercomputer, with that allocation also setup and configured from within the notebook.

Future work will seek to achieve deeper integration with Kale to achieve more detailed task and node monitoring; as well as providing more insightful visualizations; and building out the suite of tools and example notebooks for use at NERSC and for the community to build upon.

This work paves the way to understanding how human domain-expertise; automated optimization tools; and deep neural networks can be optimally combined to maximize the insight we can derive in a world of ever-growing datasets while also minimizing the time and technical knowledge necessary to achieve this on large-scale computational resources.

6   Code and Recipes

Example notebooks used in this study and recipes for running at NERSC are available at https://github.com/sparticlesteve/cori-intml-examples.

Acknowledgements. This research used resources of the National Energy Research Scientific Computing Center, a DOE Office of Science User Facility supported by the Office of Science of the U.S. Department of Energy under Contract No. DE-AC02-05CH11231. This work was in part supported by the NERSC Big Data Center; we acknowledge Cray for their funding support.

References

1. http://docs.nersc.gov/services/jupyter/
2. http://www.nersc.gov/users/computational-systems/cori/
3. https://ipyparallel.readthedocs.io/en/latest/intro.html
4. https://github.com/Jupyter-Kale/kale
5. https://ipywidgets.readthedocs.io/en/stable/
6. https://qgrid.readthedocs.io/en/latest/
7. https://bqplot.readthedocs.io/en/stable/introduction.html
8. Bhimji, W., Farrell, S.A., Kurth, T., Paganini, M., Racah, E., Prabhat: Deep neural networks for physics analysis on low-level whole-detector data at the LHC. arXiv preprint arXiv:1711.03573 (2017)
9. Chollet, F.: keras (2015). https://github.com/fchollet/keras
10. Crow, J.F.: Advantages of sexual reproduction. Genesis **15**(3), 205–213 (1994)
11. Dask Development Team: Dask: Library for dynamic task scheduling (2016). http://dask.pydata.org

12. Jaderberg, M., et al.: Population based training of neural networks. CoRR abs/1711.09846 (2017). http://arxiv.org/abs/1711.09846
13. Kluyver, T., et al.: Jupyter notebooks – a publishing format for reproducible computational workfows. In: Loizides, F., Schmidt, B. (eds.) Positioning and Power in Academic Publishing: Players, Agents and Agendas. pp. 87 – 90. IOS Press (2016)
14. LeCun, Y., Bengio, Y., Hinton, G.: Deep learning. Nature **521**(7553), 436 (2015)
15. Mendygral, P., Hill, N., Kandalla, K., Davis, M., Balma, J., Schongens, M.: High performance scalable deep learning with the cray programming environments deep learning plugin. In: Proceedings of CUG (2018)
16. Rocklin, M.: Dask: parallel computation with blocked algorithms and task scheduling. In: Huff, K., Bergstra, J. (eds.) Proceedings of the 14th Python in Science Conference, pp. 130–136 (2015)
17. Sergeev, A., Balso, M.D.: Horovod: fast and easy distributed deep learning in TensorFlow. arXiv preprint arXiv:1802.05799 (2018)

Third International Workshop on Performance Portable Programming Models for Accelerators (P^3MA 2018)

Third International Workshop on Performance Portable Programming Models for Accelerators (P^3MA 2018)

Sunita Chandrasekaran[1] and Graham Lopez[2]

[1] University of Delaware
[2] Oak Ridge National Laboratory

1 Workshop Summary

The Third International Workshop on Performance Portable Programming Models for Accelerators (P^3MA) co-located with ISC 2018 was held at Frankfurt, Germany on June 28. The workshop solicited papers on topics covering feature sets of programming models (including but not limited to C++, OpenCL, OpenMP, OpenACC, and various DSLs), their implementations, and experiences with their deployment in HPC applications on multiple architectures, performance modeling and evaluation tools, asynchronous task and event-driven execution/scheduling. We received 6 submissions in total. All submitted manuscripts were peer-reviewed. The review process was not double-blind, i.e., authors were known to reviewers. Submissions were judged on correctness, originality, technical strength, significance, quality of presentation, and interest and relevance to the conference scope. We chose 4 papers to be published in the workshop proceedings, Springer-Verlag Lecture Notes in Computer Science (LNCS) volumes.

The workshop was held for a half-day in the afternoon of June 28 at ISC and brought together researchers, vendors, users, and developers to brainstorm aspects of heterogeneous computing and its various tools and techniques. Around 45 attendees were present. All of the 4 accepted papers were presented at the workshop with topics ranging from using high-level programming models for heterogeneous systems to experiences porting legacy code to accelerators.

2 Organizing Committee

3 Steering Committee

Matthias Muller	RWTH Aachen University
Barbara Chapman	Stony Brook University
Oscar Hernandez	ORNL
Duncan Poole	OpenACC
Torsten Hoefler	ETH
Michael Wong	Codeplay Software Ltd.
Mitsuhisa Sato	University of Tsukuba
Michael Klemm	OpenMP
Kuan-Ching Li	Providence University

4 Program Chairs

Sunita Chandrasekaran	University of Delaware
Graham Lopez	Oak Ridge National Laboratory

5 Steering Committee

Xiaonan Tian	NVIDIA
John Pennycook	Intel
Swaroop Pophale	Oak Ridge National Laboratory
John Leidel	Texas Tech University
Antonio J. Peña	Barcelona Supercomputing Center (BSC)
Sandra Wienke	RWTH Aachen University
Sridutt Bhalachandra	Argonne National Laboratory
Rengan Xu	Dell EMC
Axel Huebl	Helmholtz-Zentrum Dresden-Rossendorf, Technische Universität Dresden
Kyle Friedline	University of Delaware
Antonino Tumeo	Politecnico di Milano
Suraj Prabhakaran	Intel
Adrian Jackson	The University of Edinburgh
Cheng Wang	University of Houston
Robert Searles	University of Delaware
Ray Sheppard	Indiana University Bloomington

Performance Portability of Earth System Models with User-Controlled GGDML Code Translation

Nabeeh Jum'ah[1([⊠])] and Julian Kunkel[2]

[1] Universität Hamburg, Hamburg, Germany
Jumah@informatik.uni-hamburg.de
[2] University of Reading, Reading, UK
j.m.kunkel@reading.ac.uk

Abstract. The increasing need for performance of earth system modeling and other scientific domains pushes the computing technologies in diverse architectural directions. The development of models needs technical expertise and skills of using tools that are able to exploit the hardware capabilities. The heterogeneity of architectures complicates the development and the maintainability of the models.

To improve the software development process of earth system models, we provide an approach that simplifies the code maintainability by fostering separation of concerns while providing performance portability. We propose the use of high-level language extensions that reflect scientific concepts. The scientists can use the programming language of their own choice to develop models, however, they can use the language extensions optionally wherever they need. The code translation is driven by configurations that are separated from the model source code. These configurations are prepared by scientific programmers to optimally use the machine's features.

The main contribution of this paper is the demonstration of a user-controlled source-to-source translation technique of earth system models that are written with higher-level semantics. We discuss a flexible code translation technique that is driven by the users through a configuration input that is prepared especially to transform the code, and we use this technique to produce OpenMP or OpenACC enabled codes besides MPI to support multi-node configurations.

Keywords: DSL · Meta-Compiler · Earth system modeling
Software development · Performance portability

1 Introduction

The diversity of the hardware architectures that arise to fulfill the performance needs of scientific applications represents a challenge for the scientists developing these applications. The maintainability and continuous development of applications suffers when optimizing code for several architectures. The semantics of

© Springer Nature Switzerland AG 2018
R. Yokota et al. (Eds.): ISC 2018 Workshops, LNCS 11203, pp. 693–710, 2018.
https://doi.org/10.1007/978-3-030-02465-9_50

a general-purpose language (GPL) limit the compiler's ability to exploit the underlying machine capabilities. Therefore, developers need to manually adapt the code to the target machine that will run the simulation, in order to make use of the performance capabilities of the machine. Running a model on many different machines requires to redesign the code to fit the features of the different architectures and hardware configurations. This leads to a more complicated development process where code sections are redundantly coded with machine-dependent adaptations.

Another point that complicates the development process in this context is the technical knowledge necessary during software development. Scientists developing such models need to have deep technical knowledge of the lower-level details of the computer architectures that will run the model and the necessary software development skills to exploit their features.

We suggest an approach to improve the software development process of earth system models, which are a family of high-performance scientific applications. In our approach, the model's code is written mainly with a general-purpose language. Besides, we rely on the GGDML *(General Grid Definition and Manipulation Language)* extensions from Jumah et. al [10] that can be used to write parts of the model code.

GGDML, which was previously developed as part of the approach, provides a set of semantically-higher-level extensions. As those extensions are not part of the standard syntax of the general-purpose language, we need some processing before passing the model to the general-purpose language compiler. In our approach, the source code written with GGDML syntax is passed to a source-to-source translation tool. This tool processes the code and translates it into the modeling general-purpose language. During the processing phase by the source-to-source translation tool, the semantically higher-level language extensions allow the tool to perform transformations of the source code that could not be done by a GPL compiler. An example is changing the memory layout to generate optimized code for some hardware. The transformations applied during the source-to-source translation phase are primarily defined in a configuration file which is controlled by a scientific programmer. This user-controlled source-to-source translation process is the scope of this paper.

The **main contribution** of this work is a novel user-controlled code translation technique that relies on a configurable code transformation which makes use of the higher-level semantics exhibited by the language extensions. This technique allows the user to control how the language extensions affect the code translation and optimization process. The suggested approach still permits to write manually optimized codes, e.g. using pragmas, and supports incremental rewriting to some extent. In fact, an important aspect of the approach and the technique we suggest here is the opportunity that it gives to quickly explore different configurations and options and the corresponding performance issues without the need to change the source code or rewriting the kernels.

This paper is structured as follows: First, we discuss related work in Sect. 2. We then describe the approach in Sect. 3. In Sect. 4, we review the GGDML language extensions. Next, in Sect. 5 the configuration of the code translation process is discussed. In Sect. 6, the approach is evaluated with an example application that consists of various relevant kernels. Finally, we give a summary of the work presented in this paper in Sect. 7.

2 Related Work

To exploit the performance of the underlying hardware that runs a scientific application, different techniques have been used over time. The use of libraries which provide optimized codes like BLAS/LAPACK that can be called by applications is one way to allow applications to run efficiently. Annotating an application's code and processing the annotated code is another technique that allows performance improvement by processing the annotated code in a specific way to fit the features of the hardware. Code generation and language-specific features, e.g. generic programming with templates in C++, are techniques that are used to generate code for a specific machine. Domain-specific languages (DSLs) can be developed to describe the problem, and then a machine-specific code is generated based on the problem description that is being provided by the DSL. DSLs have been used in different ways. For example, some solutions depend on writing the application code completely with a stand-alone DSL. On the contrary, some solutions use DSLs to describe specific parts of the application. In such case, the DSL drives a code generation process that results of optimized code that will then be integrated within the other parts of the application. Some DSLs extend an existing language with technical constructs that allow users to direct specific optimizations, like OpenMP/OpenACC.

Libraries are widely used to provide performance-portable code for applications. A library implements a set of functions that an application can call to provide its functionality. Libraries like ELLPACK [15], BLAS [6], Intel's MKL [9] provide a set of mathematical functions that can be used by applications to solve mathematical problems (e.g., elliptic differential equations and linear algebra). Such libraries implement the functions that they provide to the applications in a way that is aware of the architectural features and capabilities of a specific type of machines. The developers of such libraries port them to different types of machines (e.g. [18] ports the BLAS 3 to multi-GPU platforms) to allow applications to be developed for different machines while still using the hardware efficiently.

The implementations provided by the libraries are normally highly optimized, however, the calling application could still miss some optimization opportunities particularly between subsequent library calls. Such lost opportunities for optimization can be avoided when using active libraries. The source-to-source translation features in the active libraries OP2 [12] and OPS [14] analyzes the behavior of the application. An application calls the APIs that the library provides and the source-to-source translation procedure handles the optimization of the code for a specific target architecture. OPS uses its own DSL that allows the source-to-source translation process to generate optimized code.

The use of DSLs to drive the code generation of machine-specific optimized code was employed in different ways. Stella [8] for example, provides an embedded DSL for C++ that allows describing stencil codes for structured grids. The stencils and the grids are specified using the DSL, which mainly uses the C++ syntax, and the machine-specific code is generated by a special backend for the supported hardware. GridTools [2] also builds on Stella. It provides a generic C++ API to provide performance portability for grid-based codes. GridTools use a DSL for stencil computations and for halo exchange to provide codes for machines with multiple nodes.

Intel's YASK [20] is built on a DSL that enables users to define the technical decisions to control how the stencil operation is applied to the grid, including the domain decomposition of the grid over multiple nodes. The specification of stencil operations is enabled by the use of object-oriented C++ features and generic programming. The generated code is optimized for Xeon and Xeon Phi processors. Optimization techniques like vector folding [19] and cache blocking are used to optimize memory bandwidth usage.

Some DSLs are more tightly based on scientific domains, e.g., Atmol [3] and Liszt [4], in contrast to the focus on technical details. However, the move to the declarative programming needs the model developers to move to a new paradigm for software development.

In contrast to standalone DSLs, there are DSLs that added some extensions to existing general-purpose languages, e.g. Physis [11] which adds some extensions to C++, and Icon DSL [16] which adds some extensions to Fortran. [10] suggested a set of language extensions that are language neutral. The suggested DSL provides a set of extensions that can be used regardless of the general purpose language that is used to develop the model.

In code annotation techniques, descriptions can be added to the source code to provide further information about it, and to tell how it could be optimized. Such information is provided by the developers within the source code. Hybrid Fortran [13], HMPP [5], Mint [17], CLAW [1] use annotation to drive the optimization process. In Gung Ho [7] the scientific code is separated into higher level algorithms and lower-level kernels. Directives drive the generation of the code between the two layers to handle loops and parallelization. The code annotation technique needs to push the technical details within the source code. However, with these technical annotations, the scientists need to care for the lower-level optimization details.

In this paper we extend the work that has been done with the GGDML DSL [10]. We use the higher-level semantics offered by the extensions of GGDML along with a highly configurable code translation technique to transform the source code of a model into a machine-specific code that exploits the features of the underlying architecture where the model would be run.

3   Approach

In this section we review our approach to improve the software development process and discuss the user-controlled translation technique.

3.1 The General Approach

The approach is built around using higher-level language extensions. This allows to bypass the shortcomings of the lower-level semantics of the general-purpose programming languages. The higher-level semantics enable the code translation process to transform the source code in a way that exploits the capabilities of the underlying hardware. This eliminates the need to provide technical details about optimizations within the source code. Thus, the model developer, that is usually a trained scientist in the domain field, does not need to think about the hardware and performance details. In our approach we commit to the principle of separation of concerns:

– Domain scientists write the scientific problem from a scientific perspective
– Scientific programmers provide the DSL and machine-specific optimization

The scientists formulate the scientific problem within the source code based on the scientific concepts of their domain science. The GPL that the scientists generally use to build their model is used. However, the scientists can also use higher-level language extensions to write some parts of the code wherever they see that needed, although the whole code could be developed with the base language (without the extensions).

3.2 The User-Controlled Source-to-Source Code Translation

The source code is processed to translate the higher-level code into a form that is optimized with respect to a specific target machine. The code translation process described in this paper is guided by a configuration information that allows the translation process to make the necessary transformations in order to exploit the capabilities of the machine. This information is prepared by scientific programmers who have the necessary technical knowledge to harness the power of the underlying architectures and hardware configurations.

To enable the developers to use scientific concepts while programming, the language extensions of the DSL are developed in collaboration between the scientists and the scientific programmers. Then, the developed extensions are defined within the configuration information. For example, they can define type specifiers that tell some hint about a variable, e.g., that it is defined over a three-dimensional grid, which reflects a scientific attribute.

The configuration allows the user to control how the translation tool transforms the code, e.g., how to make use of the hardware to apply the computation in an iterator statement in parallel on a multicore or manycore architecture. So, a scientific programmer with expertise in GPUs for example would provide a configuration information that guides the translation tool to optimally use the GPU's processing elements to parallelize the traversal of an iterator statement over the grid elements. That information is differently written by an expert in multicore architectures to make use of the vector units and multiple cores and caching hierarchies to optimize the code for multicore processors.

The tool infrastructure is flexible allowing to design alternative DSLs while retaining some core optimizations that are independent of the frontend GPL and DSL, and the generative backend.

4 GGDML Review

In this section we review the GGDML, which was developed as one part of our approach to provide the higher-level language semantics.

The GGDML DSL has been developed as a set of language extensions to support the development of icosahedral-grid-based earth system models. Although the extensions have been developed based on the three icosahedral models Dynamico, ICON, and NICAM which are written in the Fortran language, we use the extensions to develop a testbed application in the C language. GGDML abstracts the scientific concept of the grid and provides the necessary glue code like specifiers, expressions, iterator to access and manipulate variables and grids from a scientific point of view.

GGDML offers a set of declaration specifiers that allow to mark a variable to contain values over the elements of a specific grid. The specifiers can tell, for example, that the variable has a value over each cell or edge of the grid. Although GGDML provided a set of basic specifiers, e.g., cells, edges, and vertices for the spatial position of the variables with respect to the grid, the translation technique is designed to support extending the set of specifiers. This dynamic support for the extensibility of the tool stems from the highly configurable translation technique that is described in the next section.

Besides to the hints on the scientific attributes of the variables provided by the specifiers, GGDML provides an iterator extension as a way to express the application of a computation over the variables which are defined over the elements of the grid. The iterator statement comprises an iterator index, which allows to address a specific set of grid elements. For example, to address the cells of the three-dimensional grid. To define the set of elements over which the computation that is defined by the iterator is intended to be applied, the iterator statement comprises a special expression, which is another extension that GGDML provides. Those expressions specify a set of elements of a grid through the use of grid definition operators. The code example at the end of this section illustrates the idea.

The index that is used to write the iterator represents an abstraction of a scientific concept that allows to refer to a variable at a grid element, however it does not imply any information where and how the values of the variable are stored in memory. To allow the reference to related grid elements easily, GGDML provides a basic set of operators. However, again this set is not a limited constant set, as the configurability of the translation process allows to dynamically define any operators that the developers wish to have. For example, the basic set of operators that GGDML provides includes the operator *cell.above* to refer to the cell above the cell that is being processed. Operators like *cell.neighbor* hide the indirect indices that are used in unstructured grids to refer to the related grid elements, e.g., neighbors or cell edges. Such operators abstract again the scientific concepts of the element relationships. They do not imply any information about how the data is accessed or where it is stored.

GGDML provides also a reduction expression that allows to simplify the coding of the computations that are applied within an iterator statement. The reduction expression removes code redundancy which happens so frequently within stencil codes, and at the same time, allows to write kernels independently from the grid type and the resulting numbers of neighbors.

To illustrate the use of GGDML, the following test code snippet demonstrates the use of the specifiers:

```
extern  GVAL  EDGE  3D  gv_grad;
extern  GVAL  CELL  2D  gv_o8param[3];
extern  GVAL  CELL  3D  gv_o8par2;
extern  GVAL  CELL  3D  gv_o8var;
```

The GVAL is a C-compiler define and we define it as float or double[1]. The specifiers are used as any other C specifier like extern. The following code demonstrates an iterator statement:

```
FOREACH  cell  IN  grid|height{1..(g->height-1)}
{
  GVAL  v0 = REDUCE(+,N={0..2},
       gv_o8param[N][cell] * gv_grad[cell.edge(N)]);

  GVAL  v1 = REDUCE(+,N={0..2},
       gv_o8param[N][cell] * gv_grad[cell.edge(N).below()]);

  gv_o8var[cell] = gv_o8par2[cell]* v0
                 + (1-gv_o8par2[cell]) * v1;
}
```

The iterator's grid expression here uses the GGDML grid expression modifier operator | to traverse the cells of the three-dimensional grid with the *height* dimension overridden with the boundaries 1 to one level below the last level. We can write any general-purpose language code within the iterator as a computation that will be applied over the specified grid elements. The REDUCE expression is used as follows: the value of *v*0 will be assigned the sum of the weighted values of the variable *gv_grad* multiplied by *gv_o8param* over the three edges of the cell in a triangular grid. We see here the use of multiple access operators *cell.edge(N).below()* to access the cell below a neighboring cell.

5   Machine-Specific Configuration

The extensibility of the DSL, i.e., the set of the language extensions and the configurability of the code transformation process are key parts of our approach. The basic set of language extensions provided by GGDML are not applied by the source-to-source translation process as a constant set of extensions. Instead, the translation technique allows to define new extensions and how they affect the code transformation process.

---

[1] In a future version, we will support a flexible precision of different variables that can be defined at compile time.

We mentioned in the previous section the declaration specifiers that mark the variables. The translation process accepts configuration information that defines named sets of specifiers and a set of specifiers under each set. For example, the basic set of specifiers that GGDML provides are implemented as a set of specifiers called 'loc' which includes the 'cell' and 'edge' specifiers to specify the spatial position of the variables value with respect to the grid, and another set that is called 'dim' which includes the specifiers '3D' and '2D' to specify the dimensionality of the grid over which the variable is defined. So, the specifiers are not built into the translation tool as compilers do usually. To the contrary, the users can define any set of specifiers as they need. To demonstrate the idea, the line

```
SPECIFIERS:  SPECIFIER(loc=CELL|EDGE)  SPECIFIER(dim=3D|2D)
```

shows how we configured the translation process to translate our test application.

The sets of the specifiers provide information that enables the translation tool to handle further code transformation steps. So, whenever a variable is declared with any of the defined specifiers, the tool would use that information to handle any transformations related to that variable. Among the code processing that uses such information are the allocation and deallocation of the variables' data in memory, and the transformation of the addresses of the variables' data in memory, and choosing the consistent memory layout to access the variables data.

The translation tool uses configuration information to control the allocation and the deallocation of the variables. The allocation/deallocation codes are generated based on this configuration input and the specifiers used to declare the variable.

5.1   Grid Configuration

The configuration provides information that describes the grids that are used in the model. This includes the definition of the grid's components, e.g., the cells of the three-dimensional grid or the cells of the grid's two-dimensional surface.

The tool allows the configuration to specify defaults to simplify expressing the intended grids to traverse when writing a kernel. For example, in a test code we have used the defaults to write kernels with a simple iterator expression that consists only of the word 'grid'. In the configuration that we prepared for the test application, we have

```
GLOBALDOMAIN:
   ...
  DEFAULT=CELL3D[CELL3D: cell , ce , c ][EDGE3D: edge , ed , e ]
```

This allows us to traverse the cells of the three-dimensional grid by default or when we use one of the words 'cell', 'ce' or 'c' as an iterator index. Thus, the iterator

```
foreach cell in grid
```

traverses the cells of the three-dimensional grid. Likewise, this example configuration allows to traverse the edges of the three-dimensional grid when we use one of the words 'edge', 'ed' or 'e' as an iterator index. Thus, the iterator

```
foreach edge in grid
```

traverses the edges of the three-dimensional grid. If the defaults are not intended to be used, then the name of the grid to be traversed, or additionally the grid specification operators should be used.

The definition of the grids describes the grids that are used in the model regardless of how the processing will be divided between nodes. The details of the domain decomposition and halo exchange are provided in its own part of the configuration information.

The definition of the grids allows using variables defined in the source code. For example, to define the height of the grid in a test code we defined it to take the values between 1 and *height*, which is a variable used in the source code. This allows us in the experiments to pass the height as a command line parameter to run the model with multiple heights without recompiling the code.

5.2   Configurable Access Operators

To access the value of a variable at a grid element when applying a computation within an iterator, we refer to it by the iterator's index. In stencil codes, it is essential to access the neighboring elements. To handle this, GGDML provides a basic set of operators. For example, the *cell.neighbor* allows to refer to the neighbor cell of the current cell, assuming that *cell* is the name of the iterator's index.

The set of access operators are not limited to the basic set that GGDML provides. In fact, the access operators – even the basic set of GGDML access operators – are defined in the configurations that the translation tool uses. For example, the operator *above* is defined by

```
above(): height=$height+1
```

to tell the tool how to access the element that we refer to with this operator. In a test code, besides to this operator definition, we also defined the same operator with an overloaded form that takes a parameter to specify a number of levels above the current element, e.g., the cell above some levels to allow references like *cell.above*(2). The access operators define the relationships between the grids. The connectivity of the unstructured grids is defined by the definitions of the access operators.

5.3   Memory Layout

The variables are accessed by the iterator index, which abstracts an element among a set of elements of a grid. This abstraction does not specify where the data are stored in memory and how to access them. The translation tool uses the user-provided configuration information to define the mapping and know how to access the data.

The allocation, that is guided by the configuration, allows to control the placement of the variable's data. Several information allow the translation tool to decide how to access the data of a variable: Firstly, the information about a variable that is provided by the specifiers used to declare the variable. The iterator's index and the access operators that are used to refer to the variable's data are translated into the indices that address the data in memory in a step that includes some transformations. The applied transformations use the grid definitions as part of the transformation process. Further mathematical transformations on the indices can be controlled by the configuration information. For example, the interchange of the indices, or even transforming a three-index-based address (space) into a one-index-based address according to a formula like

```
INDEX=$0*g->blkSize*g->height+$1*g->blkSize+$2
```

or even more complex formulas including functions, e.g. a filling curve, are possible. The expression

```
gv_temp[cell.above()]
```

is transformed into the three-index address

```
gv_temp[(block_index)][((height_index) + 1)][(cell_index)]
```

and applying the mentioned address transformation formula transforms the address into

```
gv_temp[(block_index) * g->blkSize * g->height +
        ((height_index) + 1) * g->blkSize + (cell_index)]
```

The example also demonstrates the use of the access operator *above* that is mentioned in Sect. 5.2.

The memory layout is a key factor to exploit hardware configurations. The choice of the transformation formulas is an important decision to improve the performance of an application. Fortunately, the simple and quick configurability of the memory layout makes the exploration of the memory layouts and the corresponding performance on different architectures a simple task.

5.4   Parallelization

The parallelization of the kernels is an important part of the code translation for the iterators. That is essential to use the hardware features to improve the performance. The translation tool allows to provide configuration information to control the parallelization process. For example, the user uses the following line

```
0:pragma omp parallel for
```

to let the tool use the OpenMP scheduler. The line tells that an OpenMP pragma is used and that the blocks are mapped to the 'for' iterations that will be run in parallel. Alternatively, on GPUs we can map the blocks to the OpenACC 'gangs' for example.

In our test codes, we have generated MPI codes with OpenMP to target multicore processors, and OpenACC to target GPU-accelerated machines. We could annotate the loops to use the cores of the multicore processors and the streaming multiprocessors of the GPUs to run the kernels in parallel. The easy configuration change of the parallelization allowed us to easily explore different parallelization alternatives to explore performance impact.

To enable the models to run on multiple nodes, the translation tool provides the necessary code translation like domain decomposition and halo exchange. The processing load of the kernels over grids that are defined in the configuration to support the model is divided between the nodes that run the model.

The code transformation of the iterators includes the grids decomposition such that each node is responsible to process its own part of the grid. As part of the code transformation, the translation tool analyzes the kernels and generates the necessary halo exchange code. However, this is controlled by the user-provided configuration information. This information controls the initialization and finalization of the communication library, and the transmission/reception of the halo data. This includes a completely configurable halo pattern definition and initialization.

In the test codes, we have used the MPI library to handle the communications of the halo data between the nodes.

6   Evaluation

In this section, we discuss some experiments to evaluate the work described in this paper. First, we describe the application that has been used as a testbed code. Then, the machines that have been used to run the tests are described. Finally, we discuss the tests results.

6.1   Test Application

A testbed code in the C-programming language is used to demonstrate and test the approach. The application is an icosahedral-grid-based code, that maps variables to the cells and edges of a three-dimensional grid. The two-dimensional surface is mapped to one dimension using a Hilbert space-filling-curve. The curve is partitioned into blocks. The testbed runs in explicit time steps during each of which the model components are called to do their computations – a component can be considered a scientific process. Each component provides a compute function that calls the necessary kernels that are needed to update some variables. All the kernels are written with the GGDML extensions. The translation tool is called to translate the application's code into the different variants to run on the test machines with different memory layouts.

6.2   Test System

Two machines have been used to run the tests. The first is the supercomputer Mistral at the German Climate Computing Center (DKRZ). Mistral offers dual socket Intel Broadwell nodes (Intel Xeon E5-2695 v4 @ 2.1 GHz). The second machine is NVIDIA's PSG cluster, where we used the Haswell CPUs (Intel(R)

Xeon(R) CPU E5-2698 v3 @ 2.30 GHz). The GPU tests were run on NVIDIA's
PSG cluster on two types of GPUs: P100 and V100.

To compile the codes and run them on Mistral we used OpenMPI version
1.8.4 and GCC version 7.1. On the PSG cluster we have used the OpenMPI
version 1.10.7 and the PGI compiler version 17.10.

6.3 Results

In the first experiment, we evaluate the application's performance for a single
node. First, we translate the source code into a serial code and run it on the
PSG cluster to evaluate the performance improvements on CPU and GPU. We
translated it again for OpenMP to run on the Haswell multicore processors. The
OpenMP version has been run with different numbers of threads. The application
was also translated to run on the two types of GPUs; the P100 and the V100.
We tested two memory layouts:

- **3D:** a three-dimensional addressing with three-dimensional array
- **3D-1D:** a transformed addressing that maps the original three-index
  addresses into an 1D index.

All the tests have been run with a 3D grid of $1024 \times 1024 \times 64$ for 100 time steps
using 32-bit floating point variables. The results for running the OpenMP tests
are shown in Table 1.

Table 1. Performance in GFLOPS on a single node CPU with OpenMP

	Serial	2 Threads	4 Threads	8 Threads	16 Threads	32 Threads
3D	1.97	3.74	7.05	13.78	24.15	46.94
3D-1D	1.99	3.95	7.59	14.43	24.98	48.87

While the change between the two chosen memory layouts have not shown
much impact on the performance on the Haswell processor, we see the impact
clear when running the same code on the GPUs. The results for running the
same code with the two different memory layouts on both GPU machines are
shown in Table 2. We also include the measured memory throughput into the
table, which we measure with NVIDIA's 'nvprof' tool.

The change of the memory layout means transforming the addresses from a
three-dimensional array indices to a one-dimensional array index, which means
cutting down the amount of the data that needs to be read from the memory
in each kernel. The caching hierarchy of the Haswell processor hides the impact
by using the cached values of the additional data that needs to be read in the
three-dimensional indices. However, the use of the code transformation to use
the one-dimensional index while translating the code to run on the GPU allowed
to get the performance gain.

Table 2. Performance in GFLOPS on a single node with a P100/V100 GPU

	Serial	P100			V100		
		Performance GFLOPS	Memory throughput GB/s		Performance GFLOPS	Memory throughput GB/s	
			Read	Write		Read	Write
3D	1.97	220.38	91.34	56.10	854.86	242.59	86.98
3D-1D	1.99	408.15	38.75	43.87	1240.19	148.49	57.12

To evaluate the scalability of the testbed code on multiple nodes with GPUs, we have translated the code for GPU-accelerated machines using MPI and we have run it on 1–4 nodes. Table 1 shows the performance of the application when it is run on the P100-accelerated machines. The figure shows the performance achieved in both cases when measuring the strong and the weak scalability. The performance has been measured to find the maximum achievable performance when no halo exchange is performed, and to find the performance of an optimized code with halo exchange. The performance gap reflects the cost of the data movement from and into the GPU's memory as limited by the PCIe3 bus and along the network using Infiniband. This gap differs according to the data placement of the elements that need to be communicated to other nodes. Thus, putting the elements in an order in which halo elements are closer to each other in memory reduces the time for the data cop from and into the GPU's memory. The scalability (both strong and weak) is shown in Table 3. The table shows how the performance improves with the nodes. Also, it shows the ratio that is achieved when running the code with respect to the maximum performance gain (that is achieved without halo exchange). The computing time spent each time step for the whole grid ($1024 \times 1024 \times 64$ elements) is measured to be 8.34 ms. The communication times spent during each time step are shown in Table 4.

The communication times between different numbers of MPI processes running in different mappings over nodes are recorded, Table 4 shows the measured values on the PSG cluster. We have run the application in 2, 4, 8, 16, 32, 64, and 128 processes over 1, 2, and 4 nodes. For multiple nodes, we mapped the MPI processes to the nodes in three ways: cyclic, blocked with balanced numbers of processes on each node, and in blocks where the processes subsequently fill the nodes. The time was measured over 1000 time steps in each case. The measured times show that optimizing the communication time is essential to achieve better performance, and that optimizing the data movement from/into the GPU's memory is essential to minimize the halo exchange time.

To evaluate the scalability of the generated code with multiple MPI processes on CPU nodes, we have run it with over 1, 4, 8, 12, 16, 20, 24, 28, 32, 36, 40, and 48 nodes. The performance is shown in Fig. 2.

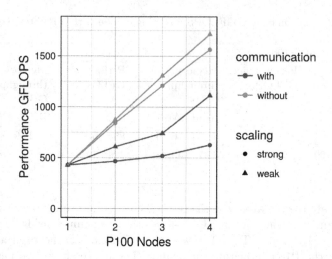

Fig. 1. Performance scalability on nodes with P100 GPUs (performance is measured in GFLOPS)

Table 3. Performance scalability on nodes with P100 GPUs (performance is measured in GFLOPS)

Number of nodes	Strong scaling			Weak scaling		
	Without communication	With communication	Ratio	Without communication	With communication	Ratio
2	1.97	1.09	55%	2.07	1.43	70%
3	2.82	1.21	43%	3.05	1.73	58%
4	3.65	1.47	40%	4.01	2.60	65%

Both the strong and the weak scalability efficiency are calculated according to the equations

$$Efficiency_{strong} = T_1/(N \cdot T_N) \cdot 100\% \tag{1}$$

$$Efficiency_{weak} = T_1/T_N \cdot 100\% \tag{2}$$

where N is the number of processes, T_1 is the execution time on one process, and T_N is the execution time on N processes. The results are shown in Fig. 3. The efficiency is slightly below 100% up to 48 MPI processes for the weak scaling measurements. The Strong scaling measurements decrease from 100% at one process to about 70% at 48 processes in a linear trend.

The performance of the generated code that uses OpenMP with the MPI is also evaluated. The code has been generated for OpenMP and MPI and run with multiple numbers of nodes and using different numbers of cores on each node. We have run the code on 1, 4, 8, 12, 16, 20, 24, 28, 32, 36, 40 nodes and 1, 2, 4, 8, 16, 32, and 36 cores per node. The measurements are shown in Fig. 4.

Table 4. Communication time per time step (in ms)

# processes	1	2 nodes			4 nodes		
		Cyclic	Block (balanced)	Block (unbalanced)	Cyclic	Block (balanced)	Block (unbalanced)
2	1.21	1.18	1.11	1.21			
4	1.03	0.93	0.86	1.18	0.88	0.90	1.24
8	1.00	0.84	0.77	1.52	0.77	0.75	1.58
16	0.80	0.83	0.56	1.59	0.69	0.54	1.60
32	1.29	0.77	0.64	1.26	0.69	0.51	1.24
64		1.33	0.82	0.78	0.84	0.52	0.77
128					1.48	1.32	1.23

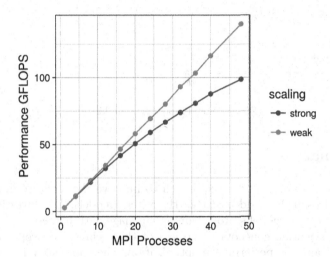

Fig. 2. MPI process scalability

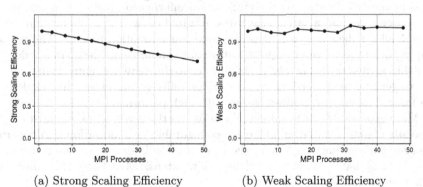

(a) Strong Scaling Efficiency   (b) Weak Scaling Efficiency

Fig. 3. Scaling efficiency

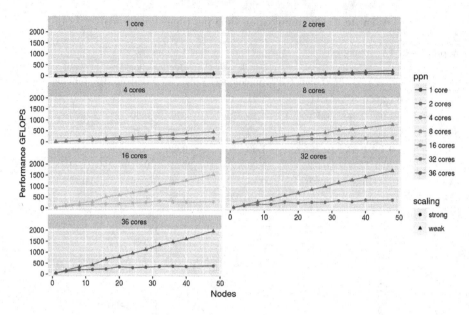

Fig. 4. MPI+OpenMP scalability

7 Summary

In this paper, we discussed an approach to improve the software development process of icosahedral-grid-based earth system models. We investigated the extensibility of the model's programming language with higher-level extensions abstracting scientific concepts regardless of the technical concepts related to the machine and the performance optimization. The approach relies on using a source-to-source translation process that uses the higher semantics of the extensions besides to user-provided configuration information together to transform the source code into a target-machine-optimized code. The configuration information allows the users to control the code transformation process. The performance portability is an important feature of the approach. The source code of a model is written once, and the translation procedure can use many configuration files to generate code versions which work on different machines while exploiting the features of those machines to run with high performance.

More extensions can be added depending on the needs of the scientists. This is possible as the translation process is configurable by information that controls the code transformation. Among the configuration information, the translation process accepts information that defines new extensions and how they affect the code transformation.

The approach is evaluated with a test application that has been written in the C language, with the use of the GGDML extensions. Different configurations were prepared to translate the source code into different targets. The resulting code versions were run on two machines. The results showed the impact of transforming the code to support different memory layouts, and the performance gain when using the cores of a multicore processor and the streaming multiprocessors of a GPU to apply the computations in parallel. In addition, the results showed the scalability when running on multiple nodes. The translation process was successfully used to generate codes that run on multiple multicore nodes and multiple GPU-accelerated nodes and the evaluation shows that the approach could provide performance portability for the software development of the models which need scalability.

7.1   Future Work

We are working further on the optimization of the halo data communication and the minimization of the communication overhead particularly to reduce the costs for the GPU version. Another important path for the research we intend to continue is the improvement of the inter-kernel and inter-module optimization. We currently provide with the translation tool some basic fusion of the kernel loops. Also, the tool currently carries out some analysis of the kernel computations. However, further work can be done to investigate the optimization opportunities over the set of kernels that are called in each time step, or even between time steps.

Acknowledgements. This work was supported in part by the German Research Foundation (DFG) through the Priority Programme 1648 "Software for Exascale Computing" (SPPEXA) (GZ: LU 1353/11-1). We would like to thank NVIDIA who supported this work with allowing to run some tests on their PSG cluster, and the German Climate Computing-Center (DKRZ) where we also have run some tests on the Mistral supercomputer.

References

1. CSCS Claw. http://www.xcalablemp.org/download/workshop/4th/Valentin.pdf. Accessed 22 Dec 2017
2. CSCS GridTools. https://pasc17.pasc-conference.org/fileadmin/user_upload/pasc17/program/post144s2.pdf. Accessed 22 Dec 2017
3. van Engelen, R.A.: Atmol: a domain-specific language for atmospheric modeling. CIT. J. Comput. Inf. Technol. **9**(4), 289–303 (2001)
4. DeVito, Z., et al.: Liszt: a domain specific language for building portable mesh-based PDE solvers. In: Proceedings of 2011 International Conference for High Performance Computing, Networking, Storage and Analysis, p. 9. ACM (2011)
5. Dolbeau, R., Bihan, S., Bodin, F.: HMPP: a hybrid multi-core parallel programming environment. In: Workshop on General Purpose Processing on Graphics Processing Units (GPGPU 2007), vol. 28 (2007)
6. Dongarra, J.J., Croz, J.D., Hammarling, S., Duff, I.S.: A set of level 3 basic linear algebra subprograms. ACM Trans. Math. Softw. (TOMS) **16**(1), 1–17 (1990)
7. Ford, R., et al.: Gung Ho: a code design for weather and climate prediction on exascale machines. In: Proceedings of the Exascale Applications and Software Conference (2013)

8. Gysi, T., Fuhrer, O., Osuna, C., Cumming, B., Schulthess, T.: Stella: a domain-specific embedded language for stencil codes on structured grids. In: EGU General Assembly Conference Abstracts, vol. 16 (2014)
9. MKL Intel. Intel Math Kernel Library (2007)
10. Jumah, N., Kunkel, J., Zängl, G., Yashiro, H., Dubos, T., Meurdesoif, Y.: GGDML: icosahedral models language extensions. J. Comput. Sci. Technol. Updates 4(1), 1–10 (2017)
11. Maruyama, N., Sato, K., Nomura, T., Matsuoka, S.: Physis: an implicitly parallel programming model for stencil computations on large-scale GPU-accelerated supercomputers. In: 2011 International Conference for High Performance Computing, Networking, Storage and Analysis (SC), pp. 1–12. IEEE (2011)
12. Mudalige, G.R., Giles, M.B., Reguly, I., Bertolli, C., Kelly, P.H.J.: Op2: an active library framework for solving unstructured mesh-based applications on multi-core and many-core architectures. In: Innovative Parallel Computing (InPar), pp. 1–12. IEEE (2012)
13. Müller, M., Aoki, T.: Hybrid Fortran: high productivity GPU porting framework applied to Japanese weather prediction model. arXiv preprint arXiv:1710.08616 (2017)
14. Reguly, I.Z., Mudalige, G.R., Giles, M.B., Curran, D., McIntosh-Smith, S.: The OPS domain specific abstraction for multi-block structured grid computations. In: 2014 Fourth International Workshop on Domain-Specific Languages and High-Level Frameworks for High Performance Computing (WOLFHPC), pp. 58–67. IEEE (2014)
15. Rice, J.R., Boisvert, R.F.: Solving Elliptic Problems Using ELLPACK, vol. 2. Springer, New York (2012). https://doi.org/10.1007/978-1-4612-5018-0
16. Torres, R., Linardakis, L., Kunkel, T.L.J., Ludwig, T.: ICON DSL: a domain-specific language for climate modeling. In: International Conference for High Performance Computing, Networking, Storage and Analysis, Denver, Colo (2013). http://sc13.supercomputing.org/sites/default/files/WorkshopsArchive/track139.html
17. Unat, D., Cai, X., Baden, S.B.: Mint: realizing CUDA performance in 3D stencil methods with annotated C. In: Proceedings of the International Conference on Supercomputing, pp. 214–224. ACM (2011)
18. Wang, L., Wu, W., Xu, Z., Xiao, J., Yang, Y.: BLASX: a high performance level-3 BLAS library for heterogeneous multi-GPU computing. In: Proceedings of the 2016 International Conference on Supercomputing, p. 20. ACM (2016)
19. Yount, C.: Vector folding: improving stencil performance via multi-dimensional SIMD-vector representation. In: 2015 IEEE 17th International Conference on High Performance Computing and Communications (HPCC), 2015 IEEE 7th International Symposium on Cyberspace Safety and Security (CSS), 2015 IEEE 12th International Conferen on Embedded Software and Systems (ICESS), pp. 865–870. IEEE (2015)
20. Yount, C.: Recipe: building and running YASK (yet another stencil kernel) on Intel® processors (2016). https://software.intel.com/en-us/articles/recipe-building-and-running-yask-yet-another-stencil-kernel-on-intel-processors. Accessed 22 Dec 2017

Evaluating Performance Portability of Accelerator Programming Models using SPEC ACCEL 1.2 Benchmarks

Swen Boehm[(⊠)], Swaroop Pophale[(⊠)], Verónica G. Vergara Larrea, and Oscar Hernandez

Oak Ridge National Laboratory, Oak Ridge, TN 37831, USA
{boehms,pophaless,vergaravg,oscar}@ornl.gov

Abstract. As heterogeneous architectures are becoming mainstream for HPC systems, application programmers are looking for programming model implementations that offer both performance and portability across platforms. Two directive-based programming models for accelerator programming that aim at doing this are OpenMP 4/4.5 and OpenACC. Many users want to know the difference between these two programming models, the state of their implementations, how to use them, and evaluate how suitable they are for their applications.

The Standard Performance Evaluation Corporation (SPEC) ACCEL benchmarks, developed by the SPEC High Performance Group (HPG), recently released SPEC ACCEL 1.2 benchmark suite to help the evaluation of OpenCL, OpenMP 4.5 and OpenACC on different platforms. In this paper we present our preliminary results that evaluates OpenMP 4.5 and OpenACC on a variety of accelerator-based systems: POWER9 with NVIDIA V100 GPUs (Summit), Intel Xeon Phi 7230 (Percival), and AMD Bulldozer Opteron with NVIDIA K20x (Titan). Comparing these benchmarks on different systems gives us insight into the support for OpenMP and OpenACC and their execution times provide insights about their quality of implementations provided by different vendors. We also compare best of OpenMP and OpenACC to see if a particular programming model favors a particular type of benchmark kernel.

1 Introduction

Benchmarks have been the backbone of performance modeling in HPC since the invention of parallel processing. They highlight key metrics that are important to a specific audience. Focusing on best practices, reproducible results and

This manuscript has been co-authored by UT-Battelle, LLC, under contract DE-AC05-00OR22725 with the US Department of Energy (DOE). The US government retains and the publisher, by accepting the article for publication, acknowledges that the US government retains a nonexclusive, paid-up, irrevocable, worldwide license to publish or reproduce the published form of this manuscript, or allow others to do so, for US government purposes. DOE will provide public access to these results of federally sponsored research in accordance with the DOE Public Access Plan (http://energy.gov/downloads/doe-public-access-plan).

© Springer Nature Switzerland AG 2018
R. Yokota et al. (Eds.): ISC 2018 Workshops, LNCS 11203, pp. 711–723, 2018.
https://doi.org/10.1007/978-3-030-02465-9_51

behavior are the main attributes that help in wide acceptance of a benchmark/
benchmark suite. Though well maintained scientific applications would be excellent candidates, applications are usually not easily available, require a lot of
domain specific information (e.g. input parameters), or are not ported to a variety of platforms. The SPEC [5] benchmark suites are a widely accepted set of
benchmarks. They are constantly improved and optimized by vendors and the
community. SPEC ACCEL benchmark suite provides a comparative measure of
parallel compute performance between accelerator platforms. The SPEC ACCEL
benchmarks are written using the offloading model in OpenCL, OpenMP and
OpenACC to program accelerators. As per guidelines set by SPEC, the use of
the benchmarks must conform to the set of rules [4] to ensure comparability and
reproducibility of results.

One of the benefit on using benchmarks is that they help us understand how a
programming model can be used and optimized to achieve good performance on a
given code, compiler, and platform combination. The SPEC ACCEL benchmark
has a set of codes that have been ported to OpenCL, OpenMP 4.5 (offload
model) and OpenACC. The members of SPEC/HPG have discussed and agreed
on the best practices to write the SPEC ACCEL benchmarks with performance
portability in mind.

We find SPEC ACCEL useful to provide answers on the quality of implementations of OpenMP and OpenACC on a variety of platforms available to us.
It can also be used to understand how programming models work and how they
are used, which is important, since there is no single programming model that
is best suited for all application domains.

The benchmarks are helpful to compare the quality of implementations across
compiler implementations on a given system and across systems. Different vendors have support for one or the other programming model. For example, PGI
has OpenACC implementations for different platforms but no OpenMP support.
So we look at the support for an implementation (OpenMP or OpenACC) for
the SPEC ACCEL 1.2 Benchmarks to see which implementations have a more
complete support for the different kernels exercised in the benchmarks. In this
paper, we focus on evaluating the OpenMP 4.5 (offload) implementations on
IBM XL, clang/LLVM, GCC, and Cray CCE, and OpenACC support in PGI
and GCC compilers. We also evaluate production closed source implementations
vs open source compiler implementations, and see how they match up in terms
of benchmark execution times.

Since compiler support for OpenMP 4.5 is work-in-progress, we use SPEC
ACCEL benchmarks (1.2) as a reference to measure where we are in terms
OpenMP and OpenACC functionality and performance support. We use the
SPEC/ACCEL benchmarks to report the execution times. None of these results
are *reportable runs* because the majority of compilers do not pass all the benchmarks. SPEC/HPG also documents official results and provides a wide range of
benchmark results for a variety of systems and compilers. Results can be found
at http://www.spec.org/accel.

2   Motivation

The OpenMP 4.0 specification [10] released in July 2013 introduced the OpenMP Accelerator Model. In the specification, the OpenMP API was extended to support accelerator and SIMD programming, allowing the user to specify regions of code that can be offloaded to one or more target devices. More recently, with the release of the OpenMP 4.5 specification [11], support for the accelerator model was further improved. Several major changes in OpenMP 4.5 affect the accelerator model including: new default data-mapping attributes, unstructured data mapping support and asynchronous execution, as well as runtime routines for memory management and extended attributes for SIMD loops, among others.

One of the goals of this paper is to evaluate the status of OpenMP 4.5 support on multiple architecture including NVIDIA GPUs and Intel Xeon Phi. We want to understand the maturity of OpenMP 4.5 offload support and how it compares to OpenACC across architectures.

Given the prescriptive nature of OpenMP, the SPEC/HPG organization designed the SPEC/ACCEL 1.2 OpenMP 4.5 benchmark implementation to rely on default behaviors to give as much freedom to the compiler and runtimes to optimize for a given architecture, without making optimization assumptions that favors one architecture over another.

For example, when a *teams* construct is executed, a league of threads is created, where the total number of teams is implementation defined but must be less than or equal to the number of teams specified by the *num_teams* clause. If the user does not specify the *num_teams* clause, then the number of teams is left completely to the implementation.

There are many concepts in the OpenMP and OpenACC specification that are implementation defined. All the implementation defined behaviors may have a significant effect on the performance of an implementation. Although deep analysis of the different OpenMP and OpenACC constructs is outside the scope of this paper, we provide the foundation by analyzing the execution times of the SPEC ACCEL 1.2 benchmarks.

3   The SPEC ACCEL Benchmark Suite

SPEC ACCEL 1.2 is a collection of the following benchmarks:

1. Stencil
   The stencil code represents an iterative Jacobi solver. The heat equation is represented by a 3-D structured grid.
2. Lattice Boltzmann Method (LBM)
   This program implements the LBM to simulate behavior of incompressible fluids in 3D. This simulation represents the most critical and computationally important part of calculations used in material science.
3. MRI-Q
   This benchmark attempts to reconstruct a MRI. This is a compute bound problem where a large set of input is processed. The result is the Q Matrix

where each element of the Q matrix is computed by the summation of contributions from all trajectory sample points.

4. Molecular Dynamics (MD)
   This benchmark performs molecular dynamics simulations of stellar objects. The simulations are applicable to all dense nuclear matter.
5. PALM
   The benchmark simulates large-eddy simulation (LES) used for atmospheric and oceanic flows.
6. Clover Leaf
   This benchmark uses domain decomposition to solve the compressible Euler Equations.
7. Conjugate Gradient (CG)
   The CG benchmark performs irregular long distance communication to solve an unstructured sparse linear system.
8. Seismic Wave Modeling
   The benchmark solves two and three dimensional isotropic or anisotropic elastic, viscoelastic or poroelastic wave equation using a finite-difference method.
9. Scalar Penta-diagonal solver(SP)
   The benchmark solves scalar, pentadiagonal equations to simulate synthetic CFD problem solver. Both Fortran and C versions of this benchmark are included in the suite.
10. Mini Ghost
    This benchmark supports Bulk Synchronous Parallel (BSP) model for finite difference stencil computation.
11. ILBDC
    The benchmark kernel is a component of a flow solver that simulates the collision-propagation routine of an advanced 3-D lattice Boltzmann flow solver.
12. Swim
    The benchmark is a weather prediction benchmark that use finite-difference approximation.
13. Block Tridiagonal (BT) Solver
    The benchmark solves a 3D discretization of Naiver-Stokes equation.

It is important to note that we use these benchmarks under the Academic license and as such the results presented here are for scientific curiosity only and may not be included as official results for the different architectures we are exploring.

4   SPEC ACCEL 1.2 Results

In this section we present our results. First we describe the systems where we run, then we report our findings on the different systems from the point of view of functionality. Then, we present the timings we found for OpenMP 4.5 offload and OpenACC. At the end we compare production closed-source implementations of OpenMP 4.5 and OpenACC versus open-source implementations.

4.1 Experimental Systems

For this study, we present results obtained on the OLCF's flagship systems:

Summit [6] is the OLCF's next generation high performance supercomputer. Summit compute nodes are IBM Power9 AC922 servers with two 22-core 3.45 GHz (turbo) IBM POWER9 processors. Each core supports 4-way SMT. Summit compute nodes have 512 GB of DDR4 memory and 96 GB of HBM2 memory, as well as 1.6 TB non-volatile memory that can be used as a burst buffer. Each compute node has 6 NVIDIA Tesla V100 Volta GPUs connected via NVLINK2 which provides up to 25 GB/s unidirectional and 50 GB/s bidirectional bandwidth between GPUs and from the CPU to the GPU. Summit compute nodes are interconnected via Mellanox EDR InifiniBand in a non-blocking fat-tree topology.

Titan [8] is the OLCF's flagship supercomputer. Titan is a Cray XK7 system with 18,688 compute nodes each with a 16-core 2.2 GHz AMD Opteron 6274 Interlagos CPU, 32 GB of RAM, and one NVIDIA Kepler K20X GPU. Titan nodes are connected via Cray's high speed Gemini interconnect.

Percival [3] is one of the supporting systems available at the OLCF and it was deployed to assist with performance portability efforts. Percival is a 168-node Cray XC40 supercomputer. Each Percival node is equipped with one 64-core 1.30GHz Intel Xeon Phi 7230 (KNL) processor and 110 GB of RAM. Percival nodes are connected via Cray's Aries proprietary interconnect in a Dragonfly topology.

We execute reportable runs (three iterations of each benchmark, with the runtime averaged over those three runs). For more details on running the SpecACCEL benchmarks see [4].

4.2 Performance

In this section we present the timing information of the benchmarks for OpenMP 4.5 and OpenACC using different compilers and platforms.

4.3 Correctness and Functionality

Table 1 shows successes and failures (Verification, Runtime, Compile time errors) of SPEC ACCEL 1.2 benchmarks on Summit, Titan and Percival. We can see that in terms of functional implementations the PGI OpenACC supports majority of the benchmarks on all of the systems. Intel compiler on Xeon Phi has the most support for OpenMP 4.5. On Summit, the XL compiler passes the most benchmarks and the Clang/LLVM compiler passes the majority of the C benchmarks. The GCC compiler is still in the early stages of supporting OpenMP 4.5 offload on NVIDIA GPUs, hence it only compiles and (correctly) executes three of the fifteen benchmarks.

Experiments on Summit are performed using CUDA 9.2.64, PGI 18.3 and XL V16.1.0 (Beta 4), GCC 7.2 and CLANG (ykt branch) where PGI and GCC provide support for OpenACC and IBM XL and CLANG provide support for

Table 1. Successes and failures of running the SPEC ACCEL 1.2 benchmarks on different architectures with OpenMP 4.5 and OpenACC. The compiler versions used are: On Summit: PGI 18.3, XL V16.1.0, Clang/LLVM (ykt branch), GCC 7.2 (gomp branch), on Titan Cray CCE 8.7.0, PGI 18.4 and Percival Intel 18.0.0.128 and PGI 18.5

	Summit (NV100 GPU)					Titan (K20X GPU)		Percival (Xeon Phi)	
	XL	PGI	GCC		Clang	PGI	CCE	PGI	Intel
	OMP	ACC	ACC	OMP	OMP	ACC	OMP	ACC	OMP
Stencil	✓	✓	✓	✓	✓	✓	✓	✓	✓
LBM	✓	✓	✓	✓	✓	✓	✓	✓	✓
MRI-Q	✓	✓	✓	✗RE	✓	✓	✓	✓	✓
MD	✗VE	✓	✓	✗RE		✓	✗RE	✓	✗CE
PALM	✗RE	✓	✓	✗RE		✗CE	✗CE	✓	✓
EP	✓	✓	✓	✗VE	✓	✓	✓	✓	✓
CLVRLEAF	✓	✓	✓	✗RE		✓	✗VE	✓	✓
CG	✓	✓	✓	✗VE	✗RE	✓	✓	✓	✓
SEISMIC	✓	✓	✓	✗RE		✓	✗RE	✓	✓
SP F	✗RE	✓	✓	✗RE		✓	✗RE	✓	✓
SP C	✗VE	✓	✓	✗RE	✓	✓	✓	✓	✓
MiniGhost	✗RE	✓	✓	✗RE		✗CE	✗RE	✗CE	✗CE
LBDC	✓	✓	✓	✓		✓	✗RE	✓	✓
Swim	✗NR	✓	✓	✗RE		✓	✗RE	✓	✓
BT	✗NR	✓	✓	✗RE	✓	✓	✓	✓	✓
Passed	8	15	15*	3	6	13	7	14	13

*GCC/OpenACC only offloads 4 out of the 15 benchmarks, the remaining 11 benchmarks utilize the CPU.
VE: Verification error
RE: Runtime error
CE: compile error
NR: benchmark excluded from run

OpenMP. Figure 1 compares the timings for SPEC ACCEL 1.2 OpenACC benchmarks when using the PGI 18.3 and GCC 7.2 (GOMP branch) compilers, both using CUDA 9.2.64. We can see that of the fifteen benchmarks PGI has better execution times for all except two (LBM and LBDC). From the timings we observe that PGI has a more optimized implementation for OpenACC. Another reason for the differences in the timing is that GCC only offloads STENCIL, LBM, MRI-Q, and LBDC to the device as GCC has only functional support for ACC kernels (without offloading) used in the remaining benchmarks. Both PGI and GCC execute all the benchmarks successfully showing that their OpenACC functionality support is complete.

Figure 2 shows the timings for SPEC ACCEL 1.2 OpenMP 4.5 (offload) benchmarks when using the XL V16.1.0 (Beta 4), the CLANG (ykt branch) and GCC 7.2 (GOMP branch). The CLANG specific version used is an IBM version loosely based on the latest CLANG version available in trunk. Clang

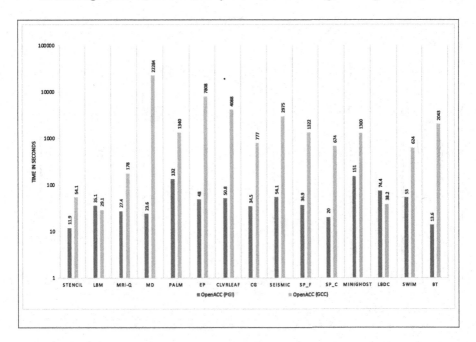

Fig. 1. Execution times of SPEC ACCEL 1.2 OpenACC using the PGI 18.3 and GCC 7.2 (GOMP branch) with CUDA 9.2.64 on Summit

compiles most of the C benchmarks (Stencil, LBM, MRI-Q, EP, CG, SP(C), BT). It produces a runtime error for CG. CLVRLEAF and Minighost are mixed C and Fortran codes, and are not supported using CLANG. The XL compiler always shows better timing results than CLANG on the sub-set of benchmarks that both implementations compile and execute correctly. However, XL does not have execution results for BT (excluded from run) and SP-C (verification error). GCC has minimal support for OpenMP 4.5 offload, as only three of the fifteen benchmarks compile and execute correctly. However we observe that for LBM it outperforms the CLANG compiler.

Figure 3 compares the execution times of SPEC ACCEL 1.2 with production implementations from PGI for OpenACC and XL for OpenMP on Summit. Both compilers use the CUDA 9.2.64 tool chains. From Fig. 3 we see that OpenACC (PGI) has better performance for four of the benchmarks (MRI-Q, EP, Clover-Leaf, CG) when compared to the OpenMP 4.5 (XL). Even when XL compiler only compiles and executes seven of the fifteen OpenACC benchmarks, three of the OpenMP 4.5 benchmarks (Stencil, LBM, Seismic) show better performance than OpenACC. This indicates that OpenMP 4.5, though newer, is promising and can have better performance compared to OpenACC. Maturity of the compiler is a relevant factor, as OpenACC implementations have been available for a longer time.

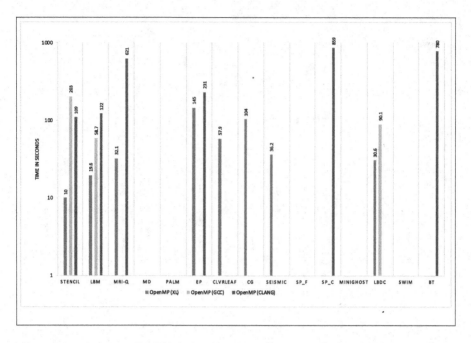

Fig. 2. Execution times of SPEC ACCEL 1.2 OpenMP 4.5 (offload) using XL V16.1.0 (Beta 4), Clang (ykt branch) and GCC 7.2 (GOMP branch) with CUDA 9.2.64 on Summit

Figure 4 shows the SPEC ACCEL 1.2 results on Titan for OpenACC and OpenMP 4.5 (offload) using the PGI 18.4 and Cray CCE 8.7.0 compilers. OpenACC has better performance on four of the benchmarks (STENCIL, MRI-Q, SP_C and BT) and OpenMP 4.5 offload has better performance on three of the benchmarks (LBM, EP, and CG). PGI fails to compile two of the benchmarks and Cray fails to pass (because of compilation, runtime and verification errors) eight of the benchmarks. This is evidence that, on Titan, the OpenACC implementation PGI provides is more mature than the OpenMP 4.5 offload implementation Cray provides when compiling the SPEC 1.2 benchmarks.

Figure 5 shows the SPEC ACCEL 1.2 benchmarks timings on Percival. On this system, OpenACC has better performance than OpenMP 4.5 offload for four of the benchmarks (Stencil, LBM, MRI-Q, MD) when using the PGI 18.5 compiler for OpenACC and the Intel 18.0.0.128 compiler for OpenMP 4.5 (offload). OpenMP 4.5 has better performance for nine of the benchmarks (EP, CLVRLEAF, CG, Seismic, SP_F, SP_C, LBDC, Swim, BT). The PGI compiler fails to produce results for two of the OpenACC benchmarks (PALM and Minighost) and Intel fails to pass one of the OpenMP benchmarks (Minighost) due to compilation errors.

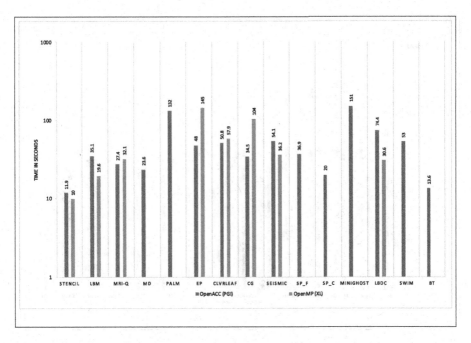

Fig. 3. Execution times of the SPEC ACCEL 1.2 OpenACC and OpenMP 4.5 (offload) benchmarks using PGI 18.3 and XL V16.1.0 (Beta 4) with CUDA 9.2.64 on Summit

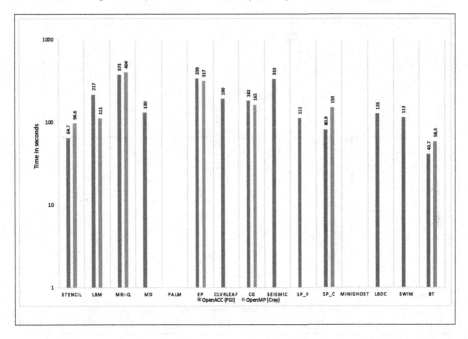

Fig. 4. Execution times of the SPEC ACCEL 1.2 OpenACC and OpenMP 4.5 (offload) benchmarks using the Cray 8.7.0 and PGI 18.4 compilers on Titan

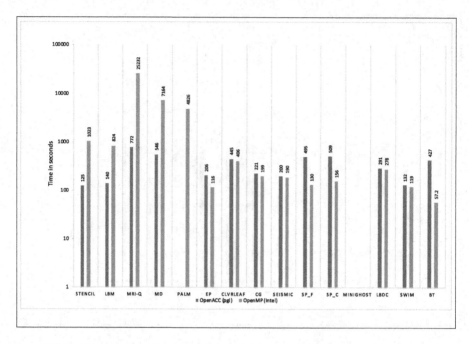

Fig. 5. Execution times of the SPEC ACCEL 1.2 OpenACC and OpenMP 4.5 (offload) benchmarks using Intel 18.0.0.128 and PGI 18.5 compilers on Percival.

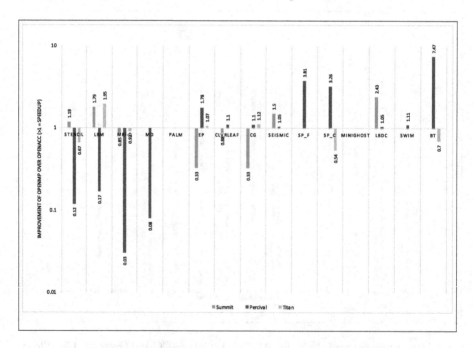

Fig. 6. OpenMP's Performance Improvement over OpenACC

4.4 OpenMP and OpenACC Performance Comparison

Since the benchmarks target the accelerator offload aspect for both OpenMP 4.5 and OpenACC, it is fair to compare the execution times as the algorithms are very similar. The performance improvement or relative speed up, shown in Fig. 6, is calculated by first choosing, for each platform, the best execution times for OpenACC and OpenMP and then dividing the OpenACC timing by the OpenMP for individual benchmarks.

For example, for Summit (Power 9 + NV100) we compare PGI's OpenACC with XL's OpenMP. For Percival we compare PGI's OpenACC and Intel's OpenMP implementations. While for Titan we use PGI's OpenACC and Cray's OpenMP implementations. From Fig. 6 it is clear that on most platforms OpenACC performs better than OpenMP 4.5 (offload). One of the reasons for it is that the OpenACC specification has been formalized for a longer time (OpenACC 1.0 was ratified in 2011), giving vendors time to optimize their implementation.

In contrast OpenMP first introduced accelerator support with OpenMP 4.0 [10] in 2013. That said, the figure also shows that for certain benchmarks like LBM OpenMP does better consistently across most platforms.

5 Related Work

EPCC has developed another suite of microbenchmarks that has both OpenMP and OpenACC variants. The OpenMP [2] versions focus on measuring the synchronization, loop scheduling and array operations overheads in the OpenMP runtime library. The benchmarks support OpenMP 3.1 API [12] and have not been modified to use `target` devices (introduced in OpenMP 4.0 and extended in OpenMP 4.5 Specification [11]). The OpenACC EPCC [1] microbenchmarks mimic kernels commonly seen in scientific codes. They focuses on low-level operations and are designed to test raw performance of compilers and hardware.

Currently there are no publicly accessible standardized OpenMP 4.5 benchmarks but an effort to build a Validation and Verification suite is underway [13] as part of a more elaborate Exascale Computing Project (ECP) - SOLVE. The OpenACC Standard [9] first introduced in 2011, focuses solely on the Application Program Interface (API) for compiler directives that offload compute kernels from a host CPU to an attached accelerator. Extensive work has been done in the field of benchmarks and validation and verification suites for OpenACC [7,14].

6 Conclusion

This paper details our findings when trying to compile and execute SPEC ACCEL 1.2 benchmarks on our production systems: Titan, Summit, and Percival.

In the findings from these experiments we can see that the OpenACC implementations are more functionally mature than the OpenMP 4.5 implementations. However, performance of OpenACC and OpenMP 4.5 (offload) varies depending on the compiler and platform. This is an indication that OpenMP 4.5 is becoming more mature and it can be at par with OpenACC implementations. Since device offloading in OpenMP is a relatively new concept it comes as no surprise that there are is more support for OpenACC than OpenMP. This is clear from the results across all systems, particularly Summit where we see fifteen OpenACC benchmarks in comparison to eight OpenMP benchmarks that have compiled and executed correctly.

For Summit we see that open source implementations of both OpenACC and OpenMP 4.5 (offload) are starting to come closer to production implementations for the case of GCC/OpenACC and CLANG/OpenMP 4.5. However, the GCC/OpenMP 4.5 (offload) is still in its early stages of supporting OpenMP 4.5 (offload) functionally and performance on GPUs.

Cray (Titan) also does not support OpenMP offloading as well as it does OpenACC, with thirteen OpenACC and only seven OpenMP benchmarks that have compiled and executed correctly.

For Intel we see that the performance gap between OpenMP and OpenACC narrows a little, with OpenACC still getting better performance for most benchmarks. But the overall high execution times with Intel and PGI compilers on Percival, when compared to other architectures, hints at the platform not being optimized to support accelerator models like OpenMP and OpenACC.

Acknowledgments. This material is based upon work supported by the U.S. Department of Energy, Office of Science, Office of Advanced Scientific Computing Research, under contract number DE-AC05-00OR22725. This research used resources of the Oak Ridge Leadership Computing Facility at the Oak Ridge National Laboratory, which is supported by the Office of Science of the U.S. Department of Energy under Contract No. DE-AC05-00OR22725.

References

1. EPCC OpenACC Microbenchmarks. https://www.epcc.ed.ac.uk/research/comp uting/performance-characterisation-and-benchmarking/epcc-openacc-benchmark-suite
2. EPCC OpenMP Microbenchmarks. https://www.epcc.ed.ac.uk/research/compu ting/performance-characterisation-and-benchmarking/epcc-openmp-micro-bench mark-suite
3. Percival quickstart guide. https://www.olcf.ornl.gov/percival-quickstart-guide/
4. SPEC ACCEL: Run and Reporting Rules. https://www.spec.org/accel/docs/runrules.html
5. Standard Performance Evaluation Corporation. https://www.spec.org/
6. Summit: Scale new heights. discover new solutions. https://www.olcf.ornl.gov/summit/

7. Friedline, K., Chandrasekaran, S., Lopez, M.G., Hernandez, O.: OpenACC 2.5 validation testsuite targeting multiple architectures. In: Kunkel, J.M., Yokota, R., Taufer, M., Shalf, J. (eds.) ISC High Performance 2017. LNCS, vol. 10524, pp. 557–575. Springer, Cham (2017). https://doi.org/10.1007/978-3-319-67630-2_39
8. Oak Ridge National Lab: Titan supercomputer. https://www.olcf.ornl.gov/titan/
9. OpenACC: OpenACC, Directives for Accelerators. http://www.openacc.org/
10. OpenMP: Openmp 4.0 specification. http://www.openmp.org/wp-content/uploads/openmp-4.0.pdf
11. OpenMP: Openmp 4.5 specification. http://www.openmp.org/wp-content/uploads/openmp-4.5.pdf
12. OpenMP Validation and Verification Suite: Openmp 3.1 Specification. https://github.com/sunitachandra/omp-validation
13. Pophale, S., Diaz, J.M., Hernandez, O., Bernholdt, D., Chandrasekaran, S.: OpenMP 4.5 Validation and Verification Suite for Device Offload. https://crpl.cis.udel.edu/ompvvsollve/
14. Wang, C., Xu, R., Chandrasekaran, S., Chapman, B., Hernandez, O.: A validation testsuite for OpenACC 1.0. In: 2014 IEEE International Parallel and Distributed Processing Symposium Workshops (IPDPSW), pp. 1407–1416. IEEE (2014)

A Beginner's Guide to Estimating and Improving Performance Portability

Henk Dreuning$^{(\boxtimes)}$, Roel Heirman, and Ana Lucia Varbanescu

University of Amsterdam, Amsterdam, The Netherlands
henk.dreuning@gmail.com, roelheirman@gmail.com, a.l.varbanescu@uva.nl

Abstract. Given the increasing diversity of multi- and many-core processors, portability is a desirable feature of applications designed and implemented for such platforms. Portability is unanimously seen as a productivity enabler, but it is also considered a major performance blocker. Thus, *performance portability* has emerged as the property of an application to preserve similar form *and* similar performance on a set of platforms; a first metric, based on extensive evaluation, has been proposed to quantify performance portability for a given application on a set of given platforms.

In this work, we explore the challenges and limitations of this *performance portability metric (PPM)* on two levels. We first use 5 OpenACC applications and 3 platforms, and we demonstrate how to compute and interpret PPM in this context. Our results indicate specific challenges in parameter selection and results interpretation. Second, we use controlled experiments to assess the impact of platform-specific optimizations on both performance and performance portability. Our results illustrate, for our 5 OpenACC applications, a clear tension between performance improvement and performance portability improvement.

Keywords: Performance portability metric
Performance optimization · OpenACC · CPU · GPU

1 Introduction

With the increased popularity of multi- and many-core processors, a new challenge emerges: different platforms seem to favor different programming models and/or styles, making it difficult to assess and compare the merits of different platforms. In this context, *portability* plays an important role: enabling the same programming model to correctly execute on different types of platforms is very appealing for productivity, but it raises concerns in terms of performance. In other words, can the concept of portability be extended to performance, too?

Ideally, and informally, *performance portability* refers to the ability of the same code to execute correctly and perform similarly on different (types of) platforms. For example, running the same OpenCL code on a CPU and a GPU, with correct results and similar performance, would deem the code *performance portable* on these two platforms.

© Springer Nature Switzerland AG 2018
R. Yokota et al. (Eds.): ISC 2018 Workshops, LNCS 11203, pp. 724–742, 2018.
https://doi.org/10.1007/978-3-030-02465-9_52

Assessing performance portability has largely focused so far on detailed comparisons, either targeting applications [12,22] or programming models [5,7,17]. Moreover, several programming models and libraries, like HPL [4], attempt to solve the performance portability by design, proposing a portable front-end, and advanced compilers that optimize the code for different hardware architectures.

Most of these scattered research efforts have introduced their own performance portability definition, often using a qualitative-only formulation. Such definitions make it very difficult to assess and interpret performance portability, or compare different platform sets or different algorithmic approaches. To alleviate this problem, Pennycook et al. [14] proposed a performance portability metric (PPM), which provides a quantitative estimate of the performance portability of a given application on a set of platforms (see Sect. 3 for more details). The proposed metric uses performance efficiency to normalize the performance per platform, and calculates a portability score as a harmonic mean of these efficiencies. The result is a *portability score* for a given application on a set of platforms.

Although the authors do provide a qualitative analysis of the challenges and implications of using this metric [15], a lot of analysis is still required to understand its merits and limitations. Therefore, in this work, *we empirically analyze the usability and usefulness of PPM, applied for OpenACC applications.* Our analysis focuses on three key aspects: (1) calculating PPM for multiple applications and platforms, (2) interpreting the results from the perspective of performance portability across devices, and (3) attempting to improve the performance portability, i.e., increase PPM. Specifically, we conduct multiple benchmarking experiments with different versions of 5 OpenACC applications, using a set of 3 hardware platforms (CPUs and GPUs). We evaluate PPM for each application, and analyze the differences between application versions and across applications.

The contribution of this work is threefold:

- We present a first in-depth study of PPM for OpenACC, using a set of 5 OpenACC applications and 3 platforms (Sects. 5 and 6).
- We present the step-by-step calculation and interpretation of PPM, and demonstrate it on our case-studies. We further show how different calculation methods are indicative of different aspects of the metric and its applicability (Sect. 5).
- We assess different ways to improve the performance portability of our case-studies using OpenACC. Our results illustrate multiple cases where a real tension between performance optimization and performance portability exists (Sect. 6).

2   Related Work

This section presents a brief analysis of related research on performance portability. Specifically, we highlight the most important studies and several proposed solutions to enable and/or enhance performance portability.

Since 2009, when OpenCL has received massive attention for its functional portability across multi-core devices, performance portability has been revisited in various studies. Such studies use empirical analysis combining different applications, programming models, and platforms, and illustrate worst-case or best-case scenarios in terms of performance portability.

For example, in [12], the authors present an investigation of a single OpenCL application, while [16, 18] focus on multiple, smaller kernels. Most studies confirm that OpenCL does not provide performance portability out-of-the-box, by simply provided counterexamples - applications where performance degrades significantly from one platform to another.

Another category of studies focuses on the ability of portable models to compete, performance-wise, against specific programming models (e.g., CUDA vs. OpenCL [5], OpenMP vs. OpenCL [17]). These studies demonstrate a rudimentary version of application efficiency (i.e., the relative performance between the portable and platform-specific code), which they use to show-case potential limitations of portable programming models. This is an idea further used by the metric proposed in [13], and, therefore, also used in our study.

Other research focuses on assessing how code should be written, using portable programming models, to ensure portability. An example for OpenCL is presented in [9], where the authors demonstrate that careful coding and some degree of specialization can provide high-performance portability for a given OpenCL code. Our work is complementary to such studies: we focus on existing code and text-book optimizations, and assess their impact on performance portability.

Going one step further, van der Sanden et al. [20] presents a performance portability study of five different OpenCL applications. Using relative performance (a form of performance efficiency), they analyze the original applications on three different platforms and notice significant discrepancies between achieved and achievable performance. They further proceed to optimize each application for each platform, and demonstrate how the selected optimizations can be platform specific, and they propose a configurable approach to writing specialized OpenCL code. Although our work uses a similar setup, our case-studies are OpenACC applications, and we take a more systematic approach to evaluating performance portability.

The studies we mentioned so far investigate performance portability in the context of a single programming model. As more programming models and tools emerged aiming to solve the performance portability challenge, an orthogonal analysis - i.e., which programming model provides more performance-portable code - can also be performed. An interesting example is [7], where no less than 5 such models have been assessed using a mini-app called TeaLeaf [19]. Their results demonstrate "reasonable levels of performance portability". Our current study only uses OpenACC, one of the models also included in [7], but discusses 5 applications and focuses on cross-platform portability.

Despite the abundance of studies on performance portability and programming models/approaches aiming to improve it, the only metric for performance portability has been proposed in [13]. Our work builds upon their results and observations, and proposes an analysis of both the merits and challenges of applying this metric in practice. More details on the metric and our evaluation process are provided further, in Sect. 3.

3   The Performance Portability Definition and Metric

This section introduces the terminology, concepts, definitions, and metrics used in this study, being a very brief summary of [14]. For a more in-depth presentation of the metric, we refer the reader to [14,15].

The definition proposed by Pennycook et al. is: "**Performance Portability** [is] a measurement of an application's performance efficiency for a given problem that can be executed correctly on all platforms in a given set".

Thus, PPM is effectively a score that *quantifies* this ability. The score is calculated using Eq. 1, where H is the set of platforms and $e_i(a, p)$ is the performance efficiency of application a, solving problem p on platform i. Note that if an application is not supported on a given platform, performance portability is reduced to 0 (according to the definition). Also note the distinction between *application* and *problem*: the application is seen as a specific instance of the problem (i.e., with given input parameters). Finally, the authors propose two different types of efficiency: *application efficiency* and *architectural efficiency*. The former quantifies the performance of the application relative to the best known version on the given platform, while the latter quantifies the performance of the application relative to the peak performance of the platform.

$$P(a, p, H) = \begin{cases} \frac{|H|}{\sum_{i \in H} \frac{1}{e_i(a,p)}} & \text{if } i \text{ is supported } \forall i \in H. \\ 0 & \text{otherwise} \end{cases} \tag{1}$$

An accurate performance portability score is heavily dependent on accurate estimates of performance efficiency. As such, we identify two major challenges in the PPM evaluation: (1) correctly benchmarking the application, and (2) correctly estimating the reference(s) to be used when computing efficiency. In the remainder of this paper, we use our 5 applications to demonstrate the conceptual and practical difficulties in computing an accurate and meaningful PPM score.

4   Experimental Setup

In this section we present the components of our experimental setup: the 5 applications and the 3 platforms.

4.1   The OpenACC Applications

We apply the performance portability metric on 5 applications, implemented in OpenACC. We have selected a small set of case studies with different computational characteristics, aiming to cover most basic patterns of modern HPC applications. Our results indeed demonstrate that the set is diverse enough to showcase different behavior types in terms of PPM (see Sects. 5 and 6). The 5 applications are[1]:

Matrix multiplication (MM): a (dense) matrix multiplication. The result of the multiplication of the $n \times m$ matrix A with the $p \times n$ matrix B is the $n \times m$ matrix C, with $C_{ij} = \sum_{k=1}^{m}(A_{ik} * B_{kj})$ for all C_{ij} in C. The input matrices are generated at runtime. For our experiments, we used input matrices of 4000×4000 single-precision floating-point elements, in order to facilitate a significant execution time. The code originates from GitHub[2].

Saxpy: combination of scalar multiplication and element-wise addition of two 1-dimensional vectors. The result is stored in one of the input vectors. A Saxpy operation on vectors A and B of length n performs $B_i = \alpha * A_i + B_i$ for all B_i in B, with V_i being the element in the ith position of vector V, and α a scalar. The input vectors are generated at runtime. We fixed the input arrays at $n = 10^9$ elements. The code is based on an implementation of vector addition from GitHub[3].

Mandelbrot (MB): calculation of the set of complex numbers c for which $f_c(z) = z^2 + c$ does not diverge when $f_c(z)$ is iteratively computed, starting from $z = 0$ (the mandelbrot set). The (scaled) x and y coordinates of elements on a grid represent the real and imaginary parts of a complex number. The application iteratively calculates $f_c(z)$ until the modulus of the complex number exceeds (or equals) 2, or until a predefined number of iterations has been executed. The grid points whose modulus has not exceeded (or equaled) 2 by the time the calculation is stopped, are assumed to correspond to complex numbers that do not diverge as explained before and thus to be in the mandelbrot set. We conducted experiments with a grid of 8192 by 8192 elements and a maximum of 255 iterations. The code originates from [2].

K-nearest neighbors (KNN): calculation of the distances between every location (represented as coordinates) in a dataset and a given input location, followed by a partial sort to find the K smallest distances and their corresponding locations. For the experiments, only the kernel that calculates distances is considered. For our experiments, the input dataset consists of a list of locations of hurricanes that is replicated until it forms a list of 21.893.120 locations. The code (and included input data) originates from the Rodinia benchmark suite[4].

Diffusion operator (Diff): simulation of heat dissipation on a cylindric surface. The cylindric surface is represented as a grid, with each cell containing a temperature value. The temperatures are iteratively updated, using a 3×3 stencil operation that calculates a weighted average of the current

---

[1] All applications use single precision floating point data types, with Diffusion Operator being the only exception.

[2] rmfarber, https://github.com/rmfarber/ParallelProgrammingWithOpenACC.

[3] Oak Ridge Leadership Computing Facility, https://github.com/olcf/vector_addition_tutorials.

[4] yuhc, https://github.com/yuhc/gpu-rodinia [3].

temperature and the temperatures of neighboring cells. The weight used in the calculation is read from a separate grid (one for each cell). The simulation stops when the difference between the lowest and highest temperature on the grid exceeds a given threshold (convergence) or when a maximum number of iterations is performed. The kernel that checks for convergence is excluded from performance measurements. For our experiments, we use a convergence threshold of 9.99999×10^5, a maximum number of 600 iterations and a grid of 5000×5000 elements. We implemented the application (and input data generator) ourselves.

4.2 The Platforms

We calculate the performance portability metric on the case-study applications using a set of three platforms: one CPU (a dual-socket Intel Xeon E5-2630-v3), and two NVIDIA GPUs (TitanX, Maxwell generation and TitanX, Pascal generation). Our platform selection is small enough to enable in-depth analysis for each application, yet diverse enough to illustrate potential inter-device performance portability problems. The relevant specifications of these platforms can be found in Tables 1 and 2. The experiments are run on the DAS5 computing cluster [1], running CentOS 7. All case-study applications are compiled using pgcc/pgc++ 17.10. CUDA applications are compiled using NVCC 9.0.176, the MKL [6] application (see Sect. 5) was compiled using ICC 15.0.4 with MKL version 11.2, and the OpenMP application was compiled using GCC 7.1.

Table 1. CPU specifications

Platform	Intel Xeon E5-2630-v3
Architecture	Haswell
# of sockets	2
# of cores (per socket)	8
# of threads (per socket)	16
Base clock frequency (GHz)	2.4
Memory bandwidth (GB/s)	48.9
SIMD support	AVX2 (256 bit)

5 Computing and Interpreting PPM

In this section, we present a systematic, step-by-step approach to calculate the PPM score, and demonstrate it for our case-study applications. We further highlight different interpretations of the results and potential sources of inaccuracy.

Table 2. GPU specifications

Platform	NVIDIA TitanX	NVIDIA TitanX
Architecture	Maxwell	Pascal
# of cores	3072	3584
Base clock frequency (MHz)	1000	1.531
Memory bandwidth (GB/s)	336.5	480
Memory size (GB)	12 (GDDR5)	12 (GDDR5X)

5.1 The PPM Calculation Workflow

Figure 1 presents the complete workflow required to assess an application's performance portability. In the following paragraphs, we present in detail each step, emphasizing the choices to be made and challenges to be overcome.

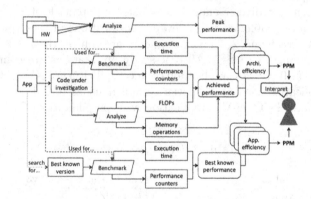

Fig. 1. The process of performance portability assessment.

We note that, although none of the steps are particularly complex, the workflow itself is. Of special interest for the accuracy of the process are correct benchmarking, selecting the right performance metrics, and selecting the correct reference performance. Of interest for the actual interpretation are the diversity of the code, and the choice between application and architectural efficiency.

5.2 Calculating Performance Efficiency

As described in Sect. 3, the PPM score is computed using $e_i(a, p)$, i.e., the performance efficiency of application a, solving problem p on platform i. Performance efficiency is a normalized metric that (implicitly) compares the achieved performance of an application, P_m, against the best possible performance, P_{peak}[5].

---

[5] In all notations with a subscript m or *peak*, **m** stands for measured, and **peak** represents a form of peak performance.

Different types of efficiencies can be defined, based on how P_{peak} is chosen. In this work, we use two metrics: architectural efficiency and application efficiency.

Architectural Efficiency. Architectural efficiency expresses the achieved application performance, P_m, as a fraction of the theoretical peak performance of the hardware, P_{peak}^{HW}.

$$e\_arch_i(a, p) = \frac{P_m}{P_{peak}^{HW}}$$

Calculating Peak Performance (P_{peak}^{HW}). Broadly speaking, the simplest two generic metrics used to estimate performance are operations throughput, measured as the number of (floating-point) operations per second (FLOP/s), and memory bandwidth, measured as the number of bytes transferred per second (B/s). We will use BW to indicate performance in terms of bandwidth, and OpT to indicate performance as operational throughput.

In the case of hardware platforms, peak performance (as specified by the datasheet) is computed assuming maximum throughput for all system components. Thus, for CPUs, the peak operational throughput is calculated as follows:

$$OpT_{peak}^{HW}(CPU) = S \times C \times W \times FLOPs/cycle \times f$$

where S is the number of sockets, C is the number of cores per socket, W is the SIMD width (in elements, thus dependent on the data size), and f is the clock frequency in Hz.

For GPUs, the theoretical peak FLOPs for single-precision calculations are determined as:

$$OpT_{peak}^{HW}(GPU) = C \times FLOPs/cycle \times f$$

where C is the number of cores, and f is the clock frequency. For double-precision applications, the peak performance depends heavily on the GPU architecture itself (i.e., different GPU architectures show a different ratio between the single- and double-precision peak FLOPs) []. Thus, we can generalize the calculation of GPU FLOPs to:

$$OpT_{peak}^{HW}(GPU) = C \times FLOPs/cycle \times f/p$$

where p corrects for different throughput of arithmetic operations when not using single precision floating point data (e.g., $p = 1$ for single precision, $p = 32$ for our TitanX GPUs, and $p = 2$ for NVIDIA V100 Volta architecture [11]).

The peak bandwidth for CPUs and GPUs can either be obtained from the platform specification sheet, or measured using a memory-bandwidth benchmark like STREAM [8].

The peak performance for our 3 platforms can be found in Table 3. The numbers are obtained by calculation for OpT and by benchmarking (using STREAM) for BW.

Table 3. Peak FLOPs and bandwidth for our selected platforms.

Platform	Intel Xeon E5-2630-v3	NVIDIA TitanX (Maxwell)	NVIDIA TitanX (Pascal)
Peak SP OpT [GFLOP/s]	614.4	6144.0	10157.0
Peak DP OpT [GFLOP/s]	307.2*	192.0	317.4
Peak BW [GB/s]	48.9**	336.5***	480.0***

*Value obtained using floating point throughput data from [11].
**Value obtained through benchmarking [8].
***Value obtained from specification sheet.

OpT or BW: Which Metric to Use? While the hardware peak performance is independent of the application under study, selecting which metric to use to calculate the architectural efficiency is an important choice: using the wrong metric may lead to overly pessimistic/optimistic numbers.

One solution for this choice is to use the same principles as the Roofline model, and choose OpT for compute-bound applications and BW for memory-bound applications. In this case, the application operational intensity (OI^{app}) - i.e., the ratio between compute operations and bytes transferred to/from memory, measured in FLOPs/Byte - is used to determine whether the application is compute- or memory-bound [21]. Specifically, we compare OI^{app} against the platform **OI** (i.e., $OI^{HW} = \frac{OpT^{HW}_{peak}}{BW^{HW}_{peak}}$). If $OI^{App} < OI^{HW}$, the application is considered memory-bound. If, on the other hand, $OI^{App} >= OI^{HW}$, the application is considered compute-bound. In both cases, the architectural efficiency is calculated as fraction of peak performance, according to Eq. 2.

$$e\_arch_i(a,p) = \begin{cases} \frac{OpT^{app}}{OpT^{HW}}, & \text{if } OI^{app} >= OI^{HW} \\ \frac{BW^{app}}{BW^{HW}}, & \text{otherwise} \end{cases} \tag{2}$$

An alternative way of calculating the architectural efficiency for memory-bound applications is to determine the actual OpT^{app} by using OI^{app}, again leveraging the Roofline model [21]. Thus, we compute $OpT^{app} = BW^{app} \times OI^{app}$. This approach simplifies the architectural efficiency calculation, allowing all analysis to be expressed in FLOPs.

We note that the two approaches are equivalent, and they both depend on the correct calculation of OI^{app}. This calculation can be done in two ways: by analyzing the source code and determining the number of floating point operations and memory accesses the application will perform during execution, or by using profiling tools to obtain these numbers. For our case-study applications, the former approach was used.

Application Efficiency. Application efficiency is the achieved performance as a fraction of the best observed performance of any implementation of the same application on that platform:

$$e\_app_i(a, p) = \frac{P_m}{P_{peak}^{app}}$$

We note that the best known performing implementation can be implemented in a different programming model than the application for which we are determining performance portability.

Also, in this case, performance can be directly observed through measurements (i.e., no approximations are needed through OI-like application features): by using the same performance metric (for example, execution time), we can directly compute application efficiency.

Application or Architectural Efficiency? Architectural efficiency offers a *theoretical upper bound* on performance, explicitly providing an indication on how much room is left for optimization. However, it does not show whether a given implementation *is actually efficient*. For example, despite reaching high architectural efficiency, an algorithm's implementation may be inefficient if it performs unnecessary memory accesses or redundant arithmetic operations (i.e., such operations may improve system utilization, but do not contribute to obtaining the result faster). Alternatively, an application might only reach low architectural efficiency, even for the best known performing implementation, due to application/data characteristics. In these cases, application efficiency uses a *practical upper bound* on performance, and it is easily computed based on direct measurements; however, it can be biased when the choice of best available implementation is poor, and it might require periodic updating. To decide whether further optimization is feasible in practice and to see whether there is more room for optimization than architectural efficiency alone can indicate, it is necessary to look at both efficiencies.

5.3 Case-Studies: PPM Results and Analysis

Using either architectural or application efficiency, PPM can be applied by filling in the efficiency in the metric. For our situation, the PPM score becomes:

$$P(a, p, H) = \frac{3}{\frac{1}{e_{Xeon}(a,p)} + \frac{1}{e_{TitanX\_M}(a,p)} + \frac{1}{e_{TitanX\_P}(a,p)}}$$

with $e_i(a, p)$ being either $e\_arch_i(a, p)$ or $e\_app_i(a, p)$.

PPM Using Architectural Efficiency. The results of applying PPM on our case study applications (described in Sect. 4), are shown in Figs. 2 and 3. The OI values obtained through our analysis, and the accompanying bounds can be found in Table 4.

Figure 2 shows the architectural efficiency and accompanying PPM score for all case-study applications. In the cases of Mandelbrot and KNN, the effect of using the harmonic mean to compute the PPM score is clearly visible: the

Table 4. OI and bounds for our case-study applications.

Mandelbrot			
Version	Platform	OI	Bound
Naive	Xeon	3329.42	Compute
	TitanX (Maxwell)	208.09	
	TitanX (Pascal)	208.09	
Coarsening	Xeon	3329.42	
	TitanX (Maxwell)	208.09	
	TitanX (Pascal)	208.09	
Load balance	Xeon	1664.71	
	TitanX (Maxwell)	208.09	
	TitanX (Pascal)	208.09	
Algebraic	Xeon	1331.77	
	TitanX (Maxwell)	166.47	
	TitanX (Pascal)	166.47	

KNN			
Version	Platform	OI	Bound
Naive	Xeon	14.83	Memory
	TitanX (Maxwell)	0.92	
	TitanX (Pascal)	0.92	
Eliminate sqrt	Xeon	9.33	
	TitanX (Maxwell)	0.58	
	TitanX (Pascal)	0.58	

Saxpy			
Version	Platform	OI	Bound
Naive	Xeon	0.17	Memory
	TitanX (Maxwell)	0.17	
	TitanX (Pascal)	0.17	
Coarsening	Xeon	0.17	
	TitanX (Maxwell)	0.17	
	TitanX (Pascal)	0.17	

Matrix multiplication			
Version	Platform	OI	Bound
Naive	Xeon	4.00	Memory
	TitanX (Maxwell)	4.00	
	TitanX (Pascal)	4.00	
Tiling	Xeon	20.16	Compute
	TitanX (Maxwell)	8.00	Memory
	TitanX (Pascal)	8.00	
Collapse	Xeon	4.00	
	TitanX (Maxwell)	4.00	
	TitanX (Pascal)	4.00	

Diffusion operator			
Version	Platform	OI	Bound
Naive	Xeon	1.17	Memory
	TitanX (Maxwell)	1.17	Compute
	TitanX (Pascal)	1.17	
Kernels	Xeon	1.17	Memory
	TitanX (Maxwell)	1.17	
	TitanX (Pascal)	1.17	

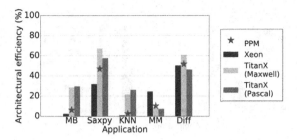

Fig. 2. Performance and PPM score based on architectural efficiency for the case-study applications.

relatively low efficiency on the CPU results in a low performance portability score, even though the efficiency on the GPUs is significantly higher. In the case of Saxpy, the performance portability score is much more positively affected by the (relatively high) architectural efficiency on the GPUs, because the efficiency on the CPU is rather high. Matrix Multiplication shows the opposite of the trend in the aforementioned applications, reaching a higher efficiency on the CPU than on both GPUs. The efficiency reached on the CPU by the Diffusion Operator application is in between the efficiencies reached on the GPUs.

PPM Using Application Efficiency. We determine application efficiency for 3 of our case-study applications: Matrix Multiplication, Saxpy, and Diffusion Operator. We select the following implementations as the best known performing ones:

Matrix multiplication: for the CPU, the implementation of dense matrix multiplication (SGEMM) in Intel's Math Kernel Library (MKL) [6] is chosen as best-known performing implementation. For the GPU, we compared with cuBLAS's [10] SGEMM implementation.

Saxpy: we compare against MKL's Saxpy implementation for the CPU, and cuBLAS's Saxpy implementation for the GPUs.

Diffusion Operator: we compare against two self-written implementations: an implementation in OpenMP for the CPU and an implementation in CUDA for the GPUs. The OpenMP implementation reaches about 58% of peak performance, while the CUDA implementation reaches between 50% and 53% of peak performance on the two GPUs.

Because we run both our case study applications and the best known performing implementations on the same platforms, we are able to use runtime as a performance metric to compute application efficiency.

Figure 3 shows the application efficiency for the three applications for which application efficiency can be computed. We see similar trends in application efficiency for these applications as we see when applying architectural efficiency, when comparing CPU and GPU performance per application. While Saxpy

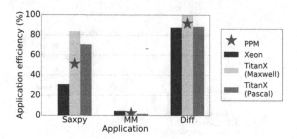

Fig. 3. Performance and PPM score based on application efficiency for Saxpy, Matrix Multiplication, and the Diffusion Operator.

reaches between approximately 30% (CPU) and 83% (GPU) of the performance of the best known implementation, Matrix Multiplication reaches no more than approximately 5% application efficiency.

Platforms Heterogeneity. Figure 4 compares the PPM scores (based on architectural efficiency) for two diffrent platform sets: one with all 3 platforms, and the second one with only the GPUs.

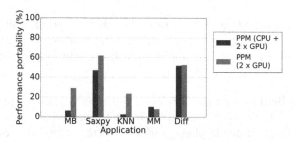

Fig. 4. Difference in PPM scores (based on architectural efficiency) when considering all 3 platforms, or only the 2 GPUs.

Figure 4 presents the PPM scores, calculated based on architectural efficiency, for two platform sets: one consisting of all three systems (CPU and GPUs), and the other consisting of only the two GPUs. Comparing the PPM scores for the two sets, we observe two types of behavior: the scores for Matrix Multiplication and Diffusion Operator change very little, while for the other three applications, excluding the CPU improves the performance portability significantly. These differences indicate that although the PPM scores are calculated for the same applications, they can lead to very different qualitative views on performance portability when there is no knowledge about the heterogeneity of the platform set. We therefore advocate the use of a metric for heterogeneity, to (at least) indicate the diversity of the platfotm set.

Further, the results in this section also support the intuition that a low PPM score is often caused by one of two things: low efficiencies overall, or big differences among platform-specific performance efficiencies. Thus, if one's aim is to improve performance portability (i.e., increase PPM), the potential performance efficiency imbalance between platforms must be investigated. If, indeed, such an imbalance exists, the optimization efforts are likely to target the underperforming platform first. Finally, the PPM score itself can serve as a threshold to decide whether optimizing the application for the underperforming platform(s) is worth it, or whether it makes more sense to drop platform(s) from the set.

6   Improving Performance Portability

After demonstrating how the PPM score can be calculated for different applications, different types of platforms, and using different performance efficiencies, we take a step further and discuss how performance portability can be improved.

6.1   Techniques for Performance Portability Improvement

When the performance portability of an application is considered too low, there are three options to improve it.

More Platforms. The first option is increasing the number of platforms supported by the application. If the application performs well on a newly added platform, the performance portability will increase. The extent to which the newly added platform improves performance portability will also depend on the efficiency of the other platforms, as we saw in the results of Sect. 5.

Furthermore, when more "similar" platforms are added, the performance portability score is very likely to increase. This scenario could be useful to show how well an application works across many devices of the same kind.

However, it is perhaps even more interesting to see what happens with performance portability when a platform of a new "type" is added - for example, adding Xeon Phi to a set of CPUs and GPUs could increase the heterogeneity of the set of platforms. To support a new platform, slight changes might need to be done to the application, and the performance portability score could still change in an unpredictable manner. In other words, increasing platform diversity can lead to subtle changes in the performance efficiency on all platforms. Nevertheless, this approach has no guaranteed behavior when plaform diversity is increased.

As a side effect of this discussion, we observe that platform diversity is not included in any way in the given metric. While it is the responsibility of the user to choose the platform mix, we argue that the PPM score should be augmented with a metric of diversity, which specify how many types of platforms exist, and how many instances of each kind there are. This would be useful when comparing mixes with similar PPM scores.

Whether it is feasible to incorporate this metric in the PPM itself, or whether it should be considered as a separate metric, in the form of a confidence score, is something we leave as future work.

Less Platforms. In case the PPM score is held back by a (type of) platform in the chosen platform set, it can make sense to remove the platform from that set. While this seems like an easy way out, it is a very useful solution when, for example, it is not effective and/or efficient to optimize the application for that platform. While this approach reduces the platform set heterogeneity, it will increase the performance portability score. Whether this solution is desirable or not depends on the actual application.

Higher Performance Efficiency. The last option for improving performance portability is to improve the performance of the application per platform, hoping for an increase of performance efficiency on the chosen platform, and little adverse effects (i.e., penalties on the performance efficiency) on the other platforms.

In reality, it is expected that applying an optimization to the application has one of the following effects: either the performance *increases on all platforms*, or *the performance increases on one platform, but decreases on another platform*. In the latter case, a genuine worst-case scenario, we observe a tension between optimizing for performance and optimizing for performance portability. The cases where such a tension arises are likely to depend on the application, programming model (and its compiler), and optimizations. However, as long as such a tension exists, a metric like PPM is useful in diagnosing it.

6.2   Case-Studies: Improving Performance Portability

We test this hypothesis by applying a number of optimizations to our case-study applications and assessing their impact on both the performance and the performance portability of the applications. Specifically, we apply the following optimizations on the naive versions of our case-study applications:

Matrix multiplication: we apply four optimizations to the original implementation. First, tiling is introduced through the use of the OpenACC *tile* clause, aiming to improve caching behavior and the memory access pattern (using tile size 32). The second optimization is to collapse the two outer loops of the Matrix Multiplication kernel through the OpenACC *collapse* clause. Additionally, two different OpenACC pragma configurations were implemented: both having *independent* clauses on the two outer loops of the kernel (indicating the iterations of the loops are independent of each other). The first configuration has a *seq* clause on the innermost loop (demanding sequential execution), while the second configuration has a *reduction* clause on the innermost loop.

Saxpy: in an attempt to improve the amount of work done per thread/granularity of work distribution/OI, a coarsening strategy is implemented for the Saxpy application. This means that multiple (specifically 4) vector elements are processed per parallel processing element.

Mandelbrot: we implement a total of three optimizations for Mandelbrot. Firstly, a coarsening approach is implemented, similar to the optimization for Saxpy (assigning 2 vector elements to each processing element). Secondly, we implement a simple load balancing (LB) strategy, by distributing the work over the parallel processing elements on a per-row basis instead of a per-element basis. Lastly, an algebraic optimization is implemented, reducing the total amount of arithmetic work that needs to be performed.

K-nearest neighbors: a single, algebraic optimization was implemented for K-nearest neighbors, eliminating the square-root operation that is performed in the distance calculation.

Diffusion operator: a single optimization is attempted for the Diffusion Operator, by adding the OpenACC *kernels* pragma to the stencil kernel, explicitly annotating the piece of code in which the OpenACC compiler should try to exploit parallelism, and that should be executed on the target device (one of our platforms).

Figure 5 shows the performance efficiency and performance portability scores before and after applying each of the optimizations above. Note that, because the results of the version of Matrix Multiplication using the *seq* and *reduce* clauses are identical to those of the naive and tiled versions, respectively, they were excluded from the figure.

Our results show a number of instances in which an optimization lead to improved performance (efficiency) on one platform, but decreased performance efficiency on a different platform. The coarsening implementation of Mandelbrot shows an improved architectural efficiency when compared to the naive implementation on the CPU, but a slightly decreased efficiency for both GPUs. Nevertheless the performance portability score is not negatively affected overall. The load balancing version exhibits the same trend: while performance on the CPU improves a bit, performance on the GPU decreases significantly. In this case, the performance portability decreases when compared to the naive version. Here is a tension between optimizing for performance on the CPU and optimizing performance portability.

Both optimizations applied to Matrix Multiplication increase architectural efficiency on one or both of the GPUs, while they decrease efficiency on the CPU. This also happens for application efficiency. Even though the application efficiency is below 5% for all implementations, the impact of the optimizations is clearly distinguishable. In all cases performance portability is negatively affected.

The impact of the optimization of Saxpy is similar for the architectural and application efficiency. In both cases, the efficiency is either equal or better than that of the naive implementation on all platforms, increasing the performance portability score. The optimization of KNN improves the architectural efficiency on all platforms, but the performance portability score increases only moderately because of the low efficiency on the CPU, when compared to the GPUs.

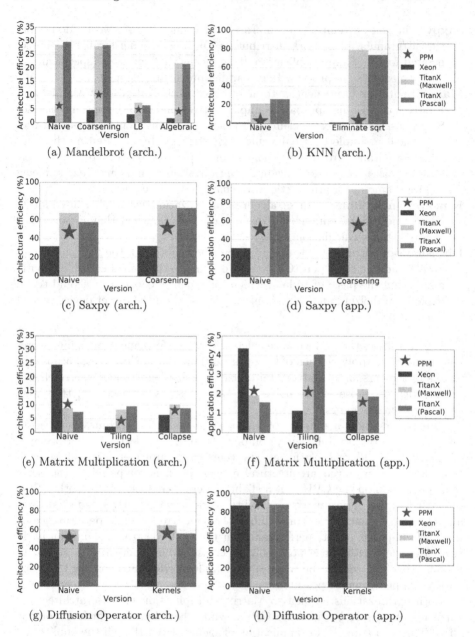

Fig. 5. Performance efficiency and performance portability effects of optimizations. Note that the vertical scales are not the same for each subfigure.

Finally, the Diffusion Operator shows a performance improvement for both GPUs after the optimization, while the CPU performance did not change. This counts for both architectural and application efficiency, and in both cases the performance portability improves. Note that the naive and kernels implementations outperformed the CUDA version that was selected as best-known performing implementation on the TitanX (Maxwell) and on both GPUs respectively. This leads to an application efficiency of 100%, since the OpenACC implementation becomes the best performing one on that platform.

7   Conclusion and Future Work

Performance portability is a desirable feature of applications running on modern multi-core systems, as it improves productivity and enables flexibility in hardware selection, even post-implementation.

In this work, we presented a step-by-step approach to compute the performance portability metric, proposed in [13], for 5 OpenACC applications, and showed the immediate challenges that need solving for a smooth process and interpretation. Although our current results could be perceived as limited by our choices (5 case-studies, the OpenACC programming model, and 3 platforms), our study has already identified two important challenges that need solving for PPM in particular, and performance portability in general: the impact of heterogeneity in the platform set, and the potential tension between performance optimizations and performance portability. Therefore, we argue for adding a heterogeneity metric to augment the PPM values, ensuring this knowledge is not lost in PPM score comparisons. We are working on integrating these two metrics into a relevant combined score. Moreover, the fact that per-platform optimizations can have different impacts on different platform mixes provides empirical evidence that some optimizations could be "more recommended than others" when performance portability is (also) a concern. To determine whether this is indeed the case, a systematic empirical analysis of different optimizations and their impact is required, to help filter optimizations as "positive" or "negative". We are actively working towards designing a systematic methodology and a prototype framework to implement such an optimization impact analysis at application level.

Acknowledgements. We would like to thank Jason Sewall and John Pennycook for their help in designing our experiments and interpreting the results.

References

1. Bal, H., et al.: A medium-scale distributed system for computer science research: infrastructure for the long term. Computer **49**(5), 54–63 (2016)
2. Bauer, S.: Accelerator Offloading mit GCC (in German) (2016). https://www.heise.de/developer/artikel/Accelerator-Offloading-mit-GCC-3317330.html?seite=3. Accessed Apr 2018
3. Che, S., et al.: Rodinia: a benchmark suite for heterogeneous computing. In: IEEE International Symposium on Workload Characterization, IISWC 2009, pp. 44–54. IEEE (2009)

4. Fabeiro, J.F.: Tools for improving performance portability in heterogeneous environments. Ph.D. thesis, Department of Computer Engineering, University of A Coruña, July 2017
5. Fang, J., Varbanescu, A.L., Sips, H.: A comprehensive performance comparison of CUDA and OpenCL. In: 2011 International Conference on Parallel Processing (ICPP), pp. 216–225. IEEE (2011)
6. Intel. Intel Math Kernel Library. https://software.intel.com/en-us/mkl. Accessed Apr 2018
7. Martineau, M., McIntosh-Smith, S., Gaudin, W.: Assessing the performance portability of modern parallel programming models using TeaLeaf. Concurrency Comput.: Pract. Exp. **29**(15), e4117 (2017)
8. McCalpin, J.D.: Memory bandwidth and machine balance in current high performance computers. In: IEEE Computer Society Technical Committee on Computer Architecture (TCCA) Newsletter, pp. 19–25, December 1995
9. McIntosh-Smith, S., Boulton, M., Curran, D., Price, J.: On the performance portability of structured grid codes on many-core computer architectures. In: Kunkel, J.M., Ludwig, T., Meuer, H.W. (eds.) ISC 2014. LNCS, vol. 8488, pp. 53–75. Springer, Cham (2014). https://doi.org/10.1007/978-3-319-07518-1_4
10. NVIDIA. cuBLAS. https://developer.nvidia.com/cublas. Accessed Apr 2018
11. NVIDIA. CUDA C Programming Guide (2018). https://docs.nvidia.com/cuda/cuda-c-programming-guide/index.html. Accessed Apr 2018
12. Pennycook, S.J., Hammond, S.D., Wright, S.A., Herdman, J.A., Miller, I., Jarvis, S.A.: An investigation of the performance portability of OpenCL. J. Parallel Distrib. Comput. **73**(11), 1439–1450 (2013)
13. Pennycook, S.J., Sewall, J.D., Lee, V.W.: A Metric for Performance Portability. arXiv preprint arXiv:1611.07409 (2016)
14. Pennycook, S.J., Sewall, J.D., Lee, V.W.: A metric for performance portability. CoRR, abs/1611.07409 (2016)
15. Pennycook, S.J., Sewall, J.D., Lee, V.W.: Implications of a metric for performance portability. Future Gener. Comput. Syst. (2017)
16. Rul, S., Vandierendonck, H., D'Haene, J., De Bosschere, K.: An experimental study on performance portability of OpenCL kernels. In: 2010 Symposium on Application Accelerators in High Performance Computing (SAAHPC 2010) (2010)
17. Shen, J., Fang, J., Sips, H., Varbanescu, A.L.: Performance gaps between OpenMP and OpenCL for multi-core CPUs. In: Proceedings of the 2012 41st International Conference on Parallel Processing Workshops, ICPPW 2012, Washington, DC, USA, pp. 116–125. IEEE Computer Society (2012)
18. Stratton, J.A., Kim, H., Jablin, T.B., Hwu, W.W.: Performance portability in accelerated parallel kernels. Center for Reliable and High-Performance Computing (2013)
19. UK-MAC. TeaLeaf (2017). http://uk-mac.github.io/TeaLeaf/
20. van der Sanden, J.: Evaluating the performance portability of OpenCL. Master's thesis, Eindhoven University of Technology, The Netherlands (2011)
21. Williams, S., Waterman, A., Patterson, D.: Roofline: an insightful visual performance model for multicore architectures. Commun. ACM **52**(4), 65–76 (2009)
22. Zhang, Y., Sinclair, M., Chien, A.A.: Improving performance portability in OpenCL programs. In: Kunkel, J.M., Ludwig, T., Meuer, H.W. (eds.) ISC 2013. LNCS, vol. 7905, pp. 136–150. Springer, Heidelberg (2013). https://doi.org/10.1007/978-3-642-38750-0_11

Profiling and Debugging Support for the Kokkos Programming Model

Simon D. Hammond[✉], Christian R. Trott, Daniel Ibanez,
and Daniel Sunderland

Center for Computing Research, Sandia National Laboratories,
Albuquerque, NM 87123, USA
sdhammo@sandia.gov

Abstract. Supercomputing hardware is undergoing a period of significant change. In order to cope with the rapid pace of hardware and, in many cases, programming model innovation, we have developed the Kokkos Programming Model – a C++-based abstraction that permits performance portability across diverse architectures. Our experience has shown that the abstractions developed can significantly frustrate debugging and profiling activities because they break expected code proximity and layout assumptions. In this paper we present the Kokkos Profiling interface, a lightweight, suite of hooks to which debugging and profiling tools can attach to gain deep insights into the execution and data structure behaviors of parallel programs written to the Kokkos interface.

Keywords: Profiling · Performance-portable · Programming models

1 Introduction

The future of supercomputing is changing. The past two decades of high-performance computing hardware have been dominated by a period of relative architectural stasis – multiple homogeneous computing nodes interconnected with a high-speed network. Leading contemporary machines and those of the next decade look almost certain to be characterized by a period of rapid architectural change, not least, in part because of a push to achieve machines capable of "Exascale" class computation (defined by the United States Department of Energy to be 50X greater application performance [16]).

Such a significant change in hardware diversity and the much greater use of computational accelerators presents a profound change for the programming models upon which scalable scientific codes are built. While we can expect the use of message-passing (MPI) based distributed memory algorithms to continue, the programming of on-node computation will change dramatically. Unfortunately, our experience to date has shown that each class of hardware often requires different approaches to programming, and in some cases, requires an outright different programming model to be employed. At Sandia National Laboratories,

© Springer Nature Switzerland AG 2018
R. Yokota et al. (Eds.): ISC 2018 Workshops, LNCS 11203, pp. 743–754, 2018.
https://doi.org/10.1007/978-3-030-02465-9_53

which is one of the largest supercomputing users in the world, and at many other HPC sites, such a position is untenable. Reprogramming of applications for each class or generation of computing architecture would require an unsustainable level of investment.

To this end, we have developed the Kokkos Programming Model [5–7] – a C++ meta-template driven approach to programming high-performance applications, that are intended to be portable across diverse computing architectures. Examples of similar approaches also include RAJA [14], Alpaka [26], Intel Thread Building Blocks (TBB) [18] and Thrust [2]. From a single C++ code base it is possible to write one version of a code and have this run efficiently on a wide range of computing architectures including multi-core processors such as Intel's Xeon [11,13,17] and IBM's POWER server-class [19,25] processor families, Intel's Knights Landing many-core processor [22,23] and GPUs from NVIDIA and AMD. Behind the scenes, the developer authored kernels are retargeted to architecture-relevant programming models using templating by a C++11 complaint compiler to utilize standard threads, OpenMP [4] threading, OpenMP offload or the CUDA programming model. Such an approach is appealing for multiple reasons: (1) we have shown our ability to rapidly port applications to novel architectures, significantly reducing development costs; (2) by providing commonly requested programming model features we have enabled application developers to reuse well crafted and optimized routines instead of writing their own, further reducing development burden and implementation bugs while also increasing runtime performance, and, (3), we have demonstrated the ability of a code base to achieve extremely agile portability while maintaining performance levels at close to that provided by native programming models. We note that, the use of native programming models will almost always provide the outright highest performance levels, but often by limiting the portability of the code to single hardware solution. Instead, we target performance at roughly 90% of a well written and optimized native implementation but, for which, our solution can provide cross-platform execution.

However, the approach pioneered in the Kokkos programming model is not without its own problems. The extensive use of C++ templating and meta-templating creates, at times, deep levels of abstraction, often implemented through traversal of internal functions and implementation header files. Further, the use of features developed within the Kokkos model exacerbate the complexity of the underlying implementation code. The anecdotal effect has been that codes developed using Kokkos have been more challenging to debug and profile than those which utilize a purely native programming model where tool support is often well tuned by the implementing vendor. A good example is the use of OpenMP on Intel platforms which is cleanly understood using the VTune Amplifier XE profiler but which struggles to disambiguate parallel regions when OpenMP is used from within the Kokkos runtime. The challenge has come in part because debugging and profiling tools are unable to efficiently handle the deepening hierarchy of calls, functions and header files implemented using Kokkos, and, further, many tools have utilized expected behavior of programs, particularly in the case of OpenMP, that parallel directive markings are directly adjacent to users code. In the case of Kokkos, this assumption is violated as lambda functions or C++ functors are given to Kokkos to map into parallel kernels.

Such observations come at potentially the worst time for developers – charged with making their code cross platform *and* performant, their need for insightful debugging and profiling tools is perhaps at its maximum as our code teams begin to understand execution behavior on the next-generation of HPC compute nodes. Our observation has been that many leading tools have failed to provide the insights needed. Failures have included: misattribution of execution timing, misrepresentation of parallel behavior on execution timelines, and, at times, sufficiently complex performance outputs that the developers are unable to wade through the results to diagnose performance/correctness issues.

This paper is laid out as follows: Sect. 2 provides a description of the Kokkos Profiling interface, including the types of events for which the system provides support. In Sect. 3, we describe several tools that have been implemented using the interface and describe how these can support application developers. We conclude the paper in Sect. 4.

2 Kokkos Profiling Tools

In this paper, we present our latest work in the development of a Kokkos profiling interface (which we often refer to as *KokkosP*) layer which is intended to provide a suite of hooks that profiling and debugging tools are able to connect to. Once attached to the predefined hooks, profiling and debugging tools are able to be called at defined events during the execution of Kokkos-based applications. This work has been developed and refined over a period of four years and has been robustly tested in large-scale production applications developed at Sandia National Laboratories. The contributions of this work include:

- **Provision of a Cross-Platform Suite of Programming Hooks** that are consistent across underlying execution hardware and baseline programming model. This provides a uniform developer experience across HPC node types and systems, enabling them to perform the same analysis activities regardless of target platform;
- **Ability to Analyze Parallel Computation and Kokkos Data Structure Allocation/Lifetime** - our hooks cover two important aspects provided by the Kokkos programming model: (1) its ability to target performance-portable execution of computational kernels using several parallel patterns (all of which have associated profiling hooks), and, (2), the ability to create multi-dimensional arrays (Kokkos "Views") and have these tracked by profiling tools from creation, to copying to/from acceleration devices and eventual destruction. In so doing, we are able to exploit deep knowledge about the Kokkos programming model handling of users direct requests, and, in the cases of the latest POWER9/Volta machines, the ability of the hardware to

perform some operations, such as data migration from the host to the GPU devices, automatically.

- **Compatibility with Leading Vendor Solutions** - we provide "connectors" which are our terminology for small layers that perform translation from a Kokkos event stream into events that can be consumed by leading vendor tools such as Intel's VTune Amplifier XE profiler, NVIDIA's NSight tool and Cray CrayPAT suite. While we provide our own basic cross-platform capable tools, which we routinely use ourselves, the ability to harness leading vendor solutions enables us to benefit from their deep hardware knowledge and ensure that Kokkos programs are correctly profiled, analyzed and represented in each tools' user environment.

User Application:

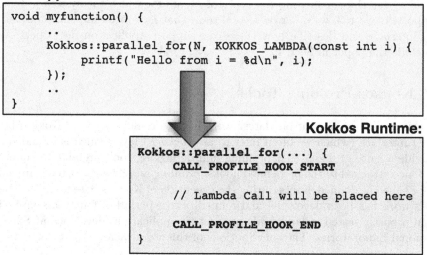

Fig. 1. Compilation of the Kokkos profiling hooks

2.1 Overview of the Kokkos Profiling Interface

Kokkos profiling hooks are implemented as a collection of function pointers which can be called when specific events of interest occur within the Kokkos runtime. Figure 1 gives a high-level overview of how the function pointer hooks would be placed into compiled code so that they would be called immediately prior and after a parallel-for loop. Profiling hooks are registered against each particular event handling function pointer through calls to the Linux dlopen interface which is utilized to load a specific profiling tool and identify the location of function calls to map into the runtime. In the event that there is no mapping from a Kokkos profiling hook to a function call within the loaded profiling tool, or that no tool is loaded for analysis, the function call is marked as empty and ignored during execution.

Unlike many profiling tools in this class, many of the Kokkos profiling hooks are automatically built into the Kokkos programming model during compilation and require no specific user/developer coding, although an extensive API is also provided where developers can provide *additional* definition of sections of their application. In general, users can consider Kokkos profiling hooks to be annotations hidden within the programming model that are compiling into the runtime by default. Through careful design we have been able to insert our hooks such that when performance tools are not running, there is no measurable overhead from the presence of the profiling hooks to running applications. However, when needed, the hooks can be connected to dynamically (through dynamic loading of a performance tool) without requiring recompilation of the application – typically an expensive operation for applications with millions of lines of source code. The effect is that applications written to use Kokkos are compiled to have an "always-on" profiling capability that has effectively zero overhead when not in use.

2.2   Event Callbacks from Kokkos

Table 1 presents the types of events which can be subscribed to via the existing implementation of the Kokkos profiling interface. Input parameters are generated by the Kokkos runtime and provided to the currently loaded profiling tool. Output parameters are provided as a pointer which the Kokkos runtime expected the tool to fill in. Three broad classes of events exist: (1) events which relate to parallel execution; (2) events relating to application segments, and, (3), events relating to data structure allocation, deallocation and copying.

Kokkos Events - Execution Dispatch. The execution dispatch events shown in Table 1 relate to the three principle kernel classes provided in the Kokkos runtime. At the time of writing, an additional mapping of tools to Kokkos task construction and dispatch is also in development. Since kernels in Kokkos can, in theory, execute asynchronously, each call to enqueue a kernel triggers an event, for which the profiling tool must provide a unique identifier. Kokkos tracks this unique identifier with the enqueued kernel and then returns it when the kernel has completed (a call to the 'end' functions). Tool developers are therefore expected to be able to track kernel timing by the unique identifier. Execution dispatch profiling hooks require no additional application code and are enabled by default (*i.e.*, unlike some instrumentation libraries, application code does not need be scattered with calls to an instrumentation library).

Kokkos Events - Application Code Segments. Our experience with developing high-performance parallel kernels for the Trilinos solver library [12] has shown that providing additional information around each kernel can aid in the

Table 1. Event types which can be subscribed to using the Kokkos profiling/debugging interface

Event type	Input parameters	Output parameters
Execution dispatch		
Begin Parallel For	Kernel Name, Device ID	Unique Kernel ID
End Parallel For	Kernel ID	None
Begin Parallel Reduce	Kernel Name, Device ID	Unique Kernel ID
End Parallel Reduce	Kernel ID	None
Begin Parallel Scan	Kernel Name, Device ID	Unique Kernel ID
End Parallel Scan	Kernel ID	None
Application code segments		
Push Region	Region Name	None
Pop Region	None	None
Create Section	Region Name	Unique Section ID
Start Section	Section ID	None
Stop Section	Section ID	None
Destroy Section	Section ID	None
Data structures		
Data Allocation	Data Space, Label, Start Address, Size	None
Data De-Allocation	Data Space, Label, Start Address, Size	None
Deep Copy Start	Origin Data Space, Origin Label, Origin Start Address Dest. Data Space, Dest. Label, Dest. Start Address, Copy Length	None
Deep Copy End	None	None

task of analyzing complex full-application behavior. This is typically made more complex in larger applications because multiple calls paths may eventually execute the same kernel and the sheer number of kernels running in an application can be difficult to locate. To this end, Kokkos provides two methods for providing a nesting/description of application structure to profiling tools: (1) code regions, and, (2) code sections.

A code region is a lightweight mechanism for describing code structure that behaves like a stack. A region is pushed onto the current structure stack and then popped once completed. The overhead associated with maintaining the stack is extremely low and so regions can be aggressively used without introducing significant extra runtime when using profiling tools. Historically, push/pop mechanisms have been well supported by vendor tools such as Intel's VTune and NVIDIA's NSight profiling tools.

Code sections have extra overhead but greater flexibility. Each section is created and assigned a unique identifier. The section can then be repeatedly started and stopped prior to its final deletion. This approach lends itself to artifacts such as user-defined timers which can execute concurrently and may not be retired by the programmer using a first-in-first out approach (that would better map to a code region). The free-form nature of sections allows them to overlap and to potentially be passed around via calls to libraries etc. if the programmer has interest in doing so. The overheads of using code sections relate to the number of concurrent sections in an application as the section identifier must be looked up by a profiling tool prior to any operation.

Both code regions and code sections require additional code to be added to the application, however, in the case of Trilinos, we have been able to hide a number of these calls in existing code structures such as timers provided by the core Teuchos utility framework [1].

Kokkos Events - Data Allocation. Data allocation events from the Kokkos runtime are triggered through the creation of structures like Kokkos multi-dimensional arrays ('Views'), through creation of parallel containers such as multi-threaded maps and vectors or through direct calls to the Kokkos `malloc` function. Since Kokkos is responsible for mapping allocations to memory spaces which can be on the host or any number of devices, a data space identifier is provided to the tools for creation and de-allocation. Such an approach is critical for systems which do not implement shared virtual addressing since a pointer address may not be unique in the system (and therefore cannot uniquely identify an allocation). A user defined label (string) is also provided to the event so that a programmer friendly name mapping to the allocations can be presented in user tools such as debuggers or profilers. These allocation labels are also utilized by Kokkos when expensive range-checking is compiled into the code to identify which data structures are being used to perform illegal accesses.

Data copying is typically an expensive but critical component of optimized host-device style execution (such as a host processor and a GPU). Since deep copies often need to be carefully profiled – in our experience they can result in significant performance penalties if not performed correctly – we provide an event immediately prior to the start of the copying operation and an event to notify the profiling/debugging tool that the copy has completed. We have used these events extensively to assess the performance of data movement traffic over the NVLINK high-performance CPU-to-GPU links [10,25] found on a number of recently installed pre-exascale platforms.

Use of data allocation events requires no additional code by the application programmer as the runtime is able to use existing allocation/deallocation and copy routines to generate the events of interest.

3   Tools for Profiling Kokkos Applications

In order to guide the design of the profiling hooks in Kokkos and provide basic functionality to developers, a small suite of basic tools have been created. This suite runs on all of the systems supported by Kokkos and additionally acts as an exemplar for the developers of larger tool suites such as TAU [21], OpenSpeed-Shop [20], Score-P [15] and HPCToolkit [24] amongst others.

3.1 Kernel Profiling

The most frequently used tool in the suite is a simple kernel timer which inter-cepts all Kokkos kernel dispatch and application structure hooks. This allows it to time each kernel running in an application as well as any application sections or regions. The output provided to the developer is a mapping of the kernel name (provided by the developer or, if none is provided, the C++ mangled name), total time taken in the kernel, the number of calls made to the kernel and then a division of these to produce an average timing. Each MPI rank in a parallel application is profiled independently and the output written to a per-process file for post execution analysis.

3.2 Parallel Time Stack Profiling

A more sophisticated variant of the kernel profiling is an MPI-aware parallel time-stack profiler. In this tool application regions and kernels are tracked in a similar manner to conventional call-tree profiling (*i.e.* nesting is preserved). Application sections are also tracked but because overlapping is permitted, nest-ing is not preserved. The output provided to the developer at the end of the run is given as a nested breakdown of execution time with inclusive and exclusive timing. Because MPI is used, we are also able to provide a measure of imbal-ance/variation across MPI ranks, giving insight into any specific rank variance that an application may experience.

3.3 Memory Event/Heap Profiling

The Memory Event profiling tool allows users to track their Kokkos data struc-ture allocations on a per-device basis. Every data allocation and deallocation is tracked, providing a Kokkos heap-usage-by-time profiling capability. We track each device in the Kokkos application independently with a separate heap. This allows application developers to inspect how much of resources such as GPU memory as being used during execution and at what times the greatest pressure is being placed on them.

4 Conclusions

The diversity of computer architectures is growing, not least because of a greater push for compute-dense accelerators to hit Exascale-class performance levels, but also, because of a much greater variety of workload drivers in the broader com-puting ecosystem. The challenge of re-programming large-scale, complex applica-tions for each architecture has been addressed, at least in some parts of the HPC community, by the adoption of C++ abstraction frameworks such as Kokkos, RAJA, Agency and Thrust. While these frameworks have been largely successful at providing the portability, and mostly the performance, required, their com-plex construction, often using aggressive templating in C++, has frustrated the use of existing profiling and debugging tools. In a number of cases, such tools have either given incorrectly attributed results or provided such complex outputs that they have become practically unusable for all but the most expert and persistent of users.

Anecdotal evidence from our use of Kokkos in the practical setting of Sandia's large-scale engineering and scientific computing workload has been that capable profiling tools in particular, are a prerequisite to handling the complex task of porting codes to next-generation architectures. Therefore, a solution to address the gap between portable C++-based abstractions, and the profiling tools offered by vendors is required.

In this paper we have provided a brief overview and discussion of KokkosP - a suite of hooks that profiling and debugging tools are able to register against to receive an event stream from an executing application written to use Kokkos for on-node parallelism. Event classes including parallel kernel dispatch, data allocation/de-allocation and varying forms of application code structure (to aid in more readable output). The hooks are intended to be compiled in to every application using Kokkos and operate with virtually zero overhead when not in active use (*i.e.*, zero overhead when any particular event type is not registered to be received by a profiling tool). Our experience with using the profiling interface over the past fours years of Kokkos development is that this is largely met and that we are able to compile the hooks in routinely. Such an approach is appealing because if any particular run of an application experiences performance issues then profiling tools can be attached to that instance of the binary – no recompilation for profiling or debugging is necessary to utilize the event stream.

Our future work will utilize the Kokkos profiling hooks to provide further information to application programmers. We are working across the DOE's Exascale Computing Project to partner with tool developers looking to utilize the Kokkos profiling hooks (such as profiling tools who want to natively profile Kokkos kernels). In addition, we expect to utilize our system to provide continuous performance monitoring through introspection of small benchmarking runs during overnight testing. The collection of data from the hundreds of runs performed each night will be able to provide timely feedback to our developer community informing them of kernels/software packages which are gradually slowing down over time or which precise kernel is experiencing performance regressions in their most recent repository changes.

The Kokkos profiling system is an extremely simple, yet practical method of addressing the complexities of profiling complex, performance portable code. Because the hooks are uniform across each architecture platform they met the Kokkos project goals of a unified user experience regardless of specific system. At the time same, they allow significant flexibility, permitting profiling using vendor providing tools on any particular piece of hardware, or a collection of cross-platform tools which will work on any system.

5   Related Work

One of the most similar approaches to ours is the OMPD and OMPT [8,9] interfaces. These build on work in [3] to add support for OpenMP debugging and profiling interfaces. These interfaces can then be used to provide a similar ability for profiling/debugging tools to connect to telemetry from the OpenMP-based runtimes. In keeping with the philisophy of Kokkos, our aim is to provide a simple, cross platform set of profiling hooks which can be used across programming models, platforms and compilers. OMPD/OMPT attempts to do the same but for a single programming model. These interfaces are now being deployed across OpenMP-complaint runtimes and have support embedded in vendor and open source tools. Similar such extensions are also being investigated for the OpenACC accelerator programming model. We expect through further work, OMPT may also be nested within KokkosP regions to provide refined profiling information.

6   Tool Availability

Kokkos Profiling hooks are built directly into the standard Kokkos runtime and require no user configuration/settings if the default build parameters are used. The profiling can be easily disabled in the event of compilation difficulties. We recommend that the profiling hooks are left on so that profiling/debugging is made easier once Kokkos is installed.

The basic Kokkos tools suite is available from the project Github repository at: https://github.com/kokkos/kokkos-tools. Bug reports and feature requests can be made using the standard Github pages.

Acknowledgements. Sandia National Laboratories is a multimission laboratory managed and operated by National Technology and Engineering Solutions of Sandia, LLC., a wholly owned subsidiary of Honeywell International, Inc., for the U.S. Department of Energy's National Nuclear Security Administration under contract DE-NA0003525.

References

1. Bartlett, R.A.: Teuchos C++ memory management classes, idioms, and related topics, the complete reference: a comprehensive strategy for safe and efficient memory management in C++ for high performance computing. Technical report, SAND2010-2234, Sandia National Laboratories (2010)
2. Bell, N., Hoberock, J.: Thrust: a productivity-oriented library for CUDA. In: GPU Computing Gems Jade Edition, pp. 359–371. Elsevier (2011)
3. Cownie, J., DelSignore, J., de Supinski, B.R., Warren, K.: DMPL: an OpenMP DLL debugging interface. In: Voss, M.J. (ed.) WOMPAT 2003. LNCS, vol. 2716, pp. 137–146. Springer, Heidelberg (2003). https://doi.org/10.1007/3-540-45009-2_11

4. Dagum, L., Menon, R.: OpenMP: an industry standard API for shared-memory programming. IEEE Comput. Sci. Eng. **5**(1), 46–55 (1998)
5. Edwards, H.C., Sunderland, D., Porter, V., Amsler, C., Mish, S.: Manycore performance-portability: kokkos multidimensional array library. Sci. Program. **20**(2), 89–114 (2012)
6. Edwards, H.C., Trott, C.R.: Kokkos: enabling performance portability across manycore architectures. In: Extreme Scaling Workshop (XSW), pp. 18–24. IEEE (2013)
7. Edwards, H.C., Trott, C.R., Sunderland, D.: Kokkos: enabling manycore performance portability through polymorphic memory access patterns. J. Parallel Distrib. Comput. **74**(12), 3202–3216 (2014)
8. Eichenberger, A., et al.: OMPT and OMPD: OpenMP tools application programming interfaces for performance analysis and debugging. In: International Workshop on OpenMP (IWOMP 2013) (2013)
9. Eichenberger, A.E., et al.: OMPT: an OpenMP tools application programming interface for performance analysis. In: Rendell, A.P., Chapman, B.M., Müller, M.S. (eds.) IWOMP 2013. LNCS, vol. 8122, pp. 171–185. Springer, Heidelberg (2013). https://doi.org/10.1007/978-3-642-40698-0_13
10. Foley, D., Danskin, J.: Ultra-performance pascal GPU and NVLink interconnect. IEEE Micro **37**(2), 7–17 (2017)
11. Hammarlund, P., et al.: Haswell: the fourth-generation intel core processor. IEEE Micro **34**(2), 6–20 (2014)
12. Heroux, M.A., et al.: An overview of the trilinos project. ACM Trans. Math. Softw. (TOMS) **31**(3), 397–423 (2005)
13. Jain, T., Agrawal, T.: The haswell microarchitecture - 4th generation processor. Int. J. Comput. Sci. Inf. Technol. **4**(3), 477–480 (2013)
14. Killian, W., Scogland, T., Kunen, A., Cavazos, J.: The design and implementation of OpenMP 4.5 and OpenACC backends for the RAJA C++ performance portability layer. In: Chandrasekaran, S., Juckeland, G. (eds.) WACCPD 2017. LNCS, vol. 10732, pp. 63–82. Springer, Cham (2018). https://doi.org/10.1007/978-3-319-74896-2_4
15. Knüpfer, A., et al.: Score-P: a joint performance measurement run-time infrastructure for Periscope, Scalasca, TAU, and Vampir. In: Brunst, H., Müller, M., Nagel, W., Resch, M. (eds.) Tools for High Performance Computing 2011, pp. 79–91. Springer, Heidelberg (2012). https://doi.org/10.1007/978-3-642-31476-6_7
16. Messina, P.: The U.S. D.O.E. Exascale Computing Project – Goals and Challenges, February 2017
17. Nalamalpu, A., et al.: Broadwell: a family of IA 14nm processors. In: 2015 Symposium on VLSI Circuits (VLSI Circuits), pp. C314–C315. IEEE (2015)
18. Pheatt, C.: Intel threading building blocks. J. Comput. Sci. Coll. **23**(4), 298–298 (2008)
19. Sadasivam, S.K., Thompto, B.W., Kalla, R., Starke, W.J.: IBM Power9 processor architecture. IEEE Micro **37**(2), 40–51 (2017). https://doi.org/10.1109/MM.2017.40
20. Schulz, M., Galarowicz, J., Maghrak, D., Hachfeld, W., Montoya, D., Cranford, S.: Open—SpeedShop: an open source infrastructure for parallel performance analysis. Sci. Programm. **16**(2–3), 105–121 (2008)
21. Shende, S.S., Malony, A.D.: The TAU parallel performance system. Int. J. High Perform. Comput. Appl. **20**(2), 287–311 (2006)
22. Sodani, A.: Knights landing (KNL): 2nd generation Intel Xeon Phi processor. In: 2015 IEEE Hot Chips 27 Symposium (HCS), pp. 1–24. IEEE (2015)

23. Sodani, A., et al.: Knights landing: second-generation Intel Xeon Phi product. IEEE Micro **36**(2), 34–46 (2016)
24. Tallent, N., Mellor-Crummey, J., Adhianto, L., Fagan, M., Krentel, M.: HPC-Toolkit: performance tools for scientific computing. In: Journal of Physics: Conference Series, vol. 125, p. 012088. IOP Publishing (2008)
25. Thompto, B.: POWER9: processor for the cognitive era. In: 2016 IEEE Hot Chips 28 Symposium (HCS), pp. 1–19. IEEE (2016)
26. Zenker, E., et al.: Alpaka-an abstraction library for parallel kernel acceleration. In: 2016 IEEE International Parallel and Distributed Processing Symposium Workshops, pp. 631–640. IEEE (2016)

Author Index

Printed in the United States
By Bookmasters